THE FAMILY
IN PERSPECTIVE

A Fourfold Analysis

SOCIOLOGY SERIES

Edited by John F. Cuber

Technology and Social Change
> By FRANCIS R. ALLEN, HORNELL HART, DELBERT C. MILLER
> WILLIAM F. OGBURN, *and* MEYER F. NIMKOFF

Sociology: A Synopsis of Principles, Fourth Edition
> By JOHN F. CUBER

Social Stratification in the United States
> By JOHN F. CUBER *and* WILLIAM F. KENKEL

Social Movements: An Introduction to Political Sociology
> By RUDOLF HEBERLE

The Sociology of Social Problems, Second Edition
> By PAUL B. HORTON *and* GERALD R. LESLIE

The Family in Perspective: A Fourfold Analysis
> By WILLIAM F. KENKEL

Making the Most of Marriage, Second Edition
> By PAUL H. LANDIS

Ethnic Relations in the United States
> By EDWARD C. MCDONAGH *and* EUGENE S. RICHARDS

American Social Structure
> By DON MARTINDALE

Population in Its Human Aspects
> By HAROLD A. PHELPS *and* DAVID HENDERSON

The Crime Problem, Second Edition
> By WALTER C. RECKLESS

Social Change in Rural Society
> By EVERETT M. ROGERS

THE FAMILY
IN PERSPECTIVE

A Fourfold Analysis

William F. Kenkel

Iowa State University

New York

APPLETON - CENTURY - CROFTS, INC.

Foreword

TEXTBOOKS as well as other serious works on the family often suffer from a pervasive fault—they confuse the reader by commingling research originating from distinct, if not incongruous, frames of reference. Unless the frame of reference is specified and understood in its more subtle implications, the theories, the conclusions from data, and even the data themselves become almost inevitably misleading. The mere piling of research upon research, authority upon authority, only compounds the confusion. Apparent corroboration may not be corroborative at all; apparent inconsistency among data or findings may actually be no inconsistency whatsoever, unless the basic assumptions and points of view are really compatible in their deeper epistomological commitments. Thus, for example, if a study based upon official divorce statistics yields "conclusions" which are discrepant from those of, say, a psychoanalytic study based upon clinical data, one has no way of ascertaining whether there is a real contradiction or not, because the two works spring from two scholarly orientations which make philosophical and methodological assumptions of vastly different—if not irreconcilable—orders. In short, the conventional concepts we use—personality, conflict, femininity, divorce, marital success—are frequently derived from diverse frames of reference, the precise nature and implications of which are rarely made explicit in textbooks, and very possibly have not been thought through by the writers. Typically one finds assembled in one bibliography, or worse yet, lumped into one footnote, several studies conceived in such diverse intellectual climates as to render agreement, corroboration, or replication virtually impossible. All that the studies have in common is that they are "about" some presumably similar topic. An astute graduate student recently remarked that given any remotely plausible cause-and-effect relationship, or correlatable variables or value position, he could document it with numerous "respectable" sources—and could do the same for its logical opposite also!

It is time, it seems, to attempt a basic sorting of our scholarly heritage of family study according to the frames of reference from which the various studies derive, to put like with like, so that the intellectually mature student can appreciate the heritage in an orderly, developmental, and logical manner. This kind of organization is the objective of Dr. Kenkel's book and is this book's distinctive contribution. It is also scholarly, well written, and objective in that it is relatively free from "bootlegged" value judgments, but these merits are manifest in varying degrees in other well-known books in the field. The singularity of this book lies in its departure from the mish-mash tradition of topical treatment and of documentation; it is a deliberate and, I think, successful attempt to introduce a needed methodological sophistication for the intermediate student. Without in any sense being self-consciously "tough," it will lead many a student to a long overdue, deepened appreciation of what the cumulative scholarship in this field really has to offer.

JOHN F. CUBER

Preface

THE SCIENTIFIC STUDY of the family has a fascinating history. Probably because of the importance of the subject matter, it has attracted excellent thinkers of many bents and persuasions and from a variety of academic disciplines. The legacy of knowledge to which the student of the family falls heir is rich. There are signs on the academic scene, however, that the contemporary student of the family all too frequently fails to receive the just portion of his scientific birthright. To help reverse this unfortunate trend is the main purpose of this book.

Two of the most widely used frames of reference for the study of the family are strictly within the discipline of sociology. The institutional approach analyzes the family, with its socially prescribed patterns of behavior and its socially endorsed values, as an important segment of society. Present, past, and changing functions of the family within a society are well suited to analysis with the institutional frame of reference. Sociologists also study the family as a social group. In essence this approach takes cognizance of the dynamics both of the family group and its individual members. Focus is on the interaction that takes place among family members as the family itself moves in its continual progression through time.

Anthropologists, historians, and sociologists have given us an amazing store of knowledge concerning the family in societies small and large and past and present. No one would claim that this knowledge is complete, but few would deny that it is significant. For reasons set forth in the first chapter, we feel that the beginning student of the family should be given an intellectual introduction to this vast store of knowledge on the family.

Almost everyone knows that psychoanalytic theories have as two of their major premises the importance of the early years of life and the effect of the family on the psychic development of the individual. In some areas, psychoanalytic theories stand as the only well-developed, systematic theories for the interpretation of the relationship between the family and individual behavior. To ignore the psychoanalytic approaches to the study of the family is tantamount to placing a film over eyes that should be clear.

The purpose of this text is to introduce the beginning student to the scientific study of the family. The first chapter consists of a general dis-

cussion of the historical-comparative approaches to the study of the family
and the values that can be gained through its use. The remaining seven
chapters in Part I deal with historic and contemporary families in a
variety of cultures. After this minimum discussion, we turn in Part II to
an institutional analysis of the American family. The time-honored family
functions of childbearing, child rearing, and the regulation of sexual
behavior are discussed within the context of the family values and practices, and changes therein, evidenced in the contemporary United States.
Part II concludes with a chapter on divorce and the implications of this
phenomenon for the institutional American family.

Part III is entitled "The Dynamics of Family Interaction." The first
chapter in this section explains our approach to the study of the family
as a social group and discusses the pivotal concepts *family life cycle* and
developmental tasks. The remaining chapters deal with personal and
interactional aspects of family living at the early married, the child-
rearing, and the later stages of the family life cycle. A psychoanalytic
approach to the study of the family is found in Part IV. An entire chapter
is devoted to a general discussion of psychoanalysis and a clarification of
key concepts of the discipline. In the next chapter, the concepts are
applied to normal personality development and the significant influences
of early family experiences on the personality of the child. The last
chapter in this section deals with psychic development during puberty
and follows through with attention directed toward mate selection and
marital interaction. Although this psychoanalytic overview of the life
cycle is necessarily incomplete, it should be suggestive at least of the
kinds of understanding of marriage and the family that can be gained
through the application of this discipline.

Our modest effort to help remove the caul of ignorance that obstructs
an understanding of the family undoubtedly will have its critics. Some,
perhaps, will decry its eclecticism. It is significant that several worthwhile
texts on the family state explicitly that they contain a "central thesis"
which is utilized throughout the entire analysis of the family. Although
eclecticism has its own difficulties, the strain toward consistency can
easily result in a one-sided approach that either ignores contributions
beyond its frame of reference or deals with them briefly out of context with
their central theories. It is our firm belief that the beginning course in
the family should be as broad as practicable. The still fluid state of the
family study seems almost to demand this. Who, really, can be sure in
which direction the next generation of family scientists will pursue the
truth?

Our intellectual indebtedness to past and present students of the
family is indeed staggering. Through the usual documentation, we have
tried to acknowledge the sources of specific facts and ideas. Full recogni-

tion can never be given to the many who knowingly or unknowingly contributed to the thoughts that are expressed on these pages.

John F. Cuber, teacher, critic, and friend, is the most important source of inspiration and motivation behind this book. His additional contributions in the capacity of Sociology Editor for Appleton-Century-Crofts are liberally displayed throughout the text. My colleagues at Iowa State College graciously consented to read portions of the manuscript and their penetrating criticisms proved most helpful. Lee Burchinal and David Fulcomer concentrated respectively on Parts II and III, and Chester Carpenter brought his training and experience in psychiatric social work to bear on the psychoanalytic approach to the study of the family.

Through their writings, enriched by personal acquaintance, we are indebted also to Ernest W. Burgess, Ruth S. Cavan, Evelyn M. Duvall, Reuben Hill, and Robert F. Winch. The list is incomplete, but it would be even more so if we failed to mention Professor Paul Shankweiler of the University of Maryland whose lively first course in marriage and the family resulted in a quest for additional knowledge. The greatest debt of all is owed my parents who in a milieu of affection fostered intellectual curiosity and an insatiable thirst for knowledge. Without these, the lessons of later years would have met with more serious obstacles than occurred despite them.

W. F. K.

Ames, Iowa

Table of Contents

PART IV

THE PSYCHOANALYTIC STUDY OF THE FAMILY

List of Tables

Part | I |

THE FAMILY
IN TIME AND SPACE

Historical and Comparative Approaches to the Study of the Family

THE FAMILY is an extremely old institution. Just how long it has been in existence no one really knows, but some form of the family undoubtedly existed many thousands of years ago. Consider, too, that the family is found in all known societies, although at the same time there are important divergences in family forms and functions from society to society. To the intellectually curious, these intriguing generalizations demand explanation. It would also seem that a foundation for the scientific study of the family would benefit greatly from the kind of perspective to be gained through historical and comparative analyses of the family.

This introductory chapter is intended merely to show how we will approach the study of families past and present. We will attempt to make explicit the values to be obtained from historical and cross-cultural examinations of the family. Before doing so, we will discuss in a general way the limitations that can serve to temper these values. Finally, we will comment on the particular societies selected for study and the reasons that prompted their selection.

POINTS OF COMPARISON

There is a great difference in the specificity, completeness, and reliability of the available information on the family in different cultures. Bounded by this limitation, we have nevertheless attempted to deal with each family type in a uniform manner. One point of comparison has to do with the structure of the family, or the personnel make-up of the usual family household. Following this we examine the roles and statuses of the different family members. In most instances, there are sufficient data to investigate at some depth the various regulations concerning who

3

may marry whom and the customs in force governing the selection of a mate.

Family systems (or structures) past and present are analyzed from the standpoint of their performance of the basic societal functions of child-bearing, child rearing, and the regulation of sexual behavior. Functions performed in addition to these are also explored. In both instances an attempt is made to go beyond a description of how the family functions are performed to the realm of values apparently embodied in the particular family institution. With this common framework for studying different family types, comparisons of various family forms should be facilitated. Then too, many of the same points of comparison will again be used when later we focus specifically on the family in the modern-day United States.

LIMITATIONS INHERENT IN HISTORICAL AND COMPARATIVE ANALYSES

The most obvious limitation of the historical and cross-cultural investigations of the family lies in the sheer impossibility of approaching completeness in the task. Even if many volumes were devoted to the family at different periods of time and the family in different contemporaneous societies, much still would be lacking. Probably we will forever be denied knowledge about many family types of antiquity. It is also true that there are numerous instances in which our knowledge of modern-day societies is wholly inadequate to allow a meaningful analysis of the family. Even if it were feasible to deal systematically with all families past and present, therefore, such a goal could not be realized. There is no way of knowing, of course, whether the families for which we lack data are more or less important, more or less relevant, or more or less worthy of study, by any criterion, than those about which we have knowledge.

The fact that some selection of families to be studied clearly is necessary should not obscure the fact that a selection has been made. From the body of knowledge on many families past and present, merely six family systems have been drawn out and made to stand apart, as it were, from the larger whole. Clearly the many historical and present family structures cannot be represented in a sample of so few, nor could they be had we examined ten times as many family institutions. What is more, some other selection of families would have promoted different values, would have had its own potential for the formulation of hypotheses, and in other important ways would have served different functions from the present selection. While it is relevant to note that probably no two sociologists would select the same six, the more important point is that certain difficulties inhere in any selection.

Serious limitations also are imposed on the cross-cultural and historical studies of the family by the kinds of materials that are available for analysis. Frequently the research reports upon which we were forced to rely did not focus specifically on the family in the society in question and it was only by consulting many such reports that the level of completeness for which we were striving could be obtained. Dozens of authorities were found, for example, who treated in some manner the historical Russian family, but none who had attempted a thorough analysis of the institution. While the necessity for consulting many researches provided a certain test of the reliability of any one, the fact that none was restricted to the family meant that detail and depth were nevertheless lacking. For the study of some other families we met almost with the opposite problem. The available material was the result of one sociologist's or anthropologist's studies and we did not have the independent replication of analyses that is sought in all scientific endeavors. Specific difficulties that arise in connection with the interpretation of historical materials, with problems of translation from one language to another, with the incompleteness of available data, and the like, will be dealt with as they apply to the particular family in question. At this point it is necessary to make explicit the more general sorts of problems that inhere in any attempt to investigate the family at different periods of time and in different societies.

VALUES AND OBJECTIVES

A study of the family over time and space is a fascinating experience. Without denying fascination, it is well to recognize that there are some important objectives that can be achieved through such studies.[1] Among these objectives we see primarily: (1) the development of an appreciation of inter-cultural variability and uniformity with respect to the family, (2) the heightening of one's objectivity as a social scientist and in particular as a student of the family, (3) the development of greater awareness of various aspects of the family in one's own society, and (4) the stimulation of curiosity leading to the formulation of specific hypotheses concerning family relationships, problems of the family, and marriage and the family generally. Brief comment on these four objectives is in order.

Appreciation of Inter-cultural Family Variability and Uniformity

Probably everyone who reads these pages "knows" that the family varies from society to society. Many may recall choice idiosyncrasies of marriage or family practices found in some "tribe" or at some time in the

[1] Compare our objectives with those set forth by Winch. See Robert F. Winch, *The Modern Family* (New York, Henry Holt & Co., Inc., 1952), pp. 19-22.

past. A true appreciation of family variability involves a great deal more than a rich store of marriage oddities. It is our thesis that only through an attempt to view a family institution *in its entirety* can one really begin to appreciate in what ways and to what degree it differs from the family in one's own group. In a similar manner, this type of analysis needs to be repeated many times before one begins to "get the feel" of the great divergencies among families past and present.

As part of the appreciation of the vastness of family variability, the lesson is almost inescapable that a great variety of marriage and family practices seem to have worked, or to be working, reasonably well. More than this, one soon begins to realize that the many workable arrangements all have loyal adherents who, at the same time, would find it difficult to imagine themselves living under some radically different family type. In the few families which we will study, for example, such competing values as polygyny versus monogamy and premarital chastity versus premarital promiscuity were found, as well as other competing ideas relating to the proper roles of family members and the goals to be pursued in rearing children. True appreciation of family variability thus means that in addition to more extensive knowledge about the divergencies in values and practices one has developed some insight into the meanings of the diverse arrangements for the people involved.

Increasing Objectivity

Anyone with an adequate exposure to the scientific method accepts the paramount necessity of achieving objectivity in scientific endeavors. But the ability to see things without prejudice or bias is not easy to achieve, particularly when sentiments, values, and loyalties are part of the data to be observed.[2] Strong loyalties and almost unshakable preconceptions abound concerning what is right or natural with respect to marriage and family practices. The frequency with which such loyalties and preconceptions blur the scientific vision of one's self and others should not be dismissed lightly. If the scientific truth about the family is worth knowing, it behooves us all to strive to overcome the hurdles that lie in the way of objectivity.

Frequently it has been found that a greater degree of objectivity can be mustered in the study of temporally and spatially distant families than in the study of the family institution of one's own society. Somehow it is easier to accept the best available knowledge on premarital unchastity

---

[2] Difficulties attending the study of the family were early observed by Groves. See Ernest R. Groves, *The American Family* (Philadelphia, J. B. Lippincott Company, 1934), pp. 14-16.

among the Trobriand Islanders, for example, than to accept the best available estimates of non-virginal brides in the United States. One's own society and others are viewed with different degrees of detachment, with the result that it is less difficult to stand back and let the facts, as best we know them, speak for themselves if we are dealing with the family in some distant society. Once this sort of scientific detachment has been gained, and once it has been developed through the analyses of many family types, it should be more possible to approach the study of the American family with the requisite degree of objectivity. The increased objectivity that can result from the study of temporally and spatially removed families is an important value to be derived from this type of study of the family.

Increased Sensitivity Toward American Family

Even after one has gained a certain degree of objectivity, it is frequently difficult to recognize the idiosyncratic features of the family in one's own society. It is the familiar problem of being too deep in the forest to see the trees. Through a study of the diverse patterns in other societies, the student of the family should find that his awareness of the institutional arrangement in his own society has been sharpened. He should begin to "see" things in his native family that heretofore escaped him.

Perhaps not until one has a real appreciation of the many different customs and practices surrounding mate selection can one grasp the significance of the dating and courtship pattern in the United States. The child-rearing practices in America, to take another example, may seem so right and normal that one fails to give them the scrutiny which they deserve. What is really our unique system may seem to be a generally endorsed pattern that inheres in the common task of producing socialized human beings. One then learns, however, that among other groups there have prevailed quite different conceptions of the nature of a child, great divergencies in the ultimate child-rearing goals, as well as disparities in the child-rearing techniques. Children have been viewed, for example, as willful, basically evil creatures whose spirit requires vigorous taming and whose inclinations need to be curbed. Perhaps only after one appreciates the significance of such conceptions of a child will questions arise concerning how we in America define the nature of a child or what actually we are striving to accomplish through our child-rearing techniques. This is the sort of awareness and sensitivity concerning the family in one's own society that can develop through historical and cross-cultural analyses.

Formulation of Hypotheses

Much of the value in studying families temporally and spatially re-moved from those of our own society relates directly to enabling the student of the family to become more perceptive, more thorough, and altogether a better analyst of the family institution. The origination of hypotheses concerning the internal workings of the family institution or how the family relates to the society in which it is found is another con-tribution to these objectives. Illustrations of such hypotheses are legion. As a result of his study of the ancient Roman family, for example, someone may develop a general hypothesis concerning the role of religion in family changes. Someone else may form a hypothesis to account for the strict taboo toward adultery among the Trobrianders as it relates to others of their sexual attitudes. The important hypotheses are those that first occur to the student as he delves into the historical and vari-cultural families. Whether these hypotheses prove to be original or commonplace, testable or untestable, is not nearly so important as the fact that scientific curiosity about the family has been stimulated and an attempt has been made to channel it.

THE FAMILIES SELECTED FOR STUDY

In selecting past and present families for detailed analyses we were obviously limited by the material that is available and by the space that could be devoted to this segment of our family study. Throughout the selection we were guided, however, by the aforementioned values that are obtainable through this type of investigation. Since one of the avowed goals is to further the appreciation of family variability, we were impelled to include families of widely different characters. The family in the Trobriand Islands, a preliterate society, the family in Russia, and the family in an Israeli kibbutz find their places in the chapters that follow. The studies of the family among the ancient Hebrews, the ancient Romans, and the early American colonists collectively span thousands of years and afford some appreciation of the family at different periods of time. In addition, an examination of these families relates to those of our goals which concern the enhancement of our perceptiveness to the modern-day American family.

In the chapter that immediately follows we deal with no one family institution. Our concern, rather, is with the various theories that surround attempts to trace the history of the family to its origins in antiquity. The disciplined student of the family would want to understand these theories and, we trust, many will be stimulated to pursue the matter further in the original source materials. A broad overview of what we know and do not know about the origins of the human family should serve also as a fitting backdrop for the more specific treatment of historical and modern families.

CHAPTER 2

Beginnings of the Human Family

IT IS only fitting that we begin our treatise on the human family by attempting to push back through time to view the family as far in the past as we are able. No one knows just when it was that humans began to live in groups that would satisfy any reasonable definition of the family, but it most certainly was thousands of years ago. If we but loosen the reins on our imaginative powers, it is not hard to develop a strong curiosity about the beginnings of the family. What, indeed, was the family like even as late as the Old Stone Age, in the days of the sabre-toothed tiger and before man knew how to create fire? Were the roles of husbands and wives as relatively fixed, and were families as relatively stable, as they are today? What were the common domestic problems, and what was the position of woman? Going further, *when* did man begin to live in families? And even more important, *why* did he decide to do so?

As stimulating as it would be to continue the above line of inquiry we must now cease, for we are only due for disappointment. The full history of the family will never be written. No one knows about the beginnings of the institution that we now consider the most important, if not the most "natural," in the world. We can trace back through recorded history, and we can study the family in simpler contemporary societies. Both such attempts, as we shall see, fall far short of a "history" of the family. Such efforts are nevertheless valuable, for, as we have pointed out, they provide a multidimensional backdrop to the stage on which the present family dramas are being enacted. In addition, even an unfulfilled effort to view the family of the past allows us to see the tremendous variability among families throughout time and over space and, at the same time, to see that there are some rather astounding similarities.

Perhaps we should also mention what our historical overview of the family does *not* purport to do. In the past, the quest for knowledge of the primal family appeared almost to be the sociological version of the once-honored search for the philosopher's stone. Not that all pockets would be filled with gold, but, rather, it was felt that once the "original family" was identified it would serve as the missing formula with which to rid the world of its matrimonial woes. Some writers, for example, have argued that in the furthest past monogamous marriage was the rule, perhaps fearing that if they did not so conclude they would be placing undue strain on the foundation of the present family.[1] Others have attempted to show that early man did not even live in what we could consider families. No wonder, it could be concluded, we have so many problems in and with our families, for the family is an "unnatural" way of life. Such searching for the "natural" would seem to lie outside the analytic discipline of sociology. At any rate, we will not designate as "natural" any family form or characteristic simply because some information of uncertain validity indicates that it existed a long time ago, or at least can be so interpreted.

In a similar manner, our presentation of various family customs, regardless of their postulated primacy, should not be taken as a subtle suggestion to adopt those that seem to work. That the ancient Hebrew family, for example, was noted for its stability does not mean that we can or should attempt to emulate its patterns in order to lower our own divorce rate. Nor does it follow that we can take the pattern of relaxed relationships between the sexes found in some primitive society out of its cultural context and install it in urban America. It is normal enough to want to improve present social conditions, in the family, the government, or other areas, and history most certainly has its place in these attempts. But there is an important difference between using history as a guide, a test, or a purveyor of hypotheses, on the one hand, and, on the other, to consider it a blanket exhortation to return to what we believe once was.

In our ponderings about the history of the family, finally, we will not attempt to assemble a quantum of information that will allow us to reconstruct in some orderly fashion the evolution of the human family. The efforts of those who have attempted this, such as Briffault, Maine, Westermarck, and Bachofen, have certainly not been in vain, and we will refer to their works from time to time.[2] But there are far too many gaps in our knowledge, and that of which we are relatively certain indicates that the changes in the human family have by no means been orderly, in the sense that all people, everywhere, have gone through certain definitive stages.

[1] Cf. Ernest R. Groves, *The American Family* (Philadelphia, J. B. Lippincott Company, 1934), p. 19.

[2] Robert Briffault, *The Mothers* (New York, The Macmillan Co., 1931); Henry S. Maine, *Ancient Law*, 3rd ed. (New York, Henry Holt & Co., Inc. 1885); Edward Westermarck, *The History of Human Marriage*, 5th ed. (London, Macmillan & Co., Ltd., 1921); and J. Bachofen, *Das Mutterrecht*, 2nd ed. (Stuttgart, 1897).

MATERIALS FOR THE STUDY OF THE EARLY FAMILY

There are various types of evidence that have been used in the attempt to study the early family. There is no type that can be labeled the best. Each, as we shall see, has its specific utility; with each also are connected certain difficulties or inadequacies which should be kept in mind.

Recorded History

Perhaps one of the first thoughts that would occur to the student about to trace the history of any institution would be to make a diligent search of "the records." Difficulties would be expected, to be sure, but the thought is frequently expressed that documents, records, or writings would somehow tell the complete story, particularly if one could but uncover the original or early ones.

A little reflection will show why doubt and uncertainty, or even downright error, can result from the perusal of ancient documents, instead of the illumination which was sought. First of all, we have the matter of accuracy. Simply because thousands of years ago someone wrote something on parchment, or for that matter carved it into stone, we cannot assume that what he wrote was true even at the time. And then we have the problem of language. Words change their meanings and entire languages drop from use. The difficulties are, of course, compounded when it becomes necessary to translate from one language to another.

The major difficulty with the use of written history for our purpose lies in the extremely short period of human history that has been recorded. A conservative estimate would place the species we call *homo sapiens* on the earth 100,000 years ago, and other species of man would date back at least a million years.[3] During the vast majority of this time, of course, nothing whatsoever was written. If we would let the height of the Washington Monument represent the length of time man has been living on this earth, then that period for which we have a written record would be equal to the thickness of a postage stamp placed on top of the monument. Obviously we cannot get very close to the earliest family by perusing the books and scrolls in our archives.

The fact that it is impossible to learn of the "original family" should not be construed to mean that documentary evidence of all sorts is utterly useless. For recent periods of time, some contain a wealth of

[3] Ralph Linton, *The Tree of Culture* (New York, Alfred A. Knopf, Inc., 1955), p. 133.

information, much of which has not been fully tapped. The Old Testament of the Bible, for example, is replete with references to family life and customs.[4] The difficulties we mentioned as applying to any written record notwithstanding, the fact remains that we do have descriptive material on one type of family that dates back four thousand or more years. A great American industrialist has said that "history is bunk," but the serious student of the family, while making allowances for its inadequacies, will not fail to recognize its worth.

Archeological Evidence

The fact that early man failed to leave a written record of his days and ways does not mean that he left no account whatsoever of himself. Archeology has contributed much to our knowledge of life in the distant past. The difficulty, however, is that so much about the habits and daily life even for those peoples for whom we have archeological data is lost or at best only can be inferred from the available evidence. We can establish, for example, when approximately it was that man first used fire and, after that, when he knew how to build a fire. But intimate knowledge of the family group that perhaps gathered at the fireside defies archeological evidence. The dwellings of early man, his clothes, the utensils used in the hunting and preparing of food, and many other artifacts can be described, and from this the student of the family is given a mere hint of the probable domestic scenes that once unfolded.

Myths and Legends

Little need be said about the reliance on myths and legends for a dependable picture of the family in the earlier days of a society. The relative recency of the times they describe must be considered as well as the obvious chance for distortion in the verbal transmission. About all we can say is that the myths and legends passed down verbally through generations *may be able* to take us back a little further than the present of a given society. Myths and legends may also prove valuable for the interpretation of present customs. On both scores, however, very careful study would be necessary and the conclusions at best would be tentative.

Existing Preliterate Societies

There are in the world today many small tribes and societies whose material culture especially lacks the complexity of one like our own.

[4] See Chapter 3.

Such societies are called *preliterate* if they do not make use of a written language. In the past, scholars have been seduced by the seeming logic in the proposition that existing preliterate groups represent early stages of human development through which the whole of the human race once passed. Through a study of contemporary primitive groups, it was reasoned, we should be able to learn about early types of human institutions, even, for example, about the original form of the family. Although it is easy to follow the reasoning of this approach, experience has taught us that for many reasons preliterate societies furnish poor ground on which to conduct a quest for early marriage and family customs.

There is, in the first place, the extreme variability in existing preliterate societies. Many quite different family forms, marriage customs, or arrangements between the sexes could be labeled the "original" if our sole criterion were that it is found in a primitive society. The most important reason why preliterate societies offer a poor guide to the habits of early man is that the terms *preliterate* and *early* are not synonymous. The simplest society found today is extremely far removed, culturally as well as chronologically, from early endeavors at group living. Again, the cultural level of a given society is relative to that of other societies. What today we label *simple* or *primitive* may, at one time, have been a quite advanced society compared to the rest of those then in existence. Despite the fact that the culture may have developed significantly over the last, let us say, one thousand years, today it could be more primitive than it was because other cultures have developed even faster. Thus, it is something of a historical accident which society is designated as primitive, and conclusions about the primacy of cultural customs based on the notion of primitiveness have a dubious basis.

The matter of cultural change needs further comment. Human institutions invariably change over time, and in this the family is no exception. Accordingly, we cannot assume that the family we find in a contemporary preliterate society is even a fair replica of the family in earlier stages of the development of that culture. We can be certain that the primitive family has changed, but in many cases we will never know *how much* or *in what direction* it has changed. There are many positive reasons, as we have seen, why the families in preliterate societies should be studied in their own right, that is, as the particular forms of a basic institution in societies whose cultures are markedly different from our own. At the same time, it is a mistake to attempt to reconstruct the history of the human family through a study of existing preliterate groups.

EARLY MARRIAGE AND FAMILY FORMS

Years ago, sociologists and anthropologists were more concerned than they are today with the original and early forms of marriage and the family. The legacy from these early writers is rich, and the serious student of the family should want at least to be acquainted with it. Our investigation of the several theories on the origin of marriage and the family is necessarily brief. For each theory, we will endeavor merely to state its major propositions, to look at the evidence that has been used to support the theory, and to bring out that evidence that can be used to refute it. Although we will not refer to it again specifically, the student should nevertheless keep in mind the previous discussion of the difficulties inherent in the various types of evidence used to support or refute the theories.

Theory of Original Promiscuity

A number of early writers on the family supported the theory that originally complete promiscuity characterized the sexual associations of men and women.[5] The theory itself is unambiguous. There were simply no regulations concerning sexual activities; men and women established sexual relationships with whomever they pleased and continued them for as long as they pleased. Since this implies no *pairing off* in any enduring sense of the term, there would be no reason why an infant would be thought of as belonging to a particular man. Although maternity would be obvious, biological paternity would be impossible to trace, even if the concept were known and considered important. Under these circumstances, children would be the immediate charges of their mothers, who, in turn, presumably would be protected by the group as a whole.

Voluminous evidence has been mustered to support the theory of original promiscuity, most notably by Bachofen, Briffault, McLennan, and Morgan. We cannot possibly recount all of the logical arguments and the supporting data of these early writers. One important argument for the theory, however, is the relaxed or outright promiscuous relationships between the sexes reported to be found in some primitive societies. Places are cited and travelers are noted who observed the near or complete absence of marriage.[6] It has been reported, for example, that it is difficult in

---

[5] See Bachofen, *op. cit.*, Briffault, *op. cit.*, and J. F. McLennan, *Studies in Ancient History* (New York, The Macmillan Co., 1896), and Lewis Morgan, *Ancient Society* (New York, Henry Holt & Co., Inc., 1878).

[6] See Briffault, *op. cit.*, p. 215.

some societies to tell whether there is such a thing as marriage or whether the people merely practice a variation of nocturnal visiting. In other places the sexual unions are described as too transitory to warrant the term *marriage*. "Marriages" may be dissolved in a few days or weeks and individuals may "marry" countless times throughout their lifetimes. In still other places, it is reported that promiscuity is the rule until the individual is well along in years. He then settles down, more or less permanently, to live out his remaining years in sterile monogamy.

It is also argued that various primitive tribes have customs which can best be explained as survivals from an earlier stage of promiscuity. The custom of wife-lending, for example, is found in such widely separated places as the Arctic and Australia.[7] This practice has been said to be a vestige of earlier times when the lending and exchanging of sexual partners was so widespread and so frequent that it most accurately could be labeled promiscuity. In some societies, again, no bride goes virginal to her husband, for it is the custom for her to spend the wedding night with the chieftain, the medicine man, the king, or whichever personage is ascribed the *jus primae noctis*. This interesting and fairly widespread practice is sometimes said to symbolize the times when the community, and not just its chief representative, would have had sexual access to any female.[8] A similar interpretation is given to the practice found in some simpler societies according to which all of the male wedding guests are granted sexual access to the bride. Survivals of this latter custom, incidentally, are said to be found in modern societies where the bride is expected to kiss or dance with all of the male guests.

It has been noted, too, that in some primitive societies, although marriage is definitely established, extramarital relations are extremely casual. It is, in fact, expected that wives will have sexual relations with friends of the husband, his guests, or others.[9] In still other places there are periods of extreme sexual license when there is a widespread exchange of wives or, more accurately, when the usual rules governing sexual relations are greatly relaxed. Thus, the reported near absence of marriage in some groups, in the sense of even a relatively exclusive and relatively enduring sexual relationship, constitutes one line of evidence for an earlier stage of general promiscuity or lack of marriage in human society.

It is probably already apparent that the various arguments for an original stage of promiscuity are open to more than one interpretation.[10]

[7] *Ibid.*, p. 260.
[8] Bachofen, *op. cit.*, pp. 12-18.
[9] Westermarck refers to many societies where wife-lending is practiced. See Westermarck, *op. cit.*, Vol. I, p. 225 n.
[10] Westermarck devotes seven chapters to challenging the theory of original promiscuity. *Ibid.*, Chs. 3-9. See also Robert H. Lowie, *Primitive Society* (New York, Liveright Publishing Corporation, 1920), pp. 49-62.

As we did with the original arguments, we can touch only briefly on the counterarguments and other evidence used to refute the theory of a primal stage of sexual communism.

To begin with, the facts themselves are frequently disputed. While one writer will state that a given tribe is sexually promiscuous, another will counter that this is but a tragic consequence of their coming into contact with civilized people. Some obscure earlier explorer had reported that they were indeed quite chaste. The proponent of one theory will try convincingly to demonstrate that most or many primitive groups behave in a certain manner, whereas another will attempt equally convincingly to demonstrate the opposite. And it is by no means easy to get to the "truth" of the matter. To be sure, we could discover with relative certainty what a specific group does now, but the proponents of contradictory theories would both agree that this would shed little light on what the group did a hundred or more years ago when the customs first were observed.

In addition to this basic disagreement with the factual evidence, there is always the matter of interpretation. Westermarck, for example, states that in a certain group premarital chastity is required and does in fact abound. To this Briffault replies that in this same group there is actually no premarital stage; the boys and girls marry at the first signs of puberty.[11] Thus it is misleading to call them chaste or unchaste during a period which for them does not exist in the usual sense. The difficulty with this particular issue could perhaps be resolved, but other matters of interpretation are not so simple. Take, for example, the custom called *jus primae noctis*. We can be fairly certain of its present meaning in those societies where it is practiced. In some cases it is not actually a "right" at all, but rather a solemn duty that must be performed to bless the marriage, to bring it honor, or perhaps to insure fertility.[12] Among other peoples it seems that the bridegroom's fear of the magic results of contamination by hymenal blood plays a part in the custom. A leader, priest, or medicine man can do with impunity what would perhaps be perilous to the common man. In the proper cultural context these explanations are straightforward enough, but it must be remembered that they deal with the present or recent meaning of the custom. The practice of *jus primae noctis* certainly does not demonstrate that all men, or even a given group, once lived in a state of sexual communism. But neither does an exposition of the present meaning of the custom prove that it did not once have a different significance.

In a similar manner, we can take the custom which requires a host to

[11] Briffault, *op. cit.*, pp. 220-221.
[12] Edward Westermarck, *A Short History of Marriage* (New York, The Macmillan Co., 1930), pp. 12-14.

give his wife as a sexual partner to a guest or traveler. To the people who practice it, this would seem to be merely a part of their general pattern of hospitality. As Westermarck points out, to call wife-lending a vestige of an early stage of sexual communism makes about as much sense as calling our present custom of feeding and housing guests a relic of an earlier stage when man did not have exclusive rights to his food or bed.[13] We will probably never be certain how customs like sexual hospitality arose. In view of this, the student of the family would do well neither to let his imagination run too freely in positing early stages of which such customs are survivals nor to dismiss the possibility that some present-day customs have changed in their meaning to the group.

The Maternal Family

Our discussion of the theory of an original stage of promiscuity is important not only in its own right but also because the theory of primordial promiscuity has been used in formulating theories on the original family. It is, in fact, one of the chief lines of evidence used to support the position that the primordial human family consisted solely of the mother and her offspring.[14] That the mother and child should form a social unit is attributed to the biological fact of the relatively long dependency period of the human infant and to an assumed "maternal instinct."[15] This instinct is said to be an older and more fundamental form of sentiment than affection between the sexes. The co-existence of sexual attraction, love, and tender feelings found today is said to be of relatively recent origin. Thus, according to the theory, there was nothing inherent in the relationships between the sexes to bring them to form any kind of an enduring group that we could call a family, while there was always a biological basis for the mother-offspring unit. As humanity advanced, it is further postulated, humans began consciously to organize into groups, with the various mother-child "families" as the important units of the larger group. This gave rise, in turn, to that form of societal organization called "Mother-right."

Rather than referring to any dominance of males by females, Mother-right is applied when the organization of an entire society has these characteristics:[16] (1) descent and kinship are reckoned exclusively through the mother; (2) rule is by men, but it is inherited and passed on along

---

[13] *Ibid.*, p. 14.
[14] McLennan, *op. cit.*, pp. 89-107.
[15] Briffault, *op. cit.*, pp. 45 ff.
[16] Edwin S. Hartland, *Primitive Society* (New York, E. P. Dutton & Co., Inc., 1921), p. 32.

the "female side" of the family; less typically rule is by women; and (3) marriages are matrilocal, that is, the husband goes to live in the home or village of his wife. The opposites of these, the patrilineal system of tracing descent, patriarchal rule, and patrilocal residence requirements, are said to have occurred at much later stages of human development.[17]

It should be noted that we have but sketched the bare outlines of the theory of the primal maternal family and the rise of Mother-right. Volumes have been written, quite literally, and data on numerous groups have been amassed to demonstrate both the truth and the falsity of the assertions. We need not again discuss the theory of an original stage of sexual communism on which a large part of the theory of the primacy of the maternal family rests. We should add, however, that the evidence on one side of the issue is no more convincing, seemingly no more valid, and no less subject to bi- or multi-interpretation than it is on the other. Although this would seem to leave our position undefined, such is not the case. We can conclude that the maternal family may have been prior to any other form in some societies and that Mother-right may have existed before its counterpart in some places. We must doubt, at the same time, that the maternal family was a universal stage in the long development of the human family.

Original Pair Marriage

In rugged opposition to the theory that sees early man in a marriage-less state and the rudimentary family as a mother-offspring unit, stands the theory that pair marriage is antedated by no other form of association between the sexes. Westermarck, the most vigorous proponent of this view, states that even in primitive times a man and a woman were accustomed to live together, to engage in sexual relations with one another, and to rear their children.[18] The man played the role of supporter and protector of his wife and children, while the woman was his helpmate and the nurse of their children. This "primeval habit" gradually grew into a full-fledged social institution, but the habit itself is said to reach back to man's earliest ancestors. Let us look at some of the arguments that have been mustered to support this assertion.

Westermarck observed, to begin with, that in some animal species the male and female, after mating, remain together until after the birth of

---

[17] For a defense of the opposing theory of the primacy of the paternal family, see Maine, *op. cit.*, pp. 128 ff.

[18] In the following section we have drawn from various of Westermarck's arguments in his *History of Human Marriage*, Vol. I, and his *Short History of Marriage*, Ch. 1.

their offspring. He was particularly impressed to find this among some man-like apes and believed that there was in them an instinctual basis for their behavior, reinforced through the process of natural selection. Such ape types found the family group beneficial in the struggle for survival, for both the female and the male were available to gather the proper quantities of food and to care for the offspring during its relatively long dependency period. It is then reasoned that early man would find the family group no more dispensable than the apes do, for is not man's diet similar to that of the apes and do not his young also have a long period of dependency? And if apes are guided by instincts in their preference for pair mating and family living, could not this be the case with man? Westermarck was led to believe it was, at least to the extent of initiating and reinforcing the habit of pair living. The supposed instinct, however, was not his only reason for accepting the original-pair-marriage theory.

A strong reason why Westermarck believed pair marriage was the primal type lay in his disbelief of the opposing theory of original promiscuity. Since we have already discussed this theory at some length, we will but add a few remarks. He challenged, first of all, the prevalence of sexual promiscuity, with or without marriage, alleged to be found in existing preliterate tribes. This challenge was strengthened by an imposing array of societies where chastity is the rule. He claimed, furthermore, that chastity was exceedingly prevalent in the most primitive tribes. He concluded that this prevalence of chastity would be expected if man, like the apes, had some instinctual basis for pair marriage. He offered, finally, substitute explanations for those customs said to be survivals of an early stage of sexual communism. Thus he was convinced that the human family did not develop from primal promiscuity, and he accepted the alternative of original pair marriage.

Male jealousy and the near-equal ratio of the sexes have also been used to support the idea of original pair marriage. It has been said that masculine sexual jealousy is a universal human trait, since the male by nature desires exclusive possession of his sexual object and becomes angered at its loss or the fear of its loss.[19] The relatively frequent custom of wife-lending and the less frequent practice of polyandry are not considered as contradictory evidence. They indicate, rather, that even "natural tendencies" can be suppressed or overruled by strong customs. In much the same manner a hungry person will refuse tabooed food.

It also has been observed that the proportion of males and females born is approximately the same and this fact has been used to bolster

[19] The universality or even prevalency of male sexual jealousy was questioned even by early writers. See, for example, Hartland's numerous examples of societies where husbands were indifferent to the sexual behavior of their wives. Edwin S. Hartland, *Primitive Paternity*, Vol. I (London, David Nutt, 1909), pp. 313 ff.

the case for the "naturalness" of pair marriage. It might, of course, be difficult to imagine how marriage customs calling for one spouse of one sex and multiple spouses of the other would arise if the sex ratio remained constant through adulthood. But it would be manifestly no more logical or natural or desirable, from the standpoint of the near-equal ratio of the sexes, to live in groups with one member of each sex than it would be to have two, five, or ten of one sex and an equal number of the other. This particular argument, then, would seem to add little to the picture.

One of basic difficulties with the theory of primordial pair marriage is its reliance on an instinctual basis for a "primeval habit" that developed into an institution. It is not that we can be sure that our human ancestors had no such instinct but, rather, that "instinct" is a slippery concept at best. If by instinct we mean a non-acquired drive or need, such as that for food, then all we can say is that it never has been demonstrated satisfactorily that modern man has an instinct for pair marriage, and the presence of it in his primal ancestors can be neither proved nor refuted. With regard to the other arguments for an original stage of pair marriage we must conclude as we did on opposing theories. Even granting the validity of most of the facts, they are certainly open to other interpretations and, what is more, an equally impressive array of facts can and has been mustered to deny what the first set claims. What, then, *was* the first form of association between the sexes? The scientist today must say: "We do not know. And what is more, we will probably never know."

If out of necessity we have abandoned our quest for the primal family, it would follow that we no longer postulate fixed, universal stages in the long development of the family institution from whatever it was to whatever it is or will be. As a matter of fact, the non-existence of such universal stages and orderly development makes greater sociological sense. Human nature as we know it is too variable and man's few fixed wants so capable of multiple satisfactions that it is difficult to imagine that complicated patterns of marriage and the family began in the same way and developed in the same order. Either man has changed more than we realize, and probably more than we would be willing to admit, or the concept of universal stages in the development of the human family is dubious. The latter is the much more tenable conclusion.

MARRIAGE AND MATE SELECTION REGULATIONS

In no society for which we have records are all unmarried persons equally eligible as mates. Some societies, on the contrary, have laid down quite detailed and restrictive rules governing who may marry whom. Our effort to investigate the family institution over time requires that some attention be given to the nature of such regulations and the theories that have arisen concerning their origin.

Two general orders of marriage regulations are: (1) *endogamous* rules, which prescribe that an individual must choose a mate *within* a certain group of which he is a member, and (2) *exogamous* rules, which establish that he must marry *outside* of a group to which he belongs. These two sets of rules are by no means contradictory, for they refer to different membership groups of the individual. In a given society, for example, a man may be required to marry someone within his own tribe while at the same time he is required to choose a woman outside his immediate clan or totem. It is as if an inner and an outer circle were drawn around a man and his fellow men; he must go beyond the inner circle in search of a mate, but he must stay within the outer one. Although all societies have endogamous and exogamous marriage rules, there is considerable variation in their specific prescriptions and restrictions.

In addition to the basic rules of endogamy and exogamy, societies have set forth regulations regarding the number of mates a person may have and concerning the permanency of his marriage. Here again we find considerable variability, but the possible variations in the number of spouses is obviously limited. Finally, there are societal regulations governing the actual selection of a spouse and there are prescribed marriage rites. Just as in our own society there are established procedures for these practices, so in societies of the past there were prescriptions to be followed even after one had assured that he had broken no endogamous or other laws.

Endogamy

The most common type of endogamy is probably tribal. Less frequently the outer circle beyond which one cannot go in search of a mate is drawn closer and marriage seldom or never takes place with a person outside some lesser division of the tribe, such as a clan or a village. In primitive societies these rules, of course, are not set down in some exposition of tribal statutes, but they are nevertheless strictly followed and rigidly enforced. An appreciation of the intensity with which such mores are held can be gleaned from the knowledge that in tribes or clans which have lived for years in close physical proximity intermarriage is rare or non-existent.

We cannot fully account for the prevalency of endogamous rules nor explain the great variability in their content. It has been suggested that tribal endogamy, for example, has its roots in the desire of the group not to lose any of its members. But if we turn the coin over, it would make equal sense to say that it is the desire not to gain members. Let us assume that patrilocal marriage prevails. Enforcing tribal endogamy assures that no woman leaves the group but just as surely assures that no "foreign" woman comes into the group. Thus it may be that a group's ethnocentrism gives rise to a certain amount of antipathy toward people with customs or habits different from their own. Such antipathy, in turn, may lead to disapproval or actual prohibition of marriage with the "strangers." It is true, too, that prohibition of marriages with those outside the group would prevent aliens from gradually infiltrating the group and acquiring or inheriting property or positions of rule. We cannot establish any basic rules that would govern the origin of endogamous regulations always and everywhere. Very likely we would have to know each group's experience, whether it would be the problem of a declining population, the proximity of warlike tribes, infiltration by strangers, or some other one, before we could explain why in the dim past certain endogamous restrictions arose. The group itself would be unlikely to know the origins of their rules and more likely than not simply would be following the practices of their forefathers to which they would have ascribed new meanings.

Racial, religious, and class endogamy also are found. Since the first two types involve contact with or at least knowledge of other groups, they would not arise in an isolated primitive tribe. Many tribes, however, do enforce class endogamy, frequently merely assuring that the rulers and the ruled do not intermarry. Like other types of endogamy, racial, religious, and class endogamy require no speculative biological explanation but probably rest to a large extent on the ethnocentric feelings of the respective groups.

Sometimes the outer circle is drawn very close around the group containing a man's eligible mates, and it is considered his duty to marry one of certain of his cousins. This is the fascinating custom called "cross-cousin marriage," and it is found, either required or allowed, in a surprising number of societies.[20] The most proper marriage, according to this system, is the one that takes place with a person and a child of either parent's cross-sex sibling. A male, for example, may be expected to marry a daughter of his father's sister or a daughter of his mother's brother. As is so often the case, the exact stipulations vary from group to group as does the rigor with which the system is enforced. At times only one type of cross-cousin marriage is allowed. For example, a man is allowed to marry the daughter of his father's sister, but the daughter of his mother's brother is ineligible to him.

[20] For a few instances of the custom, see Robert H. Lowie, *An Introduction to Cultural Anthropology*, new ed. (New York, Farrar and Rinehart, Inc., 1940), pp. 233-239. See also Westermarck, *History of Human Marriage*, Vol. II, pp. 71-79.

Various explanations have been offered for this seemingly complicated practice.[21] It is true that the practice does keep related families bound to one another and prevents too great dispersion of family property. Some have viewed it as a matter of restitution or repayal. By her marriage outside her father's family, a woman may be considered "lost" to it. She can, however, repay this loss by giving one of her daughters to her brother's son, thus returning a female to her parental family. In some societies, existing side by side with a strong preference for cross-cousin marriages lies an abhorence of marriages between other types of cousins. The reason for this lies in the method by which descent and kinship are traced; according to some systems, cross-cousins stand in a less close biological relationship than do other cousins. In general, kinship systems and residence requirements must be taken into account in order fully to explain the particular type of cross-cousin marriage that is practiced.[22]

Exogamy

Exogamous restrictions, or rules that require an individual to go outside of a certain group to choose a mate, have received greater attention from anthropologists and sociologists than have endogamous ones. Those exogamous rules that have a kinship basis, that is, that consist of a strong prohibition against marriage or sexual relations between persons believed to be within a close biological relationship, are usually called "incest taboos," while other types are frequently considered extensions of the incest taboos. Although it is accepted that all societies have incest taboos, something of a battle has raged over why this is true. But before we get into this academic warfare, let us look at the facts of the matter, the range and content of incest restrictions that exist in various societies today. We will lean heavily on the work of Murdock, who with the aid of the "cross-cultural survey" reported on a multitude of social practices in 250 different societies.[23]

It has been discovered, first of all, that in all known societies child-parent marriages are forbidden as well as brother-sister marriages. There is a *partial* exception to this in some societies where *some* of the people have been allowed to practice brother-sister marriage. Thus, in ancient Egypt the Pharaohs married their sisters, and the Ptolemies followed this prece-

---

[21] Lowie, *loc. cit.* See also George P. Murdock, *Social Structure* (New York, The Macmillan Co., 1940), pp. 172-174.

[22] Murdock, *loc. cit.* See also the excellent recent study of unilateral cross-cousin marriage, George C. Homans and David M. Schneider, *Marriage, Authority, and Final Causes* (Glencoe, Illinois, The Free Press, 1955).

[23] Murdock, *op. cit.*, pp. 284-313.

dent. Brother-sister marriage was not merely allowed but it was preferred, as it was among the royal families of the Incas and among the Hawaiian aristocracy. It is not unduly irrelevant to mention, too, the references to brother-sister marriage in Greek mythology. We find Zeus married to his sister Hera, Cronus to Rhea, and the six sons of Aeolus married to their sisters. We have called the actual cases of sibling marriage partial exceptions to the universal prohibition because in the same societies where brother-sister marriage was approved for the leaders, it was not allowed among the masses, just as it was not practiced by those who attributed incestuous behavior to their gods. So it was that the leaders or noblemen, who sometimes were ascribed god-like qualities, were exempted from a rule that was otherwise binding. The practice of brother-sister marriage assured that the aristocratic families remained untainted by the blood of commoners, and this has been suggested as one explanation for the custom.

It also has been discovered that incest taboos are never confined exclusively to the immediate family of parents and children. Although some other relatives are always included in the prohibited group, there is no specific one with whom intercourse or marriage is universally prohibited. In a few societies we find marriage allowed between cousins, aunts and nephews, half-siblings, and so on. It is interesting, too, that with the exception of the immediate family those relatives included in the incest taboo are not necessarily the closest blood relatives.

It has been discovered that incest taboos are characterized by an unusual emotional quality. So intense is the feeling regarding them that they are almost of a different order from other sexual prohibitions. In no society did Murdock discover that taboos on fornication and adultery even approached in intensity the strictest incest taboos. It should be remembered, finally, that incest taboos are broken, despite the horror with which the societal members look upon such acts. Any theory that attempts to explain the universality of incest taboos and the origin of such taboos should be in accordance with the foregoing known facts. With this in mind, let us examine some of the more commonly advanced theories.

It is frequently expressed that incest taboos have their origin in the knowledge that biological harm to the species will result from too close inbreeding. Even in our society, many laymen accept as a fact that harmful effects to the offspring will result from the marriage of close relatives. But could fear of the detrimental effects of inbreeding account for the universality of the incest taboo? For several reasons, the answer would seem to be that it could not.

The "fact" of harmful effects of inbreeding, first of all, can be challenged. It is now believed that in the offspring of near relatives recessive

traits are emphasized. Inbreeding itself, therefore, is either desirable or
undesirable, depending on the nature of the recessive traits involved. What
is more, modern scientists in various disciplines have studied and tested
the matter for years, but it is only relatively recently that we have gained
our present state of knowledge. It is difficult to imagine how primitive man
could have had the knowledge of human genetics necessary, let us say, to
allow him to conclude that it would be in the best interests of the species
to avoid inbreeding because of the detrimental effects that would occur
along with the desirable effects. On the contrary, his knowledge of human
biology has been found to be quite inadequate, reaching a low point in
those few societies where the facts of physical paternity are unknown.[24]
Yet side by side with an ignorance of the father's role in procreation exist
strong prohibitions of marriage between those defined as too closely related. It is difficult to believe that biological considerations had much to
do with the presence of incest taboos in early societies. This view is reinforced when we recall that outside of parent-child and brother-sister marriages the definition of prohibited relatives bears no relationship to their
actual blood ties.

At one time it was believed that man had a "natural horror" of incest,
in the sense that some inborn feeling directed him to avoid such relationships.[25] This belief has met with the retort that if it truly was instinctual
to avoid incestuous unions, then it would not be necessary to have strong
laws and taboos on the subject. The instinct theory, furthermore, fails to
account for the fact that, with the exception of the immediate family members, there are no blood relatives between whom a marriage is universally
defined as incestuous. The theory of an avoidance instinct does not seem
to be consistent with the peculiar intensity attached to incest taboos. If
avoidance of incest is instinctual we are left with the unexplainable conclusion that people everywhere develop an abhorrence of an impulse they
do not even possess!

Westermarck has given the instinct theory a sociological twist by
claiming that while abhorrence of incest is not innate it is learned in the
experience of family living.[26] Close association in the family, he held, dulls
the sexual appetite to the point where no erotic attraction whatsoever is

[24] For an example of such a society, see Ch. 6. See also Edwin S. Hartland,
Primitive Paternity, Vol. I, pp. 253 ff., and Arthur J. Todd, *The Primitive Family as an
Educational Agency* (New York, G. P. Putnam's Sons, 1913), pp. 70-74.
[25] Hobhouse was among the early writers who accepted this view. See L. T.
Hobhouse, G. C. Wheeler, and M. Ginsberg, *The Material Culture and Social Institutions of the Simpler Peoples* (London, Chapman Hall, Ltd., 1917). In his *Primitive
Society* (1920) the anthropologist Lowie endorsed Hobhouse's position but in a 1933
publication retracted his acceptance of an incest-avoidance instinct.
[26] Westermarck, *The History of Human Marriage*, Vol. II, pp. 192-218.

felt between those who have grown up from childhood in the same household. This theory, of course, does not account for the extension of incest taboos to non-housemates, and it completely ignores the evidence of actual incestuous unions of housemates.

Freud also saw the origin of the incest taboo in the family situation, but he posited different mechanisms through which the taboo is learned.[27] He saw the genesis of incest horror in the parental rebuffing of the child's sexual attraction. The child's impulse, although it is repressed, remains within his unconscious. The strong abhorrence of incest is the result of what is termed a *reaction-formation* to a repressed desire; a troublesome feeling sometimes can be continually repressed or denied by behavior exactly opposite to the original desire. The Freudian theory, however, fails to explain the extension of the taboos to those outside the immediate family. It fails also to account for the universal social approval of incest taboos in light of the fact that defense mechanisms other than the postulated type of reaction-formation are generally not so highly sanctioned.

Murdock feels that no one discipline is adequate to explain the universal phenomenon of incest taboos but, rather, that we must draw upon various theories in different disciplines.[28] Partly accepting Freud's explanation, he postulates how the lack of such taboos would result in sexual rivalry and competition within the family. In addition to the family's desire to avoid such conflict, it is advantageous to the society to have strong, consolidated families rather than ones weakened by the disunity resulting from sexual jealousies. Since no instinct or natural aversion is hypothesized, it is possible that not all societies came to recognize the value of reducing family conflict through incest taboos. Those that did not would lose out to those that did, so that the latter only are available for our observation. The extension of incest taboos to relatives other than the immediate family is accounted for partly by the social utility of this practice, such as the reduction of intra-group conflict by curbing sexual jealousies within the sib, clan, or village and the promotion of friendly relations with other groups through intermarriage with their members. The discussion of precise persons to whom the taboo would be extended rests on a somewhat involved explanation of the different methods of reckoning descent in various societies. Suffice it to say, then, that Murdock's explanation, which draws on the contributions of several disciplines, does take into account the major known facts of incest prohibitions. In this it stands apart from other theories.

[27] Sigmund Freud, A *General Introduction to Psychoanalysis* (Garden City, N. Y., Garden City Publishing Company, 1938), pp. 186-187 and 291-296.
[28] See Murdock, *op cit.*, pp. 292-313, for the statement and development of his theory.

Marriage Forms

There are only four possibilities for the combination of the sexes in marriage. There is the marriage of one man to one woman (monogamy), one man to plural women (polygyny), one woman to plural men (polyandry), and plural men to plural women (group marriage). Although there are but these four possibilities, there is no relative uniformity with regard to marriage forms throughout the world. Across societies there are seemingly endless variations of the basic types. But nowhere is the individual allowed to decide the matter for himself. In all societies there is a particular marriage form that is well ingrained in the culture, and most frequently there is only one form that meets with high social approval.

Group marriage. Group marriage is so exceedingly rare that some have even doubted that we can document authentic cases. In the theoretically pure type each man would be married to all of the women and each woman would be recognized as the wife of every man in the group. Each and every pair that could be formed within the group would be husband and wife, engaging in sexual relations and practicing other rights and duties in accordance with their societal customs. Among the Marquesans of Polynesia this unique matrimonial arrangement was approached, but it was more nearly a matter of a head couple with whom were living a number of men and women.[29] Although all had sexual rights with both one another and the members of the head couple, the ties of the lesser group members were somewhat more tenuous than those binding the chief couple. This would seem to indicate that something less than full married status was granted to all but the one pair.

Group marriage has also been attributed to the Todas of southern India.[30] In the days when this group practiced polyandry, there developed strong values relative to the sharing of a wife and to the inappropriateness of sexual rivalry among males. In addition, the number of available women was depressed by the practice of female infanticide. With British discouragement of infanticide, the number of women increased. Although this change might be expected to result in pair marriage, marriage practice took a different twist. A group of brothers began to take several women in common where formerly they would have taken but one. Apparently it was more difficult for men to give up their patterns of wife sharing than it was for women to make the change required of them.

[29] Ralph Linton, *The Study of Man* (New York, Appleton-Century-Crofts, Inc., 1936), pp. 181-182.
[30] *Ibid.* See also Lowie, *Primitive Society*, p. 48.

A type of group marriage, finally, has been reported among the Kain-gang of Brazil, but Murdock points out that only 8 per cent of all unions during the last one hundred years could be so classified.[31]

Some would be reluctant to consider our three examples as true group marriage, and even with a somewhat broad definition of the custom, group marriage is still an exceedingly rare phenomenon.

Polyandry. Polyandry, too, is quite rare but there are authentic cases of the practice. The previously mentioned Todas and the Tibetans are the best examples. Although the instances where polyandry is the highest-approved marriage form in a society are infrequent, it is interesting to note that such an arrangement between the sexes can be achieved. Apparently the often presumed problems of masculine jealousy and the obvious uncertainty of paternity are not insurmountable obstacles. To determine paternity, for example, the Todas had the expeditious practice whereby one of the husbands performed a simple rite while the woman was pregnant and became the legal father of that child and all other children, until in some subsequent pregnancy another of the husbands performed the rite.[32]

There has been some attempt to relate the practice of polyandry to the economic conditions and practices of a society. In Tibet, for example, the small landholdings of a family pass to all of the sons, who then take a common wife.[33] Instead of subdividing the land and attempting to make it support the individual families of brothers, each family group has the economic contributions of several males. Among the Todas the preference for polyandrous marriage has been attributed to their division of labor between the sexes.[34] To the women are assigned but minor tasks, making it advantageous for a household to consist of a number of men to assure that the many tasks assigned to males are performed. We cannot be sure, of course, that this is not reversing cause and effect and that the relatively insignificant economic role of woman is not the result of customary life in a household with several males. The absolute rarity of polyandry effectively limits our ability to reach general conclusions on this marriage form. It is significant, however, as an illustration of the versatility in man's attempts to satisfy his needs.

Polygyny. If a world-wide count of societies were made, polygyny would prove to be the favored form of marriage. The precise meaning of this statement may be missed if careful attention is not given to the unit of measure, *society*, and to the word *favored*. We are referring to the number of societies in which polygyny is the preferred form of marriage but ignor-

---

[31] Murdock, *op. cit.*, p. 24.
[32] Lowie, *Primitive Society*, pp. 47-48.
[33] Linton, *The Study of Man*, p. 183.
[34] Murdock, *op. cit.*, p. 36.

ing the gross population of the societies and even the proportion of actual plural marriages found within the groups.

If we were to judge solely on the basis of a preponderance of a given marriage form, then few, if any, societies could be classified as polygynous. Because of the near-equal ratio of the sexes, no society in the long course of its affairs could arrange for all of its males to have plural wives unless, of course, the sex ratio could somehow be upset. In the long run, for every man with two wives there would have to be a man with none. Granted we cannot insist upon a majority, how many men must have plural wives before a society can be called polygynous? Any answer would be arbitrary. How much, in addition, can a simple calculation of the prevalence of any practice really tell us about its cultural approval? The more usual procedure, therefore, is to classify as polygynous only those societies where plural wives are socially preferred. Polygyny would have to enjoy a prestige superior to any other form; it would have to be encouraged for the masses, not just permitted to them. Using the criterion of preferential marriage form, Murdock classified 193 societies in his sample as polygynous, 43 as monogamous, and 2 as polyandrous.[35]

There have been many attempts to account for the prevalence of polygyny. These probably can best be considered from the standpoint of those conditions, on the one hand, that seem to be favorable to the custom and those, on the other, which would seem to limit or discourage it.

It has been suggested that a division of labor that gives to woman an important economic function, when found in certain types of economies, is conducive to the practice of polygyny.[36] Among the Reindeer Chukchee, for example, it is said to be necessary to have a wife to care for each reindeer herd.[37] In some of the societies where women work the land it is clear that the more wives a man possesses the more land he can have under cultivation. But polygyny also has been found among groups where the economic contribution of women is not great. It would seem, then, that while some economic circumstances would be more favorable to polygyny than others, such conditions could only be called contributing causes.

In a somewhat related manner plural wives can contribute to a man's social importance. Where polygyny is esteemed, it comes to be associated with power, influence, and eminence, as well as wealth. Those who live with a single spouse are the poorer and less significant members of the group. The operation of societal values such as these obviously would go

[35] *Ibid.*, p. 28.
[36] *Ibid.*, p. 36.
[37] Westermarck, *A History of Human Marriage*, Vol. III, p. 81. Chapters 27 and 28 of this volume are devoted to a discussion of the incidence and causes of polygyny.

further in explaining why the practice tended to persist rather than how it came to arise.

The alleged inability of man to remain sexually continent has also been related to his finding favor in polygyny.[38] In some societies we find rigid taboos against engaging in sexual intercourse during a wife's menstruation, throughout her pregnancy, and sometimes during the lactation period. The more wives a man had, the greater would be his chances that always at least one would be culturally available. This view, of course, presupposes in the male something approaching a basic sexual lust which cannot be completely overridden by strong cultural taboos. In a similar manner, those theories that see in the practice of polygyny man's quest for more or for more youthful sexual partners must be met with reservations. While such interpretations may seem to some contemporary writers the only ones that make sense, they do not necessarily portray the logic of a polygynous male.

There are some circumstances that would serve to discourage the practice of polygyny. Foremost of these is the near-equal ratio of the sexes at birth. Wives, of course, could be imported into a given society either by lure or by capture, but it is difficult to imagine how such a practice could continue on a large scale over the years. Wars and dangerous pursuits may reduce the proportion of males, but not on a large enough scale or over a long enough period of time to bring about any general practice of polygyny. Another circumstance which might discourage polygyny is the widespread custom of rendering a bride price which could make a second wife a prohibitive luxury. It could also, it would seem, make matrimony a sort of financial speculation, for the greater the number of wives, the better a man's chances for daughters for whom a price could in time be collected. The practice of matrilocal residence after marriage seems to discourage polygyny since the male necessarily would become something of a circuit-riding husband, going even from village to village on his conjugal rounds.[39]

Monogamy. We will address our final remarks on marriage forms to monogamy. The fact of its secondary prestige may perhaps be new to those who through intimate association with the custom may have come to regard it as a universally preferred arrangement. It will be recalled that we are judging preference not on the basis of the prevalence of a marriage type but on the number of societies, great and small, that attach the highest value to it. Monogamy is actually the preferred form in a relatively small number of societies. It has the distinction, however, of being the only form of marriage that is permitted and recognized in every society through-

[38] *Ibid.,* pp. 64-70.
[39] A case approximating this is reported among the Yukaghir of Siberia. See Lowie, *Primitive Society,* p. 42.

out the world, despite the form of marriage that receives highest approval.[40] And, of course, the great bulk of the world's married population, by lot or by intent, are monogamously wed.

In our discussion of monogamy we have so far made no reference to the permanency of the conjugal relationship. Some would insist that we differentiate the stable from the less stable varieties. They say that there are societies in which divorce and remarriage are so prevalent that to label them monogamous would be to do semantic injustice to the term. To the marriage form in such societies, expressions like "sequential monogamy" or "installment-plan polygamy" have been applied, not always face-tiously.[41] However worthy this point of view, there would seem to be good reason for not encumbering our concept of monogamy with too rigid a definition of permanency. Whether it refers to marriages, buildings, or societies, "permanent" is a relative term. With marriage we frequently mean one that is not dissolved until the death of either spouse. Could not, however, those societies that discourage the remarriage of widows be con-sidered "more monogamous" than those that allow it? Monogamy, like polygyny and polyandry, refers only to the sex-number structure of an existing marriage. We would suggest, then, that when one man and one woman are the sole members of a marriage performed according to the laws and customs of their society we label that marriage monogamous. Whether death or divorce is destined to terminate the marriage in a fort-night or forty years, it is monogamous while it is in existence. In a similar manner, societies in which pair marriage is the preferred form would be given the unmodified classification monogamous, regardless of the fre-quency with which pair marriages are legally dissolved.

Cross-cultural data on the permanency of marriage further suggest that we consider the form and the stability of marriages separately. Divorce is not an American invention, nor is it a particularly recent one. In almost every society, preliterate as well as modern, there is a recognized procedure for releasing the partners of an unworkable marriage from their contract and for allowing them to make another.[42] No society prefers divorce to stable marriage and, furthermore, most societies actively discourage divorce. But divorce does occur and is recognized. This being so, it would be diffi-cult to find a "monogamous" society if we meant only those in which pair marriages could not be terminated.

---

[40] Cf. Linton, *The Study of Man*, p. 187.
[41] Ray E. Baber, *Marriage and the Family*, 2nd ed. (New York, McGraw-Hill Book Company, Inc., 1953), p. 486. See also Paul H. Landis, "Sequential Marriage," *Journal of Home Economics*, Vol. 42 (October, 1950), pp. 625-628.
[42] Linton, *The Study of Man*, p. 176.

MATE SELECTION PRACTICES

The methods by which men in preliterate societies obtain their spouses have figured prominently in the literature of the history of the family. This is particularly true of the more exotic practices of "wife capture" and "marriage by purchase." Around these customs, indeed, past scholars have developed theories concerning the original mode of obtaining wives. Let us look, then, at the practices themselves and the evidence used to demonstrate their primacy.

Marriage by Capture

At one time, serious consideration was given to the idea that in the very early stages of human marriage wives were obtained by force, either from within one's own group or from a neighboring tribe. The idea apparently is appealing to the modern male, if we can judge from the cartoonists' stereotyped version of mate selection among cave men. Since the captive is usually drawn as a not too unwilling victim, we can presume that the modern female can find elements of flattery in the custom. But fantasy aside, what really is known about the practice of obtaining wives by force?

There are certainly instances of women being captured and taken as concubines today, and there are even cases of them becoming the full-fledged wives of their captors. Such cases are rare, and in no known society is capture the preferred method of obtaining a spouse. With this fact there is little disagreement. It has been asserted, however, that various customs that form the marriage rites in preliterate societies had their origin in wife capture.

We could make an impressive list of societies in which some type of sham fighting or some show of struggle is part of the wedding ritual.[43] Among some African tribes, for example, the ceremony begins when the young man leads his prospective bride from her home to the midst of the waiting guests and relatives.[44] A rope is attached to her leg and a tug-of-war takes place between the members of the bride's and the bridegroom's clan. The one side struggles to retain a clanswoman, the other strives to effect a capture. When the final tug is given in the bridegroom's favor, he rushes the girl away to his father's house, keeping a safe distance ahead of her relatives, who follow in mock pursuit. Many other examples could be given in which sham fighting constitutes part of the marriage rite.

[43] Westermarck, *The History of Human Marriage*, Vol. II, pp. 254-261.
[44] *Ibid.*, p. 256.

These customs have been alleged to be survivals from the not too distant past when the combatants were in earnest.

Sometimes it is the resistance of the bride or the grief expressed by her which is believed to be a survival of wife capture. Again, it is not hard to document the existence of such customs. As part of the marriage rite in some places, a bride must run from her prospective husband and be captured only after a real or feigned struggle. In other places brides express their resistance less vigorously by actual or mock displays of impassioned grief. In still other places it is the custom to simulate a harassment of the bridal procession on its route, which could be interpreted as an attempt to prevent an imminent capture.

Granted a fanciful imagination, it is not difficult to see vestiges of wife capture in modern wedding customs. Carrying a bride over the threshhold certainly suggests forceful capture, and the wedding ring itself could be viewed as a miniature shackle to prevent the escape of a reluctant bride. One could wonder if it is not to keep them from conflict that customarily the bride's and the groom's friends are seated on opposite sides of the church. We are not seriously suggesting that these and other customs can be traced to marriage by capture. The point is that we can take almost any custom and read into it meanings which it probably never had. But we must not ignore the more straightforward interpretations.

The reluctance of a bride which is acted out in one way or another as a part of the marriage rite could be but a dramatization of actual reluctance. Even in our own society there is usually some degree of ambivalence on the part of the couple and their parents, and no one would suggest that all the tears shed at weddings are those of joy.

Wedding customs in some societies may have been suggested by actual wife capture. But this does not mean that even for those societies marriage by capture was ever general. In a warlike tribe the occasional capture of an enemy woman may have been admired, and the ordinary men may have then begun to emulate symbolically what their heroes did in practice. There is no evidence, however, that marriage by capture was at any time widespread; on the contrary, there is every reason to believe that it could not have been.[45]

Bride Price

In many preliterate societies today it is customary for the bridegroom to give something of value to the parents or relatives of his bride. The expressions "bride price" and "marriage by purchase" are used to describe

[45] See Westermarck's discussion of marriage by capture. *Ibid.*, Ch. 21.

this practice, but both are actually misnomers. Both would seem to imply a far more economic transaction than actually is the case. The payment of a bride price does not make of the woman a chattel, nor does it give to the husband the absolute control over his "property." It is rare indeed that a husband sells his wife to another man.

The payment of a bride price is an exceedingly popular custom and is found frequently in those preliterate societies where the girl upon marriage must leave her own home or village.[46] In some cases the payment of a bride price is viewed as a remuneration to her parents for the expenses incurred in rearing her and a compensation for the loss of her future services. Sometimes, however, it is seen more as a reward to the parents for having successfully guarded the virtue of their daughter; a literal translation of the native term for the payment is "the price of a virgin."[47] The practice of bride price, moreover, helps to assure that the wife will not be mistreated, for if she divorces her husband or simply returns to her parental home, the husband will have lost not only a wife but his financial investment as well. The man, too, is protected under the practice, for it is often customary to refund him the bride price if he must divorce his wife for a good reason, if she is barren, or if she should die before bearing a child. The bride price, finally, may be a token of good will or respect on the part of the bridegroom, and it may be symbolic of his willingness and ability to support a wife.

Bride-price customs vary considerably from group to group, with regard to the size of the transaction, the method in which it is negotiated, and the accompanying stipulations. We need not suppose that in every society the practice serves the functions we have mentioned or that other functions might not be realized. But it would seem that functions similar to those we have mentioned would go far in explaining the practice and that we need not see the payment of a bride price as the second stage in the evolution from marriage by capture, as has in the past been suggested. It has been reasoned, for example, that in the later stages of marriage by capture the husband found it expedient to render a gift to the bride's parents in order to appease their wrath for having carried away their daughter. In time, the payment was made before rather than after the taking of the bride. Although the payment of a bride price is probably a very old custom, there is no reason to suppose that it is merely a refined form of wife capture. Like so many other customs, any "original" or very early meaning of the custom is probably lost forever. It is difficult, however, to envision its development before a group had accumulated a

[46] Murdock, op. cit., pp. 20-21.
[47] Westermarck, The History of Human Marriage, Vol. II, p. 395.

certain amount of valuable property, so that the custom of bride price must
have developed in a period far later than the beginnings of human
marriage.[48]

Closely akin to the payment of a price for a bride is the custom of
performing some stipulated service for her parents. Marriage by service,
as it is called, is sometimes offered as an alternative to the payment of a
bride price. In any case, it would seem to serve many of the same functions,
although it would test more directly the husband's ability to provide for a
wife. Marriage by service is not, however, an extremely prevalent custom.

Marriage by Consent of Principals

It may seem that we have so far ignored the obvious method of obtaining a spouse, that is, to allow the two principals to decide the matter for
themselves. But what may seem obvious to an individualistic American is
not necessarily commonplace. In few societies, as a matter of fact, are the
nubile young given a free rein in their choice of partners.[49] When we consider the many new relationships and ties that are formed by a marriage,
it is no wonder that the parental families are reluctant to grant complete
freedom of selection. This does not mean that the wishes of the young
people are completely ignored or that they are forced into unions with
the full parental knowledge that one or the other absolutely abhors the
match.

There are societies where marriages are arranged by parents, with or
without the services of a go-between, and where the boy and girl may not
have known or even seen one another prior to the wedding day. Although
certainly such things as economic position and family background are considered by the parents, an effort is also made to insure that the couple has
reasonable potentialities for a contented union. In those instances where
the couple are acquainted, their wishes in the matter are usually elicited,
although the arrangements are all made by the parents. Perhaps the most
extreme form of arranged marriage occurs in those societies that practice
infant betrothal, particularly if an exchange of property is involved to make
the arrangement binding. Consent of the baby girl is obviously impossible,
and her future husband is not likely to be enough older for his consent to
be spoken of realistically. Even with infant betrothal, however, there is at
least a tacit provision for escape in the precedent established by strong-
willed couples of the past.

Westermarck propounded the theory that the consent of the woman

[48] For the relationship between stages of economic development and the custom of
bride price, see Hobhouse and others, *op. cit.*, p. 145.
[49] Linton, *The Study of Man*, p. 174.

was the chief requisite for her marriage in the earliest stage of the institution.[50] This would mean that marriage by consent antedated not only parental arrangement of marriages but also the practice of a husband giving a price or other consideration in exchange for his bride. Bride price and parental arrangement of marriages, according to the theory, belong to more advanced economic stages, for it was only then that families could have a sufficiently strong pecuniary interest in the matter to demand a consideration, and it was only then that enough wealth could have accumulated to assure that their demands would be met. Westermarck rests his theory largely on documentary evidence that in so-called less civilized tribes the girl's consent is frequently required whereas among the more civilized preliterates bride price is the rule. Although his alleged proof of the theory and even the concept of higher and lower civilizations may well be questioned, it is not hard to accept the idea that in the dim past the pairing off of the sexes was not a formalized economic affair. But let us close with the thought we have emphasized throughout this chapter. We do not know, and probably we will never know, what were the earliest marriage and family customs.

SELECTED READINGS

BACHOFEN, J., *Das Mutterrecht*, 2nd ed. (Stuttgart, 1897).

BRIFFAULT, ROBERT, *The Mothers*, 3 vols. (New York, The Macmillan Co., 1927).

BRIFFAULT, ROBERT, and MALINOWSKI, BRONISLAW, *Marriage: Past and Present* (Boston, Porter Sargent, Publisher, 1956).

ENGELS, FREDERICK, *The Origin of the Family* (Chicago, Charles H. Kerr and Company, 1902).

GOODSELL, WILLYSTINE, *A History of Marriage and the Family*, rev. ed. (New York, The Macmillan Co., 1934), Ch. 1.

HARTLAND, EDWIN S., *Primitive Paternity*, 2 vols. (London, David Nutt, 1909).

HOBHOUSE, L. T., WHEELER, G. C., and GINSBERG, M., *The Material Culture and Social Institutions of the Simpler Peoples* (London, Chapman & Hall, Ltd., 1917), Ch. 3.

HOWARD, GEORGE E., *History of Matrimonial Institutions*, 3 vols. (Chicago, University of Chicago Press, 1904).

MORGAN, LEWIS, *Ancient Society* (New York, Henry Holt & Co., Inc., 1878).

TODD, ARTHUR J., *The Primitive Family as an Educational Agency* (New York, G. P. Putnam's Sons, 1913).

TOZZER, ALFRED M., *Social Origins and Social Continuities* (New York, The Macmillan Co., 1925).

WESTERMARCK, EDWARD, *The History of Human Marriage*, 3 vols., 5th ed. (London, Macmillan & Co., Ltd., 1921).

[50] Westermarck, *The History of Human Marriage*, Vol. II, Ch. 22.

CHAPTER 3

The Ancient Hebrew Family

For many reasons a study of the family form and life of the ancient Hebrews is an important venture. There is, first of all, the practical matter of available data. The Old Testament of the Bible is replete with references to family customs and these references have been subjected to the scrutiny and interpretation of brilliant scholars. While the picture is by no means complete, and it is true that the scholars themselves do not always agree on interpretations, there nevertheless has emerged a body of information that can be organized to give a fair picture of marriage and family customs some twenty-five to thirty centuries ago. The fact, then, that we have this body of knowledge on a family type at a relatively early stage of history is one reason for investigating the ancient Hebrew family.

Selection of the ancient Hebrew family has been prompted also by the direct and indirect effects this family type has had on contemporary American families. Its influence on the present-day Jewish family is perhaps the most apparent. It is true that all human institutions continually change, and we are not trying to suggest that the Jewish family in the United States today is a perfect replication of the Hebrew family of long ago. But its effect on the contemporary Jewish family is by no means meager. Orthodox Jews, in particular, are governed and guided in their daily lives by the Talmud, the formal exposition of sacred law that consists of rabbinical commentaries on the basic Mosaic law over at least twenty-two hundred years.

No less significant than the direct influence of the Hebrew family on the modern Jewish family is the broader impact Hebrew culture has had, through Christianity, on the family in our own and other occidental countries. From the Hebrews came not only the founder of Christianity but also the basic system of moral philosophy in which the new religion took root. Time and again we read in the New Testament, for example, that Christ returned questions of moral principle by asking what the religious leaders of the past commanded, and many of Christ's teachings, certainly, were based on Mosaic law. Even today, most Christian religions accept the continuity of the Old and New Testaments. Referring specifically to the family, we see that the heritage from the Hebrews includes, among others, traditions concerning the proper roles of men and women, the rearing of children, and various aspects of sexual morality. It is certain that we have not accepted the Hebrew family heritage intact, and it is equally certain that there have been other important influences on the contemporary American family. The point is simply that the marriage and family patterns of the ancient Hebrews have been too important an influence to be ignored by the serious student of the family.

The Old Testament as Source Material

Because of its wider familiarity, the principal source of information on the family patterns of the ancient Hebrews that we will refer to is the Old Testament of the Bible.[1] There are, however, certain difficulties connected with the descriptive commentaries on Hebrew family life contained therein which should be made manifest. The printed document we now call the Old Testament has undergone many changes in form. After centuries, probably, of verbal transmission many of the stories appeared finally as handwritten manuscripts in an ancient tongue. To the variations that inevitably occurred in the verbal accounts were added the losses due to the poor condition of some of the manuscripts and the distortions of meaning inherent in translation. We know now, too, that the various documents which go to make up the Old Testament differ by hundreds of years from the times they describe. What we have, then, are narrative accounts of the Hebrew people over a long course of their history in which are intertwined sufficient references to allow us to obtain some appreciation of the basic pattern of their family and some of the modifications of the pattern.

The variable nature of the Old Testament accounts for much of the arduousness which accompanies the attempts to gain a picture of the Hebrew family pattern. We find a rather bewildering agglomerate of detailed genealogies, terse statements of laws, poetic descriptions, passages exhorting the masses to return to the ways of their fathers, and still others urging them to adopt new ideas. It is not always easy to determine whether a family reference is included because it deals with that which was commonplace or that which was unusual, or even because it describes life as it should be. Take, for example, Ruth's devotion to her mother-in-law, Naomi.

---

[1] All quotations have been taken from the King James version of the Old Testament. In most instances chapter and verse references apply also to the Douay version.

Was this story set forth because it portrayed an extraordinary display of loyalty that others could well emulate, or was it mentioned to reinforce attitudes that were more or less common? Perhaps it was for neither of these reasons, and reference to the daughter-in-law's devotion was somewhat incidental to the greater tale of Naomi's eventual rise above her tribulations. We have the major difficulty, finally, of trying to discern how the masses of common people ordered their family life. Moses, Lot, Abraham, and other leaders or men of wealth figure prominently in the accounts of the Hebrews' history precisely because they figured so prominently in their times. The lives of lesser men, of course, do not receive detailed attention and frequently we can only infer the behavior of the masses from the statements of their leaders. Scholars have wrestled for years over these and other problems, and they would be the last to consider that we now have anything like the "final answer." This suggests that a certain amount of scientific skepticism is in order and that we strive to make allowances for the difficulties inherent in the source materials.

Stages of Hebrew Civilization

Since, as we have seen, the documents on which the Old Testament is based were written at widely separated times we must realize that we receive no single picture of the Hebrew family, but, rather, glimpses of institutional change. The Pentateuch, which, together with the Book of Ruth, is the chief source for our reconstruction of the Hebrew family, is thought to describe times as early as 1400 B.C. and as late as 400 B.C. It should be expected that the entire Hebrew social organization underwent significant changes over the course of the one thousand years.

In the earliest period for which we have records it is clear that the Jews were a nomadic people wandering in groups across the desert. The story of Abraham and Lot deciding which of them should drive his herd across the vast country to the left, and which to the right, is representative of this period. As herdsmen in continual search for pasture and water it is fitting that their abodes were simple huts and frequently tents. At this stage, tribal feeling was strong, and substantial groups were united under the leadership and authority of the patriarch.

It was in the twelfth century, or perhaps somewhat before, that the Israelites became settled agriculturists in Canaan. Here they raised a variety of crops including wheat, barley, grapes, figs, and olives. As villages grew, a host of new occupations developed. We read of plasterers, carpenters with their rules and compasses, and later of potters and various metalsmiths. The change from a nomadic pastoral life brought a lessening of tribal ties. Village communities became important and, within them, the large family consisting of the male head, his wife, and married or unmarried children. Later we find great cities and the development of commerce and industry. Most people are probably acquainted, finally, with the Babylonian exile and the domination of the Jews by the Greeks, Egyptians, and Syrians from the fourth to the second century B.C. But these and later events are somewhat beyond our scope, for we will be concerned chiefly with the earlier stages of Hebrew civilization. The foregoing overview of the stages of Hebrew civilization has been admittedly sketchy; its purpose, however, was to give some appreciation of the long period of history covered in the Old Testament accounts of the Hebrews and the changes in their culture.

THE HEBREW FAMILY: STRUCTURE AND ROLES

Throughout the periods described above, the culture of the Hebrews prescribed a patriarchal extended family. By *patriarchal* we mean that power was vested in the male head of the household. We use the expression *extended* to indicate that the usual family group was more inclusive than the conjugal pair and their offspring. Particularly at the nomadic stage, the usual family group consisted of the patriarch, his wife or wives, his concubines, his children, slaves, and even some strangers who might have chosen to attach themselves. Married sons and their wives and children also formed part of the extended family which, at the nomadic stage, lived together in a great camp. Even at a later time we read that when Jacob moved his family from Canaan, "his sons and his sons' sons with him, his daughters, and his sons' daughters, and all his seed brought he with him into Egypt."[2]

The extended structure of the Hebrew family had much to do, of course, with the roles assigned to family members. To the male head, as we have said, was given great authority. He could choose wives for his sons and could sell his daughters into slavery, albeit not to a foreigner. Needless to say, the man had considerable control over his wife, even as Eve was told that her husband would "rule over" her.[3] So great was the authority of the patriarch that he could invalidate even a solemn vow to the Lord made by his wife or unmarried daughter.[4]

It is common, when describing a patriarchal family type, to emphasize the almost unlimited powers of the male. But granted the male had great

[2] Genesis 46:7.
[3] Genesis 3:16.
[4] Numbers 30:2-16.

authority, to him also fell commensurate responsibilities. He was the leader of what could be a sizable group, the manager of a great herding or farming enterprise, the overseer of the camp, the religious functionary, the interpreter of justice, and the public relations expert who maintained the harmony of the group. In the days when nomadic herdsmen pushed across the desert, it is likely that they found a certain strength in the numbers banded together in an extended family. Probably it was advantageous, too, to have a strong central figure to direct and guide them and have ultimate responsibility for the decisions upon which may have rested the welfare and survival of the group.

The woman, as we have seen, was in a position subordinate to man. Unless she was widowed or divorced, a woman was under the authority of some male. While she was unmarried it was the authority of her father, when married that of her husband. Husbands could not sell their wives, as fathers could their daughters, but divorce could be initiated by males alone. Within this framework of subordination, a wife had definite responsibilities and duties and if she fulfilled them well she was held in high esteem. The worth of a good wife, we are told, is "far above rubies."[5]

The Hebrew woman's role as a mother undoubtedly received greater emphasis than any of her other roles. More than anything else, it was a sacred duty for her to provide her husband with progeny "that his name be not put out of Israel." Despite the forewarning in Eden, "in sorrow thou shalt bring forth children,"[6] Hebrew women apparently accepted fully their maternal role and longed to fulfill it. "God hath taken away my reproach,"[7] cried Rachel when eventually she conceived and bore a son. We read also of the extreme sorrow of Hannah "because the Lord had shut up her womb."[8] She spoke of her childlessness as an "affliction" and vowed, if she was allowed to have a son, to give him to the service of the Lord. Thus the bearing of children was not thought of as some kind of an imposition nor as the biological sequel to sexual passion; it was seen, rather, as a sacred responsibility.

To the woman also was assigned a list of household and other tasks that might well awe, if not discourage, a contemporary wife. Proverbs spells these out with poetic succinctness:[9]

> She seeketh wool, and flax, and worketh willingly with her hands. She is like the merchant's ships; she bringeth her food from afar. She riseth also while it is yet night, and giveth meat to her household, and a portion to her maidens.

[5] Proverbs 31:10.
[6] Genesis 3:16.
[7] Genesis 30:23.
[8] I Samuel 1:6.
[9] Proverbs 31:13-27.

She considereth a field, and buyeth it: with the fruit of her hands she planteth a vineyard. She girdeth her loins with strength, and strengtheneth her arms. She perceiveth that her merchandise is good: her candle goeth not out by night. She layeth her hands to the spindle, and her hands hold the distaff. She is not afraid of the snow for her household: for all her household are clothed with scarlet. . . . She maketh fine linen, and selleth it; and delivereth girdles unto the merchant. She looketh well to the ways of her household, and eateth not the bread of idleness.

The Hebrews did not ignore the role of a woman as wife and companion to her husband and, in fact, encouraged companionship of the spouses. It was ordained, for example, that a new bridegroom should not be made to go to war or be charged with any business, "but he shall be free at home one year, and shall cheer up his wife which he hath taken."[10] Woman, indeed, was created with the companionship ideal in mind, for "It is not good that man should be alone."[11] Certainly the expression "one flesh" describes a unity and interdependence that would be difficult to surpass. And so the Hebrew woman lived out her life as a "help meet" to her husband. Even in death the unity of the pair was preserved as much as possible, for it was well established that a wife be laid to rest at the side of her husband.

To a considerable degree, the role expectations of Hebrew children are contained in the command, "Honor thy father and thy mother." Children were looked upon as willful creatures who must be trained, restrained, punished, and curbed if they were to become responsible adults righteous in the eyes of their community and their God. "He that spareth his rod hateth his son,"[12] we are told, and this thought has continued to have acceptance for thousands of years. But a father's rod was not the most severe punishment imaginable; we find death prescribed for the child who struck or cursed his parents.[13] Again, we read that if the chastisement of a "stubborn and rebellious" son should fail to remove such character defects his parents should bring him before the elders of the city, there to be stoned to death.[14]

The harsh discipline prescribed for erring children did not mean that parents were looked upon as cruel despots from whose tyrannical yoke the children longed to be delivered. Certainly the bonds of respect, loyalty, and love held parents and children together more frequently and more firmly than could be expected of sheer brutality or its threat. Isaac's willing submission to his intended sacrifice by his father, even to the point of

[10] Deuteronomy 24:5.
[11] Genesis 2:18.
[12] Proverbs 13:24.
[13] Exodus 21:15,17.
[14] Deuteronomy 21:18-21.

carrying the wood for his own holocaust, illustrates well the devotion of son to father.[15] When one reads of the grim procession of father and son up the sacrificial mountain, one cannot help think that the whole affair was carried off with more ease than some modern parents achieve when taking their child to a dentist.

We will turn, now, to other aspects of marriage and family among the Hebrews. It is well to remember, however, that the extended structure of the Hebrew family and the roles prescribed for family members had a significant influence on many aspects of their lives.

MATE SELECTION

As we have seen previously, all societies establish rules regarding who may marry whom and contain in their culture approved procedures for the execution of mate selection and marriage. Let us look at the specific form such prescriptions took among the ancient Hebrews and investigate their endogamous, exogamous, and other regulations.

Endogamous Rules

In various passages we read that the Hebrews were exhorted to marry within their own group. Numbers is particularly specific, with its command that a woman of Israel shall marry only into the tribe of her father.[16] Tribal endogamy, in this instance, is prescribed in order that the land inheritance of one tribe should not pass to another. Furthermore, before the Jews took possession of Canaan, they were cautioned against intermarriage with those already in possession of the land. Provision was made, however, for a proper marriage in the event a man "seest among the captives a beautiful woman, and hast a desire unto her."[17] Intermarriage with the Canaanites and others, nevertheless, was severely frowned upon, largely because of the fear that the Israelites would weaken in their religion and adopt the idolatrous ways of the "foreigners." We read in Genesis about the rape of Dinah by Shechem the Hittite. Although Shechem was most anxious to marry Dinah, her brothers would not allow it and explained to her suitor: "But in this we will consent: If ye be as we be, that every male of you be circumcised, then will we give our daughter unto you. And we will take your daughters to us, and we will dwell with you and become one people. But if ye will not hearken unto us, to be circumcised, then will we take our

[15] Genesis 22:5-10.
[16] Numbers 36:6-8.
[17] Deuteronomy 21:10-13.

daughter, and we will be gone."[18] As the story unfolds, of course, we learn that the sons of Jacob had no real intentions of allowing their sister to marry Shechem. The emphasis is clear that marriage with an "outsider," with someone "different," is totally unacceptable. The Hittites, furthermore, well understood this point of view and were willing to comply with the unusual request only because the son of their leader could thereby obtain the hand of Dinah. Before the period of the conquest of Canaan, therefore, it appears that endogamous regulations operated with some rigidity. There were instances, to be sure, of marriages with outsiders, but unless there were extenuating circumstances involved, they were met with strong disapproval. Moses' marriage to Zipporah, for example, apparently was accepted, but since he was a fugitive from his native land, he literally had no other choice but to marry a foreigner.

After the conquest of Canaan, it appears that endogamous restrictions became greatly relaxed. We read of Samson's marriage to the Philistine and the sons of Elimelech and Naomi marrying Moabite women. Scores of other unions are recorded, apparently without censure, between Hebrew and Canaanite, Egyptian, Hittite, and others. At a still later period there was a resurgence of interest in endogamy. The men were urged, and indeed promised, to separate from their foreign wives and leave also their children by such unions.[19] This was the period after the Babylonian exile, and it is likely that the Hebrews' experiences as captives taught them the necessity of preserving group solidarity. Throughout their history, moreover, the chief reason for the Hebrews' concern with endogamy was the fear of apostasy on the part of the Hebrew partner to a mixed-religious marriage. It is noteworthy that present-day religious leaders of all faiths express similar concern and exhort their followers to religious endogamy.

Exogamous Rules

The clearest statement of the Hebrew exogamous restrictions occurs in Leviticus.[20] It is expressly forbidden for a man to marry his mother or step-mother, his sister, his half-sister, whether the father's daughter or the mother's daughter, his paternal or maternal aunt, and his daughter-in-law. Marriage of a man to his brother's wife is also included in the list of prohibited unions, but, as we shall see later, there were circumstances when such a marriage was almost mandatory. The marriage of cousins is allowed, and there is some evidence that it may have been preferred.

[18] Genesis 34:15-17.
[19] Ezra 10:3.
[20] Leviticus 18:6-18.

Father-daughter and mother-son marriages are forbidden in these passages, and it is interesting that the prohibitions are phrased in terms of the child rather than the parent: "The nakedness of thy father, or the nakedness of thy mother, shalt thou not uncover."

Just as with our own incest prohibitions, many of which obtain their *raison d'être* from the Hebrews, we notice that closeness of biological kinship is not the only criterion of a prohibited relationship. We find among the Hebrews, for example, that a man is forbidden to marry his step-mother and his daughter-in-law. In neither case, of course, would the marriage involve blood relatives. One reason for the prohibitions would seem to be that the principals stand in too close a *social* relationship to permit their marriage. Cousins, on the other hand, might well be living in separate households or even in different villages.

As in all societies, despite the rigidity of the taboos, violations of the incest prohibitions occurred among the Hebrews. There is the well-known instance of Judah and his daughter-in-law Tamar.[21] Although Judah was unaware of the relationship and thought her to be a harlot, Tamar sought him out precisely because he was her father-in-law. Again, there is the report that the two daughters of Lot gave him wine to drink and each had sexual intercourse with him.[22] Presumably Lot himself was too much under the influence of alcohol to realize what occurred, but the same could not be said for his daughters. Finally, Abraham says of Sarah: "And yet indeed she is my sister; she is the daughter of my father, but not the daughter of my mother; and she became my wife."[23]

The Levirate Duty

Levirate, from the Latin *levir,* "a husband's brother," refers to the custom according to which a man is required to marry his brother's widow. By extension, the term would include the marriage of the widow to a more distant relative of her husband if the deceased husband had no brother or none who was willing to marry her. The explanation of the levirate duty found in Deuteronomy will allow us to discuss the custom more fully:[24]

> If brethren dwell together, and one of them die, and have no child, the wife of the dead shall not marry without unto a stranger: Her husband's brother shall go in unto her, and take her to him to wife, and perform the duty of a husband's brother unto her. And it shall be, that the firstborn which she beareth shall succeed in the name of his brother which is dead, that his name be not put out of Israel.

[21] Genesis 38:13-18.
[22] Genesis 19:30-38.
[23] Genesis 20:12.
[24] Deuteronomy 25:5-6.

It is important, first of all, to realize the special circumstances under which the levirate duty applied. Although it is not mentioned specifically in the above passage, other Old Testament references make it clear that a man who acts as levir would come into possession of his brother's land and flocks and would assume responsibility for their management. Thus, we learn that the levirate duty applies only to brothers who "live together," probably either in the same extended family or in close proximity. A man living at some distance from his brother, therefore, would not be subjected to the rather severe inconvenience involved in settling his affairs and moving to the village of his deceased brother. It is clear, too, that the levirate custom applies only if the brother died childless. Under other circumstances, as seen in the code set forth in Leviticus, marriage of a man to his sister-in-law is forbidden.

We come, then, to the meaning of the levirate to the Hebrews. It is clear from the passage, "that his name be not put out of Israel," that the principal function of the custom was to provide an heir to the deceased, albeit a pseudo-heir. To the Hebrews it was extremely important that a man not die without offspring. For a man to allow his family line to come to an end would be tantamount to precluding his immortality. The Hebrew conception of life-after-death was a living-on through one's sons. During a man's lifetime, therefore, he would go to almost any length to secure a son, and the practices of polygyny and concubinage were allowed among the Hebrews on this account. If he were unfortunate enough to die childless, it is natural that his wife and his brothers would be concerned over his fate and would attempt to remedy the situation.

The story of Judah and Tamar, to which we referred earlier, shows the lengths to which a wife will go to assure that her deceased husband's name "be not put out of Israel." When Tamar's husband died childless, the duty of a husband's brother fell to Onan. But when Onan went to his brother's wife he "spilled his seed upon the ground" and for this, we are told, the Lord slew him.[25] Thus two out of three of Judah's sons had married Tamar, and both had subsequently met their deaths. Perhaps for this reason Judah was unwilling for his last remaining son to be a levir to Tamar and begged her to go back to her father's house until Shelah was grown. But as time passed and Tamar realized that Shelah was not to be given to her, she tricked her father-in-law into having intercourse with her and, indeed, bore his twins. Nor was she censured for this, for she was using the only means available to obtain offspring by a close relative of her dead husband. Judah himself acknowledged that she behaved correctly when upon learning of the identity of the presumed harlot with whom he had relations he said:

[25] Genesis 38:9-10.

"She hath been more righteous than I; because that I gave her not to Shelah my son."[26]

We have already seen that Onan and Judah did not accept the levirate custom as a serious and sacred duty. Apparently there were more than a few men who, for various reasons, wanted to evade the responsibility. This is the inference, at least, from the fact that there existed a relatively simple, formal procedure called *chalitza*, whereby a man could be released from being a levir to his brother's wife.[27] The woman in question would initiate the procedure by complaining to the city elders that her deceased husband's brother refused "to raise up unto his brother a name in Israel." If the brother admitted that this was true, as he could do by so simple a statement as "I like not to take her," his sister-in-law would loosen his shoe and spit in his face. The chalitza would be complete when she declared, "So shall it be done unto that man that will not build up his brother's house." The chalitza ceremony thus served to clarify relationships all around. The woman was free to seek a more venturesome man from among her dead husband's lesser kin. If none were to be found, presumably she could marry a "stranger" with the realization that she had done her best to provide an heir for the deceased. Nor does the brother-in-law fare badly. Perhaps he did not want to "build up his brother's house," but would rather work on his own. Perhaps he had a personal dislike for his sister-in-law. Whatever his reason, the husband's brother was released by a simple ceremony from the task he found distasteful. The degrading aspects of the chalitza might make it appear that failure to perform the levirate duty was a serious matter and that few men would be willing to stand so accused. The fact that a formal procedure existed at all, however, means that it had become necessary to provide for a not infrequent contingency. As time went on, the practice of the levirate declined, particularly as the conjugal family replaced the extended family system. It was as late as 1879, however, that the Rabbinical Conference at Philadelphia formally declared that the custom of levirate and chalitza had lost meaning and were, therefore, no longer binding.[28]

Mate Selection and Marriage Customs

We have seen that the Hebrews had certain regulations that defined the group within which one must choose a mate and others that defined the inner kinship circle that he must go beyond to establish a non-

[26] Genesis 38:26.
[27] Deuteronomy 25:7-9.
[28] Willystine Goodsell, A *History of Marriage and the Family*, rev. ed. (New York, The Macmillan Co., 1934), p. 58.

incestuous union. The levirate custom affected who could marry whom, although, of course, it would not come into play in the majority of marriages. It remains now to investigate how mates were selected from within the defined field of eligibles and how the matter was brought to a successful close with legal marriage.

Among the ancient Hebrews marriage was conceived not as the beginning of a new family but as the continuation of one already in existence. It would follow, then, that there would be much concern over how the family was to be continued. The Hebrew father, as family representative, took an active part in the selection of his son's wife, for it was his son and his son's sons who would continue the family line. We find some writers who go as far as to claim that parental "arrangement" of marriages was a universal custom among the ancient Hebrews and that the feelings of the principals had little to do with the arrangement that was made.

It is certain that the Old Testament is replete with references to parental arrangements of marriages. We find early in Genesis, for example, that the aged Abraham charges his trusted servant with the task of finding a wife for his son Isaac. It is noted, too, that when the servant discovers a suitable girl he does not tell her his full mission. The whole business is discussed, rather, with her brother who, when he is apparently satisfied with the match, simply states: "Behold, Rebekah is before thee, take her, and go, and let her be thy master's son's wife."[29] A generation later Isaac commanded his son Jacob, "(Go) to the house of Bethuel . . . and take thee a wife."[30] We read, again, the simple statement, "And Judah took a wife for Er his firstborn, whose name was Tamar."[31] This same Judah, as we saw earlier, had the power to prevent his son Shelah from marrying Tamar, even though custom required the marriage.

Although there are ample references to parental arrangement of marriage, there are others that indicate that the wishes of the parents were ignored, even in the rather serious case of marriage to a foreigner. We see that Esau, admittedly to the grief of his parents, took two Hittite women as his wives.[32] Samson first asked his parents to get him a certain Philistine woman as a wife and acted against their wishes in the matter.[33] Examples such as these illustrate that parental control over marriages was not an unyielding custom. Formal parental consent, indeed, was not a requisite for a legal marriage. Strong custom, stemming from the importance the Hebrews attached to family line and supported by the respect

[29] Genesis 24:51.
[30] Genesis 28:1-2.
[31] Genesis 38:6.
[32] Genesis 26:34-35.
[33] Judges 14:1-10.

in which Hebrew children held their parents, probably brought about the general adherence of children to parental wishes in marriage matters. The contemporary conception of marriage as a more or less private concern of the couple, who choose one another for their own reasons and establish their own family, would have been completely foreign to the ancient Hebrews.

Formalities for Contracting Marriage

Among the Hebrews there were two distinct phases in the procedure according to which man and woman legally became husband and wife, the betrothal and the nuptials. Betrothal was a formal contract to wed and was actually more important than the wedding ceremony or nuptials. Unlike modern-day engagement, which is a promise to wed or perhaps an announcement of intention to wed, betrothal caused a man and woman to be considered "married" for many purposes. The physical consummation of the marriage, however, did not take place until after the nuptials. Betrothal was thus the ceremony by which one passed from the status of unmarried. According to various Hebrew laws, the important distinction was between the unmarried and the married, the latter almost always including the betrothed. As we will see later, for example, having sexual relations with a betrothed girl was tantamount to adultery.

The betrothal ceremony consisted of a formal declaration of marriage like "Be thou wedded to me," and the payment of the *mohar*, or bride price. Although, as we have seen, the giving of money or gifts to the bride or her relatives is not an actual "purchase" of a wife,[34] the mohar payment was a significant part of the betrothal ceremony. In Genesis we read of Shechem begging for the hand of Dinah and promising to give any gift demanded. Again, the servants of Abraham were sent forth on their mission to secure a wife for Isaac laden with valuables, which they bestowed on Rebekah as well as her brother and mother. Perhaps the most familiar Old Testament story, in this respect, is that of Jacob laboring seven years for the hand of Rachel. When his father-in-law deceived him by giving Leah instead, Jacob served another seven years for the wife he really wanted. Apparently service could be substituted for money or gifts by men of meager means. We gather that during most of the period for which we have records, the value of the mohar was not inordinately great. Its chief significance seems to have been as a symbolic gesture that formalized the contract to wed.

Although in early times there was a clear distinction between the

[34] See pp. 34-35.

betrothal and nuptial ceremonies, it was apparently unnecessary that a stipulated interval of time elapse between the two. Isaac, for example, was officially betrothed to Rebekah when the gifts were given at her home. We read next that the pair immediately traveled to his home where "Isaac brought her into his mother Sarah's tent, and took Rebekah, and she became his wife."[35] In later times, it was stipulated that a year should elapse between the betrothal of a virgin and the wedding, whereas for widows the period was reduced to three months. Since the sixteenth century the betrothal and marriage rites have been performed together as two parts of a single ceremony.

Plural Marriages

Even a superficial acquaintance with the Old Testament makes it perfectly clear that Hebrew men were allowed to have more than one wife at a time. The most important reason for sanctioning polygyny was the strong desire for offspring. It was generally assumed that if children were not forthcoming in marriage it was the woman who was sterile. The man could either divorce his wife or take an additional wife. Since the obtaining of children was the chief issue, polygyny could serve the purpose as well as divorce. The importance of offspring is well illustrated in the case of Abraham and Sarah. In this case it is the childless wife who suggests that something be done about her condition with the words, "I pray thee, go in unto my maid; it may be that I may obtain children by her."[36] It is interesting that Sarah sees this as one way in which she and Abraham can have children. We have a modern parallel to this logic in the cases of a sterile husband consenting to the artificial insemination of his wife in order that "they" might have a child. However, it is probable that Sarah would not have considered the child of her maid and her husband as her own if Abraham had taken Hagar as a full-fledged wife rather than as a concubine.

Concubinage was thus another solution to infertility and was sanctioned for this reason. Whether a man took a woman as a second wife or as a concubine largely depended on the status of the woman in question. Slaves and women captured in war usually became concubines rather than wives, but it was also possible for a wealthy man to purchase for a concubine a poorer member of his own people. The status of a concubine depended partly on how she was acquired. A purchased concubine could be bought back by her family if she proved unsatisfactory, or if her

[35] Genesis 24:67.
[36] Genesis 16:2.

family lacked the means, she even could be sold to another man. But she was generally superior to enemy captives and slaves who were taken as concubines; such concubines were more nearly property than wives. In any case, however, the status of a concubine was definitely inferior to that of a wife.

It should not be assumed that because polygyny and concubinage were allowed, either practice was encouraged for the masses or engaged in by them. The near-equal sex ratio coupled with the Hebrew endogamous restrictions would effectively prohibit the majority of men from having prior claim to more than one woman. The accounts of marriage we read in the Old Testament contain many references to leaders and kings, patriarchs and men of wealth, in short, men who could well afford plural wives or concubines. It is no rash assumption, therefore, to conclude that polygyny and concubinage were mentioned in disproportion to their actual occurrence. Nor should we conclude that a man took another woman *only* when his original wife failed to bear him a child. One need not speculate, for example, on the motives that led Solomon to assemble his harem of seven hundred wives and three hundred concubines. Since Esau, to take another example, married two Hittite women at approximately the same time, it is reasonable to assume that he had no adequate test of the fertility of the earlier wife. It is clear that Jacob took his second wife for love rather than progeny, marrying her but a week after his first matrimonial venture. As fate would have it, it was his first wife who proved the more fertile, bearing six sons and a daughter before his beloved Rachel produced a single heir. As long as plural marriage was allowed, it is not surprising that some would be motivated more by concupiscence or love than by the desire to produce heirs.

Divorce

We have said that in all known societies there is some procedure whereby the married can be released from the terms of their contract. Even at the earliest period for which we have records, the Hebrews allowed divorce. Although divorce existed prior to the time in which Deuteronomy was written, this work gives us the clearest statement of the divorce procedure: "When a man hath taken a wife, and married her, and it come to pass that she find no favor in his eyes, because he hath found some uncleanness in her: then let him write her a bill of divorcement, and give it in her hand, and send her out of his house."[37] In our own society divorce is initiated chiefly by women, but among the Hebrews it was solely the man's

[37] Deuteronomy 24:1.

prerogative to initiate and execute divorce proceedings. We learn from this passage, too, that divorce was a relatively simple, private affair. There were no "hearings," no trial, and in the early times at least, no witness to the act of divorcement was required. The husband himself terminated the marriage when he gave to his wife a simple bill of divorce with words equivalent to "Be thou divorced from me." Later, steps were taken to require witnesses to the bill of divorce, or *Get* as it came to be called, and to prevent the husband from revoking the Get once it was issued. Inability to revoke the Get assured that a remarried woman could not be charged with adultery.

Despite the ease with which a divorce could be obtained, the Hebrews strongly disapproved of divorce. Certainly the earliest Old Testament references to marriage, where we read that man should "cleave unto his wife" and that the pair shall be "one flesh," set forth the ideal of a life-long marriage. Probably the chief reason men first resorted to divorce was the barrenness of their wives. The same strong desire for immortality through heirs that made permissible polygyny, concubinage, and the levirate served to justify divorce. And once divorce was allowed and, in fact, condoned as a remedy for barrenness, it became permissible for other reasons. Adultery on the part of a wife, but not a husband, was probably early considered grounds for divorce. Although the earliest Hebrew law stipulated the death penalty for adultery and the threat of this penalty is frequently proclaimed, we read of no case in the Old Testament where an adulterer was put to death. Some references, moreover, make it plain that divorce was the usual outcome.

Just as polygyny came to serve passions other than the passion for progeny, so divorce became more widespread as grounds other than barrenness were more frequently used by men to discharge their wives. In time, some restrictions were applied to what had come to be the husband's almost unbridled right to divorce. The first restriction denied the right of divorce to a man who unjustly accused his wife of premarital unchastity.[38] If she had been found guilty, she would have suffered death by stoning; if innocent, the husband atoned for his slander by making the marriage forever indissoluble. To a serious charge is attached a serious consequence, but one can only wonder if the wife was not as much recipient of the punishment as her maligning husband. The restrictions further stipulated that a man who was discovered to have seduced an unbetrothed virgin was expected to legalize the affair through marriage.[39] Even in our own times the thought of marriage under similar circumstances has been known to cause

[38] Deuteronomy 22:13-19.
[39] Deuteronomy 22:28-29.

a sudden abatement of passion, and we can imagine that the Hebrew seducer might want to free himself from what could amount to a forced
marriage. But divorce was forever denied to him who according to Hebrew
belief irreparably altered a girl's physiological fitness for marriage.

There were restrictions on the right of a divorced person to remarry.
We are told simply that when a woman receives a bill of divorcement, "she
may go and be another man's wife." In the event the second husband also
divorced her, however, she could not under any circumstances remarry the
first. It has been suggested that this restriction was found necessary to
prevent legally sanctioned "wife-swapping." A restriction needed to prevent
wife-swapping would most assuredly not attest to a high state of sexual
morality among the Hebrews. However, it must be remembered, a breach
of marital fidelity by a woman was an extremely serious matter to the
Hebrew. Thus we read that even if death ends the second marriage a
husband cannot take back his former wife, for "after that she is defiled."
As a woman "defiled" her marriage by adultery, to a lesser extent she did
so by a second marriage subsequent to a divorce. This interpretation of
the restriction seems more plausible than that which sees it as a means to
discourage the exchanging of wives. If a curb on wife-swapping were the
only intention, it would have been unnecessary to rule that a woman could
not remarry her first husband after the death of her second husband. Few
men, we would suppose, would have agreed to a temporary exchange of
wives under the condition that the "re-exchange" take place following the
death of one of them. If we are looking for divorce legislation designed to
curb sexual immorality, a much clearer case can be found in the later
provision of the Mishnah that forbade the marriage of adulterers after
divorce from their respective spouses. We find a similar provision in four of
our states today; when adultery is used as the grounds for the divorce, the
guilty party may never marry the accomplice. The remarriage rights of a
Hebrew woman were further restricted in that she could not marry a
priest. Although statistically this is but a minor limitation on the woman's
remarriage chances, it indicates that the status of a divorcee was somewhat
lower than that of an unmarried woman.

Despite the restrictions on divorce and remarriage after divorce, it is
probable that over the years divorce became increasingly widespread. A
few hundred years before Christ we find the prophets speaking out very
strongly against divorce. Malachi, for example, reminds the people that
the God of Israel was a witness to the covenant between a man and his
wife and urges that no man "deal treacherously against the wife of his
youth."[40] These and other exhortations apparently availed little; by the

---

[40] Malachi 4:15.

time of Christ the divorce rate among the Hebrews was high, and the male had almost unlimited freedom to divorce his spouse. At about this time a strong reactionary movement arose, protesting the ease of divorce and the triviality of the grounds recognized. A controversy developed over the true meaning of the Deuteronomy passage cited earlier, and the dispute came to rest on the inclusiveness of the expression "some uncleanness" which, when discovered in a wife, gave the husband the right to divorce her. To the Shammai school, "uncleanness" meant adultery, and this school held that divorce should be allowed only in cases of adultery. The opposing Hillel school gave a broader interpretation to the passage, holding that almost anything that displeased a husband could be considered grounds for divorce. A fault, regardless how small, or an indiscretion, regardless how frivolous, could be considered "uncleanness" in the sense of a blemish on the character of a wife.

It is not surprising that a strong reactionary force developed in opposition to the conditions of the times. It would seem, nevertheless, that the School of Shammai did not have a strong case for equating "uncleanness" with adultery. Just two chapters prior to the controversial Biblical verse, it is made plain that death is the penalty for adultery: "If a man be found lying with a woman married to an husband, then they shall both of them die."[41] Although this most severe of punishments presumably was seldom meted out, the alternative of divorce is not provided. One could wonder, too, why, if adultery was meant, adultery was not said, for certainly the word or its synonyms appear many times in the Old Testament. The above-quoted verse, for example, states with native simplicity the type of behavior that is condemned. "Uncleanness" is an admittedly obscure expression, but it would be necessary to use some quite general term if flaws of character, personality quirks, and various kinds of inappropriate behavior all were grounds for divorce. Whatever the "correct" interpretation of the disputed passage may be, the less restrictive view was commonly accepted for hundreds of years. Finally, in the eleventh century A.D., a catalogue of specific grounds upon which either husband or wife could sue for divorce was substituted for the unlimited freedom of the husband to divorce his wife.

SEX MORES

From time to time we have had occasion to refer to the sexual behavior of the Hebrews. It remains, now, to bring together in one place their various sexual proscriptions. Such a cataloguing of tabooed sexual

[41] Deuteronomy 22:22.

behavior, together with comments on the punishments stipulated for would-be transgressors of the code, should give us a more complete picture of this aspect of Hebrew life. We will see, too, that the Hebrew code is not without its influence today, for from the Hebrews we have inherited a legacy of custom and taboo, which continues to make itself felt in our definitions of what is sexually permissible and what is not. Over the years we have modified, and continue to modify, our views and to stiffen or lighten the penalties prescribed for offenders, as the Hebrews themselves did. But the basic commands of Moses, together with their early interpretations, are viewed by many as a "final authority" with which should be reconciled current customs, behavior, and legislation.

A word should be said about the general Hebrew attitude toward sex which is manifest in and, in fact, forms the *raison d'être* for the more specific sexual taboos. To the Hebrews, sex was a sacred power to be used primarily as an instrument for fulfilling the command to "increase and multiply and fill the earth." Accordingly, a woman's sexuality was a vehicle for providing her husband with heirs and not a bodily resource for granting pleasure to any man of her choice. To use her sexuality outside of marriage would be a gross misuse of a sacred instrument. In a similar manner, a man's procreative powers had their use and their misuse. Behavior in keeping with the generative function of sex was basically good, and we find practices such as concubinage and polygyny justified on this account. We see, too, in the story of Onan, the fate that befell the man who "wasted his seed." Death is admittedly a severe penalty for the practice of *coitus interruptus*. The story illustrates the seriousness with which the Hebrew conception of the misuse of generative powers was held. In the normal marriage, it is doubtful that it would have occurred to a Hebrew male to practice birth control. Even Onan had a deep respect for his powers of procreation, so much so that he could not contribute his own "seed" to the increase of his brother's "house." Although the sex-for-procreation emphasis had a strong influence on the Hebrew sexual code, it is true, as we will see later, that recognition was given to a more carnal side of the male's nature.

An additional strong influence on the Hebrew sexual code was the extreme emphasis placed on family line. Any practice that would serve to confuse the issue of who was heir to whom would be unthinkable to a people with strong kinship values. It was probably for this reason that the early Hebrews made no allowance for adoption, for adoption precluded even the semi-fiction of biological relationship that we find, for example, in the levirate custom. When it is so important that a man have an heir, when, in fact, his very immortality rests thereon, it becomes important that he have no reasonable doubt of heirship. Nothing could be condoned which could serve to introduce "strange fruit" into a marriage. If the sexual code of the Hebrews, therefore, seems strict and unyielding and the punishments for transgressors severe, we can attribute this severity largely to the related influences of the Hebrew conception of the primary function of sex and their concern with biological kinship. We will see illustrations of these influences as we review the more specific sexual taboos.

Adultery

We have had ample occasion to refer to the Hebrew attitude toward adultery. The command, in this case, was unequivocal: "Thou shalt not commit adultery." The Hebrew definition of adultery included the sexual relations of a married woman with someone other than her husband and the sexual relations of a man with another man's wife. A married man who had intercourse with a single girl was not, however, considered an adulterer. As others have pointed out, a man could not sin against his own marriage but only against that of his fellow man.[42] A wife, whether her paramour be married or single, sinned against her own marriage. In either case the woman chanced the introduction of strange seed into her marriage whereas the man risked only the introduction of his seed into the family of another man.

Although death was the stipulated penalty for adultery, there are several reasons why probably it was rarely exacted. It appears, in the first place, that direct evidence of the offense was necessary. Deuteronomy prefaces the statement for the punishment of adulterers with the phrase, "If a man be found . . . ,"[43] and in the same book we learn that two witnesses, and better three, are required to establish the guilt of a man "in any sin that he sinneth."[44] It would be expected that men and women, particularly with the threat of severe punishment before them, would surround their extramarital affairs with at least a minimum of secrecy. Job himself tells us that "the eye also of the adulterer waiteth for the twilight."[45] Under these circumstances, then, it might be extremely difficult to establish the guilt of a suspected adulterer. Although a wife's pregnancy normally would be assumed to have resulted from marital intercourse, under special circumstances it might well be assumed otherwise and, in this case, witnesses to her adultery probably were not required. At

[42] David R. Mace, Hebrew Marriage (New York, Philosophical Library, 1953), p. 241.
[43] Deuteronomy 22:22.
[44] Deuteronomy 19:15.
[45] Job 24:15.

least this is the inference we can draw from the story of the widow Tamar, whose pregnancy was considered prima facie evidence that she had been "playing the harlot."[46] Indeed, her execution was ordered and presumably would have been carried out had not the prescriber of the punishment found that he was the father.

For the same reason that adultery could not be tolerated, a suspicion of it would prove unbearable to a husband. We read that if a man entertains such a suspicion, and if there are not witnesses, he should bring his wife before the priest.[47] In the course of a solemn ceremony she is then required to drink a potion of holy water that, the priest reminds her, will cause "her belly to swell and thighs to rot" if she is guilty of the charge. In the light of medical knowledge it is difficult to be sure what actually befell the guilty, but, considering the sacredness and awe of the ceremony, it is possible that the potion took on the psychological qualities of a "truth serum" and impassioned on-the-spot confessions established guilt more frequently than did subsequent rotted thighs. The Biblical passage, furthermore, recognizes that a husband may have no real basis for his charge, but merely that "the spirit of jealousy came upon him." But suspicion can play as great marital havoc as can absolute knowledge. Through the rite of the holy water, therefore, the suspicions of the husband were allayed or confirmed, not always, we would suppose, to the satisfaction of the wife.

Fornication

Fornication, or sexual relations among the unmarried, receives far less mention in the Old Testament than adultery. The principal reason for this is the early age for marriage among the Hebrews. Naturally, if girls were married shortly after puberty, the more frequent temptation to sexual irregularity would involve a married girl. Although it does not receive the attention that adultery receives, fornication, especially for the woman, was viewed as a serious transgression. The Hebrews attached a strong value to female virginity, and a woman not a virgin lacked an essential qualification for marriage.

We find that the Hebrews established different punishments for fornication depending on the circumstances under which the act took place and the status of the girl involved.[48] The first category we will refer to is

[46] Genesis 38:24-26.
[47] The "trial of jealousy" ceremony, as it is sometimes called, is described in Numbers 5:12-31.
[48] The various laws on fornication to which we refer in this section are from Deuteronomy 22.

more a matter of adultery than fornication, for it involved intercourse with a betrothed girl. If the act occurred in the city, the penalty was the same as for adultery; both partners were put to death. The woman was considered a willing participant rather than an injured victim, "because she cried not, being in the city." If, however, intercourse occurred "in the field," the girl was given the benefit of the doubt. Whether she wanted to cry for help or actually did so, no one would have heard her. Under these circumstances, the girl went unpunished, and the man alone was put to death.

If, however, a man was discovered to have seduced an unbetrothed virgin, neither received the death penalty. The man was required to marry the girl, to pay her father a stipulated sum, and not to "put her away all his days." The latter stipulation, especially, indicates the serious view taken of sexual relations among the unmarried. A single instance of uncontrollable sexual passion could precipitate an irrevocable marriage. The girl's father, however, could refuse to allow the girl to marry her lover. In this case, the man was nevertheless required to pay him the "price of a virgin." Under most circumstances, the father probably allowed the pair to marry, for the daughter's eventual marriage to some other man would be difficult to arrange. However, if a man had sexual relations with a bond-maid a mild punishment only was meted out to the couple.

The value of female virginity among the Hebrews is illustrated further by the fact that a husband who suspected his wife of premarital unchastity could bring the case to issue and obtain a morbid sort of satisfaction if she was found guilty.[49] Upon the husband's allegation that his wife came to him non-virginal, the girl's parents were expected to prove otherwise by exhibiting the "tokens of her virginity," presumably the nuptial sheet well stained with hymeneal blood. If they could not produce the sanguine evidence of virtue, the girl was brought to the door of her father's house and there stoned to death by the men of the city, among them, very likely, her premarital lover. But if virginity at marriage was established, the husband was forced to give the girl's father a hundred shekels in retribution for seriously defaming the character of his daughter. As the father was required to share in the punishment by witnessing at his doorstep the stoning of an unchaste daughter, so he was given recompense if the serious accusation was proved untrue. One can imagine that some Hebrew parents spent anxious moments on their daughter's wedding day, worried lest the insignia of virtue be not manifest. Since, as we know today, the absence of an intact hymen is not a sure sign of prior intercourse, it was possible that a false accusation could be made and "proved."

[49] *Ibid.*

The various punishments for premarital unchastity point clearly to the fact that the Hebrews took a stern view toward this type of sexual behavior. The reasons for their almost uncompromising position are the same as those that dictated similar views toward adultery. Sexually speaking, a woman belonged to one man, her lawfully wedded husband. Her sexual powers must be reserved until she could use them to provide her husband with children of undisputed origin. Premarital unchastity was thought to portend marital infidelity, a belief that may have had some factual basis.[50]

Sexual Perversions

In all societies there are some types of sexual behavior that are considered "unnatural," as opposed to those merely held to be "wrong." So completely distorted and misdirected are some uses of sex thought to be that an abhorrence of peculiar intensity is felt toward the offense and the offender. Many of our present-day definitions of sexual perversions came down to us from the Hebrews and even our laws and punishments reflect the Hebrew influence.

The Old Testament is fairly specific about what constitutes sexual perversion, and the punishments prescribed for offenders give us some appreciation of the intensity of the Hebrew attitudes. Homosexuality is expressly forbidden and was punishable by death.[51] The well-remembered story of the men of Sodom, whence came our legal term *sodomy*, indicates the strong feelings against homosexuality, for, in modern terms, the entire homosexual community was destroyed as well as the woman who ventured a last look at the city of sin.[52] It is interesting that the Old Testament contains no mention of female homosexuality, although it usually included both sexes in the mention of other perversions. Transvestism, which may or may not be accompanied by homosexuality, was condemned in both men and women, and all who would wear the clothes appropriate to the opposite sex are called "abominations."[53] Bestiality, or sexual intercourse with an animal, was punishable by death, both of the human offender, whether man or woman, and of the animal.[54] It has been suggested that the beast was destroyed to remove all memory of the odious event.

[50] See pp. 275-276.
[51] Leviticus 20:13.
[52] Genesis 19:1-11.
[53] Deuteronomy 22:15.
[54] Leviticus 20:15.

The Double Standard

Probably there has been no greater influence on our own sexual attitudes than the Hebrew "double standard" of sexual morality, so called because one standard was established for the male and a different standard existed for the female.[55] Were it not so cumbersome an expression, "double-double-standard" would be preferred for its accuracy, for in addition to the different standards for men and women, at least two categories of females were defined and each was held to a different behavioral norm. To begin with the double standard, however, it is clear that the sexual code for males was far less stringent than that for females. A married man was not considered an adulterer if he was sufficiently selective to choose an unmarried girl as his sexual partner, but any extramarital sexual behavior was viewed as adulterous for the woman. If a man merely suspected his wife of adultery, he was expected to settle the matter through a prescribed ceremony, but no parallel rite existed whereby a wife could test the fidelity of her husband. While our present-day legal definition of adultery does not differentiate between the sexes, it seems, nevertheless, that an adulterous male generally is thought of less harshly than a female. We find, for example, that a wife frequently is urged by newspaper columnist counselors not merely to forgive her errant husband but actually to reverse the guilt and determine how she failed her husband so that he found it necessary to obtain sexual satisfaction outside his marriage. It is no mere suspicion that parallel advice would seldom be given to the man and less seldom followed.

We have seen that the Hebrews held female virginity in the highest of respect, literally demanding it of a bride. There is no indication that males were expected, let alone demanded, to be virginal at marriage. For the woman there existed no counterpart of the procedure whereby a husband could charge his wife with premarital unchastity with the burden on her to prove otherwise. Since there is a partly accurate test of female virginity, surely it would not have proved too difficult to invent a test of male virginity that would have as scientific a basis as the "rite of the waters" test of a wife's adultery. Either the obviousness of male virtue or lack of concern over it made its verification unnecessary. The latter is the more tenable hypothesis. In our own times, similarly, we find a dual evaluation of virginity accepted by both females and males. Almost all studies indicate that more males than females want to marry virgins.[56] Some

---

[55] See also our discussion of the double standard, pp. 278-281.
[56] See p. 280.

studies have shown that only about one-fourth of the men were willing to marry a non-virgin while three-fourths of the women would do so. Kinsey discovered, in fact, that about a third of the females in his sample would not take a virginal mate![57] Apparently, then, the double standard finds some approval among females and is not the harsh imposition of the stronger sex that it is sometimes made out to be.

For the double standard of sexual morality to be effectively translated into action one of two conditions must prevail. Either general behavior must be at variance with the standards or there must exist a category of sexual partners to whom the standards do not apply. In order for the male to exercise his greater "freedom," there must be a female with whom he can exercise it. Among the Hebrews we find that female slaves were not held to the same standards of perfection as were higher-status women. Intercourse even with a betrothed bond-maid was met with only mild concern. Prostitution existed among the Hebrews, particularly after they settled in villages and cities, and the practitioner was no more reproached than her clients. The case of Tamar was no exception, for her sin in "playing the harlot" was not the act itself but rather that she was thought to be failing in her duty to provide an heir to her deceased husband by a close relative. The prostitute was thus in a separate class from other Hebrew women. Although her status was admittedly inferior, it placed her beyond the ordinary chastity taboos.

In our own society we find the double-double-standard operating to some extent, with a male-female dichotomy of sexual morality and a further dichotomy based on the status of the female. Males, with some frequency, divide their female age-mates into "good girls" and "bad girls," with the occasion, perhaps, defining the better companion.[58] Frequently the division is made on a class basis, and the virtue of socially inferior girls is regarded as legitimate prey whereas that of the girls of the same social rank is respected. Although this behavior toward socially inferior girls has been described as "exploitation" by the male, it would seem more accurate to assume that both male and female have favors they are willing to give in exchange for those of the other. Furthermore, social status is not always the important issue; we find the division made on the basis of ethnic status or neighborhood group.[59] Obviously when outgroup males expect the same sexual availability of ingroup girls that ingroup males expect of outgroup girls, the chastity of the ingroup girls becomes fic-

[57] Alfred C. Kinsey and others, *Sexual Behavior in the Human Female* (Philadelphia, W. B. Saunders Co., 1953), p. 344.

[58] Cf. William Foote Whyte, "A Slum Sex Code," *American Journal of Sociology*, Vol. 49 (July, 1943), pp. 24-31.

[59] *Ibid.*

titious. Nevertheless, both ingroup and outgroup may prefer fiction to reality and exhibit different attitudes and intentions toward their own as opposed to other groups of girls. Furthermore, there is some indication that the double-standard of sexual morality has begun to break down in our society. This breakdown can be caused, of course, either by the increase of the restrictions on the male or by the reduction of them for the female. From all indications we have taken the latter course. But there is much that remains of the incongruous legacy from the Hebrews.

SELECTED READINGS

CROSS, EARLE B., *The Hebrew Family* (Chicago, University of Chicago Press, 1927).

EPSTEIN, LOUIS M., *Marriage Laws in the Bible and the Talmud* (Cambridge, Harvard University Press, 1942).

FELDMAN, W. M., *The Jewish Child: Its History, Folklore, Biology, and Sociology* (London, Baillière, Tindall & Cox, 1917).

GOODMAN, PAUL, *History of the Jews* (New York, E. P. Dutton & Co., Inc., 1953).

HASTINGS, JAMES, ed., *Dictionary of the Bible* (New York, Charles Scribner's Sons, 1909).

KENNETT, R. H., *Ancient Hebrew Social Life and Custom* (London, Oxford University Press, 1933).

MACE, DAVID R., *Hebrew Marriage* (New York, Philosophical Library, 1953).

SOARES, T. G., *The Social Institutions and Ideals of the Bible* (New York, Abingdon Press, 1915).

Talmud (Boston, The Talmud Society, 1918).

THEOPHANE, SISTER M., "Family Customs in the Old Testament," *American Catholic Sociological Review*, Vol. 16 (October, 1955), pp. 198-210.

CHAPTER | 4

The Ancient Roman Family

CONSISTENT WITH our task of investigating the family at different periods, we turn now to a study of the family in ancient Rome. Legend says that Rome was founded in 753 B.C. Although little is known about the earliest period, historians have dealt at some length with the subsequent founding of the Republic, the formation and growth of the great Empire, and the eventual fall of the Roman Empire in the third century A.D.

The Roman family has gone down in history as the most complete patriarchy the world has ever seen, and for this reason alone it warrants scrutiny by the student of the family. During the nearly one thousand years which we can designate as the ancient Roman period, the family in Rome underwent some significant changes. The nature of these changes, coupled with an attempt to account for them in terms of broader societal changes, constitutes still another reason for investigating the Roman family. We have, accordingly, divided our inquiry into two sections, the first dealing with the early period of Roman history until the famous Punic Wars (264 to 202 B.C.), the second dealing with the period beginning after the wars with Carthage and continuing until the third century A.D. This division of Roman history into an "early" and a "later" period does not mean that there occurred abrupt changes in Roman family practices. It allows us, however, to study first the basic form of the ancestral Roman family and then to analyze the modifications which gradually, over a period of several hundred years, took place.

THE FAMILY IN THE EARLY ROMAN PERIOD

Structure and Functions of the Roman Family

Like the ancient Hebrew family, the early Roman family is designated as "patriarchal-extended." The usual Roman household, called *familia*,

64

consisted of a male head, *pater familias*, his wife, all unmarried children, and married sons and their children. But, unlike the Hebrews, the Romans were monogamous, and the method of obtaining heirs by plural wives was not open to them. A *pater familias* without a male heir would adopt a boy or even a grown man, who, in either case, would come under his power and be a member of his household. The adopted male, of course, benefited, for in societies in which the extended family is the rule there is little provision for a person not attached to a family. The Roman *familia* also included slaves, although in the early period slaves were not numerous. A variation of the usual practice would occur when a son was legally "emancipated," in which case he was freed from the authority of his father and was no longer compelled to live in his father's household.

Upon the death of the *pater familias*, each of the adult males who had been under his control received a share of the estate, and each might establish his own household. Although the original household was thus broken up, all households that traced their descent through males to a common male ancestor remained united in a kinship sense. Such household groupings were called *gens*, and over a period of time, of course, the *gens* could become a sizable kinship group. To the *gens* fell the responsibility of providing guardians for minor children of a deceased *pater familias* and the *gens* also took over the property of any of its members who died without an heir. The *gens* was thus no mere catalogue of "relatives," but a large kinship group that had certain recognized functions.

The Roman family constituted an economic, educational, and religious unit. In the early period most families had at least a small farm, and from it they derived not only their food but also the fiber that would be made into household linens and clothes for all of the household members. Since slaves were few, most of the hard physical work necessarily fell to the family members, and apparently the Romans of early times had a deep respect for physical labor. Some tasks, however, were not usually performed in the home, even in early times. Almost from the founding of Rome we learn of craft guilds of dyers, curriers, and metalsmiths. Interestingly enough, there were also laundries where clothes were washed and the new-spun cloth was cleaned and dressed. The Roman family, nevertheless, came close to being a self-sufficient economic unit.

Among the ancient Romans the home was the school, and the child's parents were his teachers. While the children were young, the mother had the most prominent role in the education of both boys and girls. Reverence for the gods, courage, frugality, and self-reliance were some of the lessons of childhood, taught more by example than precept. In the home were kept images and waxen masks of the deceased ancestors, whose lives and brave deeds were retold to the children. In a more formal manner, Roman mothers instructed their children in the basic skills of reading, writing, and arithmetic. The mother continued to be the sole instructor of her daughters, teaching them the usual domestic arts of the times, including the spinning and weaving of cloth.

Just as mothers prepared their daughters to assume the role of mother and wife, so the fathers prepared their sons to take on the role of an adult male in Roman society. From the time a boy was about six or seven years old, he was his father's helper and companion, following, watching, and learning as the father went about his usual tasks in the field or conducted his business in the forum. At an early age the boy was taken by his father to the forum, there to memorize the Laws of the Twelve Tables, which were to be his constant guide in public and private affairs. The father was his son's first military teacher, and it fell to him to make his sons officers of the Republic. When a boy reached sixteen, his father generally permitted him to don the *toga virilis*, or the all-white toga of the man. In a solemn ceremony, the Roman youth discarded the garb of the boy and in this way showed that he had become a man. From this time on, he took a more active part in public life and from this time, too, he was considered sufficiently mature to marry.

Religion among the ancient Romans was a family affair, centering largely about the worship of deceased ancestors.[1] According to the Romans' ancient beliefs, the soul remained with the body after death and from its living descendants demanded propitiation in the form of sacrifices, prayers, and offerings. Deep in the interior of the Roman house was the family altar where the sacred rites were performed and where the sacred fire unceasingly burned. Indeed, the fire itself was sometimes worshipped and given the name of an ancestor-god. Each Roman family thus had its own gods, and the rites and ceremonies used in worship belonged exclusively and secretly to the household. In all religious ceremonies, the father was the high-priest, offering the sacrifices and performing the rituals in the name of the family. The exclusive family rituals, songs, and ceremonies were taught by the father to his sons so that when the father himself was eventually numbered among the ancestral gods the family worship would continue in its prescribed manner. Girls and women had no major part in the family religious services but participated only through their fathers or husbands. In the early days, most girls upon marriage were taken fully into the families of their husbands and accepted those families' gods.

[1] For a discussion of religion among the ancient Romans, see James Hastings, ed., *Encyclopedia of Religion and Ethics*, Vol. V (New York, Charles Scribner's Sons, 1908-1927), pp. 746-749. See also H. L. Rogers and T. L. Harley, *Roman Home Life and Religion* (Oxford, The Clarendon Press, 1923).

Roles and Statuses of Family Members

The Roman family in the early period represented the most complete example of a patriarchal family the world has known.[2] Stemming partly from the father's role as high-priest in the family religion, the *patria potestas*, or authority of the father, was almost unlimited. The father controlled both the person and the property of those under his authority. With regard to his children, the father possessed the *jus vitae necisque*, or power of life and death, and the right of corporal punishment. He could manipulate the person of his child almost at will. At the birth of a child, the father alone was the judge of its legitimacy. He could abandon an infant child or condemn to death a full-grown child. Although he was required to summon a council of his relatives before putting a child to death, the council acted merely in an advisory capacity and the decision remained with the father. The father could sell his children or transfer them to another family by adoption, and, in a similar manner, the father could adopt sons without the consent of his wife. He could arrange marriages for his sons and daughters and secure divorces for them with or without their consent.

Children were not able to hold property separate from their father. Everything that the son acquired became the property of the father. In a reciprocal manner, the *pater familias* was responsible for the misdemeanors of his sons, although he could surrender the offending son in full satisfaction of the damage. Prior to his father's death, there were only three ways in which a son could be released from the authority of his father, by his adoption by another family, by his sale, or by his emancipation, all of which, again, were controlled by the father. Under normal circumstances the sale of a son or adoption by another family were probably not frequent, for too great was the desire for heirs. Emancipation of a son was formalized by a mock sale, ritualistically repeated three times. After the ceremony the son became independent of all authority except the state's. At the same time, the emancipated son lost all legal relationship with his family and could not share in the estate of his father.

Females were even more controlled than males. Girls and women lived out their entire lives under the power of some male. While girls, they were under the *potestas* of their father and upon marriage usually came under that of their husband, or, if the husband was *in potestate*, under

[2] Cf. Herbert N. Couch, "Woman in Early Roman Law," *Harvard Law Review*, Vol. 8 (April, 1894), pp. 40-41. For those aspects of the roles and statuses of family members reflected in the law, see Sir Henry Maine, *Ancient Law* (New York, Henry Holt & Co., Inc., 1894), pp. 123-268.

the control of the husband's father. A male guardian was appointed for the girl who had neither husband nor father. There was no legal provision, furthermore, for the emancipation of daughters. The Public Law of early Rome did not recognize the woman as a legal person. She was ineligible as a witness in court and was unable to make a will. Although she could inherit from her father, if she was unmarried, or from her husband, the inheritance was hers in name only and was controlled by the male under whose power she was. For her misdeeds the woman was answerable to her father or husband. Cato the Censor describes the judicial power the male held over his wife:[3] "The husband is the judge of his wife. If she has committed a fault, he punishes her; if she has drunk wine, he condemns her; if she has been guilty of adultery, he kills her." In still another passage he says:[4] "If you were to catch your wife in adultery, you would kill her with impunity without trial; but if she were to catch you, she would not dare to lay a finger upon you, and indeed she has no right."

It is something of a paradox that the woman of ancient Rome was legally so thoroughly submerged, while at the same time she held a place of high esteem in private and social life.[5] She was not confined to her own quarters within the home, as were the women of ancient Greece. A Roman wife could mingle with her husband's guests, attend banquets and festivals at his side, frequent the public places and theaters. In short, she was quite unrestricted in her social activities. At the time of her marriage, when her husband carried her over the threshold of his home, the wife was accustomed to say: "Where thou art Lord, I am Lady." These were no idle words. Within the home she was truly the mistress, occupying the *atrium*, the most important room of the dwelling. There she planned the household management and attended to the well-respected tasks of spinning and weaving. In wealthier households she managed the slaves, who released her from the more onerous domestic duties.

Marriage Regulations

The various regulations on marriage imposed by the ancient Romans reflect their conception of the purpose of marriage and the family and the nature of the marriage contract. Neither the personal happiness of the couple nor their own inclinations or aspirations were considered essentially relevant to the purpose of marriage. The purpose of marriage was exterior to those so intimately involved in it.[6] In the first place, marriage was simply

[3] Couch, *op. cit.*, p. 46.
[4] *Ibid.*
[5] *Ibid.*, pp. 49-50.
[6] Cf. Guglielmo Ferreo, "Woman and Marriage in Ancient Rome," *Century*, Vol. 82 (May, 1911), pp. 6-7.

considered the proper and normal state for an adult of either sex. It was felt, in addition, to be almost a duty to the state to marry and beget children. Among the aristocracy, marriage was also an instrument for political domination. Through marriage, the aristrocratic families increased in size and maintained and strengthened their position of dominance.

Roman marriage was a purely private act. No state or other official performed the marriage, and no registration of marriage was required. Indeed, there was no prescribed rite that had to be followed in order to enter into a valid marriage. Marriage was a contract between a man and a woman, and the essential ingredient of the contract was their verbal or tacit consent to it. As early as 449 B.C., when the Laws of the Twelve Tables were enacted, we find consent to be the only essential requisite to a valid marriage. There is reason to believe that the private contract nature of marriage existed before this time.[7]

We have seen that in Roman society children of both sexes were under the authority of their fathers. Since daughters and non-emancipated sons were incapable of independent acts, it would not seem that their consent was necessary for a valid marriage. But only in a limited sense was this the case. Consent of the principals was indeed necessary, but it was given for them by the only one who had the authority to do so, usually the father. It is doubtful, however, that a father could force a son or daughter to marry, for all parties would be aware of, and generally would respect, the conception of marriage summed up in the Roman dictum, "Marriage is contracted by consent only."

Another seeming contradiction is that families, through the father, played a major part in the selection of mates for their sons and daughters. Marriages, in the early days, were most frequently arranged between families, and a girl of seven could be betrothed by her father. To account for this contradiction, we must return to the Roman conception of the *purpose* of marriage. Since the purpose of marriage was exterior to the couple and since so much more than a legalized mating of two individuals was involved, parents were necessarily concerned with the spouses taken by their children. Although marriages might well be arranged between the families, for a valid contract the principals had to consent to the arrangement. In view of the patriarchal-authoritarian nature of the Roman family, however, it is probable that not too many children acted contrary to the wishes of their fathers. Nevertheless, the fact that consent was, theoretically at least, the sole requisite for a marriage set the stage for more casual marriages at a later time.

In Roman society there were three classes of persons: the patrician, or

[7] James Bryce, "Marriage and Divorce in Roman and in English Law," *Studies in History and Jurisprudence* (New York, Oxford University Press, 1901), p. 786.

full citizen; the plebeian; and the slave. In early times, a marriage within the class was necessary for a *matrimonium justum,* the recognized form of marriage, which conferred full rights to the husband and children. Only in *matrimonium justum* was it possible, although not necessary, for the wife to come under the power of her husband. Marriage of a patrician to a slave was scarcely considered, and it simply was not possible for a patrician to have a recognized marriage with a freed slave. A marriage between those of unequal social rank was called *matrimonium non justum* and, although legally binding, was not a fully recognized marriage. The offspring of such a marriage were ascribed the status of whichever parent had the lower social rank. In *matrimonium non justum,* furthermore, the wife always remained under the power of her father or guardian.

In 422 B.C. these endogamous rules were modified to the extent of granting the right of intermarriage of patricians and plebeians.[8] Later still the right of intermarriage, or *conubium,* was extended to other groups, including soldiers who took foreign brides. Concerning age regulations, girls could legally marry when they reached twelve years of age, and boys could marry whenever their fathers or guardians allowed them to put on the *toga virilis,* usually at about age sixteen.

For couples who met all the requirements for a valid marriage, the next step was the betrothal ceremony. At this time the amount of the wife's dowry was set. A verbal ritual was exchanged between the man and the father of his bride-to-be. The young man would say, "Do you promise to give your daughter to me to be my wedded wife?", to which the father would reply, "The gods bring luck! I betroth her." The man then gave his fiancée a ring, to be worn on the third finger of her left hand. To the Romans, betrothal was a contract to marry, but the contract was not legally binding. Either party might repudiate the engagement simply by notifying the other, and each was entitled to reclaim any gifts he had bestowed on the other.

Marriage Ceremonies

Although a perfectly valid marriage could be enacted without any ceremony at all, in the early period there existed certain wedding rites which were generally followed.[9] These rites, followed for religious reasons and by virtue of custom and tradition, were peripheral to the validity of the marriage contract. One of their major functions was to provide a

[8] James Donaldson, *Woman: Her Position and Influence in Ancient Greece and Rome and among the Early Christians* (London, Longmans, Green & Co., Inc., 1907), p. 81.

[9] For a brief discussion of the various marriage rites, see Couch, *op. cit.,* pp. 44-45.

means for transferring the wife from the power of her father to that of her husband. If the marriage was contracted *cum mano*, the wife then came under the hand or power of her husband; otherwise she remained under the authority of her father. Marriages, even those contracted with the ceremonial embellishments of the traditional wedding rites, could be contracted with or without *manus*.

It is likely that in the earliest times most marriages were performed *cum mano*. The ancient religion almost required this, for the special household gods could be worshipped only by family members.[10] If a wife was not fully taken into the family of her husband, she could neither share in the usual religious rites nor take part in the family religious festivals. She would be required, furthermore, to return to her father's home for religious worship at certain times. Over the years, religion became an increasingly less important influence, and eventually many of the families completely gave up the worship of their family gods. Marriage *cum mano* thus lost its religious significance. Since it was never essential to the marriage contract that a woman come under the power of her husband, it proved to be a simple matter merely to omit the rite that had usually been performed at the time the marriage was contracted.

Under the kings and during the early years of the Republic, the patrician was almost always married with the ceremony called *confarreatio*. This was a religious rite in which a cake of spelt, a type of wheat, was employed. The name of the ceremony was derived from the Latin term for the grain, *farreus panis*. The *confarreatio* ceremony was conducted in the evening at the home of the groom. In a procession led by torchbearers and flageolet players, the bride-to-be was escorted to her husband's home. If the bride and groom were sufficiently well known, the streets on their route would be gaily decorated and lined with well-wishers, whose shouts of encouragement might well be labeled crude by today's standards. Once at the home of the groom, the bride was carried over the threshold, and it was at this point that she would turn to her husband with the words, "Where thou art Lord, I am Lady." The actual *confarreatio* ceremony then began. In the presence of the *pontifex maximus* (chief of the college of priests or pontiffs) and ten witnesses, who probably were symbolic of the ten guardians of ancient Rome, the bride and groom together would eat the sacred wedding cake. Their hands were next joined, and traditional words repeated. A sheep was sacrificed upon the family altar, and its skin was laid over two seats, upon which the bride and groom seated themselves. This ritual symbolized the unity of the two personalities. A banquet in which all the guests participated followed the ceremony, and

[10] Donaldson, *op. cit.*, p. 106.

after this the bride was led by her attendants to the marriage couch. After the bride was joined by her husband, the attendants remained outside the bridal chamber to sing hymns of marriage; the native simplicity of the words of these songs and the nature of the messages they carried would scarcely make them appropriate at modern-day weddings.

Another form of marriage ceremony, called *coemptio*, was also used by the Romans, probably at first chiefly by plebeians. The preliminaries to the *confarreatio* ceremony, that is, the torch-lit parade and the carrying of the bride over the threshold, could take place before the *coemptio* rite as well. Unlike the religious *confarreatio* service, the *coemptio* rite consisted of a fictitious sale of the bride in the presence of five witnesses, all necessarily Roman citizens above the age of puberty. Usually a single coin was ceremonially placed on a balance to symbolize the transfer of the bride, for a consideration, from the hands of the father to those of the husband.

The third recognized manner whereby a wife could come under the power of her husband was called *usus*. This involved no ceremony at all, merely the continuous cohabitation of a man and a woman for one year. Just as according to Roman law a man would gain control of some movable chattel by the undisturbed possession of it for a year, so he achieved full marital power over his wife under similar circumstances. If the wife, however, absented herself from her husband's house for three consecutive nights out of a year, she thwarted the prospective *usus*. In this early period, marriage by *usus* was largely confined to the plebeian class. The element of consent, essential for a Roman marriage, was in the case of *usus* tacitly assumed of the woman who voluntarily lived with a man for the stipulated period and of the man who permitted her to do so.

Divorce

It is clear that from very early times divorce was allowed among the Romans. The Laws of the Twelve Tables set forth the simple form of words to be used by the man repudiating his wife. "Take thy property to thyself" (*Tuas res tibi habeto*). Although the state was little involved in divorce regulations and procedure, Roman divorce was encumbered by religion and custom.[11] If the marriage had been performed with the religious ceremony *confarreatio*, it could be dissolved only by the corresponding divorce ceremony of *diffareatio*. In this opposite rite, the husband and wife rejected the sacred cake in the presence of a priest and witnesses.

---

[11] The account of Roman divorce that follows is based on Couch, *op. cit.*, pp. 46-47.

Generally, all those present at the wedding were invited to the religious rite for the dissolution of the marriage. In a similar manner, marriage by *coemptio* was dissolved by *remancipatio*. This rite simply amounted to the symbolic resale of the wife to her father or some other male relative. Just as *usus* was the least ceremonious way to be married, so the breaking of such a marriage was simple and direct. The marriage ceased to exist when the husband ordered his wife to leave his house.

In all cases of contemplated divorce, custom required the husband to call together a council of his own and his wife's relatives and explain to them his reason for seeking a divorce.[12] The recognized grounds for divorce were committing adultery, concocting poison, drinking wine, and counterfeiting the household keys. Presumably the council to which the husband brought his divorce petition acted in an advisory capacity only, but the husband would probably be socially rebuked if he did not follow the recommendation of the council. Traditionally Spurius Carrilius Ruga, in 231 B.C., was the first Roman to divorce his wife, and this tradition was accepted by writers just a few generations after Ruga. Historians tend to doubt the story but believe, rather, that he was the first to divorce his wife for other than the customary grounds.[13]

In the early Roman period, divorce was infrequent, was procedurally somewhat complicated, and was frowned upon by custom. Nevertheless, in the Roman conception of divorce were the seeds of a much laxer code. The only essential ingredient for a divorce was the breaking of the marriage contract by the husband using the simple formula contained in the Laws of the Twelve Tables. Just as marriage was a private contract between consenting agents, so divorce was a breaking of the private contract, controlled somewhat by custom and religion but not formalized by the state.

THE FAMILY IN THE LATER ROMAN PERIOD

While there was no sharp break in the cultural history of Rome, there is good reason to select the close of the Punic Wars as the beginning of a new era in Roman family practices and ideals. Both the conditions of the long wars with Carthage and the sequelae of the victory had important effects upon the Roman family. For over thirty years a sizable proportion of the men were away from their homes and engaged in actual fighting. Women had complete responsibility and control of household and estate. For long periods of time they managed the estates and performed other tasks previously thought beyond their capabilities. What is more, women

---

[12] Donaldson, *op. cit.*, p. 109.
[13] Couch, *op. cit.*, p. 47.

were temporarily freed from the authority of husbands and fathers. Although her new responsibilities were temporarily delegated and her new freedom from control was by necessity rather than design, the woman nevertheless demonstrated her capabilities to herself and others and tasted the fruit of independence. These experiences contributed to the change in the status of women that was to follow.

After the Punic Wars, the conquests of Rome became extensive. From the conquered peoples was exacted heavy tribute, and the wealth that came into Rome gradually accumulated in influential families. Wealthy men wished to provide for their daughters as well as their sons and were reluctant to see their daughters pass under the hand of a husband. As long as a marriage was performed with *manus*, the property a wife brought to marriage became her husband's; it is not surprising, therefore, that marriage with *manus* declined. In the upper classes there were many women who came to marriage with some wealth, sometimes with sufficient means to provide for themselves for life. With wealth came influence and importance, for such, as we shall see, were the values of the times. Marriage without *manus* further meant that women were capable of inheriting from their fathers, and, with or without *manus*, husbands could leave large sums to their wives. Unmarried daughters inherited equally with sons. In time there arose a class of women, unmarried or widowed, who were wealthy in their own right and who were under the close supervision of no man. It is true that fathers legally controlled their daughters and that guardians were appointed for the fatherless, but in both instances the duties were interpreted with increasing laxity.

The Punic Wars likewise affected the status of sons and led to a weakening of the *patria potestas*. Prior to this time, sons under the authority of their fathers were incapable of owing property independent of their fathers, with the exception of certain modest savings, called *Peculium*, which sons did not have to contribute to the household account. In the early years of the Empire, the acquisitions soldiers obtained in the course of the wars were removed from control of the father and were considered to be part of a son's permissive property or *Castrense Peculium*.[14] Three hundred years later the privilege of private ownership of property of sons under power was extended to the earnings of those employed by the state (*Quasi-Castrense Peculium*). Thus the early provision for extremely limited ownership by sons under power provided the machinery for the gradual reduction of fathers' control over their sons' property.

Following the Punic Wars, we find also some modification of a father's control over his son's person. Although a father could still expose an infant,

[14] Maine, *op. cit.*, p. 187.

in which case the child was more likely to die than to be found by another, he could no longer deliberately put his son to death. Nor could a father sell any but a young child and then only if he was unable to support him. There was much that remained, of course, of the *patria potestas*, but the extreme rights of fathers were at least tempered. Perhaps even more amazing than any decline of the *patria potestas* was the fact that the ingrained custom remained so much intact despite the fact that many sons, as soldiers, had been away from home for years and had acquired possessions of their own.

The broader social changes in Roman society following the wars with Carthage affected the family every bit as much as the more direct influence of the changing status of women and sons. The unprecedented influx of wealth seemed to breed a desire for more wealth. Money-making came to be a major pursuit, and money itself came to be viewed as the ultimate good, whence were to be derived prestige, power, and respect. Such were the conditions that prompted Juvenal to satirize:[15] "Be it that to Gold the Fiend we have no temples, no altars to the jingling coin, yet Mammon is enthroned supreme God." Despite the absences of "altars to the jingling coin," the attitude toward wealth permeated the entire society and was not without its effects on the family. Mercenary considerations for marriage, childlessness, legacy-hunting, and refusal to marry were some of the direct or indirect results, as we shall see later, of the presence of wealth and more particularly of the societal importance attached to wealth.

Probably little else of Roman life in the era preceding the decline of the Empire has received the attention given to the leisure-time pursuits and the lavish expenditures of the upper classes. Costly banquets with great quantities of food, some rare and imported, were one way of consuming and displaying wealth. Indeed, a certain notoriety was attached to him who had a reputation for overindulgence. Martial tells a youth of his day, "You are not content, Tucca, to *be* a glutton. You long to be *called* and to appear a glutton."[16] Lavish entertainment was wont to accompany the Roman banquet. Lyre and flute playing, recitals, dancing girls, clowns, and mimics indulging in obscenities came to be expected at fashionable dinner parties.[17] The meal was frequently followed by a gambling session, perhaps continuing until daybreak, and large fortunes are reported to have changed hands.

The purchase and maintenance of costly homes and villas were yet

[15] Quoted in Ludwig Friedländer, *Roman Life and Manners under the Early Empire,* Vol. I, 7th ed. (New York, E. P. Dutton & Co., Inc., 1908), p. 213.
[16] Quoted in William S. Davis, *Influence of Wealth in Imperial Rome* (New York, The Macmillan Co., 1910), pp. 175-176.
[17] Friedländer, *op. cit.,* p. 218.

other ways to enjoy and demonstrate affluence. Cicero is reported to have had no less than eight expensive villas in addition to smaller homes along the principal roads, which, as was the custom among the rich, he maintained for convenience when traveling.[18] Something of a contest for bigger and costlier dwellings raged among the elite. Maximus relates (near the end of Tiberius' reign) that a palace with its gardens, walks, libraries, and galleries which extended only over four acres made for decidedly cramped living![19] From the ruins that have been unearthed, we gather that the tales of luxurious baths with their crystal ceilings, marble pillars and statues, and water flowing from silver faucets are no exaggeration. Seneca the philosopher reported that a man would feel like a beggar if his bath did not "sparkle with costly stones." Such were the values of the wealthy men of that time.

Although it has become common to equate wealth with moral decadence and to decry the behavior of the "idle rich," perhaps too little attention has been given to the effect of a wealthy class on the rest of society. In Rome, less gifted emulators of the rich increasingly filled the ranks of debtors and spendthrifts, and, even more important, the example of successful men led to a general acceptance of wealth as the supreme social goal. The attitude toward riches of the impoverished many probably had more to do with the changes in marriage and the family than the ignoble example of the oppulent few. That there was a relationship between wealth and the state of the Roman family, few will deny.

Marriage

We have already referred to the decline of marriage *cum mano* and the lessening appeal of the traditional wedding ceremonies. These changes may be regarded as indications of fundamental changes in the nature and conception of marriage which were reflected also in the motives for marrying, the marriage rate, the permanency of marriage, and the general respect for marriage and its institutional partner, the family.

Gradually the wealth-seeking values of Roman society were reflected in the motives for marriage. It became entirely honorable for a member of the aristocracy to marry a rich woman in order to further his political career or even to fulfill the social obligations attached to his rank. But economic motives for marriage were by no means limited to the political aristocracy. Young women with a substantial dowry, and rich widows, particularly if old or in poor health, were the object of much attention

---

[18] Davis, *op. cit.*, p. 171.
[19] *Ibid.*, pp. 169-170.

by speculative men. Martial relates the courtship of one Gemellus: "He begs, he beseeches, he makes splendid gifts, and yet there is no creature in the world that is uglier than she. Where the charm then?—She has a bad cough."[20] But it must not be concluded that the economic motives for marriage resulted in an entirely one-sided bargain. If the man was socially or politically prominent, by a simple step a rich woman could translate her wealth into prestige. Again, a wealthy widow could gain the convenience of marriage, and little other than reasonable discreteness was expected of her. Without marriage *cum mano* and with women financing the matrimonial venture, it is not surprising that women sometimes became the real heads of the family, ruling their husbands and even openly keeping lovers. "She bought her husband for a million sesterces—that is the price at which he calls her chaste," satirizes Juvenal.[21] The tyranny and infidelity of rich wives received much comment. The man, of course, could divorce his wife, but the exchange of poverty for release was not always considered a wise bargain. Then, too, unless the husband could clearly demonstrate the faults of his wife he would be required, after a divorce, to return her dowry in a lump sum, which often enough he was simply unable to do. Cicero, who at the age of 63 divorced his wife after thirty years of marriage, solved the problem by marrying his wealthy ward.[22] With the fortune of this seventeen-year-old girl, he not only repaid the dowry of his first wife but liquidated his rather large accumulation of debts.

The economic and political motives for marriage reflected the change in the general attitude toward marrying and remaining married. Although we have no precise records, it is clear that there was a general disinclination to marry. With their greater wealth and freedom, women were often enough unable to see any advantage in taking a husband. Men of the upper classes regarded marriage as a burden and an interference with their liberty. They attributed their lack of interest in marriage to the general extravagance of women, their infidelity, and to the difficulty of running a family with two masters. Undoubtedly the morality of the times had much to do with the decline in the marriage rate. Adultery, although officially condemned, was more or less openly practiced. No longer could a man be certain of the origin of his reputed progeny. Pliny the Elder reports that in a single year two consuls bore a striking resemblance to gladiators who performed before them, and Juvenal claims that many an aristocrat's son was in actuality the son of a gladiator or a popular flute player.[23] Husbands were no more virtuous than their wives. Prostitution flourished openly, and

---

[20] Quoted in Davis, *op. cit.*, p. 290.
[21] *Ibid.*, p. 292.
[22] Ferreo, *op. cit.*, p. 10.
[23] Davis, *op. cit.*, p. 300.

since the prostitutes frequently were recruited from the ranks of slaves and former slaves their services were inexpensive and well within the reach of the common man.

Part of the picture of the waning value of marriage was the decreasing desire to have and rear children. In the older days it would have been an intolerable calamity for a man to die childless, for his name and his family religion would thus come to an end. In the days when the ancient religion, with its emphasis on ancestor worship, was strongly imbued in the society, adoption was utilized by the childless to insure that the souls of the deceased family members would not lack for worship or propitiation. In these later times, by contrast, childlessness became an enviable state, and abortion, infanticide, and the abandonment of infants were resorted to when unwanted children were conceived. Abortion was defended on the grounds that the widespread infidelity of wives made paternity uncertain and that it was better to prevent the birth of a child of dubious origin. Infanticide was condoned for the same reason. But adulterous wives alone cannot be held to account for the sharp decline in the birth rate and the sometimes wholesale abandonment of infants. In the city of Rome, for example, it is reported that yearly hundreds of infants were abandoned.[24] Those who withstood the exposure were picked up by unscrupulous venturers to be raised as prostitutes or sold into slavery. All of this points to a basic devaluation of the worth of a child.

Not only were children considered a burden and expense, but remaining childless came to have a positive advantage. It had become common in Rome for the wealthy to remember their friends in their testaments. In view of the pecuniary values of the society, one can imagine that before long friendships were nurtured with one eye on a possible inheritance. Legacy hunting became a systematic art, and the unmarried and childless, of course, made particularly suitable prey. The elderly rich were flattered, waited upon, and bestowed with gifts. Their every whim was satisfied by a hovering group of self-appointed attendants; their idle words were given serious consideration. Such were the conditions that enabled Seneca to comfort a mother who had lost a promising son with the singular reminder that "childlessness gives more power than it takes away."[25] There was always something of a gaming air about the occupation of legacy hunting. Wills would be opened, and the most ardent attendant to the deceased would find that he had not been remembered. It was always possible, of course, that the man might last longer than his money and that years of personal

[24] Willystine Goodsell, A History of Marriage and the Family, rev. ed. (New York, The Macmillan Co., 1934), p. 178.
[25] Friedländer, op. cit., p. 216.

attention by friends would be for naught. Some of the hunted, in turn, were said to reverse the procedure and angle their friends for service, attention, and gifts, with no real intention of rewarding them in their wills. Martial tells of a wealthy man who ten times fell sick and just as many times recovered.[26] Each time his entourage of legacy hunters would give him splendid gifts in mock joy at his recovery. When at last the gentleman succumbed, he left to his friends nothing but the right to weep at his tomb! In the intriguing game of legacy hunting, it is not surprising that wealthy bachelors without close relatives became the favored object of the chase. But it should not be assumed that legacy hunting caused celibacy and childlessness. The lapsing of the ancient religion, the development of pecuniary values fostered by the flow of wealth into Rome, and the changing sexual morality all helped to make children unwanted and unnecessary. The services and attentions of professional legacy hunters gave a positive charm to those without close kin and encouraged celibacy and childlessness once they came into vogue.

Although we have referred to it only indirectly, that enduring marriages were scarcely the mark of this second period of Roman history has probably already become apparent. Just how high the divorce rate reached no one knows, for divorce, like marriage, traditionally was considered a private affair beyond close judiciary supervision. There is no doubt, however, that divorce and remarriage were quite frequent occurrences and that the public attitude toward divorce had changed much over the years. Juvenal, whose remarks must be tempered with allowance for his usual cynicism, talks of a woman who had eight husbands in five years.[27] But others report similarly. Seneca claims that a number of the wealthier women remembered the years not by the names of the consuls but by the names of their husbands. Martial tells of a woman married to her tenth husband. People who had married so often were undoubtedly rare; the mere fact that they elicited enough attention to be recorded suggests that they were not commonplace. The extremes, nevertheless, tell something of the general attitudes toward the permanency of marriage.

To provide an explanation for the high divorce rate and the greater acceptance of divorce, we must again return to the reasons for the marked change in the general attitudes toward marriage and the family. Divorce was but another indication of the more fundamental changes. For the same reasons that men were disinclined to marry, and we need not repeat these reasons, some were prompted to return to the ranks of the unmarried. Paradoxically, some of the same reasons that motivated men to marry in-

[26] Reported in Davis, op. cit., p. 312.
[27] This and the two cases that follow quoted in Donaldson, op. cit., pp. 118-119.

fluenced their subsequent divorce. When economic and similar motives
become important in mate selection, it is but an easy step to forsake one
venture if an even more promising one appears. Women, as we have seen,
were socially more independent than in the past and many could remain
financially independent of any man for much of their lives. If marriage
proved too burdensome, why continue it? Were it not for the general
levity with which marriage was viewed, of course, only the exceptional
couple would define marriage as "too burdensome." It is an important
lesson of history that social problems, almost however defined, can most
adequately be dealt with by attempting to discover and treat the more
fundamental conditions rather than the apparent symptoms. If divorce
is but one indication of the more general levity with which marriage and
the family were viewed, how do we account for the devaluation of marriage and the family? If the wars and their immediate and later effects
contributed to the declining significance of marriage and the family, how,
then, should the society reckon with such effects? Today's sociologist would
continue this line of analysis and would try to isolate basic causative conditions, which, in turn, would suggest alternative ameliorative programs.
But let us see what attempts were made by the Romans to alter the conditions which the people or their leaders defined as undesirable.

Laws Strengthening the Family

Beginning almost with the close of the Punic Wars, various laws were
passed in an attempt to discourage luxurious and extravagant living. While
these measures were aimed at the conditions themselves and were not
designed to strengthen the family, the course of the history of the Roman
family undoubtedly would have been altered had the laws produced their
intended results. As early as 184 B.C. Cato the Censor ordained that jewelry, dresses, carriages, and the like that exceeded a certain value would be
assessed, for tax purposes, at ten times their worth. A few years later the
Les Orchia, which attempted to limit the number of banquet guests a man
could entertain, was enacted. From time to time other laws were passed
to curb what was defined as extravagant living; now the maximum price of
a banquet was set forth, now the amount of food to be served was regulated, now the quantity of fish and meat was limited, now some imported
foods were forbidden altogether. At a later time Julius Caesar directed
guards to seize prohibited meats at the market and limited the use of
litters and the wearing of purple robes and jewels to persons of certain ages
and ranks. His foster son Augustus attempted once again to put an upper
limit on the cost of banquets. As late as A.D. 16 a law was passed which

forbade men to wear silk clothing or gold jewelry except at religious festivals. Still further legislation was to follow. Generally speaking, each new law met with the same lack of success as did its forerunner. It is not that laws never have an effect on human behavior, but that often enough either the folkways and mores prove to be the stronger force or the laws deal with behavior so difficult to detect and control that the laws are practically unenforceable. Both of these conditions apparently were true with regard to the Roman laws that sought to curb expensive personal habits and entertainment.

The long-run ill effects of childlessness, celibacy, and frequent divorce were recognized by at least one Roman lawmaker as early as 131 B.C.[28] Metellus, after observing that ". . . we cannot live comfortably with our wives, or live at all without them . . . ," urged men, in their family and matrimonial life, to consider the welfare and future of the society and not merely their personal, immediate inclinations. No laws were enacted, however, and none were to be passed for over a hundred years. In 18 B.C. Augustus first proposed legislation encouraging marriage and the rearing of children. His proposals were rejected, and it was not until A.D. 3 when they were re-introduced with increased rewards for the married and for parents and with less stringent penalties for the celibate and childless, that they were enacted as laws. Some additions and refinements were made in the following few years by the consuls Papius and Poppaeus.

The *Lex Julia et Papia Poppaea,* the legislation that combined the measures of Augustus and the later consuls, sought to encourage marriage by rewarding the married and penalizing the single. A married candidate for public office was given preference over an unmarried. Unmarried men and women over twenty were subject to special fines and taxes. Later it was ordained that when an unmarried man reached sixty years of age and an unmarried woman fifty they were to be considered celibates for life, regardless of any subsequent marriage. The unmarried, in addition, could not inherit unless they were related to the testator within the sixth degree of kindred. These laws against the unmarried led to certain abuses. There are cases on record, for example, of office seekers who married shortly before taking office and divorced their wives shortly after their appointment. Marriages in name only were sometimes contracted to avoid the legal penalties of celibacy. But presumably the advantages of the unmarried state continued to outweigh the disadvantages, for the population as a whole had no greater propensity to marry after than before the *Lex Julia et Papia Poppaea.*

---

[28] For a brief account of the various legislative measures affecting the family, see Davis, *op. cit.,* pp. 302 ff. See also Donaldson, *op. cit.,* pp. 144 ff.

This same legislation contained measures to persuade the married to have children. A married woman who was childless could receive only one tenth of what was assigned to her in her husband's will. The childless, like the unmarried, could receive a legacy only from those to whom they were related within the sixth degree. A man need have only a single child to escape the penalty of noninheritance, but a free woman was required to have three children and a freedwoman four. Free women with three children and freedwomen with four children, furthermore, were released from the guardianship of their husband or father. Candidates for public office, finally, were given preference according to the number of their children, and the man with children was allowed to hold office at a younger age than the man who was unmarried or childless. Although in individual cases a man seeking office or a woman wanting release from guardianship may have been induced to have children, the laws had practically no effect on the Roman birth rate. Making the laws even more futile, later emperors conferred the "privilege of three children" (*jus trium liberorum*) on those with fewer or with no children at all.[29] In time, almost anyone with some influence at court could obtain the "privilege of three children."

Certain other laws were designed to curb excessive divorce and marital infidelity. Augustus required the party initiating the divorce to serve a written notice of divorce to his mate in the presence of seven witnesses. Divorced persons were obligated to wait eighteen months before marrying again. Although adultery was common enough for Juvenal to comment that "a good wife was rarer than a white crow," the stipulated penalties for adultery were severe. The *Lex Julia de Adulteriis*, enacted under Augustus, compelled a husband to divorce his adulterous wife, and he who failed to do so was guilty of a crime. The guilty woman lost half of her dowry, one third of any other property, and could be banished to an island used for the confinement of state criminals. It is an amazing commentary on the times that Julia, the daughter of the emperor who passed the laws on adultery, was herself guilty of breaking them and died in banishment under the *Lex Julia de Adulteriis*. A man found guilty of adultery lost half of his property, was compelled to return his wife's dowry in full, and was subject to banishment. In spite of these strict laws, however, we learn of a generally permissive attitude toward sexual behavior outside of marriage. Early in history, we are thus given a vivid illustration of the extreme difficulty, if not impossibility, of enforcing laws that run contrary to strong public feelings.

[29] Thomas G. Tucker, *Life in the Roman World of Nero and Saint Paul* (New York, The Macmillan Co., 1910), p. 315.

SELECTED READINGS

BRYCE, JAMES, "Marriage and Divorce in Roman and in English Law," in *Studies in History and Jurisprudence* (New York, Oxford University Press, 1901).

CARCOPINO, JAMES, *Daily Life in Ancient Rome* (New Haven, Yale University Press, 1940).

COUCH, HERBERT N., "Woman in Early Roman Law," *Harvard Law Review*, Vol. 8 (April, 1894), pp. 39-50.

DAVIS, WILLIAM S., *The Influence of Wealth in Imperial Rome* (New York, The Macmillan Co., 1910).

DONALDSON, JAMES, *Woman: Her Position and Influence in Ancient Greece and Rome and among the Early Christians* (London, Longmans, Green & Co., Ltd., 1907).

FERREO, GUGLIELMO, *Ancient Rome and Modern America* (New York, G. P. Putnam's Sons, 1914).

———, "Woman and Marriage in Ancient Rome," *Century*, Vol. 82 (May, 1911), pp. 3-14.

FRIEDLÄNDER, LUDWIG, *Roman Life and Manners under the Early Empire*, 4 vols. (New York, E. P. Dutton & Co., Inc., 1908-1913).

JOHNSTON, HAROLD W., *The Private Life of the Romans* (Chicago, Scott, Foresman & Company, 1903).

LEFFINGWELL, GEORGIA W., *Social and Private Life at Rome in the Time of Plautus and Terrance* (New York, Columbia University Press, 1918).

MAINE, SIR HENRY, *Ancient Law* (New York, Henry Holt & Co., Inc., 1894).

McDANIEL, WALTON B., *Roman Private Life and Its Survivals* (Francestown, N. H., Marshall Jones Company, 1924).

PRESTON, HARRIET W., and DODGE, LOUISE, *Private Life of the Romans* (New York, Leach, Sheinell, and Sondborn, 1894).

ROGERS, H. L., and HARLEY, T. R., *Roman Home Life and Religion* (Oxford, The Clarendon Press, 1923).

SCHUSTER, E. J., *The Wife in Ancient and Modern Times* (London, Williams & Norgate, Ltd., 1911).

TUCKER, THOMAS G., *Life in the Roman World of Nero and Saint Paul* (New York, The Macmillan Co., 1910).

CHAPTER 5

The Family in the Early New England Colonies

THERE ARE, at once, both advantages and difficulties in dealing with the family life of the early New England colonists. Temporally and culturally we are coming "closer to home," with the result that interest should be keen in the mores of our social, or even biological, forefathers. Then too, most Americans have studied the colonial period in some detail and should not find it difficult to see the family institution in its proper perspective, merged with the physical conditions, the way of life, and the happenings of the times. Since later we will investigate the modern American family, our present exploration will serve both as a background and a point of comparison for our discussion of the contemporary family. At times the contrasts between the colonial and present-day family will seem vivid; at times the cultural continuity will be striking; but always in our modern institution we will see the basic form of the colonial family over which have been draped cloaks of many other customs, with a resulting change in outward appearance.

Several difficulties inhere in the study of the family during the colonial period. In the first place we must reckon with our societal attitudes toward this period and the people who lived it. While not seriously wishing to experience the rugged life and hardships of colonial days, we tend to surround the period with an unrealistic aura of virtue and to attribute superhuman qualities of character and body to those who lived it. They who discover evidence incongruent with the cultural myth are expected, like the worthy sons of Noah, to approach with downcast eyes and quietly to cover the nakedness of their forefathers. Those who are able to observe with open eyes and relate what they have observed to their "brethren without" are all too often judged deficient in filial respect.

A further difficulty in our venture is that too many may expect too much by way of an accurate analysis of the family in colonial times. It is true that we are now dealing with a relatively recent period of history, a mere several hundred years ago, and it is equally true that there are histories and biographies, diaries and official documents, all in our own language and pertaining to our own land. Although these records profitably can be perused for insights into family life at the time, we must not expect too much. Information concerning the colonial family frequently is sketchy and impressionistic. We do not have the kind of information, or enough of it, to allow us to make a point-by-point comparative analysis of the family in our own and in colonial times. From the sundry records available we can reconstruct a reasonably accurate picture of the colonial family, but it necessarily will lack specificity and detail.

FAMILY STRUCTURE AND FUNCTIONS

While the colonial family was not the extended type of the Hebrews and Romans, its structure and size differed markedly from the family of today. In addition to the married pair and their unmarried children, the household usually contained unmarried adult relatives or others who were almost forced to attach themselves to some family group. Not only was there little place for a single person without family ties, but it was regarded morally wrong to allow the single to escape the watchful eyes of a settled family. Frequently enough the court would assign a bachelor to a given family household,[1] and even when he was allowed to choose a family, his choice was restricted to a family approved and licensed by the magistrate.[2] Single women most often remained at their parents' home until they married or their services were needed at the home of a married brother or sister. Maiden aunts, not necessarily old in years, became permanent members of not a few families and, forsaking their own chances for marriage, settled down to help raise the children and run the households of their adopted families.

The early colonial family thus included more categories of potential members than the present-day family. In addition, the number of children in a family was sometimes unbelievably large by today's standards. There are recorded cases of twenty-six children by a single mother, and families of from fifteen to twenty children can be found with little difficulty.[3] A document of 1675 claimed that the average family household

[1] Arthur W. Calhoun, A Social History of the American Family, Vol. I (Glendale, California, The Arthur H. Clark Co., 1917), p. 67.
[2] Ray E. Baber, Marriage and the Family, 2nd ed. (New York, McGraw-Hill Book Company, Inc., 1953), p. 27.
[3] C. M. Andrews, Colonial Folkways, Vol. 9 (New Haven, Yale University Press, 1919), p. 87.

consisted of 9.02 persons, almost three times as many as today's household.[4] Although records of the early period are unprecise, and we must not place too much emphasis on extreme instances, there can be no doubt that the colonial families were considerably larger than those of today.

Economic Function

Because of the unique conditions under which it found itself and because of the interpretation of these conditions, the early colonial family took on certain features that distinguished it from its Old World cultural progenitors. In all societies the family performs an economic function,[5] that is to say, through the performance of tasks in and outside of the home the family members are maintained. Societies differ considerably, however, in the degree to which the family constitutes a self-sufficient unit of economic production. At times, almost all of the goods and services required to meet the needs of family members are produced within the family through an age-sex-status division of labor among almost all family members. At other times, economic production is restricted to only one or two family members who go outside the family unit and through their labors in a non-family work group gain the means for maintaining themselves and the other members of the family. In any ultimate sense there is no one best way for the family to satisfy the maintenance needs of its members. The kind of economy, whether pastoral, agricultural, or industrial, and the level of development within these broad types quite obviously affect the extent to which the family can operate as an independent productive unit.

Perhaps the most distinctive feature of the early colonial family was that economically it was an almost self-sufficient group. For a time at least, much of what was needed by the family was produced by its own members. Nearly all food was obtained from the family farm, with only salt, spices, and sugar procured otherwise. But even maple sugar and molasses were often enough produced on the family farm. The building and furnishing of the home, certainly no mean tasks, were also the family's responsibility. Clothes and linen were produced in the family for the family. Fuel for cooking and heat was provided by the family, and candles of tallow or bayberry were made within the home. In time, of course, these family tasks gradually came to be performed outside the home. As late as 1790, however, 95 per cent of the population was classified as rural. For the vast majority of people, the family was at this time still the unit in

[4] Referred to in Willystine Goodsell, A *History of Marriage and the Family*, rev. ed. (New York, The Macmillan Co., 1934), p. 298.
[5] An exception may be found in the modern Israeli kibbutzim. For a discussion of this point see Ch. 8, particularly pp. 172 & 176.

which production took place, even though the degree of their self-sufficiency had been reduced.

The fact that the family in colonial times was an almost complete economic unit had important implications for family life, family customs, and family values. It affected both the propensity to marry and the considerations taken into account in a particular match. Certainly there were few places in the society for the single and unattached. When a man took a wife, he took a "help meet" in the most literal sense, for each partner made a direct contribution in his own sphere to the productive economy of the family. In a similar manner, children were an economic asset. We are told that widows with many children were sought out as marriage partners because of the entourage of willing workers a man thereby obtained at marriage. When later we investigate familial roles, we will see that the economic functions of the colonial family affected to a substantial degree what was expected and demanded of its members.

It has been only a little more than three hundred years since the first important English settlement on this continent. During most of this time, the family has been the major economic unit and the various family members, with little children excepted, have each had his role to play in the productive economy. This tradition continues to affect, indeed sometimes to plague, the modern family, for it is all too frequently asserted that because such conditions *were*, they *should be*. Changes in either the self-sufficiency of families or the emphasis on economically productive roles for family members within the family commonly have been labeled "losses." To be sure, they *are* losses, in the sense that families no longer perform these functions, but it is often suggested that these changes also constitute a moral loss, and that the self-sufficient family with jobs for all was somehow ethically superior to our present-day family. Obviously expressions like "superior" and "better" demand definitions; we need to know for whom the self-sufficient family allegedly was better, for what purposes, and under what conditions, before we can even begin to reckon with the return-to-the-family-of-the-past advocates. However, it is not our purpose at this time to evaluate the institutional success of the modern family but, rather, to point out some of the ramifications of the economic organization of the colonial period. Among these ramifications, certainly, we must number the doubtful legacy of family values we have received from the colonial family.

Educational Function

It is no doubt true that the colonial family functioned more as an educational agency than does the family of today. The family took a significant part in preparing its children to play the roles of adult males and females. The emphasis was on teaching children the practical skills necessary in everyday life, as opposed to more formal academic education. It was no educational philosophy that governed this choice, but the practical necessity of adjusting to the rigors of life in an undeveloped land. Accordingly, boys had to learn how to carry on the work of their fathers in clearing the land, building homes, and farming. The great demands on women in a nearly self-sufficient family meant that girls had to learn to cook and sew, knit and weave, as well as to perform some of the farm chores. Most frequently the industrial training of children took place in their own home, with their parents as their teachers. Very early, however, provision was made for "binding out" orphans and children of poorer families to families of better means. Boys so apprenticed were taught trades or special skills and in return for their training and maintenance worked long hours in the shop or fields of their master. Girls "bound out" to a family were taught how to perform the usual domestic tasks of the day, which, no doubt, they had ample opportunity to practice in their substitute home.

While the early colonists necessarily emphasized practical education, almost from the beginning the need for some formal education outside the home was recognized. As early as 1647, the law of Massachusetts Colony stated that all towns of fifty families should provide a school where children could be taught to read and write.[6] Towns of one hundred or more families were required to furnish a grammar school. These schools were public, that is, open to all, but the students' parents had to bear the expense, and frequently even to furnish the wood to heat the school. Formal education thus existed and, to some extent, was encouraged, but schools were few and poorly attended. Frequently girls were not allowed to attend school or, in some places, went to special classes before and after the usual school day. The majority of children of both sexes received most of their education from their family.

Although there is much that is taught and learned in today's home, the child's major preparation for life's work takes place outside the family. Nor are most parents intimately aware of what is taught their children, how it is taught, or even why it is taught. The modern school system, with its complex bureaucracy, is many steps removed from the village schoolmaster who was personally hired, paid, and fired by the parents of his charges. Perhaps because of the utter infeasibility of the suggestion, scarcely anyone wants to return to the family-centered and family-influenced educational system of colonial days. If pressed on the matter, most would

[6] Cf. Goodsell, op. cit., p. 420.

admit that the family has lost much of its educational function, but almost all would add that this loss is not a loss, but a decided gain. To be sure, there are occasional disputes over whether home or school or church is the rightful sphere for teaching this or that. But no one seriously contends that most of our present generation can adequately be prepared for life without the schools. Few bemoan the passing of the educational function from the family or attempt to demonstrate that the family is disintegrating because it has lost this function. If in other areas we were equally willing to accept change and to evaluate new practices in the light of the new societal conditions, there would be far less talk about the disorganization of the modern American family.

Religious Training in the Home

The role the early colonial family took in the religious training of children scarcely can be discussed without giving some attention to the nature of the dominant religion. Indeed, much of New England colonial life, and particularly family life, was flavored by religious teachings and practices. Puritanism was a composite of theological, social, and ethical ideals. Hard work in and of itself was good, just as idleness was intrinsically evil. Theologically, the doctrines of original sin, infant damnation, predestination, and the belief in a material hell of dire proportions were emphasized. All personal life was to be ordered about these grim realities and lived in strict obedience to the diverse laws of God as interpreted from the Bible.

The colonial family was the center of the religious training of children. At very early ages children learned of their innate baseness, and of death, judgment, and the fiery hereafter that awaited those who persisted in their evil ways. It is impossible to estimate how great were the effects or how many children were affected by the fervent religious teachings in the home. From the pages of Judge Sewall's diary we learn some of the impact on his own eight-year-old daughter:[7]

> When I came in, past 7 at night, my wife met me in the Entry and told me Betty had surprised them. I was surprised with the Abruptness of the Relation. It seems Betty Sewall had given some signs of dejection and sorrow; but a little while after dinner she burst into an amazing cry which caus'd all the family to cry too. Her Mother ask'd the Reason, she gave none; at last said she was afraid she should go to Hell, her Sins were not pardon'd. She was first wounded by my reading a sermon of Mr. Norton's; Text, Ye shall seek me and shall not find me. And these words in the Sermon, Ye shall seek me and die in your

[7] Quoted in Alice Morse Earle, *Child Life in Colonial Days* (New York, The Macmillan Co., 1889), p. 238.

Sins, ran in her Mind and terrified her greatly. And staying at home, she read out of Mr. Cotton Mather—Why hath Satan filled thy Heart? which increased her Fear. Her Mother asked her whether she pray'd. She answered Yes, but fear'd her prayers were not heard, because her sins were not pardoned.

In another section of his diary, the good Judge relates his difficulty in bringing his son Sam to see the "need he had to prepare for Death." The boy seemed unimpressed and spent the instruction period nibbling on an apple. But later, his father relates, "he burst out into a bitter Cry and said he was afraid he should die." We then read how the father comforted his small son with such appropriate scriptural readings as "O death, where is thy sting?" Cotton Mather, the minister whose words so impressed Betty Sewall, tells how he performed his fatherly duty toward his four-year-old daughter:[8]

I took my little daughter Katy into my Study and then I told my child I am to dye Shortly and shee must, when I am Dead, remember Everything I now said unto her. I sett before her the sinful Condition of her Nature, and I charged her to pray in Secret Places every Day. That God for the sake of Jesus Christ would give her a New Heart.

Mather lived on for thirty years, long surviving the little girl whom he so arduously sought to save from perdition.

The impact of Puritan teachings on the bulk of colonial children can be inferred from personal documents such as those quoted above and, perhaps even better, from the books and other materials read to and by children of the times. Old-time alphabet books have been found which began, "With Adam's fall, we sinned all" and continued on with twenty-five more "suitable" little lessons for children. We are told that the most popular and widely read children's books were Joneway's A Token for Children, being an Exact Account of the Conversion, Holy and Exemplary Lives and Joyful Deaths of Several Young Children, and its companion volume, A Token for the Children of New England; or, Some Examples of Children in whom the Fear of God was remarkably Budding before they died.[9] Later we see titles like The Prodigal Daughter; or, The Disobedient Daughter Reclaimed and The Afflicted Parents; or, The Undutiful Child Punished.[10] The last-named child's book tells of a boy who killed his sister for her attempts to persuade him to lead a good life. The reader is taken through the boy's capture, trial, sentencing, and eventual execution. When he is cut down, the boy comes back to life, only to be hanged once more as a double warning to wayward children.

[8] Ibid., p. 236.
[9] Ibid., p. 249.
[10] Ibid., pp. 256-257.

The spirit of Puritanism proved to be hardy, for at about the time of the Revolution we still find children's books filled with the familiar accounts of sinfulness, judgment, and death-bed scenes. In *The History of the Fairchild Family* we learn of the prayer young Lucy was wont to repeat:[11]

My heart is so exceedingly wicked, so vile, so full of sin, that even when I appear to be tolerably good, even then I am sinning. When I am praying, or reading the Bible, or hearing other people read the Bible, even then I sin. When I speak, I sin; when I am silent, I sin.

This same work relates in gruesome and realistic detail how the Fairchild children were taken by their father to view a corpse hung in chains on the gibbet in order, in their father's words, "to show them something which I think they will remember as long as they live, that they may love each other with perfect and heavenly love."[12] The author apparently found it unnecessary to explain how the gruesome object lesson was to enhance in the little Fairchilds the tender sentiment of love.

It is scarcely necessary to note that the family of today no longer instructs its children along the same religious lines as did the colonial family. It is true, too, that the family is less intimately involved in the religious training of their young. Some there undoubtedly are who profess regret at the decline of religious teaching in the home. Many Americans, however, probably are willing to concede that the passing of religious instruction from the family to specialized functionaries is a requisite of our secondary society.

ROLES AND STATUSES OF FAMILY MEMBERS

The Father in the Colonial Family

Among the Puritans, the father was considered the actual and legal head of the family. Ample justification for their belief in the sacredness and naturalness of the partriarchal family organization was found in the basic Mosaic laws. The colonial husband had extensive, but not complete, control over the property and person of his wife and children. Upon marriage, all of the wife's chattels, movable property, earnings, and even personal effects became the husband's property during his lifetime and could be disposed of as he saw fit. If a wife inherited some property, this too was controlled by the husband, who could use any profits from it

[11] *Ibid.,* p. 297.
[12] *Ibid.*

throughout the duration of the marriage. In a reciprocal manner, the law required the husband to support his wife and made him responsible for her debts acquired during or even before marriage. It was generally accepted that if the marriage took place on the king's highway with the wife clothed only in her chemise the husband would not be responsible for her antenuptial debts. Many such "shift marriages" were recorded, and it is said that some women omitted their chemise, the better to demonstrate symbolically that as the husband received no worldly goods, so he was not responsible for previous debts.[13]

The colonial husband's control over his wife's person was not as complete as in the Hebrew and Roman type of patriarchal family. By law and custom in the colonies the husband could exact obedience from his wife. The husband determined the legal residence of the family. In old papers we occasionally find notices of run-away wives who, if found, legally could be forced to return to their husbands. Nowhere in the colonies, however, could a husband put his wife to death, and in most places he was likewise forbidden to lash her, either physically or verbally. Wives with a "shrewish tongue" were punished by the community rather than by their husbands. Throughout New England the ducking-stool was prominently displayed and was used to punish the willful woman who verbally accosted her husband.

The strictest obedience was demanded of colonial children by their parents, especially their father. Here again justification for the child's submission to his father's will was taken from Hebraic law and custom. Several of the colonies had laws that stipulated the death penalty for a disobedient child, and both the content and the phraseology of the laws bear a close resemblance to the appropriate Old Testament passages. Such a law was that of the Ptscataqua Colony which read:[14]

If any child or children above 16 yrs. old of competent understanding, shall curse or smite their natural father or mother, he or they shall be put to death unless it can be sufficiently testified that the parents have been unchristianly negligent of the education of such children. . . . If any man have a rebellious or stubborne son of sufficient years and understanding, viz. 16 years of age or upwards, which shall not obey the voice of his father or the voice of his mother, yt when they have chastened him will not hearken unto them . . . such son shall be put to death, or otherwise severely punished.

There is no record of a rebellious son being put to death, but the existence of such strong laws succinctly summarizes the dominant relationship of parents to children in colonial days.

[13] William B. Weeden, *Economic and Social History of New England, 1620-1789*, Vol. 2 (Boston, Houghton Mifflin Co., 1890), p. 538.
[14] Quoted in Calhoun, *op. cit.*, pp. 120-121.

The Colonial Woman

Although much of the position of colonial women can be inferred from the status of the male, there are two important aspects of the colonial wife's role that deserve further special attention. A married woman was expected to rear children and to care for the family household. But in both of these spheres the actual demands are sometimes difficult for the present generation to imagine. Childbearing and child rearing were extremely difficult matters under the severe and primitive conditions of colonial times. The physical strain of frequent pregnancy and childbearing exacted a heavy toll from the colonial mother. The precise statistics on maternal deaths are unknown for the early colonial period, but there are other types of records which give us an all-too-vivid picture of the price exacted for the peopling of our continent. A tabulation of the graves of youthful mothers, though lacking in precision and completeness, provides an estimate of the maternal death rate.[15] A crude headstone inscribed, "Here lies . . . with her six little children," tells its own story. In a small burying plot near Bath, Maine, there were found the graves of ten women, all but two of whom had died between the ages of twenty-two and thirty.[16] The following excerpt from a man's tribute to his deceased wife is a telling account of the reproductive function of the colonial mother:[17]

She always went through the difficulties of childbearing with a remarkable steadfastness, faith, patience, and decency . . . Indeed she would sometimes say to me that bearing, tending and burying children was hard work, and that she had done a great deal of it for one of her age, (she had six children, whereof she buried four, and died in the 24 year of her age.) yet she would say it was the work she was made for, and what God in his providence had called her to, and she could freely do it all for Him.

Few would disagree that "bearing, tending and burying" children was hard physical work. We can scarcely imagine, however, the cruel psychological price paid by the colonial woman in performing the last of her motherly duties. From the records of her great-grandfather's progeny in the family Bible, Mrs. Earle writes:[18]

He had sixteen children. When the first child was a year and a half old the second child was born. The baby was but four days old when the older child died. Five times did that mother's heart bear a similar cruel loss when she had a baby in her arms; therefore when she had been nine years married she had one living child, and five little graves bore record of her sorrow.

[15] This method was utilized in Frederic L. Paxon, *History of the American Frontier* (Boston, Houghton Mifflin Co., 1924).
[16] Andrews, *loc. cit.*
[17] Calhoun, *op. cit.*, p. 90.
[18] Earle, *op. cit.*, p. 5.

We must not neglect, in our discussion of women's roles, the usual household tasks of colonial wives, for these tasks at once affected and were affected by her childbearing tasks. Large families required a lot of hard physical work. What is more, this work was performed under all the primitiveness of a frontier society. Just the preparation of the daily three meals, using crude pots and pans and an open fire, would seem to be a full-time occupation. But there were cloth to be spun, clothes to be made and patched, and the rustic abode to be kept clean. Always there were some farm chores that fell to the woman. Calhoun cautions that we should not overrate the labor performed by the colonial wife.[19] He reminds us of the indisputable fact that there were several categories of "mother's helpers," that is, older children, maiden aunts, or even neighbor's daughters, who would share in the household responsibilities. The high infant mortality rate, realistically, meant that not all children born would have to be reared. Undoubtedly some of the large families, because of the high maternal death rate, were the product of more than one mother; that meant that the second or third wife would have the assistance of older children. It is well to take all this into account. It is nevertheless no rash conclusion that there were ample hours of hard, physical work for most women in colonial households.

The Child in the Colonial Family

Growing up in early colonial days could most succinctly be described as a curtailment of freedom in a milieu of submission. Child life in colonial times was strongly flavored by the "three R's" of repression, religion, and respect. We have already seen the fate that could befall a disobedient child. The strong Puritan beliefs not only demanded filial respect but fostered a work-for-the-sake-of-work attitude and had much to do with the repression of what today would be labeled normal childhood tendencies.

The concept of original sin was interpreted by the Puritans to mean that a child was innately base and sinful. His "natural" tendencies, therefore, would be toward evil, and only by diligent training and rigid discipline could the "Old Adam" be kept in reasonable submission. Parents, teachers, and other adults were in grim agreement that beating was the best way to curb the sinful inclinations of children. The entry in Judge Sewall's diary on the beating of his son gives some of the religious flavor that accompanied the punishment:[20]

[19] Calhoun, *op. cit.*, pp. 97-98.
[20] Quoted in Earle, *op. cit.*, p. 208.

1692, Nov. 6, Joseph threw a knob of Brass, and hit his sister Betty upon the forehead so as to make it bleed; upon which, and for his playing at Prayer-time, and eating when Return Thanks I whip'd him pretty smartly. When I first went in, call'd by his Grandmother, he sought to shadow and hide himself from me behind the head of the Cradle, which gave me the sorrowful remembrance of Adam's carriage.

In Joseph's attempt to hide from his disciplinarian, his father was thus reminded of Adam, after the fall, cringing before the Lord. No doubt this comparison made it easier for the Judge to perform his fatherly duty, but one can only speculate on the effect it had on the child, who more than likely was made aware of his resemblance to the original sinner.

It is well known that teachers were empowered, and indeed expected, to whip their charges. An early Pilgrim teacher has recorded his views on the requisite first educational step. "Surely," he writes, "there is in all children (though not alike) a stubbernes and stoutnes of minde arising from natural pride which must in the first place be broken and beaten down that so the foundation of their education being layd in humilitie and tractablenes other virtues may in their time be built thereon."[21] This describes with fair accuracy the general attitude toward the nature of children, and how it should be dealt with. Some towns gave commissioners the power to sentence to be whipped those children who behaved "disobediently and disorderly toward their parents, masters, and governours."[22] In church there was the tithing-man who was required to "watch over youths of disorderly carriage, and see they behave themselves comelie, and use such raps and blows as in his discretion meet."[23]

The use and threat of strong disciplinary measures, perhaps needless to say, did not produce a generation of little Puritan saints. Boys proved to be particularly troublesome, and time and again we are given instances of "incorrigible" and "wicked" youths. The following account of the "evil ways" of a small boy was recorded in church by a Connecticut justice of the peace:[24]

A Rude and Ideal Behaver in the meeting hous. Such as Smiling and Larfing and Intiseing others to the Same Evil. Such as Larfing or Smiling or puling the hair of his nayber Benoni Simkins in the time of Publick Worship. Such as throwing Sister Penticost Perkins on the Ice, it being Saboth day, between the meeting hous and his plaes of abode.

Despite this serious indictment, we are not told of the fate that befell this obviously wicked youth. A similar instance was recorded in Massachusetts

[21] Ibid., p. 192.
[22] Ibid., p. 205.
[23] Alice Morse Earle, Home Life in Colonial Days (New York, The Macmillan Co., 1898), p. 372.
[24] Ibid., p. 373.

of a boy who was brought before the magistrate with the charge that in church he "sported and played, and by Indecent gestures and wry faces caused laughter and misbehavior in the beholders."[25]

Of course it was doubly damning for a child to misbehave on the Sabbath. But even in their daily family lives there were restrictions on children that portrayed the familiar "be seen and not heard" attitude. A little etiquette book for children contained the following instructions for children's proper behavior at the table:[26]

Never sit down at the table till asked, and after the blessing. Ask for nothing; tarry till it be offered thee. Speak not. Bite not thy bread but break it. Take salt only with a clean knife. Dip not the meat in the same. Hold not thy knife upright but sloping, and lay it down at right hand of plate with blade on plate. Look not earnestly at any other that is eating. When moderately satisfied leave the table. Sing not, hum not, wriggle not. Spit no where in the room but in the corner . . .

The examples we have cited of colonial measures circumscribing the freedom of expression of children could be increased many fold. Today's generation perhaps would conclude that colonial children were not allowed to be children. In still another sense would this be true, for, by today's standards, the colonial child was grossly overworked. No doubt the struggle for existence under pioneer conditions forced a certain amount of work on all capable hands. The Puritan belief in the sin of idleness provided a spiritual justification for work, with the result that children from an early age were expected to perform relatively arduous labor about the home and farm. As one writer has concluded, being a child was a serious business in colonial days.[27]

COURTSHIP AND MARRIAGE

Exogamous and Endogamous Rules

As in all societies, the New England colonies had certain regulations regarding who may marry whom, and there was a prescribed manner for entering legally into the state of marriage. In view of the Puritan's theological reliance on the Old Testament of the Bible, it is not surprising that the basic exogamous rules of colonial New England resembled the Levitical code. The Puritan's definition of what constituted incest in marriage or sexual relations was quite similar to the law of Moses. Some of the colonial

[25] *Ibid.*
[26] Quoted in Earle, *Child Life in Colonial Days*, p. 215.
[27] Baber, *op. cit.*, p. 43.

exogamous provisions, deriving their spiritual justification from the basic law of Moses, were culturally reinforced by the unique conditions of the times. Such was the provision that a man could not marry his wife's sister. It was not uncommon, it will be recalled, for unmarried women to live in the home of their married brother or sister. Such women, whether sister or sister-in-law, could by no means be viewed by the wife as sexual rivals or possible successors.[28]

The records are exceedingly meager with regard to violations of exogamous restrictions. Although most records do not contain mention of violation of parent-child or brother-sister type of restrictions, it does not mean that such violations never occurred. Later we will have occasion to refer to an instance of a man who married his brother's widow in open defiance of the code. It is likely that there were other violations of the incest restrictions, for in Massachusetts at least the penalty for incest was carefully set forth and included the wearing of a capital *I* by the offender.[29]

It is interesting that the early colonists were so little concerned with endogamous rules. It was not until 1705 that Massachusetts forbade Negro-white marriages, and intermarriage with Indians was allowed legally until 1786.[30] In the early years, of course, there were few Negroes in New England, and those few were socially set apart from the rest of the population. Any history will attest that intermarriage with Indians occurred with some frequency, particularly after contact with them became more friendly and more frequent. Not until frontier conditions had long passed and something of a stable society was in force were the laws against miscegenation enacted.

Parental Consent

Quite generally throughout the New England colonies consent of the girl's father or guardian was a necessary requisite for marriage. Usually a suitor was expected to obtain parental approval before even initiating courtship, and this requirement was written into the laws of the Connecticut and New Haven colonies. The control of parents over the selection of mates was not, however, absolute. In the first place, it was not considered proper for a father to attempt to force his daughter to marry a suitor of his choice; the ultimate decision to marry or not rested with the principals. A father could merely withhold his consent and thereby exercise a sort of veto power over his daughter's choice. A young couple, however, could appeal to the

[28] Calhoun, *op. cit.*, p. 99.
[29] Stuart A. Queen and John B. Adams, *The Family in Various Cultures* (Philadelphia, J. B. Lippincott Company, 1952), p. 245.
[30] *Ibid.*

magistrate if they considered that their parents had been unreasonable in withholding consent. In a new country, with a premium on numbers, unjustifiable discouragement of natural increase was not viewed lightly.

Publication of Banns

After the permission of the girl's father was secured, courtship usually proceeded swiftly. Before marriage, however, it was required that there be an announcement of the intention to marry. Banns were usually read three times at a public meeting, or a notice of intent to marry was posted for two weeks in a public place. It was sometimes possible, however, to avoid the necessity for publication by payment of two guineas for a license.

Marriage Ceremony

The early New England colonists were by and large Puritans, who, it will be recalled, were not in harmony with the Church of England. To the Puritans, marriage was a civil contract rather than a sacrament, and it was early ordained in New England that only civil authorities had the power to perform a marriage. In 1646 the Massachusetts Bay Colony enacted that "no person whatsoever in this jurisdiction, shall joyne any persons together in Marriage, but the Magistrate, or such other as the General Court or Court of Assistants shal Authorize in such place, where no Magistrate is neer."[31] Similar laws were passed in the Plymouth, New Haven, and Connecticut colonies. The marriage ceremony usually took place at the bride's home rather than the church. After the early necessity for frugality had passed, marriages became quite elaborate affairs with feasting, dancing, and drinking extending over a period of two or three days. An entry in an early diary candidly describes the festivities of one wedding: "At noon went to William Jones to drink punch, met several of my friends and got decently drunk. The groom could not be accused of the same fault."[32]

Marriage Registration

Almost all of the colonies made some provision for the official recording of marriages. Frequently a fine was stipulated if the parties to a marriage failed to have the marriage duly registered. Despite the rather

[31] George E. Howard, A History of Matrimonial Institutions, Vol. II (Chicago, University of Chicago Press, 1904), p. 133.

[32] Alice Morse Earle, Colonial Dames and Good Wives (Boston, Houghton Mifflin Co., 1895), p. 201.

rigid marriage laws governing parental consent, publication of banns, the marriage ceremony, and registration, there were those who chose to flout the laws and enter into an illegal marriage. Cases of self-betrothal were frequent enough to prove bothersome to the authorities. A number of such marriages were undoubtedly between Quakers, whose religion provided for a mutual-contract marriage ceremony. But there were others who simply lived as man and wife beyond the pale of the law. The case is recorded, for example, of a New Haven couple who scandalized the community by their open defiance of the law. The issue was resolved somewhat circumspectly when the magistrate met them on the street and engaged them in the following "conversation":[33]

"John Rogers, do you persist in calling this woman, a servant, so much younger than yourself, your wife?" "Yes, I do," retorted John. "And do you, Mary, wish such an old man as this to be your husband?" "Indeed I do," she said. "Then, by the laws of God and this commonwealth," was the disconcerting reply, "I, as magistrate, pronounce you man and wife."

Mate Selection and Courtship

The various marriage laws to which we have referred, defined, in a general way, who could marry whom and set forth the proper procedure for entering into a legal marriage. Within this legal framework, how were mates actually selected? How long was the usual courtship, and how was it conducted? What qualities did the Puritan male look for in his bride and she in him? It would be difficult to answer these queries in terms of present-day society, let alone for the colonial days of several hundred years ago. From diaries, letters, and some public records, however, we are able to piece together something of the more personal side of colonial courtship and marriage.

Few accounts of early New England fail to mention the mercenary element that pervaded colonial courtship. Prospective husbands would haggle and bargain with the girls' fathers over the proposed dowry, and there are cases recorded where, after marriage, a man sued his father-in-law for an agreed-upon dowry that had not been paid in full. The courtships of Judge Sewall, who outlived two wives and experienced some difficulty in finding a suitable third, read more like business than matrimonial ventures. In a letter to Widow Gibbs, who was to become his third wife, he proposes marriage and sets forth the conditions:[34]

[33] Calhoun, op. cit., p. 61.
[34] Goodsell, op. cit., pp. 376-377.

For your children, or some in their behalf, to give Bond to indemnify me from all debts contracted by you before the Marriage; and from all matters respecting the Administration. This, I told you (in a previous letter) I peremptorily insisted upon. I was to secure you Forty pounds per annum during the term of your natural life in case of your Survival.

Perhaps the ultimate in economic considerations for marriage was reached in the case of a certain John Brown who married a widow and then sued the government for his predecessor's back salary, the value of the first husband's escaped slave, and the worth of the horse on which the slave escaped.[35]

Courtships were not expected to be long-drawn-out affairs, but once begun led quickly to an offer of marriage. In some instances, indeed, there could scarcely be said to have been any courtship at all, for the man called at the door of a girl he had never seen, told of his need for a housekeeper, proposed marriage, and published the banns all in the same day.[36] Once parental consent had been obtained, there was little chaperonage of the couple. Young men escorted girls to dances and parties and accompanied them home at the end of the evening.[37]

No account of colonial courtship would be complete without some mention of "bundling." According to this fascinating practice, a young man and woman would spend the evening or perhaps the entire night lying in bed together, without undressing. No doubt there was an economic basis for the custom. In harsh times, needless consumption of fuel was avoided whenever possible. Bundling afforded the couple an opportunity for relatively private, comfortable, and, we trust, not unpleasant courtship. Yet bundling persisted in New England for almost two hundred years, long after it was economically "necessary." Although most historians agree that bundling was more prevalent in the lower classes, it was certainly not unknown among the more well-to-do.

The various practices for restricting the intimacy between bundlers suggest that bundling was not always the "innocent" courtship procedure it is often made out to be. Sometimes a low board or bolster was used to keep the couple discretely separated, and some mothers even took the precaution of tying a daughter's ankles together before she was allowed to bundle.[38] Some historians believe that at no time was bundling particularly conducive to chastity,[39] but Calhoun claims that it was after the men

[35] Earle, *Colonial Dames and Good Wives,* p. 39.
[36] Calhoun, *op. cit.,* p. 52.
[37] Earle, *Colonial Dames and Good Wives,* p. 201.
[38] E. S. Turner, *A History of Courting* (New York, E. P. Dutton & Co., Inc., 1955), p. 126.
[39] This is brought out in Adams' discussion of the custom. See Charles F. Adams, Jr., "Some Phases of Sexual Morality and Church Discipline in Colonial New England," in *The Proceedings of the Massachusetts Historical Society* (Cambridge, Massachusetts, John Wilson and Son, 1891), pp. 504-509.

returned from the French and Indian wars that they "stripped bundling of its innocence."[40] One minister defended the unique practice with the assertion that "bundling has prevailed 160 years in New England, and, I verily believe, with ten times more chastity than sitting on a sofa."[41] Other ministers were equally vociferous in their condemnation of the custom. Bundling was still prevalent in New England in the middle of the eighteenth century but seems to have declined rather rapidly after that time. A New York court, in 1804, settled an alleged seduction case by ruling that since the girl's parents had permitted the couple to bundle they could not legally complain about the consequences which "naturally followed it." Perhaps at a much earlier date the innocence of bundling was assumed, but by this time it was associated with the more carnal types of courtship.

Permanency of Marriage

There is much concern today with "broken homes" and with the effect of this phenomenon on children, the spouses, and even society in general. Although we are not suggesting that Americans should be unconcerned with these problems, it seems to us that there is a current conviction that broken marriages and incomplete families are the recent invention of a morally decadent society. Let us look at such facts as we are able to muster on the permanency of marriage in colonial days.

There are two basic ways for a marriage to be broken, by death and by divorce.[42] It is obvious, of course, that death eventually breaks all marriages not previously severed by divorce. Sooner or later one of the partners dies, and at that time the marriage is broken and the family group no longer complete. A marriage may also be broken prematurely by the early death of one of the spouses. Any chronicle of colonial times is replete with instances of broken families caused by the premature death of one of the spouses. There are many cases of mothers who died in the prime of their life, leaving behind several young children. Colonial life was also hard on males; we are told that in 1698 Boston was full of widows.[43]

In the case of the death of a spouse, remarriage generally was accomplished swiftly. Something of a record for prompt remarriage was probably established by a certain Isaac Winslow who proposed marriage anew on the evening of the day he buried his wife and was married within the

---

[40] Calhoun, *op. cit.*, p. 130.
[41] Baber, *op. cit.*, p. 31.
[42] Separation, either legal or privately arranged, accounts for only a very small proportion of "broken" marriages.
[43] Calhoun, *op. cit.*, p. 70.

week.[44] The first marriage in Plymouth colony, it appears, was between a widower of seven weeks and a woman who had lost her husband less than twelve weeks previously.[45] Occasionally the unkind fates would repeatedly conspire against the same man or woman. We read of Peter Sargent, for example, who had three wives in his lifetime. The second had been twice a widow. The third wife had lost her first husband, survived Sargent, married again, and lost her third husband. Her last husband, incidentally, had lost three previous wives.[46] Although we have no accurate records on the matter, it is certain that broken families, due to the premature death of a husband or wife, were a common phenomenon.

In colonial days divorce was less frequently responsible for broken families than premature death. The Puritans had a fairly liberal attitude toward divorce, but actual cases were not many. In Massachusetts the power to grant divorces was vested in the Court of Assistants, and there are available records of the cases handled by this body during the years 1639-1692, 1739-1760, and 1760-1786.[47] During the earliest period there were thirty-six suits for divorce and four annulment cases. Seventy per cent of the suits were brought by women, a proportion very close to today's. Adultery and desertion were the common complaints, but adultery alone, on the part of the husband, was insufficient cause for divorce. Twenty-three of the divorce and two of the four annulment petitions were granted.

The records are missing for the years 1692-1739. From 1739 to 1760 we find eleven petitions for the dissolution of marriage. Six were brought by the wife. There were granted three full divorces and two separations from bed and board (*a mensa et toro*). During the twenty-seven years of the latest period, 1760 to 1786, there were ninety-six petitioners for divorce and of these seventy-six were granted complete divorce. Fifty-six of the petitioners were women, forty were men. Adultery, the sole complaint in seventeen cases and one of the complaints in fifty-one other cases, was the most common allegation.

The Puritans' relatively liberal attitude toward divorce may, at first, seem out of keeping with their general marriage and sex codes. Conducive, in part, to their attitude toward divorce was the fact that marriage was viewed as a civil contract and not a sacrament. Undoubtedly the Puritans were influenced, too, by the very real difficulty for either a man or a woman to live alone or in an incomplete family. Some writers consider that the

[44] Andrews, *op. cit.*, p. 87.
[45] Calhoun, *op. cit.*, p. 70.
[46] Earle, *Colonial Dames and Good Wives*, p. 32.
[47] The data on divorce are reported in Goodsell, *op. cit.*, p. 393.

number of men who had left their wives in the old country to start life anew in the colonies also was responsible for a liberal divorce policy.[48]

SEX MORES

It is common today to equate "Puritanism" with the most severe sort of sexual repression. Although, as we have seen, Puritan doctrine involved much more than sexual morality, it is true that religious beliefs accounted for their definitions of the purpose of sexual behavior and their absorbing interest in behavior in any way related to sexual morality.

According to Puritan doctrine, the sole purpose of sex was procreation within marriage. All non-marital sexual behavior was condemned with a vigor that before or since scarcely has been matched. What is more, sexual behavior was considered low and base, even within marriage and for procreation. It was considered improper, for example, for a man and wife to have sexual relations on the Sabbath. Some ministers went so far as to refuse baptism to any child born on a Sabbath because of the belief that he was conceived on the same day of the week.[49] Under some conditions, therefore, sexual relations between a husband and wife were so sinful that their child, in accordance with Puritan belief, could be condemned to eternal damnation because of it. It is no wonder that the strenuousness of the Puritan views toward non-marital sexual relations almost defies description.

Apparently much time and effort were spent in guarding against transgressions of the rigid sexual code and in ferreting out guilty parties. Many of the sexual offenses of Puritan times seem trivial today, and we are amazed to learn that not so long ago they were considered serious matters. There is an instance of a certain Captain Dremble who in 1656 sat two hours in the public stocks in punishment for "lewd and unseemly behavior" that consisted in his having kissed his wife "publicquely" on the Sabbath at the doorstep of his home.[50] The captain, it should be added, had just returned from a voyage of three years! In another case, action for slander was taken against the woman who spread the malicious gossip that one Anneke Bogardus lifted her petticoats when crossing the street and exposed her ankles in unseemly fashion.[51] Fortunately for the woman accused of such corrupt behavior, witnesses were produced who swore that Anneke had raised her petticoats no more than was necessary to avoid the mud! Many other examples of the close concern with sexual decency could be

[48] Calhoun, op. cit., p. 149.
[49] Adams, op. cit., p. 494.
[50] Earle, Colonial Dames and Good Wives, pp. 135-136.
[51] Ibid., pp. 90-91.

provided. In the efforts to eliminate sexual stimulation, even the Maypole came under Puritanical attack. An early instance of "banning in Boston" occurred in 1715 when the representatives sought an act to prohibit stage plays which "may have a Tendency to corrupt youth."[52]

The penalties for breaking the stern sexual code were indeed severe. In all of the New England colonies except Rhode Island and Plymouth death was the prescribed punishment for adultery, and there are recorded several cases in which the punishment was exacted. The practice of requiring adulterers to wear a scarlet A became law in Plymouth in 1658. Even before this time, this particular form of public degradation was used. There is recorded the case of a woman who in 1639 was so required to advertise her infidelity with the stipulation that if she ventured forth without her ignominious badge she was to be "burned in the face with a hot iron."[53] Another erring wife was required to stand on display in the Boston market place wearing a sign: "Thus I stand for my adulterous and whorish carriage."[54]

Sexual relations among the unmarried were dealt with less severely than adultery. Fining and whipping were generally prescribed for fornication, and we are told that in Massachusetts "hardly a day went by without some convictions."[55] Interestingly enough, one of the "punishments" for premarital sex relations was the enforced marriage of the couple. The Connecticut Code of Laws of 1650 ordered that ". . . if any man shall commit fornication with any single woman they shall be punished either by enjoining to marriage, or fine, or corporal punishment, or all or any of these, as the Court of Magistrates shall appoint, most agreeable to the word of God."[56] The New Haven records of 1642 contain the entry, "Samuel Hoskings and Elizabeth Cleverley, for their filthy dalliance together, which was confessed by them both, they were both severely whipped."[57] A few days later the pair was back before the court, this time requesting permission to marry. The later entry in the court's records reads:[58]

Samuel Hoskings and Elizabeth Cleverley, being desirous to join together in the state of marriage, and not being able to make proof of their parents' consent, but seeing they both affirm they have the consent of their parents, and with all having entered into contract, sinfully and wickedly defiled each other in filthy dalliance and unclean passages, by which they have made themselves unfit for any other, and for which they have both received public corrections, upon these considerations granted them liberty to marry.

[52] Weeden, *op. cit.*, p. 549.
[53] Howard, *op. cit.*, p. 172.
[54] Calhoun, *op. cit.*, p. 138.
[55] *Ibid.*, p. 136.
[56] Turner, *op. cit.*, p. 74.
[57] *Ibid.*, p. 73.
[58] *Ibid.*, p. 74.

Perhaps this case partly explains the later provision that a couple found guilty of fornication be required, not just allowed, to marry. By their action the pair was judged to have rendered themselves unfit for marriage, but to avoid the possibility of future "sinful dalliance" and its concomitant scandal to the community, it was considered best to get them legally wed.

The punishment most difficult for the contemporary student to comprehend, perhaps, was the public confession often required of those who had committed a sexual transgression. Standing in the broad aisle of the church, the guilty couple would announce their sinfulness to the entire congregation, sparing none of the details of their particular offense. Many such soul-bearing sessions disclosed premarital sexual relations between a man and woman who had later married. The following case, recorded by the pastor of the Braintree church in 1683, is typical of many similar ones on record:[59]

Temperance, the daughter of Brother F . . . , now the wife of John B . . . , having been guilty of the sin of Fornication with him that is now her husband, was called forth in the open Congregation, and presented a paper containing a full acknowledgment of her great sin and wickedness,—publickly bewayled her disobedience to parents, pride, unprofitableness under the means of grace, as the cause that might provoke God to punish her with sin, and warning all to take heed of such sins, begging the church's prayers, that God would humble her, and give a sound repentance, etc. Which confession being read, after some debate, the brethren did generally if not unanimously judge that she ought to be admonished; and accordingly she was solemnly admonished of her great sin, which was spread before her in divers particulars, and charged to search her own heart wayes and to make thorough work in her Repentance, &c. from which she was released by the church vote unanimously on April 11th 1698.

Within the Puritan church itself can be found the compelling force that prompted confessions such as this one. The colonial church, it should be pointed out, was a social as well as a religious organization; much of the social activity in the early days centered about the church. A person excluded from the church, therefore, became a social, as well as a spiritual, outcast. A number of churches in the early colonies, furthermore, refused to baptize an infant conceived before his parents' marriage unless the parents had atoned for the sinful circumstances of his origin by public confession. Typical of the regulations of the times was that of the Groton church:[60]

The Church then voted with regard to Baptizing children of persons newly married, That those parents that have not a child till seven yearly months

---

[59] Adams, *op. cit.*, p. 481.
[60] *Ibid.*, p. 493.

after Marriage are subjects of our Christian Charity, and (if in a judgment of Charity otherwise qualified) shall have the privilege of Baptism for their infants without being questioned as to their Honesty.

Although in "Christian Charity" allowance could be made for premature births, the Puritanical brand of charity apparently knew definite bounds. Parents who refused to acknowledge their sexual transgressions, when proof of it was apparent under the "seven month's rule," signed the spiritual death warrant for their child. With baptism considered essential for salvation, the unrepentant parent thus sentenced his child to all the eternal torments of a Puritan hell.

In view of the stern attitudes toward non-marital sex behavior and the severe punishment that awaited transgressors, it might be assumed that a new level of sexual morality was reached in colonial America. We do not, of course, have any real way of knowing how many violated the sexual code or how frequently they did so. We have only some records of those *discovered* to have broken the law, which all but the naïve will agree is quite a different matter.

The original records of the Groton, Massachusetts, church reveal that of the two hundred persons owning the baptismal covenant between 1761 and 1775, sixty-six had confessed to fornication. In three later years sixteen couples were admitted to full communion; permanently inscribed after the names of nine of them are the letters *C.F.* (confessed fornication). The records of the Braintree, Massachusetts, church also have been examined. Many confessions to fornication are recorded. Most frequently the parties were husband and wife and their confession involved sexual relations with each other before marriage. The small town of Dedham, finally, averaged a public confession to unlawful sexual relations a year for a period of twenty-five years. The records of these few towns are by no means unique but are thought to give a typical picture of New England during the eighteenth century.[61]

Not all of the discovered cases of illicit sex relations involved a couple who ultimately married. There is a case mentioned in the Braintree documents, for example, of a Josiah Owen who married his brother's widow in violation of the Levitical code. Josiah was beseeched by the elders to come to church in order to hear the sermon directed against him and the prayers in his behalf. But Josiah failed to appear on the following Sabbath, and in the records we read that the brethren agreed to his excommunication and voted him to be ". . . an impenitent, scandalous, wicked, incestuous sinner . . ."[62] In another case, an unmarried woman admitted to a church

[61] The cases referred to above, as well as others, can be found in Adams, *op. cit.*, pp. 490 ff., and Calhoun, *op. cit.*, pp. 132 ff.

[62] Adams, *op. cit.*, p. 484.

committee that called upon her that "she had been delivered of two bastard children since she had made confession to the church of the sin of fornication."[63] She refused, however, to come to church and make proper atonement and for this reason was suspended from communion. These isolated cases notwithstanding, it is nevertheless true that most of of the reported sexual irregularities concerned the premarital unchastity of future spouses with each other. One historian has described the sexual morality of the times as "peculiar rather than bad,"[64] for though there evidently was much incontinence there was little promiscuity.

As difficult as it is to uncover the facts on sexual behavior in colonial times, it is still more difficult to explain the so-called "peculiar" conditions. The rigid Puritanical sexual code, the harsh punishment for transgressors, and the open publicity for offenders might be thought to act as deterrents to the tabooed behavior, but we should not dismiss the possibility that the effect was opposite. It is not beyond comprehension that the constant and strong focus on sexual wrongs gave to this type of behavior all the psychological qualities of forbidden fruit and actually increased the behavior it purported to control. Certainly the public confessions were intense emotional experiences for both participants and observers. We can only guess how frequently men and women were drawn into the sin-penitence-salvation cycle because of the high degree of emotional satisfaction attendant on its completion.

It has become common to talk of the "preoccupation with sex" in the modern-day United States, as if it were a unique and recent phenomenon. Apparently our colonial forefathers were also well engrossed in the subject. Although the contemporary emphasis sometimes borders on the hedonistic, the Puritans' had elements of perversity. Who is to say which emphasis is less "natural"?

SELECTED READINGS

ADAMS, CHARLES F., JR., "Some Phases of Sexual Morality and Church Discipline in Colonial New England," in *The Proceedings of the Massachusetts Historical Society* (Cambridge, John Wilson and Son, 1891), pp. 477-516.

ANDREWS, C. M., *Colonial Folkways*, Vol. 9 (New Haven, Yale University Press, 1919).

BRUCE, HENRY A., *Woman in the Making of America* (Boston, Little, Brown & Co., 1912).

CALHOUN, ARTHUR W., *A Social History of the American Family*, Vol. 1 (Glendale, California, The Arthur H. Clark Company, 1917).

[63] *Ibid.*, p. 490.
[64] *Ibid.*, p. 503.

108 THE FAMILY IN TIME AND SPACE

CRAWFORD, MARY C., *Social Life in Old New England* (Boston, Little, Brown & Co., 1914), Chs. 5 and 6.

EARLE, ALICE MORSE, *Child Life in Colonial Days* (New York, The Macmillan Co., 1889).

——, *Colonial Dames and Good Wives* (Boston, Houghton Mifflin Co., 1895).

——, *Home Life in Colonial Days* (New York, The Macmillan Co., 1898).

HOWARD, GEORGE E., *A History of Matrimonial Institutions* (Chicago, University of Chicago Press, 1904), Chs. 12-15.

LAWRENCE, HENRY W., *The Not-Quite Puritans* (Boston, Little, Brown & Co., 1928), Chs. 3-9.

TRUMBULL, JAMES H., ed., *True Blue Laws of Connecticut* (Hartford, American Publishing Company, 1876).

TURNER, E. S., *A History of Courting* (New York, E. P. Dutton & Co., Inc., 1955).

WEEDEN, WILLIAM B., *Economic and Social History of New England, 1620-1789*, Vol. 2 (Boston, Houghton Mifflin Co., 1890).

WHARTON, ANNE H., *Colonial Days and Dames* (Philadelphia, J. P. Lippincott Company, 1895).

CHAPTER 6

The Trobriand Family

WE WILL venture, at this time, into an analysis of marriage and the family in a contemporary preliterate society.[1] While not the simplest group that could be found, the Trobriand Islanders are culturally far removed from modern Western society. There are several distinct advantages in studying the family among our contemporary primitives. Such a study should contribute to our goal of learning to appreciate the society-to-society variation in the institution of the family. It should increase the objectivity of the student of the family. However unusual the family practices among primitives may strike us or however "odd" they may seem, they are found in a functioning society. Frequently it is easier to be objective when we are dealing with a land and a people remote from our own, for we have fewer preconceived ideas about their culture and are less likely already to have evaluated their institutions.

Two competing views of preliterate societies are frequently found among laymen, sometimes even in the same person. There are those who view preliterates as happy-go-lucky children of nature, living in aboriginal bliss in prodigiously endowed tropical lands. The "natives" are inclined to be lazy, perhaps, but they are more or less "free" and "natural" in everything from their work habits to their sexual lives. Coexisting with this somewhat idyllic view of preliterates is the view that stresses their ignorance and baseness. Strange customs are looked upon as inferior, and any practice not usually the topic of conversation at middle-class American dining tables is used as proof of the moral turpitude of non-literate people. It is the "white man's burden" somehow to educate and civilize these

---

[1] Our account of the Trobriand family is based entirely on Bronislaw Malinowski, *The Sexual Life of Savages* (New York, Eugenics Publishing Company, 1929). Page references to the original work are given for major sections of the chapter only.

Although the account is written in the present tense, it should be pointed out that Malinowski's work grew out of his expeditions to the Trobriand Islands between 1914 and 1918. The interested student will want to consult the original account as well as Malinowski's *Argonauts of the Western Pacific* (New York, E. P. Dutton & Co., Inc., 1922).

untutored aborigines in faraway places. The sociologist, of course, can subscribe to neither the "lazy-but-free" nor the "morally depraved" view of people whose culture happens to be different from our own. As scientists we can investigate these cultures and study such institutions as the family in order to further our knowledge and insight concerning human behavior. But we must at all times strive neither to adopt a condescending attitude toward preliterate peoples nor to be beguiled by the seeming simplicity and freedom of their lives.

THE TROBRIAND ISLANDERS

About two hundred miles off the northeast coast of New Guinea lies the Trobriand Archipelago, a group of coral islands surrounding a wide lagoon. The fertile islands are rather densely populated by people of Papus-Melanesian stock. There is a great variety in their physical appearance. Some are tall and have aquiline noses and high foreheads. Skin color ranges from medium to dark brown while hair type varies from straight to frizzy. Their dress is of the slightest. Men wear only a pubic leaf fastened to a narrow belt while women wear short fiber skirts. Both men and women wear earrings and adorn themselves with armlets and necklaces.

Economic activities in the Trobriand Islands center about agriculture and fishing. Yam vines, taro, and sugar cane are planted in small gardens, which are meticulously cared for by their owners. Men of the coastal villages spend much time on fishing trips, and some of the catch is always exchanged, through an intricate system of barter, for vegetables produced in the inland villages. Various arts and crafts are practiced, for there are always fishing canoes to be built, clothing to be made, jewelry and ornaments to be fashioned, homes and storehouses to be constructed, and so on. Perhaps even this simple sketch of Trobriand society whets the intellectual appetite for more knowledge of the people and their family institution. In a number of important respects, as we shall see subsequently, the sex-marriage-family pattern of the Trobrianders is radically different from any we have so far encountered.

FAMILY ORGANIZATION AND ROLES

Kinship and Descent

The Trobriand is a matrilineal society with patrilocal residence requirements.[2] Both of these attributes profoundly affect the sexual lives of the people, their choice of marriage partners, and the roles of family mem-

[2] Bronislaw Malinowski, *The Sexual Life of Savages*, pp. 3 and 6-7.

bers. Since the society is matrilineal all kinship and descent are reckoned solely through the mother. A child is not considered biologically related to his father, for, in native belief, the father has no procreative function. In accordance with the particular application of the matrilineal kinship system in Trobriand society, any hereditary office or social position is passed on exclusively through the mother-line. In a given generation there are some powers and functions, such as those accompanying the role of chief, which are vested in the male. But these, it must be remembered, are always transmitted by the female. Thus when the chief of a village dies it is the son of his sister who becomes the new chief. The old chief received the power of his office because the hereditary position was in his "mother's family," so to speak, and upon his death it is returned to his mother's family to be taken by the son of his mother's daughter. The working of the kinship rules can further be observed at a time of bereavement. The intricate social regulations governing mourning, burial, and food distribution at a time of death stem from the principle that those related in the mother-line form a close kinship group. Those "unrelated" to the deceased man, such as his children, can anoint and bury the corpse with impunity, but these services are tabooed to the dead man's "real kinsmen," that is, his maternal relatives. And in all spheres of tribal life the bond between mother and child is clearly recognized and used as the basis for reckoning kinship and no bond whatsoever is recognized between a child and his father.

Residence Requirements

The requirement that a couple at marriage must live in the man's village influences and sometimes complicates the marriage and family life of the Trobrianders. Since marriage is patrilocal, at time of marriage the woman moves from her village. Because of the kinship system, however, the offspring of this marriage will actually belong to the woman's village. They will live, of course, with their mother in her husband's village but will always be reckoned as belonging to the mother's village. A son, for example, will take his wife and live in his "own," that is his mother's, village. The operation of the matrilineal kinship system and the patrilocal residence requirement will become clearer as we investigate the structure of the Trobriand family and the roles of family members.

The Family Group and Their Roles

The usual Trobriand household consists of the husband and wife and their immature children. There is a well-defined division of labor between the sexes, with regard to the care of the home and family as well as the economic pursuits outside of the home.[3] The woman must prepare and cook the food. Women are completely in charge of the family's water supply. Each morning the women of the village assemble at the water-hole and amid chatting and gossiping clean and fill their water vessels. In general, the heavier tasks and those requiring absence from home belong to the male. Overseas fishing expeditions, trading, canoe building, and the gathering of timber are customarily performed only by men. Both sexes work the gardens, but the more arduous tasks of building fences and cutting the brush are male tasks. The father has a considerable share in the care of young children. He bathes the baby, feeds it mashed vegetables, and will carry it about for hours at a time. He is genuinely fond of children and is a close companion to them while they are young.

As the child grows older, certain changes in his relationship with his father appear. He learns, first of all, that he is not biologically related to his father and that while he and his mother belong to the same clan, the father-husband is an outsider. The child learns that his "real" village is that of his mother, which may be some distance from where he is living. Nevertheless, that is the place where he can lawfully claim citizenship, where he will have property, and where all his true kinsmen are dwelling. Gradually, as the child grows up, his father's authority over him is diminished, and his father's place is taken by the mother's brother. The mother's brother, as a true kinsman, is more responsible for the upbringing of the child than is the child's father. The maternal uncle can demand certain services of his sister's child and can grant or withhold permission to the child in some spheres of his daily life.

One of the most fascinating aspects of Trobriand society is found in the above described role of the father. The natives stoutly maintain that he is unrelated to the children of his wife. Yet there is an important functional role for him in the family. In addition to his economic activities, the husband-father shares in the upbringing of the children and has certain household tasks. It is clear that the role of father is socially rather than biologically derived. He has definite rights and privileges and duties not because he has fathered the children but because he is the husband of the children's mother.

Despite the seeming confusion introduced by the father's lack of kinship to his children, the Trobriand family functions as a closely knit group. The family members will spend their leisure time together, or as a group they will visit with another family. A typical scene at the end of the day is that of the entire family in front of their hut. The mother is perhaps preparing the food, the older children are playing, and the father is caring

[3] *Ibid.*, pp. 19-20 and 25-27.

for the baby. The love and affection of family members for one another, and the ability of the family to operate as a closely knit group, are due to the relationships between members that are socially, rather than biologically, defined.

MARRIAGE REGULATIONS AND MATE SELECTION PRACTICES

Perhaps in no instance does the practice of designating preliterate groups as "simple societies" seem less appropriate than when dealing with their marriage mores. Among the Trobrianders, for example, there are intricate exogamous and endogamous rules governing the selections of mates. When a mate finally has been selected in accordance with these rules, a whole series of prescribed rites are dutifully followed before the marriage of the man and woman is fully accomplished. In Trobriand society, as in other preliterate groups, the various marriage regulations are not found as a written and codified body of law. But custom, the desire to do what is "right," and the fear of group censure for behaving contrary to the mores are all strong motivating forces. With the exception of occasional infractions, the marriage rules are almost always followed, and they are held by the natives as the only right way of acting.

Exogamous Rules

According to Trobriand belief, all humanity is divided into four totemic clans. Totemic nature is a real and pervasive characteristic of an individual roughly analogous, in its immutability and importance, to his sex. A person is born into a certain clan, he can never change clan membership, and even after death his clan identification will remain. Each of the four clans recognized by the Trobrianders is composed of sub-clans which are also important groups. Members of the same sub-clan consider themselves real kinsmen, they live together in the same village or in the same section of a larger village, and they are considered by themselves and others as having the same social rank.

In order of increasing stringency of taboo, marriage is tabooed between members of the same clan, the same sub-clan, and between those who trace descent to a common close ancestor on the mother-line.[4] Intra-clan marriage is considered incest and a serious breach of tribal law. Cases of intra-clan marriage have been recorded, however, and apparently the group does not actively interfere with the transgressors once the marriage has been

[4] *Ibid.*, pp. 82-83 and 455.

contracted. It is considered in distinctly bad taste to refer to the incestuous nature of such a marriage in the presence of the couple or their relatives. It seems, then, that when a breach of clan exogamy occurs it is tacitly ignored to avoid having to punish the offenders. All realize that it is something that should never be done, however, and there are supernatural sanctions which help to keep this type of incest at a minimum. Partners to an intra-clan union are reported to fall ill with a certain "incest disease" unless they avail themselves of the prophylactic magic that will counteract the effect of their moral breach.

Malinowski tells us that marriage within a sub-clan is "impossible."[5] The same could be said of mother-son and brother-sister marriage. Interestingly enough, a man may not marry his daughter, not because she is related to him, for in tribal belief she is not, but because a man's daughter is his wife's closest kinswoman. In a similar manner, a man may not marry his wife's mother or his wife's sister. Although marriage with a daughter, mother-in-law, or sister-in-law is strictly forbidden, and even unthinkable, there is not associated with such relationships the same moral repugnance that is attached to marriage with a close kinsman. The "supreme taboo," as Malinowski terms it, operates with respect to marriage or sexual relations between a man and his sister.

Endogamous Rules

In addition to the exogamous rules governing mate selection, there are regulations defining the group within which a marriage partner should be secured.[6] These endogamous rules are not extremely restrictive. In general, mates should not differ greatly in social rank, and they should be roughly of the same age. Their native villages should be within the same district, an area consisting of some ten to twelve villages. This latter rule is not rigidly enforced except with respect to a district in the northwest corner of the island. The inhabitants of this district are almost completely endogamous because they are defined as inferior by the rest of the Trobrianders, who therefore refuse to marry with them.

Patrilateral Cross-Cousin Marriage

In Trobriand society there is an additional restriction on mate selection that we have not yet considered. This is the custom and strong preference

[5] *Ibid.*, p. 513.
[6] *Ibid.*, pp. 82-83, 458, and 499.

for patrilateral cross-cousin marriage. Let us see what is involved in this practice and explore the functions it serves.

A person's cross-cousin is the child of his mother's brother or the child of his father's sister. In some societies an individual may marry either of his cross-cousins, that is, either the daughter of his paternal aunt or the daughter of his maternal uncle. Such a system is referred to as bilateral cross-cousin marriage. In a very few societies there is unilateral cross-cousin marriage. In this case it is expected that a man marry only the daughter of his father's sister or only the mother's brother's daughter. In the first instance we speak of patrilateral and in the second matrilateral cross-cousin marriage.

Among the Trobrianders, as we have said, there is a strong preference for patrilateral cross-cousin marriage. Such cross-cousins are said to be the best possible mates for one another, and cross-cousins standing in this relationship are almost required to marry one another. It should be made clear that the preferred relationship is only between a man and his father's sister's daughter. Other cousins, whether parallel or cross, are not in the special category of preferred mates.

Preferential unilateral cross-cousin marriage is a rare phenomenon in human societies and deserves explanatory attention. Homans and Schneider have shown a relationship between the type of unilateral cross-cousin marriage practices, that is, whether it is patrilateral or matrilateral, and the system of reckoning descent in the society.[7] In general, marriage to the mother's brother's daughter was found in patrilineal societies and marriage to father's sister's daughter in matrilineal society. This theory is consistent with what is found in the Trobriand Islands. Since descent is reckoned only through females a woman's son cannot marry her brother's daughter, for they are close kinsmen. Since the father and son belong to different clans, others in the father's clan, including his sister and her children, are not closely related to the man's son. But the Trobriand custom of patrilateral cross-cousin marriage is more than a matter of *permitting* certain cousins to marry because they are not unduly closely related. This type of marriage actually is strongly *preferred* and, therefore, must serve some definite, positive functions.

Malinowski sees the explanation for the Trobriand cross-cousin marriage preference as a reconciliation of father-love and the tribal law of matriliny.[8] For purposes of illustration, let us use the village chief and his family. The chief enjoys certain rights and privileges and is a man of

[7] George C. Homans and David M. Schneider, *Marriage, Authority, and Final Causes: A Study of Unilateral Cross-Cousin Marriage* (Glencoe, Illinois, The Free Press, 1955).
[8] Malinowski, *op. cit.*, pp. 95-97.

extraordinary wealth. His rank and title, and all else that goes with chieftainship, will pass at his death to the son of his sister. The reigning man is chief because he is the son of a certain woman and the chieftainship will stay in this woman's family, passed on through the females but acted out by the males. If the chief arranges for his sister's daughter to marry his son, however, the boy will at the same time be marrying the next chief's sister. Brother-in-law to the chief is a very influential and secure position for the boy, for, as we shall see later, men are required to contribute economically to their sisters' households. The present chief's son would thus be closely linked to and largely supported by the next chief. In a similar manner, a father of lesser means can indirectly transmit property to his son by arranging a marriage with the boy's proper cross-cousin. All his adult life the father has contributed substantially to his sister's household, and whatever wealth has accumulated goes from the woman to her daughter. With a patrilateral cross-cousin marriage, the wealth can be enjoyed by the contributor's own son.

The Trobrianders express still another reason for preferring cross-cousin marriage and that is the desire to have a daughter-in-law who is at the same time a real kinswoman.[9] A man in his old age may have to rely on his son and his son's wife. But in the Trobriand kinship system the man and his son belong to different clans and sub-clans and are not actually related. A man and his sister, and thus the sister's daughter, are reckoned as close kin. If a man's daughter-in-law is also his sister's child there is a close kinship tie between them and the man in his old age can expect better treatment from her than from a "stranger."

Although we have merely sketched the operation of preferential cross-cousin marriage and have only stated other restrictive mate selection proscriptions, perhaps enough has been said to show that the selection of a marriage partner in Trobriand society is governed by rather exacting rules. We will turn now to the actual choice of mates, that is, how boys and girls eligible to one another as marriage partners eventually pair off and become man and wife.

Courtship and Marriage

To appreciate fully Trobriand courtship and marriage, we must begin with the sexual lives of young children and follow them through early and late adolescence and finally into marriage. (Sexual behavior will be dealt with in more detail at a later point.) Since sexual activity plays such an

[9] *Ibid.*, p. 103.

important part in the preliminaries to marriage, it is necessary to present a brief sketch of the Trobriand sex life at this point.

In the Trobriand Islands premarital chastity is not considered a virtue and is practically non-existent. From an early age children indulge in sexual play and attempted intercourse, with the approval of their elders.[10] This generally free attitude toward premarital sexual behavior continues into adolescence. At this time, however, young people become more selective in their choice of sexual partners, and the intrigues assume a more enduring character. Sexual intercourse thus ceases to be a type of play and takes on a more serious, and at the same time a more passionate, quality.

The sexual pairing-off during adolescence represents an institutionalized phase of prenuptial life.[11] Since this stage functions as a prelude to marriage and a means of mate selection, it clearly requires societal control. If it were the custom in our society, for example, for marriage to be preceded by a sort of trial sexual life, we would expect to find some rules and regulations governing the practice, some specified place where the pair could sexually cohabit, and so on. Among the Trobrianders there is the institution of the bachelors' house. There are usually several to a couple of dozen bachelors' houses in every village. Each house is generally owned by about four or five late-adolescent boys each of whom has a bunk in the house. When one of these boys is seriously interested in a girl with whom he has already been having sexual intrigue, he invites her to sleep with him in the bachelors' house.

It must be understood that couples sleeping in a bachelors' house are in no way setting up a temporary household. Strict tribal law dictates that the couple must not eat together, and consequently both return to their parents' homes for all meals. In the bachelors' house, furthermore, there is strict decorum and etiquette. There is no exchange of partners, and it is decidedly bad form to watch another couple engaged in love-making. Sleeping together in the bachelors' house, finally, is in no way binding on the couple. They will continue the arrangement only as long as it is mutually agreeable. Sooner or later either the couple will decide to marry or will break off their relationship.

If the couple decide to marry, they are expected to spend many of their daytime hours together in public; this practice serves as a kind of societal notice that they are "settling down" to one another.[12] Even at this stage, however, it is not considered wrong for each of the pair to have sexual relations with some other person, as long as it does not occur too openly or too frequently. One night the boy and girl will not go to the

[10] *Ibid.*, pp. 51-52 ff.
[11] *Ibid.*, pp. 62-75.
[12] *Ibid.*, pp. 84-93.

bachelors' house as usual, but will spend the night together in the boy's parental home. In the morning the girl's parents will bring a small gift of food. The couple then eats together for the first time, and the word is passed that they are married. There follows an elaborate exchange of gifts between the families which continues until the first harvest. After this last gift exchange, the couple will set up its independent household.

The usual marriage rite in Trobriand society is thus a quite simple one, consisting of the girl remaining overnight with the boy in his parents' home, the girl's parents indicating their consent by the initial gift of food, and the couple sharing a meal at the boy's home. Although the rite is simple, it serves to announce to the community that the two are wed and has a binding force on the principals.

There is another way of arranging marriages in Trobriand society in which particularly the preliminary stage differs from the usual custom. In the case of cross-cousins only, Trobrianders practice infant betrothal.[13] During the children's infancy or early childhood, their parents agree that the cousins will marry one another, and the children grow up in full realization of this relationship. The betrothed pair is expected to lead a sexually restricted life. Although no one anticipates that they will remain prenuptially chaste, a certain amount of discretion is demanded. The girl, for example, is not supposed to sleep with her betrothed or anyone else in the bachelors' house, and the boy is not expected to have an open and lasting sexual relationship with a girl other than his future wife. Unfaithfulness between the betrothed can and does occur, but as long as reasonable secrecy is observed there is no scandal and no censure from the group. Cross-cousins betrothed in infancy, therefore, have limited sexual experience before marriage, and they do not have the opportunity for prolonged sexual liaisons. When cross-cousins reach marriageable age, they must go through the usual marriage rite, that is, they must sleep together in the boy's home and share a meal there. The ordinary exchange of gifts between the two families at the time of marriage is reduced, because part of the exchange took place when the pair were promised to one another as infants.

Those imbued with a culture that fosters the ideal of premarital chastity and defines marriage as the ultimate in sex fulfillment may find it difficult to understand the motives for marriage in a society like that of the Trobriand Islands. In the Trobriand Islands, as we have seen, after a generally unrestricted sexual life a couple falls in love and thenceforth restrict their sexual relations to one another. Their premarital sexual lives meet with complete approval of their parents and other adults. There is

[13] *Ibid.*, pp. 94 ff.

even an institutionalized arrangement, the bachelors' house and the rules governing its use, where the unmarried couples can conduct their affairs with a modicum of privacy and convenience. Adultery, furthermore, is severely frowned upon among the Trobrianders with the result that marriage, instead of granting new sexual freedom, actually curtails the sexual experience of Trobriand youths. What, then, induces the young people to marry? Why do not some or even all of them choose to remain single, maintaining an exclusive sexual relationship as long as it is mutually agreeable and going on to another if perchance they fall out of love?[14]

We have already noted that Trobriand men have a strong affection for their children and spend a great deal of time with them. The only way to fulfill the desire for children, which is strong in both men and women, is through marriage. It is considered morally wrong and quite reprehensible for an unmarried girl to have a child. Even if a child were born to an unmarried girl, which happens rarely despite the extensive sexual activity, the male would still be thwarted in his desire for fatherhood, for no man would suspect that he had anything to do with the girl's pregnancy. The only way to achieve fatherhood, according to Trobriand belief, is to marry and wait until one's wife, operating with biological independence, presents him with an heir.

Another motive for marriage is the urge of the Trobriander to establish his own household. Merely sleeping together is not enough. Couples truly in love want to live their lives together, sharing their meals, cooperating in household tasks, and enjoying the more extensive companionship that only marriage affords. From the male's standpoint, there is a distinct economic advantage in marriage. All males, as we have already noted, contribute to the support of their married sister's household so that the single man is contributing economically to a family without in turn having a family that is supported by someone else. The Trobriander has the final inducement of conforming to group expectations. This inducement operates in a circular fashion. Since most people desire to marry and do so, marriage becomes the accepted way of adult life, and once it is so accepted it serves as an added impetus to marry.

There are important lessons to be learned from the Trobriand incentives for marriage. It is obvious that not all peoples of the world look upon marriage as the culmination of a romantic love affair in a legitimate and exclusive sex relationship. In the Trobriand Islands love affairs among the unmarried are frequent and passionate, and it is usual for them to involve sexual intercourse. Yet young people do marry. It is clear that a man's culture can teach him to expect and to need certain satisfactions that are

14 *Ibid.*, pp. 78-82.

found in that society only in marriage. In Trobriand society these satisfactions happen to be the pleasures of child rearing, the full companionship with a member of the other sex, and the maintenance of one's own household. Clearly sexual privilege is not a strong motive for marriage. The Trobriand youth gives up a life of relative freedom, sexually and otherwise, to embark on one of greater responsibility. He does this because he has learned that the normal adult role includes marriage and that there are even greater satisfactions in this role than in his previous one. Personal attraction between the mates is part of the picture, of course, but it is not the major consideration in marriage. If it were possible to obtain completely honest answers about the matter, we might find that in our own society the wish to conform to group standards, to live as most adults live, is a stronger motivating force for marriage than is realized. Undoubtedly the desire to be married is often confused with the desire to marry a certain person.

THE CHILDBEARING FUNCTION OF THE TROBRIAND FAMILY

An extremely fascinating area of Trobriand culture is the whole pattern of beliefs and behaviors concerning childbirth.[15] Their beliefs pertaining to the mechanism of reproduction are most assuredly unique. We have already hinted at these beliefs with our remarks that the father is not considered biologically related to his offspring and the observation that unmarried Trobriand girls, although engaging in sexual intercourse, do not as a rule conceive. The pregnancy rites in Trobriand society are equally interesting.[16] The preparation for a baby is no less complicated than, although admittedly different from, the pregnancy rites of modern American society, more frequently termed prenatal care.

The Mechanism of Reproduction

In Trobriand belief, paradoxically, life begins with death. When a Trobriander dies his spirit leaves the body and is removed to Tuma, the Island of the Dead. All is happiness in Tuma, and through a process of perpetual rejuvenation, the spirits live as youthful adults. But by and by a spirit may wish to return to life, that is, to the Trobriand Islands. To do this it must first accelerate the process of rejuvenation and become a spirit-child. Then it casts itself off the Island of the Dead to become an

15 Ibid., pp. 164-203.
16Ibid., pp. 211-232.

unborn infant in the Trobriand Islands. In this it is helped by an adult spirit, called a *baloma*, who is generally a relative of a Trobriand mother-to-be.

When the baloma sees a spirit-child floating on a drift log or debris, she may notice that it is good-looking and that it belongs to the same clan and sub-clan as one of her relatives in the Trobriands. At night, while the woman is sleeping, the baloma will place the spirit-child on the head of the mother-to-be. Blood from the woman's abdomen immediately rushes to her head, and as it descends again the spirit-child is carried on the sanguinal tide to the womb. The same blood builds up and nourishes the body of the spirit-child. That is why, according to native physiology, when a woman is pregnant her menstrual flow ceases. When a Trobriand woman notices that her menses no longer "ebb and flow with the moon," she realizes that the blood has been otherwise utilized and that a thoughtful baloma has brought her a child.

The essentials of the foregoing account of the mechanism of reproduction are known and believed by all Trobrianders. There are occasional, less authoritative, variations. A few hold that conception takes place through the vagina rather than the head. This version still involves the baloma and the spirit-child, and it is only the avenue of entry that differs from the more commonly held account. In still another version more spontaneity is attributed to the spirit-child, who is said to seek out its relative and enter her body without the assistance of a baloma. Basically, a woman becomes pregnant when a spirit, who had a former existence in the Trobriand Islands, somehow enters her body. In this belief there is complete concurrence.

The Trobriand conception of reincarnation, it should be noted, is strictly an impersonal one. They do not claim to know who in some previous existence had the spirit now used by themselves. The spirit is the life-giving substance and as such animates first one body and after its death another. All that is known about the spirit is that it has always belonged to one's own clan.

The male is conspicuously absent in the Trobriand account of reproduction. He is not considered essential for conception to take place, and the natives see no causal link between sexual intercourse and pregnancy. The Trobrianders have come into contact with "foreigners" and are well aware that "missionary talk" states that conception is caused by sexual intercourse and that the male, therefore, has a definite causative role in reproduction. They consider this "theory" completely unreasonable and have forceful, if not always logical, arguments to demonstrate its utter absurdity.

One of the strongest arguments used to discount the "missionary talk" concerning physiological paternity is the observation that although unmarried girls have extensive sexual experience they rarely, if ever, become pregnant. If sexual intercourse causes pregnancy, it is argued, why do not these girls become pregnant? The natives point out that night after night, over a period of years, the unmarried girls have sexual intercourse. It is an observable fact, moreover, that premarital pregnancy is a rare phenomenon. Just why this is so we will investigate later. In this simple observation of the lack of a relationship between sexual intercourse and conception among the unmarried, the Trobrianders have a strong argument for their own views and one which is difficult to ignore.

The Trobrianders define some women as completely unsuitable as sexual or marriage partners. In this category would fall albinos and those who are hideously deformed or diseased. No one, it is asserted, would even consider having intercourse with such a woman. Yet there have been a few cases where women of this kind have conceived and borne a child. Surely this demonstrates that pregnancy is unrelated to sexual intercourse! At least one Trobriand male knows full well that someone has been having intercourse with the albino or deformed woman. In view of the taboo against it, he is understandably disinclined to make his relationship known to his fellow men. And so the Trobrianders have another forceful argument favoring their supernatural explanation of pregnancy.

When we observe the Trobrianders in their everyday life, it becomes clear that they are firm in their repudiation of physiological paternity. There are several instances, for example, in which a husband had been absent from home for well over a year and upon his return found a newborn baby in his home. Instead of accusing their wives of adultery, a serious offense in the islands, these men were genuinely pleased that the spirit-gods had visited in their absence. One of the husbands involved in such a situation offered it as positive proof that sexual relations had nothing whatsoever to do with childbearing!

Among the Trobrianders there is a strong taboo against eating wild pig, while pigs kept tame in the villages are considered a delicacy. It is considered an insult, or at best a bad joke, to accuse a person of eating bush pig. Yet the male domesticated pigs are castrated, and to the outsider the only reason why the females continue to produce young is to be found in their misbehavior with the bush pigs. To the Trobrianders, who know full well that no self-respecting person would eat a wild pig or its descendant, the fecundity of their pigs proves that even among animals copulation is unnecessary for reproduction.

There is a final line of argument that demonstrates the tenacity with which the Trobrianders hold to their beliefs concerning the absurdity of physical paternity. Among these people it is morally reprehensible for an unmarried girl to bear a child. It is only right and proper that a child be born into a complete family, where there is both a mother and a father to take care of him. If on occasion a spirit-child is brought, by mistake, to a single girl the natives are unquestionably awed. It is morally wrong and dishonorable to bring a child into the world when there is no husband to help with its care and rearing. A boy may be having an exclusive and extended sexual affair leading up to marriage, and he would be the first to claim that no one else was having sexual relations with his partner. If the girl became pregnant, however, he would refuse to marry her because of her impending motherhood, a despicable event for an unmarried girl.

Perhaps we have dealt sufficiently with the evidence of the Trobrianders' lack of knowledge of the male's role in reproduction and the reasoning they employ when proffering their unique views on how conception actually takes place. Let us return briefly to the cogent argument based on the extremely low incidence of premarital motherhood. Surely this is beyond all reasonable expectations in a society which grants extreme sexual license to the unmarried.

Malinowski states that he is certain the Trobrianders use no type of contraceptive. He believes they are aware of a mechanical method of abortion but rarely make use of it. Certainly if the unmarried girls regularly conceived and used abortion to terminate their pregnancies, it would be difficult to conceal the fact that abortions were being performed. Even granting that abortion is occasionally practiced, we have cleared up but little of the puzzle. We know that the Trobrianders are post-pubertal at time of marriage. It is possible, nevertheless, that in view of their relatively early marriage, many of the girls or boys, or both, are sterile before marriage or at least of low fertility. It may be fortuitous that the Trobrianders' age at marriage coincides so neatly with the rising fertility section of the natural fertility cycle. Indeed, we cannot push this explanation too far, for in every society there are many individual variations in the age at which reproductive capacity is reached. Among the Trobrianders, furthermore, not everyone marries at exactly the same age. We would expect, then, that there would always be those girls who, either because they married at a later age or because they were biologically precocious, did not marry until well after they were able to bear children. Nevertheless we can think of the young age at marriage as a partial explanation of why Trobriand girls do not conceive before marriage despite their full sexual experience. Perhaps age even explains a large part of the enigma. But it does not solve the entire puzzle.

In a few instances it is possible that conception takes place before marriage, but only just before marriage. The Trobriands diagnose pregnancy by the swelling of the breasts and the darkening of the nipples. When after this a woman misses two or three menstrual periods, they are reasonably sure that the spirit-gods have brought her a child. It could be that now and then a woman who happens not to manifest the early signs of pregnancy could marry unaware of her condition or at least manage to keep her husband-to-be ignorant of it. This, frankly, is not a strong explanation at all. Marriage shortly after conception adds a little, but only a little, to our attempt to account for the low illegitimacy rate.

It must be remembered, finally, that occasionally unmarried Trobrianders do bear children. The incidence is low, but it does happen. In a society, like the Trobriand, that severely frowns on illegitimacy, every attempt would be made to conceal the true incidence. Making allowance even for purposive obscuration, however, Malinowski reported only a few cases of unmarried mothers. These few can, however, be deducted from the total number of prenuptial girls for whom an explanation of infertility is required.

The question that remains is whether or not we have fully accounted for the fact that the sexually active unmarried Trobriand girls rarely bear children. To a large extent this phenomenon is probably due to their age at marriage, and to a much lesser extent it may be due to the practice of abortion or marriage shortly after pregnancy. But can all the cases be explained in this way? Some probably feel that somehow these explanations *must* account for the complete picture. Others, perhaps the more romantically inclined, will choose to believe that not all of the pieces of the perplexing puzzle have been found and that there is still some undiscovered reason why the majority of unmarried Trobriand girls do not conceive. And we cannot be sure that there is not.

Pregnancy and Childbirth

Shortly after the first signs of pregnancy, that is, the swelling of the breasts and the discoloring of the nipples, the Trobriand woman usually has a dream. In this dream she sees the baloma, the spirit of one of her kinswomen who is bringing her a child. Four lunar months after the dream, according to native embryology, the woman's abdomen begins to swell. If this is the woman's first pregnancy, a series of special pregnancy rites soon commence to assure the well-being of the mother and her unborn child.

Kinswomen of the mother-to-be's father construct for her special long, flowing pregnancy robes made of frayed banana leaves. Then, by a formula known always to some of the village women, the robes are imbued with magical qualities which improve the personal appearance of the wearer. On the morning following the construction of the pregnancy robes, the same female relatives of the pregnant woman accompany her to the sea-shore. The women arrange themselves in two rows, extending outward into the water. Facing one another, they join hands and the prospective mother walks along the human bridge. After she passes, the end pair move to the front thus extending the column. Eventually the pregnant woman is allowed to jump into the water, and, in a playful mood, her companions thoroughly wash her. After this they carry her ashore and with an elaborate magical rite invest her in her pregnancy robe. She is then carried to her father's house where for the rest of the day she remains immobile and unspeaking on a specially erected platform.

The pregnancy rites described above are performed only during a woman's first pregnancy. In subsequent pregnancies the flowing cloak is worn, but it is made by the woman herself and put on without ceremony. At about the fifth month of any pregnancy certain taboos become operative. Various foods are never eaten by pregnant women because of the harmful effect they are alleged to have on her or her unborn child. If a mother-to-be were to eat certain fish with sharp and poisonous fins, for example, her child would undoubtedly be bad-tempered and would cry constantly. As the woman's pregnancy progresses, she rigorously refrains from sexual intercourse, for, as the natives put it, "the penis would kill the child." During the seventh or eighth month the woman moves to her father's or her maternal uncle's home. Her husband and her maternal kinsmen nightly keep a vigil outside the hut to guard against possible sorcerers intent on working evil.

When the woman's time approaches, as indicated by the first pains, she is made to squat over a very low fire in order to liquefy her blood and help her delivery. During actual labor she will sit on a mat with her legs apart and her knees up-raised. Bearing down on her shoulders is her sister or some other close maternal relative. The baby is allowed to fall on the mat, and only then is it touched by one of the assistants. If labor is difficult, the natives realize that it is due to evil magic, and the assistants send for someone who knows the appropriate countermagic. In the event that the afterbirth is not soon forthcoming after delivery, a stone is tied to the umbilical cord, and the woman is made to stand, in the hope that the weight of the stone and the frenzied incantations of countermagic will free the placenta.

So it is that the return of an ancestral spirit from the Island of the

Dead culminates in new life in the Trobriand Islands. During her pregnancy and confinement the parturient woman is carefully cared for and in particular is protected from evil magic and sorcery. These same precautions continue after her delivery. The newly born child is bathed daily and anointed with oils. Children are breast-fed, but almost from their first days of life they are given well-boiled taro, carefully chewed first by the mother. The child will be weaned when he is about two years old or, as the Trobrianders express it, when he is able to say clearly that he wants something to eat or drink.

THE REGULATION OF SEXUAL BEHAVIOR

It has been necessary, from time to time, to refer to different aspects of the sexual lives of the Trobrianders. Undoubtedly the impression has been gained that the mores of this group grant considerable sexual freedom to the individual before he is married. This impression is essentially correct. But there are regulations on sexual behavior. Neither in Trobriand society nor anywhere else can an unmarried person engage in sexual intercourse whenever and with whomever he pleases, even if the other party is willing. The Trobriands, like other societies, have placed certain restraints and taboos on marital sex as well as on extramarital relations. It is our task, at this point, briefly to sketch the sexual history of the typical Trobriander, paying particular attention to the regulations governing his sexual activity.[17] This will allow us to fill in the gaps in their sexual lives and, with this more complete picture, better to understand their sexual values and behaviors.

Sexual Life of Children

The confines of a native one-room hut do not conduce to privacy. From an early age, consequently, Trobriand children are aware of the sexual side of marriage. Propriety requires that children should not watch their parents in marital embrace. Too inquisitive youngsters are gently chided and told to cover their eyes with a mat. No attempt is made to exclude children from the sexual talk and joking of adults, and even young children seem to understand such repartee. Little girls accompany their fathers on fishing trips at which time it is the habit for all men to remove their pubic leaves. Of course there is no sexual connotation to nakedness at such a time; it is simply considered a matter of necessity. Young girls, nevertheless, receive an education in the sexual anatomy of the adult male.

[17] *Ibid.*, pp. 51-75, 114-120, and 438-536.

Since relationship is reckoned along maternal lines, the early application of incest taboos means that boys are prohibited from any contact with their mothers or sisters that is in the least way sexually tinged.

Young boys and girls alike find among their companions ready tutors in sexual matters. Somewhat older children allow them to witness their amorous behavior and may even introduce them more directly to the mysteries of pre-pubertal sex. Earnest, if not effective, sexual activity begins at an incredibly early age. The natives claim that girls of five attempt and even accomplish intercourse with somewhat older boys, but Malinowski suggests that we add a few years to the ages of both sexes. Parents and other adults are fully aware of the sexual practices of children. Indeed, sexual practice is regarded as the normal play of children. There is one important exception to the tolerant attitude of parents. The little boy who attempts to romp with his sister or makes any advance that can be ascribed an erotic overtone by suspicious adults is swiftly and sternly rebuked. The expressions of genuine horror on his parents' faces together with their unusual roughness early teaches the child the "supreme taboo" against erotic involvement of brother and sister.

Malinowski sees in the sexual behavior of children something of an aesthetic touch, for it always involves more than the physical act of sex. Intercourse, or attempted intercourse, may follow group games many of which have a strong sexual flavor. The children may "play house," imitating even the sexual side of married life, or perhaps sexual activity follows a little hike to the seashore or into the jungle. As the child approaches puberty, sexual activity ceases to be looked upon as play. He is expected to have a steady sexual partner, although no one expects that this relation will eventually terminate in marriage. The pubertal youth is required to observe the tribal sexual taboos. In general, those girls who are forbidden as marriage partners are also tabooed as premarital sex partners. With the exception of brothers and sisters, however, the premarital sex taboos are not as rigidly enforced as the parallel taboos pertaining to marriage. A man is forbidden to marry or to have intercourse with his maternal cousins, for example, and although the marriage taboo is strictly followed the prohibited type of premarital intercourse is actually a frequent occurrence.

Sexual Taboos for the Married

We have already traced the sex life of the post-pubertal youth and have seen that it involves longer and more exclusive intrigues. Eventually he chooses to marry a girl with whom he has been regularly having sexual relations. Looking back over the premarital sexual history of the typical

Trobriander, we see that never was he completely unrestricted in his sexual behavior. Gradually, the restrictions were increased, and he was expected to be more and more faithful to one sexual partner as he approached marriage. Rigid sexual taboos come into force after marriage. Adultery is severely frowned upon, and the deviations from the standards that occur are never condoned. If a man or wife accuses his mate of adultery in public, the guilty party will feel a great sense of shame and very likely commit suicide by jumping from a tall palm tree.

In addition to the expectations of strict fidelity among the married, there are other contrasts in the Trobriander's general attitude toward marital and premarital sex. The sexual life of a married couple is considered a strictly tabooed subject. No one dare make reference to it or even imply in a general way that sexual intercourse is engaged in by the married pair. It is perfectly acceptable, on the other hand, to talk and even joke about the sexual intrigues of the unmarried. A married couple, once again, must observe strict decorum in public. It is considered wrong for a man and wife to walk hand in hand or with their arms about one another as premarital lovers are wont to do. Husband and wife never refer to their own or to the other's premarital lovers although, of course, each knows the other party has come to marriage with extensive sexual experience and each could probably cite a number of the persons with whom the other's sexual experience was obtained.

It is interesting to view the differential attitudes toward premarital and marital sex of the Trobrianders in the light of those of our own society. Although we do, of course, have a taboo against adultery, and no doubt it is considered more severe that the prohibition against premarital sex, in other respects relations between the sexes are greatly relaxed after marriage. Sexual jokes can be told in "mixed company" as long as "everyone's married anyway." Even personal references to the nocturnal pursuits of the married can be made, if they are not "too personal." Sexually tinged teasing or mimic attempts at seduction can take place between married persons not married to each other provided, of course, that such teasing does not go "too far." Some couples discuss with friends their problems in controlling conception, and still other couples ask advice about their bedroom difficulties of total strangers. All of this would be totally tabooed in the Trobriand Islands and would be considered perfectly reprehensible behavior for married people. The Trobrianders unquestionably would be shocked to learn that people across the sea are so "sexually loose" after marriage. Perhaps the realization of how we could be judged will allow us to achieve a greater objectivity concerning the sexual values of the Trobrianders.

THE ECONOMIC FUNCTION OF THE
TROBRIAND FAMILY

In some societies the family operates as a relatively self-sufficient economic unit. The family members produce nearly all that is required to meet their needs and consume nearly all that is produced. We often associate this near economic self-sufficiency of families with non-industrialized societies. In the Trobriand Islands, however, we find the family performing its economic function in a unique manner.[18] Family members consume and the adult members are economic producers, but the nuclear family, the husband, wife, and their offspring, is not the most important economic unit. Through a fairly intricate arrangement, a family receives half or more of its support from the wife's brother. The husband of the family in question is, in turn, supporting his sister's family or the family of some close maternal relative. Particularly today, when it is popular to decry the decreasing functioning of the family as an economic unit, it is worth while to realize that there is much variation in the ways in which societies assign economic tasks to families and family members. It is well to realize, too, that motivation for productive activity is not restricted to cultures that emphasize the individual and his immediate family.

From the time that the bride's family indicates, by sending the first gift, that they give consent to the marriage, they assume a permanent obligation to support the new family. The obligation is generally fulfilled by the bride's brother each year at harvest time. After the yams produced in the family gardens are dug and cleaned, a large portion of them are arranged in a huge conical heap near the home. These are the yams that are to be delivered to the man's sister's household. But first they must remain at his home for all of his friends and fellow villagers to inspect and to admire. Indeed, people will come from neighboring communities, and all who see the yam heaps will realize how good a gardener a man is and how adequate a provider he is for his sister's household.

After the yams have been on display for a few days to a week, they are loaded into baskets and taken to the sister's village. The transporting of the harvest can be a quite difficult task, for, since marriages are patrilocal, the sister may well be living in a village some distance from the brother's. In a festive mood, a procession of men, women, and children, all carrying baskets of yams, sets out for the sister's village. At the home of her husband the yams are reheaped before the family storehouse. Here they remain for the friends of the man and his wife to inspect and thus to judge the

18 *Ibid.*, pp. 121-129.

economic acumen of the wife's provider-brother. In addition to this major gift, the sister's household will receive a number of smaller ones, consisting of several baskets of vegetables, from others of her maternal kinsmen. The sister's husband retains a small portion of his own harvest for the needs of his household and this portion, when combined with the substantial gifts from the wife's relatives, generally makes up a total more than sufficient for his family's needs. Variations from the usual economic arrangement among the Trobrianders can and do occur. The household of a woman with no brothers, for example, would receive its support from some other close relative of the woman. A man with many sisters, and no brothers, would probably not single-handedly support them all but would be assisted by other kinsmen. One can well imagine the distinct economic advantage for a Trobriander to marry a girl with many brothers.

In our own society it is customary to see the motivation and compelling force for "work" in the desire for a person to maintain himself and particularly, perhaps, his immediate family. Motives like power, prestige, and affluence are recognized, of course, but there seems to be the underlying feeling that the great bulk of men work hard at their jobs so that "the wife and kids" will have a "decent life." We are not denying that this *is* the case for many Americans. The lesson from the Trobrianders, however, is that there are other motivations which have been employed by an on-going society for many, many years. Given the proper motivation and reward, men will work, and will work hard, so that the households of their sisters will be well supplied. Feelings of shame and loss of respect in one's group can be cruel punishments, indeed, and the opposite emotions of pride and esteem can be satisfactory rewards. Together they operate to keep the typical Trobriand male hard at work for the economic well-being of his sister's household. From Trobriand society we learn also that man can invent many ways to satisfy his needs. As difficult as it may have been to appreciate the economic arrangements of the Trobriand family, other areas of Trobriand culture may have been even more difficult to accept. Variability in family structures, value systems, and ways of behaving is the big lesson of cross-cultural studies of the family.

SELECTED READINGS

BENEDICT, RUTH, *Patterns of Culture* (New York, Houghton Mifflin Co., 1934).

DENNIS, WAYNE, *The Hopi Child* (New York, Appleton-Century-Crofts, Inc., 1940).

MALINOWSKI, BRONISLAW, *Argonauts of the Western Pacific* (New York, E. P. Dutton & Co., Inc., 1922).

————, *The Father in Primitive Psychology* (New York, W. W. Norton & Company, Inc., 1927).

————, *Sex and Repression in Savage Society* (New York, Harcourt, Brace & Company, Inc., 1927).

————, *The Sexual Life of Savages* (New York, Eugenics Publishing Company, 1929).

MEAD, MARGARET, *Coming of Age in Samoa* (New York, William Morrow & Company, 1928).

————, *Growing Up in New Guinea* (New York, William Morrow & Company, 1930).

WHITING, JOHN W. M., *Becoming a Kwoma* (New Haven, Yale University Press, 1941).

CHAPTER | 7

The Russian Family

IN FEBRUARY 1917 Nicholas II, Czar of Russia, was arrested by the revolutionary force that a week earlier had seized his government. The eyes of the world turned toward Russia and saw the subsequent execution of the Czar and the imperial family, revolution and counter-revolution, countless peasant rebellions, and in October of the same year, the seizure of power by the Bolsheviks. The world had never witnessed a more radical upheaval than that which soon reached into every crevice of economic and social life of Russian society. Perhaps we should begin our study of the Russian family at this point, for the Russia most familiar to contemporary students originated in 1917. But just as the present-day family in the United States traces back beyond the American Revolution, so the family in the U.S.S.R. has been influenced by hundreds of years of cultural development. The swift and dramatic changes in the family following the Bolshevik revolution can be appreciated best when viewed against the early Russian family and the internal and external forces that over the years shaped it.

It has been posited that in the dim past of Russian history, and we cannot accurately date this period, a matriarchal-matrilineal family was common, particularly among the Slavs. Elnett tells us that "women enjoyed full independence in holding large possessions, being the heads of families and even of tribes, choosing their husbands and lovers."[1] The evidence used by Russian and other writers to support the theory of an early Russian matriarchal-matrilineal system is sketchy at best. Reliance is placed on such inferential data as the linguistic roots of the early words for mother and father and on reports of the early system of blood-revenge rights which seem to indicate that those who traced descent to a common female had the right to avenge the murder of one another. Although the meager evidence may suggest a matriarchy, the form and structure of the

---

[1] Elaine Elnett, *Historic Origin and Social Development of Family Life in Russia* (New York, Columbia University Press, 1926), p. 1.

earliest Russian family remain an enigma shrouded by long years of unrecorded history.

As the Russian Slavs became more truly an agricultural people, the patriarchal extended family began slowly to develop. The size of the extended family seemed to be conducive to accomplishing the physical work connected with agriculture, and the relationship of the members served to facilitate co-ordinated effort. At this time, Russian society was loosely organized under the control of a number of princes, who were the overlords of the land on which the bulk of the people lived. Although there was considerable cultural diversity even among the Slavic peasants, there prevailed the economically self-sufficient, extended family system. There is very little evidence of matriarchy at this period, and the relative position of the sexes probably approached equality.

Near the end of the tenth century the Russian princes, following the lead of Prince Vladimir, were converted to Christianity and embraced the Greek Orthodox religion. With the aid of the princes, the church grew in wealth and authority, and gradually its influence reached the daily lives of the masses. It has been said that "the introduction of Christianity in Russia was one of the most potent factors in bringing about a state of shameful subjection for the Russian woman."[2] It is true that the teachings of the Greek Orthodox Church recognized the superiority of males, who, guided by the male priests, were to head their families in worldly and spiritual affairs. Woman was said to be morally weak and inferior, as was the first woman, and ever since that day in Eden the devil has had a particular affinity for the female of the species. These views on the innate baseness of women were new to Russia, but gradually they were accepted along with the other teachings, the rituals, and the pageantry of the Byzantine religion.

In the thirteenth century the Mongol horde from the East swept over Russia and soon brought most of it into submission. For two hundred years Russia was under the "Tartar Yoke," and the intermingling and intermarriage with the Mongols produced a certain amount of cultural change. From the standpoint of the family, a significant effect of the Mongol invasion was the reinforcement and further development of the strong patriarchal family, which had long been the custom in the Asiatic countries whence the invaders came. But the Mongol conquest also led to broader changes which were to have their effect on the Russian family. Since the Tartars were interested in revenue rather than domination, to the Russian princes they delegated much authority and made them responsible for collecting tribute from the people. Ivan of Moscow was appointed

[2] Ibid., p. 21.

Grand Prince by the Mongol kahn. For two hundred years Russians became accustomed to the central authority of a Moscow prince. When the Mongols were driven out under the rule of Ivan III, he declared himself the first czar of Russia. It remained for his successor, Ivan the Terrible, to break the control of the other princes and fully to establish an autocracy. Over the years the czars became increasingly powerful, a feat in which they were assisted by their break with the Greek Orthodox Church. The newly formed Russian Orthodox Church held that the czar derived his authority directly from God, and the role of the church was to support and assist the government of the czar. Meanwhile more severe demands were made on the peasantry, and they found themselves increasingly bound to the land. Gradually two hereditary classes of landowners and workers developed, and we have the beginning of true serfdom.

Serfdom in Russia reached its peak in the seventeenth and eighteenth centuries. Misery, hard work, and oppression increasingly became the lot of the serf. Landowners assumed the right to order serfs beaten, to sell them apart from the land, to dictate the terms of their marriages, and to increase the amount of work and tribute required of them. The conditions of serfdom and the social organization of the period greatly affected the Russian family. Landowners allocated land not to individuals or families but to village communes, which became the unit for the land payments. Within the communes we find the extended Russian family consisting of a male head and wife, their unmarried children, and married sons with their families. The bolshak, or head of the household, assumed increasingly more authority, determining the amount and kind of work to be done by the various family members. Centralization of power in the bolshak was encouraged by the landowners and the state for administrative reasons. Land payments and taxes could be collected and soldiers could be conscripted more efficiently by working through a powerful central head. The dominance of the male and subordination of wife and children found support of the Russian Church, which, like the Byzantine Church before it, likened the father's role to that of the Almighty. The father was just and forgiving, perhaps, but definitely the all-powerful, single authority who demanded strict obedience.

The father's authority over his children was extensive and could be exercised in various ways. Disinheritance or its threat, which was well within the rights of the bolshak, could be used to control a willful son. In extreme cases the father could drive the disobedient son from home with nothing but the clothes on his back and his crucifix. The father, as spiritual head of the family, could direct God's wrath toward the wayward son or refuse to bestow the parental blessing. In view of the church's teaching, even the most willful of sons would anticipate great misfortune if his father cursed him or withdrew his blessing. Again, a disobedient or unfavored son could be the one selected by the father for military conscription. The Domostroy, a code of Russian family practices drawn up in the sixteenth century, strongly advocates the corporal punishment of sons:[3]

> Beat your son in his youth, and he will comfort you in your old age and will give beauty to your soul. And do not weaken in beating the child. Beating with a rod will not kill him, but will make him healthier, for hitting his body you are saving his soul from death. Loving your son, inflict more wounds on him and you will rejoice afterward. . . . Bring your child up used to denials and you will find in him rest and blessing. Do not smile at him when playing with him; if you will be weak in his childhood, he will make you suffer when he grows up, will set your soul on edge. And give him no power in youth but crush his ribs while he is growing, because when he is big he will not obey you, and you will feel annoyed and ill at heart, and your house will be ruined, and your neighbors will reproach you, and your enemies will rejoice at your misfortune.

We have every reason to believe that the harsh prescriptions of the Domostroy were followed and that the whip became standard household equipment. The Russian folk proverb, "If he does not obey his father, he will obey the whip," is a succinct and probably not too unrealistic description of father-son relations at this period.

Wives fared little better than children during the rise and development of the extended patriarchal family under serfdom. Indeed, "The husband is father to his wife," the folk proverb tells us. Obedience, respect, and complete self-abnegation were demanded of the wife. Turning to the Domostroy again, we learn the prescribed means for insuring the obedience of a wife:[4]

> The husband ought to teach his wife with love and sensible punishment. The wife should ask her husband about all matters of decorum; how to save her soul, how to please the husband and God; how to keep the house in good order. And to obey him in everything. Whatever the husband orders, she must accept lovingly; listen to him with fear and do as he bids.
> . . . And if the husband finds that his wife or servants do not keep everything in order, or the way he wants the things done, he should reason with her and instruct her. If she obeys, he should love her and be good to her. If she does not obey, or does not know everything herself and teach the servants properly, then the husband should punish his wife and fill her with fear, and punish her with love. . . . And no matter how guilty the wife is, the husband should not hit her eyes or ears, nor beat her with his fist or feet under the heart; nor strike her with his staff or with anything made of iron or wood; whoever beats

[3] *Ibid.*, pp. 32-33.
[4] *Ibid.*, pp. 33-35.

that way in his wrath or grief—causes much trouble; blindness, deafness, broken hands and feet, headache and toothache, injury to the unborn child if the woman is pregnant. But to beat carefully, with a whip, is sensible, painful, fear-inspiring and healthy. . . . In case of a grave offense, pull off her shirt and whip politely, holding her by the hands and saying: "Don't be angry; the people should not know or hear about it; there should be no complaints."

Such were family conditions under serfdom. Although we have referred most frequently to the peasant family, conditions were similar among the laboring classes of the cities. The Domostroy, in fact, was originally drawn up as a code for the urban families, when it was found that the wives and children showed tendencies to resist fulfilling the approved familial roles. Only in the small upper classes do we find mitigation of the intense subjugation of women and their harsh treatment.

In 1861 Czar Alexander II officially abolished serfdom. Generally, however, the emancipation provisions favored the landowner, and the peasant found himself bound still to his village commune and under the authority of the head of his household. He could be refused a travel passport or forced to return home if the household head so desired. Large-scale industrial development did not begin in Russia until the 1870's when more of the peasants migrated to the cities. For the oppressive conditions of peasantry they substituted long hours of work, poor working conditions, low wages, and sub-standard living arrangements. In the years that followed we find large-scale strikes and unorganized peasant uprisings. The aristocracy, meanwhile, and the small class of wealthy urbanites continued to enjoy great luxuries, to pursue the cultural life of the theater and music, and to indulge in lavish entertainment. In this era of stark contrasts, revolutionary parties arose to protest the plight of the masses. The most remembered of these was the Social Democratic Party, which was formed in 1898 and which drew its doctrines from the writings of Karl Marx. Five years later a split in the party gave birth to the Menshevik (minority) and Bolshevik (majority) factions.

Throughout the nineteenth century there had developed in Russia a strong feminist movement. The women, recruited largely from among the bourgeois, advocated complete equality of the sexes in political, economic, and social spheres. It is not surprising that in the early twentieth century the feminists aligned themselves with the male revolutionaries who, following the dictates of Marx, preached a similar doctrine. The stage was now set for the events of 1917.

THE RUSSIAN REVOLUTION AND THE FAMILY

We have said that the Revolution of 1917 resulted in a radical social and economic upheaval. Indeed, it was an upheaval in the literal sense, for out of the depths rose the poorest and the most exploited, the weakest and the most oppressed. Workers became the new elite, rulers became the ruled, and owners found themselves without property. It is manifestly impossible to wipe clean the slate on which is recorded thousands of years of cultural history, but the revolutionaries were willing at least to try. Nothing was considered too sacred to change, nothing so deeply ingrained that in time it could not be altered. The post-revolutionary era was thus a time of rapid and sweeping change. But it was change for a purpose. The new society was to be largely patterned after the ideal communist state envisioned by Marx and Engels. We will investigate, in this section, the changes in the Russian family in the revolutionary and immediate post-revolutionary period, taking into account not merely what changes occurred but why, in the light of new Russian ideals, such changes were made or attempted.

Views on Marriage and the Family

To begin with, it can rightly be asked just what kind of marriage and family the new regime wanted. Engels, in his *Origin of the Family,* leaves no doubt about *his* views of the type of family found in capitalistic societies at the time.[5] He sees monogamy as but one stage in the history of marriage and the family. Rather than some kind of an evolutionary pinnacle at which is found the maximum happiness, the monogamous stage is said to have ushered in the greatest subjugation of one sex by the other the world had ever seen. "The modern monogamous family," we are told, "is founded on the open or disguised domestic slavery of women."[6] And if this is not strong enough, in still another passage Engels likens conventional marriage to prostitution. A wife differs from a common prostitute "only in that she does not offer her body for money by the hour like a commodity, but sells it into slavery for once and all."[7] Engels' views must be considered, of course, in their cultural context and specifically in the light of the conventional patriarchal family of which he spoke. It is no wonder that Engels' words found a receptive audience in Russia, for probably at that time in no

[5] Friedrich Engels, *The Origin of the Family, Private Property, and the State* (Chicago, Charles H. Kerr and Company, c. 1902).
[6] *Ibid.,* p. 89.
[7] *Ibid.,* p. 86.

society was the patriarchal family more fully entrenched, complete, as we have seen, with the actual subjugation of women. Words like *oppression, subjugation,* and *inequality* had all too clear a ring, for they described with much accuracy the position of Russian women.

After the Bolshevik Revolution, a certain faction came to the fore which not only embraced Engels' view toward the family but embellished it with their own trappings derived, not necessarily with logic, from communist ideology. Marriage and the family were viewed as institutional twins whose early demise was to be sought by any means. The liaison between the sexes replacing marriage and the reproductive unit replacing the family were not to be cluttered up with such bourgeois proprietary concepts as "my husband," "our children," and "our home." Love was to be "free" and sexual relations stripped of the emotions that lead to possessiveness. And so we have the much-remembered "glass of water" theory of sexual intercourse. As thirst arises naturally and is quenched unemotionally, so be it with the sexual appetite. Unfortunately, from the standpoint of accuracy, these views of marriage, family, and sex received the greatest attention in the non-communist world. At the time, many in the West did not realize that this radical view of the family was the expression of a minority, largely composed of the earlier feminists who had aligned themselves with the Bolshevik cause and small numbers of others attracted to the extreme position. What, then, was the official post-revolutionary position on the family?

Ironically enough, from the standpoint of recent history, personal freedom for the average man was a major broad goal of the October revolution. In the area of the family this was interpreted to mean that within very broad limits everyone should have the right to marry if he pleased, whom he pleased, and to remain married only as long as he pleased.[8] Neither state nor church nor custom should be allowed to encroach on the personal liberty of the individual. No longer, then, must children be made to obtain the permission of their parents in order to marry, and no longer could lords be allowed to dictate marriage terms to the peasants. Mutual consent of the principals was established as the prime requisite for a valid marriage. Freedom from control of the church was likewise legislated. Shortly after the October revolution it was officially decreed that civil marriages only were recognized. Although it was not against the law to be a partner to a religious marriage ceremony, neither did such a ceremony give the couple the legal and other rights of the married. Marriage was made as completely secular as possible. The couple

[8] For a discussion of the main points of the Family Code of 1918, see G. M. Sverdlov, "Milestones in the Development of Soviet Family Law," *American Review on the Soviet Union,* Vol. 9 (August, 1948), pp. 10 ff.

needed only to state their intentions at the Registry Office and acknowledge that they were aware of the health of one another. The marriage was then recorded and from that moment was considered in force. It is significant that no one pronounced the pair man and wife. Indeed, it was not essential that both partners even be present; either could register the marriage if he brought with him the necessary documents. Marriage, therefore, was considered a private affair, a free agreement between a man and a woman, which the state merely recorded.

As a corollary to the goal for personal freedom, the new socialist government sought to remove from marriage and the family anything that resembled inequality between the sexes. But to pronounce equality is not the same as to achieve it, and so we find that many sorts of economic and social changes were deemed necessary to assure the equality of the sexes. The Orthodox Church sanctioned and encouraged the patriarchal family, so this was yet another reason to remove marriage from the influence of the church. Various prevailing marriage customs were interpreted as placing the woman in a position inferior to the male. No longer, then, need the wife assume her husband's name, but the couple must decide whether the bride's or bridegroom's surname became their matrimonial name or whether, indeed, it was to be a combination of their two names. No longer was it true that the husband alone decided where the family should live and that a wife's legal residence was that of her husband. Although most frequently it could be expected that the pair would agree on a mutual residence, it was decreed that a change of residence on the part of one of the spouses did not obligate the other to follow. It was further stipulated that if either party was in need, and unable to work, he or she was entitled to support from the other. Thus equal rights carried with them equal responsibilities. But still other modifications of the traditional marriage and the family were necessary before the type of equality sought became a reality.

Attitude Toward Divorce

If the world was shocked by the minority extreme views on marriage and sex, it was no less disturbed by the official position on divorce. Just as the new marriage laws enabled individuals freely to enter the married state, so the intent of the new divorce laws was to allow them to abandon it with equal ease. To this end, everything possible was done to make the securing of a divorce a simple matter. There were no divorce suits, and no reasons for the divorce were required. The original family code decreed that the mutual consent of the spouses, as well as the desire of only one of

them, was all that was necessary to dissolve a marriage. The concept of a
"guilty" and an "innocent" party was thus unknown. In the case of mutual
agreement to the divorce, the couple need only appear at the Registry
Office and present their personal identification and proof of marriage.
Each had to state what surname he would use in the future, and in the
event a decision could not be reached each was reassigned the name he
used before marriage. The divorce was then recorded, read back to the
couple, and signed by them. In a matter of a few minutes, and at no
cost to the couple, the whole business was completed. Divorce, like marriage, was a private affair. When a couple, for reasons they need disclose to
no one, desired a divorce, they simply stated their decision and the state
recorded it.

Divorce proceedings were a little more complicated if one party alone
wanted the marriage dissolved. Here we have the difficult case of trying to
protect the rights of two "free agents," one of whom wants a divorce while
the other wants to remain married. The wishes of both, quite obviously,
could not simultaneously be honored. The solution was to allow the one
party to register the divorce but, at the same time, to protect the other
party as much as possible. The one registering the divorce had so to inform
the other party by mail within three days, or if the address was unknown,
the Registry Office inserted a notice in the newspaper. The former procedure soon excited notice in the West, where it was dubbed "postcard
divorce," and frequently it was fancied that many a Russian spouse's first
awareness of marital discord came from the casual postal notice that his
mate had divorced him. But in all probability divorce by mutual consent was
by far the more common course of events. The law provided that either
husband or wife could demand the support of the other for one year after
the divorce if he was unable to work and for six months if able-bodied but
unemployed. Thus economic reasons for wanting to remain married when
one's mate wanted a divorce were reduced. It is doubtful that there were
many cases of strong emotional one-way ties, for in Russia as elsewhere, it is
difficult to imagine that a normal man or woman can live in marital
serenity with a mate who would very much like to be free. It appears that
the indignant finger-pointing and acrimonious words directed at Russia for
having reached a new moral depth with its "postcard divorce" were at least
overdone.

The family code contained, as would be expected, provisions for the
maintenance and education of children of divorced parents. If the couple
agreed on which of them should assume the responsibility, it was so recorded at the time of divorce registration. But children, through the
courts, could fall back on the legal provision which made both parents,

even after divorce, equally responsible for their maintenance. If the original agreement was not respected or if no agreement could be reached, the court would determine who should have custody of the child and would fix the amount of support required of the other party. If, in the interest of the child, it was deemed necessary to place him in a children's home, each parent, in accordance with his ability to provide it, was responsible for up to half of the child's support. Although the laws aimed at the protection of children of divorced parents were put into force when needed, the usual practice was for the children to remain with the mother.

Employment and the Changing Status of Women

We have already seen something of the emphasis placed on equality of the sexes in the post-revolutionary period. Although the new marriage and divorce laws helped to bring about the much-sought-for equality, even more drastic changes were considered necessary before the sexes would be completely equal. Engels tells us that the supremacy of men is assured as long as women's activity is confined to household tasks. "The emancipation of women becomes feasible," he writes, "only when women are enabled to take part extensively in social production, and when domestic duties require their attention in a minor degree."[9] It was important, therefore, not merely to allow women to be employed but actively to encourage them to work outside the home and make it possible for them to do so. Once women took their place next to men in the industrial world, the patriarchal family and the traditional subjugation of women were expected to wither of their own accord.

In addition to the strong ideological motive for drawing women from the home, there was the practical reason that women were sorely needed in industry. It was Stalin who later said that Russia in 1917 was fifty to a hundred years behind the rest of the industrialized world and that it was attempting to "catch up" in a few decades. Full employment of women, if possible, would practically double the size of the labor force. In the years following the revolution women began streaming through the factory gates, slowly at first but after the mid-twenties in great numbers. Trades that formerly were closed to women now became accessible to them. Nowhere were women more welcomed than in the new industries that were literally pleading for workers. By the mid-thirties over two-thirds of the able-bodied women of working age were employed outside the home.[10]

[9] Engels, op. cit., p. 196.
[10] Susan M. Kingsbury and Mildred Fairchild, Factory, Family and Woman in the Soviet Union (New York, G. P. Putnam's Sons, 1935), p. 33.

Although the dream of equality was not yet a fact, the large-scale employment of women was making it increasingly possible.

Much has been written about the nature of work performed by women in Russia, sometimes implying that the dirtiest, least pleasant, most menial jobs were reserved for the weaker sex. This scarcely would be equality! It is true that women were found chiefly in the ranks of the unskilled and semi-skilled workers. Women took their places in heavy construction and farm work, were employed as stevedores and dock workers, worked in the mines, and swept the streets. But this was from necessity and not by design. Each worker, male or female, was expected to find a role in the economy commensurate with his abilities. Since women had less training and experience, the less skilled jobs, for a time, fell disproportionately to them.

At the time of the revolution, it must be remembered, the Russian masses were not an educated lot. Some place the illiteracy rate at 70 per cent of the population.[11] Others claim it was not this high, but all agree that women were grossly overrepresented among the illiterate. It has been estimated, for example, that even by 1926 75 per cent of the illiterates were women.[12] It is little wonder that about this same time women workers were earning only about two-thirds as much as men. But coeducation, begun only after the Revolution, gradually changed the employment picture. Women began increasingly to be found in skilled jobs and in the professions. The point was reached, as a matter of fact, where three-fourths of all of the medical students in universities were women. Equal education for women allowed them to compete more realistically with men for available jobs and thus to achieve the equality they were promised.

Even while women were encouraged to seek their place in the working world, it was admitted that it would not be profitable to hire women workers on the same terms as men. To sacrifice the future to immediate industrial expansion would have been remarkably shortsighted. Russia needed a new generation of workers, more numerous, healthier, and better educated than ever before. In an effort to encourage the employed woman to bear children, the Labor Code contained provisions for the protection of women workers, which involved some expense and somewhat reduced women's efficiency as workers. It was stated that no employer could refuse work to a woman because she was married or pregnant. Nor could he discharge her during pregnancy or during the time she was nursing her child. Pregnant women and nursing mothers were exempted from overtime and night work. A woman worker received leave with pay for a period before and after the birth of her child. When she returned to work she was allowed time off to

[11] *Ibid.*, p. 177.
[12] *Ibid.*, p. 169.

nurse her child, who might well be cared for in the crèche maintained by the factory. Most of these services and privileges cost the woman worker nothing, but they were expensive for the state to provide. In the interest of obtaining the productive efforts of women and of thereby enabling them to achieve a status equal to men, they were considered worth the cost.

A new role, therefore, was created for women in a remarkably short time. The woman who saw her role only as a homemaker and mother no longer was considered the most useful citizen. To be fully accepted she must also make a direct economic contribution to society and must take her part in civic and public life. From all indications, the new worker-mother role became increasingly accepted by Russian women. In order better to understand their motivation to take on the double task of worker-mother one must remember that the masses of Russian women came from a background of hard work and oppression. Their grandmothers and in some cases their mothers had been ignorant and untrained serfs, who performed the most menial of farm tasks. The women who formed the group of workers had been accustomed to privation, heavy labor, and exploitation whether they had worked in a peasant commune or in the cities. Then too, as Halle puts it, it was "anything but a pleasure to be a housewife in Soviet Russia."[13] Housing was almost unbelievably inadequate; overcrowding, dilapidated construction, and the lack of basic equipment were usual. Add to this the extreme shortages of food and the usual consumer goods used in the maintenance of a home, and it is understandable why the job of homemaker was unattractive. Woman's new role offered at least freedom and hope—freedom from the oppression of the past, and hope, through her own efforts, for a higher level of living in the future.

Changing Family Functions

It will come as no surprise to learn that the new role of women in Russia necessitated a revamping of the traditional functions of the family. As women began to take a direct place in the productive economy, other institutions had to perform some of the functions formerly taken care of by the family, and as these institutions arose and flourished more and more people found it desirable to delegate to them some of the traditional family tasks. But there was more to changing the functions of the family than providing an opportunity for women to work. Partly, as we shall see, the changes reflected the Soviet ideology regarding the role of the family in society. We will direct our attention chiefly to the functions of (1) main-

[13] Fannina W. Halle, *Women in Soviet Russia* (New York, The Viking Press, Inc., 1935), p. 368.

tenance and protection of family members, (2) childbearing, and (3) child
rearing, for the changes in these areas were some of the most dramatic and
had far-reaching effects on the entire Soviet family.

Protection and maintenance of family members. The feeding, care, and
protection of family members are frequently labeled "traditional" functions of the family, for though other agencies *could* perform these functions,
in the past they have most frequently fallen to the family. Changes in
traditional family maintenance functions have occurred in many societies,
but change was more sudden in Soviet Russia than elsewhere, and in some
respects it was more drastic.

An admittedly radical element of Soviet society wanted to remove entirely from the home the responsibility for feeding family members. Only
then would a true collectivistic life be possible. The case was bolstered by
citing the expense of constructing private houses each duplicating the cooking and eating facilities of the other. Centralized communal kitchens and
dining halls could get the same job done with more efficient use of equipment and personnel. In addition, women would be freed from "household
slavery" and would be able to make a more substantial contribution to
the economy. In time, it was expected by the radical minority, the family
would completely lose the responsibility for feeding and caring for its members, as well as other functions, and would then wither away from sheer
lack of anything useful to do. As one Russian sociologist envisioned it, the
atrophied family eventually would come to rest in its particular niche in
the "Museum of Antiquities."[14]

It would be a mistake to assume that the above represented the majority or even the official views on the fate of the family. To be sure, it
was deemed necessary for the state to take over some family functions,
including the feeding of family members. To this end communal dining
halls were erected, and many families in which both husband and wife
worked undoubtedly found them desirable. From all indications, however,
communal feeding never became extremely popular. Although we are told
that "the separation of the kitchen from marriage is an event of yet greater
historical importance than the separation of church and state,"[15] the
former separation never became as complete as the latter. In order further
to lessen the need of woman's labor in the home, public baths and laundries
were provided in the new factory communities, the older cities, and even
in the smaller towns. Although the use of these services was encouraged,
they were not fully accepted or utilized by the masses.

[14] Quoted in Rudolph Schlesinger, ed., *Changing Attitudes in Soviet Russia: The
Family in the U.S.S.R.* (London, Routledge and Kegan Paul, Ltd., 1949), p. 346.
[15] Reported in Halle, *op. cit.,* p. 366.

Perhaps the most drastic modification of traditional family functions was realized in the state's assuming responsibility for the care and protection of those unable to provide for themselves. An extremely broad social insurance program provided aid literally from the cradle to the grave. We have already mentioned the maternity leaves with pay and the payment of hospital costs of delivery. In addition, workers were entitled to medical care at no cost to themselves as well as payments to compensate for the loss of earnings while sick. Continued treatment in sanatoria was likewise provided as well as periods of rest in convalescent homes. The permanently disabled and the aged were given pensions. Finally, burial grants and aid to the families of deceased workers were made available when necessary. Generally speaking, the various insurance benefits were not large and the pensions, computed as a percentage of earnings, favored the more productive and higher-skilled worker. The social insurance program nevertheless constituted an important transfer of functions from the family to the state, for traditionally it was considered the family's responsibility to provide the health and other services for its members.

The services for women and children loomed large in the picture of state-provided protective and maintenance services. Soon after the Bolsheviks came into power, they formed the Institute for the Protection of Mother and Child. It eventually included a whole network of organizations and services, including maternity hospitals, homes for children, medical and legal consultation centers, crèches, and nurseries. Beginning with the twenty-seven institutions or centers established in 1917, a total of almost five thousand were in operation in 1929.[16] In that same year, about $54,000,000 was spent in the protection of women and children.[17] Even this sum was insufficient, of course, to furnish every woman and child with the services of the Institute. Most of the centers were found in large cities such as Moscow, Leningrad, and Kiev, where a great reduction in infant and maternal mortality followed their establishment.[18] Whatever else can be said about the Russian state's "taking over" the traditional functions of the family, it is nevertheless clear that family members reaped definite benefits from the transfer of functions. The goal of the Soviet state was to give to all citizens a feeling of security against sickness, poverty, and suffering. The comprehensive social insurance program and the special services for women and children contributed to this goal directly, whereas the transfer

[16] Kingsbury and Fairchild, op. cit., p. 153.
[17] Alice W. Field, Protection of Women and Children in Soviet Russia (New York, E. P. Dutton & Co., Inc., 1932), p. 51.
[18] Child mortality has been reported to have dropped from 257 per 1,000 in 1913 to 141 per 1,000 in 1930. See Sir Arthur Newsholme and John A. Kingsbury, Red Medicine (Garden City, N. Y., Doubleday & Company, Inc., 1933), p. 202.

of some domestic tasks, such as cooking and laundering, was designed to result in a higher level of living for the masses.

The function of childbearing. All societies that wish to perpetuate themselves obviously must arrange for the birth of young. With extremely few exceptions childbearing has been considered a function of the family. Although this too may at first seem obvious, one must remember that the biology of reproduction does not demand that parents be legally wed and living in a family group. Almost universally, however, societies have failed to approve of childbearing outside of the family. Societies differ, on the other hand, in the extent to which they disapprove of childbearing outside of the family and the degree to which they encourage it within the family.

In early czarist Russia an illegitimate child was not considered related to either its mother or its father. The peasants called them "self-sown children." This concept may have eased the conscience of biologically naïve lovers, but it had unfortunate implications for the status of the child. After 1902 an illegitimate child was recognized as related to his mother only. Through the original Family Code of 1918 illegitimacy was eliminated by fiat. No legal or social distinction was made between a child born in and out of wedlock. "Actual descent is regarded as the basis of the family," the law read. Any child, therefore, was entitled to the support of his biological parents. In order to provide for the contingency that some fathers would not claim a child born outside of marriage, the law stated that an unmarried pregnant women should report her condition at the Registry Office no later than three months before the birth of the child. She had to state the time of conception and the father's name and address. The man was notified, usually by postcard, that he was being registered as the father. If he did not communicate his objections within a month, his silence was taken as an admission of paternity. If the man named as father objected, a paternity suit would be initiated and would have to be settled in court. In some cases the alleged father might plead *exceptio plurium*, that is, that various men had intercourse with the woman close to the time of conception and that, accordingly, it was impossible to determine which one was the father. Guided more by justice than by biological reality, the state considered all the men the father in the sense that all were liable for the expense of delivery and support of the child. Since the child might object to his collective paternity, one man only was officially registered as the child's father.

Such were the views on illegitimacy immediately after the Revolution. Although much was done to reduce the stigma of bastardy as well as legally to equate children born in and outside of the family, there remained what would seem to be the degrading practice of paternity suits. Childbearing outside of the family, moreover, was definitely not officially encouraged by the new regime. Although the legal provisions for support of illegitimate children made the unwed mother's role easier and thus might be construed as unofficial encouragement of the practice, the same provisions would seem to have discouraged cost-conscious males from becoming unmarried fathers. At this stage of history, therefore, Soviet society recognized the family as the only approved unit for childbearing, although steps were taken to aid children whose parents broke with approved behavior.

The Russian state, as we have seen, by no means sought to remove the function of childbearing from the family. But how much, on the other hand, did it actively encourage childbearing within the family? The many state-provided services for children and working mothers most certainly indicate a positive view toward married fertility. But the Soviet experiment with free and legal abortion also should be considered in its relation to the child-bearing function of the family. Let us look, first, at the official decree on abortions of 1920:[19]

> During the past decades the number of women resorting to artificial discontinuation of pregnancy has grown both in the West and in this country. The legislation of all countries combats this evil by punishing the woman who chooses to have an abortion and the doctor who performs it. Without leading to favorable results, this method of combating abortions has driven the operation underground and made the woman a victim of mercenary and often ignorant quacks who make a profession of secret operations. As a result, up to 50 percent of such women are infected in the course of the operation, and up to 4 percent of them die.
>
> The Workers' and Peasants' Government is conscious of this serious evil to the community. It combats this evil by propaganda against abortions among working women. By working for socialism, and by introducing the protection of maternity and infancy on an extensive scale, it feels assured of achieving the gradual disappearance of this evil. But as the moral survivals of the past and the difficult economic conditions of the present still compel many women to resort to this operation, the People's Commissariat of Health and Justice, anxious to protect the health of the women and considering that the method of repression in this field fails entirely to achieve this aim, have decided:
>
> (1) To permit such operations to be performed freely and without any charge in Soviet hospitals, where conditions are assured of minimizing the harm of the operation.
>
> (2) Absolutely to forbid anyone but a doctor to carry out this operation.
>
> (3) Any nurse or midwife found guilty of making such an operation will be deprived of the right to practice, and tried by a People's Court.
>
> (4) A doctor carrying out an abortion in his private practice with mercenary aims will be called to account by a People's Court.

It is clear from the above document that abortion was recognized as a serious evil. The greater evil, however, was thought to lie in allowing women intent on having abortions to risk and lose their lives in the process.

---

[19] Quoted in Schlesinger, *op. cit.*, p. 44.

For humane reasons the new government *allowed* abortion; that is not the same, of course, as *encouraging* it. Nevertheless, by almost any standards, there were abuses. The government built special hospitals for abortions, called *abortoria,* but it was difficult to meet the ever-increasing demand. In Moscow, in 1924, twenty-seven abortions were performed for every one hundred live births. In 1930 there were 175,000 abortions performed in Moscow alone, 55,000 of them in a single abortorium. Doctors sought to discourage women seeking abortions, posters proclaimed the dangers of the operation even under the best of conditions, and the papers spoke out against the "evil." But still the women flocked to the abortoria. Most of the women applying for an abortion were married and had borne children. The most common reasons for seeking abortions were "social," largely the inability to support the child. The feminists hailed legal abortion as another gain in women's rights and sex equality, inasmuch as it gave women the privilege to decide whether or not to bear a child and allowed women, like men, to enjoy sexual pleasures without necessarily accepting their biological consequences. This view, however, received almost no official support. An abortion during a first pregnancy was allowed only for strong medical reasons. It is probable that few abortions were performed to destroy the fruit of sexual indiscretion among the unmarried. It is evident, in sum, that Russia was not striving to destroy the childbearing function of the family through state-sanctioned abortion. Whatever our personal views on the matter, it is important to remember not only that Russia experimented with legal abortion but why she felt compelled to do so.

The function of child rearing. In all societies the family plays some part in the socialization of the young; in no society is the family *alone* responsible for the performance of this function. We want to investigate, then, the extent to which the state, after the Bolshevik Revolution, became involved in the socialization of the Russian young. The transfer of child-rearing functions from the family to the state would be a matter of extreme importance, for the children of today are the adults of tomorrow, and the lessons of childhood are most surely reflected in adult personality. Too great significance can scarcely be attached to who guides, directs, educates, and cares for the children and how these things are accomplished. It is little wonder, then, that the new Soviet society, intent as it was on producing a new generation conditioned to collectivistic living, became increasingly involved in the rearing of children. Then too, what the state did, the family need not do, and this meant that more mothers were enabled to work outside the home. And so, soon after the Revolution, we find children of all ages coming more and more under the watchful eyes of agencies other than the family. Crèches and kindergartens were established, school attendance was made compulsory, and supervised play, summer camps, and formal youth organizations became the approved recreational outlets. All of these services undoubtedly had definite influences on the minds of Soviet children and youth. We will be concerned, however, chiefly with the state services for very young children not because the early years are necessarily more important but because such services are the least familiar in our own society and in some respects their provision represented the most radical facet in the partial transfer of child rearing from the family to society.

There is no American counterpart of the Russian state-supported crèche, or day nursery for children from two months to about three years of age.[20] One function of the crèche was to provide the working mother with a place to leave her infant or young child. But the crèche was more than a state-furnished mass baby-sitter. It soon became a multi-function institution, feeding and clothing the children under its care, checking on their health, instructing parents in proper methods of child care, and carefully supervising play activities. "But above all," we are told, "the crèche aims to lay foundations for the formation of a functioning communal society by training children from their birth to be social beings in the Communist sense."[21] In the course of all of its activities, the crèche was governed by the principles underlying Communism, which had been arduously worked out and applied to the crèche situation by pediatricians and child psychologists.

The typical crèche day began before seven-thirty in the morning when the mother brought her child on the way to her work. The mother undressed the child and then was relieved of responsibility for it until after work, unless she returned periodically to nurse it. The child was next examined briefly for signs of illness, was bathed, dressed in state clothes, and placed in a small age-graded group. It is particularly with the somewhat older children, those of about one to three, that we notice the definite attempts to manipulate personal and social development. Play activity must be in accord with the broad aim of Soviet education, to produce an active worker in the collectivistic structure. Some of the primary goals for the younger child included training in responsibility, collectivistic living, and communal ownership of property. In accord with the first goal, a sign in every crèche reminded attendants, "Do Not Do Anything for a Child Which He Can Do for Himself."[22] The child's environment, of course, was so constructed that there was much that he could do for himself. Tables,

[20] For a good discussion of the purposes, types, and functioning of the crèches, see Vera Fediaevsky, *Nursery School and Parent Education in Soviet Russia* (New York, E. P. Dutton & Co., Inc., 1936). See also Field, *op. cit.*, pp. 107-142.

[21] Field, *op. cit.*, p. 107.

[22] Reported in Field, *op. cit.*, p. 115.

wash basins, and other equipment were child-size, and clothes were fashioned so that he could easily undress himself as soon as he had the proper co-ordination. Training for resourcefulness and work was further evident in children's games. Play was not to be purposeless, and it is reported that children accordingly were encouraged to play at chopping wood, setting tables, ironing clothes, in short, anything that would help train their minds and muscles and at the same time help fit them to live in the workers' society. The reading of fairy tales to children was strictly forbidden, for not only are the morals drawn in them frequently inappropriate to a collectivistic society but the stories themselves are not realistic. Revolutionary figures and the children in other lands were the heroes of the substituted "real life" stories which no doubt contained their own moral lessons.

True ingenuity was sometimes required to develop crèche-level lessons for living in a collectivistic world. An infant was seldom placed alone in a play pen, but two or three babies were made to share the restricted environment. Play and other activities had to be so arranged that a child would find the most pleasure in co-operation and joint undertakings. Children's blocks, for example, were made so large that a child could not easily handle one by himself, but two children could lift a block while a third guided it into place! In a similar manner, children were shown how to help one another with undressing and other tasks. And so at a very young age the child was supposed to learn that it is more fun and more effective to work with others than alone.

Communal ownership of property was likewise taught at the crèche. Some of the toys of children were replicas of the new social reality, and children could be seen building and playing with co-operative stores, collectivized farms, and state factories. But there were other lessons to be learned from play. The child was taught that he could play with a given toy for as long as he wished, but it was not *his* toy. When he was finished with it he could not "keep it," "lend it" to another, or otherwise indicate that he "owned" the toy. Whether twenty years later the man will feel about factories and houses as the boy was taught about rocking horses is an important but unanswered question.

The Russian peasants had a proverb, "What the mother puts into the child's head, the father will not knock out." Perhaps we should paraphrase it to read, "What the crèche mother-substitute puts into the child's head, and is reinforced at home, *nobody* can knock out!" It is evident that the crèche movement had an effect on the lives and personalities of the children involved; how much an influence it is impossible to tell. However the number of children who came under the guidance of a crèche is small. It is estimated that even by 1932 there were only about 600,00 permanent places in crèches. Not many families, therefore, were involved in this aspect of the transfer of child rearing from the home to the state. From the stand-point of the nature and intent of crèche activities, however, the movement is extremely fascinating as well as significant.

Still other agencies arose to care for Russian children. The point was reached where, in the cities at least, a working mother could be relieved of the responsibility for her child for a large part of every day throughout the year. When he became too old for the crèche, the child was immediately eligible for kindergarten and then school. After school hours there were parks and playgrounds, supervised by well-disciplined Soviet workers, where the child could remain until his parents came home from work. There was the Komsomols, or Young Communist League, for youths of fourteen and over, and later the Young Pioneers and Octoberists were established for younger children. These groups, under Communist leadership, provided fellowship and recreation outside the home, and at the same time they helped to mold the youth for collectivistic life in accord with Communist ideals. On her day off, the working mother could take her child to a Park of Culture and Rest and there leave him at the supervised play school while she enjoyed other attractions of the park. In the summer months the older child could go to a camp directed by trained personnel who were assisted by Komsomols. Younger children could be sent to one of the many seasonal crèches established in the country. Most of these outside-the-home services for children have their counterpart in our own and other industrialized so-cieties. There is a big difference, however, in the degree of philosophical agreement between the various programs for children. In our own society, for example, private agencies of diverse ideologies compete among them-selves and with public agencies for the time of the child. Children may well divide their free time among religious groups, character-building organiza-tions, school clubs, and community-sponsored recreation programs. The child who does so quite obviously receives nothing akin to the monolithic ideology imparted to his Russian age-mate from crèche to Komsomol. In neither country, of course, is any organization other than school compul-sory, but we are suggesting that the agencies engaged in child rearing have the potential for greater influence on the child in Soviet Russia than in our own society. In neither society, again, has child rearing ceased to be chiefly a family function, but it would seem that Russia provided more ex-tensive services to complement, or perhaps counteract, the family's training.

Sex Mores after the Revolution

With true ambivalence, many Westerners bitterly condemned what they avidly read about the "sexual communism," "free love," and "socialized women" reported to exist in Russia. Many such reports were pure fiction and others were nearly so, but fiction which passes for fact has a unique fascination. By the time more accurate information on Russian sex mores became available, it was an anticlimax to a world conditioned to the salacious.

Within the younger generation arising after the Bolshevik Revolution, there developed a faction with a concerned "lack of concern" for matters sexual. Sexual relations, they contended, should be simple and direct and not embellished with strong emotional attachments that smacked of reactionary possessiveness. They said that in sexual relations a stimulus was received, a response produced. Chastity or any sexual restrictiveness that placed men above the level of tomcats was labeled "petty bourgeois." No good Communist, some of the young Communists told one another, would deny members of the opposite sex the pleasure of his body, for it was just a physical act, which should carry no deeper meaning than does escorting and being escorted to the cinema. This was the faction that developed the renowned "glass of water" theory of sex to which we have earlier referred. The young radicals found the support and encouragement, and indeed the provocation, of the older radicals, particularly the feminists. It is difficult to determine how large or how small a proportion of Russian society endorsed the "glass of water" view of sex and well-nigh impossible to know how many of those who did accept it practiced open promiscuity. In all probability, the new view of sex was shared by a minority, and certainly the leaders of Russia did not subscribe to the minority position. Lenin himself minced no words in the statement of his views on the matter:[23]

I consider the famous "glass of water theory" to be utterly un-Marxian, and, moreover, unsocial. . . . Of course thirst cries out to be quenched. But will a normal person under normal conditions lie down in the dirt on the road and drink from a puddle? Or even from a glass with a rim greasy from many lips? But most important of all is the social aspect. Drinking water really is an individual concern. Love involves two, and a third, a new life, may come into being. That implies an interest on the part of society, a duty to the community.

Lenin's remarks, of course, did not immediately put to an end the "un-Marxian" views of sex. For a time, emotional nihilism was avidly discussed, and a poll revealed that a large proportion of students were influenced by the current philosophy of sex-without-love.[24] It is nevertheless clear that this was not the accepted Communist philosophy of sex.

Marxists have always taken a strong stand against prostitution, especially for its connotation of exploitation of the weak. What is more, prostitution has been linked with the capitalistic economic system, which, it is

[23] Quoted in Halle, op. cit., p. 113.
[24] Ibid., p. 116.

charged, forces some to sell themselves into slavery while enabling others to buy the body of a human being. Marxists have been particularly vehement in their condemnation of the hypocrisy accompanying prostitution. They state that the same class of men who through their purchases of the service made prostitution a profitable undertaking was the one responsible for insisting on public surveillance and criminal prosecution of prostitutes. It is no wonder, then, that the oldest profession was to have no place in the newest social order.

The goals of the new Russian regime were to eliminate prostitution and prevent, through improved social and economic conditions, its recurrence.[25] Operators of brothels, procurers, and others who encouraged prostitution were punished severely, as were incorrigible prostitutes. Most prostitutes, however, were not punished but were simply provided with employment, for they were considered more as exploited unfortunates than criminals. In the years following the Revolution, it is reported, prostitution practically vanished.

In the early twenties, the growing unemployment affected more women than men, for many of the women were still untutored and unskilled. The prostitution problem returned and called for vigorous counteraction. The guiding principle in the new action was that "under no circumstances must the war against prostitution degenerate into a war against prostitutes."[26] Accordingly, emphasis was placed on the rehabilitation of prostitutes, and the first of the famous prophylactoria came into being. A prophylactorium is a combination home-clinic-workshop where prostitutes are treated for venereal infections, kept at work, and educated. Entrance is voluntary and the patients pay a part of their earnings in the prophylactorium shop for their upkeep. At the same time the former prostitutes are re-educated so that they can see themselves in occupations more useful to the workers' society. When a girl leaves a prophylactorium, she is found a job and a place to live, to assure that of necessity she will not return to the street. From all reports, most of the ex-prostitutes "make good" after leaving the prophylactorium, and this institution, as well as other measures, helped drastically to reduce the prostitution problem. In the space of a few years, for example, the number of prostitutes in Moscow was reported to have dropped from 3,000 to 400.[27] Although prostitution did not disappear, perhaps the essential point is to recognize the attitude taken toward it by the Russians. Prostitution was considered a degrading practice for both the buyer and the seller of sexual pleasure, and vigorous efforts have been made to eradicate the practice and to prevent its renaissance.

[25] See Field, *op. cit.*, pp. 195-198, and Halle, *op. cit.*, pp. 218-266.
[26] Halle, *op. cit.*, p. 226.
[27] *Ibid.*, p. 254.

CHANGES IN FAMILY POLICY OVER THE YEARS

In the foregoing section we have dealt with the family in Russia during the period from the Revolution of 1917 to about the mid-twenties. Our next major point of inquiry will be the family in Russia during and since World War II. But some important changes in family law and policy occurred in the almost two decades that intervened between these two periods.

It will be recalled that the original post-revolution family code made marriage a private contract. It was necessary, however, for the couple to register the marriage with the state if they wished to claim the rights and privileges of the married. Yet in Russia as elsewhere there were those who flouted the laws of society and merely lived together. In the days of the czars, peasants spoke of such couples as married "without a priest, without a cross, around a fir tree." More technically such liaisons came to be called "de facto marriages," for marriages they were in some respect. In the post-revolution period, de facto marriages were not considered valid. To be sure, all children were granted the same rights regardless of the marital status of their parents, but spouses were protected only if the union had been duly registered.

Experience with the original family code indicated that some changes were necessary. Accordingly, in 1925 a draft of a new family code was prepared by the People's Commissariat of Justice and submitted to the All-Russian Central Executive. In the draft, the new code recognized de facto marriage, equating it with registered marriage as far as the rights and responsibilities of all family members were concerned. So lengthy was the discussion of the new code in the Executive that it was decided to obtain the views of the masses on the new proposals.[28] For over a year, workers' groups, peasants, men and women, young and old, discussed the proposed code point by point. Some 6,000 formal reports of the discussion were sent to the People's Commissariat, and we are told that thousands of other discussions took place.[29] The opinions and supporting logic of the people were no less fascinating than the procedure for obtaining them.

Several objections to the recognition of de facto marriage seemed to recur. Some felt that making it unnecessary to register a marriage would serve to strengthen religious marriages. In a sense, a religious marriage and a registered marriage would be equated. After a church ceremony, not followed or preceded by registration of the marriage, couples might con-

[28] For a brief report of the discussion of the proposed family code, see Schlesinger, *op. cit.*, p. 81, and Halle, *op. cit.*, pp. 117 ff.
[29] Halle, *op. cit.*, p. 118.

sider themselves married and live accordingly. Others objected to de facto marriage on the ground that it would make for too relaxed relations between the sexes. The difference between a budding de facto marriage and a casual relationship might be slim indeed, and all sorts of abuses were predicted. Still others, on the other hand, claimed that the recognition of de facto marriage would unduly coerce the population to virginity and virtue, since one party might construe even a temporary sexual interlude as marriage and later claim support privileges.

The proponents of recognition of de facto marriage likewise had strong arguments to support their views. In the first place, it was held that the closer Russia came to the ideal Communist society, the more marriage should be liberated from controls and obligations of all sorts. Why, under the ideal Communist order, should the state be told who contracts a marriage with whom? It was pointed out, again, that the proposed code simply was taking account of reality. Thousands of de facto marriages existed, and the women particularly were not receiving just protection under the law. Especially was this true in the so-called "seasonal marriages" in which women were taken as de facto wives at the harvest season only to be sent on their way when their services were no longer required. Legalization of de facto marriage would help to put an end to such exploitation. It was argued, finally, that requiring marriages to be registered would do little to stabilize sexual relationships, for divorce was free, easy to obtain, and no attempt was made to limit subsequent remarriage.

The majority of those registering their opinion, it appeared, were in favor of the recognition of de facto marriage. At any rate, the proposed code became law in 1926.[30] Registered marriage was preferred, de facto marriage accepted. With the courts rested the ultimate decision whether or not the relationship of a given couple was close enough to a recognized marital relationship to be called a de facto marriage. Factors such as cohabitation in a common household, the couple's admission of their status to a third party, mutual support, joint raising of children, and the like were to be considered by the court in determining whether the couple was married de facto.

Ten years later we again find important family legislation. At this time state socialism had advanced considerably and the standard of living of the masses had improved. In view of the increased well-being of the people, a law was introduced prohibiting abortion and containing other measures to strengthen the Russian family.

The Soviet experiment with legal abortion had had mixed effects. The

[30] For the final version of this code, adopted in 1926, see Sverdlov, *op. cit.*, pp. 13-16, and Schlesinger, *op. cit.*, p. 154.

new regime, it must be remembered, had never approved of abortion but merely tolerated it. It allowed abortions to be performed openly and without cost at state-financed abortoria partly to eliminate unskilled practitioners working under unsanitary conditions. In one respect the legal abortion experiment was a success; it was reported that secret abortions had all but vanished and the death rate from abortion and attempted abortion had become negligible. On the other hand, for a state not approving of abortion is was discouraging to see the tremendous demand for the operation and the abuses to which legal abortion were put. Large abortoria were constructed and abortions were performed on a mass-production basis, within the limits of approved medical practice. But still the number of women seeking abortions exceeded the number of hospital beds available. It is not surprising, then, that the Family Law of 1936 forbade abortions except for serious medical considerations.[31] Economically, the Soviet state had sufficiently improved that none but medical reasons were considered valid reasons for a woman not to bear a child she had conceived.

The 1936 amendments to the family code also broadened considerably the state aid to mothers and children.[32] The allowance for the purchase of a layette was increased, as were the payments to nursing mothers. An annual allowance for large families was introduced at this time, providing 2,000 rubles per year for five years for each child from the seventh to the tenth child in the family. Beginning with the eleventh child, a special 5,000 ruble "bonus" was given the family during his first year, and the annual allowance was 3,000 rubles for four years thereafter. Provision was also made for the expansion of maternity homes, crèches, and kindergartens, in a number of instances calling for a doubling of the available facilities. Through the 1936 family code amendments, therefore, much was done to ease the burden of mothers and to encourage childbearing. Although the new code gave evidence of a positive view toward the family, little was done legally to discourage divorce. What changes were made in the divorce laws were prefaced by the admission that there was evidence of "light-minded attitudes towards the family and family obligations." Some would consider this a gross understatement, for the divorce rate was high. Some years before it had reached the point in Moscow where there were actually more divorces than marriages in one month.[33] To combat such "light-minded attitudes" it was decreed that 50 rubles be charged for the first divorce, 150 for the second, and 300 rubles for each subsequent

[31] Schlesinger, op. cit., p. 251.
[32] For a discussion of the 1936 family code, see Rose Maurer, "Recent Trends in the Soviet Family," American Sociological Review, Vol. 9 (June, 1944), pp. 242-249.
[33] Reported in Helen G. Pratt and Harriet L. Moore, Russia: A Short History (New York, John Day Company, 1947), p. 188.

divorce. Both parties, furthermore, had to appear at the Registry Office, and the fact of a divorce was recorded on their passports. Some steps were taken, therefore, to discourage divorce, but the far-reaching measures to combat divorce were not to come until a later period.

WORLD WAR II AND THE SOVIET FAMILY

World War II represents an important milestone in the course of Russian family policy. It is almost tautological to say that wars have a disruptive effect on families, separating family members temporarily or permanently and affecting the economy upon which the material base of family living rests. Most Americans are probably aware of the tremendous price Russia paid for its part in the successful completion of World War II. An estimated 20,000,000 Russians lost their lives, more than half of them civilians.[34] In the Ukraine alone half of the means of production was destroyed.[35] It is obviously no small matter for a society to lose half of all its factories and ships, half of its machinery and tools, half of its farm equipment, port facilities, and railroad stock. In addition, 82,000 schools, in which 15,000,000 children had previously been enrolled, were destroyed, to say nothing of the homes and personal possessions of Russian citizens.[36] Wars are always destructive, but it is well to realize just how much destruction World War II wrought in Russia, for the wartime and subsequent changes in family policy stem partly from the effects of the human and property losses.

Even while engaged in conducting the war, the Soviet government turned toward the immediate and foreseeable family problems the war was producing. The family legislation of 1944 was prefaced by the following policy statement:[37]

Concern for children and mothers and for strengthening the family has always been one of the most important tasks of the Soviet State. . . . During wartime and afterwards, when for many families material difficulties are more considerable, a further widening of measures of State aid is needed.

The family legislation of 1944 was thus seen as being called for by the unique wartime and postwar conditions, and, at the same time, it purported to reflect the usual attitude toward the family. But as we investigate some of the legislative changes with respect to marriage, divorce, aid to

[34] *Ibid.*, p. 246.
[35] *Ibid.*, p. 247.
[36] Rose Maurer, "The Behavior of Soviet School Children," *American Review on the Soviet Union*, Vol. 9 (March, 1948), p. 3n.
[37] Sverdlov, *op. cit.*, p. 21.

unwed mothers, and the like, we will see that it is more accurate to say a new policy toward the family was contained in the 1944 promulgations.

Increased Regularization of Marriage

One method of strengthening the family, it was felt, was to regularize marriage and bring it under the control of the state. In the 1944 family code, accordingly, was the stipulation that from that time on registered marriages only would be valid. Having admitted that de facto marriage was practiced by thousands, having submitted the question of whether or not to recognize de facto marriage to public discussion, and, finally, having given official recognition to unregistered marriage, the state now, not quite twenty years later, officially decreed that "only registered marriage confers the rights and obligations of the spouses."[38] Of course, in the phrase "twenty years later" is contained part of the explanation for the new legislation. The previous recognition of de facto marriage was prompted partly by the deleterious effects common-law marriage was having on women. Over the years conditions had changed. The exploitation of women was thought to be less of a threat since women had come closer to achieving equality with men socially, educationally, and occupationally. We are told, in addition, that a higher level of cultural and moral demands increasingly had been made on each individual, particularly with regard to family relationships.[39] It was possible, in short, to do away with de facto marriage in order to strengthen family stability.

The law removing the official recognition of de facto marriage casts a curious ideological glow. In the ultimate communistic state, marriage was to be a private affair of the individual, and even in the embryo socialistic state of 1917 only its registration was required. As socialism advanced and the goal of a communistic state presumably came more into view, compulsory marriage registration was abandoned. The change was defended by those who had accepted Lenin's injunction "to march in the van and not lag behind in the rear ranks" in the progressive march to full communism. Regardless of the practical reasons for first accepting and then rejecting de facto marriage, the new family code represented an ideological retreat. In 1944 marriage became less of a free contract between spouses than it had been in the preceding period. Only registered marriage afforded legal rights to the couple and, as we shall see later, even the child was denied the right to support by his parents unless they were officially married.

[38] *Ibid.*, p. 23.
[39] *Ibid.*, p. 22.

1944 Divorce Legislation

Fundamental changes were contained in the 1944 divorce legislation.[40] Once again, the intent was to increase family stability, and to this end divorce was made more difficult to obtain. Where once divorce was a private concern and the couple need not state their reasons for dissolving the marriage, now the state stepped in to inquire their reasons for dissolving the marriage, to establish the guilt of the respective parties, and to attempt to effect a reconciliation. Where once divorce was free, now a charge of from 500 to 2,000 rubles was made. Where once it was a simple matter to obtain a divorce, it now became an involved procedure. The People's Court, the first step in what could be a lengthy procedure, investigated the motives for divorce and in the course of so doing could call witnesses, interview friends of the couple, and the like. The People's Court was also expected to attempt a reconciliation, and even such major steps as securing job transfers were reported to have occurred in this connection.[41] The People's Court could, in the end, simply refuse to recommend that a divorce be granted, in which case appeals to successively higher courts were the only recourse of the couple. All in all, it became extremely difficult to obtain a divorce in Russia following the 1944 legislation, and consequently the divorce rate dropped sharply. In one locality, for example, there was an eleven-fold reduction in the number of divorces.[42] Obviously the fewer divorces the more families there are intact in a legal sense, and in this respect the law produced the desired effects. But at the same time the 1944 divorce law represented a reversal of the one-time position on the nature of divorce in a socialistic state.

Measures to Encourage Childbearing

Partly to compensate for the tremendous population loss due to the war and partly further to implement the new views toward the family, the 1944 family law contained strong measures designed to encourage childbearing.[43] Financial rewards to mothers were increased, honorific awards were established, and childlessness was discouraged through taxation.[44]

[40] Ibid., p. 23.
[41] Ibid., p. 24.
[42] Ibid.
[43] For the text of the 1944 family code, see American Review on the Soviet Union, Vol. 6 (November, 1944), pp. 69-76. A 1947 decree reduced by half the financial aid to mothers. See American Review on the Soviet Union, Vol. 9 (March, 1948), pp. 69-70.
[44] A discussion of these and other aids to parents, including some changes subsequent to the 1944 code, can be found in Mark G. Field, "Social Services for the Family in the Soviet Union," Marriage and Family Living, Vol. 17 (August, 1955), pp. 244-249.

The fact that greater provision was also made for the unmarried mother at this time would seem to indicate that strengthening the family was not the sole objective of the family code amendments.

Instead of the earlier regulation that provided state aid at the birth of a seventh child, the new law stated that birth payments were to begin with the third child. The amount paid increased with family size, ranging from 400 rubles for the third child up to 5,000 rubles for the tenth and subsequent children. State monthly payments began with the fourth child and likewise increased in amount according to the number of children in the family. Articles 12 to 15 of the 1944 family law established the famed honorific rewards for mothers of large families. A "Motherhood Medal," first and second class, is awarded to those who have brought up six and five children respectively. The Order of Motherhood Glory is awarded, in three classes, to mothers who have reared seven, eight and nine children. The birth of a tenth child makes its mother eligible for the title "Heroine Mother."

The financial and honorific awards to mothers should be considered in the light of their bearing on the new Soviet policy toward the family and the role of women. It is doubtful that many American women could be persuaded to have a houseful of children in order to obtain a medal, a citation, and a title, and we are not suggesting that the masses of Russian women were in fierce competition to become Heroine Mothers. But certainly the various rewards indicate an official encouragement of childbearing and a recognition of its importance. The financial rewards made it economically more feasible to have children, and the honorific awards show that it was commendable for a woman to raise a family, perhaps more so than to work at the local factory. After all of the state's efforts to lure woman from the home, now she is beseeched to return.

The 1944 family code included also some changes with regard to unwed mothers. The former practice of the court's determining, when necessary, the legal father of the child was abandoned. Henceforth the unmarried mother was entitled to receive support only from the state and not from the child's father. The new method undoubtedly benefited the mother, for the state payments would probably be easier to obtain, more consistently received, and in a lot of cases more substantial than those from the father. At the same time, the new policy would seem to encourage childbearing outside of marriage; at any rate it would not discourage the practice. The new policy eased the burden on the "lonely mother," as the Russian term is sometimes translated, for not only was she now more likely to receive adequate support for the child, but she was spared the bother and possible humiliation of attempting to establish the child's paternity.

A child was a child, and if he had no social father in the sense of a man married to his mother then the state assumed responsibility for his maintenance. At the time when new lives were needed to replace the millions lost in the war and when the sex ratio was such that there were not nearly as many men as women, it was thought neither wise nor expedient to insist that each woman have a legal husband before she could have a child.

The New Family Law and the Status of Women

It has undoubtedly occurred to the student that none-too-subtle changes in the status and role of women were to follow the activation of the 1944 family code. From various legislative acts it is apparent that according to the new outlook woman's role is foremost that of a mother. The new role includes homemaking and housekeeping but not necessarily employment outside of the home. While women are not actively discouraged from employment, the number employed outside the home had decreased, and, what is more important, the increased financial aid to mothers would make outside work less necessary.

A change in Russian educational policy throws additional light on the new role of woman. After the Revolution coeducation was established in Russia. At this time it was lauded as a necessary and fitting move to enable women to become the economic and social equals of men. In 1943 coeducation was abolished.[45] Separate education of the sexes was tried in Moscow, and success there prompted the 1943 decision. It was more than a matter of housing boys and girls in separate school buildings, for we read that the sexes were to have different curricula. To the girl's curriculum were added courses in child care, domestic science, personal hygiene, and needlework; in short, girls were to be prepared for the role of homemaker and mother. The 1943 statement concerning the abolition of coeducation pointed out, as an illustration, that the geography course for boys was to be "different" from that for girls, presumably because the boys might be the warriors of the future for whom a knowledge of topography and map reading would be valuable. Although it is true that military training was added to the boys' curriculum, coeducation was not abolished only or even chiefly to facilitate military education of the males. What was envisioned was truly a different type of education for girls and for boys. It was more or less assumed that girls were to become mothers and homemakers and boys were to be the family providers, and the sexes were tutored accordingly.

[45] For a discussion of this law, see "Education Notes," *American Review on the Soviet Union*, Vol. 8 (March, 1947), pp. 79-84.

In the days of the czars the peasants proverbially said that "a chicken is not a bird and a woman is not a human being." After the Revolution every step was taken to remove the negative from that part of the proverb that applied to women. The peasant proverb required still further modification in 1944 so that it would read, as it were, "a chicken is one type of bird, equal to other types, and a woman is one type of human, equal to the other type." The ideal roles of the sexes were to be different, but neither was inferior to the other, the familiar concept of "separate-but-equal." But is it really possible to implement the concept of "separate-but-equal" whether we are talking about bird species, races, or the sexes? Certainly it is difficult when one of the separate categories was traditionally considered inferior. In this respect Soviet Russia would seem to have an advantage, for since 1917 equality of sexes has been preached much and practiced almost as much. But if the separation of kitchen and marriage was so important to bring about equality of the sexes, what is to happen when they are reunited with the blessing of the state? It will be interesting to see whether in the "workers' society," with its accent on economic performance, the role of homemaker-mother can be given sufficient social importance to place it on a par with a role more directly related to production.

THE FUTURE OF THE SOVIET FAMILY

Throughout this chapter we have been hampered in our remarks by a lack of data sufficient to tell us all we would like to know about the Russian family. If the dearth of information has limited our discussion of the past, so much more does it restrict our remarks about the future. But with the past as an imperfect prologue we shall make a few cautious predictions.

The Russian family is not going to "wither away." In the immediate future, the state will probably continue to spend lavishly on aid and services to the family, women, and children, to the extent that economic conditions make it necessary to do so. Once it was said that "the saucepan is the enemy of the party cell"; now it is recognized that the family is *the* important cell of society, and efforts will probably be continued to strengthen this cell. As economic conditions become better, and unless other forces such as a war arise, women probably will move closer to their new mother-homemaker role. At the same time, we will venture to say that women will not lose their hard-won equality with males. The Russian family of the future, despite the lure of Mother Heroine medals, probably will be smaller, not larger, than in the past, because of the continuing growth of industrialization and urbanization. This, at least, has been the experience of most of the rest of the world.

Although we can learn little about interpersonal relations of family members, the family since the Revolution seems to have furnished satisfying experiences and to have been a source of security to its members.[46] By those ideologically separated from the regime, the family has been described as "a refuge or retreat from a threatening life situation."[47] Where family members all share the ideals of the new society, they probably serve as psychological props to one another on the sometimes difficult path to the ideals. Cases of denunciation of parents by children never actually were frequent, and since the parents of today have known only the new system they and their children should be at political and economic odds even less frequently than in the past. Despite crèches and collectivization, the Russian family should hold and further its place as the important source of satisfaction for the Russian masses.

SELECTED READINGS

Elnett, Elaine, *Historic Origin and Social Development of Family Life in Russia* (New York, Columbia University Press, 1926).

Fediaevsky, Vera, *Nursery School and Parent Education in Soviet Russia* (New York, E. P. Dutton & Co., Inc., 1936).

Field, Alice W., *Protection of Women and Children in Soviet Russia* (New York, E. P. Dutton & Co., Inc., 1932).

Field, Mark G., "Social Services for the Family in the Soviet Union," *Marriage and Family Living*, Vol. 17 (August, 1955), pp. 244-249.

Geiger, Kent, "Deprivation and Solidarity in the Soviet Urban Family," *American Sociological Review*, Vol. 20 (February, 1955), pp. 57-68.

Geiger, Kent, and Inkeles, Alex, "The Family in the U.S.S.R." *Marriage and Family Living*, Vol. 16 (November, 1954), pp. 397-404.

Halle, Fannina W., *Women in the Soviet East* (New York, E. P. Dutton & Co., Inc., 1938).

——, *Women in Soviet Russia* (New York, The Viking Press, Inc., 1935).

Kingsbury, Susan M., and Fairchild, Mildred, *Factory, Family and Woman in the Soviet Union* (New York, G. P. Putnam's Sons, 1935).

Mead, Margaret, and Calas, Elena, "Child-Training Ideals in a Post-Revolutionary Context: Soviet Russia," *Childhood in Contemporary Cultures*, Margaret Mead and Martha Wolfenstein, eds. (Chicago, University of Chicago Press, 1955), Ch. 11.

Meisel, James H., and Kozera, Edward S., eds., *Materials for the Study of the Soviet System* (Ann Arbor, Michigan, George Wahr Publishing Co., 1953).

---

[46] For two reports which deal in part with Russian family relationships, see Kent Geiger, "Deprivation and Solidarity in the Soviet Urban Family," *American Sociological Review*, Vol. 20 (February, 1955), pp. 57-68, and Kent Geiger and Alex Inkeles, "The Family in the U.S.S.R.," *Marriage and Family Living*, Vol. 16 (November, 1954), pp. 397-404.

[47] Geiger and Inkeles, *op. cit.*, p. 404.

NEWSHOLME, SIR ARTHUR, and KINGSBURY, J. A., *Red Medicine* (New York, Doubleday & Company, Inc., 1933).

RAPPOPORT, A. S., *Home Life in Russia* (New York, The Macmillan Co., 1913).

SCHLESINGER, RUDOLPH, ed., *Changing Attitudes in Soviet Russia: The Family in the U.S.S.R.* (London, Routledge and Kegan Paul, Ltd., 1949).

CHAPTER 8

The Family in the Israeli Kibbutz

In Hebrew, *kibbutz* means "a gathering" or "a company." Since 1921, kibbutz has come to mean a particular type of "gathering," that is, a collective settlement or village in what is now the state of Israel. There are at present over 227 separate kibbutzim and their total population numbers over 75,000. Sired by the ideologies of Zionism and socialism, kibbutzim have existed in spite of the stark realities of physical hardships, depleted and non-arable lands, warfare, and the scarcity of funds. But the kibbutz *has* lived. In the past four decades the kibbutz has passed from a dream to a fact. Kibbutzim, therefore, are no "wild schemes" or utopian visions. They are functioning and growing communal settlements, which have adopted some of the most unique social arrangements the world has recently witnessed.

A look at some of the general characteristics of a kibbutz is necessary to appreciate the importance of studying the family in this unique society. A kibbutz is a co-operative society in the fullest sense of the term. There is almost no private property. The house in which a person lives belongs to the kibbutz. The food he eats at the communal dining hall is furnished by the kibbutz. Each member receives his clothes and personal effects from the community storeroom. Medical bills are paid by the group, and even a small vacation allowance is furnished each member. All the goods and services that an individual needs are supplied, without the necessity for payment, by his kibbutz.

In the type of kibbutz with which we will be dealing the rearing of children is a community responsibility. Children live not with their parents but in special children's homes, where they are cared for and educated by special nurses and teachers. Like adults, children receive all of the necessities of life and all of the "luxuries" that the society can provide from the kibbutz. Parents have no direct responsibility for the economic needs of their children.

There is a job for every able-bodied adult in the kibbutz. Some work in the fields, others in the various industrial shops, others care for the children, and still others perform the necessary service work, such as laundering, repairing, and cleaning. No one is paid for his work. All profits from the sale of agricultural and industrial products belong to the kibbutz as a group and are used to meet the bills of the society. In short, the group, rather than the individual or the family, is the unit through which the production and distribution of economic services and goods takes place.

In kibbutz society the family as a social unit is most certainly de-emphasized. It is for this reason that the kibbutz family warrants special attention from the family sociologist. What function *does* the family serve when the traditional family responsibilities are borne by the group? Family members do not even live together in a common household, nor are children reared by their parents. Some have gone so far as to say that there is no marriage and no family in the kibbutz. If this were true, and we will return to this matter later, the kibbutzim would be the only enduring societies in which marriage and the family have not been found. Whatever else it is economically and socially, to the family sociologist the kibbutz is a fascinating experiment that demands serious investigation. Could it be that our generalizations concerning the universality of marriage and the family require modification? And, if so, how shall we modify our dicta to take account of these unusual experiments? Before turning specifically to the family in the kibbutz, it is well to explore the ideological forerunners of the kibbutz movement and briefly to trace the history of the social experiment. Such an exploration will enable us better to understand and interpret the daily life in the kibbutzim and the admittedly unique form of social organization of these communities.

BACKGROUND OF THE KIBBUTZ MOVEMENT

For over nineteen centuries the Jewish people were without a "home" in the sense of a publicly recognized national state. The hope and dream of somehow, someday, returning to Zion, or Palestine, was always present among the millions of Jews in many parts of the world. From the suffering and discontent of the Jews in Russia during the 1880's there arose the active idea that in the return to Palestine lay the solution to their economic and social ills. Zionism as an active movement can be said to have begun in 1897 with the First Zionist Congress. As set forth at this convention, the basic aim of Zionism was to establish a "publicly recognized and legally assured home in Palestine."[1] It was felt that the historic claim of the Jews

[1] Esther Tauber, *Molding Society to Man* (New York, Bloch Publishing Company, 1955), p. 9.

to Palestine was not enough. Only through reuniting themselves with the land itself, by working and rebuilding the soil with their own labor, could their right to the ancient homeland be renewed. Some groups at the First Zionist Congress linked the Jewish problem with social and economic injustices and saw in socialism the way to a better society. A synthesis of the two ideologies gradually emerged. Zionism, the reconstruction of a national state in Palestine, was the goal, and socialism was considered the best social organization for a new nation dedicated to the principles of social equality and justice.

Even before the First Zionist Congress there was a small migration to Palestine of Jews from Russia and the countries of Eastern Europe. The first Jewish farming village was established in Palestine in 1882. Economically it was unsuccessful and had to be subsidized by the wealthy Baron de Rothschild. This village, and a few established later, were managed by hired professional farm experts. A group of workers on one of the national farms became dissatisfied with the management system and asked for the chance to experiment with a self-managed farm. Thus was the *kvutza* born in 1909.

The *kvutza* (Hebrew for "group") plan was to establish a strict communal society. The group as a whole was to be responsible for all work and was to provide for the needs of the individual members. For several reasons its founders felt that this method offered the only hope for extensive colonization in Palestine. In the first place, most of the immigrants were inexperienced in farming and would scarcely be willing, let alone able, to undertake settlement on an individual farming basis. Not only that, but most of the settlers were poor. There was also the matter of defense against the Arab marauders. It was believed that a compact group, pooling their efforts and their talents, might succeed where a number of individual family settlements would fail. And the *kvutza* settlements did succeed. Until 1921 they remained the only form of Zionist farm settlement.

From the *kvutza* experiences there emerged two new ideas, each thought by its proponents to hold the greater promise for continued and widespread colonization in Palestine. One plan would combine private ownership with co-operative management; the other sought to retain the communal basis of society but to diversify its economic activities. The latter group held that only by extending communal activities into industries and crafts could the growing body of immigrants best be absorbed. In 1921 the 12th Zionist Congress gave its permission to a group of settlers to experiment with the new expanded collective settlement, or kibbutz, as it came to be called.

Although communal living arose largely from necessity, it gradually developed a strong ideological value. Foremost in this ideology is what has been termed the "moral value of labor."[2] Work is not just necessary for life, it is in itself good. All work is important. On the practical level of kibbutz life, this meant that no "outside" help was to be hired to perform work necessary for kibbutz life. In the early years, too, all jobs were rotated to further emphasize the goodness and importance of the most unskilled and menial jobs as well as the more demanding ones. A second aspect of the developing kibbutz ideology was the principle of equality.[3] If all roles in society were equally good and if all were necessary, then there should be equal rewards for their incumbents. Collective ownership of all property and communal living were thought to be the means for insuring that social and economic inequalities would not arise. No one is paid for the work he performs in a kibbutz, but, of course, money is unnecessary, for everything the individual needs is supplied by the kibbutz. As nearly as possible all share equally in the profits of the group, although the principle of equality is tempered by that of need, as in the case of the member who requires a special diet.

The third principle of the working ideology of kibbutzim deals with the importance of the group and group living.[4] The group is held to be both the source of individual happiness and a worth-while entity in its own right. The group is something more than a mere aggregate of personalities. The welfare and survival of the group require that the ambitions and interests of the individual must be in accord with those of the group, and if need be subordinate to them. Preservation of the group further demands that each individual feel responsible for the welfare of each other person, as well as for the group itself. In the kibbutzim, finally, the emphasis on the group has had the effect that group experiences, whether in living arrangements, working, or leisure, are valued higher than the individual experiences. A person who seeks an undue amount of solitude or privacy is considered too individual-centered and even somewhat odd.

From the early adjustment of the settlers, therefore, there arose certain convictions concerning the best ways to accomplish the goals of Zionism. Today some of these convictions are strong motivating forces for the thousands who live in kibbutzim and for those who yearly seek membership in a kibbutz because of the better way of life that it promises. An understanding of the value system of the kibbutz and the intensity with which some of the values are held is essential for an accurate interpreta-

[2] Melford E. Spiro, Kibbutz: Venture in Utopia (Cambridge, Harvard University Press, 1956), p. 11. See also Tauber, op. cit., pp. 12-13.
[3] Spiro, op. cit., pp. 19 ff.
[4] Ibid., p. 29.

tion and appreciation of the family in the kibbutz. We will return now to our central issue, the investigation of marriage and the family in the kibbutz.

MARRIAGE

By some definitions of the concept, there is no marriage in the kibbutz. There is, however, a relationship between adult members of the two sexes that certainly resembles marriage. We could, of course, simply supply a definition of marriage that would include the kibbutz-type relationship and let the matter rest at that. But the existence or non-existence of marriage in society is not a matter to be solved by semantic quibbling and hair-splitting definitions. It deserves more serious attention. We can get closer to the root of the matter by investigating the regulation of sexual behavior in the kibbutz, ignoring for the time being the question of marriage.

All societies have established a relatively enduring social relationship between one or more men and one or more women within which relationship the principals are expected to find their chief source of sexual satisfaction. More than sexual privilege is associated with the relationship, of course, but the point is that everywhere the socially approved relationship we are describing does provide for the sexual gratification of the people involved in it. Society further prescribes who may enter into such a relationship, in terms of kinship and age, how many can enter into a single such relationship and the means by which the relationship can be terminated. Quite generally, too, there is a ceremony or ritual which marks the beginning of the relationship and following this the principals are assigned a new status in the society.

Sexual behavior outside of marriage is sometimes tolerated and sometimes disapproved, depending on the society and, within the society, on such factors as the age, marital status, and kinship relationship of the couple. Although there is considerable variation in the specific arrangements, all societies place some restrictions on the sexual behavior of their members and all recognize a relatively enduring sexual association of one or more men and one or more women. With these generalizations in mind, we will investigate the regulation of sexual behavior in the kibbutz.

The early kibbutz settlers were chiefly young people in their late teens and early twenties. Displeased with what they called the "false" sexual morality of the European cities from which they came, they set about to establish a rational sexual code.[5] A rebellion against the inequality

[5] *Ibid.*, p. 111.

of the sexes permeated the new code. Let us turn to the contemporary kibbutz and observe how this new code is implemented in the lives of the kibbutz members.

In many of the kibbutzim children are housed separately from their parents. Through high school there is no separation of the sexes in the dormitories, and up until high school the sexes use a common shower. Young children are discouraged from engaging in sexual play, however, and high school youths are discouraged from engaging in sexual relations and even from forming strong emotional attachments with one another. These things are frowned on because it is felt that such activities divert interests from the group and interfere with school and cultural activities.

A young person does not become a full-fledged member of the kibbutz until he has graduated from high school. From this time on, sexual affairs among the single are their own concern.[6] There are no taboos against sexual intercourse between these young people. In the private room of either the boy or the girl, or at some other convenient place, transitory sexual affairs take place as frequently as the couple desires. Young people at this stage of their lives have all privileges of other adults in the community and, as long as they are able to find a partner, can obtain whatever degree of sexual satisfaction they desire. One might speculate, then, that there would be no further changes in the sexual lives of the kibbutz members. But such is not the case.

Most commonly there is a "pairing off" among the young people.[7] A couple decides that they are "in love" and wish to live together in a relatively permanent, relatively exclusive relationship. At this time they ask permission of the group for a double room. The term *marriage* is not used to describe this relationship, but once a man and woman have moved into a common room they are referred to as a "pair" or a "couple." The woman talks of her "companion" or her "young man," and the man uses comparable terms when referring to her. Sexual relations involving one of the pair and another party are definitely frowned upon, although not forbidden. The pair relationship can be terminated as easily as it was commenced. The couple simply makes it known to the kibbutz housing committee that they desire single rooms once again, and the pair relationship is then considered broken. Most pairs stay together, however. At one period it was estimated that the proportion of pair break-ups was a little less than the then current divorce rate in the United States.

One may well ask how this admittedly unusual arrangement between the sexes came into being. The answer is to be found in the kibbutz

[6] *Ibid.*, p. 113.
[7] *Ibid.*, pp. 113-116.

settlers' strong negative reaction to the traditional subordinate position of women and the corresponding dominant role of men. In the kibbutz, women, as well as men, are assigned a role in the productive economy. With the communal eating facilities and the common rearing of children there is no need for a woman to be "tied to the home." The equality of the sexes made possible in this manner was thought to be enhanced by the kibbutz-type "marriage." Selection of mates is purely a matter of the personal attraction of one for the other. There is no need for permission from the group, and the traditional Hebrew marriage ceremony has been eliminated. The woman, as an equal of the man, does not assume the man's name at the time of their "marriage," for this could be construed as a symbol of her inferior position. There are no legal ties between the couple as far as the kibbutz is concerned. Nor does a woman, or for that matter a man, benefit economically from the marriage. Each is entitled to his support solely because he is a member of the kibbutz. In a similar manner, a woman's importance and prestige in the group is derived solely from her own accomplishments. Whether he be a leader or a dullard, the man's reputation and prestige are in no way ascribed to his mate. Equality of the sexes is reflected, finally, in the kibbutz provisions for terminating the "marriage" relationship. No woman need remain with a man she does not love simply because she would have difficulty maintaining herself otherwise, and no man need fear alimony and support payments which sometimes can prohibit remarriage. Just as the two join together because they are attracted to one another, so they are free to separate when they no longer like the arrangement.

The question that remains is whether this arrangement between the sexes can or should be called "marriage." Sociologically, of course, it makes little difference by what name the relationship is called in the kibbutz or whether the couple uses the conventional forms of address, husband and wife. What is important is whether or not the kibbutz pair relationship serves most of the same functions and has most of the usual attributes of what we commonly call marriage. Let us review the case.

In the kibbutz there is a relatively enduring sexual relationship between two persons of the opposite sex. There is a ceremony that marks the beginning of this relationship. It matters not, of course, whether a society requires the principals to a marriage to join their hands, exchange gifts, or dance around an oak tree in the nude. The point is that if a culture truly contains differentiated statuses for the married and the single there is usually a way to mark the transition from one to the other, a way of announcing to the group, so to speak, that a person has changed his status. In the kibbutz we have the request for a double room and the moving of beds into it, certainly a straightforward and self-evident way of proclaiming that a sexual relationship is being established!

There would seem to be in the kibbutz a discernible differentiation of status between the single and couples. Presumably the pair, after the bed-moving ceremony, consider themselves a social unit, and they are so considered by the rest of the group. The term used to describe the pair relationship is not used for lovers or those who are engaged in a transitory affair.[8]

What else, then, must we have before we can say that there is marriage in the kibbutz? The anthropologist Murdock found in his studies of some 250 societies that marriage was characterized by a relatively enduring sexual relationship plus economic co-operation between the married members of the opposite sex. In all of the societies there was some kind of division of labor within the marriage, so that the married pair or group constituted an economic unit. Murdock concludes that ". . . marriage exists only when the economic and the sexual (activities) are united in one relationship, and this combination occurs only in marriage."[9] In the kibbutz, as we have seen, there is no economic co-operation between the parties to a marriage. The division of labor takes place within the larger group, the kibbutz itself. In short, marriage in the kibbutz seems to serve no economic function whatsoever.

Despite the fact that everywhere else marriage has been found to involve economic co-operation, we would venture to conclude that there *is* marriage in the kibbutzim. These pioneer settlements have an admittedly unique economic organization, one which happens to preclude a division of labor between mates. But there *is* a socially sanctioned sexual relationship, sufficiently enduring to make possible the procreation and birth of children. This would seem to constitute the essence of marriage, whatever other functions it usually serves.

It should be pointed out that what we have chosen to call "marriage" in the kibbutz does serve functions other than providing for the sexual satisfaction of the mates. These functions are difficult to define and describe, but one of them would seem to be the provision for a close and intimate type of companionship not otherwise available in the kibbutz.[10] Whether by nature or by nurture, members of the kibbutz seem to need this kind of intimacy or at least derive sufficient satisfaction from it to help motivate them to marry. In the kibbutz sexual intercourse can, of course, be obtained outside of marriage with apparently no group censure.

[8] *Ibid.*, pp. 118-119.
[9] George P. Murdock, *Social Structure* (New York, The Macmillan Co., 1949), p. 8.
[10] Melford E. Spiro, "Is the Family Universal?," *American Anthropologist*, Vol. 56 (October, 1954), p. 842.

But it would seem that the sexual association provided in marriage is sufficiently more satisfying and that the psychological security found in marriage is sufficiently rewarding that, taken together, they create a powerful incentive to marry. Most adult members of the kibbutz *are* married, and there are other indications that most seem to think of the married state as the preferred way of life. In short, marriage seems to serve sufficiently important functions in the kibbutz that it is an institutionalized part of the kibbutz life.

FAMILY FUNCTIONS IN THE KIBBUTZ

As in all societies, kibbutz husbands and wives produce children whom they recognize as their "own." In a biological sense, then, there are families in the kibbutz, consisting of the married pair and their offspring. But there is more to the concept of family than biological relationship, which, indeed, is not always required to allow a group to be classified as a family.

The family is a social unit consisting of married adults and their biological or adopted children. Defined in this way, the family is also a reproductive unit. A man and wife without children would not constitute a family but would be referred to as a married couple or a married pair. It is common for the social and reproductive unit we have called the family to maintain a common residence, to provide for the rearing of children, and to be characterized by economic co-operation among its members. Some would refuse to label a family the mere biological group of parents and their immature children unless the group did maintain a common residence and did perform the economic and socialization functions.[11]

In some of the Israeli kibbutzim, parents and their offspring do not live in a common household. Parents have but a minor part in the socialization of their children, and they have no direct part whatsoever in the satisfaction of their children's economic needs. Is it correct, then, to speak of the biological unit of parents and children as a family? If we choose not to, the kibbutz would constitute the only known society without a family. Our approach to the question of whether or not the family exists in the kibbutz will be two-fold. We will investigate, first, how the socialization and economic functions are being performed. This will allow us to see the possible societal arrangements for the performance of traditional family functions. We will turn, then, to the family itself and attempt to discover what functions it *does* serve. In other words, if the family neither rears its children nor provides for the maintenance of family members, what, indeed, does it do? With these two approaches to the

[11] Cf. Murdock, *op. cit.*, p. 10.

functions of the family in the kibbutz, we should be in a position to evaluate the case for and against labeling the parent-child group a true family. Furthermore, the investigation should provide insights into an admittedly unique form of social organization and an admittedly unusual family, if such we come to call it.

Child Rearing in the Kibbutz

Most kibbutzim provide excellent medical care for mothers. Children are usually born in a hospital, away from the kibbutz, and are brought home with their mothers about four days after birth. It then becomes the responsibility of the group to care for the child and to mold him into a functioning adult member of the society.[12] The child will always live apart from his parents. He will pass, along with his age mates, through a series of children's houses where he will be cared for and educated.

The long period of socialization begins when the four-day-old infant is taken to the Infants' House. Here there will be no more than sixteen babies, all usually under a year old, under the care of full-time nurses. Most children are breast fed and are gradually weaned when they are about eight months old. A child's mother, therefore, has considerable contact with her infant during this period. There is a visiting hour at the Infants' House each afternoon during which time the father can be with his child. When the child is six months old, his parents may take him to their room each afternoon for an hour.

When the child is about a year old, he is moved to the Toddlers' House. Here he will be one of eight children. Two nurses will care for the children and teach them the skills appropriate to their stage of development. The child will learn to feed and dress himself and gradually will be toilet-trained. He will come under the guidance of a specially trained nursery school teacher when he is between two and a half and three years of age. While living in the Toddlers' House, children may visit their parents' room for as long as two hours a day.

Children leave the Toddlers' House sometime after they are four years old and before they are five. Two groups of Toddlers are combined to form a group of sixteen children, known as a *kevutza*, who will remain together until they reach high school. Buildings for the kindergarten age group contain classrooms as well as the usual eating and sleeping facilities, for it is the philosophy of the kibbutz that formal education should be integrated as much as possible with the child's life. Special kindergarten

[12] For a discussion of kibbutz child-rearing practices, see Spiro, *Kibbutz: Venture in Utopia*, p. 128 ff., Tauber, *op. cit.*, pp. 62 ff., and Murray Weingarten, *Life in a Kibbutz* (New York, The Reconstruction Press, 1955), pp. 80 ff.

teachers are employed for the children. The remainder of the day the children are under the supervision of their nurses. After the evening meal, children may spend two hours with their parents. When they are returned to the dormitory, the nurses supervise their showers, tell them a story, and put them to bed.

After kindergarten, the children again move into a new dormitory-school. Although each kevutza retains its identity, in the sense of having its own classroom and bedroom, there may be several or more groups of sixteen children in the school at the same time. The child must now learn to see himself as part of a larger group. When the child completes grade school, he enters high school and comes under the special guidance of his "educator." This person combines the roles of home-room teacher, counselor, and parent-substitute. He teaches academic subjects, guides the children, and listens to their problems. If at all possible, he remains with the same kevutza until its members graduate from high school. While in grade school and high school the child can and does continue to visit with his parents in their room. High school children, however, gradually visit their parents less frequently and spend more of their time with their age-mates. After graduation from high school the youth does not automatically become a full-fledged member of the kibbutz but must ask for admission into the group. It is significant that in the kibbutz studied intensively by Spiro not one child has failed to announce his candidacy for membership.[13]

As we review the child's life from the time he enters the Infants' House until he graduates from High School, it is apparent that the significant adults in his life have not been his parents. From an early age on he has been fed, bathed, and otherwise cared for by his nurses. It is the nurses, and not his mother, who have comforted him when he was hurt, watched over him in his play, and tucked him in bed when the day was over. Under the guidance of his nurses and teachers he has learned to get along within his kevutza, and he has learned the major lessons of life and living from these adults. What the child is, and what he will become, is to a great extent determined by the various non-parent adults so intimately involved in his life.

It is true, of course, that after the age of six months children can spend a little time each day with their parents. Nevertheless it seems that the parents' influence on the socialization of their children is not great. The time spent in the parents' room more nearly resembles a visit.[14] Some have claimed that most kibbutz children are spoiled because so short

[13] Spiro, Kibbutz: Venture in Utopia, p. 139.
[14] The father has been likened to a "grown-up playmate" of his child. See Henrik F. Infield, Co-operative Living in Palestine (New York, The Dryden Press, Inc., 1944), p. 103.

is the visiting period allowed them that parents are not prone to reprimand or punish their children but indulge their whims as far as possible. Parents and children may spend some time together, but the actual rearing of the children takes place outside the family.

The Economic Function of the Family

The child *in* a kibbutz is quite literally a child *of* the kibbutz. Not only is he guided and educated by group-selected functionaries, but he secures his maintenance from the group. Food, clothing, and shelter are supplied him by the kibbutz. Should he become sick, the kibbutz will furnish him the best medical care possible. The kibbutz provides his education and many kinds of recreation. All of these goods and services, as well as many others, are made available to the child because he is a child of the kibbutz. It matters not what contribution the child's parents make to the group. Each child is entitled to the same maintenance and education. Since there is practically no private property in the kibbutz, there is no such thing as inheritance. Parents owning nothing can pass nothing on to their children.

It is clear that the family serves no economic function as far as its children are concerned. We have seen, too, that the adult members of the family, the husband and the wife, have all of their economic needs met outside the family. By no stretch of the imagination, then, can it be said that the family constitutes an economic unit. For both ideological and practical reasons, this is a purposeful arrangement in the kibbutz. Just as the settlers were opposed to the position of woman in bourgeois society, so, in a similar manner, they protested against the position of the child. A major reason for the subjection of the child in the traditional patriarchal family, it was thought, was the economic dependence of the child on his family, particularly his father. By removing the economic dependence, the authority of the father would be definitely weakened, if not eliminated. Nearly the ultimate in economic independence of children from their individual family is found in the kibbutz.

There is yet another ideological reason for not allowing the kibbutz family to become an economic unit and for not permitting family members to live together. The kibbutz, it will be recalled, emphasizes two entities, the group and the individual. The group has a reality and identity of its own and is something more than a collection of co-operating individuals. It is considered important, furthermore, to preserve the group and to do everything possible to maintain its identity. The individual, too, is extremely important. His needs and wants and happiness are most definitely taken into account. It is felt, however, that in the long run it is through the continued existence of the group that the individual will find his greatest satisfaction and fulfillment. The kibbutz's emphasis on the identities of the person and the group is interpreted by its members to mean that the existence of other entities would be detrimental to the important two. Any formal, enduring subdivision of the kibbutz which maintained a stable body of personnel and established and fostered its own identity would be thought to detract from the emphasis on the larger group. And so the family as an entity intermediate between the individual and the kibbutz has been de-emphasized. The family has been stripped of its usual functions of child rearing and maintenance of its members, and children are separated physically from their parents.

We have said that there were practical reasons for the housing of children apart from their parents and for the communal rearing of children. Much hard, physical labor was needed when the early settlers first came to Israel. Every person who could be spared was needed to till the land and construct the necessary buildings. Collective child rearing freed most of the women for work on the farm[15] and made possible an efficient building program in the kibbutz. As soon as possible, suitable living quarters were erected for the children and next came a communal adult dining hall, which could be used also for a meeting place and for recreation. In many of the kibbutzim the adults lived in tents for a number of years, until gradually better housing was provided them. Such a building plan was thought to be more satisfactory than an attempt to erect permanent individual homes for each family.

There can be little doubt but that the communal living arrangements and rearing of children were efficient methods for the early kibbutzim. The children especially benefited from it, for almost from the beginning they had a decent place to live and could be provided a better diet than the adults allowed themselves. But many of the kibbutzim are now well beyond the subsistence stage of economy. It is questionable whether the communal system is necessarily more efficient at the more advanced stage. Most of the women no longer work in fields but are doing the service work, such as caring for the children, teaching, cleaning, and working in the laundry. Perhaps there is a resemblance between the occupation of women in the established kibbutzim and that of middle-class housewives who decide to earn money by taking in one another's laundry. Although no one disputes the necessity of the work performed, the arrangement adds nothing to the economic production of the group. In the kibbutz we find one woman caring for eight children, while another is

[15] Tauber, *op. cit.*, p. 103.

mending eight sets of clothes, another cleaning eight rooms, and so on. Is this necessarily more efficient than each woman performing all of the tasks for her own family? Apparently the system does not allow a large proportion of the women to be released from the usual home-making tasks and to take their place in the productive economy.[16] In the days when many of the niceties of living had to be foregone, communal child rearing enabled many mothers to make a direct contribution to the production of the group. Today, it would seem safe to conclude, communal child rearing is retained largely for ideological reasons, that is, simply because the people want it that way, rather than because it is necessarily much more efficient.

The Family as a Social Unit

There is evidence that the biological group of parents and their offspring constitutes, however, a distinct and recognizable social group-ing that performs definite functions for all of its members. Parents and children consider themselves a unit and speak of belonging to a family. All the members of the kibbutz recognize the parent-child unit and use the Hebrew term for *family* when referring to it.[17] No one is confused about whether he belongs to a family, or to which family he belongs, or why he belongs to one. He realizes he is in a particular family because he is the offspring of a particular adult pair, that there is no other way of gaining membership into his family, and that he cannot leave his family to become a member of another.

The members of a family constitute a social unit in the sense that they interact with one another, presumably in an intimate manner. Al-though not housed together, the family members do get together and interact, usually privately, at certain definite times. The entire kibbutz regularly breaks down, so to speak, into these interacting family groups. One must not, of course, place too great emphasis merely on the amount of time spent in the family group. On a working-day basis, the kibbutz father probably sees more than, or at least as much of his young child as does his suburban American counterpart, who has but a short time between his arrival home and the child's bedtime to be with his child and who frequently, we might add, is too tired to utilize all of it. The same would be true of the working mother in our society. It is true that our suburban parents and their children spend the night together under the same roof, but, if the parents can arrange it, there is no interaction during this time.

---

[16] *Ibid.*, p. 60.
[17] Spiro, *Kibbutz: Venture in Utopia*, p. 123.

Rather than dwell on the amount of time that the kibbutz family is together, let us see what we can learn about the type of family interaction that takes place.

Kibbutz parents and children are greatly attached to one another. Spiro tells us that "for most parents, the entire day is a prelude to the brief period in the late afternoon when they are joined by their children."[18] So important is this family time that all work in the kibbutz regularly ceases. Apparently, family members derive satisfactions from one another that are not attained outside the family and that are desirable to all concerned. If we must give these satisfactions a label, let us call them security and affection. From the children's standpoint, there seems to be a deep satisfaction in being emotionally tethered to a small, intimate group. Here there is practically no competition for affection, and here the child does not have to share the adult's love with fifteen other unrelated children. As the child moves from nursery school, to kindergarten, to grammar school, and so on, he must transfer his affection for one nurse to a new one. But his parents are always his own. His parents' room becomes a sort of psychological home to the child, and it is, indeed, to the parents' room that a child is referring when he speaks of "my room."[19] For parents, the family provides the counterpart of the needs they satisfy in their children. Parents can give freely of their love. They derive the satisfaction of providing comfort and security to their children. There is a "need to be needed" in most of us which a child of our own can meet in a uniquely positive manner. Probably all would agree that "home" means something more than a place to live and to have one's economic needs met and that "family" means something more than a group that co-operates in meeting these economic needs. It is this "something more," this emotional and interactional side of the family, that is present in the kibbutz family and that constitutes, as a matter of fact, about all there is to the family. Perhaps the strong emotional involvement and the satisfaction of deep-seated psychological needs are sufficiently important that they alone will allow us to speak of the parent-child kinship group found in the kibbutz as a "family." At any rate, it does not seem to us an injustice to the sociological concept to say that the kibbutz culture does contain an institutionalized family.

It is of more than passing interest, of course, that in all societies save the Israeli kibbutzim the family is characterized by economic co-operation among its members and the sharing of a common residence.

[18] Ibid., p. 124.
[19] Ibid., p. 125.

Spiro sees as the explanation of this the fact that the kibbutz itself is perceived by its members as a large extended "family," of which the parent-child group is but a part.[20] He supports this view with the finding that members of a given kibbutz tend to avoid marriage with one another and choose their marriage partners from a near-by group. Although a kibbutz undoubtedly has some family-like characteristics, it would seem that the concept "family" would have to be unduly stretched so to label an entire kibbutz. It seems, rather, that we must modify our long-standing generalizations concerning the universal functions of the family. The kibbutz experiment has demonstrated that there are unique types of social organization in which the family is not required to perform the functions most commonly assigned to it. How successful the kibbutz venture is, will be our next inquiry.

EVALUATION OF THE KIBBUTZ SOCIETY

It is one thing to conclude that a society can be so organized that the family does not perform the functions usually assigned to it. It is quite another thing to conclude that such a system is "just as good" as any other from the standpoint of the welfare and the survival of the society. The issue is crucial and it is a touchy one. Does the family really need to perform its time-honored functions, including the socialization of its young, or can these functions be performed equally well in some other manner? Regardless of our conclusions, of course, we are advocating neither one system nor the other. We will deal with the question not as a matter of "should be," but as scientific fact, and fact, indeed, in which the student of the family will be most concerned.

The *survival of society* is a difficult concept. What exactly has to be going on within a society in order to claim that it is "surviving"? Perhaps we should turn the question around and ask what conditions are indications that the survival of the group is in jeopardy. Practices that bring about the disintegration of the society, so that it no longer exists as a separate entity, obviously do not conduce to the society's survival. Such practices could be many, and they either could cause a dispersal of the society's members, their death, or could so radically alter the group's organization, value system, and way of life that a new society could be said to have come into existence. The death of a society, furthermore, need not occur suddenly. Practices that are clearly operating to produce this result in the future are operating against the survival of the society just as surely as those that bring about the group's immediate

[20] Spiro, "Is the Family Universal?," p. 846.

destruction. Survival of a society, finally, does not imply that it increase in numbers or in wealth, although growth in both of these spheres *may be* qualities conducive to survival.

The concept of the *welfare of society* is related to, but different from, the *survival of society*. Theoretically one could imagine an unhealthy society whose survival was not threatened in the foreseeable future. Unfortunately we lack precise standards by which we can judge the health of a society. Let us try to envision some of the characteristics of an unhealthy society and the types of practices that might bring them about.

A society would not be healthy if it produced a very great number of unhealthy people, be they physically or mentally ill or deviants from the group's own standards. Nor would a society be healthy if it forced too great a proportion of its members to withdraw from it. Theoretically such a society could continue to exist if it somehow managed to attract a sufficient number of replacements. But few would disagree that there was "something wrong" in the society that regularly forced a large proportion of its members to leave. These are admittedly crude indices of the welfare of a society. But coupled with the criteria for the survival of a society, they will serve as a rough basis for evaluating the success of the kibbutzim.

The first kibbutz was founded in 1921. Since that time the kibbutz movement has been marked by continual expansion. By 1936 there were already 92 settlements with a total population of almost 23,000. Today there are over 75,000 people living in some 227 kibbutzim. The settlements have developed various industries, including the manufacture of machinery, chemicals, textiles, wood products, and metal wares.[21] Nearly all of the kibbutzim established before World War II have already paid off their debts and have achieved a high standard of living. Meanwhile, under emergency conditions, the kibbutz villages have absorbed immigrants beyond their intended capacities. Of all the Israeli settlements, the kibbutzim have furnished the largest number of men and women for the defense forces, and they have suffered a loss of personnel and property at the hands of the Arabs. To achieve solvency and a high standard of living under such conditions is an indication that the kibbutz movement has so far proved to be economically sound.

Among the original kibbutz settlers there has been a certain amount of discontent, leading sometimes to withdrawal from the group.[22] There have been those who became disillusioned with collectivism in principle and decided that some other type of settlement was in reality better for

[21] Tauber, *op. cit.*, pp. 77 ff.
[22] See Infield, *op. cit.*, p. 69, and Weingarten, *op. cit.*, pp. 156-157.

Palestine. Others found themselves personally unsuited for the collective way of life. They resented the separation from their children, the relative lack of privacy in the kibbutz, and the complete reliance on group decisions. Some women became dissatisfied when they discovered how the equality of the sexes worked out in practice. Having left home and housekeeping tasks behind, many found that they were assigned to these same housekeeping tasks in the kibbutz. Despite these and other reasons for resigning from the kibbutz, the movement has kept far more people that it has lost. Membership in a kibbutz is entirely voluntary, so it is no rash assumption to say that those who remain are reasonably satisfied with their life. It should be added, finally, that the kibbutz continues to attract new members from the outside.

The socialization system of the kibbutz seems to be effective. Kibbutz-born children have developed a strong sense of loyalty to the movement and their particular community. Most of the youths were, and are, given a chance to live outside the kibbutz for a year or have served in the army for an even longer period. The great bulk of them have elected to return to their kibbutz or to follow their mates to a similar one.[23] Some kibbutz-born youths have become the core of new kibbutz settlements. The kibbutz value system seems to be well preserved in successive generations. There have been changes in the kibbutz way of life, to be sure, but the basic kibbutz spirit lives on.

We must conclude, it seems, that the welfare and survival of the kibbutz are not in jeopardy. In a certain type of social organization, it appears that the family can be stripped of its economic functions at no detriment to the society. Even the socialization of the young can be performed outside of the family with apparent effectiveness. But the twin institutions of marriage and the family, devoid of some of the functions they serve in all other known societies, nevertheless live on in the Israeli kibbutzim.

SELECTED READINGS

Aurbach, Herbert A., "Social Stratification in Israel's Collective," *Rural Sociology*, Vol. 18 (March, 1953), pp. 25-34.

Baratz, Joseph, A *Village by the Jordan: The Story of Degania* (London, The Harvill Press, 1954).

Infield, Henrik F., *Co-operative Living in Palestine* (New York, The Dryden Press, Inc., 1944).

Kurland, Samuel, *Co-operative Palestine* (New York, Sharon Books, 1947).

Levensohn, Lotta, *Outline of Zionist History* (New York, Scopus, 1941).

[23] Tauber, *op. cit.*, p. 107.

Spiro, Melford E., "Education in a Communal Village in Israel," *American Journal of Orthopsychiatry*, Vol. 25 (April, 1955), pp. 283-292.

————, "Is the Family Universal?," *American Anthropologist*, Vol. 56 (October, 1954), pp. 839-846.

————, *Kibbutz: Venture in Utopia* (Cambridge, Harvard University Press, 1956).

Tauber, Esther, *Molding Society to Man* (New York, Block Publishing Co., Inc., 1955).

Weingarten, Murray, *Life in a Kibbutz* (New York, The Reconstruction Press, 1955).

Part II

INSTITUTIONAL ANALYSIS
OF THE AMERICAN FAMILY

9

The Family as an Institution

In the foregoing chapters we have investigated the family in a variety of cultures. From the study of cultures past and present, one learns to appreciate the amount of diversity that is associated with the family. The structure of the family group, the values embodied in family living, the way in which the bearing and rearing of children are provided for, and the like vary to a greater or lesser degree from society to society. At the same time, a certain similarity is evident in the family at different times and in widely separated places. It is time now to turn our analytic attention to the American family.

Just as in our cross-cultural studies we largely ignored the relationships in specific families and the behavior of individual family members, so in the institutional approach to the American family we will focus on the idea or concept of family rather than on the internal workings of particular family groups. In order to do this we need first to examine the concept of "institution" generally and next to apply the concept to the study of the family. This should help to clarify what is meant by the institutional analysis of the family, to demonstrate the particular level of the study of the family for which this approach is suited, and to distinguish institutional analysis from other analytic studies of the family.

THE CONCEPT OF INSTITUTION

Everyone realizes that in order for a number of people to function as a social group some rules of behavior are necessary. More than this, there must be some degree of consensus about the societal rules. Just as an organized game would be impossible unless the players knew the rules, agreed upon them, and agreed to abide by them, so orderly social living would be well nigh impossible unless similar conditions prevailed.

Many of the societal rules governing behavior are crystallized in some organized pattern of behavior that is expected or demanded of people in certain positions in society. The societal definition of the rights and duties belonging to the individual who fills a certain position in society is termed *role*. Clearly there is need in any society to delineate various roles and to define how they relate to one another. Orderly social living would be difficult to imagine unless each individual had at least a general idea of what was expected of him and what he, in turn, could expect of others.

The various prescriptions and roles of a society relate in some manner to what the people hold important or essential. The role behavior that is specified and the rules that are in force to assure proper behavior in a society thus represent the expression of values people hold in common. Taken together, the values, the behavioral prescriptions, and the methods of enforcing the behavioral norms serve to shape and direct the activity of a society's members. Areas of social activity that are so regulated and controlled are said to be *institutionalized*.[1] The American family pattern is one institution, while our educational system, our governmental system, and the general pattern of our religion are others.

It is important to realize that the term *institution* is an abstraction. As such, it can be considered apart from any people or objects and can be used without reference to them. We can think of the abstractions "blue-ness" or "cold," for example, without having any particular object in mind even though we cannot observe these abstractions. We can see a blue sky and we can taste a cold drink, but we cannot perceive blueness or cold in the abstract. In a similar manner, we cannot observe government or family in the abstract even though we can observe a particular government or a specific family. It is necessary to keep in mind this distinction between the institutional pattern or system and any specific group through which it finds expression. There is a definite and close relationship, however, between an institutional pattern and the particular sphere of social activity that comes under its regulation. Considered together, all of the families in a society tend to embody what is contained in the institution of the family, and each specific family embodies the institution to some degree. As a matter of fact, the internal organization of an institution can be inferred from the study of the many groups that embody it. Although an institution and the groups through which it is expressed are closely related, therefore, the two phenomena are nevertheless distinct.

[1] For other conceptions of an institution in the sociological sense, see Robin M. Williams, Jr., *American Society* (New York, Alfred A. Knopf, Inc., 1952), pp. 29-31 and references cited therein. See also Robert C. Angell, *The Integration of American Society* (New York, McGraw-Hill Book Company, Inc., 1941), pp. 25-27.

An institution can be defined as *an organized system of practices and roles, developed about a value or a cluster of values, and the machinery designed to regulate and control the affected areas of behavior.*[2] There is a deep sense of loyalty to these systems of social relationships because they are judged to embody the values essential to group welfare and survival.[3] The analysis of any institution necessarily must be concerned with the salient concepts in this definition. Analyses would be in terms of the series of values, the behavioral prescriptions designed to implement the values, and the methods used to regulate behavior, which collectively comprise the institution, as well as in terms of the degree of loyalty manifested toward the institution. Let us determine how this method of analysis can be applied to the institution of the family.

THE INSTITUTION OF THE FAMILY

Values

A *value* is the meaning or definition of worth that is attached to any object, condition, principle, or idea.[4] Values are relative, that is, greater or lesser degrees of worth can be attached to different ideas by the same person or to the same idea by various individuals. When we talk of the ultimate values embodied in the institution of the family, we are obviously referring to values extremely high in the hierarchy of all values. Hertzler[5] talks of institutions being involved in the satisfaction of "compelling social needs" and "eminently desirable social ends," whereas Cooley[6] thinks of an institution as meeting "some persistent need or want." In various other ways it is expressed that the ultimate values embodied in an institution relate to ideas judged extremely important by a society and thought by its members to be essential to the survival of the society and its well-being.

One way of delineating the ultimate values embodied in the institution of the family is to attempt to define the functions that the family serves that are considered essential to the well-being and survival of the

[2] Adapted from Edward B. Reuter, *Handbook of Sociology* (New York, The Dryden Press, Inc., 1941), p. 129.

[3] Cf. Angell, *op. cit.*, p. 25.

[4] For an excellent discussion of the concept of value and its significance, see Williams, *op. cit.*, Ch. 11.

[5] Joyce D. Hertzler, *Social Institutions* (New York, McGraw-Hill Book Company, Inc., 1929), p. 67.

[6] Charles H. Cooley and others, *Introductory Sociology* (New York, Charles Scribner's Sons, 1933), p. 402.

society. With this restriction, we arrive at the functions of childbearing, child rearing, and the regulation of sexual behavior. We and others have referred to these as "time-honored" functions of the family, for it seems that whatever other functions the family may serve or has served, always and everywhere to it is relegated the societal tasks of reproducing young, caring for and socializing them, and providing, through the adjunct institution of marriage, an outlet for and control over sexual relations.[7] In American society at the present time, all other functions performed by the family are considered of secondary importance to the basic three in terms of their relation to the welfare and survival of the society.

It is important to distinguish between the societal functions performed by an institution and the personal satisfactions accruing to one or many individuals who live in a particular institutional group. A man may enjoy helping to rear children and may derive many satisfactions from it. The personal functions that a family serves for the individual who lives in it logically should be separated from the societal functions served by the particular *type* of family the society has institutionalized. The personal values realized through various aspects of family living are important, and they are related to societal values expressed in the institution, but the two orders of values are not identical. In subsequent chapters where we analyze more thoroughly the institution of the family, we will be concerned with the *societal* functions, reproduction of the species, socialization of the young, and regulation of sexual behavior.

Systems of Social Practices

The social practices developed about a cluster of institutional values are more obvious than the values themselves. The practices of a society that relate to the reproductive function of the family can be observed, measured, and even predicted with some accuracy. Practices relevant to the regulation of sexual behavior are at least possible to observe and measure. In a similar manner, the way in which families socialize their young is determinable.

Around each of the basic family functions there clusters a series of intermediate values, which can be inferred from intensive and extensive analyses of the various practices in the several areas of family living. From birth rates, rates of childlessness, and similar data, for example, we learn of the childbearing patterns in American society, and from these patterns it is possible to infer the degree of worth that is attached to bear-

---

[7] See, however, the modifications of this point when we take into account the family in the Israeli kibbutz. See Ch. 8.

ing children or to bearing certain numbers of children. Subsidiary values such as these cluster around the presumably universally endorsed value that reproduction of the species is better than societal extinction. The various subsidiary values thus represent the particular society's refinement and definition of the ultimate value of reproduction, and they can be translated into goals toward which the society's members can legitimately aspire. Our analysis of the family institution necessarily rests to a considerable degree on the systems of practices that have been developed about the ultimate societal values expressed through the family.

Regulatory Machinery

The machinery that has evolved to standardize behavior toward the common family values can be formal or informal, simple or complex.[8] The codified statements of rules that fall under the heading *laws* are perhaps the most recognizable of the instruments developed by a society to bring the goals and values of the family into the world of action. In our society, for example, we believe that only those with certain qualifications should be allowed to form a marriage. Various formal rules, such as the necessity for obtaining the state's consent to a marriage, have been designed to insure that only those deemed qualified to marry can do so. Other segments of the legal structure provide for the detection of violations of the law and the punishment of offenders. Less formally, the customs and mores of society serve to implement the same values.

The totality of the ways and means developed to standardize behavior toward even one specific family value can be an extraordinary conglomerate. Various symbols, rituals, laws, mores, customs, and systems of rewards and punishments surround the ideal, for example, of monogamous marriage. As difficult as it would be fully to analyze the regulatory machinery, there are important reasons for making attempts to do so. Several societies may support the same family values, but they may have developed quite different methods of controlling behavior in keeping with the values. Just as surely can a society retain a certain value in its family institution while developing new social machinery to regulate behavior toward the traditional value. Thorough investigation of an institution, therefore, demands that some attention be directed to what we have

[8] Some sociologists would no doubt prefer to exclude regulatory machinery, particularly formal laws, from the concept of institution. As we discuss various types of regulatory machinery in the paragraphs that follow and in subsequent chapters, it should become evident that such machinery bears directly on the family in a society and should not be ignored in the study of the family. Following Reuter, we prefer to consider it an integral part of the family institution. Cf. Reuter, *loc. cit.*

termed the regulatory machinery. The regulatory machinery alone may be in a state of change, or change in the institutional machinery may be indicative of change in values.

LOYALTY TO THE FAMILY INSTITUTION

We have said that there is in a society a deep sense of loyalty to institutionalized arrangements because they are believed to embody some common, ultimate values. The degree of loyalty to various aspects of an institution, therefore, has certain relevancy for the condition or state of the institution in its entirety. Loyalty to an institution is difficult to assess.[9] Individual lack of participation in groups tending to embody the institution is not necessarily evidence of disloyalty to the institution. The mother of an illegitimate child, for example, may agree with other Americans that children should be born and reared within a family. A bachelor may accept the notion of marriage as a basic societal good.

When the behavior of a growing proportion of people is directed toward goals competitive with the traditional ones, this can reasonably be interpreted as evidence of waning loyalty to the traditional value. It is necessary, however, not to confuse *any* amount of deviancy with disloyalty to the institution. A certain amount of institutional flexibility is probably necessary for the smooth functioning of a society.[10] It has been asserted, for instance, that if every traffic law was enforced literally in any of our large cities, vehicular and pedestrian movement would be hopelessly snarled. In a similar manner, the exceptions and permissible variations from institutionalized arrangements may have more to do with the maintenance of the basic structure of the family institution than is realized. At any rate, the presence of condoned deviations and even, within limits, an increase in the extent of condoned deviations are not unmistakable signs of a growing disloyalty to the institution.

CHANGE IN THE FAMILY INSTITUTION

Every student of sociology has learned that institutional change is inevitable. Whether the change is major or barely perceptible and whether its effects are more or less disturbing, we must recognize that some change in the institution of the family has occurred and is now occurring.

[9] For a discussion of the meaning of loyalty to an institution, see Angell, *op. cit.*, pp. 25 ff.

[10] Stouffer suggests that it may be the provision for some flexibility or "social slippage" that makes behavior in groups possible. See Samuel A. Stouffer, "An Analysis of Conflicting Social Norms," *American Sociological Review*, Vol. 14 (December, 1949), pp. 707-717.

For the sake of analysis, family change can be investigated at several different levels. There is change that takes place in the values embodied in the family institution. Surely it must be admitted that the definitions of the proper size of families and of the correct role of women in the family, for example, have undergone change from colonial times to our own. Less dramatic value changes and changes that are in process are admittedly more difficult to determine and to measure. Nevertheless, when a sizable proportion of a society's membership seems to aspire to family goals different from the traditional ones and attempts through their behavior to achieve the new goals, it is reasonable to conclude that family values have changed in that society.

It is possible for societal practices to change somewhat independent of the values which they express. A society may for some years espouse the child-rearing value of "a healthy personality for every child" (conceivably it could define "healthy" similarly throughout the period of time). Over the years they may develop different child-rearing techniques or new conceptions of parent-child relationships to implement the cherished goal of "a healthy personality for every child." Although the new conceptions can themselves be thought of as values, they are more specifically fresh practices designed to implement a traditional goal. It is cautioned, therefore, that changes in family values can be incorrectly, as well as correctly, inferred from the changing practices of a society.

Institutional change can likewise occur in the social machinery that is designed to enforce the practices surrounding a particular family value. A discernible amount of such change undoubtedly has occurred in the area controlling sexual behavior. The stocks and pillories and public degradation of colonial times have disappeared as approved methods of regulating sexual behavior, and they are rapidly being joined by the threats and fears of a less distant past. This particular area of institutional change is a complicated one, for it is likely that changes in values have occurred as well as changes in methods of regulation. Value changes, or the extent of value change, nevertheless may be improperly adduced from changes in society's attempts to regulate behavior. It is quite possible that the changes in non-marital sexual behavior in our society and the changes in the values we espouse with regard to such behavior are consistently exaggerated because of the very real changes that are taking place in enforcement of prescribed practices.

The interrelationship of institutional values, practices, and regulatory machinery, and the fact that change can occur at any and all levels, make it exceedingly difficult to delineate accurately the kinds of changes that have occurred. The institutional approach to the study of the family, nevertheless, provides a framework for a meaningful analysis of family change. Accordingly, we will address ourselves to the change that has occurred and seems to be occurring with respect to the basic family functions as we deal with them separately in the subsequent chapters.

It is important to realize that there is a fundamental distinction between institutional change and institutional decline. Although change can both strengthen and weaken an institution, it does not necessarily do either. An area of social activity, the family or any other, can remain institutionalized in the face of even pronounced changes. When new family values displace traditional ones, the institution clearly has undergone change. It does not for this reason alone become less of an institution. We will return to the implications of institutional change when, with the aid of a more intensive analysis of the separate family functions, we can evaluate the matter more concretely.

SELECTED READINGS

ANGELL, ROBERT C., *The Integration of American Society* (New York, McGraw-Hill Book Company, Inc., 1941).

COOLEY, CHARLES H., *Social Organization* (New York, Charles Scribner's Sons, 1909).

COOLEY, CHARLES H., AND OTHERS, *Introductory Sociology* (New York, Charles Scribner's Sons, 1933).

HERTZLER, JOYCE D., *Social Institutions* (New York, McGraw-Hill Book Company, Inc., 1929).

PARSONS, TALCOTT, AND OTHERS, *Family, Socialization, and Interaction Process* (Glencoe, Illinois, The Free Press, 1955), Ch. 1.

WILLIAMS, ROBIN M., JR., *American Society* (New York, Alfred A. Knopf, Inc., 1952), Chs. 3 and 4.

CHAPTER 10

The Childbearing Function of the Family

ALL SOCIETIES that wish to be sure of continued existence must provide for and encourage the birth of young. For a relatively short period of time, and this may cover many generations, a society could replace its losses by drawing members from other societies. The religious sect of Shakers, for example, espoused the value of strict celibacy and had no arrangement for childbearing within the group. For over a hundred years the society grew in numbers both in England and in the United States. No one society can be certain, however, of its continued ability to replace its membership from other societies, and it is obvious that every society in the world could not endorse celibacy and the globe remain populated!

There is nothing in the process of reproduction that demands that it take place only in families. We have no record of a continuing society, however, that failed to give the highest approval to childbearing within the family as opposed to childbearing outside of it. Societies differ in the extent to which they disapprove of reproduction outside of the family, and some, indeed, encourage a certain amount of childbearing by the unmarried. Some of the current practices in Soviet Russia reward what our society calls "illegitimacy," and we do not have to look that far from home.[1] In the relief-payment policies of some of our states that give increased payments according to number of children whether or not the mother is married, some see a financial inducement for the unmarried woman to have children. To what extent these policies have this effect, no one knows, but we are certain that they were not *designed* to encourage childbearing outside of the family. The existence of a few instances of encouragement of some childbearing among the unmarried and the more frequent instances of tolerating the cases that occur do not detract from the major point: well entrenched in the value system of every society is the idea that childbearing should take place within a family.

[1] See Ch. 7, particularly pp. 160-161.

Although societies universally agree that reproduction should take place within families, among societies we find considerable variation in such reproductive practices as the number of children the married women give birth to and the ages at which they begin to bear children. We find variation, too, in the methods by which groups attempt to restrict child-bearing to the family, the methods used to accomplish it within the family, and the success they meet in both of these respects. It is clear that although all societies accept the general values that replacement is better than ex-tinction and that the family should provide for the replacement, there is cross-cultural divergency in a number of subsidiary values. Furthermore, a society can alter its values concerning how it should perform the function of reproducing itself and can develop new methods for putting its goals into force.

These are the matters with which we shall deal in discussing the re-productive function of the family in the United States. We will treat, first of all, the reproductive practices of American families and the changes, trends, and differences with respect to these practices. We will deal also with reproduction outside of the family. In all cases we will attempt to see beyond mere numbers and rates into their meanings for the reproductive values in our society.

REPRODUCTIVE PRACTICES

There are many different ways of measuring and describing the repro-ductive patterns of a society. Although all have to do with the number of children that are born, the measurements tell us different things about the childbearing habits in the society. Some focus on the society and allow us to determine what has been the long-term trend in the number of children born within the group as a whole. Other measures are useful for compar-ing the fertility of different segments of the population, and we employ still others when our focus of attention is on families and their size. It is well for the student of the family to be familiar with the indices of reproduc-tion commonly used in the United States.

Crude Birth Rate

One of the simplest measures of the births in a society is to relate the number of births at a given time to the number of people in the society at that time. This is called the *crude birth rate*, and it is usually expressed as the number of births per thousand of the population. Although the utility of this rate is limited, it is useful for purposes of comparison within the society at different periods of time.

TABLE 1. Crude Birth Rate, 1915-1958

Year	Births per 1,000 Population	Year	Births per 1,000 Population
1915	25.0	1943	21.5
1920	23.7	1944	20.2
1925	21.3	1945	19.5
1930	18.9	1946	23.3
1931	18.0	1947	25.8
1932	17.4	1948	24.2
1933	16.6	1949	23.9
1934	17.2	1950	23.6
1935	16.9	1951	24.9
1936	16.7	1952	25.0
1937	17.1	1953	25.1
1938	17.6	1954	25.3
1939	17.3	1955	24.6
1940	17.9	1956	24.9
1941	18.8	1957	25.0
1942	20.8	1958	24.3

SOURCE: U.S. Department of Health, Education, and Welfare, *Vital Statistics of the United States: 1950*, Vol. I (Washington, D.C., U.S. Government Printing Office, 1950), p. 77; *Monthly Vital Statistics Report*, Vol. 5, No. 13; Vol. 6, No. 13; and Vol. 7, No. 10. Rate for 1958 based on first nine months.

It is clear that over the period for which data are available for the United States, the crude birth rate first declined, and, after reaching its lowest point in the depression years, began steadily to rise. The slight dip in 1944-1945 reflects the absence of men because of military service outside the country. In 1947, when the men had returned, we note an unusual spurt in the birth rate. Since that time the rate has been rising at a modest rate.

The crude birth rate for the United States is obtainable only for the years since 1915. For earlier periods, and to get a broader look at trends, we must rely on a different computation, the number of children under five years of age per 1,000 women of childbearing age. Since almost all of the additions to the 0-4 age group are from births, these data give us a rough index of the birth rate in our society for earlier years. They are complicated, however, by the fact that they also reflect the death rates. Over a given period, for example, the ratio of children to women could remain the same even if the birth rate went down so long as the death rate for that age group of children also decreased. Taking this into account, we nevertheless note a consistent decrease over the years 1800 to 1950 in the number of children under five years of age per 1,000 women aged sixteen to forty-four. The inescapable conclusion is that over this period increasingly fewer children were born in proportion to the number of women who were capable of bearing children.

TABLE 2.   Number of Children Under Five Years
per 1,000 Women Aged 16 to 44, 1800-1950

Year	Children 0-4 yrs. per 1,000 Women	Year	Children 0-4 yrs. per 1,000 Women
1800	1,000	1880	635
1810	976	1890	554
1820	928	1900	541
1830	877	1910	508
1840	835	1920	489
1850	699	1930	407
1860	714	1940	342
1870	649	1950	488

SOURCE: Walter F. Wilcox, *Studies in American Demography* (Ithaca, N.Y., Cornell University Press, 1940), p. 267; U.S. Bureau of Census, *Statistical Abstract of the United States: 1954* (Washington, D.C., 1954); and U.S. Bureau of Census, *Current Population Reports,* Series P-20, Nos. 26 and 46.

Net Reproduction Rate

We could imagine a society in which year after year the women faithfully bore children only to have them die before maturity. The crude birth rate would be exceedingly high in our hypothetical case, but the society would soon cease to exist because none of the female infants lived long enough to bear children. In the United States we have approached the opposite situation. Despite the fact that for many years the crude birth rate dropped, the total population increased. The death rate becomes extremely important, therefore, when we are trying to assess the extent to which a society's birth rate allows it to replace its numbers. The *net reproduction rate* has been developed to measure the combined effects of births and deaths as they relate to the stability of a population. The net reproduction rate is 1,000 times the ratio of (*a*) the number of daughters 1,000 women born at the same time would bear if birth and death rates remained fixed to (*b*) the number of female infants in the original group. If, for example, under given conditions of fertility and mortality 1,000 female infants could be expected to bear 1,200 daughters, the net reproduction rate would be 1,200. A net reproduction rate over 1,000 indicates a potentially increasing population, one under 1,000 a potentially decreasing population. While it deals only with female births and deaths, the net reproduction rate is nevertheless a rough measure of how the size of one generation compares to the size of the generation that produced it.

For ten years of the period shown in Table 3, the net reproduction

TABLE 3. Net Reproduction Rate, 1935-1956

Year	Net Reproduction Rate	Year	Net Reproduction Rate
1935	975	1946	1,344
1936	962	1947	1,505
1937	980	1948	1,435
1938	1,011	1949	1,439
1939	992	1950	1,435
1940	1,027	1951	1,519
1941	1,075	1952	1,561
1942	1,185	1953	1,594
1943	1,228	1954	1,654
1944	1,163	1955	1,673
1945	1,132	1956	1,724

SOURCE: U.S. Department of Health, Education, and Welfare, *Vital Statistics—Special Reports,* Vol. 48, No. 17 (November 20, 1958), p. 492.

rate hovered around the 1,000 level, dipping as low as 962 in 1936. Although it is a value judgment to say that a society *should* retain its population level, it is a statistical fact that the net reproduction rate of our country for several years indicated a *potentially* declining population. If the rate had continued at a sufficiently low level for a long enough time, it could have been said that the family was failing to provide for the replacement of the society.[2] Beginning with the World War II period, however, we note a general upswing in the net reproduction rate. The current birth rate is obviously well above the level necessary to maintain a stable population. Quantitatively speaking, in other words, the family is performing more than adequately its function of reproducing the society.

Size of Families

The foregoing data furnish a general picture of what is happening to the population of our society because of the reproductive practices of American families. Only by inference, however, can we learn anything from these data about the trend in size of families.

There are two different ways of considering family size.[3] One deals

[2] The net reproduction rate is not generally considered a reliable indicator of the extent of population growth since it does not take into account fluctuations in such variables as marriage rate, age at marriage, and duration of marriage. Although caution should be used in interpreting the rate of any one year, a long-term analysis of the net reproduction rate nevertheless gives an indication of the direction of population change. For a detailed discussion of the nature and utility of the net reproduction rate see Population Association of America, *Population Index,* Vol. 15 (April, 1949), pp. 114-128.

[3] Cf. Paul C. Glick, *American Families* (New York, John Wiley & Sons, Inc., 1957), pp. 29 ff.

with the numerical composition of families at a given time. It is an enumeration of all of the members, adults as well as children, who share a common household. The size composition of families, of course, can be studied over a period of time and we can determine whether families are becoming larger or smaller in the sense of the size of the group that lives together. *Family size* is also used in the sense of the number of children a woman bears throughout her married life, the fertility pattern of married women or couples. Examination of trends of this kind will allow us to ascertain whether the total number of children ultimately born to married couples is getting larger or smaller.

The distinction between these two usages of *family size* can be clarified by the hypothetical case of a married couple who had six children. If all of the children lived to maturity, it is still possible that at no time were they all living together with their parents. Before the sixth child was born, the oldest one or two may have already left home and established families of their own. In the sense of their fertility level, this couple had a family of six children. In terms of the group that lived together, that interacted with one another, that had to be supported, and so on, this couple never had a six-child family. Both ways of reckoning family size are useful, but they describe different kinds of family size.

TABLE 4.   Average Number of Persons per Family Household, 1790-1960

Year	Persons per Household
1790	5.7
1850	5.6
1900	4.8
1910	4.5
1920	4.3
1930	4.1
1940	3.8
1950	3.5
1955	3.4
1960 (projected)	3.4

SOURCE: Data assembled from U.S. Bureau of Census reports: *A Century of Population Growth from the First Census of the United States to the Twelfth, 1790-1900*, p. 96, and *Statistical Abstract of the United States: 1957*, p. 45.

In a little over a hundred years, as shown in Table 4, the average family household has lost two members. In our society, with its custom of establishing new households at the time of marriage, the theoretical upper-limit of a family household is comparably low. The addition or subtraction of one or two members assumes greater significance in terms of the proportional growth or decline of families. The family of sixty years ago, for example, was 40 per cent larger than that of today and a little over a hundred years ago, in 1850, there were 65 per cent more people in the average household than there are now.

TABLE 5.　Per Cent of U.S. Families with Specified
Number of Persons, 1790-1956

Number of Persons	1790	1900	1930	1940	1950	1953	1956
2................	8.1	15.8	26.1	28.6	32.8	33.5	32.5
3................	12.1	18.5	22.5	24.4	25.2	24.2	22.8
4................	14.3	17.8	18.8	19.5	19.8	20.3	20.9
5................	14.4	15.0	12.8	11.8	11.1	11.4	12.3
6 or more........	50.8	32.8	19.7	15.7	11.0	10.6	11.6

SOURCE: Data assembled from Bureau of Census Reports: *A Century of Population Growth from the First Census of the United States to the Twelfth, 1790-1900*, p. 98, *Statistical Abstract of the United States: 1954*, p. 54, and *Statistical Abstract of the United States: 1957*, p. 47. Also from census data reported in Paul C. Glick, *American Families* (New York, John Wiley & Sons, Inc., 1957), p. 30.

If, instead of dealing with averages, we consider the percentage distribution of different family sizes, we get a more complete picture of the change in the American family. One of the most dramatic changes that has occurred over the years is the pronounced drop in families of six or more members. Fully half of all the families in existence in 1790 were large families (six or more members), and a little over fifty years ago every third family was this large. Today, by contrast, only about 10 per cent of all families have six or more members. The small two- or three-person family has shown a corresponding increase from 20 per cent of all families in 1790, to 34 per cent in 1900, and to 55 per cent of all families in 1956. We can sum up the change by pointing out that in 1790 80 per cent of all families in our society contained *four or more* members, whereas in 1956 almost 80 per cent had *four or fewer* people.

TABLE 6.　Number of Children Ever Born to Women of
Recently Completed Fertility*

Year	Per Cent Childless	Average Number of Children per Woman
1940	16.8	3.00
1950	20.4	2.49
1952	19.4	2.35
1954	19.0	2.34
1957	17.7	2.40

SOURCE: U.S. Bureau of Census, *Current Population Reports*, Series P-20, No. 84 (August 8, 1958), p. 7.
* Ever-married women aged 45 to 49.

A good measure of family size, in the sense of the total number of children born to families, is the census computation of the number of children ever born to married women of completed fertility. Age forty-four is defined as the last reproductive year. If we restrict our analyses to women aged forty-five to forty-nine, we can then ascertain the final number of children a group of women born within a five-year period gave birth to during their entire married life. A comparison can be made, then, of the total number of children born to women who had just passed their reproductive years at one period of time and those who had recently passed their childbearing years at another period of time. In Table 6 we note that the women of completed fertility in the years since 1950 averaged fewer children than those who had completed their fertility in 1940. There was a higher percentage of childlessness among the women who reached forty-five to forty-nine years of age between 1950 and 1957 than among those who were that age in 1940. The women who passed their childbearing years between 1950 and 1954 were born at about the turn of the century. Even the oldest of them had not been married long before the economic depression of the thirties, the years, as we have seen, when the crude birth rates were the lowest. On the average, each of these women bore about 2.4 children as contrasted with the average of three children born to the women twelve years their senior. Family size, in terms of the total number of children born, quite definitely decreased over this relatively short period.

The women of recently completed fertility in 1957 were born between 1912 and 1916. The oldest of them were thus about thirty-five years of age at the time of the spurt in the birth rate after World War II. As a group, therefore, their fertility pattern resembles more that of prewar years. Although by 1957 childlessness had decreased from its high point in 1950, it had not quite reached the 1940 level.

The women who are marrying today obviously have many potential childbearing years ahead of them. We will not know the ultimate size of their families until they pass the age when it would be rare for any of them to have a child. We can, however, learn much about their reproductive pattern and compare their pattern with past generations by examining the data on order of births. In addition to how many babies are born, almost all places also keep records on whether each baby born alive is his mother's first child, her second, third, and so on. For a given year, we can ascertain the rate of specific birth orders and determine what proportion of all children born were, for example, first-, second-, or third-order children. With birth order data we can also examine the trend in family size. It is evident from such data whether there are more or fewer higher-order births today than there were in the past.

TABLE 7. Live Births per 1,000 Women Aged 15 to 44 by Specified
Order of Birth, 1920-1956

YEAR	TOTAL	LIVE-BIRTH ORDER					
		1st	2nd	3rd	4th	5th	6th and Over
1920..........109		35	23	16	11	7	16
1922..........104		32	24	15	10	7	16
1924..........104		32	23	16	10	7	16
1926.......... 96		30	22	14	10	6	14
1928.......... 90		29	20	13	9	6	13
1930.......... 86		29	20	12	8	6	12
1932.......... 79		26	18	11	7	5	11
1934.......... 76		26	18	11	7	5	9
1936.......... 74		28	18	10	6	4	9
1938.......... 78		31	19	10	6	4	9
1940.......... 78		30	20	11	6	4	7
1942.......... 92		40	24	12	6	4	7
1944.......... 89		32	25	14	7	4	8
1946..........103		41	29	15	7	4	7
1948..........106		41	31	16	8	4	6
1950..........103		34	32	18	8	4	5
1952..........110		34	33	21	10	5	6
1954..........114		33	33	23	12	6	7
1956..........116		33	32	23	13	7	8

SOURCE: U.S. Department of Health, Education, and Welfare, *Vital Statistics—Special Reports,* Vol. 48, No. 17 (November 20, 1958), p. 491.

The birth order data in Table 7 contradict, in part, some of the popular beliefs that modern-day Americans are "going back to large families." Much depends, of course, on the definition of *large* and on the base year to which the present birth order data are compared. Third-order births have shown a steady climb since 1940 and the rate today is higher than it was nearly forty years ago. The rate of fourth-order births is about the same now as forty years ago, and it has risen substantially from its low in the thirties and forties. Out of every 1,000 births, more are currently fourth births than were twenty years ago. Only a slight increase is evidenced in fifth-order births over the last two decades, and they are no more numerous than they were in the early 1920's. Sixth-order and higher-order births are fewer than in 1930 and fewer still than in 1920. Putting these various data together, we see that, compared to the recent past, more couples are now having a third and a fourth child. On the basis of birth-order information, we would conclude that the trend is toward an increasing number of moderate-sized families. Large families, if by that we mean those with six or more children, are less common today than thirty or forty years ago and no more common than twenty years ago.

DIFFERENTIAL FERTILITY

In the foregoing sections we have been concerned with broad trends in the reproductive pattern of American families. For a long time it has been recognized in this and other countries that all groups and classes of the population do not enter equally into the prevailing fertility trends. It is meaningful, therefore, to investigate the differential fertility patterns in our society and to examine them with respect to changes in their trends. Only then can we attempt an explanation for the varying birth rates in different segments of the population.

Socio-Economic Status and Fertility

It has been observed that "ye have the poor with you always." To many it has seemed an unwritten corollary that society is destined to absorb a disproportionately larger number of the children of the poor than of those in better circumstances. From time to time the thought or realization of a differential fertility rate by socio-economic status has been disturbing to moralists and leaders of society. Some have seen in the fertility differentials elements of race suicide because the presumed least fit reproduce more of their kind than the better equipped members of society. Others have censured the better educated and the wealthier for not assuming their "fair responsibility" in the bearing and rearing of the next generation. Before we get involved in the effects and the causes of socio-economic differentials in fertility, we need to ascertain the extent to which these differentials have prevailed and continue to prevail in our society.

Differential fertility is no new phenomenon. An early study, reported in 1906, dealt with the differential birth rate in four European cities during the last decade of the nineteenth century. When the women of Paris, Berlin, Vienna, and London were classified on a six-point scale ranging from "very rich" to "very poor," it was found that there were two to three times as many births per thousand women in the lowest class as there were in the highest.[4] In all of the cities, there was a steady decline in the number of births as economic circumstances improved. With due recognition of the methodological difficulties of this early study, we nevertheless can

---

[4] Sir Arthur Newsholme and T. H. Stevenson, "The Decline in Human Fertility as Shown by Corrected Birth Rates," *Journal of the Royal Statistical Society*, Vol. 69 (March, 1906), pp. 34-38.

conclude that over fifty years ago there already was evidence of an inverse relationship between socio-economic status and fertility in Europe.

Accurate information on socio-economic differential fertility for the entire United States is not available for the years prior to 1910. Recently, however, an analysis was made of some data from the New York State Census of 1865 in which each woman who was or had ever been married was asked the total number of children she had ever borne.[5] Information was also obtained on some social and economic characteristics of the family. In general, it was found that occupational and economic status were inversely related to fertility. Among the women of completed fertility in 1865, those whose husbands had white-collar occupations had had fewer children than the wives of skilled workers, who, in turn, had had fewer than the wives of unskilled laborers. Rural occupations presented much the same picture. Farm owners had had fewer children than farm tenants and laborers. Economic status, as measured by the value of the family dwelling, showed a similar inverse relationship to the number of children ever born. The findings of the New York study suggest that as early as the close of the Civil War there was already evidence of class differentials in fertility. The women who were forty-five to sixty-four years of age in 1865 were born, of course, between 1801 and 1820. We can further conclude, therefore, that beginning with the marriages formed about 1820, socio-economic differentials in fertility prevailed in the New York county studied.

TABLE 8. Occupational Class and Number of Children Ever Born per 1,000 Women of Completed Fertility

OCCUPATIONAL CLASS OF HUSBAND	NUMBER OF CHILDREN			
	1910	1940	1952	1957
Professional	3559	2155	1710	1908
Proprietors, managers, officials	3803	2410	2104	2273
Clerical and sales	3524	2175	1932	2107
Skilled workers	4458	2878	2575	2564
Semi-skilled	4643	3087	2828	2791
Unskilled	5251	3561	2991	3337
Service workers	4391	2824	2636	2701

SOURCE: U.S. Census data reported in Charles F. Westoff, "Differential Fertility in the United States: 1900-1952," *American Sociological Review*, Vol. 19 (October, 1954), p. 557, and U.S. Bureau of Census, *Current Population Reports*, Series P-20, No. 84 (August 8, 1958), p. 11.

In Table 8 we have presented data on the number of children ever born to women of completed fertility in 1910, 1940, 1952, and 1957. There is a clear inverse relationship between fertility and the occupational class of the husband for all of the periods. Further inspection shows that the

[5] Wendell H. Bash, "Differential Fertility in Madison County, New York, 1865," *Milbank Memorial Fund Quarterly*, Vol. 33 (April, 1955), pp. 161-186.

differentials among the occupational classes actually have widened slightly over the forty-seven-year period. In 1910 the rate for the professional group was about 68 per cent that of the unskilled laborer group, while by 1940 it was down to 61 per cent. In both 1952 and 1957 professional workers had a birth rate 57 per cent of that of the unskilled worker. Although the completed fertility of all occupational groups dropped over the forty-seven-year period, the three higher occupational groups showed more of a reduction than the lower ones. As early as 1910 and as late as 1957, we find that the higher the occupational class of the husband the fewer are the children born in his family. For women of completed fertility, the nearly five-decade trend in class differentials became somewhat more pronounced.

It must be remembered that most of the women forty-five years of age and older in 1957 did not have many childbearing years in which to take part in the so-called baby boom since World War II. The foregoing analysis, therefore, tells us little about the current class differentials in fertility. Since age at marriage varies, and since how long after marriage children are born can be controlled to some extent, the only accurate account of the total reproductive performance of women marrying since World War II will be obtained as these women reach the end of their childbearing years. Beginning in the mid 1960's the women who married early in the 1940's will reach forty-five years of age, and only then will we know for certain whether class fertility differentials still pertain and, if so, to what extent. We can obtain an indication of the direction in which current fertility differentials are moving, however, by comparing the reproductive records of the women now in their childbearing period with those of the women in the same age group at earlier periods of time.

TABLE 9. Occupational Class and Number of Children Ever Born
per 1,000 Married Women of Childbearing Age

OCCUPATIONAL CLASS OF HUSBAND	NUMBER OF CHILDREN			
	1910	1940	1952	1957
Professional	1818	1266	1653	1939
Proprietors, managers, officials	2164	1459	1759	2085
Clerical and sales	1887	1325	1555	1982
Skilled workers	2575	1842	1932	2282
Semi-skilled	2765	2001	2076	2454
Unskilled	3131	2283	2380	2699
Service workers	2256	1645	1805	2229

SOURCE: U.S. Census data reported in Charles F. Westoff, "Differential Fertility in the United States: 1900-1952," *American Sociological Review*, Vol. 19 (October, 1954), p. 558, and U.S. Bureau of Census, *Current Population Reports*, Series P-20, No. 84 (August 8, 1958), p. 11.

It is evident from Table 9 that in 1957 there was an inverse relationship between occupational status and fertility of women then in their reproductive period. We also note a general drop in the fertility rate between 1910 and 1940 and then a rise since 1940. Closer inspection reveals that women whose husbands were in the higher occupational classes experienced the greatest increase in fertility between 1940 and 1952. During this twelve-year period the fertility rate of wives whose husbands were in the professional class increased 31 per cent; the next two classes increased 21 and 17 per cent, in that order. The three lower occupational groups, by contrast, showed an average increase in fertility of about 4 per cent.

Between 1952 and 1957, the increases in fertility rates for professionals, proprietors, skilled laborers, and semi-skilled laborers were almost exactly the same. The clerical group and the service workers showed a greater increase in fertility, but the unskilled workers showed a somewhat lower rate of increase. In other words, the narrowing of the class differentials in fertility that took place between 1940 and 1952 did not continue into 1957. Not only is there still an inverse relationship between the number of children born and occupational status, but the fertility patterns of the top and bottom of the occupational hierarchy are not much closer now than they were in 1952.

When income is used as a measure of socio-economic status we find the familiar inverse relationship between status and fertility. The relationship is clear and consistent; the higher the husband's income, the fewer were the children born to women of completed fertility in 1957. The married women in the three higher income groups bore, on the average, only slightly more than two children, not quite enough to replace themselves and their husbands if allowance is made for the pre-adult death of some of the children, and not enough to replace all people in their income classes if the unmarried further are taken into account.

The relationship between income and number of children born to

TABLE 10. Annual Income and Average Number of Children Born per Married Woman, 1957

INCOME OF HUSBAND IN 1956	AVERAGE NUMBER OF CHILDREN PER WOMAN	
	Women 15-44 yrs.	Women 45 yrs. and over
Under $1,000	2.86	3.83
$1,000-1,999	2.67	3.41
2,000-2,999	2.33	3.04
3,000-3,999	2.27	2.80
4,000-4,999	2.23	2.40
5,000-6,999	2.31	2.30
7,000 & over	2.38	2.13

SOURCE: U.S. Bureau of Census, *Current Population Reports,* Series P-20, No. 84 (August 8, 1958), p. 12.

date among women still in their childbearing period is an interesting one. While we note in Table 10 that current fertility decreases with increased income over the lower five income categories, there is a reversal of the relationship in the two higher classes. Women in the two higher income classes, of course, do not have as many children as do the women in the two lower income groups. We note, too, that the differences among the income groups are not as large for the women in their reproductive period as they are for women of completed fertility. This narrowing of the differentials in fertility will be intriguing to study in the future. We are as yet too close to the changing pattern to make any predictions except on a simple extrapolation basis.

TABLE 11.   Educational Level and Number of Children Born per
1,000 Married Women 15 Years of Age and Older

EDUCATION	CHILDREN BORN PER 1,000 WOMEN		PER CENT INCREASE
	1957	1950	
College, 4 years or more.........	1,601	1,236	29.5
College, 1 to 3 years............	1,727	1,350	27.9
High School, 4 years............	1,833	1,423	28.8
High School, 1 to 3 years........	2,217	1,738	27.6
Elementary School, 8 years.......	2,127	1,827	16.4
Elementary School, less than 8 yrs.	2,792	2,094	33.3

SOURCE: U.S. Bureau of Census, *Current Population Reports,* Series P-20, No. 84 (August 8, 1958), p. 10.

Our final index of socio-economic status is the educational attainment of the wife. The long-run trend, for the periods for which we have records, has been for family size to vary inversely with years of schooling of the mother. We see, for example, that this is true for the married women both in 1950 and in 1957. Other data indicate that between 1940 and 1950 the fertility rate of the better-educated women increased more rapidly than that of the less-educated ones. Since 1950, as shown in Table 11, the family size of college graduates did not continue to increase more rapidly than that of other educational groups. If the recent data are a valid indication of future trends, then the temporary decrease of the traditional negative relationship between education and number of children born would not be expected to continue.

Let us summarize our conclusions on class differentials in fertility, taking into account the three measures of socio-economic status we have employed:

1. Over the last fifty years, and possibly for much longer than this, there has been an inverse relationship between family size and socio-economic

status. The wealthier, better-educated, higher occupational-status groups have consistently had fewer children than those with less money, less education, and lower occupational prestige.

2. For the bulk of this period, class differentials in fertility have widened slightly or remained the same.

3. The increase in the fertility rate of higher status women between 1940 and 1950 led to a narrowing of the class fertility differentials. During recent years, however, there has been little indication of substantial further reduction of the differentials in fertility. Fertility rate according to family income may prove to be an exception to this latter trend.

Class Differentials in Fertility Explained

The most common explanation for the class differentials in fertility is that there has been an uneven spread in contraceptive knowledge and use in our society. We can document with many studies the position that the higher the socio-economic status the greater the use of contraceptives.[6] It has been discovered also that the higher status groups are more likely to be practicing contraception effectively, in the sense of controlling both the number and the spacing of their children.[7] But we must not be too quick to attribute the differential birth rate solely to the use of contraceptives. When considering the effect of contraceptive knowledge and practice on family size, we must, first of all, take into account the relatively long period of time over which class fertility differentials have prevailed. Certainly methods of preventing conception or birth have been known for a long time, but the widespread use of contraceptives by any class or group seems to have begun several generations *after* class differentials in fertility were already in force.[8] We must also take into account the findings of the Indianapolis study that show that in the group which planned the number and spacing of their families fertility varied directly, instead of inversely, with socio-economic status.[9] Since this group comprised only about 20 per cent of the sample, since the effective planners were chiefly of higher socio-economic status, and since the fertility of the effective planners was rel-

[6] See, for example, Clyde V. Kiser and Pascal K. Whelpton, "Social and Psychological Factors Affecting Fertility, IX: Fertility Planning and Fertility Rates by Socio-Economic Status," *Milbank Memorial Fund Quarterly,* Vol. 27 (April, 1949), pp. 188-244.

[7] *Ibid.* Essentially the same conclusions were reached in a study over a decade earlier. See Raymond Pearl, *The Natural History of Population* (Oxford, Oxford University Press, 1939), pp. 215 ff.

[8] For a general discussion of the types and extent of contraception see Norman Himes, *Medical History of Contraception* (Baltimore, Williams & Wilkins, Inc.,) 1936.

[9] Kiser and Whelpton, *op. cit.,* p. 242.

atively low, we cannot attribute too much significance to the finding. But it cannot be ignored.

The desire to limit family size and the means of doing so are sometimes confused as causes of reduced fertility. It would be difficult to imagine that a people would seriously and for a long time desire to limit their numbers if they knew of no way, or no acceptable way, of doing so. In a sense, then, the fact that contraceptive knowledge is available helps to make people desire to control fertility.[10] However, it is possible that a strong desire to limit reproduction may motivate a group to find a way to achieve its goal. Consider the situation in Ireland. For many years this rural, predominantly Roman Catholic country has had a stationary or declining population. The Irish have avoided overpopulation largely by late marriage, celibacy, and emigration.[11] The desire to avoid overpopulation was strong, and acceptable means were found to achieve this goal.[12] In avoiding overpopulation the means of controlling fertility are, perhaps, less necessary than deeper motivations. It is thought that we will come closer to the real reasons for decreasing births, whether in an entire society or in segments of a society, by looking to the values, attitudes, and the ways of life of a group which make it want to restrict its numbers. With respect to class differentials in the United States, the kind of motivational research we need has not yet been done.[13] All we really know is that for a long time people of higher status have desired to keep their fertility low and have been able, recently through the use of contraceptives, to do so.

[10] The ways of controlling fertility apparently are many and well known. See Himes, *op. cit.* For a briefer discussion of the subject see Warren S. Thompson, *Population Problems*, 4th ed. (New York, McGraw-Hill Book Company, Inc., 1953), Ch. 1.

[11] For a good discussion of the value system of the rural Irish family, see C. M. Arensberg and S. T. Kimball, *Family and Community in Ireland* (Cambridge, Harvard University Press, 1940).

[12] Among the married, the desire for children apparently is strong. See Arensberg and Kimball, *op. cit.*, pp. 137 and 208.

[13] More accurately, not enough motivational research has been done. For a few of the studies that investigated some of the value and attitudinal influences on fertility, see H. V. Muhsam and Clyde V. Kiser, "Social and Psychological Factors Affecting Fertility, XXXII: The Number of Children Desired at the Time of Marriage," *Milbank Memorial Fund Quarterly*, Vol. 34 (July, 1956), pp. 287-312; Robert J. Potter, Jr., and John F. Kanter, "Social and Psychological Factors Affecting Fertility, XXVIII: The Influence of Siblings and Friends on Fertility," *Milbank Memorial Fund Quarterly*, Vol. 33 (July, 1955), pp. 246-267; Lois Pratt and Pascal K. Whelpton, "Social and Psychological Factors Affecting Fertility, XXX: Extra-Familial Participation of Wives in Relation to Interest and Liking for Children, Fertility Planning, and Actual and Desired Family Size," *Milbank Memorial Fund Quarterly*, Vol. 34 (January, 1956), pp. 44-79; Ruth Riemer and Pascal K. Whelpton, "Social and Psychological Factors Affecting Fertility, XXVII: Attitudes Toward Restriction of Personal Freedom in Relation to Fertility Planning and Fertility," *Milbank Memorial Fund Quarterly*, Vol. 33 (January, 1955), pp. 63-111; and Edwin S. Solomon, Jeanne E. Clare, and Charles F. Westoff, "Social and Psychological Factors Affecting Fertility, XXXI: Fear of Childlessness, Desire to Avoid an Only Child, and Children's Desires for Siblings," *Milbank Memorial Fund Quarterly*, Vol. 34 (April, 1956), pp. 160-177.

Not yet explained is the narrowing of class fertility differentials since 1940. Undoubtedly the earlier age at marriage of higher-status people has had some effect.[14] Although the better educated and potentially wealthier segments of the population now have more reproductive years in their marriages than formerly, they would not necessarily have larger families unless they were unable to control family size. We have seen, however, that the upper-status people are the very ones most likely to have contraceptive knowledge and most likely to use contraceptives effectively. It seems reasonable, then, that we may be witnessing a genuine shift in values concerning size of family desired by the upper classes of society. This view is partially substantiated by the evidence that the "ideal" family size mentioned by Detroit women was directly, rather than inversely, related to three separate measures of socio-economic status.[15] More penetrating analyses need to be made of the desires of higher-status couples, and their stated desires need to be compared with their actual reproductive performance.

Rural-Urban Fertility Differentials

It has generally been accepted that rural people have a higher fertility rate than urban people. How long this differential has existed we cannot be sure, but it was noted as early as the seventeenth century in the writings of British demographers.[16] The data in Table 12 show the trend in the rural-urban differential for women of completed fertility. Although the differential has persisted over the forty-seven years covered in the table, there have been some broad changes in the degree to which the rural fertility rate was higher than the urban. In 1910 the rural-farm fertility rate was 32 per cent higher than the urban rate, but by 1940 the farm rate was 52 per cent higher than the urban. There was actually a widening, therefore, of the rural-urban differential because of the unequal fertility decline of the groups. During the four decades the fertility rates dropped more severely for urban than for rural non-farm dwellers and more for rural non-farm than for farm dwellers.

Between 1940 and 1952 there was a contraction of the rural-urban

[14] John Hajnal, "Differential Changes in Marriage Patterns," *American Sociological Review*, Vol. 19 (April, 1954), pp. 153-154.

[15] Ronald Freedman, David Goldberg, and Harry Sharp, " 'Ideals' about Family Size in Detroit Metropolitan Area: 1954," *Milbank Memorial Fund Quarterly*, Vol. 33 (April, 1955), p. 188.

[16] Reported in Anne Anastasi, "Intelligence and Size of Family," *Psychological Bulletin*, Vol. 53 (May, 1956), p. 187. See also John Graunt, "Of the Difference between Burials and Christenings" (1662), in T. Lynn Smith and C. A. McMahan, *The Sociology of Urban Life* (New York, The Dryden Press, Inc., 1951), pp. 250-252.

TABLE 12.   Rural-Urban Differences in Fertility: Ever-Married
Women of Completed Fertility

| | CHILDREN EVER BORN PER 1,000 WOMEN | | | |
	1910	1940	1952	1957
Urban	4,526	2,912	2,571	2,514
Rural non-farm	5,001	3,558	3,089	3,069
Rural farm	5,988	4,449	3,645	3,910

SOURCE: U.S. Census data reported in Charles F. Westoff, "Differential Fertility in the United States: 1900-1952," *American Sociological Review,* Vol. 19 (October, 1954), p. 553, and U.S. Bureau of Census, *Current Population Reports,* Series P-20, No. 84 (August 8, 1958), p. 10.

fertility differential but the fertility difference was nevertheless greater than it had been in 1910. Between 1952 and 1957, however, the only fertility rate that increased was that of the farm women of completed fertility. The difference between urban and farm women was back about to where it was in 1940.

TABLE 13.   Rural-Urban Differences in Fertility:
Married Women Aged 15 to 44

| | CHILDREN EVER BORN PER 1,000 WOMEN | | |
	1940	1952	1957
Urban	1,592	1,747	2,035
Rural non-farm	2,027	2,155	2,356
Rural farm	2,624	2,790	3,009

SOURCE: U.S. Bureau of Census reports, *Fertility, Special Report,* Series P-E, No.5C (1955), pp. 23-24, *Statistical Abstract of the United States: 1954,* p. 50, and *Current Population Reports,* Series P-20, No. 84 (August 8, 1958), p. 10.

For the effect of the postwar upsurge in the birth rate on the rural-urban differential we turn to the data in Table 13 on women within their childbearing years in 1940, 1952, and 1957. Although the usual differential obtains for this period, differences have become less because of the greater postwar increase in the urban than non-farm or farm birth rates. The trend toward contraction of the differential began to occur in the 1940's and is still evident at the present. If the trend continues, there will be increasingly less difference between the fertility rates of rural and urban women.

Another way of viewing the rural-urban fertility differential is through a comparison of the net reproduction rates of the two groups. A rate of 1,000, it will be recalled, indicates a potentially stable population. Even in the first decades of the century the urban birth-to-death ratio indicated a potentially declining population.[17] The rural net reproduction rates never dropped below the 1,000 mark even in the depression years of the 1930's.[18] Since World War II all three population groups have shown net reproduction rates characteristic of potentially increasing populations, while the traditional rural-urban differential has remained in force.

It has been said that in the country children are counted as "helping hands" but in the city as "hungry mouths." In this difference between the economic function of rural and urban children lies part of the explanation of the rural-urban differential fertility. On the farm a child, even at an early age, can contribute *something* to the productive economy of the enterprise. The tasks he performs contribute directly or indirectly to the productivity of the farm and thus to the standard of living of the family. In cities, the child is for the most part economically unproductive. Even if "jobs" can be found for him around the apartment, house, or yard, it is difficult to make a case that he is thereby contributing to the income of the family. Under urban conditions each child in the family is responsible for a substantial sum of money on the debit side of the family ledger, which seldom is even partially balanced by his economic contributions. It is little wonder that urban families typically are smaller than rural ones.

Urban living in itself is scarcely conducive to large families. Adequate space in which children can live and play not only is extremely expensive but frequently cannot be found at any price within the city. The move to the suburbs and exurbs is one way to find room, but it is a costly one, both in direct expenses and the increased traveling time for the breadwinner. What is more, our modern suburbs are seldom built with the large family in mind. Whether he chooses to remain in the city or to move his family "out a ways," the urban worker will find that, cost aside, it is extremely difficult to find adequate living space to meet the various needs of a family of six or more children. It is a simple fact that small families are better suited to urban and suburban living than large ones.

The employment of married women outside the home must be considered in relation to the rural-urban fertility differential. Industrialization has both created jobs outside the home for women and created the need for jobs. Let us consider first the latter effect. In a non-farming economy, almost anyone who is not employed outside of the home is, to some extent, an economic liability on someone else. Industrialization has robbed women of economically productive roles in the home. Most of the making of clothes, much of the processing and preparation of food,

---

[17] U.S. Bureau of Census, *Statistical Abstract of the United States: 1954* (Washington, D.C., U.S. Government Printing Office, 1954), p. 70.
    [18] *Ibid.*

and many other tasks formerly performed by women in the home are now performed in the factory. When we consider the availability of jobs for women in the city, we begin to see why a significantly larger proportion of urban than rural wives are employed outside the home. Among the married women with husbands present we find that 25 per cent of the urban wives, 20 per cent of the rural non-farm, and 13 per cent of the farm wives were in the labor force in 1950.[19] Employment of women, furthermore, is related to fertility. Both among the women in their child-bearing years and the women of completed fertility the average number of children born is lower for wives in the labor force than for other wives.[20] Co-ordinately, the extent of childlessness is greater among the working wives than among those not in the labor force. It appears, then, that three major factors account for a large part of the difference in fertility of urban as opposed to rural women: (1) the greater proportion of urban wives employed outside the home and the concomitant negative effect on fertility, (2) the apparent unsuitability of the city or suburb as a place to rear large families, and (3) the burden of supporting many family members who make no contribution to the productive economy of the family.

It has probably already become apparent that our attempts to explain rural-urban differential fertility can be applied to the changes in the broad fertility pattern of our country over the last one hundred years or more. In 1790 about 95 per cent of our population was living in rural areas. There was no city in the United States of over 50,000 population and over two-thirds of the urban people were living in cities under 25,000 population. It is little wonder that our fertility pattern had a distinctly rural flavor. Today, by contrast, about two-thirds of our population live in cities and over half of this group live in places of 50,000 population or more. Over the last century and a half, in other words, the fertility pattern in the United States has responded to the twin forces of urbanization and industrialization and the correlative forces of declining economic importance of children, inadequate facilities for the rearing of children, and growing proportion of married women in the labor force. The tremendous rural-to-urban population shift that we have witnessed has given a distinctly urban mark to our national fertility pattern.

Race Differentials in Fertility

Since in our country almost all non-whites are Negro, any discussion of race differentials in fertility necessarily revolve around Negro-white varia-

[19] U.S. Bureau of Census, *Fertility—Special Report*, P-E, No. 5C (Washington, D.C., U.S. Government Printing Office, 1955), pp. 84-85.

[20] *Ibid.* Working women also express a lower "ideal" family size than do other women. See Freedman, Goldberg, and Sharp, *op. cit.*

tions. All of the fertility indices, for as long as we have adequate records, indicate that there are a greater number of children born to Negro than to white women.[21] The differential is consistent whether we utilize the crude birth rate, the number of children born to women of completed fertility, or the pattern for the current generation as indicated by the fertility rates for women now within their childbearing years. The Negro-white differential, furthermore, cuts across differences in class and residence.[22] Although urban Negroes have lower fertility rates than rural Negroes, both groups generally have had greater fertility rates than their counterparts in the white group. Among Negroes there is an inverse relationship between occupational status and fertility, just as there is among whites, but at each occupational level Negroes show a higher fertility rate than whites. Negroes are somewhat more likely to be found in rural than in urban areas, and they are distinctly more prevalent in the ranks of the high-fertility unskilled and semi-skilled workers. As a group, therefore, Negroes can be expected to have a higher fertility rate than whites, irrespective of the difference associated with race in and of itself.

The trend in racial differentials in fertility is not clear-cut. Up until about 1920 there was an observable, but not great, lessening of the differences between white and Negro fertility. The gap appeared to have stabilized for a few decades but then seemed to widen again. Negroes, in other words, proportionately contributed slightly more to the postwar upsurge in the birth rate than did whites.

It is paradoxical that over a long period of history Negroes have had a higher birth rate than whites but the proportion of the population that is Negro has actually been decreasing. To a large extent the answer lies in the significantly higher death rates of Negroes, particularly the rates of infant and maternal deaths. As the Negro death rate approaches that of whites, we can expect an increase in the proportion of our Negro population regardless of the race fertility differential.

Religious Fertility Differentials

Over 30,000,000 Americans claim membership in the Roman Catholic Church, a religious body that officially condemns the use of contraceptives and gives positive sanction to large families. To what extent have these and other influences created a religious differential in fertility?

Every adequate study that has sought information on the birth rate in relation to religious affiliation has discovered a higher Catholic than non-

[21] Wilson H. Grabill, Clyde V. Kiser, and Pascal K. Whelpton, *The Fertility of American Women* (New York, John Wiley & Sons, Inc., 1958), Chs. 4, 5, and 6.
[22] U.S. Bureau of Census, *Fertility*, Special Report, P-E, No. 5C, p. 25.

Catholic birth rate.[23] Although simple observation might have suggested this conclusion, it is necessary to investigate the magnitude and the trend of the differential. Both of these matters are extremely complicated because fertility measures by religion are not available over any extended period of time. We must necessarily rely, therefore, on spot studies restricted to certain populations and on the statistics collected by the Catholic Church.[24]

A careful analysis of the records has led one investigator to the conclusion that in 1953 the fertility rate of Catholic women aged fifteen to thirty-four was 46 per cent higher than that of non-Catholic white women in the same age group.[25] In the 1930's it was thought that the gap between non-Catholic and Catholic fertility seemed to be narrowing; recent analysis suggests that this has not occurred. From 1920 to 1949, between 21 and 24 per cent of all births were Catholic. In 1953 the proportion had risen to 27.3. Although we lack the data to make precise comparisons of the fertility patterns of different religious groups, we can state our conclusions in general terms: (1) there is now, and there has been for some time, a sizable difference in the birth rates of Catholics as compared with others, and (2) at present, there is no evidence that this differential is decreasing but there is some indication that it may be increasing.

REPRODUCTION OUTSIDE OF THE FAMILY

For as long as we have had marriage, we have had children born outside of marriage. Our concern with this age-old problem is a limited one. We are interested in the incidence of illegitimacy only in our own society and only in those respects that help round out the picture of the reproductive function of the American family. Loyalty to the reproductive practices and values of a society can be inferred both from the extent to which childbearing occurs within families and the extent to which it occurs outside of families. The illegitimacy pattern in our society can be used as a rough indication of how much childbearing outside of the family competes and, in a quantitative sense, detracts from childbearing within families.

There are three common measures of the extent of illegitimacy. Each looks at the phenomenon from a somewhat different angle and each, accordingly, tells us something unique about it. There is, first of all, the

[23] What is more, studies in Detroit in 1952 and 1954 discovered that Catholics in all socio-economic strata indicated a significantly higher "ideal" family size than comparable Protestants. See Freedman, Goldberg, and Sharp, *op. cit.*

[24] For national statistics collected by the Catholic Church, see *Official Catholic Directory* (New York, P. J. Kenedy and Sons, yearly).

[25] Dudley Kirk, "Recent Trends of Catholic Fertility in the United States," in *Current Research in Human Fertility* (New York, Milbank Memorial Fund, 1954), pp. 93-105.

sheer volume of illegitimate births or the number of children born each year to unmarried parents. Such a measurement describes the magnitude of the problem in a statistical sense; it tells how many illegitimate infants have to be cared for or otherwise reckoned with, how many unmarried fathers and mothers we have, and so on. Obviously it makes a difference whether as a society we must deal with the present number of over 190,000 children born out of wedlock each year, or a fourth this number, or four times this number. But, of course, the number of illegitimate births is partly dependent on the size of the population, particularly the size of the unmarried, postpubertal population. A convenient measure of illegitimacy, called the *illegitimacy rate*, relates the number of illegitimate births to the number of unmarried women between the ages of fifteen and forty-four. It thus compares the number of illegitimate births to the number of women who are socially capable of bearing an illegitimate child by virtue of their unmarried status and who are capable biologically because they are within the childbearing ages. The illegitimacy rate takes into account fluctuations in the age at marriage and the proportion of the population married.

The *illegitimacy ratio* is the number of illegitimate live births per 1,000 live births in a specified population. It describes the extent of illegitimacy in terms of the proportion of all births in a society, a class, or an age group. From the illegitimacy ratio we learn how much of the total reproduction of the species is carried on within marriage and how much outside of it.

TABLE 14. Illegitimate Births, Illegitimacy Rates, and
Illegitimacy Ratios, 1938-1956

YEAR	ILLEGITIMATE BIRTHS	ILLEGITIMACY RATE*	ILLEGITIMACY RATIO†		
			Total	*White*	*Nonwhite*
1938	87,900	7.0	38.5	20.5	166.5
1940	89,500	7.1	37.9	19.5	168.3
1942	96,500	7.9	34.3	16.9	169.2
1944	105,200	8.9	37.6	20.2	163.4
1946	125,200	11.0	38.1	21.1	170.1
1948	129,700	12.7	36.7	17.8	164.7
1950	141,600	14.2	39.8	17.5	179.6
1952	150,300	15.2	39.1	16.3	183.4
1954	176,600	18.3	44.0	18.2	198.5
1956	193,500	20.2	46.5	19.0	204.0

SOURCE: U.S. Department of Health, Education, and Welfare, *Vital Statistics of the United States*: 1956, Part I (Washington, D.C., U.S. Government Printing Office, 1956), *Vital Statistics—Special Reports*, Vol. 44, No. 3, and Vol. 42, No. 11.
* Illegitimate live births per 1,000 unmarried women aged 15-44.
† Illegitimate live births per 1,000 live births.

Over the past twenty years we have had a decided increase in the number of illegitimate births. The annual rate of about 88,000 in the late 1930's has more than doubled and it now rests at more than 190,000 such births each year. Table 14 also indicates that the illegitimacy ratio has been relatively stable for the last twenty years. For most of this period slightly less than four out of every hundred births were illegitimate; for recent years the ratio has been greater than four in a hundred. The illegitimacy ratios for the races differ significantly. Whereas in recent years two or fewer out of every one hundred white births have been illegitimate, the ratio is about twenty out of every one hundred Negro births.

Turning to the illegitimacy rate, we note a marked rise, beginning about 1945, and rising consistently since that time. During most of the war and postwar years we experienced a high marriage rate and a tendency to marry at younger ages, thus decreasing the total unmarried population. But the number of illegitimate births actually increased. There has been a real increase in illegitimacy in the sense of the number of births occurring outside of marriage as compared with the number that could have occurred. For practical purposes it is only the single girls and women who bear an illegitimate child. In recent years, then, a greater proportion of the unmarried women have been having children than in the past. We are left with the paradox that when the economic and other conditions of our society are such that more people can marry and can marry at younger ages, we nevertheless experience an increase in illegitimacy!

TABLE 15. Illegitimate Births and Illegitimacy Ratios
by Race and Age of Mother, 1956

| | | | ILLEGITIMACY RATIO | |
AGE OF MOTHER	ILLEGITIMATE BIRTHS	Total	White	Nonwhite
Under 15 yrs.	4,200	660.8	425.9	798.4
15-19 yrs.	72,800	139.9	62.6	404.8
15-17 yrs.	37,000	230.4	101.6	529.0
18-19 yrs.	35,800	99.8	47.8	317.9
20-24 yrs.	58,800	44.4	19.6	189.7
25-29 yrs.	29,400	26.0	9.6	136.0
30-34 yrs.	17,000	23.4	8.5	123.4
35-39 yrs.	8,800	24.8	10.4	116.7
40 yrs. & over	2,500	26.4	13.5	111.6

SOURCE: U.S. Department of Health, Education, and Welfare, *Vital Statistics of the United States: 1956*, Part I (Washington, D.C., U.S. Government Printing Office, 1956).

The illegitimacy pattern for specific age groups is particularly illuminating. In 1956 about 40 per cent of all illegitimate children were born to women under twenty years of age; in over 4,000 cases the mother was less than fifteen years old. About two-thirds of all the babies born to mothers who are under fifteen years of age are illegitimate, and almost one out of four of the babies of fifteen- to seventeen-year-old mothers are illegitimate. For the nonwhite group, fully 80 per cent of the children born to mothers under fifteen are illegitimate. Since relatively few girls are married and bearing children at the younger ages, their proportion of all births that are illegitimate could be expected to be high. When we use the illegitimacy rate, which takes into account the number of unmarried women at each age level, we find that illegitimacy is highest for the age group twenty to twenty-four and has been since 1938. This age group, and the ones immediately older, have recently shown a considerably higher increase in illegitimacy than others and thus have contributed far more than the younger girls to the war and postwar increase in illegitimacy.

It should be borne in mind that all of the official estimates of the extent of illegitimacy are undoubtedly lower than the true extent. In a society that stigmatizes the child born out of wedlock and severely condemns his mother, the pressures to conceal illegitimacy are intense. What is more, there is quite likely a consistent bias in the reported illegitimacy data.[26] The less-educated, the younger, and the less wealthy are not as likely to be able to conceal illegitimacy even if they want to do so, and those from groups where the stigma of bastardy is not as pronounced are not as likely to want to conceal it. To an unascertainable extent, therefore, illegitimacy is under-reported in our society, and it is more under-reported among whites than Negroes, among older than the younger mothers, and among the better-educated than the less-educated.[27]

How, finally, should we interpret the illegitimacy pattern in our society and its trend? From the standpoint of its effect on the reproductive function of the American family, the number of children born out of wedlock and the proportion of all births that are illegitimate have had an almost negligible effect. The increase in illegitimacy in the last decade, as sharp as it is from some standpoints, by no means indicates that the reproductive function of the family is being threatened by a willingness to bear children outside of the family. No one knows how many, but certainly a large proportion of unmarried parents hold loyally to the value that reproduction should take place only in the family, probably even more so after their own experience than before it. And if, as in recent years,

[26] Cf. U.S. Department of Health, Education, and Welfare, *Vital Statistics—Special Reports*, Vol. 33, No. 5 (February 15, 1950), p. 81.

[27] For one attempt to determine the direction and magnitude of the bias in reported illegitimacy, see Clark E. Vincent, "The Unwed Mother and Sampling Bias," *American Sociological Review*, Vol. 19 (October, 1954), pp. 562-567.

we have come to regard the unmarried mother as more in need of therapy than censure and her child more needful of help than condemnation to a life of jeopardy and shame, it does not mean that we are giving tacit approval to childbearing outside of marriage. Although there is evidence of some change in our methods of discouraging childbearing outside of the family, in the direction of making the controls both more humane and more in keeping with sociological and psychiatric knowledge, there seems to be no evidence of change in the basic value of the reproductive function of the family.

CHILDLESSNESS

The extent of childless marriages in our society bears investigation as evidence of loyalty or disloyalty to the reproductive function of the family. If a sizable proportion of all women, for example, never in the course of their married life bore a child, we would be forced to conclude that the reproductive function of the family was statistically unimportant. In a similar manner, an ever-growing proportion of permanently childless marriages could only mean that the childbearing function of the family was becoming less significant or, if one prefers, that the family was losing this function. In this section, then, we want to investigate the current rate and trend of childless marriages in the United States.

TABLE 16.   Childlessness among Women Ever Married

| | Per Cent Childless | | |
Age	1940	1950	1957
15-44	26.5	22.8	15.9
15-19	54.6	52.8	47.9
20-24	39.9	33.3	26.9
25-29	30.1	21.1	13.1
30-34	23.3	17.3	11.3
35-39	19.9	19.1	12.3
40-44	17.4	20.0	14.1
45-49	16.8	20.4	17.7
50 and over	16.6	18.1	17.8

Source: U.S. Bureau of Census, *Current Population Reports,* Series P-20, No. 84 (August 8, 1958), p. 7.

There is no doubt that the long-run trend in childlessness has been upward. In 1890 about 8 per cent of all married women of completed fertility had never borne a child; in 1952, the figure was 19 per cent. It seems, however, that we are witnessing a dramatic reversal in the upswing of childlessness. The bulk of women who married since World War II were, in 1957, below thirty-five years of age. We can, therefore, compare the extent of childlessness in the group who were under thirty-five in 1957 with that of the women who were under thirty-five in 1940 and obtain a preview of the ultimate fertility pattern of the war and postwar wives. Fewer of the women married during and after World War II are childless as compared with the women married in the previous decade. Only 11 per cent of the women who were thirty to thirty-four in 1957 were childless in what was then about ten years after their marriage. It is likely that a number of these women, perhaps as many as a third of them, will yet bear a child. This would reduce childlessness to about 8 per cent of all marriages, the same proportion as prevailed in the 1890's. Already these women and even those in the next-younger age group have a lower proportion of childlessness than their seniors who have had ten and fifteen additional years in which to bear children. The future has already happened. Childlessness has decreased; we need only to wait until the younger women pass through their childbearing years to determine the *extent* to which it has decreased.

Since we are concerned with the basic value of reproduction in the family and loyalty to this value, it is of considerable importance to determine the extent to which childlessness is a voluntary or involuntary phenomenon. It makes a difference, in other words, whether the childless couples have chosen not to bear children or whether they have been forced to accept this condition. It is by no means easy, however, to determine the proportion of all childlessness that is voluntary. In the first place, we have the matter of a suitable definition. Although at first it might seem to be a simple matter to define voluntary childlessness, a moment's reflection will indicate that such is not the case. Since the only certain test of fertility is successful parturition, it is entirely possible that some couples who are actively taking measures to prevent conception could not have a child in any case. Despite the fact that, unknown to themselves, they are biologically incapable of reproduction, we would perhaps be prone to label such couples voluntarily childless. But what of the couples who in the early years of marriage actively try to prevent conception only to find that when they abandon the measures they remain childless? Are these couples voluntarily or involuntarily childless, or both, depending on when in their married life their condition is being defined? No one knows, of course, whether in their younger years these particular couples could have conceived, and this question further contributes to our definitional dilemma. Among those classified as "voluntarily childless" we have some who are physiologically incapable of bearing a child, and among the "involuntarily childless" are those who at the time of marriage when their chances of conception were highest sought to prevent it. Adequate knowledge of the proportion of all childlessness that is voluntary is further hampered by the lack of large-scale studies, embracing various age, class, and other groups. The best estimate to date, taking into account the various difficulties we have mentioned, is that about half of all childless couples are voluntarily so.

Among the relatively small proportion of all couples who are voluntarily childless are those of many bents and persuasions. Whatever the reasons for their desires, whether they believe themselves to be economically incapable of having children or temperamentally unsuited as parents, many in this group are basically loyal to the reproductive values of our society. They are loyal in the same sense that a bachelor is loyal to the institution of marriage and does not want to reshape our mating system around the principles of free love. They are loyal in the same sense that some non-churchgoers and some people non-religious by almost any definition nevertheless feel strongly that religion is an important societal institution. Despite the fact that only a small segment of our married population believes that parenthood is not for them, there seems to be no real evidence that reproduction is, or is becoming, a less essential part of the American family than ever it was.

SUMMARY

In the opening pages of this chapter the point was made that although societies everywhere espouse the basic value of reproduction of the species within the family, there is considerable cross-cultural variation in the way this value is interpreted and the practices designed to implement it. At the present juncture the student is no doubt convinced that there is "considerable variation" even within his own society, and he may have wondered more than once whether we can speak of basic values concerning the reproductive function of the American family. This impression may partly be the result of our purposefully segmentalized approach in which we took apart, so to speak, the fabric of a specific family function and examined it strand by strand and sometimes thread by thread. We will now attempt to reverse the operation, aided by the insights and knowledge gained in the original procedure.

To a certain small extent reproduction of the species occurs outside of the family in our society. Some families, moreover, serve no reproductive function whatsoever. But the vast majority of women never bear a child outside of marriage. Over 90 per cent of both sexes marry sometime in their life, and to over 80 per cent of married couples there is born at least one child. What is more, these facts have obtained year after year after year. The very obviousness of these generalizations obscures their meaning. Perhaps only an observer from a family-less culture could grasp the impressive regularities of the reproductive patterns of our society. Such an observer, we would suppose, would be struck at once by the tenacity with which we have held to these values through the famines, feasts, and floods of many years. So impressed would our observer be with the basic similarity over time of the reproductive pattern of our society that he would probably fail to notice the myriad changes in the less basic attitudes. Nor is it merely an exercise in fantasy to attempt the completely detached viewpoint of the mythical observer. After all, we have never "abolished" childbearing even for so short a period as a year or a decade, and we have never experimented with having, for example, half of the children in society born outside of the family and half within it. Truly there has been in our society an essential similarity in the reproductive values and practices concerning whether or not reproduction should take place within the family. These values are so basic, so nearly unanimously held, that it is hard sometimes to view them as the points of agreement they are.

Throughout the present chapter we have noticed, on the other hand, a certain variability in the reproductive practices both over time and, at a given time, within the many sub-groups that make up our society. Much of this variation in reproductive practices undoubtedly is a reflection of value differences. Within the strongly held framework of reproductive values, we allow competitive values to be held and to be put into practice. We have, to some extent, institutionalized our variation and formalized our divergency. Finally, we have more or less tolerated a certain small amount of deviation. It is difficult to see how any or all of this can be construed as a "loss" in the reproductive function of the family in any important sense. Change we have had, and change we will continue to have, but reproduction of the species remains an extremely important function of the family, unthreatened by change and unharmed by divergency.

SELECTED READINGS

Bernett, Eleanor, *America's Children* (New York, John Wiley & Sons, Inc., 1958).

Eugenics Quarterly. (Pertinent articles appear in every volume.)

Frazier, E. Franklin, *The Negro Family in the United States*, rev. ed. (New York, The Dryden Press, Inc., 1948).

Glick, Paul C., *American Families* (New York, John Wiley & Sons, Inc., 1957).

GRABILL, WILSON H., KISER, CLYDE V., and WHELPTON, PASCAL K., *The Fertility of American Woman* (New York, John Wiley & Sons, Inc., 1958).

KISER, CLYDE V., and WHELPTON, PASCAL K., "Résumé of the Indianapolis Study of Social and Psychological Factors Affecting Fertility," *Population Studies*, Vol. 7 (November, 1953), pp. 95-110.

Milbank Memorial Fund Quarterly. (Pertinent articles in every volume.)

U. S. Bureau of the Census, *Current Population Reports—Population Characteristics,* Series P-20 (Washington, D.C., U.S. Government Printing Office).

———, *Fertility,* Special Report, P-E, No. 5C (Washington, D.C., U.S. Government Printing Office, 1955).

U. S. Department of Health, Education, and Welfare, *Vital Statistics of the United States* (Washington, D.C., U.S. Government Printing Office, yearly).

———, *Vital Statistics—Special Reports* (Washington, D.C., U.S. Government Printing Office).

CHAPTER 11

The Function of Socialization

IN ONE SENSE, the reproduction of the human species is not accomplished with the birth of a child. It is begun, but it is not completed. If he is to replace a social being, the infant must be submitted to a relatively long period of training, instruction, and indoctrination, and only then will he be sufficiently human to take his place in a society with other humans. The whole process is so gradual and much of it is so subtle that it is difficult to grasp and appreciate the dramatic metamorphoses involved in an infant's becoming a social adult. Our first objective in this chapter, therefore, is to gain a more thorough understanding of the nature of socialization. We will then be in a better position to discuss qualitative and quantitative aspects of the American family's role in the socialization of its young.

THE NATURE OF SOCIALIZATION

Sociologists use the concept *socialization* to refer to the process through which an infant is prepared eventually to take his place in the group into which he was born.[1] Socialization is the process of learning the group's mores and standards and learning to conform to them, of learning the group's traditions, of becoming imbued with a sense of oneness with the group, and of doing all of this to a degree sufficient to command at least the tolerance of one's fellow men. A socialized being has acquired, furthermore, a myriad of physical, mental, and social skills that take their form and content from the culture in which they are found. Socialization is thus education in its broadest sense; it includes all of the results of learning from other people, whether the learning takes place formally or informally and, indeed, whether or not the teacher and the learner know that it is happening.

[1] Cf. Kimball Young, *Social Psychology* (New York, Appleton-Century-Crofts, Inc., 1944), p. 564.

Even from our brief discussion of the nature of socialization its importance should be manifest. No society could long endure if socialization were not performed. So accustomed are we to living and interacting with socialized beings that we find it almost impossible to imagine a member of our species, with unimpaired capacity to learn, who had learned absolutely nothing from fellow humans. So accustomed are we, too, to dealing with members of our own and similar societies that we sometimes fail to comprehend the range of variation that can be wrought through different systems of socialization. Cross-cultural comparisons, therefore, can teach us much about the significance of socialization by allowing us to examine the results of socialization that differs in content from that of our own society. But even when what is taught and learned is quite different from that of our own society, there is still socialization. The people, however different, are nevertheless social beings. Perhaps the import of socialization could be grasped most quickly and dramatically if we could discover completely unsocialized humans.

No social scientist would suggest that we devise an experiment involving the deliberate seclusion of a human infant from all human contact for a number of years merely to determine the effects it might have on his personality and social development. There have been instances, however, when such an experiment unwittingly has been approached. Probably everyone has heard something about the so-called "wild men" or "wolf children" who are known or assumed to have been reared from infancy by wolves, bears, or other animals. The discovery of *ferals*, as such individuals are technically called, provides us with a glimpse of human beings as nearly unaffected by their fellows as it is possible to imagine. From time to time, moreover, children are discovered who have been reared by their parents or others in what approached complete isolation. Such *isolates* have had a minimum of human attention and interaction, just barely enough to keep them alive. By turning our attention first to ferals and then to isolates, we will be able to get some idea of the nature of socialization and its utter necessity in producing an individual whom we would deign to call human.

Ferals

Legend says that Romulus and Remus, abandoned by their parents, were suckled by a she-wolf, who reared them until they were able to fend for themselves. Accounts similar to this, varying only in details, are found with remarkable regularity in the myths and folklore of many peoples. Perhaps beneath the surface of what we label myth is a stratum of reality in the sense that actual cases provided the substance around which the legends were embellished. But, myths aside, there are a few instances in which we can be reasonably sure that a child was reared by a sub-human animal. Such is the case of the "wolf-girls" of India, given the names Amala and Kamala, who were found by a missionary and taken to his orphanage.[2] This case is unique in that the same person observed the girls in the company of wolves, subsequently captured them, reared them and, what is more, kept a running account of their post-capture activities. The diary and pictures of the girls at various stages of re-development have been examined by a number of responsible experts. No less an authority than Arnold Gesell concluded that the pictures could not have been faked and stated that "there can be no doubt whatever that Amala and Kamala early in life were adopted by a nursing wolf."[3]

On his missionary rounds in a jungle area of India, the Rev. Mr. Singh learned of a strange "man-ghost" that frightened the natives by its nocturnal appearances. Mr. Singh had a platform erected in a tree near where the "man-ghost" had been seen, and in his diary the missionary tells us what he observed from that vantage point:[4]

The same Saturday, October 9, 1920, evening, long before dusk, at about 4:30 or 5:00 P.M., we stealthily boarded the machan and anxiously waited there for an hour or so. All of a sudden, a grown-up wolf came out from one of the holes, which was very smooth on account of their constant egress and ingress. This animal was followed by another of the same size and kind. The second was followed by a third, closely followed by two cubs one after the other. The holes did not permit two together.

Close after the cubs came the ghost—a hideous-looking being—hand, foot, and body like a human being; but the head was a big ball of something covering the shoulders and the upper portion of the bust, leaving only a sharp contour of the face visible, and it was human. Close at its heels there came another awful creature exactly like the first, but smaller in size. Their eyes were bright and piercing, unlike human eyes. I at once came to the conclusion that these were human beings.

[2] A report of this case has been prepared both by the missionary and by Arnold Gesell. See J. A. L. Singh and Robert M. Zingg, Wolf-Children and Feral Man (New York, Harper & Brothers, 1939), and Arnold Gesell, Wolf Child and Human Child (New York, Harper & Brothers, 1940).

[3] Singh and Zingg, op. cit., p. xvii. The authenticity of this case recently has been challenged by Bettelheim. The essence of his argument seems that since the behavior of Kamala (he accepts Singh's account of her behavior) resembled that of non-feral autistic children at a treatment center, Kamala was autistic and had not been reared by wolves. Bettelheim seems to ignore the account of Singh and others who observed Kamala in the company of wolves. See, however, Bruno Bettelheim, "Feral Children and Autistic Children," American Journal of Sociology, Vol. 64 (March, 1959), pp. 455-467.

[4] Singh and Zingg, op. cit., p. 5.

The wolf-children were observed on a second night and in the morning were captured by the missionary and his assistants. Amala, the younger of the girls, was thought to be about one and a half years old and the older girl was judged to be about eight years old. There is no reason to believe that they were sisters. Amala died about a year after her capture, but Kamala lived for almost nine years. Much of the missionary's account, therefore, is concerned with the older girl.

In the early accounts of the girls, one is struck at once by their utter lack of human traits. They could not stand erect or walk at all. They moved either by running on all fours or by crawling on their knees. When first taken to the orphanage they showed extreme fear in the presence of humans and would huddle, for hours at a time, mute and still in a corner of the room. In the following passage, Mr. Singh describes their uncanny nocturnal howling, which was the only sound that was heard from them.[5]

This cry was a peculiar one; it began with a hoarse voice and ended in a shrill wailing, very loud and continuous. It had a piercing note of a very high pitch. It was neither human nor animal. I presumed it was a call to their companions, the wolves, or the cubs. . . . Almost every night they used to cry regularly three times, once at about ten o'clock in the evening, once at one o'clock, and once at three o'clock in the morning. . . . It could be heard from a good distance. . . . They went on crying at regular intervals. Later they used to cry now and then, but always at dead of night and never during the day.

The food habits of Amala and Kamala were scarcely human, whether we consider their method of eating or their preferred diet. They did not use their hands to take food but lowered their mouths to the plate on the floor. Kamala, we are told, would eat from the same plate with the dogs whenever she was not prevented from doing so. Recorded in the diary about a year after the girls were brought to the orphanage is this commentary on Kamala's eating preferences:[6]

Not only did she eat carrion, but she even attacked the vultures and crows and drove them from a carcass in the field. After driving them away, she commenced eating the meat very ferociously. At times, she dragged the dead body to and fro, and if the vultures approached it, she drove them away again and again, with a peculiar harsh noise proceeding from the mouth and nose.

Before this, it was noticed, when she found a dead chicken lying in the courtyard, that she at once took it in her mouth and ran out on all fours so quickly that she could not be overtaken. She hid herself inside the lantana bushes, and was not found till she herself came out after finishing the chicken. A feather and particles of meat were found on her lips and on the sides of her cheek.

[5] Ibid., p. 45.
[6] Ibid., p. 77.

Under the affectionate and patient care of Mrs. Singh, Kamala began to lose many of her wolf-like characteristics. It was almost three years, however, before Kamala could stand upright. She never learned to run except on all fours. Six years after her capture we find the first mention of her desire to be clothed and then only when she went out-of-doors. Kamala said her first word after about three years of living in the Singh's orphanage and at the time of her death had a vocabulary of about forty words.

No one can be sure for how long Kamala had lived with the wolves, although the presumption is that it had been since early infancy. Although we know nothing of her hereditary background, the case does furnish us an appreciation of the importance of human contact in the early years of life in order to develop into a normal, social being. Any doubts we may have had concerning the necessity and importance of socialization as a basic societal function are dramatically dispelled. Certainly a literal interpretation of Rosseau's classic statement, "Man is born free, but everywhere he is in chains," seems untenable. Whatever were the potentialities of Amala and Kamala, it is safe to assume that they achieved them to only an infinitesimally small degree because they were bound from infancy by the chains of freedom from human association. It is more than a play on words to conclude that the only reason human beings have personalities is that they have been reared by persons!

Isolates

From time to time children are discovered who have lived for many years, even from infancy, locked in storage rooms or attics and whose life has been devoid of all but the minimum of human contact. Although interaction of a sort took place with others, in some of these cases there was never established a close, intimate relationship with the child. Such children who are physically, socially, and emotionally removed from their fellows are called isolates. A study of isolates complements the study of ferals in our quest for more complete knowledge of the importance of socialization. Although presumably great physical and other demands are made of a feral to adjust to the rigors of wilderness life, almost no demands are made on the isolate, vegetating in his solitary prison. Ferals and isolates present different problems when once discovered. Amala and Kamala, for example, had much unlearning to do before they could acquire human traits. With the extreme isolate, it is almost as if nothing had been learned. The following cases of isolates, given the names of Anna and Isabelle, were first described by Kingsley Davis.[7]

Anna was born in the private home of a nurse in 1932. She was the second illegitimate child of a presumably moronic daughter of a Pennsylvania farmer. After her birth, Anna was taken to a children's home and later she was boarded for a time with a practical nurse. All who saw her and cared for her, we are told, said that she seemed to be a perfectly normal baby and, indeed, quite a beautiful child. Between the time she was six and ten months old she was returned to her mother's home, where she was destined to remain for the next five years, imprisoned in an upstairs room.

Apparently Anna spent her entire days and nights in a semi-slouched position in a broken chair. Possibly before she became apathetic she was even tied to the chair. For almost five years she was fed only milk. No one bothered to train her in any way, to bathe her, to play with her, or to caress her. Anna was barely kept alive and received what must have approached an absolute minimum of human care. Anna was discovered in 1938, shortly before her sixth birthday, and was taken to a county home. The following passage describes her condition at that time:[8]

When first brought to the county home she had been completely apathetic—had lain in a limp, supine position, immobile, expressionless, indifferent to everything. Her flaccid feet had fallen forward, making almost a straight line with the skeleton-like legs, indicating that the child had long lain on her back to the point of exhaustion and atrophy of her foot muscles. She was believed to be deaf and possibly blind.

Though her eyes surveyed the room, especially the ceiling, it was difficult to tell if she was looking at anything in particular. She neither smiled nor cried in our presence, and the only sound she made—a slight sucking intake of breath with the lips—occurred rarely. She did frown or scowl occasionally in response to no observable stimulus; otherwise she remained expressionless.

Anna remained at the county home for about nine months, during which time she received little training. She was placed in a foster home for another nine months and ended up in an institution for mental defectives. Anna died in 1942, when she was about ten and a half years old. The reports prior to her death indicate that she had made remarkable improvement in the four years after her discovery. At the same time, it seemed that there was little possibility that she would ever attain mental and social normality. Anna could walk well but ran clumsily. She could dress

[7] The account that follows is based on Kingsley Davis, "Extreme Social Isolation of a Child," *American Journal of Sociology*, Vol. 45 (January, 1940), copyright 1940 by the University of Chicago, pp. 554-565, and Kingsley Davis, "Final Note on a Case of Extreme Isolation," *American Journal of Sociology*, Vol. 52 (March, 1947), pp. 432-437.

[8] Davis, "Extreme Social Isolation of a Child," pp. 555-556.

herself but could not fasten buttons, and she could not manipulate a knife and fork in eating. Amazingly enough, she did learn how to talk, but her speech was arrested at about the two-year-old level. No one knows how nearly normal Anna would have become had she lived to maturity, and no one knows whether if real efforts at training had been made after her discovery she would have responded any differently. We are shown vividly, however, what the lack of adequate care in a setting of personal and intimate relations produced in a human being.

Another case of an extreme isolate came to light just nine months after the discovery of Anna.[9] This case shows some remarkable similarities to the previous one. The girl, given the pseudonym Isabelle, was born within a month of Anna. Isabelle, too, was illegitimate and was secluded with her deaf-mute mother in a dark room of the mother's parental home. Apparently there was some communication between Isabelle and her mother but only by simple gestures. When Isabelle was discovered at the age of six and a half, she could scarcely make a sound and her lack of any response made it difficult to determine whether or not she could hear. "Her behavior toward strangers, especially men, was almost that of a wild animal, manifesting much fear and hostility."[10] Specialists believed her to be feeble-minded.

Despite the unfavorable prognosis, a systematic and skillful program of training was begun for Isabelle. After a slow start, she developed by leaps and bounds. Two years later her speech and mental development were judged normal. She entered grade school, and in a few years it was reported that she was doing well and was participating in all school activities.

Isabelle's case shows clearly how far from being socialized a normal human being is when he is kept from human interaction and prevented from acquiring an adequate method of communication. It shows, too, that even six years of such isolation does not preclude the possibility of becoming a socialized being with proper treatment. Nevertheless, we see vividly that the mere presence of another person is not sufficient to transform an infant into a socialized child with behavior, skills, and attitudes appropriate for his age level. From the study of discovered isolates we begin to appreciate the vast amount of learning from others that is involved in the production of a social being. There is simply no possible way for a society to avoid completely its task of socializing its young and continue as a society. Whether the young should be socialized is never the question; the issue becomes how and by whom this task should be performed.

[9] Reported in Davis, "Final Note on a Case of Extreme Isolation."
[10] *Ibid.*, p. 436.

Influences on Socialization

Earlier we said that the only reason a human has a personality is that he has been reared by persons. The studies of ferals and isolates have shown only too clearly what happens when an individual is not socialized. If the fact of having a human personality is dependent on socialization, it is reasonable to suppose that the nature of personality would be related to the nature or content of socialization. For a long time scientists have been concerned with the relative influence of individual characteristics and of socialization and other environmental factors on personality. Research work in which the disciplines of psychology, sociology, and anthropology meet is the most recent attempt to understand personality development. Systematic studies of the interrelations of the individual, society, and the culture of the society leave little doubt of the plasticity of original nature and of the effects of early socialization on the personality outcome of a human being. In a simplified manner, we can sum up our level of knowledge as follows:

1. In some important respects, each normal man is like every other normal man; in other respects, no man is like any other man.
2. There is a basic similarity in the personality of all normal people in any given society, with the consequent result of a cross-societal dissimilarity.
3. The members of any society show considerable variation in personality, so that there is an overlapping and concordance of personality types from society to society.

An understanding of the nature of socialization, and of the importance of the family's role in the process, demands that we investigate the foregoing principles.

Individual characteristics. Almost everyone accepts the fact that individuals are different. At times it seems that nothing has been more exaggerated or more misunderstood than the notion of individual differences. A given man shares with every other normal man a remarkable number of characteristics. This lesson is easiest to see at the level of the physical apparatus that makes up the human body. All normal humans have the same number and type of organs which perform identical functions, and once we become accustomed to looking for similarities instead of differences we note a remarkable structural sameness among all men, everywhere. Men everywhere have the same basic organic needs. Despite the fact that culture defines, directs, and channels these needs, all men continue to be driven by the needs for food, for sleep, for protection against bodily harm, and for sexual satisfaction. There are, in addition, certain orders of psychic needs, or whole series of psychological requirements, that are universally found. Linton suggests that a broad classification of universally found psychic needs would include the need for emotional response from other individuals, the need for security of a long-term sort, and the need for novelty of experience.[11] Whether these psychic needs are innate or acquired is unimportant for they are found everywhere.

Just as surely as there is an essential sameness among humans, no two humans are exactly alike. Individuals differ in such essentials as muscular capacity, mental ability, and glandular functioning, and any of these, alone or in combination with another, will affect personality. The unique characteristics of a normal human establish a range within which his personality type will fall. The range is exceedingly wide, despite the ultimate limits set by inherited, presumably immutable, unique characteristics. Recognition of the fact of individual differences accounts for the second part of our first principle: "No man is exactly like any other man." It indicates, furthermore, that there are limits imposed on socialization by the nature of the raw material that is to be fashioned into a social being.

Culture. We have said that there is a basic similarity in the personality of all normal people in any given society. However, the delineation of personality similarity in a society is a difficult and crucial issue. Frenchmen, for example, are similar in that they speak French and that they have certain dietary preferences, but in how many other ways, and which other ways, are Frenchmen similar? Anthropologists have begun to speak of a Basic Personality Type for a society as a whole.[12] The Basic Personality Type consists of the personality traits that appear to be compatible with the cultural demands of the society. It is thus an abstraction derived from the study of a culture rather than from a study of individuals who participate in the culture. The extent to which the societal Basic Personality Type represents also the common denominator of the personalities of those who participate in the culture has not been demonstrated. The concept Basic Personality Type nevertheless constitutes a valuable analytic tool

[11] Ralph Linton, *The Cultural Background of Personality* (New York, Appleton-Century-Crofts, Inc., 1945), pp. 6-9.

[12] For a few representative studies in which the concept Basic Personality Type, by that or some other designation, has been utilized, see Abram Kardiner, *The Individual and His Society* (New York, Columbia University Press, 1939); Abram Kardiner and others, *The Psychological Frontiers of Society* (New York, Columbia University Press, 1945); Ralph Linton and others, *Culture and Personality* (Washington, D.C., American Council on Education, 1941); and S. S. Sargent, ed., *Culture and Personality* (New York, The Viking Fund, Inc., 1949).

for examining the relationship between the culture of a group and the personalities of the group members.[13]

Culture, then, is the key concept for understanding the broad configurations of behavior patterns that vary from society to society. The simplest definition of culture is the "way of life" of a society, and an expansion of this definition shows that it includes an almost infinite number of specifics concerning what to do and how to do it, and even what and how to think. The common feature of the multitude of cultural prescriptions is that they represent an approved response to a particular situation. By precept and example, by observation and instruction in the approved responses to situations, the individuals of any given society begin from their early years to have a certain commonality of personality organization. The common experience of society members during their formative years is thought to produce an essential sameness of personality. Since cultures vary one from the other, no society offers its members the totality of experience that is offered in another society.

It is generally accepted that the first years of life are extremely important to the formation of the inner core of an individual's personality.[14] For this reason, we look particularly to certain cultural features to explain the existence of the basic personality type found in the society. No list of early situations that influence personality would be complete, but great stress is generally placed on the behavior and attitudes associated with feeding, with bodily elimination, and with the handling of the basic emotions. One of the earliest introductions the infant has to the people in the world about him is gained through their responses to his persistent and recurring need for food. We would be extremely interested in determining, therefore, the culturally patterned teachings associated with the regularity of infant feeding, the encouragement or discouragement of breast feeding, the length of the nursing experience, and the manner of weaning. Food cannot be denied the infant if he is to be kept alive, but the socially approved methods of infant feeding can produce in the child a general satisfaction with respect to the quantity of food given, its frequency, and the conditions under which it is offered. Within a given society, particularly within small, homogeneous societies, the child-rearing patterns associated with feeding tend to be similar, although not identical. To the extent, therefore, that these techniques have an effect on the basic per-

[13] For a penetrating critique of the concept Basic Personality Type and culture-personality studies in general, see A. R. Lindesmith and A. L. Strauss, "A Critique of Culture-Personality Writings," *American Sociological Review*, Vol. 15 (October, 1950), pp. 587-600.

[14] See, for example, Fisher's remarks in Ralph Linton and others, *Culture and Personality*, pp. 24 ff. Psychoanalytic theory places great stress on the function of the early years of life in personality formation. See our Chs. 18, 19, and 20.

sonality structure of the individuals, the members of a society will come to have elements of personality in common.

Bodily elimination is an automatic process to the infant. By rewards, punishments, or merely by example, he is trained to bring this automatic act under conscious control. When and by what means sphincter control is effected is generally considered another strong influence on personality development. The patterns associated with the development of sphincter control vary from society to society. In some respects the practices concerned with training for sphincter control lend themselves to greater variability than those in the feeding area. We find, in some societies, that bowel training is begun well before the child is a year old and the child is rather severely punished for slow or incomplete mastery. Other times toilet training is delayed until the child is over two years old. Among the Japanese, typically, great stress is placed on excretory functions and punishment is in the nature of shame or the threat of ridicule from outsiders.[15] In some other societies the child learns to control and exercise his need for elimination by example and imitation only, and punishment for early childhood failures is not considered necessary. One does not have to be well steeped in psychoanalytic theory to sense that the differences in this particular aspect of child rearing can be important.

A third area of child-rearing practices of extreme importance in the development of personality is the manner in which the emotions of love and hate, of sympathy and hostility, are taught and displayed within the family. There can be no doubt that the expressions of these emotions vary from society to society.[16] In some societies the children are greatly loved and indulged. Infants receive loving, gentle care from all about them. Sympathy, love, and affection continue to be expressed throughout childhood. In other places we find a quite different pattern. Very little affection may be displayed toward the child by his mother or anyone else, rivalry among siblings may be encouraged, and children may be teased, ridiculed, or threatened with loss of love or security to make them "behave." In a similar manner, children can be taught to express their aggression or to conceal it, to co-operate or to compete, and to fear or not to fear the external world in which they find themselves.

Despite the wealth of data that has accumulated from culture-personality studies, we are far from understanding the dynamics involved in the relationship between culturally patterned child-rearing practices and

[15] For cross-cultural comparisons of this and other child-rearing practices, see Young, *op. cit.*, pp. 50-57.
[16] Various of Margaret Mead's studies illustrate this point well. See particularly Margaret Mead, *Sex and Temperament in Three Primitive Societies* (New York, William Morrow & Co., Inc., 1935).

the formation of a basic group personality type. Already we can be sure that no one-to-one relationship between techniques and personality traits prevails in the sense that abrupt weaning plus late toilet training produces such and such a personality. The mechanism is far more complicated than this. Increasingly more attention is being turned to the less tangible feeling tones that accompany, and thus form a part of, the infant and child care. It is the sum total of what is done to a child and how it is done, rather than the more specific child-rearing techniques, that influences the child's personality. If the child is more or less constantly confronted with tasks he cannot achieve and goals he cannot reach, if, through experience in many areas of life, the child learns that adults are unfriendly or hostile, we would expect a more or less lasting effect on his personality. So it is that the various culturally patterned child-rearing techniques and accompanying attitudes and emotions, particularly, but not only, those we have emphasized, in combination one with the other, work so great an influence that we are able to speak of a basic personality system of a society containing traits of suspicion or trust, hostility or friendliness, and competitiveness or co-operativeness. These and other characteristics are deeply seated in the individual and are relatively immutable once they have been established. Although these traits are expressed differently in different social situations, they are expressed sufficiently clearly in most situations and by a sufficient number of normal adults for us to speak of them as characteristic, or typical, of the personality structure in a given society.

The family. We have said that within any society there is a diversity of personality types. Partly, of course, this is accounted for by the individual differences with which people are born, that is, the dissimilarities in the basic bio-psychic equipment which is utilized in the process of personality formation. We must look also, however, to the particular family group which is attempting to accomplish the socialization of the child. The role of culture in personality formation can go only so far. Some agent is needed to put into practice the cultural prescriptions and to interpret and to transmit the culture to the child. The child-rearing prescriptions about which we have talked do not simply descend on a child and influence his personality; they must be acted out by someone, usually his parents. And the mandates of culture, in these and other respects, are only imperfectly followed. This is the way it must be. Because of their own uniqueness, no two individuals interpret the demands of their culture in exactly the same way, and even when interpretations are close no two individuals are able to act out the cultural demands in precisely the same manner. Certain it is that the various attitudes and beliefs of a society, their fears and taboos, their systems of thinking, and their values, all have an influence on personality development. Before they affect the child, however, they are filtered through the interpreting and transmitting agents of socialization. The child does not come into contact with culture. He comes into contact with people, whose behavior toward him and toward one another imperfectly embodies the culture of the group of which they are a part. For the young child such indirect contacts with the culture of his group are limited to the members of his family.[17]

The family has a unique advantage in being the first cultural agent to attempt to socialize the child. Never again in his life will the individual be as pliable or as malleable as he is at the time that his family receives him. However, it is not as if the child responded to parental influence as wax to the thumb. The point is, rather, that the child will never be more susceptible to being shaped or molded, or for that matter warped or twisted. Some have felt that the influences of the early years on personality development have been grossly exaggerated.[18] It is true that the experiences of youth and adulthood give meaning and significance to the events of childhood and that later experiences must be considered as important formative forces. Surely, however, the experiences of childhood help to determine the importance of subsequent personality influences. A personality trait cannot be reinforced or even modified if it is not present in the first place, and the personality changes that are made in later life must reckon with the existing personality traits, whether modifying them, building on them, or counteracting them. The fact that personalities continue to change to some extent and that people and events in the post-childhood period have an influence on personality development by no means detracts from the important role of the family as the first socializing agent to affect the child.

The family as a socializing agency is favored by another advantage, less tangible than that of primacy of contact but no less important. This advantage is the peculiar emotional quality that is fostered through the generally close and intimate association among family members. The importance of this psychological dimension of the family group is difficult to determine. Infants seem actually to fare better, psychologically and even physiologically, when reared in an atmosphere of love and emotional response of an adult, as communicated to the infant by holding, hugging, cuddling, and otherwise "mothering" him. Much of the evidence for this

[17] The importance of the family as a socializing agency is stressed by various family sociologists. See Willard Waller and Reuben Hill, *The Family*, rev. ed. (New York, The Dryden Press, Inc., 1951), Ch. 2, and Ernest W. Burgess and Harvey J. Locke, *The Family*, 2nd ed. (New York, American Book Company, 1953), pp. 194-202.

[18] See, for example, L. Guy Brown, *Social Pathology* (New York, Appleton-Century-Crofts, Inc., 1942), p. 11.

theory has come from the study of infants reared in hospitals or other institutions and therefore deprived of psychological mothering. Ribble and others claim that this deprivation can have serious effects and see in it the cause for the disorder "marasmus," a slow dying and wasting away of infants despite proper diet and adequate physical care.[19] Ribble suggests, too, that even among the infants that survive, permanent damage may be done to the emotional capacity of those who have been denied the intimacy of "mothering." It is necessary to add that the findings and theories of Ribble and others have been severely challenged, particularly as they refer to the dire physiological consequences of psychological deprivation.[20]

However necessary for physical survival the intimate association of mother and child may prove to be, it is likely that in a broader sense the intimacy and emotional quality of family living is extremely important. It constitutes a distinct advantage of the family as an agency for teaching behavior and instilling in the young important attitudes and values. The family has the potential for being and remaining the most important reference group for all of its members. What is taught and learned from those who stand in the closest emotional relationship to the child has the potential for becoming an integral part of his basic personality structure.

Another characteristic of the family as a socializing agency is the duration of its contacts with the child. In our own society, for example, the family is practically the only agency that reaches the very young child. Any others that "get to" the child can be screened by and, indeed, intercepted by the child's parents. As the child gets older, he spends more and more time away from his family. But almost every day, for as many as eighteen years or even longer, he does return to the family and spends some part of his time with them. The very repetitiveness of family contacts constitutes a distinct advantage in shaping and fixing the personality of the child. However basic elements of the personality like security, hostility, and a generalized attitude toward sex are introduced, they stand a good chance of being incorporated into the basic personality system of the individual if they find continual and long-term reinforcement in the family. When we consider that the family typically gets children first, retains at least some influence over them for almost all of their immature years, and is characterized by a peculiar intimacy which facilitates the transference of basic attitudes and values, we begin to appreciate the paramount significance of the family in the shaping of the personalities entrusted to it.

[19] Margaret A. Ribble, *The Rights of Infants* (New York, Columbia University Press, 1943). See also René A. Spitz, "Hospitalism," *The Psychoanalytic Study of the Child*, Vol. I (New York, International Universities Press, Inc., 1945).

[20] Samuel R. Pinneau, "A Critique on the Articles by Margaret Ribble," *Child Development*, Vol. 21 (December, 1950), pp. 203-228.

FAMILY SOCIALIZATION IN THE UNITED STATES

Everyone has heard that "the hand that rocks the cradle rules the world." We need not insist on a literal interpretation of this proverb to be convinced of the societal importance of the function of socialization. Our remarks on the nature of socialization and the import of the family's role in it should make it patently clear that we cannot analyze the contemporary family without reference to the manner in which it performs the basic function of socialization of the young. Any meaningful evaluation of the modern family, furthermore, must in part rest on how and how well it is doing its part in the replacement of society which comes only when a sufficiently well-socialized adult is produced.

No student of sociology needs to be reminded that ours is a complex, heterogeneous, and rapidly changing society. Because of these traits, which are no less true because they are oft-repeated, the task of describing the American socialization pattern becomes extremely difficult. So numerous and varied are the competing values and techniques that some would even question whether it is at all meaningful to talk about *the* socialization pattern in the United States. Nevertheless, there are reasons for attempting to set forth the common core of techniques and attitudes, for it is such that distinguishes our socialization process from that of similar societies. The undertaking, furthermore, will provide a conceptual device for analyzing changes in socialization goals and practices. At the same time, we will not neglect the important differences in the socialization patterns, at least those that are found with some frequency and are found to be relatively distinct in certain large segments of the population.

Child Rearing in America: Past and Present

Parental anxious-uncertainty. Despite the specific child-rearing techniques used and despite the particular values a given family is attempting to inculcate in its young, there is a pervading attitude toward child rearing that in some respects is distinctly American.[21] We can speak of this as an anxious-uncertainty that colors the various specifics of child rearing.

At one time, mothers in our society were fairly certain about how children should be raised. To a large degree it was exactly as they themselves had been reared. There was good consensus on what a child was like, what he was to become, and how to produce the desired metamorphosis

[21] For several of the general points concerning child rearing in the United States, we are indebted to Gorer's national character study. See Geoffrey Gorer, *The American People* (New York, W. W. Norton & Company, Inc., 1948), particularly Ch. 3.

from child to man. Whether these prevailing ideas were valid, whether they were "good" for the child, and whether the prescribed techniques really produced the sought-for results are other matters. The point is that a young mother approached child rearing with a sense of security fostered by the certain knowledge that her mother, her grandmother, her older sisters, the midwives, and the neighbors all were in basic agreement on what should be done to, for, and with the child.

For a number of years, but particularly over the last thirty or forty, mothers seem to have become increasingly anxious about the kind of job they are doing in raising their children and how it should be done. Few mothers seem completely able to approach child rearing with the spontaneity and the naturalness that stem from an inner sense of assurance that they are doing what is best for the child. The exact manifestations of the underlying anxious-uncertainty are many, but the basic attitude is evidenced with a certain regularity that crosses barriers of class and race and is exhibited in a wide range of specific habits and techniques.

Perhaps in no other area is the anxious-uncertainty of American mothers so obvious and so prevalent as it is with respect to feeding habits. Most mothers are deeply concerned that their babies be fed the correct diet in the correct manner. But here, of course, is the rub. In each case, who is to say what is "correct"? There are too many "authorities." Feeding fads come and go and meanwhile this authority disagrees with that one, and neither of them happens to think very highly of the way in which the mother herself was reared. Each competing "system," of course, is hailed as the very latest and best for the infantile hero in our tragedy-comedy of kaleidoscopic fashions. First breast feeding is condemned because it is impossible "scientifically" to control the "formula" and sometimes even the quantity of nourishment. Now breast feeding is encouraged because it affords an opportunity for expressing mother-love, and above all else a baby needs love. First a rigid ounce-interval feeding schedule is drawn up because "science knows best" what the normal infant requires and when. Today, parents are urged to feed on "demand" because baby, rather than science, knows when he is hungry! It is little wonder that the modern mother feels confused and that child psychologists are deluged with children, or rather mothers, with "feeding problems."[22] Amazingly enough, the underlying anxiety toward feeding finds expression regardless of the specific techniques that happen to be in vogue. We find it today, despite the emphasis on permissiveness and self-demand, just as surely as we found

---

[22] Changes in the area of feeding and weaning are, of course, part of more general changes in infant care. For a short summary of such general changes during six recent decades, see Clark E. Vincent, "Trends in Infant Care Ideas," *Child Development*, Vol. 22 (September, 1951), pp. 199-209.

it when mothers expected their babies to run like little clocks. Of course the outward symptom is different. Today we find the "compulsively permissive" mother who makes a fault of flexibility and freedom by almost abdicating her job as mother. Others grit their teeth in the face of unreasonable self-demand schedules and probably communicate to the child their feelings of anxiety and dislike as readily as if they made him "cry it out" until the next feeding time.

Food anxiety is not restricted to infancy. As the child becomes older, he is faced with all the complexities of the ever-changing "balanced diet," which belies its name by requiring liberal supplements of pills or tonics or capsules. Even the most permissive mother becomes more than a little anxious when her child goes for five days "without touching his eggs" or when inadvertently she forgets his daily dose of fish oil. Undoubtedly children are quick to grasp parental concern over food, including the practiced mimicry of unconcern.

No one would seriously suggest that we have described all American mothers or even the vague "typical" mother. The feeding anxiety we have described, rather, is thought to be sufficiently common, in greater or lesser degree, to be considered a characteristic of our child-rearing practices. Whatever the effect of feeding anxiety, more children fall under its spell than manage to escape it entirely.

In other areas of child rearing the underlying anxious-uncertainty of American parents finds expression. It frequently seems as if they were trying too hard to be good parents. In the area of toilet training, there are those who attempt to follow the latest dictum on relatively late and permissive training but are afraid to trust it too completely because of the real or anticipated derision of neighbors, friends, or parents. Others resolve that they will use "common sense" and not take the latest fads too seriously but have at least occasional pangs of guilt about what the effect will be on their child. The "compulsive permissiveness" so pronounced in feeding practices characterizes toilet training as well. By trying so hard not to try too hard to train the child in all the niceties of bathroom conduct, a mother can communicate to the child that this is a special kind of behavior and that she is particularly concerned with the child's behavior in this area.

It is perhaps in the area of infant and child sexuality that anxious-uncertainty finds its greatest manifestation. Once again, it is not so much that parents are demonstrably rearing their children "wrong," but that parents are not sure whether they are wrong or right. In various and subtle ways they communicate to the child that sex is a most special area of behavior and one that is not altogether "nice." They teach their children the "proper" words for sexual organs and are shocked when they use them too frequently or outside of the immediate family. They tell their children "the story of fertilization" and then are concerned lest they are making them wise beyond their years. They awkwardly allow, or sometimes insist, that children view other family members in a state of nudity and are surprised when this does not put an end, once and for all, to sexual curiosity. The child, of course, is learning all of the lessons, both the factual origin-of-babies and names-of-organs reports and the feelings of concern and anxiety exhibited by his parents. Very few parents, it seems, are able to approach the normal sexuality of children with the matter-of-factness that indicates that they are sure of what they are doing.

Conformity.   Almost any comparative study of the American socialization pattern would note that it is characterized by an unusual expectation of conformity to ill-defined group standards. American parents seem perennially concerned that their children "adjust" and "get along" with their peers. So that they may not feel "left out" or "different," children must have the same toys, watch the same television programs, and wear the same type of clothing as the meaningful "everybody elses" in their lives. We are proud of our "rugged individualism," but parents seem to do everything they possibly can to discourage any semblance of it. It is significant that an American psychiatrist asks of the American readers, *Must You Conform?*[23] Others, too, are concerned with the tendency to overstress conformity at the expense of individuality.

It is very likely that the emphasis on conformity stems from the basic anxiety and uncertainty of American parents to which we have earlier referred. So long as the standards and techniques of child rearing change with predictable regularity and so long as few feel comfortable in their approach to child rearing, each individual parent can always find refuge in what the masses are doing. Whether late weaning is good or bad, whether permissive toilet training produces normals or neurotics, and whether the methods of handling childhood sexuality lead to frigidity or precocity, many parents do not know. But at least "everybody else is doing it." Uncertainty, it seems, is another lover of company.

It has become commonplace to stress the competitiveness of American society and to point to evidence of competitiveness in the child-rearing practices of our society. American society is competitive, and various of our child-rearing practices are infused with competition. If we examine the matter more carefully, however, we find that it is a peculiar breed of

[23] Robert Linder, *Must You Conform?* (New York, Rinehart & Company, Inc., 1956). See also his *Prescription for Rebellion* (New York, Rinehart & Company, Inc., 1953).

competition. We plead guilty to oversimplification, but it sometimes seems as if every American parent would like to see his child excel in what "everybody else" is doing. If "the group" is emphasizing football, parental pressures will be brought to bear to insure that Junior is the best football player and not a good gardener, pianist, or, for that matter, discus hurler. Competition we have, but it is a tightly circumscribed, neatly delimited type of competition. To excel is a strong American desire, but in one's search for areas of excellence one must not depart too far from the areas of endeavor of the vague "everybody else."

Dominant role of the mother. A further idiosyncratic feature of American child rearing is the major role assigned to the mother. In most families it is the mother who rewards and punishes the child and who not only tells him to "be good" but who defines "good" for him. All of the effects of this tendency in our society are not known, but it requires little speculation to conclude that the adult personalities produced in America are in some important degrees different from those produced in societies where the rearing of children is more of a joint task of the parents or is done primarily by the male.[24] Whatever is done to personality development because of the dominant role of the mother in early child rearing finds reinforcement in our educational system, which places children of both sexes predominantly under the influence of women from nursery school to high school. Some writers have emphasized the effects of a female-dominated training system on the male personality. Novelists have dramatized the vampire-like qualities of maternal overprotection,[25] and psychiatrists have placed the blame for the unusually high number of psychiatric misfits discovered during World War II squarely on the shoulders of American mothers.[26] Gorer has described the American conscience as "feminine" because both sexes have internalized more of the "do's" and don't's" of their mothers than of their fathers.[27] He claims that, for the man, this has led to a peculiar ambivalent attitude toward women and a latent fear of being too much like a woman. The effect of the dominant role of the mother on the personality formation of girls has received less attention. Despite the fact that girls will someday be women, they are going to have to live in a society where half of the people are male, they are going to have to marry a man, and they are going to have to rear

[24] For an interesting and sophisticated account of child rearing in various modern and preliterate societies, see Margaret Mead and Martha Wolfenstein, eds., *Childhood in Contemporary Cultures* (Chicago, University of Chicago Press, 1955).

[25] Wylie's trenchant discourse on "momism" probably is well known. Philip Wylie, *Generation of Vipers* (New York, Rinehart & Company, Inc., 1942).

[26] Edward A. Strecker, *Their Mothers' Sons* (Philadelphia, J. B. Lippincott Company, 1946).

[27] Gorer, *op. cit.*, Ch. 4.

male children. It should be obvious that the modern-day woman has a unique approach to these male-oriented areas of life because her own upbringing was predominated by women. There is undoubtedly much more to be learned and understood about the effects of the dominant role of the mother in child rearing on the personality development of both sexes. The general pattern of the dominant role of the mother in child rearing is nevertheless a peculiarity of American society.

Class Differentials in Child Rearing

In the foregoing section we have attempted to deal with the broad generalities of child-rearing practices in the United States. Our task at this point is to look for the differences in child rearing within our society. American society contains two major races, many ethnic groups, scores of religious groups, and all of these groups are enveloped in a system of differential social status. One might well expect to find important differences in the United States with regard to child-rearing values and methods. There is a dearth of substantial research, however, of the kind necessary to allow us to generalize about the socialization practices of various segments of our society.[28] We have elected to concentrate on the social status differentials in child rearing partly because this area has attracted more research but largely because of the more pervasive nature of the stratification system.

All known societies have a system of differential status. To a greater or lesser degree, rewards, power, privilege, and prestige are distributed unequally in every society, with the result that each member of society has a certain determinable rank relative to other members in his society. In the United States alone, hundreds of studies have demonstrated that a person's position in the status hierarchy is related to scores of important social and personal characteristics. One effort to understand further the socialization function of the American family has been concerned with the differences in child rearing at different status levels of our society. This is an extremely important area of investigation. To the extent that there are important differences in the socialization process among people of different statuses, we should expect to find important differences in the adult personalities. Despite the extensive work that has been done in this area, the present state of our knowledge is far from satisfactory.[29] The many

[28] A forthright study that helps fill the void in research on child rearing is Robert E. Sears, Eleanor E. Maccoby, and Harry Levin, *Patterns of Childrearing* (Evanston, Illinois, Row, Peterson & Company, 1957).

[29] It is manifestly impossible even to list the research work that has been done in this area. An unpublished bibliography compiled by Lee Burchinal, Iowa State University, lists over 275 items, published before 1956, that have some bearing on class differentials in child rearing.

reasons for the present inadequacy of our knowledge are the difficulties of conceptualization and measurement of the three essential variables: (1) social status, (2) socialization practices, and (3) personality. A review of the major difficulties in these areas will also allow us to describe the kind of studies of class differentials in child rearing that have been conducted.

Social status. Most of the studies of the relationship between socialization techniques and social status have employed some type of categorical theory of social stratification. In the studies, that is, social status is conceived of as a discrete variable with the result that individuals possessing various status characteristics can be collectively thought of as belonging to or being in a particular social class. Most frequently, child-rearing patterns are studied as a class rather than individual phenomena, as if the social classes were real and functioning groups that to some extent shared a common culture. Perhaps this categorical conception of social status has hampered our successful acquisition of knowledge more than we realize. The existence of social classes in this sense is itself a theory, and not a fact. A competing view of social stratification holds that social status is a continuous variable and that the status hierarchy of our society can most accurately be envisioned as an arrangement of individuals along a gradient of status.[30] It is conceivable, but not yet demonstrable, that greater utilization of the continuum theory of stratification would affect the nature of our findings on the relationship between social status and child rearing. It may well be, for example, that we would find a direct linear relationship between a certain child-rearing practice and social status but, at the same time, we would *not* be able to speak of a lower-class or a middle-class practice in the sense that it would be found typically in that class but not in any others.

A second difficulty lies in the measurement of social status. In any bibliography on the relationship between social status and child rearing will be found studies employing an extremely wide variety of techniques for assessing the status of the study group. Occupation has been used both by itself and in combination with other characteristics, and so have income and education. Social class scales have been employed. One study separated its respondents into upper and middle class on the basis of whether they attended a private or a public high school. And so on and on. No one would seriously contend that the various studies are measuring entirely different characteristics, but neither are they measuring exactly the same ones. Statistical tests show that there is a correlation between and among any num-

[30] For a more thorough treatment of the distinction between the categorical and continuum theories of social stratification, see John F. Cuber and William F. Kenkel, *Social Stratification in the United States* (New York, Appleton-Century-Crofts, Inc., 1954), especially Chs. 2 and 7.

ber of specific status factors, but the relationships have never yet been reported as perfect.[31] Even two different occupational scales do not result in exactly the same status placement of all respondents. More refined and more standardized techniques for measuring social status are needed.

A third major difficulty with the studies of socialization practices and social status is that they have been restricted to certain segments of the status hierarchy. Almost always the upper classes have been ignored and most studies have failed to study people of the very lowest status. The comparative studies, therefore, have dealt largely with what most of them call the "working class" and the "middle class." It is true that most people are at neither the extreme top nor the extreme bottom of the status hierarchy but somewhere in between. Particularly because of our crude research techniques, however, it is possible that if our research dealt with more nearly the entire range of status differences it would uncover trends that are ignored in dealing only with the middle segment. Even if new trends were not discovered, the knowledge of socialization practices at the upper and lower extremities of society would fill a void in our understanding of the American family.

If we were to scrutinize the methodologies of specific studies, our list of difficulties would become unduly extensive. We would find, for example, that some studies have failed to control one or more variables, such as ethnic status or stage in the family life cycle,[32] when attempting to determine the relationship between social status and child-rearing practices. We would certainly have ample opportunity for lamenting the use of the same label, for example, *lower class*, to stand for apparently different segments of society. But we will have to be content with a brief discussion of some of the more important conceptual and methodological difficulties connected with the status variable in the studies of class differentials in child rearing.

Child-rearing variables. At the risk of oversimplification, we can divide the studies of social status and child rearing into two groups, those that have emphasized parental behavior or behavior patterns, and those that have concentrated on parental attitudes or feelings toward their children. It is more than an assumption, of course, that there is some relationship between attitudes and overt behavior. The sets of findings from one type of study, however, are not always comparable with those of the other type. What may appear to be contradictory results may more nearly be that two or more different dimensions of child-rearing roles have

---

[31] Cuber and Kenkel, *op. cit.*, Ch. 6.

[32] An appreciation of the necessity for controlling on family life-cycle status can be gained from our discussion of this concept in Ch. 14.

been tapped. It becomes exceedingly difficult to generalize, therefore, about the child-rearing practices of any one status level, particularly if we attempt to use such summarizing concepts as "permissiveness," "hostility," "rigidity," and so on.

The sheer volume of studies on child rearing preclude any systematic review of their findings.[33] We can use Davis and Havighurst's classical study as point of departure.[34] This study was conducted in Chicago over ten years ago. The white sample consisted of 100 families classified as middle or lower class on the basis of parents' occupation and education, property ownership, organizational membership, and the section of the city in which the family lived.

In Table 17 we have presented an abridged summary of the findings of

TABLE 17. Social Class and Child-Rearing Practices: Chicago, Boston, and Eugene Studies

Practice	Middle Class			Lower Class		
	C	B	E	C	B	E
Percentage children breast-fed only	6	—	15	17	—	17
Median months old when weaning completed	10.3	12	13.2	12.3	12.6	14.1
Percentage children fed when hungry	4	—	—	44	—	—
Median months old when bowel training begun	7.5	9.6	11.5	9.1	9.9	11.8
Remedial practices for soiling:						
Percentage spank, whip	13	—	6	40	—	11
Percentage scold	11	—	8	14	—	11
Mean score, severity of toilet training (1: mild; 9: severe)	—	3.8	—	—	4.6	—
Percentage reporting household chores and rules expected of children	76	38	62	78	40	58
Mean score, permissiveness regarding child's sexual behavior (1: permissive; 9: severe)	—	4.3	3.6	—	5.7	4.9

SOURCE: Adapted from Richard A. Littman, Robert C. A. Moore, and John Pierce-Jones, "Social Class Differences in Child Rearing: A Third Community for Comparison with Chicago and Newton," *American Sociological Review*, Vol. 22 (December, 1957), pp. 694-704.

[33] Burchinal, *op. cit.*

[34] All references to this study in the following pages are from Allison Davis and Robert J. Havighurst, "Social Class and Color Differences in Child Rearing," *American Sociological Review*, Vol. 11 (December, 1946), pp. 698-710.

the Chicago, Boston, and Eugene studies of class differences in child rearing. With respect to feeding and weaning, it appears that the Chicago lower class was exhibiting the behavior that is approved in most pediatric circles today. As compared with the middle class, lower-class mothers were more likely to breast feed their children, to wean them later, and to feed them when they were hungry rather than on "schedule." It was discovered that the use of "pacifiers" (reminiscent of the older practice of providing "sugar teats" for infants) was more prevalent in the lower class. Whatever else lower-class parents were doing, it would seem that they were presenting their children with fewer feeding and sucking frustrations at the time when the infant had few pleasure-seeking alternatives. Conversely, middle-class children would seem to be encountering greater frustrations. Some substantiation for this view is found in the discovery that three times as many middle-class children were reported to suck their thumbs.

Interestingly enough, later studies in Boston and Eugene failed to find any significant differences between lower- and middle-class infant feeding practices.[35] Mothers at both status levels were similar with respect to whether or not they breast-fed their child and when and how severely they effected weaning. Regional and time differences may well account for some of the discrepancy in the findings of the three studies. Not to be overlooked, however, is the fact that a greater proportion of the Chicago's lower class fell in the lowest sub-categories than did in the Eugene and Boston samples.[36] In other words, although all three studies used the term *lower class*, it would seem that we cannot assume that they were referring to the same relative social level of their respective cities.

The Chicago study did not agree with either the Eugene or Boston study on class differentials in toilet training. Although Chicago middle-class mothers began bowel training earlier than lower-class mothers, there was little difference in this facet of child rearing among the Boston or Eugene mothers. All three studies, however, found the lower class to use more severe training methods.

Davis and Havighurst found that middle-class children were expected to be able to go downtown alone at an earlier age than lower-class children. Middle-class girls, as compared with others, were expected to begin to

[35] All references to the Boston and Eugene studies are from Richard A. Littman, Robert C. A. Moore, and John Pierce-Jones, "Social Class Differences in Child Rearing: A Third Community for Comparison with Chicago and Newton," *American Sociological Review*, Vol. 22 (December, 1957), pp. 694-704.

[36] Maccoby states that a fourth of the Boston "lower class" included what Warner would term "lower middle class." Eleanor E. Maccoby and others, "Methods of Child-Rearing in Two Social Classes," William E. Martin and Celia B. Stendler, eds., *Readings in Child Development* (New York, Harcourt, Brace & Company, Inc., 1954), pp. 380-396.

cook, sew, and care for younger children at an earlier age. On the other hand, lower-class children were allowed to attend the movies alone at an earlier age and were not expected to be in the house as early as were the middle-class children. Lower-class boys and girls, furthermore, were likely to be expected either to quit school and go to work or to get a job after school at earlier ages. The Boston study did not include comparable information, but found no significant differences between the middle and lower classes with respect to giving the child at least one regular job to do around the house and requiring him to be neat and orderly. There was no great difference between the proportion of lower- and middle-class Eugene mothers who reported that they required children to perform certain chores around the house.

It is not our intent to rationalize the discrepancies between and among the Chicago, Boston, and Eugene child-rearing studies. Taken together, the three illustrate the serious difficulties of our child-rearing studies.[37] Foremost of the difficulties is the interpretation of the findings. Even if we assume that each set of findings is reasonably accurate for its own setting and time, what does any one set really mean? Which class, for example, actually encourages their children to assume "responsibility"? The lower-class child is earlier taught to assume the responsibility for caring for himself outside of the house after dark, to select and attend a movie by himself, and to take a job outside the home. The middle-class girl is taught domestic arts at an earlier age, and she is expected to know how to negotiate the intricacies of public transportation by herself. Which class, then, is actually encouraging greater "responsibility" among its children? It depends, obviously, on how we define our term. The definition of "proper responsibility" for children seems itself status linked! It would seem to be more important to discover *why* the respective mothers are doing what they do and the effect of the maternal behavior on the children. Does the lower-class mother allow her children to attend evening movies alone because she wants to give them a certain amount of "freedom" or because she wants to rid herself of their noisy presence? Does the child feel elated in his freedom and secure in the knowledge that his parents can provide him the wherewithal to attend the movies, or does he feel rejected? In a similar manner, does a middle-class mother teach her children to travel downtown alone to enrich their social experience or to prepare them to do errands for her? Lower-class mothers, to take an example in a different area, have been found to use more severe methods in toilet train-

---

[37] An attempt to explain the discrepancies in terms of changes over time and reference-group differences of middle- and lower-class mothers can be found in Martha Strum White, "Social Class, Child Rearing Practices, and Child Behavior," *American Sociological Review*, Vol. 22 (December, 1957), pp. 704-712.

ing, with *severe* being defined as use of physical punishment. But what, really, does a smart smack on the buttocks *mean* to the young child? Perhaps it is actually *less severe* than the middle-class method of withholding praise, if withholding praise is interpreted by the child as withholding love. There can be no doubt that we have needed, and that we need still more, studies designed to discover the specific techniques of child rearing utilized by parents of different social status. Further research may well discover, however, that there are more important dimensions of child rearing than those that can be tapped by the study of behavioral specifics.

There have been a number of studies concerned with the parental attitudes in child rearing and the general emotional orientation of parents towards their children. The technique of Duvall and others, asking parents for a description of a "good child" and a "good mother" (or father), shows promise of attacking a meaningful dimension of child rearing.[38] The few studies that involved parents of different social status have discovered that lower-class parents tend to give more "traditional" responses and middle-class parents use more "developmental" terms in their descriptions.[39] The relationship of parental responses to actual child-rearing behavior has largely been ignored. Although it may be reasonable to assume that there is a relationship, even a normal degree of scientific skepticism would insist that it be demonstrated. At any rate, until we can be sure that "developmental" and "traditional" mothers differ in what they do to their children and what feelings they get across to them, we cannot make a strong case for the traditional-developmental split being an important difference among families of different social statuses.

Personality. There are serious difficulties, too, with the third variable in our scheme. The issue can be stated succinctly: even if there are meaningful differences in child rearing among people of different statuses, what kinds of personality effects, if any, can be traced to these different systems of socialization? The first approach to this crucial problem lies in the determination of whether or not there are personality differences at different status levels. We would need to determine, next, whether any personality differences discovered were causally related to the methods of family socialization at the various class levels.

The major difficulty with the problem of personality differences is again definitional. At one level of personality, we can be reasonably sure that there *are* personality differences at various status levels. Many studies have demonstrated, for example, that political, economic, racial, religious,

[38] Duvall's original study and later studies using similar formulations are reported in Evelyn M. Duvall, *Family Development* (Philadelphia, J. B. Lippincott Company, 1957), pp. 47-57.
[39] Duvall, *op. cit.*, p. 51.

and other attitudes vary by social status.[40] Fifteen years ago Cattell reviewed a number of studies in class differences in responses to personality-trait tests and found that at that level of attitudes, values, and habits the studies were in basic agreement that class differentials existed.[41] Auld has reviewed studies in class differences in responses to personality tests.[42] Most of the studies did show differences by social status. Even when differences in the total scores were slight, moreover, there were often many specific test items that indicated a marked social class differential. On every personality test that showed a difference, the direction of the status differential was always the same: middle-class subjects had more favorable scores than the lower-class, indicating that the middle class had better adjusted personalities than the lower. At one level of personality traits, therefore, we can be reasonably sure that status differentials are present.

It becomes exceedingly difficult to assess whether or not there are any major differences in basic personality structure across status lines. If we assume that the Rorschach Test and the Thematic Apperception Test are getting at a level of personality deeper than that tapped by the usual personality questionnaire, then the few studies utilizing these methods would suggest basic personality differences at different status levels.[43] Some are inclined to infer status differences in basic personality structure from the discoveries that lower-status individuals are more likely to contract some types of mental illness than people at other levels of society. At present, however, our all-too-meager knowledge makes it impossible to conclude whether there are or are not major and meaningful differences in basic personality structure among people of different statuses.[44]

We have the germane question, finally, of the relationship between personality and child rearing. A few studies have discovered no significant differences between the mothers' memory of childhood training methods, such as gradual or abrupt weaning, scheduled or self-demand feeding, and type of punishment used in toilet training, on the one hand, and the personality scores of their children on a standard personality questionnaire, on the other.[45] Clinical evidence, however, strongly suggests that such child-

[40] See Cuber and Kenkel, op. cit., Chs. 7, 9, and 10 and references cited therein.

[41] R. B. Cattell, "The Cultural Functions of Social Stratification, II: Regarding Individual and Group Dynamics," Journal of Social Psychology, Vol. 21 (February, 1945), pp. 25-26.

[42] Frank Auld, Jr., "Influence of Social Class on Personality Test Responses," Psychology Bulletin, Vol. 49 (July, 1952), pp. 318-332.

[43] For example, Charles McArthur, "Personality Differences between Middle and Upper Classes," Journal of Abnormal and Social Psychology, Vol. 50 (March, 1955), p. 247-254.

[44] Cf. Robert J. Havighurst, "Social Class and Basic Personality Structure," Sociology and Social Research, Vol. 36 (July-August, 1952), pp. 355-363.

[45] William H. Sewell, "Infant Training and the Personality of the Child," American Journal of Sociology, Vol. 58 (September, 1952), pp. 150-159.

hood experiences have significant and lasting effects.[46] Ignoring the weaknesses in both lines of evidence, we have the problem of which child-rearing traits are meaningful, at which age, and for which phase of personality. It is possible, too, that the very child-training methods found unrelated to later responses to personality tests actually do have a strong bearing on personality formation but the effect is not yet measurable at all stages of personality growth, at least not by the methods in use today. Nevertheless, until we can establish at least general patterns of relationships between certain socializing methods and personality development, the investigation of child-rearing differentials among families of different status will remain relatively sterile. Whether we come to find few or many differences in child-rearing specifics, we will need sound evidence of the effect and significance of these specifics on personality formation.

CHANGES IN SOCIALIZATION

The fact that ours is a rapidly changing society has hampered the foregoing discussion of both the similarities and the differences in socialization practices. Studies have to be recent and broad in their scope and sampling before we can be sure that what yesterday appeared to be a tendency is not today a confirmed habit, or what seemed to be a waning practice is not gone altogether. Since throughout this chapter our main purpose has been further to understand the nature of socialization and the family's role in it, we will restrict ourselves to a discussion of some broad areas of change in the socialization function of the American family. Accordingly, we have selected (1) the family's role in the total socialization process, and (2) the goals sought in socialization, as two significant areas where change is taking place.

The Family's Role in Socialization

It has become commonplace to refer to the decreasing importance of the family in the total socialization of the child. Many are the writers who stress the lessening importance of the family in the total process and who then go on to make the point that this is but another indication of the weakening of the family because of its gradual loss of functions. In a certain quantitative sense, of course, it is perfectly obvious that the family has lost part of its role in the socialization of the young. But the matter is decidedly more complicated than a mere account of who spends how many hours socializing the immature members of society would indicate. Perhaps what

[46] See Ch. 18.

is needed is a fresh approach to the problem of the family's role in the socialization of the young. How does our society compare with others in the shifting emphasis on the family in socialization? How can we account for the changes in the family's role? And, most important, what effect are these changes having on the personality development of the child?

The studies of many varied societies can once again help place the American family in its proper perspective. In no society, however simple or complex, is the family entrusted with the entire job of socializing the young. In the simplest societies the non-family agencies of socialization are not as a rule formalized, but always there are persons other than the immediate family who help prepare the child to fill an adult role in his society. Sometimes the various members of the child's extended family, in addition to the immediate family, have an important role in the socialization of a child. In a less obvious manner, many, many adults help to socialize the child. This is perhaps easiest to see with respect to the learning of physical skills. The Trobriand boy, for example, does not learn how to construct a native hut solely by observing his father or maternal uncle. Every male he has watched build a hut, and to a certain extent every hut that is standing in his village, may very well add to his knowledge or reinforce what he has already learned. When the Trobriand youth becomes a man, he will be able to build a dwelling that is remarkably similar to those that have been built on the islands for many years. But who, really, has taught him this art, and who has had the most important role in his learning it? In a similar manner it would become well-nigh impossible to trace all of the influences on the child's ideas of the supernatural, his conception of ideal family life, or his evaluation of warfare. No one is denying that the family has an important role in the socialization of the young. But the family is not the only agency of socialization.

When societies are viewed over space, or the same society is viewed over time, it becomes apparent that to describe the family's part in the socialization of the young we must utilize relative terms. In some of the Israeli kibbutzim, for example, the family has a relatively minor role in socializing its children, but it has a role. In some primitive societies the family may constitute a very important agency of socialization, but it is not the only agency. So in our own society we have gone from a time when the family had a more extensive role in the socialization process to a time when it has a less-pronounced one. Certain it is, to take but one extra-familial socializing agency, that the school system gets children earlier and keeps them longer. Organized nursery schools will take the toddler of two or two and a half and the child can remain in some type of school well beyond puberty. Not only that, but more and more children are coming under the socializing influence of the school system. Each year an increasingly greater proportion of American children are enrolled at each and every educational level. Since it is literally true that when the child is coming under the influence of an extra-familial agency he is not at the same time coming under the influence of the family, it would be easy to demonstrate that quantitatively the family of today has a less important role in the socialization of its young than it did in colonial times.

We must not lose sight, however, of the end product of socialization, the production of an adult who is able to function adequately in his society as he will find it by the time he is an adult. In a relatively simple, relatively unchanging society, perhaps the family can retain for generations a significant part of the socialization of the young and still produce a requisite number of socialized adults. The very complexity of our industrialized society requires that the socialization be broader than almost any family could itself perform. Then there is the matter of the type of mature personality sought. It is apparent that there are some changes in the kind of adult personality our society would like to produce. It would seem, furthermore, that changes in socialization techniques are mandatory if we are to produce the type of personality for which we seek and that, furthermore, many of these changes involve transferring some of the traditional socializing functions from the family to an outside agency. In sum, there would seem to be room for another way of looking at the loss of the socialization function of the American family. It is a loss only in the sense that the American family no longer is the dominant socializing agency it once was. This loss to the family is a decided gain for the society in the sense that the newer arrangement for socialization more nearly produces the kind of individual we want in view of the kind of society in which we anticipate he will have to live. No one is trying to rob the family of its sacred function or usurp its time-honored responsibility. Change and time and new understandings and a host of other factors have altered our conceptions of a well-adjusted child and a mature adult. Agencies and institutions other than the family are more important than in previous times because the experiences they have to offer are in accord with today's goals for the mature personality.

Changing Child-Rearing Goals

There is some indication that we are in the midst of a change in our conception of what a normal child should do and should be like. Where the impetus for the new conception arose is difficult to say. We can see be-

ginnings of the new view before the turn of the century in the writings
of John Dewey and in the Progressive Education Association's formulation
in 1919 in "freedom for children to develop."[47] In the mid 1940's Evelyn
Duvall attempted to get at parents' conceptions of what they wanted to
produce in their children by asking a sample of mothers, "What are five
things a good child does?"[48] She discovered that the many answers, given
in the mothers' own words, clustered around two conceptions of a "good
child." One she called the *traditional* conception because it emphasized
the qualities and characteristics of a child that have been held important
for a long time in our society. Traditional parents stressed that a good child
is obedient, respectful, truthful, polite, and a willing worker around the
home. The newer conception of a good child focused on the child's personal
and social development and hence was labeled the *developmental*
emphasis. Parents holding the developmental conception stressed that a
good child is cheerful and happy, expresses himself well and asks questions,
grows in his ability to handle himself in different situations, and likes and
gets along well with other children.

The temptation should be resisted to consider the developmental-
traditional split as a rigid one or to assume that one is always the polar
opposite of the other. Mothers with the developmental philosophy are
not striving to produce disrespectful liars nor are traditional mothers
totally unconcerned with the child's cheerfulness or ability to get along
with others. A traditional mother, for example, will stress that a child
should not be destructive whereas a developmental parent likes to see
her child get along well with others. It is no mere suspicion that a destructive child would have difficulty in finding acceptance in almost any group
save a demolition team. Or again, in an over-simplified case, both kinds of
mothers would be concerned if their youngster deliberately hit his friend's
tricycle with a baseball bat. The traditional mother would be concerned
with the "character defect" shown by his disrespect for property, whereas
the developmental mother would be more concerned with the social im-
maturity evidenced by his choice of an inappropriate tension release. Yet
even in this example we see the difference in emphasis: the traditional approach seems to get across the idea of conformity to adult notions of respect for property, whereas the developmental view focuses on the
personal and social adjustment of the child. It is this type of difference in

---

[47] A summary of the changes in general attitudes toward children and child rearing occurring from the 1880's to the 1950's, and the key people or events associated with
the changes, can be found in Duvall, *op. cit.*, pp. 44-46. See also Grace Langdon and
Irving Stout, *The Discipline of Well-Adjusted Children* (New York, The John Day
Company, Inc., 1952), Ch. 1.
[48] Duvall, *op. cit.*, p. 47.

emphasis that is discovered when mothers are asked to describe a good child. The fact that a certain set of traits is mentioned first and that this set comes to mind at all out of possibly hundreds of ideas about a good child is thought to reveal differences in basic philosophy of child rearing. At the present time there are very real difficulties in rigidly defining and adequately measuring the different orientations to child rearing. The results of other studies since Duvall's pioneer work seem to indicate that the developmental-traditional concept, nevertheless, provides a meaningful basis for distinguishing between two general approaches to child rearing.[49]

There is some evidence, therefore, that we have in our society two relatively distinct, and in a sense competitive, views of what a child should be like. We are much less certain how widely held each conception is and how extensive has been the change from the traditional to the developmental orientation. Apparently many parents exhibit a mixture of *both* types. In the various studies, mothers whose responses were largely traditional nevertheless had some developmental ideas and, conversely, those mothers who had a predominantly developmental approach to child rearing had some conceptions that were classified as traditional. There is no way of knowing, furthermore, exactly what proportion of all American parents could be classified even as "predominantly developmental" or "predominantly traditional." Duvall suggests "that developmental attitudes are more frequent among family members with the advantages of education and the privileges of middle class status."[50] This would seem to indicate that these attitudes are held by a minority of parents. A few intergenerational studies show that developmental conceptions are finding greater acceptance, but the evidence is sketchy at best.[51]

SUMMARY

We began our treatment of socialization with a description of ferals and isolates, and we have concluded with a few remarks on the changing child-rearing goals in the United States. Some attention also was given to the personal, family, and cultural influences on socialization as well as to the studies of class differentials in socialization in present-day America. It is possible to abstract from this discussion of socialization two broad ideas:

[49] For example, Robert O. Blood, "A Situational Approach to the Study of Permissiveness in Child Rearing," *American Sociological Review*, Vol. 18 (February, 1953), pp. 84-87. See also Rachel A. Elder, "Traditional and Developmental Conceptions of Fatherhood," *Marriage and Family Living*, Vol. 11 (Summer, 1949), pp. 98-100.

[50] Duvall, *op. cit.*, p. 67.

[51] For example, Ruth Connor, Theodore B. Johannis, Jr., and James Walters, "Intra-Familial Conceptions of Good Father, Good Mother, and Good Child," *Journal of Home Economics*, Vol. 46 (March, 1954), pp. 187-191.

(1) socialization of the young is an extremely important societal function, and (2) the culture of a group and those who interpret the culture in socializing their young have a significant impact on the personality of the individual. Any attempt to evaluate the efficacy of the American family in its performance of the basic function of socialization should reckon with these central ideas.

In any ultimate sense, it is impossible to evaluate the kind of job the American family is doing in socializing its young. Any judgment would have to rest on a combination of qualitative and quantitative measures that would allow us to answer with some surety how well how many children are being prepared to enter society as reasonably acceptable adults. It is certain that the American family is not failing miserably in these respects, but we lack the kind of data to demonstrate how well it is succeeding. As we have shown, the American family retains a significant role in the total socialization of society's young. The family has exhibited a remarkable degree of resiliency and adaptability in its performance of this basic function in the face of change and uncertainty. The strength and importance of the family as an institution seems unthreatened by those changes in socialization that require increasing utilization of non-family personnel. Once again, it becomes crucial not to confuse change over time, or even a certain amount of variation at a given time, with institutional decline. Unless one insists upon judging today's family on how well it performs yesteryear's tasks, one is forced to conclude that the American family is performing well its function of socializing society's young.

SELECTED READINGS

BARKER, ROGER G., and WRIGHT, HERBERT F., *Midwest and Its Children* (Evanston, Illinois, Row, Peterson & Company, 1954).

BRODY, SYLVIA, *Patterns of Mothering* (New York, International Universities Press, Inc., 1956).

DAVIS, W. ALLISON, and HAVIGHURST, ROBERT J., *Father of the Man* (Boston, Houghton Mifflin Co., 1947).

GESELL, ARNOLD, *Wolf Child and Human Child* (New York, Harper & Brothers, 1940).

LINTON, RALPH, *The Cultural Background of Personality* (New York, Appleton-Century-Crofts, Inc., 1945).

MEAD, MARGARET, and WOLFENSTEIN, MARTHA, eds., *Childhood in Contemporary Cultures* (Chicago, University of Chicago Press, 1955).

MILLER, DANIEL R., and SWANSON, GUY E., *The Changing American Parent* (New York, John Wiley & Sons, Inc., 1958).

ORLANSKY, HAROLD, "Infant Care and Personality," *Psychological Bulletin*, Vol. 46 (January, 1949), pp. 1-48.

RIBBLE, MARGARET A., *The Rights of Infants* (New York, Columbia University Press, 1943).

SEARS, ROBERT R., MACCOBY, ELEANOR E., and LEVIN, HARRY, *Patterns of Child Rearing* (Evanston, Illinois, Row, Peterson & Company, 1957).

SEWELL, WILLIAM H., "Infant Training and the Personality of the Child," *American Journal of Sociology*, Vol. 58 (September, 1952), pp. 150-159.

SINGH, J. A. L., and ZINGG, ROBERT M., *Wolf-Children and Feral Man* (New York, Harper & Brothers, 1939).

WHITING, JOHN W. M., and CHILD, IRVIN L., *Child Training and Personality* (New Haven, Yale University Press, 1953).

CHAPTER 12

The Regulation of Sexual Behavior

No SOCIETY has ever been discovered that is completely indifferent concerning the sexual behavior of its members. All societies provide some restraints on sexual behavior and all provide for sexual expression on the part of their adult members. These sociological universals require explanation.

Man shares with lower animals an inborn sexual urge. No healthy, postpubertal person needs to be told this, nor is it probably necessary to remind him that the sexual urge in humans is a powerful force. Society is interested in the sexual behavior of its members, and establishes restraints upon it, because it feels that the welfare and survival of the group would be in jeopardy if this strong impulse were left in its unbridled form. A completely indifferent attitude to all types of sexual behavior is thought to be well-nigh impossible for an enduring society. Perhaps at some time a group had this hypothesized indifferent attitude and for this reason, or for some other, failed in the struggle for survival. The fact remains that all known societies apparently consider it too great a disruptive risk to allow their members to have sexual relations whenever and with whomever they please.

At the same time, however, the survival and welfare of the group would most assuredly be jeopardized if it did not make provision for some sexual behavior on the part of its adult members. Under usual circumstances, the group would soon die out from lack of replacements. Such a society, too, would run the risk of personality maladjustment and discontent among its members. We are not denying that the sex drive, as powerful as it is, can be sublimated or suppressed, nor are we asserting that the lack of sexual expression dooms an individual to neurosis. The *risk* of great malcontent and of personality difficulties would nevertheless be present in any society that attempted to prohibit *all* types of sexual behavior for *all* of its members. As our cross-cultural studies have shown, every society has established a relatively enduring social relationship between one or more men and one or more women within which relationship the principals are expected to find their chief source of sexual satisfaction. Marriage involves more than sexual privilege, of course, but the point is that all societies have institutionalized an arrangement that should provide for the sexual needs of most of their adult members. No society has been completely success-ful, however, in restricting the sexual behavior of its members to marriage; furthermore, it seems that some societies are more concerned with attempt-ing to do so than are others.

All societies have had to find their way between the perplexing alternatives of too lax and too severe restrictions on sexual behavior. In attempting to reach this satisfactory balance, different societies have come to endorse a wide variety of sexual values. It is as if there were many different definitions of the careful balance between too little and too great sexual freedom. Among the Trobrianders,[1] there are far fewer restrictions on premarital sexual intercourse than in our society. In the present-day United States, however, extramarital relations probably occur with greater frequency and are less seriously condemned than among the Trobrianders,[2] the ancient Hebrews,[3] or, for that matter, among the early New England colonists.[4] Premarital sex relations are frowned upon in the Israeli kibbut-zim for persons of high school age but not for the unmarried after their schooling is completed.[5] And so, culture by culture, we can catalogue the mores and taboos, and we are forced to admit that there is great variability in what is permitted sexually and for whom it is allowed.

Just as we have observed variation in sexual values and behavior among groups, so there are variations within a given group. First of all, values change over time. A group may come to alter its values concerning sexual activity and will prescribe new rules of conduct for its members. In heterogeneous societies, moreover, it is not unusual to find different subcultures each with its own somewhat different set of behavioral norms. A third type of intrasocietal variation occurs because of the deviation from societal norms that is allowed. In other words, even when there is good consensus on what people "should" do, society is seldom successful in de-manding that everyone's behavior be in strict accordance with the norms or approach normative behavior to the same degree. The toleration, within limits, of some non-normative behavior means that we should anticipate behavioral variation in a society.

Three aspects of societal attempts to regulate sexual behavior can be

[1] See pp. 126-127.
[2] See p. 128.
[3] See pp. 57-59.
[4] See pp. 104-107.
[5] See p. 170.

isolated. We can, first of all, attempt to determine what people are doing sexually. This is admittedly an imposing task and becomes increasingly more difficult as we refine our analysis in terms of types of sexual behavior and the characteristics of the behaving people. Then we must come to grips with the matter of sexual values and attempt to discover what the society considers important in the area of sexual behavior. In the consideration of sexual values it is appropriate, too, to investigate the degree of stability or change that is manifested in the society. The final area of analysis is concerned with what we have called the machinery utilized by a society to regulate behavior in accordance with its values. It should be clear that the established patterns of behavior, the values, and the methods used to regulate behavior in accordance with the values are all intricately intertwined. For analytical purposes, however, they can be separated. In our analysis of the regulation of sexual behavior in American society, we will focus separately on the three institutional aspects we have defined. Although we could start the analysis at any of the three levels, we believe there are advantages in attempting first to discover what are the patterns of sexual behavior in the United States.

SEXUAL BEHAVIOR IN THE UNITED STATES

In our own and other societies, the type of heterosexual behavior that meets with highest social approval is that which occurs within marriage. Non-marital sexual intercourse certainly occurs, and an investigation of the extent to which it does will assist us in determining the values that surround this behavior in our society. We are aware that at the present time sexual behavior outside of marriage cannot be analyzed completely or to the degree of accuracy which we prefer. Although it is a more than trite remark that "more research is needed," it is sometimes amazing how much work has been done in this admittedly hard-to-research area. Specificity and detail are lacking, some areas have barely been studied at all, and we are not always sure how much confidence we can place in this or that finding of a specific study. At the same time, however, there are some aspects of non-marital sexual behavior in our society about which we can be reasonably sure.

In our discussion of the extent of non-marital sexual intercourse in America, we will rely almost entirely on the two works of the late Dr. Kinsey and his staff. We do this, first of all, because we firmly believe that whatever the weaknesses of the Kinsey studies there are no better ones available for our purposes. But since there are weaknesses in the studies, as Kinsey himself has admitted, the more important of these should be made explicit. It is not our intention to give a critique of the Kinsey studies. A 1954 bibliography of published material *about* the Kinsey reports contained 260 items and its compilers mention that 600 additional items were excluded.[6] Most of these articles and books criticized, pro or con, the methods, findings, or interpretations of one of the studies. To go into all of the comments is manifestly impossible and unwise. For our purposes it is only necessary to point out the more important methodological and other inadequacies and, among these, only the ones that have a direct bearing on the data that we will use.

Although the Kinsey studies utilized information from over 5,000 persons of each sex, the cases were not selected according to a statistically acceptable sampling plan. Kinsey pleads that the refusal rate would have made a probability sampling technique prohibitively costly. Some of his critics say that he should have used a probability sample or that he should have at least tried.[7] He did not do so, however, and this creates difficulties with respect to the representativeness of his sample. If we cannot estimate how representative of a total population a given sample is, then there is the chance that the sample for some reason is an unusual or atypical segment of that population.

Kinsey utilized what is technically called a self-selected sample. This means that whether or not a person was included in the study depended to some extent on whether or not that person was willing to be interviewed. It was not a volunteer sample, in the sense that Kinsey took the first 10,000 people who offered to be interviewed. It is nevertheless true that the men and women Kinsey studied differ from those who refused to be interviewed, or who would have refused to be interviewed if asked, in willingness to co-operate with a sex researcher. We are yet uncertain, however, whether willingness to be interviewed about sexual behavior is related to sexual behavior, or how it is, or to what types of behavior it may be related. Some have assumed that those who are the more inhibited at the behavioral level would be the more inhibited in discussing their sex lives,[8] but those who have "nothing to hide" may be the very ones who least mind talking about it. The matter, of course, should be thoroughly tested and until then we can only recognize it as a possible source of bias.[9] Kinsey

[6] Jerome Himelhoch and Sylvia F. Fava, eds., *Sexual Behavior in American Society: An Appraisal of the First Two Kinsey Reports* (New York, W. W. Norton & Company, Inc., 1955), pp. 417-435.

[7] Harvey J. Locke, "Are Volunteer Interviewees Representative?," in Himelhoch and Fava, *op. cit.*, p. 114.

[8] John A. Calusen, "Biological Bias and Methodological Limitations in the Kinsey Studies," in Himelhoch and Fava, *op. cit.*, p. 41.

[9] Some attempt has been made to discover the differences between those who would permit themselves to be interviewed by the Kinsey staff and those who would not. See Aron W. Siegman, "Responses to a Personality Questionnaire by Volunteers

attempted to overcome this bias by selecting groups, such as college fraternities, women's clubs, and the like, and attempting to get all of the people in the group to contribute their sexual histories. This corrected for self-selection error within the groups, but not among groups that would and would not co-operate to this extent.[10]

The reliance upon memory or recall in the Kinsey studies is another potential source of difficulty. Unless behavior is observed while it is occurring, we must, of course, rely on the ability of the individual to recall what actually happened. Just as we cannot assume that self-selection is related to all types of sexual behavior, even if it may be related to some, so the inability of the subject to remember his behavior is in all likelihood only a problem with respect to some types of behavior. It seems highly unlikely, for example, that even a woman fifty-five years old would not remember whether or not she had sexual relations before she was married. Unless her experience was highly unusual, it seems much more likely that a woman of this age would know for a fact if she had had pre-marital relations, would probably be certain of the number of men with whom she had had them, and could give a reasonably accurate estimate of how many times it had occurred. No great intuitive knowledge of American society is required to suspect strongly that fornication and adultery are not the sort of things about which most people simply cannot remember. It is a little different, on the other hand, to trust implicitly a sixty-year-old man's estimate of how frequently he masturbated when he was fifteen, but even in this case the distortion may not be as great as might be imagined. Recognizing the potential source of bias in recall data, however, we can make allowance for it in the sense of the confidence we place in *some* types of Kinsey's data.

There are other difficulties with the Kinsey methodology which either need not concern us or for which we make allowance in our subsequent presentation. Examples of the first category would be Kinsey's definition of *adolescence* and his use of sexual orgasm as a criterion of sexual adjustment. We will not be dealing with matters that rely on either of these measures. It is apparent, to take another example, that Catholics and Jews are underrepresented in the Kinsey samples. Accordingly, our major comments on sexual behavior as related to religious devoutness are restricted to Protestants. We have attempted, in sum, to use only the data about which we

---

and Nonvolunteers to a Kinsey Interview," *Journal of Abnormal and Social Psychology*, Vol. 52 (March, 1956), pp. 280-281. See also Abraham H. Moslow and James M. Sakoda, "Volunteer-Error in the Kinsey Study," in Himelhoch and Fava, *op. cit.*, pp. 119-125.

[10] Utilizing entire groups may have introduced other sources of error, such as those due to discussion by group members. Cf. Locke, *op. cit.*, p. 116.

can be reasonably confident. In the task of selecting these data we have been guided by the findings of other studies rather than what we feel personally "really" is going on sexually in America. We chose Kinsey's, as opposed to the previous studies, because of their recency, their completeness, and the fact that the methodologies, despite their weaknesses, are the best yet utilized in a large-scale study of sexual behavior. The committee appointed by the Commission on Statistical Standards of the American Statistical Association has stated:[11]

> The statistical and methodological aspects of KPM's work [Kinsey, Pomeroy, and Martin, *Sexual Behavior in the Human Male*] are outstanding in comparison with other leading sex studies. In a comparison with nine other leading sex studies . . . KPM's were superior to all others in the systematic coverage of their material, in the number of items which they covered, in the composition of their sample as regards its age, educational, religious, rural-urban, occupational, and geographic representation, in the number and variety of methodological checks which they employed, and in their statistical analyses. So far as we can judge from our present knowledge, or from the critical evaluation of a number of other qualified specialists, their interviewing was of the best.

Our comments concerning the Kinsey studies have been somewhat lengthy. Keeping in mind the various difficulties we have mentioned, let us now turn to the discovered facts on non-marital sexual behavior in America.

Premarital Sexual Behavior among Males

We will use the expression "premarital sexual intercourse" to refer to all heterosexual intercourse among unmarried males. Some have objected to this usage on the undeniable grounds that sexual intercourse among men who will never marry is not "premarital" at all. Nevertheless over 90 per cent of all men who live to age forty are or have been married by that time in their life and, what is more, not all of the remaining have had heterosexual experience. It is true that there is a difference between the male who engages in sex relations for a period of a few years before he is married and another who more or less adopts sexual relations outside of marriage as his way of life in place of marrying. But since almost all males with sexual experience eventually marry and since our data do not allow us to distinguish those who eventually marry from those who do not, we will label both types of sexual experience "premarital."

---

[11] William G. Cochran, Frederick Mosteller, and John W. Tukey, "Statistical Problems of the Kinsey Report," *Journal of the American Statistical Association*, Vol. 48 (December, 1953), p. 674.

Even a cursory acquaintance with Kinsey's and others' data makes it obvious that there is no monolithic pattern of sexual behavior among the unmarried males in the United States. Indeed, this can be considered an important contribution of the various studies of sexual behavior. Instead of simply asking what unmarried males are doing, we must inquire which males, and with whom, and at what age. In general, differences in premarital sex behavior are found according to educational level, residence (whether rural or urban), and religious devoutness. Within each of these categories, furthermore, there are different rates of activity by age.

Social status. The amount of a man's education, or potential education, was found more closely related to premarital sex experience than any other social characteristic measured by Kinsey. We can summarize the data in Table 18 succinctly: (1) the lower the education level, the earlier the male begins his premarital sexual activity, and (2) the lower the educational level, the more males, at every age, are ultimately involved in premarital sexual intercourse. More than four times as many boys who will

TABLE 18. Premarital Sexual Intercourse among Males by Educational Level

| Some Experience by Age: | Per Cent at Educational Level | | |
	0-8 years of Education	9-12 years of Education	13 or more years of Education
15	42.2	44.7	9.5
18	76.1	73.7	30.8
21	83.6	76.7	49.1
25	89.9	83.8	64.4

Source: Alfred C. Kinsey, Wardell B. Pomeroy, and Clyde E. Martin, *Sexual Behavior in the Human Male* (Philadelphia, W. B. Saunders Co., 1948), p. 550.

end their education with grade school begin their heterosexual life by age fifteen as compared with those who will eventually attend college. By age twenty-five, at which age a large proportion of all males will have ended their premarital life by virtue of their marriage, we note that a smaller proportion of the college-educated have had premarital sexual relations than the high school group, which, in turn, is smaller than those who did not go beyond grade school.

Better-educated males are less sexually active than their less-educated peers in still another sense. Age for age, the college male who did have premarital sexual intercourse experienced it less frequently than high school and grade school graduates. For the five-year period covering ages sixteen through twenty, for example, the average male who did not go beyond grade school, and who was experiencing some sexual intercourse, experienced it slightly over four times a month. The average high school male had premarital sexual intercourse three times a month, whereas among the college males who had intercourse the frequency was slightly more than once a month.[12]

TABLE 19. Premarital Intercourse among Males Aged 16 to 20
by Occupational Class*

Occupational Class	Per Cent with Experience	Median Frequency per Week
2 (lowest)	79.3	.88
3	77.4	1.07
4	66.3	.63
5	38.8	.27
6	39.4	.20
7 (highest)	35.3	.21

SOURCE: Alfred C. Kinsey, Wardell B. Pomeroy, and Clyde E. Martin, *Sexual Behavior in the Human Male* (Philadelphia, W. B. Saunders Co., 1948), pp. 430-431.
* Data restricted to cases where respondent remained in occupational class of his parents. Premarital intercourse with prostitutes not included.

All in all, then, there is a fairly sharp and consistent relationship between education and sexual activity among males. Whether we consider age at first premarital intercourse, the percentage involved at a given age level, or the frequency of premarital intercourse, it is clear that the less educated are the most sexually active. Apparently, however, it is not "just education" that accounts for the differences in sexual behavior, for when individuals are classified by their own or their parents' occupational status a fairly consistent pattern emerges: (1) the lower the occupational status, the higher is the proportion that engage in sexual relations, and (2) among those with premarital experience, the lower the occupational status the greater is the frequency with which they engage in it. Education and occupation are both important indices of a more generalized social status. Although we should not overlook the possibility that factors in the educational and occupational experiences themselves help to account for the discovered behavioral differences, it seems more likely that the influences are more subtle and are to be found in the more general differences in the value systems of people of different statuses. Whether we infer social status from education or occupation or some other characteristic, the broader value differences should manifest themselves.

Religion. It is scarcely necessary to note that the Judeo-Christian moral code strongly condemns non-marital sexual relations. In earlier

[12] *Average* refers to the median case of all males in the category. Half of the males, therefore, had more frequent sexual intercourse and half experienced it less frequently. Data are from Alfred C. Kinsey, Wardell B. Pomeroy, and Clyde E. Martin, *Sexual Behavior in the Human Male* (Philadelphia, W. B. Saunders Co., 1948), pp. 348 and 350.

chapters we have seen the rigor with which such behavior was condemned and the severity of the punishments for transgressors of the code among both the ancient Hebrews and the Puritans of New England. Although times have certainly changed since these periods, it is nevertheless true that the various Protestant denominations, the Catholic Church, and Judaism all consider sexual intercourse before marriage as morally wrong. But how effective have the teachings of the churches been in controlling behavior? In an attempt to answer this question, Kinsey classified his sample of males as Protestant, Catholic, or Jewish, and within these categories as devout or inactive, according to church attendance and participation in church activities.

TABLE 20. Premarital Intercourse and Religious Background
of Males Aged 16 to 20

YEARS OF EDUCATION	PER CENT WITH SOME EXPERIENCE		MEDIAN FREQUENCY PER WEEK	
	Devout Protestants	Inactive Protestants	Devout Protestants	Inactive Protestants
0-8	70.4	90.5	.56	1.12
9-12	67.4	80.4	.67	.94
13 or more	27.3	45.0	.09	.20

SOURCE: Alfred C. Kinsey, Wardell B. Pomeroy, and Clyde E. Martin, *Sexual Behavior in the Hnman Male* (Philadelphia, W. B. Saunders Co., 1948), p. 480.

At each educational level, as shown in Table 20, the devout Protestant male was less likely to engage in premarital sexual intercourse, and to engage in it less frequently, than the inactive church member. But the differences between devout and inactive Protestants do not approach the differences by educational level. The devout Protestant who did not go beyond eighth grade, for example, engaged in premarital intercourse about half as frequently as the inactive Protestant of similar education, but six times *more* frequently than the religiously devout college-educated man. Apparently religious devoutness does make a difference with respect to sexual activity but it is not as influential as social status. In other words, we could predict with greater accuracy which males would have premarital intercourse if we knew their eventual social status than if we knew their religious activity. Knowing both characteristics, of course, would increase the accuracy of our predictions.

Extramarital Relations among Males

It is usual to define sexual relations between a married person and someone other than his or her spouse as extramarital intercourse. Kinsey found that the married males in his sample showed considerable interest in this topic. Many were quite concerned with what "really" is going on in this area, presumably, according to Kinsey, because of their own behavior or desires.[13] At the same time, Kinsey reported that his male subjects were more reticent about their extramarital sexual history than about any other aspect of their sexual experience, including homosexual behavior and animal contacts.[14] He believes it is likely that a certain proportion of his sample falsified their reports by not admitting to extramarital affairs.[15]

Allowing for falsification, Kinsey suggests that about half of all married men have intercourse with women other than their wives at some time during their married life.[16] The incidence at any one age level would not, of course, be this high. The estimate, furthermore, makes no reference to the frequency of the experience. It includes the one-time experience of the young husband who has not yet "settled down," the single or infrequent venture of the married serviceman alone in a foreign land, as well as the more extensive experiences of a man who more or less openly keeps a mistress over a period of years. Nevertheless, many Americans were quite shocked when they heard this estimate. They found it almost unbelievable that, statistically, every other married man had already or would sometime commit adultery.

TABLE 21. Extramarital Relations among Males by Education
and Age at Time of Experience

	PER CENT WITH EXPERIENCE	
AGE	0-8 Years of Education	13 or more Years of Education
16-20	44.6	19.6
21-25	34.5	14.2
26-30	35.7	19.5
31-35	31.7	24.6
36-40	26.6	29.6
41-45	21.0	23.9
46-50	18.6	27.2

SOURCE: Alfred C. Kinsey, Wardell B. Pomeroy, and Clyde E. Martin, *Sexual Behavior in the Human Male* (Philadelphia, W. B. Saunders Co., 1948), p. 348.

When we examine the data on extramarital relations, we find a rather close relationship with social status. The least and best educated groups differ to some extent on whether they have extramarital intercourse and rather markedly on when in their married life they have it. The grade school male, as indicated in Table 21, is more likely to have extramarital relations

[13] *Ibid.*, p. 584.
[14] *Ibid.*, p. 585.
[15] *Ibid.*
[16] *Ibid.*

in the early years of marriage than at any other time. Gradually, the percentage of grade school males involved in extramarital affairs drops until it reaches its lowest point among the forty-six- to fifty-year-old males. The pattern is exactly opposite for the college-bred male. The incidence of extramarital intercourse is higher in the later years of marriage, as judged by the age of the husband, than it was in the early years.

The different patterns of extramarital behavior by men of different social status is not at all easy to explain. Kinsey sees a relationship between the lower-status male's greater premarital sexual experience and his propensity for extramarital intercourse early in his marriage.[17] The college-bred man, sexually more inhibited in his youth, retains these inhibitions for non-marital sex until after he has been married for some time. Left unexplained, however, is the gradual decreasing proportion of less educated males who have extramarital relations as they grow older. More thorough investigation of such factors as differential opportunities for extramarital affairs, and more information on the partners in the extramarital intrigues, would undoubtedly shed some light on the divergent patterns by educational level.

As impressive as the differences in extramarital relations by education are the similarities in the incidences by certain age groups. Actually, after age thirty the differences between the percentages of extramarital experiences in the extreme types of educational groups are not large. This drawing closer together of males of admittedly divergent backgrounds is something that was not found with regard to premarital intercourse. In that case, it will be recalled, age for age, more of the less educated males had premarital relations than did the better-educated.

Religious activity was found to be inversely related to extramarital relations. At various ages, the "inactive Protestant" group was from two to three times more likely to engage in this type of intercourse than the regular church attenders. The relative crudity of the devout-inactive breakdown, the lumping together of all Protestant sects, the absence of comparable data on Jews and Catholics, and the failure to have a category for those who are not simply inactive but who profess no religion whatsoever, all effectively prohibit us from trying to investigate the causes of the relationship between religious background and extramarital sexual relations.

Stability of Male Sexual Patterns

Whether it is viewed with tolerance, indifference, or alarm, almost everyone believes that non-marital sexual behavior has increased in recent years. One of the most startling findings of the first Kinsey study was that,

[17] Ibid., p. 587.

basically, this is not the case at all. The similarity of the behavior of two generations of males is far more striking than any of the discovered differences.

We see in Table 22 that behavior in the two generations is almost identical for each of the extreme educational levels. By age twenty-five, about the same percentage of both groups of males had at some time in their life experienced premarital intercourse, and about the same proportion had had at least one experience with a prostitute. Kinsey did discover, however, a significant increase in the proportion of grade school boys who by age sixteen had had sexual relations at least once.[18] The fact that the less educated males now begin their heterosexual lives earlier than a generation ago is one of the few changes in premarital sexual patterns observed by Kinsey.

TABLE 22. Two Generations of Males: Percentage with Any Premarital Intercourse and Any Intercourse with Prostitutes by Age 25

Years of Education	Intercourse with Prostitutes		All Premarital Intercourse	
	Per Cent of Older Generation	Per Cent of Younger Generation	Per Cent of Older Generation	Per Cent of Younger Generation
0-8	65.7	63.6	90.3	88.9
13 or more	28.3	28.9	62.0	65.9

SOURCE: Alfred C. Kinsey, Wardell B. Pomeroy, and Clyde E. Martin, *Sexual Behavior in the Human Male* (Philadelphia, W. B. Saunders Co., 1948), pp. 402 and 404.

Although it is true that the proportion of both the younger and older generations who have had sexual relations with prostitutes seems not to have changed, the reported frequency of this type of premarital intercourse has quite definitely been reduced. At every age and at every educational level the average number of contacts with prostitutes is markedly less today than a generation ago.[19] But since the total amount of premarital sexual intercourse has remained about the same, it can only mean that intercourse with non-prostitutes has replaced that with prostitutes. Taking into account their entire premarital history, Kinsey concludes that fully a third to a half of the sexual intercourse males used to have with prostitutes they now have with other girls.[20]

Kinsey's data reveal no orderly trend with respect to the extent to which the two generations of males engaged in extramarital relations.[21] A somewhat lower proportion of college-bred males in the younger genera-

[18] *Ibid.*, p. 404.
[19] *Ibid.*, p. 410.
[20] *Ibid.*, p. 413.
[21] *Ibid.*, p. 410.

tion have had extramarital relations than those in the older generation. Among the grade school and high school groups, however, more of the younger males have had extramarital intercourse than have the older married men. Although these differences exist, they are not extremely great and once again we are struck more by the similarity of behavior than by the divergence.

Premarital Sexual Behavior of Females

For the very obvious reason that "it takes two," we have already learned something of female sexual experience from our previous discussion of the male. To deal with the matter more completely, however, we need to investigate the various social characteristics associated with non-marital sexual behavior among females. Just as we did with respect to the male, in this section we will largely be concerned with presenting the various "facts" of non-marital sexual behavior among females. Later, we will attempt to tie all these data together, for male as well as female, and to relate them to the current sexual values in the United States and any changes therein.

Of all the females in the Kinsey sample, nearly half had sexual intercourse sometime before they were married.[22] Although this proportion is considerably higher than that discovered in some earlier studies, it is only a little higher than that discovered in other studies, and is actually lower than that found in one study. To a large extent the discrepancies in the findings of the various studies reflect the social characteristics of the populations studied. Kinsey alone attempted to get a cross-section of American females and even he was not successful. Because of the make-up of Kinsey's sample, the data in which we can place the most confidence are those that concern the white, urban female who is college-educated. Other segments of the population are represented, but not always sufficiently so to allow detailed comparisons. With these cautions in mind, we will turn to Kinsey's findings.

Social status. Since lower-status males are more likely to engage in premarital intercourse than other males, one might immediately expect that a similar relationship between social status and sexual behavior would prevail among females. This belief would be strengthened by the realization that there is a tendency for men to choose as sexual partners women who are of their own or a lower social status. In general, it does seem that

[22] Alfred C. Kinsey, Wardell B. Pomeroy, Clyde E. Martin, and Paul H. Gebhard, *Sexual Behavior in the Human Female* (Philadelphia, W. B. Saunders Co., 1953), p. 286. (Hereafter referred to as Kinsey, *Female.*)

the lower the educational level of the woman the more likely she is to engage in premarital intercourse. The relationship between social status and sexual experience before marriage is not, however, as strong among females as among males.

TABLE 23. Premarital Intercourse among Females
by Age and Education

SOME EXPERIENCE BY AGE:	PER CENT AT EDUCATIONAL LEVEL		
	0-8 years of Education	9-12 years of Education	13-16 years of Education
15	18	5	2
20	25	26	20
25	26	37	39

SOURCE: Alfred C. Kinsey, Wardell B. Pomeroy, Clyde E. Martin, and Paul H. Gebhard, *Sexual Behavior in the Human Female* (Philadelphia, W. B. Saunders Co., 1953), p. 333.

From Table 23 we note that before age twenty-five, and particularly before age twenty, the girl destined to complete her education with grade school is more likely to be engaging in sexual relations than are other girls. At age fifteen, for example, almost none of the college-bound girls have had intercourse, whereas almost 20 per cent of the grade school girls have had at least one experience. As age increases, the proportion levels off.

Table 23 also shows that by age twenty-five more of the better-educated women have had premarital intercourse than the lesser-educated women. It is now believed that this particular finding is misleading and that, more accurately, the proportion of women who have premarital intercourse increases with age, regardless of social status. Probably there were too few women in the sample who had not gone beyond the eighth grade in school and who were still available, by virtue of their unmarried status, for premarital intercourse. More recent studies by the same research staff give a different picture of the lower-status girls and women.[23] It is now thought that the incidence and frequency of premarital intercourse is greater among lower-status females but that the relationship between social status and premarital experience becomes less pronounced with increasing age.

The relationship between age at marriage and age at first premarital intercourse also has a bearing on the differential sexual behavior at different status levels. Generally speaking, the earlier in her life a girl has premarital intercourse, the younger she will be at time of marriage. Of all the girls who married between the ages sixteen and twenty, for example, 30 per cent

[23] Paul H. Gebhard and others, *Pregnancy, Birth and Abortion* (New York, Harper & Brothers, 1958).

TABLE 24. Premarital Intercourse among Females
and Age at Marriage

Per Cent with Experience by Age:	Age at Marriage		
	16-20	21-25	26-30
16	15	4	2
18	30	13	8
20	47	26	14
25	—	42	38
28	—	—	56

Source: Alfred C. Kinsey, Wardell B. Pomeroy, Clyde E. Martin, and Paul H. Gebhard, *Sexual Behavior in the Human Female* (Philadelphia, W. B. Saunders Co., 1953), p. 337.

had had premarital coitus by age eighteen. Only 13 per cent of the girls who married in the next five-year age group and only 8 per cent of those who married between the ages of twenty-six and thirty had had sexual relations by age eighteen. Apparently, then, most of the premarital sexual activity of girls and women occurs one to a few years before their marriage. Since lower-status girls marry at younger ages than others, it follows that their premarital intercourse also occurs at younger ages.

TABLE 25. Sexual Partners of Married Women with Premarital Sexual Intercourse

Partner	Percentage
With fiancé only	46
With other males only	13
With fiancé and others	41

Source: Alfred C. Kinsey, Wardell B. Pomeroy, Clyde E. Martin, and Paul H. Gebhard, *Sexual Behavior in the Human Female* (Philadelphia, W. B. Saunders Co., 1953), p. 336.

The close relationship between age at first premarital intercourse and age at marriage suggests that the sexual relations were had with the girl's future husband, possibly even during engagement. In more than half of the sample, however, this was not the case. Table 25 is based on Kinsey's data on married women who had experienced premarital intercourse. Their premarital history is therefore completed. Fifty-four per cent of women who were not virgins at the time of marriage had had intercourse with some man other than the one they married. In the large group, 41 per cent of the total, that had sexual relations both with their fiancé and others it is most likely that the relations with the "others" occurred before those with the fiancé. It is quite probable, therefore, that among the non-virgins at time of marriage at least half lost their virginity by some man other than their future husband. Premarital intercourse for the female is more than a matter of an occasional sexual act with the man she is about to marry. Although almost half of the girls with intercourse experience before marriage did restrict it to their future husband, it is well to recognize that more did not. This, of course, brings the female sexual statistics more in line with those on the male, for surely the many males reporting premarital relations have had them with *some* girl!

Religious background. With respect to religious background, Kinsey found that females behaved in a similar manner to males. Age for age, as shown in Table 26, the devout Protestant girls were about half as likely to have engaged in premarital intercourse as the religiously inactive ones. While the data are incomplete, the general trend is the same for the Catholic and the Jewish group. The devout girls who did have sexual intercourse, furthermore, generally had it less frequently than the others and were more likely to express regret over the experience.[24]

TABLE 26. Premarital Intercourse among Females
by Religious Background

| Age | Accumulated Per Cent with Experience | |
	Devout Protestants	Inactive Protestants
15	3	5
20	14	25
25	22	44
30	26	55
35	30	63

Source: Alfred C. Kinsey, Wardell B. Pomeroy, Clyde E. Martin, and Paul H. Gebhard, *Sexual Behavior in the Human Female* (Philadelphia, W. B. Saunders Co., 1953), p. 342.

Extramarital Relations among Females

Whether we call it by the harsher term *adultery* or by the more morally neutral expression *extramarital relations*, probably everyone realizes that sexual relations between married persons and those other than their spouses do occur. Since it has been estimated that fully half of the married males have at least one experience of extramarital intercourse and since it is unreasonable to assume that all of these males found unmarried partners or sought the paid embraces of a prostitute, we should expect to find that a sizable proportion of married women have had extramarital intercourse. Indeed, of all the married women in Kinsey's sample, 26 per cent, or about one out of four, had had extramarital relations by the time they were forty years old. There were variations, as might be expected, by the women's

[24] Kinsey, *Female*, pp. 304-307.

age, educational attainment, religious background, and premarital sexual experience.

TABLE 27. Extramarital Relations among Females by
Educational Level

YEARS OF EDUCATION	PER CENT WITH EXPERIENCE BY AGE:		
	20	30	40
9-12	7	16	24
13 or more	6	17	29

SOURCE: Alfred C. Kinsey, Wardell B. Pomeroy, Clyde E. Martin, and Paul H. Gebhard, *Sexual Behavior in the Human Female* (Philadelphia, W. B. Saunders Co., 1953), p. 440.

Educational level is not actually an extremely discriminating factor with respect to female extramarital intercourse. Although at the younger ages, as shown in Table 27, the college and high school group behaved similarly, fewer of the less educated women ultimately were involved in extramarital intercourse. The difference, however, is not great. The variation that we notice most is the increase in extramarital activity with the age of the woman. In most cases, of course, the older woman had been married longer and consequently had had more time over which to engage in extramarital relations. Nevertheless both the highest proportion of women who engaged in extramarital intercourse and the highest frequency with which they experienced it were found among women in their middle thirties to the middle forties.[25] The stereotyped version of extramarital affairs, with its lure of younger women figuring prominently, is certainly not borne out by these findings.

Religious background was more definitely related to whether or not a woman engaged in extramarital relations than was any other factor examined by Kinsey. At each age level, the inactive Protestant woman was from three to four times more likely to be experiencing extramarital intercourse than the devout one. Between the ages thirty-one and thirty-five 7 per cent of devout women but 28 per cent of the inactive Protestants had at least one extramarital affair.[26] The corresponding figures for the age group thirty-six to forty were 8 and 23 per cent.[27]

The common belief that if a woman engages in sexual relations before her marriage, she is more likely to have intercourse with someone other than her husband after marriage is borne out statistically by Kinsey's findings. Most of the women who had extramarital intercourse experienced it for the first time before they were forty-five years old. By this age, only

[25] *Ibid.*, p. 417.
[26] *Ibid.*, p. 443.
[27] *Ibid.*

TABLE 28.   The Relationship between Premarital and Extra-marital Intercourse among Females

	PER CENT WITH EXTRAMARITAL INTERCOURSE		
	by Age 35	by Age 40	by Age 45
Without Premarital Intercourse	16	20	20
With Premarital Intercourse	33	39	40

SOURCE: Alfred C. Kinsey, Wardell B. Pomeroy, Clyde E. Martin, and Paul H. Gebhard, *Sexual Behavior in the Human Female* (Philadelphia, W. B. Saunders Co., 1953), p. 427.

20 per cent of women with no history of premarital coitus had had at least one extramarital affair as contrasted with 40 per cent of those who had intercourse before marriage. At other ages the relationship was similar; those with premarital sexual experience were definitely more likely to have extramarital intercourse. Other studies, such as Landis'[28] and Hamilton's,[29] discovered a similar relationship between premarital and extramarital intercourse, and Terman[30] found that those who had had premarital coitus were more likely to *desire* an extramarital affair. It seems, then, that the attitude of tolerance toward non-marital sexual behavior is carried over into marriage. If we could investigate such things as whether or not premarital intercourse was had with future husband only, frequency of premarital intercourse, and the like, we would be in a better position to consider a causal relationship between the incidence of premarital and extramarital relations.

Stability of Female Sexual Pattern

One of the most dramatic changes that has occurred with regard to non-marital sexual behavior is the increased proportion of females in America who have had premarital intercourse. The big change seems to have occurred in the group of women born since the turn of the century. These were the women who reached adolescence and early adulthood about the time of World War I and the subsequent "roaring twenties." Since that time, the proportion of women who have had intercourse before marriage has remained more or less stable.

[28] Carney Landis, *Sex in Development* (New York, Paul B. Hoeber, Inc., 1940), p. 98.

[29] G. V. Hamilton, *A Research in Marriage* (New York, Albert and Charles Boni, Inc., 1929), p. 346.

[30] Lewis M. Terman and others, *Psychological Factors in Marital Happiness* (New York, McGraw-Hill Book Company, Inc., 1938), p. 340.

TABLE 29. Premarital Intercourse among Females
by Decade of Birth

SOME EXPERIENCE BY AGE:	PER CENT BY DECADE OF BIRTH			
	Before 1900	1900-1909	1910-1919	1920-1929
15	2	2	3	4
20	8	18	23	21
25	14	36	39	37
30	26	53	48	—
35	35	56	54	—

SOURCE: Alfred C. Kinsey, Wardell B. Pomeroy, Clyde E. Martin, and Paul H. Gebhard, *Sexual Behavior in the Human Female* (Philadelphia, W. B. Saunders Co., 1953), p. 339.

Studies other than Kinsey's have discovered similar proportions of women reporting premarital intercourse and have found the same relationship between decade of birth and percentage of women involved. Terman, for example, found that fully 86 per cent of the women born before 1890 were virgins at time of marriage.[31] Of those born after 1900, only about a half were virgins.[32] The proportion continued to drop, but his study included too few women born after 1910 to make the analysis entirely reliable. Terman pointed out that if the drop continued at the same rate, virginity at marriage would be close to the "vanishing point" for females born after 1940.[33] Kinsey's data, however, seem to indicate that the rate of non-virgins at marriage did not continue to drop among those born during the thirty-year period following 1900.

The change in women's premarital sexual behavior is consistent with, and helps explain, the change in the males' premarital experience. Although the number of males who have had premarital intercourse has remained relatively stable and the frequency of their total experiences has not materially changed, there has been a decided drop in the frequency of sexual intercourse with prostitutes. It is apparent, then, that non-prostitutes supply the male with much of the premarital intercourse that formerly he had with prostitutes. We should therefore expect to find, as indeed we do, that a higher proportion of women have had sexual intercourse before marriage than in the past.

The findings on female extramarital intercourse show a general increase among the women born since 1900. We are hampered in our analysis of this trend, however, by virtue of the fact that the post-marital histories

[31] *Ibid.*, p. 323.
[32] *Ibid.* See also the findings regarding the relationship between premarital sexual experience and decade of birth in Ernest W. Burgess and Paul Wallin, *Engagement and Marriage* (Philadelphia, J. B. Lippincott Company, 1953), pp. 331-333.
[33] Terman, *op. cit.*, p. 323.

of women born since 1920 are not yet completed. We have already observed that there is a relationship between engaging in premarital intercourse and extramarital coitus, and we discovered, too, that there has been an increase in premarital intercourse. It is statistically reasonable, therefore, to expect a concomitant increase in the proportion of women who at some time have extramarital relations.

AMERICAN SEXUAL VALUES

In the foregoing sections we have presented facts and more facts about sexual behavior in American society. To the extent that these data are reliable, we should have a fairly comprehensive picture of non-marital heterosexual behavior. There remains now the task of tying together the various data on sexual behavior and of trying to relate them to the sexual values of our society.

Although overt behavior never perfectly reflects a group's values, certainly there is some relationship between the kind of life a group wants and the way its people act. When a significant number of people begin to behave in a manner contradictory to traditional goals, we should at least investigate the possibility that their goals may already have changed or are changing. What, then, do we know about the sexual values in our society? Are we approaching the point of altering them, or at least some of them? In some areas, perhaps, we have already passed this point, and new sexual values have replaced the traditional ones. What can we say, furthermore, about the efficacy of the family institution in its task of regulating the sexual activity of society members? And what do we know, finally, about the ways in which we attempt to regulate sexual activity today? These are the types of generalizing questions with which we will now be concerned. We will consider them under three broad topics: (1) the double standard of sexual morality, (2) the "new" single standard, and (3) the machinery for regulating sexual behavior.

The Double Standard

Strictly speaking, we have never actually had a double standard of sexual morality in our society. "Double standard" means simply that one code of sexual conduct is in force for one sex and a different one governs the behavior of the other.[34] In the past in our society, this has taken the form of strictly forbidding non-marital sex for women while condoning

[34] For a good discussion of the double standard, its implications, and its present status, see Ira L. Reiss, "The Double Standard in Premarital Sexual Intercourse," Social Forces, Vol. 34 (March, 1956), pp. 224-230.

or allowing it for males. Such a double code, of course, would be an utter impossibility if rigidly enforced, for the males would have no one with whom to engage in non-marital intercourse. In practical affairs, the dilemma was partially solved by establishing a category of women who were beyond the pale of the usual feminine code. The most obvious membership in the ranks of permissible deviants were prostitutes, but a "fallen woman," that is, a known unmarried non-virgin, was frequently included. The logic seemed to be that any woman who by a single action departed from the norms for "respectable" women could thereafter be treated by males as if the conduct norms no longer applied to her. Apparently there was always a certain amount of confusion over to whom the norms applied, for someone must have considered the "fallen woman" a potential non-virgin or she could never have attained the actual status.

If a society had a sufficient number of females to whom the usual code did not apply, be they prostitutes, slaves, available and agreeable foreigners, or what have you, it would be theoretically possible to have a permissive sexual code for males and a rigid one for the women whom these males would select as wives. In the past, as we have indicated, we approached but never reached this state of affairs. There is no indication that all males ever restricted all of their premarital intercourse to a more or less institutionalized group of permissible deviants. On the attitudinal level, there is no indication that all males actually defined all girls, except a publicly recognized category, as completely inaccessible to them as partners in non-marital intercourse. On both the behavioral and attitudinal levels, however, we came much closer to the theoretically pure type of double standard fifty years ago than we do today. The decline of the double standard has been one of the more impressive changes in American sexual values.

A little reflection makes it plain that there are at least two ways a society could remove the kind of double sexual standard we have been discussing. It could either insist that men adopt the restrictive code of women, or it could allow women to practice the more permissive code of men. Apparently we have chosen the latter course. It is quite evident, as we have shown, that the premarital sexual behavior among females is approaching that among males. Although there are still more virginal brides than grooms, an estimated 50 per cent of all girls have intercourse before marriage. The frequency of premarital relations with prostitutes has declined, whereas the total frequency of male sexual intercourse has remained relatively stable. Premarital sex partners are apparently chosen from a fairly broad range of *all* girls and are not restricted to a smaller category defined as being beyond the usual taboos. The picture is similar with respect to extramarital relations. A significantly larger proportion of today's married women have sexual relations with someone other than their husbands than in the past. The rate of female extramarital relations approaches that of males.

Although we can be reasonably sure about what people are doing sexually, it is more difficult to discover how they think and feel about sex. We do not have sufficient studies, but those that have been made seem to indicate an increasing willingness among males to marry non-virgins.[35] The male is saying, in effect, that having intercourse before marriage is not "bad" enough to disqualify a girl for marriage, even to himself. One of the highest rates of males verbally accepting the single standard was found by Landis and Landis, who reported that three-fourths of the college men in their sample would be willing to marry a non-virgin.[36] The actual behavior of American females plus the intellectual acceptance of their behavior by American males constitutes the bulk of our evidence that the double standard of sexual morality has declined as a working value in our society.

It should be obvious, on the other hand, that the traditional double standard has not yet joined company with the dodo. The bulk of American girls and women still behave differently from the bulk of males, whether we consider the proportion involved in non-marital intercourse or the frequency with which it occurs. This can only mean that a smaller group of women are making up the difference, so to speak, and thus allowing something of the double standard to continue. More men than women, furthermore, want to marry a virginal spouse and, conversely, more women than men would be willing to marry a non-virgin, an indication that both sexes still expect differential behavior of one another.[37] Prostitution does still exist and, as Ehrmann has pointed out, there is still a tendency for males to seek sexual partners from social levels lower than their own.[38] Although this latter practice is undoubtedly waning, what remains of it serves to indicate that some males still divide females into those with whom they are

[35] Actually, different studies have discovered a rather surprising variability with respect to the desire to marry a virgin. See Wayne C. Neely, "Family Attitudes of Denominational College and University Students, 1929-1936," *American Sociological Review*, Vol. 5 (August, 1940), pp. 516-522; Judson T. Landis and Mary G. Landis, *Building a Successful Marriage*, 3rd. ed. (Englewood Cliffs, New Jersey, Prentice-Hall, Inc., 1958), pp. 224-226; Kinsey and others, *Male*, p. 364, and Kinsey and others, *Female*, p. 323.

[36] Landis and Landis, *op. cit.*, p. 226. Note, however, that engaged men were less tolerant of premarital sexual experience for a prospective wife and, also, that both groups of men said they would not marry a girl who had had sexual relations with *several* different men.

[37] See n. 35, above.

[38] Winston W. Ehrmann, "Influence of Comparative Social Class of Companion upon Premarital Heterosexual Behavior," *Marriage and Family Living*, Vol. 17 (February, 1955), pp. 48-53.

willing to have premarital sexual relations and those they are willing to marry. The double standard is going. But it is not yet gone.

The objective social scientist, viewing the matter over the last one hundred years, may not find it too difficult to see the decline of an old value and the emergence of the new. But to the person trying desperately to find a guide for action, the remnants of the old and the preludes of the new form a queer and perplexing combination. A certain amount of doubt, confusion, and uncertainty seem almost inevitable because of lack of clear and explicit values in this area. The male, for example, who attempts to live by the double standard believes that it is permissible for him to remove female virginity, and at the same time he expects to marry a virgin. Since we do not have a complete double standard, sooner or later many such males will come face to face with what can be rather cruel facts of life. They will realize that someone will marry these "bad girls" with whom they have been having intercourse, and, reciprocally, that other men have been having intercourse with the group of "good girls" from which they will choose wives. It is a simple fact today that a sizable proportion of males should expect to marry non-virgins. Although virginity is not yet the "unattainable commodity" of Terman's prediction,[39] Kinsey's data indicate that half of American girls have had premarital sexual relations. Intellectually many men realize that the proportion of non-virgins must be close to this or else the reports of their friends and acquaintances are sheer fabrications. Emotionally, however, a sizable proportion cannot accept the facts as they apply to their wife or future wife.

It is no less difficult for the girl to determine what the double-standard confusion requires of her. She is taught on all sides that today she can vote, pursue a career outside the home, enter a bar, and, in short, do almost anything a man can do. If she attempts to apply this to her sexual life, she may come to find that the one man she cares most about unfortunately has not learned the "modern" code. Perhaps she decides to wait until engagement before having sexual relations, "to be sure it's love," only to find that engagements have a way of being broken, the more so, according to one study, when sex relations are involved.[40] If she refuses to accept the "new code," she hears on many sides how prudish and Victorian she is and her own observations will show her that her "modern" companions seem not to have jeopardized their chances for marriage and motherhood by their premarital experience. Who and what *is* she to believe? In the present state of confused sexual values the answer is simple but harsh: We do not know.

[39] Terman, *op. cit.*, p. 329.
[40] Burgess and Wallin, *op. cit.*, pp. 357-358.

The New Single Standard

Even if our society were somehow able to exorcise the ghosts of the double standard that seem so reluctant to leave, we would still have the tremendous task of deciding what the *single* standard should be. Granting for the moment that goose and gander will be expected to behave alike, what kind of behavior should we reasonably expect and attempt to enforce? There are indications that our society does not know the answer to this question.

To judge by the accumulated verbiage on the matter, our society certainly disapproves of non-marital sexual relations of all types. The organized religions stand out as the most consistent and adamant defenders of the anti-fornication and anti-adultery values. *Sin* and *sex*, as a matter of fact, have almost become semantically interchangeable, implying that the "big sin" is a sexual one. Religious leaders seem solidly against sexual sin and attempt to inculcate this value in all that can be brought under their influence. Religious leaders are not alone in extolling the desirability of virginity and marital fidelity. We have the traditionalists who are not sure why non-marital sex is bad but feel that somehow it must be, because it always has been. The old-fashioned girl who married Dad, we are reminded, was a *good* old-fashioned girl, and the fact that non-marital sex was bad then is a good enough reason for so considering it today. Still others verbally support the sex-outside-of-marriage-is-wrong value from a vague sense that it is socially desirable to take this position. Although they are not too sure *why* it is socially desirable, or what would happen to society if we endorsed other values, these social disapprovers of non-marital sex can be as vociferous in their pronouncements and denouncements as the religious and traditionalist defenders of "chastity for all."

We find competing with these anti-sex expressions an overwhelming mass of evidence that Americans approve of non-marital sexual relations. We have seen that a sizable proportion of Americans engage in sexual relations outside of marriage. Whatever the "true" proportion is, it is high enough to indicate that the sex-is-for-marriage-only value is not a literally accepted guide for a large number of men and women. But there is other evidence of a favorable attitude toward non-marital sex. Our stage plays, films, and novels abound with references to sexual relations among the unmarried, and only the most extremely naïve will miss the point that sex outside of marriage is often portrayed as thrilling, enjoyable, and all in all "quite the thing to do." The avowed purpose of fiction is to entertain, but it *is* meaningful that Americans find entertaining a favorable attitude toward non-marital sexual relations.

A popular reason for justifying premarital sexual relations is that what is wrong under some circumstances is permissible under others. Being "very much in love," whether or not accompanied by formal engagement, seems to be the most agreed-upon circumstance under which sexual intercourse is permissible. There are other circumstances, of course, such as "going away to war" and the seemingly endless peacetime variations of this theme, but even in such cases the couple should be "very much in love." The same action that would be vigorously condemned if the couple admitted it was done only because both found it pleasurable is frequently condoned or at least considered a pardonable indiscretion for the couple "in love." First we state that intercourse outside of marriage is bad, then we admit that it is not *always* bad, or not always *so* bad.

A certain amount of confusion in our sexual values is due to the presence of competing values, or at least contradictory behavior, within various sub-groups of our society. We have seen that if and when a male engages in premarital relations and when he has extramarital intercourse are related to his social status. When during her lifetime a girl has premarital relations is most definitely related to social class, and among both sexes the more devoutly religious behave differently from the less devout. It is very likely that there are regional and ethnic differences in evaluations of sexual behavior as well. Certainly there are different standards for different occupational groups, such as the ministry and professional actors. To the extent that these many groups develop characteristic and standardized ways of thinking and behaving they can be said to have a culture of their own. We are not suggesting that the norms and values of the various sub-cultures in our society are all radically different, but rather that a certain amount of variability exists in these respects.

The various areas of cultural confusion about what we really value in sexual behavior has caused a certain amount of conflict and doubt at the level of individual behavior and decisions. There are those who experience sex outside of marriage and feel guilty about it ever afterwards. There are others who hold strictly to the traditional code while envying their fellows who dare to break it. The boy or girl who decides to have sexual relations only if he is in love is no better off. He is on his own to decide whether or not he is *that* much in love and to deal with his conscience if suddenly he falls out of love. And what if "something happens" to his second, or fourth, or sixth, "true love" affair?

In a similar manner, trying to conform to the expectations of one's several important reference groups can be a baffling task. Should a person try to live up to the standards of his social class or his church group or of the devout members of his church group at his status level? And what if his ethnic group fosters still other values or the occupation to which he aspires proposes still another code of behavior? The truth of the matter, of course, is that a person must live in all these groups, and, what is more, he is likely to come into contact with competing standards of still other groups. We are not contending that it is impossible today to choose a course of sexual action and to be reasonably satisfied that it is right. It is difficult, however, to do this. Perhaps it is less puzzling to discover that some have failed to make a choice they are willing to live with than that others have managed to do so.

Regulation of Sexual Behavior

Our discussion of sex in American society would not be complete without mention of the methods used for regulating sexual behavior. Although for discussion purposes we can separate how we regulate behavior from the standards we hold, the two are intricately related. It has probably already been anticipated that the confusion in our sexual values makes it difficult to find appropriate enforcement techniques. But the cause and effect relationship also works the other way around. Knowing the methods we do *not* want to use to control behavior, and not always knowing what methods we prefer to substitute, makes it exceedingly difficult to determine the standards of behavior we can reasonably expect to enforce.

It may well be that as a society we have been so concerned with real or alleged changes in sexual behavior that we have missed a more dramatic change that seems to have occurred. With respect to the way in which we will attempt to regulate behavior, we have come to good agreement, but by no means unanimity, on what we do *not* want. Gone or going fast are the repressive measures of the past with the three big clubs of "infection, conception, and detection" dangled over the heads of youth. What is more, it is distinctly unpopular to bemoan their demise. Most people, regardless of what standards they wish to enforce, believe that there must be better, more rational methods of enforcement than fear. Some see the reason for the decline of the big fears in our modern technology, in the sense that penicillin, contraceptives, and automobiles make the traditional threats too unrealistic to be effective. Whatever the role of these changes may be, it is also evident that severe repressive measures of all types are not in keeping with the kinds of personalities we wish to create today and the ways in which we want to mold them.

Although we generally agree that we do not want to frighten one another into living virtuous lives, we are far from agreeing on what methods of control we should substitute. There seems to be a vague notion that somehow "education" must be the answer, but who is to educate, and how, are as ill-defined as what values should be taught and learned. The so-called sex education of the schools is a good case in point. All too frequently this becomes an elementary course in human embryology with little or no attention given to the relationships between the sexes and particularly the norms of sexual conduct. One is no longer surprised to hear a young school boy discourse on human reproduction with a fair degree of accuracy and using technical terms. Unfortunately too many believe that now that the youngsters know all about ova and testicles and Fallopian tubes they will be able to understand and handle their sexual *emotions* about which nobody much bothered to talk. Even when some attempt is made to deal with standards of behavior for the relationship between the sexes, it frequently falls short of providing adequate guides for action. Chiefly lacking is a meaningful rationale for the proffered code. If as a society we are going to substitute education for coercion and appeal to tradition, we had better be prepared to answer the provocative "why's" that the educational approach invites. Could it be that, like the young child, we are looking for someone to tell us why we want what we want?

One big task facing American society, in conclusion, is to come to grips with the question of what are its sexual values. The second lies in determining how to implement these values, whatever they come to be. The alternative to solving these problems, it would seem, is to continue in our present maelstrom of confusion with its competing and contradictory values, its inconsistencies between preachment and practice, and its seemingly ineffective methods of regulating behavior.

SELECTED READINGS

BURGESS, ERNEST W., and WALLIN, PAUL, *Engagement and Marriage* (New York, J. B. Lippincott Company, 1953), Chs. 11 and 12.

CALVERTON, V. F., and SCHMALHAUSE, S. D., eds., *Sex in Civilization* (New York, The Macaulay Company, 1929).

DAVIS, KATHERINE B., *Factors in the Sex Life of Twenty-two Hundred Women* (New York, Harper & Brothers, 1929).

DUVALL, SYLVANUS M., *Men, Women, and Morals* (New York, Association Press, 1952).

ELLIS, ALBERT, *The Folklore of Sex* (New York, Charles Boni, 1951).

FORD, CLELLAN S., and BEACH, FRANK A., *Patterns of Sexual Behavior* (New York, Harper & Brothers, 1953).

HAMILTON, G. V., *A Research in Marriage* (New York, Albert and Charles Boni, Inc., 1929).

HIMELHOCH, JEROME, and FAVA, SYLVIA F., eds., *Sexual Behavior in American Society: An Appraisal of the First Two Kinsey Reports* (New York, W. W. Norton & Company, Inc., 1955).

KINSEY, ALFRED C., POMEROY, WARDELL B., and MARTIN, CLYDE E., *Sexual Behavior in the Human Male* (Philadelphia, W. B. Saunders Co., 1948).

KINSEY, ALFRED, C., POMEROY, WARDELL B., MARTIN, CLYDE E., and GEB-HARD, PAUL H., *Sexual Behavior in the Human Female* (Philadelphia, W. B. Saunders Co., 1953).

SEWARD, GEORGENE H., *Sex and the Social Order* (New York, McGraw-Hill Book Company, Inc., 1946).

CHAPTER 13

Divorce

THE CYNIC contends that the only real cause of divorce is marriage. Whatever else was its intended meaning, the statement contains a certain truth in one of its meanings. The institution of marriage consists of an approved method of establishing a mating relationship, and it defines the status of the married pair, elaborating their individual and joint responsibilities and obligations. Divorce, sociologically, is thus the reciprocal of marriage. It is the societally sanctioned means of terminating a marriage and redefining the statuses of the couple involved. Just as all societies institutionalize marriage, every society that allows the termination of marriage prior to death surrounds the termination with customs and laws that serve to announce to the group that the pair is no longer married. Relationships and statuses once established by marriage necessarily are redefined at its termination.

CROSS-CULTURAL VIEW OF DIVORCE

Divorce is neither an American invention nor monopoly. Although it is true that almost everywhere marriage is contracted for life or for an indefinite period, it is equally true that most societies provide a way of terminating marriages prior to the death of either spouse. The absolute frequency of divorce, as any student of sociology would well imagine, varies considerably from society to society. Perhaps a quick overview of divorce in other societies, both preliterate and modern, would serve as a fitting prologue to our more detailed analysis of divorce in the United States.

In some few societies marriage is regarded as an irrevocable contract, and its termination prior to death is not permitted for any reason. Hobhouse, writing several decades ago, noted that among 271 preliterate groups about 4 per cent did not allow divorce under any condition.[1] There is little

[1] Leonard T. Hobhouse, G. C. Wheeler, and M. Ginsberg, *The Material Culture and Social Institutions of Simpler Peoples* (London, Chapman & Hall, Ltd., 1917), pp. 159 ff.

recent cross-cultural information that adds much to this estimate. About the best we can conclude is that apparently the indissoluble conception of marriage is a rare phenomenon among preliterate groups. Among the societies that allow divorce, Hobhouse discovered that 48 per cent permitted it at the will of either party, 23 per cent at the husband's wish alone, and less than 1 per cent only on the wife's desire. The remaining groups, some 24 per cent, permitted divorce only under certain specified conditions, and not merely because one or both of the spouses desired to terminate the marriage.[2]

If all of the "just causes" for divorce found in various primitive societies were grouped together, we would have a bewildering array of reasons for terminating marriage.[3] Adultery on the part of the wife is commonly a basis for divorce, but there are those societies which do not allow divorce for adultery even though they allow it for other reasons.[4] A wife's barrenness frequently is considered a cause for divorce. Laziness, failure to cook food properly, bad temper, and suspected witchcraft in some groups allow a man to divorce his wife. A wife, in turn, may in some places secure a divorce because her husband is cruel or neglectful, because he failed to sew her clothes properly, or because he attempted to sell her to a stranger. In primitive society the marital complaints justifying divorce range from the serious to the trivial, by almost anyone's definition of the terms. It must be remembered, however, that in many preliterate societies the parties to a marriage can divorce for their own reasons and no one demands that they expound on the frailties of one another.

The relative ease of divorce in some preliterate societies does not necessarily mean that divorce is extremely frequent. It has been suggested that the payment of a bride price serves as an economic inducement to remain married.[5] A more important stabilizing practice is the custom of vesting parents with the right to choose marriage partners for their sons and daughters. However great an affront to romanticism this custom may be, it does seem that experienced parents are quite successful in arranging durable matches for their children. Despite the stabilizing effects of arranged marriage, bride price, and public opinion favorable to marriage stability, the divorce rate in some preliterate societies is quite high. We cannot, of course, make neat statistical comparisons between the frequency

[2] Ibid.
[3] Ibid., See also G. E. Howard, A History of Matrimonial Institutions, Vol. I (Chicago, University of Chicago Press, 1904), Ch. 5, and Edward Westermarck, A Short History of Marriage (New York, The Macmillan Co., 1930), Ch. 11.
[4] Edward Westermarck, The History of Human Marriage, 3 vols., 5th ed. (London, Macmillan & Co., Ltd., 1921), p. 277.
[5] George P. Murdock, Social Structure (New York, The Macmillan Co., 1949), pp. 197-198.

of divorce in our society and among the Chuckchee, the Karaya, the Zulu, or any other primitive group. Using the best data available, however, some anthropologists have concluded that in general the family in primitive society is a less stable unit than our own.[6] The near-universality of divorce and its sometimes high frequency in primitive societies does not make it "right" if one is arguing from some unalterable set of moral principles, nor does it mitigate the problems of divorce in contemporary America. One important lesson is, however, that in any sizable sample of preliterate societies we find great differences in attitude toward divorce, frequency of divorce, and the manner in which divorce is executed. It is wise to realize, too, that even simple, folk societies far removed from the stresses of urbanization and rapid social change have found it necessary to make concessions to human frailty by providing for release from intolerable marriages.

TABLE 30. Divorces per 1,000 Population in Selected Countries

	1910-1914	1930-1934	1950
United States	1.0	1.5	2.5
Canada	.05[1]	.1	.4
Denmark	.3	.7	1.6
England & Wales	.05	.1	.7
Finland	.1	.3	.9
France	.3	.6	.8
Germany	.3	.6	1.6
Netherlands	.2	.4	.6
Norway	.2	.4	.6
Portugal	—[4]	.1	.1
Sweden	.1	.4	1.1
Switzerland	.4	.7	.9
Japan	1.1	.8	1.0
Israel[2]	—[4]	5.8[3]	2.1

SOURCE: Metropolitan Life Insurance Company, *Statistical Bulletin,* Vol. 33 (June, 1952), p. 7.
[1] Less than .05 per thousand
[2] Jewish population only
[3] Rate for 1935-1939
[4] Data not available

A rapid survey of the divorce rate in contemporary modern societies should broaden our perspective of the divorce picture in the United States. Table 30 does indeed give support to the popular belief that "we lead the civilized world in divorce." With a few exceptions, such as Japan in the early period and more recently Israel, the United States has held the lead in divorce for the last half century. The rate of change over the forty-year period must also be considered. It is apparent that the general world trend has been toward an ever-higher divorce rate. Divorce in the United States,

[6] *Ibid.,* p. 197. See also Robert H. Lowie, *Primitive Society* (New York, Liveright Publishing Corporation, 1920), pp. 68-70.

as a matter of fact, has increased less than in most of the countries for which we have data, particularly Canada, England, and Sweden. Statistically speaking, the divorce rate in the United States showed greater discrepancy from the rest of the world forty years ago than it does today. Germany and Denmark, for example, now have rates almost two-thirds of our own, where once they were only about a third. One should not conclude from our cross-cultural comparison that nothing can or should be done about our admittedly high rate of divorce. The recognition that divorce is not exclusively American should afford us a more realistic view of our divorce problems and their amelioration.

DIVORCE RATES AND FREQUENCIES

Shortly after the close of the Civil War, about 10,000 couples were divorced each year. We passed the 100,000 per year mark in 1914, and in recent years almost 400,000 divorces have been granted annually. Simple addition produces an even more staggering picture. Just in the last ten years, over *four million* marriages ended in divorce. Making no allowance for those who secured more than one divorce in the decade, approximately *eight million* individuals went through the experience of divorce. A mere counting of the number of divorces each year and a comparison with the number in previous years tell us much about the divorce phenomenon in our society. We can observe, for example, the low point in divorces during the depression years of the early thirties and the peak that was reached after World War II. But sheer numbers tell only part of the story.

As everyone knows, the population of our society has been on the upswing. We should expect that the number of divorces would show a corresponding increase. The question becomes, of course, whether or not the number of divorces has increased relative to the population growth. The crude divorce rate, which is the ratio of the number of divorces to each 1,000 persons, provides us with the answer. It is clear from Table 31 that divorces have definitely increased relatively more than the total population. After the breakup between 1944 and 1946 of the so-called "furlough marriages" formed during World War II, the crude divorce rate settled back close to, but a little higher than, its pre-war level. Discounting the World War II spurt in divorces and the subsequent decline from this high point, we see that over a long period the divorce rate has been gradually increasing.

One of the main disadvantages of the crude divorce rate is that it can be easily "upset" by changes in the birth rate. A sudden increase in births, such as our society has experienced recently, adds to the population base on which the rate is computed and tends to deflate the divorce rate even

TABLE 31. Divorces and Divorce Rates, United States, 1870-1956

Year	Number of Divorces	Divorces per 1,000 population	Divorces per 100 Marriages Performed in Year
1870	10,962	.3	3.1
1880	19,663	.4	4.3
1890	33,461	.5	5.9
1900	55,751	.7	7.9
1910	83,045	.9	8.8
1920	170,505	1.6	13.4
1930	195,961	1.6	17.4
1932	164,241	1.3	16.7
1934	204,000	1.6	15.7
1936	236,000	1.8	17.2
1938	244,000	1.9	18.5
1940	264,000	2.0	16.5
1942	321,000	2.4	18.1
1944	400,000	2.9	27.5
1946	610,000	4.3	26.6
1948	408,000	2.8	22.5
1950	385,144	2.6	23.0
1952	392,000	2.5	25.5
1954	379,000	2.4	25.4
1956	377,000	2.3	24.0

SOURCE: Data from, and computed data in, U.S. Department of Health, Education, and Welfare, *Vital Statistics—Special Reports,* Vol. 46, No. 12 (July 23, 1957), pp. 325, and Vol. 36, No. 2 (June 5, 1951), p. 25; also from *Monthly Vital Statistics Report,* Vol 5, No. 13 (March 12, 1957), p. 4.

though the number of divorces has remained the same or risen. Another type of divorce rate relates the number of divorces to a given number of married females during a certain period of time. This rate takes cognizance of the obvious fact that it takes a marriage to have a divorce. It relates the number of divorces that actually occur in a given year to the number of people married.

A common method of describing the divorce incidence is based on the relationship between the number of divorces in a given year and the number of marriages in the same year. This measure, as in Table 31, is usually expressed as the number of divorces per 100 marriages. This method of computation also has given rise to statements on the proportions of all marriages which will end in divorce. When the divorce rate was 3.1, for example, it could have been said that one out of every thirty-three marriages would end in divorce. Today, when the rate is around 25, we hear that one in every four marriages will end in divorce. Such statements are not entirely accurate, however, since the divorces granted in a given year deal almost entirely with marriages that were not contracted in the same year. In the long run, unless there is a great fluctuation of either the marriage or divorce rate, the estimate of marriages that will end in divorce made on this basis is fairly reliable. If, for example, every year for a generation beginning in 1950 twenty-five couples were granted a divorce for every one hundred who were married, then it would be reasonable to say that one out of four 1950 marriages ended in divorce. Whenever the marriage rate shoots up, it should be noted, the ratio of divorces to marriages makes it *appear* that the divorce rate has gone down. Caution should therefore be exercised in making year-to-year comparisons of this and other divorce rates. We should strive instead to determine the more general trend.

Some interesting results are obtained when, as in Table 32, we compare the recent trends in the various measures of divorce. According to the crude divorce rate, divorce has increased about 44 per cent since 1920, but the ratio of divorces to the number of married women has increased only about 16 per cent for the same period. Without going into detail, the discrepancy can be accounted for in the different age and marital-status compositions of the population at the two periods of time. The actual number of divorces has increased 121 per cent since 1920, but the number of divorces per 100 marriages has gone up only 25 per cent. Clearly a great deal of caution is required in interpreting divorce statistics. It is essential to be cognizant of what facet of the divorce picture is being described and what type of measure is being utilized. Despite the difficulties with the various measures of divorce, it is clear that divorce has been increasing in our society. The estimate that currently about one in every four marriages will end in divorce is more than likely a little low.

DIFFERENTIAL TENDENCY TO DIVORCE

In our mass society, with its many social differences and social types, it is at once predictable and understandable that all segments do not enter equally into the divorce phenomenon. An investigation of the differentials in the divorce rate by various social groups is an important first step in gaining a greater understanding of divorce. Were our information more complete, knowledge of divorce differentials should put us one step closer to the causative factors for at least some divorces. Once we can be reasonably sure, for example, in which income group, which race, and which educational level divorce is more likely to occur, we can go on to ask what it is about these groups that increases their members' chances of divorce. Unfortunately, we do not have the kind of national data that we need. We must perforce restrict our analysis to major categories of the population and, even so, utilize limited surveys rather than national enumerations.

TABLE 32. A Comparison of Types of Divorce Rates, United States, 1920-1955

Year	Number of Divorces	Cumulative Per Cent Change	Divorces per 1,000 Total Population	Cumulative Per Cent Change	Divorces Per 100 Marriages Performed	Cumulative Per Cent Change	Divorces per 1,000 Married Female Population	Cumulative Per Cent Change
1920	170,505	....	1.6	....	13.4	....	8.0	....
1930	195,961	14.9	1.6	0.0	17.4	29.9	7.5	−6.2
1940	264,000	54.8	2.0	25.0	16.5	23.1	8.8	10.0
1950	385,144	125.9	2.6	62.5	23.0	71.6	10.3	28.8
1955	377,000	121.1	2.3	43.8	24.6	83.6	9.3	16.3

SOURCE: Data from, and computed from data in, U.S. Department of Health, Education, and Welfare, *Vital Statistics—Special Reports*, Vol. 46, No. 12 (July 23, 1957), pp. 325, 330, and Vol. 36, No. 2 (June 5, 1951), p. 25.

Socio-Economic Status Differentials in Divorce

In polygynous societies there is frequently a direct relationship between plural marriage and wealth. Only the wealthier men, usually, can afford to obtain and support more than one wife. In our own society, where plural marriage is practiced consecutively rather than contemporaneously, it is sometimes assumed that much the same relationship prevails, that is, that divorce and remarriage are more frequently found among the wealthier members of society. The divorces of those people who are in the public eye have strengthened this impression. No great journalistic wisdom is needed, however, to recognize that the divorce of one entertainer is worth far more newsprint than the divorces of a thousand factory workers. And if the divorce of the celebrity is attended with intrigue, bitter contestation, and an elaborate alimony settlement, the public is all the more likely to associate marriage instability with wealth and prominence. But the facts tell us something else. Regardless of the measure of status, the general trend is the lower the socio-economic status, the more divorce. Since our aim is understanding, in addition to indicating, relationships we should investigate this phenomenon more carefully.

Occupation. Several recent studies agree that divorce varies inversely with occupational prestige. The general pattern discovered by Monahan among the non-rural occupations in the entire state of Iowa was found by Kephart in Philadelphia and Goode in Detroit.[7] There seems to be good evidence to conclude that the upper occupational levels contribute less than their share of divorces, the middle levels a proportionate share, whereas the lower occupational groups are over-represented in divorce cases.[8] The relationship is far more complex than our general conclusion may indicate. Within each occupational group there is sometimes considerable variation in the divorce rates of different occupations. Among professionals, for example, physicians are more prone to divorce than dentists and considerably more likely to secure a divorce than teachers.[9] Taxi drivers have a

[7] Thomas P. Monahan, "Divorce by Occupational Level," *Marriage and Family Living,* Vol. 17 (November, 1955), pp. 322-324; William M. Kephart, "Occupational Level and Marital Disruption," *American Sociological Review,* Vol. 20 (August, 1955), pp. 456-465; and William J. Goode, "Economic Factors and Mental Stability," *American Sociological Review,* Vol. 16 (December, 1951), pp. 802-812.

[8] From his study of "marriage instability," which included divorce, separation, desertion, and marital conflict, Hollingshead concluded that greater instability is found in the working and lower classes. In his study, unlike the divorce studies, marriage instability was found next most frequently in the lower upper class. See August B. Hollingshead, "Class Differences and Family Stability," *Annals of the American Society of Political and Social Science,* Vol. 272 (November, 1950), pp. 39-46.

[9] Monahan, *op. cit.*

higher divorce rate than truck drivers, cooks divorce more frequently than waiters, and so on.[10] Unfortunately we do not have adequate data to make any real analysis of divorce by specific occupations.

Income. A comparison of the incomes of divorced and married men gives some indication of the economic levels most vulnerable to divorce. It should be made clear, however, that the data in Table 33 refer to men divorced *at the time of the census* and not to all men who have ever been divorced. But the trend is clear. A higher percentage of divorced men, as opposed to married men, have little or no income, and more married than divorced men earn over $4,000 annually. We can conclude that there is a general inverse relationship between economic position and divorce.

TABLE 33. Annual Income of Divorced and Married Males, 1950

Income	Per Cent Married Males	Per Cent Divorced Males
No income	3.7	5.6
$ 1.-999	11.8	19.1
1,000-1,999	15.9	18.5
2,000-2,999	22.9	20.8
3,000-3,999	22.4	18.9
4,000 and over	23.2	17.1

SOURCE: U.S. Bureau of the Census, *Marital Status, Special Reports,* P-E, No. 2D (Washington, D.C., U.S. Government Printing Office, 1955), p. 47.

Education. A somewhat circuitous way of determining the relationship between education and divorce is to relate the previous marital status and educational status of people marrying during a specified period. Particularly in the younger age groups, the great bulk of remarriages follow the divorce rather than the death of a spouse. Table 34 shows a considerable difference according to educational levels of persons with first marriages and remarriages. For both males and females, the educational achievement of those remarrying between 1947 and 1954 was definitely lower than for those marrying for the first time. As education increases, the frequency of remarriage decreases. Census data on currently divorced women indicate a relationship between educational level and divorce similar to that inferred from the remarriage pattern.[11]

In one sense the foregoing discussion indicates that divorce is no respecter of economic or social status. Although marriage instability exists at all socio-economic levels, we have seen ample evidence that the general

[10] *Ibid.*

[11] See, for example, U. S. Bureau of Census, *Duration of Current Marital Status,* Special Reports P-E, No. 2E (Washington, D. C., U. S. Government Printing Office, 1955), p. 44.

TABLE 34. First Marriages and Remarriages by
Educational Attainment, 1947-1954

	Elementary, 8 years or less	High School, 1-4 years	College, 1 year or more
Male			
First marriage	22.9	56.0	21.1
Remarriage	40.6	45.0	14.3
Female			
First marriage	15.2	67.4	17.3
Remarriage	36.1	54.5	9.4

SOURCE: U.S. Department of Health, Education, and Welfare, *Vital Statistics—Special Reports,* Vol. 45, No. 12 (September 9, 1957), p. 301.

trend is for marriage breakup to be more pronounced at the lower status levels of our society. Our attempts to explain this phenomenon will take the form of a broad answer to the query, "What is there about low socio-economic status that accounts for a propensity to divorce?" Admittedly this will be but a partial explanation of the divorce phenomenon, for it purposefully excludes the divorces among the higher-status individuals.[12]

Economic difficulties of the lower classes. So often do we hear that money is not essential for "true happiness" that perhaps we have become callous to the effects of poverty. Consider the wife in the low-income family. Daily she attempts to make a home out of a house which, never very good, seems to vie with the neighborhood for speed in deterioration. The low-income homemaker is less likely to have such things as a freezer, automatic washer, dryer, and so on. It is certain that many women have and do get along without these devices, but if there is any truth at all in their popular designation these devices do save labor. Furthermore there are still families living without indoor toilets and running water and more families without running hot water. In general, cheap furnaces or stoves and a low fuel budget produce little comfort in winter. Inexpensive housing usually is draftier, dustier, and more crowded than better housing. If any can find it a pleasure to be a low-income housewife, it must be in spite of the poor housing and cooking facilities.

Low income would seem to have a great potential for producing problems and conflict in family living. It is not hard to imagine that when there is insufficient money for essentials, "extravagances" or "frivolous purchases" by one spouse may lead to bitter recrimination by the other. Car,

[12] For a more detailed presentation of socio-economic factors associated with divorce and a discussion thereof, see William J. Goode, *After Divorce* (Glencoe, Illinois, The Free Press, 1956), pp. 43-67.

house, and equipment are likely to need repairs that cannot be afforded. Almost anyone could continue to list the many ways in which inadequate income could produce short tempers and discontent. If about nothing else, the low-income husband and wife could always argue about unpaid bills.

It is almost a truism that it is not just the lack of money but what it means to the couple that produces problems which may lead to divorce. Even a cursory glance at some of the many effects of poverty will illustrate why the low-income group is more prone to divorce. The inability to provide an adequate living may touch deep at the heart of a man and destroy his faith in himself as a husband and father, a provider, and as a man. The problem is not alleviated if he manages to project the blame onto his wife. Similarly a woman may lose respect for herself or her husband. In an age of relative plenty, the defeat, if it is so defined, would seem to have a double sting. Although economic wants seem always to find a way of outdistancing financial ability, it may well be that there is greater discrepancy between the wants and the ability to satisfy them among the less than among the more affluent segments of society.

It must be remembered that more lower-class people remain married than get divorced. Whatever strains low income is capable of producing, many are able to deflect them, accept them, or at least to avoid letting them produce a permanent rupture in their marriage. We are suggesting, nevertheless, that inherent in low income is a potential for problems and difficulties. Terman discovered that insufficient income was the most frequently mentioned grievance of both husbands and wives in his sample.[13] In addition, Harmsworth and Minnis found that a sample of lawyers considered financial problems as the most frequent real cause of divorce, regardless of the statutory grounds used in the cases.[14] It is quite possible that in some cases economic marital conflicts are but symptoms of difficulties in other areas or even of basic incompatibility. On the other hand, it is equally probable that financial problems lead to other types of marital problems.

Non-economic difficulties of the lower classes. In previous chapters we have seen that sexual behavior, family size, and child-rearing practices all have some relationship to socio-economic status. It is impossible to discuss the many areas of life in which important differences based on social status have been discovered. We do not know, furthermore, which of the social and psychological differences among status groups are the most important as far as their effect on divorce is concerned. There are many char-

[13] Lewis M. Terman and others, *Psychological Factors in Marital Happiness* (New York, McGraw-Hill Book Company, Inc., 1938), p. 96.
[14] Harry C. Harmsworth and Mhyra Minnis, "Non-Statutory Causes of Divorce: The Lawyer's Point of View," *Marriage and Family Living*, Vol. 17 (November, 1955), pp. 316-321.

acteristics of the lower classes, however, which seem to constitute real liabilities, in the sense that they have a potential for an adverse effect on marital relations and stability. Mental illness, infant mortality, and conviction of crime are three types of crises more prevalent at lower socioeconomic levels than others.[15] We are not suggesting that these crises in themselves lead to divorce but, rather, that these and other troubles can place a severe strain on the best of marital relationships. Chronic illness, industrial accidents, and some types of physical diseases further tend to favor the already overburdened lower classes.[16] One study of low-income families found pronounced changes, following various types of troubles, in the family dominance patterns, home routine, children's discipline, and the sexual activity of the spouses.[17] Some families, of course, adjust well and quickly to trouble and even to repeated difficulties. We are merely suggesting that it is more than a statistical accident that the segment of our society most vulnerable to many types of troubles is also most prone to divorce.

Various other types of liabilities of the lower classes most certainly could be imagined. Their presumed lower skill, because of less formal education, in effective communication and in formulating and solving everyday problems immediately suggests itself. Again, no one knows how great an adverse effect the internalized feeling of inferiority of some lower-class people has on interpersonal relations. To have failed in the race for status, wealth, and achievements, surface rationalizations to the contrary, may constitute a severe psychological impediment in various areas of human interaction. Only when more research is devoted to the sum total of differences among people at different status levels will we be able to move closer to the discovery of the factors that make the lower classes more vulnerable to divorce. Considering these differences in terms of the economic, social, and personal lack of privilege of the lower classes is but a start in this direction.

Rural-Urban Divorce Differentials

It is frequently asserted that in rural areas there is a pronounced taboo against divorce with a consequent lower rate of marriage instability. National and regional data generally lend support to this assertion. In our

[15] John F. Cuber, Robert A. Harper, and William F. Kenkel, *Problems of American Society*, 3rd ed. (New York, Henry Holt & Co., Inc., 1956), pp. 77, and 143-144.
[16] *Ibid.*, pp. 100-101.
[17] Earl L. Koos, *Families in Trouble* (New York, King's Crown Press, 1946), pp. 91-106. See also Mirra Komarovsky, *The Unemployed Man and His Family* (New York, The Dryden Press, Inc., 1940).

compilations in Table 35 we show that although farm women constitute about 10 per cent of the population only about 3 per cent of them are found among the women currently divorced. Looking at it in another way, we note that less than 1 per cent of the farm women in the age group were divorced, whereas between 1.4 and 2.9 per cent of all other women were divorced at the time of the enumeration.

TABLE 35. Divorced Women Aged 14 and Over, by Residence, 1958

	Per Cent Total Population	Per Cent Women Currently Divorced	Per Cent of All Divorced Women
Urban	64.6	2.9	81.4
Rural non-farm	24.6	1.4	15.3
Rural farm	10.6	.7	3.3

SOURCE: Computed from U.S. Bureau of Census, *Current Population Reports,* Series 20, No. 87 (November 14, 1958), pp. 11-12.

Since the data in Table 35 deal with current residence and current marital status, we do not know from them how many of the divorced urban women were living on farms at the time of or just prior to their divorce. It would seem reasonable that economic and other pressures would force many women from the farm when their marriages terminated in divorce. We must avoid, on the other hand, overcompensating for post-divorce migration. We can assume that divorced men would not feel the same economic necessity to move from the farm as do divorced women. Monahan discovered, however, that over a third of all Iowa's employed males but only 9 per cent of the divorced males were farmers.[18] The fact that farmers contribute less than their share of all divorces makes it appear that the occupation-residence factor has a real and not spurious relation to divorce.

Race Differentials in Divorce

There seems to be sound evidence that family stability is greater among the white than the Negro portion of American society. This condition, moreover, probably has prevailed for the last sixty or seventy years. Goode has computed that for every U.S. Census period since 1890, with exception of 1940, the proportion of Negroes divorced was higher than that of whites.[19] These rates refer to the percentages of both races that had the status "divorced" at the time of the censuses and not to those who had ever been divorced.

[18] Monahan, *op. cit.*, p. 323.
[19] Goode, *After Divorce*, pp. 48-49.

TABLE 36.   Percentage of Population Divorced
at Time of Census, by Race

Color	1890	1900	1910	1920	1930	1940	1950	1958
White	.29	.37	.51	.67	1.2	1.5	2.2	2.1
Non-white	.36	.62	.85	1.02	1.8	1.4	2.3	2.6
Difference	.07	.25	.34	.35	.6	−.1	.1	.5

SOURCE: Data for 1890 to 1950 reported in William J. Goode, *After Divorce* (Glencoe, Illinois, The Free Press, 1956), p. 49; 1958 data computed from U.S. Bureau of Census, *Current Population Reports*, Series 20, No. 87 (November 14, 1958), pp. 9-13.

The Negro-white differential in divorce is also quite apparent when we contrast the remarriage rates of the two races. Of all the white men who married between 1947 and 1954, 82 per cent were entering their first marriage; the comparable figure for Negro men was 71 per cent. Among females, 75 per cent of the Negro were contracting a first marriage during this period as compared with 80 per cent of the white women. It is also noted that third and higher-order marriages were more frequent among Negroes of both sexes than among whites, although, of course, the proportion of higher-order marriages is in every case quite low.

TABLE 37.   Number of Times Married for Persons Marrying
between 1947 and 1954

NUMBER OF TIMES MARRIED	WHITE		NON-WHITE	
	Male	Female	Male	Female
Once	81.5	79.9	71.4	74.8
Twice	16.7	17.4	22.8	21.7
Three times or more	1.7	2.7	5.9	3.5

SOURCE: U.S. Department of Health, Education, and Welfare, *Vital Statistics—Special Reports,* Vol. 45, No. 12 (September 9, 1957).

It should be apparent that the racial difference in rate of divorce, although clear, is not extremely great. The extent of impermanence of marriage, however, is considerably greater among the non-whites than whites. The Negro separation rate is fully four times as high as that of the total population.[20] Since separation can be viewed as an alternative to divorce, it must be considered with racial differences in marital stability. The races apparently exhibit different patterns with respect to utilization of divorce

[20] William M. Kephart and Thomas P. Monahan, "Desertion and Divorce in Philadelphia," *American Sociological Review*, Vol. 17 (December, 1952), pp. 710-727. See also the later study, Kephart, "Occupational Level and Marital Disruption," *American Sociological Review*, Vol. 20 (August, 1955), pp. 456-465.

versus separation. We will not even attempt to go into the complex historical, social, and economic factors that help account for the lower stability of Negro marriages. Perhaps we can do no better than to refer the interested reader to Frazier's monumental work on the Negro family in the United States.[21]

Other Divorce Differentials

The foregoing discussion demonstrates that various categories of the population of our society contribute differentially to the divorce rate. Within each of these broad groups, though not necessarily to the same degree, certain social and psychological characteristics of the married couple or the circumstances of their marriage have been discovered to affect their proneness to divorce.

Repeatedly it has been discovered that the younger the age at marriage, the more likely it is that the marriage will end in divorce.[22] Although we can be reasonably certain of this general relationship, our knowledge of why it is true is meager. Is it due to the poor financial condition of youthful marriages, the couple's lack of readiness for marriage, or simply the longer period of time during which a divorce can occur, or have their presumably fewer years of dating been insufficient to allow them to choose a mate wisely? The recent trend toward younger age at marriage suggests that our society may be interested in finding the answers to questions such as these.[23]

Other studies have found that premarital pregnancy does not augur well for success in marriage.[24] It has been discovered, too, that mixed religious marriages have a better chance of ending in divorce than others.[25] It is well to investigate these and other situations that are likely to lead to divorce. It is reasonable to suppose that the better we are able to isolate

[21] E. Franklin Frazier, *The Negro Family in the United States*, rev. ed. (New York, The Dryden Press, Inc., 1951).

[22] See, for example, Thomas P. Monahan, "Does Age at Marriage Matter in Divorce?," *Social Forces*, Vol. 32 (October, 1953), pp. 81-87; and Harvey J. Locke, *Predicting Adjustment in Marriage* (New York, Henry Holt & Co., Inc., 1951), pp. 101-102.

[23] For an investigation of the economic base of youthful marriages and an attempt to relate this to their chances for success, see Lee G. Burchinal, "How Successful Are School-Age Marriages?," *Iowa Farm Science*, Vol. 13 (March, 1959), pp. 7-10.

[24] Harold T. Christensen and Hanna H. Meissner, "Studies in Child Spacing, III: Premarital Pregnancy as a Factor in Divorce," *American Sociological Review*, Vol. 18 (December, 1953), pp. 641-644.

[25] Loren E. Chancellor and Thomas P. Monahan, "Religious Preference and Inter-religious Mixtures in Marriages and Divorces in Iowa," *American Journal of Sociology*, Vol. 61 (November, 1955), pp. 233-239. See also Thomas P. Monahan and William M. Kephart, "Divorces and Desertion by Religious and Mixed-Religious Groups," *American Journal of Sociology*, Vol. 59 (March, 1954), pp. 454-465.

the potential sources of difficulty in high-risk marriages, the greater will be the possibility that the risks can be compensated for or at least reduced.

CHILDREN AND DIVORCE

The effect of divorce on children is a much-talked-about subject. There are those who forecast nothing but psychological doom for the child of divorce. The outlook is no less pessimistic among those who shift the issue to marital unhappiness and contend that it is this, rather than the formal dissolution of marriage, that foredooms a child to a lifetime of misery. Others glibly assert that "it all depends," presumably on the individual child and the specific marriage. Although this assertion may be technically accurate, it is not far from being utterly useless unless one goes on to delineate and explain the conditions upon which so much "depends." In our efforts to cut through the mass of accumulated verbiage on children of divorce, we will be forced to uncover some admittedly ugly facts of life, but we refuse to join forces with those who know before they look what the effect of a divorce will be. It is necessary, first, to gain some appreciation of the magnitude of the problem.

Once it was commonplace to temper remarks on divorce by the observation that in most instances no children were involved. We have witnessed a real change in this respect. Over the past twenty-five years the proportion of all divorces involving at least one child has risen from 38 to almost 50 per cent. The average number of children per divorced family reporting any children at all has remained the same or, if anything, risen slightly. Jacobson reported that in 1922, 1932, and 1948 there was an average of 1.8 children for each divorce that involved a child or more.[26] Data from twenty-two states in 1955 indicate that the average is 1.9.[27] Since the proportion of divorces involving children has risen while the average number of children per divorced parent has remained about the same, the total number of children yearly affected by divorce has increased. About twenty-five years ago, for every 100 divorces granted 68 children became divorce-orphans.[28] By 1948 the figure had risen to 74, and today 95 children are involved in every 100 divorces. Even if the number of divorces had remained constant over this period it would still be true that more and more children are yearly involved in divorce. But, as we have seen, the sheer number of divorces and the divorce rate have shown a gen-

[26] Paul H. Jacobson, "Differentials in Divorce by Duration of Marriage and Size of Family," *American Sociological Review*, Vol. 15 (April, 1950), pp. 235-244.
[27] U. S. Department of Health, Education, and Welfare, *Vital Statistics—Special Reports*, Vol. 46, No. 4 (April 9, 1957), pp. 94-95.
[28] Reported in Jacobson, *op. cit.*, pp. 239-240.

eral increase. The result is that annually a staggering 350,000 children are experiencing divorce.

TABLE 38.   Divorce and Children Under 18 Years Old, 1955

Number of Divorces	Number of Chil- dren Reported	Children per 100 Divorces	Average Number of Children per Divorce with Children
377,000	347,000	95	1.9

SOURCE: U.S. Department of Health, Education, and Welfare, *Vital Statistics—Special Reports,* Vol. 46, No. 4 (April 9, 1957), pp. 94-95 and 101.

It should be pointed out, too, that most of the children annually affected by divorce are under ten years of age. Earlier studies have indicated that from 63 to 69 per cent of children of divorce were less than ten years old, because of the prevalency of divorce in the relatively early years of marriage.[29] A conservative estimate would be that currently over two million children under eighteen years of age have at some time in their life experienced divorce. There is no reason, of course, to assume that the divorce of parents does not matter to older children or that the effects of divorce, whatever they may be, are automatically erased on the child's eighteenth birthday. A fuller appreciation of the numerical importance of the effect of divorce on children could be gained by obtaining the sum total of all people living today who as children experienced divorce, regardless of how old they are today. However we count and tally them, the children of divorce are a sizable group. Many of them do or have experienced divorce when still quite young.

TABLE 39.   Divorce by Specified Number of Children
Under 18 Years Old, 1955

		NUMBER OF CHILDREN						
	None	1	2	3	4	5	6	7 or more
Per Cent of Divorces	51.9	22.8	14.5	6.8	2.3	.9	.4	.4

SOURCE: U.S. Department of Health, Education, and Welfare, *Vital Statistics—Special Reports,* Vol. 46, No. 4 (April 9, 1957), pp. 94-95.

Each of the 350,000 children under eighteen who were parties to a divorce last year represents an individual case with unique problems. Differences in age, sex, perception of the divorce, and family relations before the divorce are a few of the contingencies that must be added to the

[29] *Ibid.,* pp. 241 ff.

basic differences in personality among the children. In one sense, no two of these children experienced exactly the same divorce, not even if they came from the same divorced family. It is also true, however, that there is a certain commonality in most divorces. Inherent in the divorce situation, almost regardless of who is getting divorced or why, are potentialities for serious difficulties for the child or children. How and if these potentialities are realized depends on the personalities of all the people involved in the divorce and the peculiarities that are added to the common divorce situation. The effects of divorce on children nevertheless can be considered from the standpoint of the situational features of divorce and the broad areas of commonly found situational differences.

Whatever else happens at divorce, the family unit is broken. This can happen because of death or desertion and undoubtedly it occurs in some cases of extreme marital discord that do not end in divorce. It is difficult to appreciate what family disruption means to a child. Play groups change, neighbors come and go, his class in school changes membership or teacher, but always a child's family is there, the significant reference group in his young life. To grow up with an optimum amount of self-confidence and security every child needs to feel that he is wanted and loved and that he "belongs" to somebody. Clinical evidence makes it apparent that young children have a real grasp of their basic helplessness and as a result can experience extreme fear when the security of the sort we are talking about is threatened.[30] Adults too, of course, have been known to have severe emotional reactions to death and other situations that leave them psychologically alone in the world. Few adults can probably imagine the fear-ridden void experienced by a child who perceives divorce as parental abandonment. This is why it has been called a "dangerous illusion" to assume that children will automatically adjust to divorce.[31] Many do, of course, and some do so admirably, but the point is that almost every divorce *threatens* the basic security of almost every child involved.

Some children of divorce remain insecure, lonely, anxious individuals for all of their lives, although many more, we trust, go on to regain their sense of security. Some situations aggravate the threat of security loss and others help to relieve it. Being a ward of the state while parents work out or dispute custody arrangements or learning that neither parent really wants him and that "arrangements" have been made for him to live with this or that relative can inflict deep psychic wounds, which if healed at all will show ugly scars for many years. On the other hand, a well ordered life

[30] J. Louise Despert, *Children of Divorce* (Garden City, New York, Doubleday & Company, Inc., 1953), p. 33.

[31] Edmund Bergler, *Divorce Won't Help* (New York, Harper & Brothers, 1948), p. 162.

with an emotionally stable parent or full acceptance in a new family formed by the parent's remarriage may do much to help the child achieve a sense of belonging and being loved once again. Under favorable conditions, time may blur the picture so that only the memory of the hurt, and not the hurt itself, will remain. Every divorce means that mother, father, and children will no longer live together, and it is this disruption of the family that is a potential threat to the inner security of the immature members of the broken family.

A great deal of insight into the children's problem can be obtained from parents who have experienced divorce. Perhaps only parents who have searched hard for the answers can know what it means to explain to a young child that although both parents love him very much one of them is leaving the home for good. It is difficult to answer the child who reasons that since family ties are so tenuous and adult emotions so fickle perhaps someday his parents will fall out of love with him, or have already done so. Is there anything at all that a father can say as he permanently removes himself from the family circle? Or how can a mother explain that the child's father will never live with them again but he still loves the child and will take him for a walk two Saturdays a month if he takes full advantage of the court's visiting order? Looking at these problems from the parents' point of view is another way of imagining the doubt, confusion, and fear that rests in their children.

A grave problem in divorce involving children is the child's perception of cause and blame for the affair. Surely things as important as family disruption do not "just happen," and the child demands to know, whether he asks or not, why it occurred in his family and whose fault it is that it did. Sometimes one parent succeeds in creating for the child a pretty damning picture of the other. Such a child may find it difficult ever again to be totally at peace with the accused parent, the sex and role he represents, or often, for that matter, with anyone else in the world. Then, of course, the whole case may be emotionally reopened when the insights of advancing maturity force the child to ponder about the other side of the story he once accepted. Some parents take great pains not to destroy in the child the love and respect he feels for each of them. Perhaps they are reasonably successful, and the child does not center blame on either of them. But he is left to his own devices to riddle out why such nice, righteous, upstanding people, as his parents represent one another to be, failed to get along together.

Clinicians not infrequently report that children assume the blame for their parents' marital difficulties.[32] Sometimes they are able to verbalize

[32] See, for example, Despert, *op. cit.*, p. 32.

their feelings of guilt, but more frequently they remain as inner gnawings, which the child finds difficult to admit to anyone, least of all to himself. Once again, there are conditions that aggravate children's feelings of self-blame for their parents' divorce. Perhaps the child has heard his parents arguing about him, his behavior, or what to do with him after the divorce. Young children may see in their own misbehavior, of which every child is guilty in his parents' eyes, the main cause for the family unrest that culminated in divorce. Guilt amounting to self-loathing may well result if, in addition, the child has rightly or wrongly perceived that his parents never wanted him in the first place. The guilt of a child can be greatly relieved, on the other hand, by parents who are able to see further than their own urgent problems to those of the child. Even when he is given every assurance to the contrary, however, the child searching for an explanation for the fate that is befalling his family may still toy with the idea that basically he is at fault.

Different post-divorce circumstances contain the potential for different effects on children quite as much as do the circumstances of the divorce itself. A few examples will illustrate the range of post-divorce situations and their differential effects. Much may depend on which parent is awarded custody, and although it is usually the mother who is to rear the child, it is not always the mother. The parent who is awarded custody may or may not remarry, although, again, most of them will remarry. There are several kinds of problems for a child whose mother does not remarry, that is, problems that are not found either in most complete families or in families where the child's mother has remarried. The divorced mother attempting to rear a child or children alone may well find herself in severe financial straits. Alimony and support payments when awarded are rarely sufficient to provide for the needs of mother and children. Working outside the home may solve the financial problems but create others. The child in the incomplete family is socially and psychologically deprived of a father figure, either to emulate directly or to serve as a model of the opposite sex.

If the divorced mother remarries, whole areas of problems may be removed, but others may be created. Even in the least complicated case, the child's adjustment to his mother's husband may not be easy. All children may not be able to work things out in their own minds with the seeming simplicity of the little boy who spoke of his "real daddy" and "the daddy I live with." There are more complex cases, of course, as exemplified by the probably mythical case of the frantic remarried mother who complained to her also remarried husband that "your children and my children always pick on our children." We see, once again, that the post-divorce family situations can be many and varied. Nor have we even touched on most of them. Perhaps we have furnished sufficient illustrations to demonstrate our major point: divorce and post-divorce situations, by their very nature, contain the potential for grave difficulties for children. That these potentials are so frequently realized is one of the tragedies of divorce.

The picture of the child of divorce we have presented is admittedly unpleasant. The all-too-frequent alternative, life in a home torn apart by marital discord, can be equally unpleasant. Children are quick to perceive trouble and discord and have a deeper grasp of the whole emotional climate of the home than parents may think. Everything we know about human behavior forces us to the conclusion that the marital relationship does have an effect on children. Life with a tyrannical father can warp a boy's or girl's entire conception of manhood. Nor would we expect much good to come from being reared by an indulgent mother who is compensating for her lack of marital love by fostering overdependency in her children. The child's definition of his own and the other sex's status, his conception of normal marital relationships, in short, his whole conception of normal and proper family life comes first from life in his own family. When by any reasonable definition these first learnings are twisted and confused, subsequent experiences may find a shaky base on which to build more healthy attitudes.

We can grant that the ideal situation would be for every child to grow up in a complete family marked by harmonious relations and love. It becomes exceedingly difficult to decide whether it is better for a child to be reared in a home broken by divorce or in one of intense marital conflict. One recent study, for example, discovered that the adjustment of adolescents was similar in three behavior areas whether they came from unhappy complete homes or from broken homes, but in three other areas of adjustment the youths from broken homes showed better adjustment.[33] The adolescent living only with his mother scored higher in parent-child relationships, but in other ways he had an adjustment level similar to youths whose divorced mother had remarried. Apparently there is much yet to be learned concerning the factors in a marriage and family situation that affect the personal adjustment of a child. The "best interests of the child" is a worthy goal; the difficulty lies in assessing in just which direction the best interests lie.

[33] F. Ivan Nye, "Child Adjustment in Broken and in Unhappy Unbroken Homes," *Marriage and Family Living*, Vol. 19 (November, 1957), pp. 356-361.

REMARRIAGE AFTER DIVORCE

Landis has pointed out that a higher proportion of people in contemporary America experience plural marriage than in *some* societies classified as polygynous.[34] Since in our society the sexual and other privileges of
plural marriage are experienced consecutively rather than concurrently, it
has been suggested that our marriage form be designated as "sequential
polygamy." One could argue, of course, that the proportion of all marriages
that are plural is not the essential criterion to use in designating marriage
forms, and we could point out, too, that in *most* societies classified as
polygynous the proportion of plural marriages exceeds that in the United
States.[35] If calling our marriage form "sequential polygamy" draws attention to the relatively high rate of remarriage, the term is a suitable one.
We want to go beyond recognition of the extent of remarriage following
divorce, however, and investigate the factors associated with remarriage
and the success of this type of marriage.

TABLE 40.   First Marriage and Remarriage Rates by
Age and Sex, 1950-1953

AGE	FIRST MARRIAGES PER 1,000 SINGLE		REMARRIAGES PER 1,000 DIVORCED		REMARRIAGES PER 1,000 WIDOWED	
	Male	Female	Male	Female	Male	Female
20-24 years	160	180	...	...	...	...
25-29	151	122	341	340	...	182
30-34	91	72	269	264	...	104
35-44	35	42	244	146	88	47
45-54	20	7	99	112	79	19
55-64	9	2	69	59	36	5
65 and over	4	1	23	40	8	2

SOURCE: Reported in Paul C. Glick, *American Families* (New York, John Wiley & Sons, Inc.,
1957), p. 136.

Most divorcees ultimately remarry and many marry quite soon after
their divorce. It has been frequently pointed out that, age for age, the
marriage rate of divorcees is higher than that of the single or the widowed.
The precise meaning of such a statement is sometimes missed, for it is
well recognized that the majority of all marriages occurring during a given
year are first marriages. Of every 1,000 single women between twenty-five
and twenty-nine years of age, for example, 122 will marry during a given
year; 340 of every 1,000 divorced women of the same ages will marry during

[34] Paul H. Landis, "Sequential Marriage," *Journal of Home Economics*, Vol. 42
(October, 1950), pp. 625-628.
[35] Cf. pp. 29-30. See also Murdock, *op. cit.*, p. 28.

the same period of time. In terms of the number who are capable of
marriage by virtue of their unmarried status, therefore, the divorced show a
greater willingness to marry than the single. This relationship holds true
for men as well as women, and the statistical advantage of the divorced
person in the marriage market increases with age. One may reason, of
course, that the relatively low marriage rate of the single people who are
middle-aged and older is to be expected. Those who wanted to and were
able to marry did so earlier in their lifetime so that the single, middle-
aged constitute, either by intent or by fate, largely an unmarriageable
residue. Divorcees, on the other hand, have demonstrated their willingness
and ability to attract mates. The relatively high remarriage rate further
demonstrates that divorcees have not become disillusioned with marriage
as a way of life. Each year a sizable proportion of the divorced demonstrate
by their remarriage that basically marriage agrees with them even though
their first spouse did not. How many more would like to remarry if they
could, we do not know, just as we do not know how many single persons
would like to enter into a first marriage.

TABLE 41. Duration of Divorce Before Remarriage*

Duration of Divorce Before Remarriage	Per Cent
Less than 1 year	12.1
1 year	24.1
2 years	20.0
3 years	12.4
4 years	8.6
5 years	5.6
6 years	2.6
7 years	2.2
8 years	2.0
9 years	1.8
10 years or more	8.6
Median years divorced before remarriage	2.7

Source: Reported in Paul C. Glick, *American Families* (New York, John Wiley & Sons, Inc.,
1957), p. 139.
* For persons with remarriages between 1950 and 1953.

Glick has computed that under current conditions about two-thirds of
all women who divorce will eventually remarry.[36] Close to three-fourths of
all divorced men will someday remarry. Of all the divorced people remarrying during any one year, most have not been divorced for a very
long time. A full 12 per cent, as shown in Table 41, remarried within the

[36] Paul C. Glick, *American Families* (New York, John Wiley & Sons, Inc., 1957),
p. 139.

year of their divorce and in over a third of the remarriages the parties had been divorced no more than a year. It has been suggested that the relatively quick remarriage of divorcees may mean that we have discounted too heavily the possibility that many divorces take place so that one or the other party may marry an already selected person.[37] An alternative hypothesis is simply that the divorced person is strongly motivated to remarry, even though he has no specific person in mind, and that he is quite able soon to find another mate. The difficulty in making new friends or adjusting to a couple-centered social life, the inability to make a satisfactory sexual adjustment, the desire to experience home life again or to provide one's children with a surrogate parent are a few of the post-divorce conditions that can strongly motivate a person to remarry. This does not mean that we should ignore the familiar triangle as a precipitant to divorce, but rather that other forces may also press a person to early remarriage.

Selective Factors in Remarriage

There is no single path leading out of the conflict of marriage and formal divorce upon which the new divorcees travel. Sooner or later, it is true, many will reach the goal of remarriage, but the routes they traverse are varied. Others choose or are thrust upon a still different path which does not lead to another marriage. What causes this difference in post-divorce behavior? What do we know about the personal and social characteristics of those who remarry and those who do not? Although admittedly we do not know as much as we would like to, there are some characteristics that operate in a statistical sense to select from all divorcees those headed for another marriage.

The age of a divorced person is very strongly associated with his likelihood of remarriage. The younger a person is at the time of divorce, the more likely it is that he will remarry. An appreciation of the strength of the age factor can be gained by comparing the remarriage rate of those in the extreme age categories. Turning back to Table 40, we see that the marriage rate is over eight times as high for the younger divorced men and women as it is for those over age fifty-five. As age progresses, there is a steady drop in the rate of remarriage. Goode's valuable study of divorced mothers supplies some of the missing dynamics in the association between age and remarriage rate.[38] He found, to begin with, that a positive attitude toward love and marriage, frequency of dating, and receiving help from parents and friends in meeting eligible men were all conducive to remar-

---

[37] Landis, op. cit., p. 626.
[38] Goode, After Divorce, Chs. 18 and 19.

riage. All of these factors were found to be more frequently characteristic of the young divorced mother than the older ones. Youth itself, however, was a favorable characteristic for remarriage independent of the other factors. In other words, it is partly just being young that steers some women into a second matrimonial venture, although the younger women have greater opportunities for dating and meeting eligible men and are likely to have a better attitude toward love and marriage. Perhaps factors like these operate as well among divorced women without children and among men. They help to explain, at any rate, part of the high association between age at divorce and remarriage rate.

It might well be supposed that in an era when children are considered an economic liability they would adversely affect a divorced woman's chances of remarriage. We have seen, too, that frequent dating is associated with prompt remarriage, and one might imagine that the divorcee without children would find it somewhat easier to date. Divorced mothers, on the other hand, might seem to be the most interested in remarriage, for added to any desires for companionship would be the wish for a normal home and a surrogate father for their children. Then, too, the divorced mother could be said to be the more firmly committed to home and family life, and thus more inclined to remarry, than the divorcee without children. As is so frequently the case, sheer "logic" can be made to defend opposing positions.

TABLE 42.   Remarriages per 1,000 Women by Number of Children Ever Born

Number of Children Ever Born	Unstandardized Remarriage Rate	Remarriage Rate Standardized for Age
No children	102	84
1 or 2 children	83	76
3 or more children	53	81

Source: Reported in Paul C. Glick, *American Families* (New York, John Wiley & Sons, Inc., 1957), p. 138.

Data on remarriage rates by number of children support the position that the childless remarry with greater frequency. Much of the relationship seems to be explained by the age factor. The longer a marriage endures, in other words, the greater is the chance that children will be born and, of course, the older are the marriage partners. When we limit our study to young women, the divorcees without children have only a slightly better chance for remarriage than the divorced mothers. Not yet explained is why those with three or more children have a somewhat higher rate of remarriage than the mothers of one or two children. Perhaps such unknowns as the ages of the children and the number of children living at home, instead of the number ever born, help to obscure the picture. It would seem, however, that the mere fact of having children does not complicate greatly the divorced woman's chances for remarriage.

Further and more detailed research is necessary before we can understand the mechanisms involved in other remarriage differentials. Education, residence, and labor-force status, for example, have been investigated as selective factors, but there is a certain interrelationship among these factors. Careful studies designed to test the independent nature of apparent selective factors, as well as their strength, are sorely needed. We must not lose sight of the fact, however, that the bulk of divorced men and women ultimately do remarry.

Success of Remarriages

A little thought makes it apparent that there are many obstacles in the way of the success of a remarriage. These obstacles can be thought of as the personal and situational factors that have the potential for weakening or disrupting the remarriage relationship. Divorce leaves some men and women with a sense of failure, a feeling of inadequacy, or at least the gnawing thought that they are incapable of successful marriage. Others manage to shift the blame wholly to their spouse but are left with the inescapable conclusion that they are poor choosers. Perhaps the inner voices that speak of inferiority in being or selecting a good marriage partner can be quieted fully and forever. But when they cannot they would seem to constitute a psychological liability in a second marriage. Various studies have shown that a certain proportion of all divorced persons still love their former mates and would like to remarry them. Undoubtedly there are not many cases in which these feelings are strong at the time of marriage to someone other than the former spouse. Where they remain at all or where they have been exorcised only with difficulty, they would seem not to be the sort of emotional equipment for successful remarriage.

We should not ignore the motives for remarriage. Many remarry for reasons that are normal by any standards, but since we are talking of obstacles in the way of success of remarriage we must admit that there are unhealthy motives for marrying again. Remarriage, for some, is necessary to prove to themselves that they are still as capable of eliciting love as they would like to think, despite the fact that someone previously rejected them. Others may respond, in their selection of a second marriage partner, to immediate and strongly felt pressures, like the need for financial support or for sexual outlet, and may pay too little attention to other traits of the new mate. As harsh as it sounds, we must also admit that the remarrying group contains a certain proportion of individuals who are seemingly incapable of a happy marriage.[39] Neurotics, like the poor, we seem to have with us always, and for some of them divorce and remarriage are either the result of their emotional instability or a direct expression of it. Nor are neurotic elements in mate selection limited to the obviously unstable. Even the layman would suspect, for example, that when a woman chooses three alcoholics as successive husbands it is not only the men in question who are emotionally sick. Bernard suggests that about a third of the divorced population is neurotic and lacking in "marital aptitude."[40] Whether or not we accept this estimate as correct, it is nevertheless true that the personality of some of those entering a remarriage stands as an obstacle to its success.

Apart from the personalities of the marriage partners, there are situational factors in remarriage that are capable of creating strain and tension. We will mention but a few as illustrative of the kinds of situations found in remarriage and seldom in first marriage. More likely lacking in remarriage is the support of the community, friends, and family, and more likely present are the reservations and the attitude of "let's wait and see how *this* one turns out." To the lack of full approval is added, in many cases of remarriage following divorce, the adjustment of one or both of the spouses to the other's children. There may be financial problems due to the divorced husband's alimony or support payments. Family routines may be upset by visiting privileges to the children by the ex-husband or wife. Any of these situations could take different forms which would have different effects on the marriage and, of course, other situations could well be imagined. The point is that inherent in the remarriages of the divorced are possibilities for stresses and strains not found in first marriages. Whether these potentialities result in less success among remarriages is our next point of inquiry.

One way of discovering the success of remarriages is through comparative studies of the happiness or adjustment level of remarriages and first marriages. The same or similar tests have been administered to both the first-married and the remarried; we need not concern ourselves with the items utilized in the tests or how well the tests measure what they purport to measure. The important question, rather, is how the remarried group compares with the other group if we use the test scores as our criterion of

---

[39] Bergler emphasizes that for neurotics divorce is futile unless the underlying cause of their inability to have a successful marriage, that is, their neurosis, is removed. See Bergler, *op. cit.*, particularly Ch. 2.

[40] Jessie Bernard, *Remarriage: A Study of Marriage* (New York, The Dryden Press, Inc., 1956), p. 108.

success in marriage. Bernard has summarized a number of studies of marital success, and the results show no clear-cut pattern of less success among the remarried.[41] We have chosen Locke's study for illustration since it is more recent than some and since both the previously divorced and the married-once groups were given the same test, the Burgess-Cottrell marital adjustment test.[42] Although a few more of the previously divorced fall into the "poor adjustment" category, as indicated in Table 43, it seems that the two groups were basically similar. We must freely admit that there are methodological difficulties with this study as well as with the others to which we have referred. In the comparative studies, however, there is no reason to suppose that sampling or other biases worked systematically for or against the previously divorced groups as opposed to the others. Taking the studies at face value, we would conclude that a large proportion of marriages involving a previously divorced person are successful, almost to the same degree as are first marriages.

TABLE 43.   Marital Adjustment of Married-Once and
Divorced-Remarried Groups

| | MARITAL ADJUSTMENT | | |
MARITAL STATUS	Per Cent "Good"	Per Cent "Fair"	Per Cent "Poor"
Married once	50.0	39.1	10.9
Divorced-remarried	44.7	38.3	17.0

SOURCE: Harvey J. Locke, *Predicting Adjustment in Marriage* (New York, Henry Holt and Company, Inc., 1951), p. 307.

Divorce statistics on the previously divorced are another way of estimating the success of remarriages.[43] In a given year, about 40 per cent of all divorces are granted to those who have been married two or more times. At the younger ages particularly, it is more than likely that the marriage or marriages preceding the one currently ending in divorce also were broken by divorce and not by death. The relatively high proportion of all divorces granted to the previously divorced, then, puts one immediately on guard concerning the stability of remarriages. A more thorough approach is to analyze the marriage and divorce rates according to previous marital experience. In 1955, never-married persons constituted about 78 per cent of all marriages. In that same year, however, the once-married group accounted for but 61 per cent of all divorces. The previously married, on the other hand, made up about 16 per cent of all marriages in a given year but

[41] Bernard, *op. cit.*, pp. 109-112.
[42] Locke, *op. cit.*
[43] The divorce and marriage statistics that follow were computed from U. S. Department of Health, Education, and Welfare, *Vital Statistics: 1955*, Vol. I (Washington, D. C., U. S. Government Printing Office, 1957), pp. 67 and 78.

accounted for more than twice that proportion of all divorces. Although we do not have as complete data as we would like, it would seem clear enough that the previously divorced contribute more than their share of all divorces. This same conclusion was reached by Monahan after intensive study of marriage and divorce patterns in two states.[44]

Putting together both the studies of marital happiness and of divorce among the remarried leaves us with an interesting picture. The two sorts of evidence are not, of course, contradictory. A probable interpretation of the seeming paradox is that those remarriages that last are about as happy as first marriages. On the other hand, the once-divorced seem particularly reluctant to put up with marital conflict. They know from experience the social and other costs of divorce and choose this alternative to remaining in what they consider an unworkable marriage. After the least happy and the least adjusted couples have ended their remarriage, there is left a core of remarriages that is much like all other marriages as far as its representation of happy and unhappy couples is concerned.

DIVORCE AND THE INSTITUTION OF THE FAMILY

In preceding sections of this chapter we have concentrated on gaining an understanding of the phenomenon called divorce. We have seen figures and rates dealing with divorce as it was, as it is now, and as it exists in different segments of the population. The issue that must be faced squarely is concerned with the meaning of divorce, not to *a* family or even *most* families, but to *the family*. Are we to believe the soothsayers who see in current divorce practices the picture of a decadent family institution speeding on its path toward utter disintegration? In our attempts to answer this type of question we will necessarily touch on some of the reasons for divorce, but our primary purpose is to suggest a way of relating divorce to the status of the American family.

It is our thesis that divorce is the price we are paying for having the kind of marriage that we have and presumably we want. This does not mean that divorce cannot be reduced without destroying our marriage system nor that a few simple changes in the marriage pattern will eliminate divorce once and for all. We mean, rather, that freedom to divorce is granted by a significant proportion of Americans precisely because it fits in well with the values they cherish in marriage. The goals sought in marriage and the preferred method of mate selection are two basic values that seem to have a bearing on the society's tolerance of divorce.

Whatever else Americans are looking for in marriage, most think of it

[44] Thomas P. Monahan, "How Stable Are Remarriages?," *American Journal of Sociology*. Vol. 58 (November, 1952), pp. 280-288.

as a way to personal happiness. We can point to specific motives like companionship, sexual satisfaction, or love, but when we examine them more carefully it must be admitted that these things are desired because they produce or are a part of happiness. In their personal motives for marriage, Americans scarcely consider that marriage and the family are socially required for the reproduction of the species and would cast a jaundiced eye on anyone who claimed he was marrying for this reason. Economic considerations, in the sense of marriage constituting an efficient symbiotic pair relationship in the struggle for existence, are today greatly reduced if not gone entirely. Almost any man or woman can sustain himself without a mate and without children. Few people feel any sense of duty to society to marry and have children. Each year thousands do both because they believe that in marriage and parenthood they will find a happier, fuller, and more meaningful life. When so much of the impetus for marriage comes from the promise of close, satisfying, interpersonal relations, it places this aspect of marriage in a vulnerable spot. When the all-important happiness is not found, or is not found in sufficient degree, there are few felt imperatives to remain married.

A second characteristic of American marriage that seems to play a part in our divorce pattern is the freedom in mate selection that is almost literally demanded. This freedom seems almost necessary as long as the goal of marriage emphasizes so strongly personal compatibility and personal happiness. Each individual feels that he alone is capable of choosing a mate with whom he will find happiness. This is not to say that parental and community pressures are never brought to bear in mate selection. It is interesting, however, that unless the arrangement is too unusual, such as one that involves a great disparity in age, the community will often support the couple against the parents, for "everyone deserves a chance at happiness." For some, of course, the chance turns out to be nothing more than an opportunity to make their own mistakes. Nevertheless the personal choice in mate selection is one of the assumed freedoms for many Americans. A moment's reflection will indicate the tremendous burden our system places on the individual. With all too little preparation, he is expected at a fairly young age to choose a partner with whom to embark on the life-long venture in happiness his culture so blatantly promises him. All in all, it is no wonder that some discover that freedom of choice carries no assurance that the choice will be a wise one.

To a certain extent the freedom of divorce follows from the current conception of marriage. If marriage is for happiness and if the individual is free to pursue happiness in this direction, should not he be also free to flee from unhappiness? A sizable proportion of Americans seem to answer affirmatively. To a large extent, it would seem that this type of reasoning accounts for the greater acceptance of divorce. We submit that the very marriage system that is cherished in our society practically implies that there will be some divorce. The societal definition of a successful marriage almost assures that some marriages will be unsuccessful, and the insistence that all be allowed to choose their own mates for their own reasons means that some will choose unwisely. All of this adds up to an important change in the institution of marriage. With the rise of values like personal happiness, companionship, and individual development, and the de-emphasis of stability in and of itself, economic and educational functions, the complexion of marriage has undergone a decided change. If the new values sought in marriage seem to imply greater freedom to divorce, then this too must be considered as a change in the institutionalized pattern of mate relationships in our society. In earlier sections of this chapter we have, if anything, overstressed the harmful, unpleasant, and otherwise negative effects of divorce on those involved in it. This does not mean that we can legitimately point out similar harmful effects of divorce on the institution of marriage or speak of the modern family as being in a state of disorganization. If the new values around which modern marriage is organized seem strange, need they be considered intrinsically inferior? As long as the changes in the values and practices associated with marriage and the family are not intrinsically incompatible with the time-honored functions of regulation of sexual behavior and the bearing and rearing of children, it is difficult to maintain that the changes have led to a disruption of the family institution.

SELECTED READINGS

BERGLER, EDMUND, *Divorce Won't Help* (New York, Harper & Brothers, 1948).

BERNARD, JESSIE, *Remarriage: A Study of Marriage* (New York, The Dryden Press, Inc., 1956).

DESPERT, J. LOUISE, *Children of Divorce* (Garden City, New York, Doubleday & Company, Inc., 1953).

GLICK, PAUL C., *American Families* (New York, John Wiley & Sons, Inc., 1957), Chs. 6, 7, and 8.

GOODE, WILLIAM J., *After Divorce* (Glencoe, Illinois, The Free Press, 1956).

LICHTENBERGER, JAMES P., *Divorce* (New York, McGraw-Hill Book Company, Inc., 1931).

MURDOCK, GEORGE P., "Family Stability in Non-European Cultures," *The Annals of the American Society of Political and Social Science*, Vol. 272 (October, 1950), pp. 195-201.

PLOSCOWE, MORRIS, *The Truth about Divorce* (New York, Hawthorn Books, Inc., 1955).

Rothenberg, Charles, *Postscript to Marriage* (New York, Greenberg: Publisher, 1946).

U.S. Bureau of the Census, *Duration of Current Marital Status*, Special Report, P-E, No. 2E (Washington, D.C., U.S. Government Printing Office, 1955).

U.S. Department of Health, Education, and Welfare, "Divorces and Annulments: Detailed Statistics for Reporting Areas, 1955," *Vital Statistics—Special Reports*, Vol. 46, No. 4 (April 9, 1957).

Waller, Willard, *The Old Love and the New* (New York, Liveright Publishing Corporation, 1930).

Part III

THE DYNAMICS OF
FAMILY INTERACTION

CHAPTER 14

Basic Concepts: The Family Life Cycle and Developmental Tasks

A FAMILY is a group. A family is a *primary* group. These words are not strange even to those with a limited acquaintance with sociology. But the concepts "group" and particularly "primary group" are pivotal to the interactional approach to the study of the family.

A beginning course in sociology usually teaches that a group is "any number of human beings in reciprocal communication."[1] It is then explained that the network of communication that binds group member to group member gives rise, to some degree, to a mutual sense of belonging together so that the interacting individuals can be thought of as a unity or a whole. A primary group, in the words of the early sociologist who developed the concept, is "characterized by intimate face-to-face association and cooperation."[2] Cooley states that *primary* is a fitting designation because such groups "are fundamental in forming the social nature and ideals of the individual."[3] He goes on to point out that the result of the intimate association in a primary group is "a certain fusion of individualities in a common whole, so that one's very self, for many purposes at least, is the common life and purpose of the group."[4] In the light of this definition, it is understandable that the family has been termed the primary group *par excellence.*

When we state, then, that our focus in this section is on the family as a primary group, we have already told much about the approach. It indicates that we will be concerned with the personal interaction that takes place in the family group. The approach takes cognizance, too, of

[1] John F. Cuber, *Sociology,* 4th ed. (New York, Appleton-Century-Crofts, Inc., 1959), p. 297.
[2] Charles H. Cooley, *Social Organization* (New York, Charles Scribner's Sons, 1909), p. 23.
[3] *Ibid.*
[4] *Ibid.*

Cooley's remarks on the result of primary group living on the personalities of the individuals comprising the social unity. With this approach, therefore, we attempt to get inside the family group and analyze its functions as far as they involve interaction between and among members. Since our emphasis is on the interaction that takes place within the family, we must perforce pay some attention to the individuals who are doing the acting and reacting. What each family member is and what each will become is, to some extent, affected by the family group to which he belongs. The family, in turn, affects what each member is and does, both now and in the future.

Adding slightly to the words of Burgess, we can speak of the family as "a dynamic unity of interacting personalities."[5] *Dynamic* pertains to activity, change, and movement, and is therefore most apt in reference to the family. If we stop the movement of the family at any one time, we can see that the group has had a past and has a future, just as each of the individuals comprising the group has. Each family member can thus be viewed as a developing member of a changing group. Simply stated, then, our focus in this section is on the interaction that takes place between and among family members as the family itself moves on in its continual progression through time.

Getting at the internal workings of families is not a simple task. At the same time, it can be one of the most rewarding emphases in the study of the family. The approach recognizes the family as something more than a collection of people, but it does not ignore the individuals who make up the family. It takes cognizance of a similarity, at one level, of all families, but it leaves room for recognition of the myriad differences among them. Far from ignoring the fact that family interaction takes place in the context of a specific community within a broader society, the dynamic interactional approach incorporates the social and cultural factors that affect the demands made on families and family members. For those whose orientation primarily involves ameliorating the ills of family life, the dynamic interactional approach allows them to isolate and specify the potential sources of difficulty experienced by family members as they relate themselves to one another and to their society. We do not claim that we will do all these things in the few chapters that follow. Our aim is to explore a framework for studying family interaction, to sketch its outlines, and to fill in some of the more salient features. Two concepts, *family life cycle* and *developmental task*, are crucial to our approach to family interaction and warrant a general exploration.

[5] Ernest W. Burgess and Harvey J. Locke, *The Family*, 2nd ed. (New York, American Book Company, 1953), p. 293.

FAMILY LIFE CYCLE

Families have a beginning, they grow in numbers, their membership next declines, and eventually the original family exists no longer. The individual is born, he grows, enters a period of decline, and inevitably passes from the scene. The striking parallel between the life pattern of a normal individual and the history of a typical family gave rise to the concept *family life cycle*. The concept, we believe, is an extremely useful one. Partly because of its apparent simplicity, it can also be one of the more confusing concepts in family sociology.

Barring accident or disease, the individual human follows without major deviation the life cycle of the species. The normal human is born with an inherent growth system, and after birth he will enter into a period of growth for a period of time characteristic of the species. He will next reach sexual maturity, and he will remain sexually fertile during a certain span of his life. Decline and senility follow maturity and lead inevitably to death. Each normal human being who escapes accident and disease at early stages goes through precisely the same life cycle. No individual departs at all from the sequence of life's stages, and there is relatively minor deviation from the characteristic times at which the stages are reached by each biologically normal member of the species. The metabolic system common to the species demands that this is so.

It should be apparent that families *do not* have a life cycle in the same sense that an individual does. Surely it would be senseless to say that a family matures in the literal sense, for had not two of its members been sexually mature from the beginning it probably would not have been formed and scarcely could have grown. More serious difficulties with applying the life cycle concept to the family are found in the ideas of uniformity and regularity of the stages of development. The family is not an organism, and it does not contain the determinant of a relatively rigid life pattern analogous to the metabolic system of the individual. All couples do not go beyond the married-pair stage, and it would be difficult to say that they are for this reason stunted or freak anomalies of the genus family. The stages of family life, furthermore, do not unfold in some kind of predetermined, regular sequence. Childbearing or its imminence can precede, and, of course, precipitate, the married-pair stage. A man and woman may marry after both have passed the period of fertility, and although the family will have a beginning, a life's history, and a death, it cannot go through the usual stages identified in a family life cycle.

It is well to recognize that "family life cycle" is a metaphorical expression that suggests a likeness to the life cycle of the individual organism. It does not demand that all the characteristic features of the one phenomenon be found in the other. By recognizing this we will avoid pushing the analogy too far. It is impossible for a human being to start life mature, but there is nothing pathological or freakish about a family that starts with an older couple, although it is statistically not common. It is evidence of pathology if an individual's growth remains stunted at an immature state, but a married couple that never goes through the childbearing stage does not for this reason constitute an unhealthy, stunted, or pathologically abnormal family.

Family life cycle, although not a literal analogy, is a fitting and useful concept. There is a characteristic way for families to begin and that is with marriage. There are typical or usual stages through which families go, even though deviation from them is no evidence of pathology. Families, once formed, typically enter into a period of growth as children are born and grow older. A contracting stage is reached when the mature children leave the family to begin adult lives of their own. The married pair, if each has managed to escape premature death, are alone together once again. Inevitably one of the pair dies and at this point the family that started with their marriage can be said to have reached the end of its life cycle.

The concept family life cycle provides more than a descriptive identification of families at different periods during their married life. It is, rather, a sociological frame of reference that allows us to identify a changing set of family-life attributes that have a demonstrable effect on individual behavior and interaction within the family. As the family life cycle status shifts, for example, from the early married to the child-rearing stage, the adult family members are required to modify their roles. Whereas once they were only husband and wife, now they are both mates and parents. Different demands are made on the time of each, new skills need to be learned, new attitudes appropriated, and in many other ways the couple's life undergoes significant changes as the family moves on to a new stage in its life cycle. There is more involved for the couple making this family life cycle shift than simply retaining earlier roles and adding new ones. Being a husband to a woman who is also a mother is different from just being a husband. The ways and times of demonstrating affection may have to be changed, the values of companionship and shared activities may have to be re-evaluated, and so on. Family life cycle status is a crucial variable and one that explains to a considerable extent the demands and expectations of family interaction.

The readjustment of roles required when the married pair become parents is but one in a continuing process of changing role demands. There is no reason even to assume that it is the most important or the most drastic shift required. Adequate parents of young children may undergo severe strain as parents of noisy adolescents and even greater strain when, as the children leave, they are in a sense parents no longer. A woman may experience greater difficulty being a wife to a husband in retirement than she experienced at any other time of her married life. Each and every shift in family life cycle status demands a readjustment in each aspect of the roles of all family members. These shifts are necessary if the parents and children are to meet the expectations of one another and to "play the parts" they are expected to play in accordance with the life cycle status of the family.

There is some evidence from research that demonstrates the utility of the family life cycle concept for understanding and predicting human behavior. Family income and spending habits have been found to be related not merely to family size but to the stage of the family cycle as determined by the ages of the youngest and oldest children.[6] Whether or not a wife works outside the home is related not just to the presence or absence of children but to their ages.[7] The role reorganization necessitated by the disruption of a family because of the death of a spouse apparently has a generally adverse effect on personal adjustment in old age.[8] What is more, widowhood status is directly related to self-conceptions of being old and of being treated as old by others in our society.[9] Widowhood status, finally, goes much further in explaining the giving up of home ownership by older people than age alone.[10] Although a gradual leveling off and slight decrease in home ownership has been discovered with respect to increasing age, a pronounced drop has been found among the older people who are widowed. The foregoing are but a few of the specific findings that demonstrate the importance of family life cycle status for understanding many types of behavior.[11]

It is probably already apparent that there is a relationship between age and family life cycle status. Age is not the crucial feature of family life cycle stage, however, even though the two characteristics may compare neatly and progress steadily for many couples. A couple can be at the

[6] John B. Lansing and Leslie Kish, "Family Life Cycle as an Independent Variable," *American Sociological Review*, Vol. 22 (October, 1957), pp. 512-519.

[7] *Ibid.* See also Paul C. Glick, "The Life Cycle of the Family," *Marriage and Family Living*, Vol. 17 (February, 1955), p. 8.

[8] Bernard S. Phillips, "A Role Theory Approach to Adjustment in Old Age," *American Sociological Review*, Vol. 22 (April, 1957), p. 215.

[9] *Ibid.*, pp. 215-216.

[10] Lansing and Kish, *op. cit.*

[11] See also James H. S. Bossard and Eleanor S. Boll, "Marital Unhappiness in the Life Cycle," *Marriage and Family Living*, Vol. 17 (February, 1955), pp. 10-14.

"early married" stage at almost any age, and there can be at least a twenty-five-year difference between two couples each with a young child. For a fairly large span of the typical family life cycle it is convenient to reckon stages in terms of the ages of the children. We speak, for example, of families with young children or of families with adolescents. The fact that a child has lived sixteen years is not nearly as crucial as the fact that in our society the role of adolescent carries with it the responsibility for imminent departure from the family and that this, in turn, requires a reordering of the roles of the parents. It is the roles thrust upon family members by the structure of their family, therefore, that is the essential variable in reckoning the stages of family life cycle.

DEVELOPMENTAL TASKS

From embryology we learn that a living organism begins as a single cell. Through the process of cell division, the single cell becomes many, integrated into a system in which different cells take on specific forms and functions. Normally the development and growth of the human embryo takes place in an orderly fashion with each organ having its time of origin and ascendancy as well as its proper place. Studies of fetal development, both human and non-human, point to the extreme importance of timing in the formation of organs.[12] If the heart, for example, fails to develop at the time prescribed for its rapid growth, it will not be able at a later time to come into dominance and develop fully. It has missed its apportioned time of ascendancy and other biological formations will dominate the latent tendency toward heart development. Not only will the heart be malformed, but the entire cardio-vascular system is likely to be affected by the failure of the heart to develop at its proper time. Fetal development can thus be viewed as a long series of tasks that must be completed, involving the orderly differentiation of cells to take on particular forms and functions and the orderly sequential development of the specialized parts.

Let us shift now to post-natal life and away from the biological sphere to personal and social development. Normal healthy development involves the learning of many things. There are a multitude of tasks that must be accomplished in order for the individual to be considered, and to consider himself, a reasonably successful member of society. These tasks that the individual must learn if he is to achieve self-satisfacton and societal approval have come to be called *developmental tasks*. As Havighurst defines it:[13] "*A developmental task is a task which arises at or about a certain*

[12] John J. B. Morgan, *Child Psychology*, 3rd ed. (New York, Rinehart & Company, Inc., 1942), pp. 39-60.
[13] Robert J. Havighurst, *Developmental Tasks and Education* (Chicago, University of Chicago Press, 1948), p. 6. Copyright 1948 by the University of Chicago.

*period in the life of the individual and successful achievement of which
leads to his happiness and to success with later tasks, while failure leads to
unhappiness in the individual, disapproval by the society, and difficulty
with later tasks."* The parallel between this definition and our brief discussion of biological formation of the embryo is immediately striking. Both
emphasize the factor of timing and in both it is clear that failure to achieve
an appointed task has adverse effects on later development and on the
entire organism. In our further investigation of the nature of developmental
tasks we will use as a point of reference the process of embryonic development.

Nature of Developmental Tasks

The term *task* in the expression *developmental task* conveys the idea
of compulsion or necessity and has the obvious connotation of work. To a
degree both of these connotations are intended and are accurate. A developmental task *is* work in the sense that it involves something that must
be "worked on" or learned. A reflex, like the eye-blink, is not a developmental task. *Task* also seems to imply something that should or almost
has to be done. There is this element of relative compulsion in a developmental task. Various skills, such as walking, reading, and eating with
utensils, have to be learned if an individual is to be considered a normal,
successful member of society. Just as work in the sense of a daily job must
be performed if one desires certain rewards, so the developmental tasks
must be learned or worked on if certain definite end products are desired.

We must be careful not to stress too greatly the compulsive nature
of developmental tasks. Stating that these tasks must be accomplished
does not imply that all of them be done in the same way in every society
or even in the same society. Some few developmental tasks are universal.[14]
Everywhere a normal human is expected to walk upright, and everywhere
it is expected that the normal person has the skill to communicate verbally
with his fellows. Many more developmental tasks take their form and substance from the culture of the society in which the person lives. In some
societies the individual only shortly after puberty is expected to have
learned the role of an adult and to be able to take on the tasks of marriage
and parenthood. In some societies, again, the task of choosing a vocation
can hardly be said to exist or exists only in a rudimentary form. All adults
of one sex are expected to have a certain set of basic skills, and there is
little specialization to be found. In our own society, by contrast, choosing
a life's work is quite a necessary task, made difficult for many by the sheer

---

[14] Cf. Robert J. Havighurst, *Human Development and Education* (New York,
Longmans, Green & Co., Inc., 1953), p. 26.

volume of choices before them. So far we have said that some developmental tasks are everywhere necessary, whereas others are necessary only in some societies, in both instances *necessary* to the end product of a normal, successful, happy member of society.

Even within our own society there is considerable variation in the nature of some, but not all, developmental tasks. Presumably there is a common core of tasks such as learning a general appreciation of such notions as the democratic process and the worth of the individual. The kinds of behavior that are frequently classified as etiquette immediately suggest themselves as illustrative of the variation in the number and nature of developmental tasks. It is not farfetched to state that at some levels of society happiness, self-satisfaction, and success as judged by others demand that the individual master the ritualistic niceties accompanying a formal dinner party. Many in our society escape this task, as well as such other specific ones as learning to interview and hire a butler, knowing what duties are usually assigned to the upstairs maid, or learning the expected role relationship between a man and his chauffeur. Within our society there is great variation in what is involved in the task called "preparing for one's life work." There is variation in the timing of some developmental tasks. At lower status levels, for example, the task of becoming an economically self-sufficient adult must be met at a younger age than at higher status levels. A similar difference exists with regard to preparation for the adult roles accompanying marriage and parenthood. Unlike the tasks implicit in normal embryonic development, the learnings we have called developmental tasks are not all required for everyone within the same society. Even when similar tasks are required, they may come to the fore at different stages of the individual's life cycle.

In the biological development of the fetus, the factor of timing is emphasized. Each organ, as we have pointed out, has its time of ascendancy, and if it fails to develop at its proper time the chances are great that it will be malformed and that the failure will produce adverse effects on the total organism. For some developmental tasks there is likewise a special time in life when accomplishment is required, and there are adverse results if the task is not learned at its appropriate time. Toilet training is one example. Up to a certain age the young child is incapable of developing conscious control over his eliminatory functions. Later, as his sphincter muscles develop, it is time for him to learn to exert conscious control over his bowel movements. Prior to the proper time it is literally impossible to bowel-train a child, although, of course, a mother can train herself to anticipate the child's action and in this way get him to use the toilet most of the time. Attempting to train a child previous to the time allotted

for this task is not only futile but can be an extremely frustrating experience
for the child.[15] Very early in his life he meets with repeated failure and
learns that, in a sense, he has been tried and found wanting by those whose
love he wants and needs.

Less common in our society is the opposite failure of allowing the
teachable moment to pass by without helping the child to gain sphincter
control. Failure to initiate toilet training early enough also can produce a
sense of failure in the child. By a certain age the child seems to internalize
the norms of eliminatory practices, which he has observed among his parents and his young play group. He seems to know what he "should" be
doing even though no one has tried to train him and no one censures him
for his noncomformity. Failure to begin bowel training early enough, furthermore, can make eventual learning of the task more difficult, for as
time goes by the child may find it increasingly difficult to give up the infantile pleasures associated with uncontrolled elimination, even though a
part of him greatly desires to do so. Although there is more leeway than
the expression "teachable moment" may imply, it is nevertheless true that
there is a proper time for accomplishing some developmental tasks, in the
sense of both when society expects it to be done and when the individual
is physically and psychologically ready to accomplish the task.

With some other developmental tasks there is in actuality no teachable moment, for the tasks themselves persist over a large portion of an
individual's lifetime. There is no element of completion in the task of
learning to get along with one's peers. It is a persistent task of group living.
The young child meets it when first he begins to interact meaningfully with
other children, the middle-aged housewife must work out her relationships
with neighbors and friends, and the retired plumber must develop new roles
and new self-concepts in keeping with his withdrawal from the world of
those who daily work their trades. For many decades, to take another example, maintaining a satisfactory affectional relationship with one's spouse
continues to be one of the developmental tasks of the majority of adults.
Although the need for the skills and attitudes arises first at a specified point
in time, it is not a task that can be completed once and for all. It does not
even have the relative finality of the task of choosing a life's occupation.
There may be times in married life when particular strains arise with respect to the couple's affectional relationship, but always there is the need
to evaluate anew one's response patterns, to continue to try to understand
the needs of one's mate, and otherwise to work on the affectional aspects

[15] Cf. the psychoanalytic viewpoint on toilet training and its importance. See
pp. 425-427.

of marriage. There are other instances, as will be shown in the chapters to follow, of recurrent and almost continuous developmental tasks.

A further aspect of the factor of timing in the achievement of developmental tasks has to do with the sequence or order in which some tasks in a series of tasks must be performed. Failure to meet the demands of one stage of development may make it exceedingly difficult to perform the tasks of a later stage. Physical maturation alone, for example, is insufficient to meet the task of learning to run. Before the child can practice running and eventually accomplish this physical skill, which is one usually expected of him, he must have reached at least a certain level of expertness in standing and walking. Skill in the various games of older children, particularly boys, will depend in part on a minimum accomplishment of the task of learning to run. In other areas of life we find a similar orderly progression through what are really a series of related developmental tasks. The success which an adolescent meets in learning attitudes toward sexual behavior appropriate to his stage of life will almost surely have an effect on the ease with which he is able to meet the attitudinal and behavioral tasks associated with his marital sex life. Later, as a parent, the task of helping his children to achieve a wholesome attitude toward sex will be greatly complicated for the person who is experiencing severe frustration or who is deep in the throes of serious sexual conflict. Stage by stage, some developmental tasks build one upon the other. Failure with a task late in a sequence of tasks frequently can be traced to unsuccessful completion of some earlier one.

Classification of Developmental Tasks

The term *task* in the expression *developmental task* may seem at first to be an unnecessarily vague expression. Some such general term is needed, however, to stand for the variety of behaviors, both covert and overt, that are included in our concept. Developmental tasks are sometimes broken down into categories like physical abilities, mental skills, and attitudes. A look at the sorts of behavior that are included in each of these categories will constitute our final attempt in the clarification of the concept.

Physical abilities. Actions or behavior patterns that involve primarily the use of the body, its parts, or its functions are commonly said to require "physical ability." Only those physical abilities in which there is a demonstrable amount of learning could be classified as developmental tasks. Learning to walk is a developmental task, so is learning to play, to climb stairs, and no doubt in many segments of society so is learning to drive an automobile. The ability to see is not a developmental task, but the physical aspects of learning to read most certainly are. Not all learned physical abilities are developmental tasks. Painting a picture in water colors, erecting a scaffolding around a building, and joining two sections of lead pipe are obviously learned, physical abilities. They may be requirements for a job, and at least two in the list could also be skills demanded by one's hobby. But none are developmental tasks in the sense of physical skills that must be acquired in the course of normal, healthy, and satisfactory growth in our society.

Mental skills. A certain level of proficiency in reasoning, computing, evaluating, and in other skills involving primarily the use of the mind is demanded in our society. Failure to come up to the required level in various specific mental skills will most certainly meet with societal disapproval and will complicate the achievement of later developmental tasks. The specific mental skills required of a person before he can be judged by his society as a reasonably adequate person are many and, as would be expected, they increase in level of difficulty as one advances in the stages of life. The young child, even before he is able to talk, is expected to respond to his name and to indicate that he has begun to develop a concept of self, that is, that he has begun to separate himself from all of the non-selves in the world about him. Soon he is expected to associate names with various objects about the home, to remember these names, and to use them correctly. He is expected later to understand the difference between fantasy of his own creation and the real world in which he lives. Later comes the necessity for learning simple arithmetic computations and still later the requirement for a minimum level of abstract thinking. Meanwhile he is supposed to be learning and remembering a whole body of "facts" about the society and the world in which he lives, to be amassing, in other words, the body of so-called "everyday knowledge." The foregoing examples of specific mental skills should serve to illustrate the rather wide range of intellectual activity that is included in this category and the differences in this particular kind of task at different stages of development. Any mental skill that can be said to be required in order for an individual to be considered a normal member of society would fall within our designation of developmental task.

Attitudes. An attitude is defined as a readiness or a predisposition to act. All attitudes are learned. There are some attitudes or orientations toward people, objects, situations, or even self that are considered appropriate at one or another stage of life. There are attitudes toward an adult that a child should have if he is to be considered a satisfactory child, and adequate parents should exhibit certain attitudes toward children. These are the sorts of attitudes that are also developmental tasks.

It is easy enough to see that becoming married necessitates the learning of new skills. There are communication problems to be worked out, the sharing of physical facilities to be arranged, and the common plans to be formed. Each of these and other activities of married life is accompanied by, and to some extent dependent on, certain feeling states or attitudes. As difficult as it may be to spell them out, there are attitudes that should be incorporated into the personality of every married person if he is to be successful in his marriage. A feeling of being married should come about, an appropriate mental set toward in-laws needs to be developed, and there is an acceptance of the mate's personal idiosyncrasies that must be learned. An acceptable older person, to take a different example, is one who has developed new ways of looking at leisure, feels differently from the young person about physical prowess, and so on. In short, the "thinkings and feelings" that make for a good adjustment at a given stage of development and serve as satisfactory bases for continued development are the sorts of attitudes we would consider developmental tasks.

DEVELOPMENTAL TASKS AND THE FAMILY LIFE CYCLE

A meaningful analysis of family interaction can be built around the simultaneous application of the pivotal concepts "family life cycle" and "developmental tasks." One way, in other words, to get inside the family group and to understand its mechanics is to study the developmental tasks of each family member at the various times in the family life cycle. In striving to accomplish his developmental tasks, each family member is in repetitive interaction with all other members, each of them striving to accomplish his own tasks. Each member of the family is thus seen as an individual, but none is viewed in isolation. The dynamics both of the individual and the family become evident.

The accomplishment of developmental tasks at the different stages of the family life cycle should not be looked upon as an all-or-none proposition. Indeed, there would be some merit in speaking of developmental strivings instead of developmental tasks, for the former expression conveys the idea of aiming toward and approaching a goal rather than fully achieving it. The demands for new learnings by family members have a way, sometimes, of following one another with swiftness and persistence.[16] It is no wonder that seldom in the life cycle of any family are all of its members "caught up with themselves" and with what is required of them. Knowing the

[16] Cf. Evelyn M. Duvall, *Family Development* (Philadelphia, J. B. Lippincott Company, 1957), pp. 110-113.

developmental demands placed on family members at the different stages of the life cycle of the group allows us to evaluate the family in a relative rather than in an absolute manner. The better equipped a family is for each of its members to meet his developmental tasks and the closer each comes to accomplishing them, the more successful is the family.

Living means changing. No family or individual is exactly the same one day as it was the one previous. For purposes of study, it is useful to divide the ever-changing cycle of the family with its accompanying ever-changing demands on its members into a number of periods or stages. The division system we will employ is based primarily on the times in the family life cycle when major new role learnings are first necessitated. Accordingly, our investigation will center around the family at the following periods of development: (1) the married-pair stage, (2) the child-rearing stage, (3) the middle years of family life, and (4) the later years of family life.

It should be clear that the continuous cycle of family living could be divided in many ways. No system, furthermore, is completely adequate, for none can take cognizance of the differences among families due to the varying ages at which couples marry, the different intervals between marriage and the arrival of the first child, the different number of children eventually born, and so on.[17] It is defensible to reckon the phase in the family life cycle by the stage of development of the oldest child, for many of the reorganizations of roles in the family first are required by his development. Realistically, of course, many families that grow into a new phase with their oldest child remain also at previous stages with other children. Regardless of the number of stages into which the family cycle is divided and despite the overlapping of family cycle stages, the unique utility of the family life cycle concept will be realized if the dynamic continuity of family living is recognized.

SELECTED READINGS

Bossard, James H. S., and Boll, Eleanor S., "Marital Unhappiness in the Life Cycle," *Marriage and Family Living*, Vol. 17 (February, 1955), pp. 10-14.

Duvall, Evelyn, *Family Development* (Philadelphia, J. B. Lippincott Company, 1957), Chs. 1 and 5.

———, "Implications for Education through the Family Life Cycle," *Marriage and Family Living*, Vol. 20 (November, 1958), pp. 334-342.

Glick, Paul C., "The Family Cycle," *American Sociological Review*, Vol. 12 (April, 1947), pp. 164-174.

[17] Duvall, *op. cit.*, pp. 6-10.

————, "The Life Cycle of the Family," *Marriage and Family Living*, Vol. 17 (February, 1955), pp. 3-9.

HAVIGHURST, ROBERT J., *Developmental Tasks and Education* (Chicago, University of Chicago Press, 1948).

————, *Human Development and Education* (New York, Longmans, Green & Co., Inc., 1953).

LANSING, JOHN B., and KISH, LESLIE, "Family Life Cycle as an Independent Variable," *American Sociological Review*, Vol. 22 (October, 1957), pp. 512-519.

PHILLIPS, BERNARD S., "A Role Theory Approach to Adjustment in Old Age," *American Sociological Review*, Vol. 22 (April, 1957), pp. 212-217.

STOTT, LELAND H., "The Longitudinal Approach to the Study of Family Life," *Journal of Home Economics*, Vol. 46 (February, 1954), pp. 79-82.

CHAPTER 15

Developmental Tasks of the Married Pair

THE FIRST STAGE of the family life cycle, which begins with the marriage of the pair, is for many couples a happy, carefree period. Youth, health, and vigor are generally on their side. The longings and desires of engagement can now find fulfillment, and the busy years of babies are not yet upon them. At the same time, there is ample evidence that many couples find the early years of marriage anything but rewarding.[1] Fully half of all divorces occur within the first five years of marriage. Thus the alienation and growing apart began not long after marriage.[2] Of all divorces, about half are granted to childless couples, many of whom perforce have not been married long. What makes this difference in the experiences of the early married years? There is no simple answer to the question, but part of it can be found by understanding the developmental tasks facing couples at this stage of the family life cycle and the demands these tasks place on marriage partners.

There are many complex developmental tasks that arise for the first time at the early-married stage. In a very real sense it is unwise to rank them in any order of importance, for successful and happy marriage demands that they all be met, at least to some degree. A partial list of these tasks would be the following:[3]

1. Developing competency in decision making.

---

[1] This is not to say that the early years of marriage are necessarily the most critical ones. For those whose marriage does not end in divorce, there is some indication that the peak of marital unhappiness comes at a later stage. See James H. Bossard and Eleanor S. Boll, "Marital Unhappiness in the Life Cycle," *Marriage and Family Living*, Vol. 17 (February, 1955), pp. 10-14.

[2] See Paul H. Jacobson, "Differentials in Divorce by Duration of Marriage and Size of Family," *American Sociological Review*, Vol. 15 (April, 1950), pp. 235-244.

[3] Compare our list of developmental tasks with those of Duvall. See Evelyn M. Duvall, *Family Development* (Philadelphia, J. B. Lippincott Company, 1957), p. 128. See also the discussion of this stage of the family life cycle in Evelyn M. Duvall and Reuben Hill, eds., *Report of the Committee on Dynamics of Family Interaction* (National Conference on Family Life, Inc., 1948). (Mimeographed.)

2. Working out mutually satisfying and realistic systems for getting and spending the family income.
3. Achieving a satisfactory sexual relationship.
4. Developing a readiness for parenthood.
5. Achieving and enjoying the status of "married" in the community and among friends and relatives.
6. Developing ways of expressing and accommodating differences creatively.
7. Developing satisfactory relationships with relatives, particularly husband's and wife's parents.
8. Learning the co-operation required in intimate pair living.
9. Working out satisfactory household routines and schedules that facilitate smooth functioning in the world of work and pleasure.

We have selected the first four developmental tasks from the above list for further analysis. For each of the four task areas we will attempt to do three things: (1) to describe the nature of the task, that is, what exactly is required with respect to the learnings of attitudes or skills, (2) to comment on the importance of the specific task in the total marriage relationship, and (3) to discuss the common sources of difficulty in achieving the developmental task. A more thorough understanding of the early marriage stage would demand that this sort of analysis be carried out for each developmental task that arises at this stage of the family life cycle.

DEVELOPING COMPETENCY IN DECISION MAKING

Everyone comes to marriage with some practice in decision making. Most people probably have had some experience in group decision making, whether as children and young adults in their families or in some other situation. Some even have had extensive experience in family decision making. Beginning with early childhood they have had a part, in keeping with their abilities, in reaching decisions that affected the entire family group. Individuals thus differ widely in the nature and extent of the experience in decision making that they bring with them to marriage. Regardless of their preparation, they face a common task when they enter the first stage of the family life cycle; they need to learn a system of decision making that is satisfactory to both of them and that is good for each of them and for the marriage. This is a complex developmental task and, like so many others occurring at the early stage, the degree to which it is accomplished is important throughout the life cycle of the family.

It is useful to distinguish three distinct aspects of family decision making: (1) the content, or what is decided, (2) the process, or how decisions are reached, and (3) the roles assumed by husband and wife in the decision-making process.

The first aspect is concerned with the nature of the solution to a problem or the course of action decided upon by the couple. Families differ widely with regard to the "wisdom" or "rationality" of their choices. The only meaningful evaluation of the content of family decisions is that which is made within the context of the goals and values of the particular family. As we will indicate in our discussion of spending decisions, there is no reason why families have to allocate their financial resources in a certain prescribed manner. It may be very wise for a specific family to spend considerably more than most families on food, for another to spend less on recreation, or for a third to allocate a large portion of its income to housing. These and a host of other decisions that so obviously affect the family must be judged against the wants and needs of the family, most of which are not vital in any ultimate sense but depend on the hierarchy of values of the particular family. Perhaps the crucial developmental task in this instance is the recognition of the fact that, in many areas of life, worth and importance are relative attributes which derive their meaning from the individual. The corollary to the idea of relative worth should be a greater willingness to accept divergent values and systems of values. Such acceptances do not immediately solve all of the problems of the young married couple, but they should facilitate reaching a common decision on the allocation of time, money, and other family resources.

The second aspect of family decision making we have labeled *process*. This has to do with the procedure or strategy that a family uses in order to reach a decision. Fifty years ago John Dewey spelled out what he termed the "steps in problem solving" to explain the cognitive process an individual goes through in solving a problem or making a decision.[4] The years have seen many adaptations of Dewey's phases of problem solving to such special areas as family decision making and farmers' decisions to adopt new agricultural ideas.[5] In essence each describes the kind of thought process that takes place from the stage where it is recognized that

[4] John Dewey, *How We Think* (New York, D. C. Heath & Company, 1910), pp. 72 ff.
[5] See Orville G. Brim, Jr., David C. Glass, and David E. Lavin, "Child Rearing Decisions by Husbands and Wives" (paper presented at annual meeting of the American Sociological Society, 1958). See also George M. Beal and Joe M. Bohlen, *How Farm People Accept New Ideas* (Ames, Iowa, Agricultural Extension Service, Special Report 15, November, 1955).

a decision is necessary to the stage where a course of action is selected. A typical scheme of the stages of decision making would be as follows:

1. Recognizing and clarifying the decision that has to be made.
2. Exploring and evaluating alternative courses of action.
3. Choosing and carrying out a course of action.
4. Evaluating the course of action in the light of intended results.

It is feasible to think of evaluating couples in terms of the rationality of their decision-making process. Just as some ways of searching for a lost object in a field are more sensible than others, so some methods of decision making are superior to others. How couples make decisions could be judged against such criteria as the likelihood of reaching a decision when it is possible to do so, the efficiency of the system, or the couple's satisfaction with decisions that are reached. It would seem to be more rational or logical for a couple to attempt to exhaust and to explore the possible alternatives of action before choosing one. Appraising the decided-upon course of action in the light of intended purposes would seem to be a rational follow-up to decision making. Thus we can consider a developmental task the acquisition and use of a rational system for making choices and solving problems. Although some couples find it helpful to make the process explicit, even to the point of listing goals and developing written lists of alternatives, others find this too burdensome or unnecessary. The use of some rational and efficient system of decision making, however, is a valuable skill to develop and practice at the early stage of the family life cycle.[6]

The decision-making process we have outlined is used by individuals as well as by couples or other groups. The third aspect of family decision making is concerned with the roles that are taken by family members in reaching decisions that have an effect on the family as a whole. In a given family, for example, the father may determine almost alone how the family income is to be spent, whereas in another the mother may decide where and when the family is to spend its vacation. In both instances, the decision affecting the family may be quite rational. If in investigating alternatives the wishes of the other members were somehow accurately assessed, there is good possibility that all would be satisfied with the family decision made by one member.

Although families differ considerably in the roles taken by their members in reaching decisions affecting the group, there has come to be a "preferred" method of family decision making. For want of a better term, we can call it "democratic family decision making." The essence

[6] See also Blood's discussion of problem-solving methods and the seven-stage scheme suggested by him in Robert O. Blood, *Anticipating Your Marriage* (Glencoe, Illinois, The Free Press, 1955), pp. 225-250.

of this process is that all members of the family group enter into various phases of the decision-making process in keeping with their abilities to do so. If we restrict our illustrations to the married pair, in democratic decision making it would not be assumed that either husband or wife had some inherent right to greater influence or was necessarily more skillful than the other. Democratic decision making does not imply equality in performance. Perhaps in one situation the husband is more skillful at suggesting alternatives, whereas the wife is better able to evaluate the consequences of the suggested lines of action. In another situation their roles may be reversed or they may show similar skill in these areas but differ in their ability to state the problem. To the extent that the value of democracy is reflected in family decision making, there would be lack of rigid role assignments in joint problem-solving tasks. Although experience in this type of decision making should increase each of the pair's competence, there may nevertheless remain types of decisions or phases of the decision-making process in which one or the other exhibits the greater skill.

Many couples entering marriage are unprepared to practice democratic family decision making. Probably the most common source of difficulty in achieving it is the tradition of authoritarian decision making which holds that each spouse must hold himself to certain spheres of activity and that the man has an inherent right to "final say" in matters affecting the couple. Role differentiation in decision making, in this tradition, rests not on the skill or knowledge of the participants but proceeds along established lines reflecting the status of the family members. Individuals coming to marriage may have experienced this type of decision making in their own families, or for other reasons they may be more comfortable in traditional family roles.[7] A case can be made, however, for the conclusion that it is good for most couples to practice democratic decision making. This implies a common allegiance to certain values. It assumes that personality growth, in particular an increasing ability in judgment and a greater creative skill, is worth while for the husband, for the wife, and, at later stages of the family life cycle, for the children. The case for democratic family decision making is strengthened by recognition of the fact that the skills required are increasingly expected, in our society, in non-family situations.[8] The matter could

---

[7] For an indication of the extent to which a sample of married college students operated in traditional roles in decision making, see William F. Kenkel and Dean K. Hoffman, "Real and Conceived Roles in Family Decision Making," *Marriage and Family Living*, Vol. 18 (November, 1956), pp. 311-316.

[8] For some broader implications of the desirability for skill in decision making and related tasks, see Nelson N. Foote and Leonard S. Cottrell, Jr., *Identity and Interpersonal Competence* (Chicago, University of Chicago Press, 1955), particularly Chs. 2 and 5.

be put like this: given the kind of societal expectations for individuals, both within and outside of the family, and assuming the value of certain personality traits, democratic family decision making shows promise of being the most appropriate system for today's family. If research bears out the posited relationship between personality growth and experience in democratic decision making, then we would conclude that developing competency in democratic decision making is an important developmental task facing the young married couple.

GETTING AND SPENDING THE FAMILY INCOME

Regardless of lofty expressions about the best things of life being free, in modern-day America many of the essentials of life cost money. Barring unusual times or circumstances, a successful family in the eyes of the community is expected to acquire sufficient money and to use it with sufficient wisdom to provide the essentials of life. More than this is required. Certain comforts in the home, adequacies of dress, and so on, all are considered necessary for a "decent" standard of living. Still further economic demands are placed on those who aspire to be accepted at the higher levels of society. No family wholly escapes the tasks connected with getting and spending resources, and these tasks begin at the time of marriage and are never actually completed.

There are several lines of evidence that point to the importance of learning the developmental tasks associated with getting and spending money. Some, but not all, studies of marital happiness have found a relationship between general marital harmony and various economic factors. Terman, for example, found that 56.3 per cent of husbands and 50.6 per cent of wives with low happiness scores, as opposed to 22.0 per cent and 17.8 per cent of those with high scores, cited insufficient income as a definite source of unhappiness.[9] Since the amount of income was *not* found to be related to marital happiness,[10] it appears that the happy and unhappy couples must have reacted differently to similar amounts of income. This observation is borne out by Locke, who found that a larger proportion of divorced than happily married women felt that their income was inadequate to meet the economic needs of the family.[11] Divorced women showed a general tendency to devalue the economic

[9] Lewis M. Terman and others, *Psychological Factors in Marital Happiness* (New York, McGraw-Hill Book Company, Inc., 1938), pp. 85 and 87.
[10] *Ibid.*, pp. 169 ff.
[11] Harvey J. Locke, *Predicting Adjustment in Marriage* (New York, Henry Holt & Co., Inc., 1951), p. 280.

ability of their husbands, fully half of them rating the ex-husband's efforts as unsatisfactory or very unsatisfactory.[12] In some cases this was probably an accurate description of the husband's attempts to earn a living, in others it probably tells less about the man's efforts than it does about the woman's wants. Both instances, however, illustrate the relationship between economic problems and marital unhappiness. A recent analysis of the cases of a marriage counseling clinic discovered that economic problems were evident in 79 per cent of the families.[13] Next to sexual relations, Landis found that spending the family income was the most common area in which couples had problems of adjustment.[14] Bit by bit, the evidence has accumulated to substantiate the point that the broad area of getting and spending the family income is an important aspect of family life. Failure to learn the developmental tasks associated with this area can have immediate adverse effects on the happiness of the couple and ramifications for the later tasks they will meet as they progress through the family life cycle. In the following section we will deal separately with the developmental tasks associated with getting the family income and those associated with spending it.

Developmental Tasks Associated with Acquiring Income

In almost all families it is expected that the husband will furnish at least a substantial part of the family income. An important developmental learning facing most husbands, therefore, is the full acceptance of the idea that he is, and will continue to be, responsible for a major portion or all of the family support. Ideas he has of advancing in his occupation, of changing jobs, or of furthering his training or education for a better position, all must somehow be reconciled with the family responsibility he has assumed at the time of marriage. The young husband, too, must come to grips with the realities of his occupation as they affect his marital roles and married life. Jobs and occupations make varying demands in terms of the hours of work required, the necessity for changing location periodically or for traveling, and the regularity of employment. Many of these things must be accepted, but there is frequently some possibility of modifying the demands. The young physician, for example, can limit his practice to a particular field or he can enter into a group-practice arrangement if he wants to modify to some extent the

[12] *Ibid.*, p. 286.
[13] John R. Cavanaugh, *Fundamental Marriage Counseling* (Milwaukee, Bruce Publishing Company, 1957), p. 420.
[14] Judson T. Landis, "Adjustments after Marriage," *Marriage and Family Living,* Vol. 9 (May, 1947), p. 33.

demands of his profession for long and irregular hours. The electrician can seek employment in industry if he wishes to get away from seasonal peaks and low points still found in the building trades. The point is that the young husband must recognize the demands of his job and decide which he will accept and which he will attempt to modify. The income features of his job, both in terms of the present remuneration and the potential, need now to be evaluated in terms of *family* income. Many will find it necessary to accept and to adjust to the limitations of the income, however great they may be, but in some cases it is realistic to consider basic changes in the way in which to support the family. The rewards and demands of a man's job affect in so many ways his total way of life. The task facing the young husband, therefore, is to relate these aspects of his job to his married life. We are not implying that every husband will be forced to make stoic choices between "love" and "duty," but rather that there must be a certain amount of acceptance of the realities of the workaday world.

There are certain developmental learnings facing the young wife which relate to the way in which her husband performs his role as income provider. In some respects her learnings are more difficult than those of her husband, for frequently she must learn to accept and to adjust, with no possibility of modifying her husband's job arrangements. She must learn to live comfortably with the fact that her husband's ability, training, and even personality needs place definite limitations on the kind of work he can do and hence on his present and potential earnings. The alternative to this kind of acceptance is a lifetime of futile nagging at him to be "like other husbands" or to give up his chosen career for "something really worth while," or hostile accusations about his disregard for his family because he chooses to remain in a job that requires traveling or night work or whatever else fails to conform to her conception of what some vague group of "other men" do for a living. Just as the young husband must begin to see his job in relation to his marriage and to the needs of his wife, so the young wife must learn to accept those relatively unmodifiable demands of her husband's job and the style of living it affords them.

Full acceptance of the realities of the husband's occupation does not mean, in these times, that the young couple must consider the husband's earnings coterminus with family income. Increasingly, families are adding to their total income through the full or part-time, temporary or more or less permanent, employment of the wife. Changing conditions of American society have thus created a new developmental task.

A few generations ago hardly any married couple was really faced with the task of deciding whether or not the wife would seek employment outside the home. It was well understood that "woman's place was in the home" and that was that. A mere 5.6 per cent of all married women held jobs in 1900.[15] Today, by contrast, fully 30 per cent of all married women work outside the home. The proportion of working wives is even higher at the stage of the family life cycle with which we are dealing—just about 57 per cent of all young wives without children are in the labor force. As shown in Table 44, the employment status of the wife shifts with changes in family life cycle status. Married women tend to drop out of the labor force while there are young children at home, but many return after their youngest child is in school. The pronounced increase in the proportion of employed married women, the very high percentage of working wives at the early stage of the family cycle, and the relatively high proportion at later stages, all point to the fact that the reaching of a mutually acceptable decision on the wife's employment constitutes a new developmental task for young married couples today. Unsuccessful completion of this task could have not only immediate effects but could make for difficulties at later stages of the family cycle. It may well be, for example, that the failure of the wife to work after marriage and before there are children may effectively reduce her chances of employment after the children are in school or grown. This does not mean that all brides should seek employment, but it does mean that the decision whether to or not can have far-reaching implications.[16]

TABLE 44. Employment of Married Women at Different Stages in the Family Life Cycle

Stage in Family Life Cycle	Percentage of Working Wives
Early married, no children	57.2
Child rearing, youngest child under 6 years	21.0
Child rearing, youngest child over 6 years	39.6
Middle and later years	27.1

SOURCE: Adapted from John B. Lansing and Leslie Kish, "Family Life Cycle as an Independent Variable," *American Sociological Review*, Vol. 22 (October, 1957), p. 514.

[15] For number and per cent of married women workers in the years from 1900 to 1954, assembled from Census reports, see John F. Cuber, Robert A. Harper, and William F. Kenkel, *Problems of American Society*, 3rd ed. (New York, Henry Holt & Co., Inc., 1956), p. 355.

[16] For some of these implications, see Alva Myrdal and Viola Klein, *Women's Two Roles* (London, Routledge and Kegan Paul, 1956).

There are many factors that make it difficult for young husbands and wives to reach a satisfactory decision on the wife's employment and still others that make it hard to live with the decision once it is reached. The difference between making and living with a decision is largely the reason for including this task at the young-married stage. Although, increasingly, engaged couples reach a conclusion on the woman's postmarital employment, and there is every good reason why they should do so, only the married have the opportunity to act out the decision and discover its implications.

Employment of the wife can be thought of as making certain demands on and requiring certain learnings of both the husband and the wife. It is up to the couple to be realistic about these demands and requirements in their attempts to reach a decision on the issue. For optimum adjustment to the wife's employment, the husband, first of all, must be able emotionally to accept the idea of the wife's work.[17] Some husbands find it no threat to their masculinity or their feeling of self-worth to admit to themselves and others that they are not the sole providers for the family. Others can scarcely harbor such a thought without exhibiting symptoms of near-panic. To them, such a recognition is tantamount to an admission of failure. It strikes at the core of their masculinity and the more the wife earns the less a "real man" they feel. The majority of men probably fall between the two extremes. Their society has fairly well conditioned them to prefer that husbands and wives remain in their traditional roles, but there are no deep-seated emotional blockings to relearning. Even when the decision on the wife's employment takes into account the emotional make-up of the husband, the decision itself is far from easy. Few would agree that destruction of the husband's self-confidence is worth the financial rewards of the wife's work. It is no wiser to bargain away the wife's personal development, her opportunity for self-expression, or her confidence, to preserve a private definition of masculinity that excludes women from economic pursuits. Discovering what is best for the husband, the wife, and the marriage describes the true nature of the task facing the young married couple.

The developmental tasks facing the employed wife parallel those of her husband. Can she earn as much or more money than her husband and think no less of him as a man and a husband and, for that matter, no less of herself as a woman? Is she emotionally able to trust her and her husband's decision in the face of possible criticism from parents, friends,

[17] See Artie Gianopulos and Howard E. Mitchell, "Marital Disagreement as a Function of Husband's Attitude Toward Wife's Employment," *Marriage and Family Living*, Vol. 19 (November, 1957), pp. 373-378.

or neighbors? It is not uncommon for working wives to report that the "admiration" and "praise" expressed by others can have a none-too-subtle sting. Can the wife, finally, make the adjustments required of her if she is to perform successfully her dual role? It may well be necessary, for example, for her to change her standards of housekeeping perfection and to relinquish some household tasks to her husband. The working wife may have to accept a curtailment of social activity. Both partners being in the labor force can make for a "killing pace" for both husband and wife, or it can be a challenge to be accepted generously and worked on with intelligence. Although the type of work both do is important, much also depends on the attitudes they bring to marriage and the flexibility they can muster in meeting the demands of the situation.

Developmental Tasks Associated with Spending the Family Income

The new learnings required of husband and wife for the tasks of developing a satisfactory system of spending the family income can be every bit as difficult as those connected with earning it.[18] There are many good systems of spending money, and there are also many poor systems. The essential feature of the kind of system we would label "good" is the acceptability of the system to the couple. Not many families are at a bare subsistence level of living. Conflict, discontent, and unhappiness, when they occur, center around the larger portion of the income that can be spent for things other than the necessities.

As unusual as it may at first sound, one of the chief lessons for the young couple to learn is that their family income is theirs, to be spent on the items they wish, decided upon in the manner most acceptable to them. Pressures to do otherwise are many, and sometimes they are difficult to resist. The advice and standards of parents, friends, and relatives play more of a role than is frequently realized and may have a greater influence on the couple than either would like to admit. There is an abundance of books and charts setting forth norms and averages of family expenditures. It is one thing for a young couple to use this information as a guide or as a means of learning more about the relative cost of the components of the cost of living. It is quite another to develop a sort of slavish worship of average percentages and conclude that it is somehow "wrong" to spend more on food or less on clothes than does the statistical myth of an average family. Nor can we ignore the sort of high-pressure advertising and selling that seems determined to get people to buy things

[18] A general treatment of this topic can be found in Irma Gross and E. W. Crandall, *Management for Modern Families* (New York, Appleton-Century-Crofts, Inc., 1954).

that they do not really want at prices they cannot afford to pay. Some couples seem to find themselves perennially enmeshed in a web of pressures to spend their money, and this is reflected in the financial condition of their marriage. Others, at all but the lowest income levels, claim that the important needs and wants of their family are usually satisfied and the process of balancing out-go with in-come is neither terrifying nor terribly painful. This is the difference between learning and failing to learn the developmental tasks associated with a satisfactory system of spending the family income.

ACHIEVING A SATISFACTORY SEXUAL ADJUSTMENT

It has been said that although some things in this world are more wonderful than sexual intercourse, there is nothing *exactly like* it. This same statement, of course, could be made about popcorn, a *very* dry martini, and a trip down the Grand Canyon on muleback. But the original statement was not meant entirely facetiously. It implies that there are different tastes in sexual experience and also that there is room for personal judgment on the importance of sex in marriage. These are essential points to keep in mind throughout our discussion of the developmental task we have called "achieving a satisfactory sexual adjustment."

The Importance of Sex in Marriage

It is easy to take an extreme view of the importance of sexual relations in marriage. There are those who practically equate sexual intercourse with the whole of married life, and there are others who greatly devalue sexual experience by overstressing the "many, many other things" that are important in the typical marriage. As in so many cases, right and accuracy are not entirely on either side of the issue. The sexual side of marriage *is* important. There is many a couple who find it a richly satisfying and rewarding part of marriage and the ultimate in the expression of mutual love. Grief and sorrow, trial and pain, are all part of life, and married life is no exception. Happiness, love, and pleasure are also part of life, and it is on this side of the emotional ledger that a satisfying sexual relationship falls. This is at least partly what is meant when couples, in the face of tribulations, somewhat stoically proclaim, "At least we have each other." If they really do have each other, in the sense of being partners to a pleasant sex life full of lively satisfaction, such a couple has very much indeed.

As enjoyable as the sexual side of marriage can be, marriage is not all sex, and certainly not all of the happiness in marriage comes from sex fulfillment. There is the bond of love between the couple which, while it includes the sexual attraction, goes far beyond it. In well-matched couples there is the kind of sharing of inner thoughts and ambitions that can take place only between those who accept and care very much for one another. There is enjoyment in planning and dreaming and the reward that comes from mutual effort, even if the goals themselves are never reached. These things, and many others, are important in married life. To recognize that there are other extremely satisfying facets of marriage, however, is not to discredit sex. A satisfactory sexual relationship between a man and wife is one, but only one, of the rewarding aspects of marriage.[19] It is worth striving to achieve.

One way of estimating the importance of sex in marriage is through the studies of the relationship between sexual satisfaction in marriage and the total outlook of marriage happiness. Psychiatrists, marriage counselors, and other clinicians regularly report a high incidence of sexual complaints among people with marital difficulties.[20] What is more, in a rather high number of divorce actions sexual maladjustments are specifically mentioned, suprisingly so since one would expect couples to stick to more stereotyped, conventional grounds in the legal appeal.[21] In some, probably even many, cases serious complaints in other areas of marriage produce dissatisfaction in a sexual life that previously had been adequate. In other cases, some common situation brought about dissatisfaction in several areas of married life, among them the sexual life of the couple. There are some cases, however, in which cause and effect are reversed, and the basic incompatibility in marriage is the sexual one. What is more, the other cases we have mentioned at least seem to indicate that sex is a peculiarly sensitive barometer of marital adjustment. Whether the sexual relationship more frequently produces or reflects a change in the emotional state

[19] Perhaps no better discussion of the role of sexual relations in marriage and the nature of a satisfactory sexual adjustment can be found than Levy and Munroe's. See John Levy and Ruth Munroe, *The Happy Family* (New York, Alfred A. Knopf, Inc., 1938), pp. 108 ff.

[20] See, for example, the various cases referred to in Edmund Bergler, *Divorce Won't Help* (New York, Harper & Brothers, 1948), and Victor Eisenstein, ed., *Neurotic Interaction in Marriage* (New York, Basic Books, Inc., 1956).

[21] William M. Kephart, "Some Variables in Cases of Reported Sexual Maladjustment," *Marriage and Family Living*, Vol. 16 (August, 1954), pp. 241-243. See also Harry C. Harmsworth and Mhyra Minnis, "Non-Statutory Causes of Divorce: The Lawyer's Point of View," *Marriage and Family Living*, Vol. 17 (November, 1955), pp. 316-321.

of marriage is difficult to determine. Both possibilities demonstrate clearly the very real importance of the sexual side of marriage.

The Developmental Tasks in Achieving a Satisfactory Sexual Adjustment

Some no doubt would object to the word *satisfactory* in our label of this developmental task. Satisfaction always implies a balance between what is expected and what is achieved. Satisfaction can be reached either by getting what you want or by learning to want what you happen to get. It is what the poet means when he says that a man who is poor and content is rich, and rich enough. We used the word *satisfactory* advisedly, for in so many respects it is impossible to describe a "good" or "adequate" or "successful" sexual life without reference to the specific pair and their needs and wishes. Indeed, we would go as far as to say that the learning of the highly individualized nature of a good sexual relationship constitutes an extremely important developmental task of the newly married couple. The very nature of a satisfactory sexual adjustment would seem to demand that some husbands and wives learn to discard earlier notions and preconceived ideas about what is "normal" or "average" or "right." Among couples who report a good sexual adjustment, great variation is found not only with respect to frequency of intercourse but with regard to a preference for darkness or light, time of day at which intercourse takes place, and other specifics of their sexual life. Variation is also reported with respect to the emotional tone of marital intercourse. At times, the sexual act will be a soul-reaching emotional experience bringing forth deeper and more intense passions than either thought possible and leaving them in a state of ecstatic euphoria that only slowly abates to pleasantness and a sense of well-being. Just as surely will many well-adjusted couples experience times when the pleasure level of sexual intercourse is routine and when they obtain a physical relief with no deep psychological meaning to either of them. There will be times, too, when their sexual relations will have an air of gaiety and playfulness expressed in teasing, in mock seduction, or in some other way a couple in the mood for fun will invent. All of this the well-adjusted couple is able to accept. Their sexual life is good even though there will be occasions when the desires and needs of one fail utterly to coincide with those of the other. They have learned the flexibility of outlook that facilitates the working out of a satisfactory sexual life. They have learned to accept that what they find good is good for them. They have learned how to communicate to one another enough of their feelings to allow them to discover what will make for them a satisfactory sexual life. The developmental learnings associated with achieving a satisfactory sexual adjustment are many, and they are among the most difficult adjustments required of a young married couple.

Factors Interfering with Good Sexual Adjustment

Failure to achieve a satisfactory sexual adjustment is as much an individual matter as a successful adjustment. Almost anything can bring disharmony into the sexual life of a couple. Dissatisfactions in other areas of married life, such as great disappointments in the spouse in roles not primarily sexual, are almost sure to be reflected in the sexual relationship. The particular experiences of the couple may lie at the root of their sexual difficulties, for example, the inability of one or both to forgive premarital indiscretions. A partner may have revealed his indiscretions in a desperate effort to relieve guilt or in the hope that revelation would somehow bring the pair together, only to find that an irrevocable barrier to intimacy has been raised. Although these particular experiences and others are not at all uncommon, they are highly unique to the couple and are not the sort of general obstacles to sexual adjustment that require attention here.

Sheer ignorance must be labeled one of the causes of sexual difficulties. In these days when sex education is considered a sort of panacea to various human ills from divorce to delinquency, it is difficult to imagine how much ignorance still abounds.[22] Much which passes for sex education, it seems, is restricted almost exclusively to the cold physiological facts of reproduction and the intricacies of sexual anatomy.[23] No one has ever demonstrated, of course, that there is any causal relationship between the ability to label the parts of the male sex organ in cross-section and a satisfactory sexual adjustment in marriage. Well primed with physiological facts, many women still enter marriage woefully ignorant of the psychology of the male and attribute to all men the emotional depth of a forest wolf. Men, on their part, are equally naïve about the sexual make-up of women. The same man who has an adequate knowledge of reproduction may never learn, or learn only with difficulty, that women are capable of strong sexual passion or that it is scarcely reasonable to judge a woman "wanton" because she makes obvious sexual advances to her own husband! Possibly because they have had some sex education, men and women

---

[22] A crude estimate of the amount of ignorance and unanswered questions in this area can be made from the discovery that 87 per cent of the letters to a newspaper "advice column" showed a need for sex information other than birth control. See Christine H. Hillman, "An Advice Column's Challenge for Family-Life Education," *Marriage and Family Living*, Vol. 16 (February, 1954), pp. 51-54.

[23] Robert A. Harper and Frances Harper, "Are Educators Afraid of Sex?," *The Humanist*, Vol. 16 (May-June, 1956), pp. 122-128.

delude themselves into believing that they know all about sex and proceed confidently to act out their ignorance in marriage.

A particular obstacle to good sexual adjustment in marriage is the concern couples have about the normality of their sexual life.[24] Some, frankly, expect too much too soon and quickly conclude that either the wife is frigid or the man inadequate if sexual intercourse does not unfailingly lift them to the dizzy heights of gods. Others have fairly well committed to memory a so-called sex manual and despair because they do not have intercourse as frequently as the "average" couple or because they do not enjoy the intricate positions for intercourse so vividly portrayed. Some couples do enjoy a certain variation in their sexual life, and some regularly prefer less usual positions and circumstances in expressing their sexual love. These couples are normal, and so are those who cannot mix sex and acrobatics or who simply do not enjoy turning their marital couch into a miniature gymnasium.

A large number of people worry about normality with regard to the female orgasm. With the realization that women are capable of full sexual release has come a change in the definition of virility.[25] Where once a man was considered virile if he was capable of enjoying sex, perhaps with some unclearly specified frequency, now he has the added responsibility or arousing and stimulating his wife so that she too may experience orgasm. Here again the difference between expectation and achievement may prove disastrous. Some women are indeed capable of explosive, almost violent orgasm, whereas others experience a milder reaction at the peak of their sexual pleasure. Still others state quite frankly that they seldom or never experience orgasm but still enjoy sexual relations. All of these women are capable of working out a satisfactory sexual adjustment in marriage.[26] Some will find it difficult to do so if failure to achieve a positive orgasm threatens the masculinity of the husband or bestows on themselves the ignoble label *frigid*.

The foregoing discussion should make it clear that achieving a satisfactory sexual adjustment is not a simple developmental task of early marriage. It should come as no surprise to learn that frequently the task takes time. Although some couples apparently work out an adjustment from the beginning of marriage, others require months before they are able to dis-

[24] Levy and Munroe, *op. cit.*, p. 135.
[25] Helen M. Hacker, "New Burdens on Masculinity," *Marriage and Family Living,* Vol. 19 (August, 1957), p. 231.
[26] Terman found that almost half of those wives who seldom or never experienced orgasm nevertheless felt that they received complete or nearly complete satisfaction from intercourse. Lewis M. Terman, "Correlates of Orgasm Adequacy in a Group of 556 Wives," *Journal of Psychology*, Vol. 32 (October, 1951), p. 128.

cover what is right for them.[27] An important learning involved in the developmental task of reaching a satisfactory sex relationship is the acceptance of the idea that marital sex adjustment takes time and is not something that descends on a couple at the close of the wedding ceremony. Success in achieving the adjustment can be one of the most rewarding experiences in the early married period. Failure to do so can adversely affect both other developmental tasks at this stage of the family life cycle and tasks of later stages.

PREPARING FOR PARENTHOOD

Most young couples want at some time to have children. About eight out of ten married couples have a child, and in about half of the remaining cases the childlessness apparently is involuntary.[28] To have children seems to be a common expectation of married couples, and there is some indication that the desire for children augurs well for marital happiness. Biologically speaking, most married couples find it easy to become parents. There are, however, a series of new learnings associated with becoming parents. There is the planning for children, and there are various psychological and physical preparations for parenthood to be made.

Preparing for parenthood begins before pregnancy. It is not unrealistic to expect couples to come to grips with the idea of children in the family and to reach at least tentative conclusions concerning how many children they would like to have and when they would like to have them. Understandably, many couples prefer to have some time together, to work on other developmental tasks, and to learn to live as a pair before "settling down" to raise children. One authority suggests that this process may take several months.[29] Judging by the average length of time between marriage and conception, however, we infer that it would be well not to delay too long the general sort of planning for children about which we are talking.

The idea unfortunately has arisen that the essence of planning for parenthood is the selection of appropriate means of controlling conception. Although for many couples in American society planning for parenthood does include this task, there is much more to the matter than this. Perhaps the difficulty has arisen because of the confusion between the concepts "planned children" and "wanted children." We would most assuredly agree that being wanted is the minimum expectation a child can have of

[27] Judson T. Landis, "Length of Time Required to Achieve Adjustment in Marriage," *American Sociological Review*, Vol. 11 (December, 1946), pp. 666-677.
[28] See p. 221.
[29] Evelyn M. Duvall and Reuben Hill, *When You Marry*, rev. ed. (New York, D. C. Heath & Company, 1953), p. 341.

his parents. This does not mean that we should consider unwanted any child whose start in life was not preceded by a deliberate abandonment of contraceptives. The estimates of unplanned pregnancies, even among well-educated couples, run high. Two studies of college marriages, one at Michigan State University, the other at Purdue University, revealed that only about a third of the pregnancies were planned.[30] It is no rash judgment that a larger proporton of these couples developed during pregnancy highly positive attitudes toward the forthcoming parenthood and wanted the child in a very real sense. Controlling which month conception takes place is no sure indication that the couple had healthy reasons for wanting a child in the first place, nor does the inability to control conception necessarily result in a child unwanted and unloved.

Planning for parenthood should include some exploration by the couple of why they want a child or children. To be sure most couples will not be able to delve very deeply into their own motivations, but there is every good reason for trying to determine why children are wanted. A child deserves to start out life being wanted, and he deserves to be wanted for his own sake and not because of pressures put on his parents by friends or relatives. Wanting a child for his own sake undoubtedly facilitates the later task of accepting the child. Conversely, those who are motivated to parenthood by such things as the desire for an eventual junior partner in the family business may find it difficult to accept the sex, the intelligence, or the personality of the child they produce.

Planning for parenthood includes the development of realistic attitudes toward what children will mean to the family. It would imply an acceptance of the fact that changes in family routine will occur and an acceptance of the financial facts of parenthood. Children do cost money, and all but the very wealthy will notice the cost in their family budget. Some alterations in the couple's daily routine will almost always be necessary, and many will find themselves modifying their recreational, visiting, or other patterns. Children require room, and so in preparing for parenthood some couples will find it advisable to move to a larger home. The exact consequences of the addition of a child depend much on the situation of the couple. Nevertheless, it is a requisite task of pre-parenthood to develop realistic attitudes toward the coming of a child and the modifications in the family's way of life his coming will require.

Once the wife becomes pregnant there are other concrete develop-

[30] Judson T. Landis and Thomas and Shirley Poffenberger, "The Effects of First Pregnancy upon the Sexual Adjustment of 212 Couples," *American Sociological Review*, Vol. 15 (December, 1950), pp. 766-772. Harold T. Christensen and Robert E. Philbrick, "Family Size as a Factor in the Marital Adjustments of College Couples," *American Sociological Review*, Vol. 18 (June, 1952), pp. 306-312.

mental tasks facing the couple. Some of these are associated with the pregnancy period, and others can be viewed as preparation for the role of parent. To people in some other societies it would indeed seem unusual to consider a developmental task the accepting of the idea that pregnancy is a natural state and childbirth is a normal bodily function. Unintentionally our society has done much to foster the opposite idea. For this reason some doctors are in favor of establishing "Mother's Homes" for prenatal and obstetrical care, where much of the routine work of obstetricians would be done by women who were trained as doctors' helpers.[31] Some question, frankly, whether *healthy* mothers with *normal* pregnancies need the continued services of a person trained in the treatment of disease, and whether the hospital, which exists primarily for the treatment of disease and injury, is the proper locale for normal childbirth. As worth while as the growing use of physicians and hospitals has been for reducing infant and maternal mortality, medical care has neverthless helped to usher in the notion that pregnancy is almost a pathological condition. Ridding themselves of such an idea will not be easy for most "modern" couples well steeped in the lore of drugs and tests and expert attendance at delivery. Unless they can somehow learn to accept pregnancy and childbirth as normal biological functions, however, they are likely to experience difficulty with the other developmental tasks of the expectant parenthood phase. The average woman today spends over two years of her life pregnant, and the mother of four children has spent three years in pregnancies. At the beginning stage of the family life cycle, it would seem to behoove couples to do what they can to develop healthy attitudes toward pregnancy.

Accepting the normality of pregnancy does not mean that there will be no problems to be faced or adjustments to be made. It should mean, however, that couples will be able to take any modifications of routine or change in recreational habits necessitated by pregnancy more or less in their stride. Although it may be true that tobogganing is a little risky in later stages of pregnancy and even the most accepting woman might wonder about square dancing in her eighth month, the couple that fully accepts the normality of pregnancy will be able to find many sources of recreation while awaiting the birth of their child. Problems of the over-protective husband should be reduced, while at the same time the man will realize that his wife may be experiencing some discomforts. The prospective mother can discover the happy medium between considering herself a near invalid and so completely ignoring her condition as to harm herself or her child. Getting adequate exercise and rest, watching her diet, and

[31] Niles Newton, *Maternal Emotions* (New York, Paul B. Hoeber, Inc., 1955), pp. 68-69.

even curtailing some social activities if necessary will require a little work and attention, but they will not be looked upon as troublesome chores by the couple accepting the essential normality of pregnancy.

One of the most difficult developmental tasks of the expectant parenthood stage is that concerned with the couple's sexual behavior. Some of the difficulty in meeting this task can be traced to sheer ignorance about the kind and amount of modification of sexual activity that is really necessary in normal pregnancy. Probably every counselor has met couples who drastically restrict sexual intercourse during most of pregnancy and give it up entirely several months before the birth of the child, because of some fuzzy notion that allowing their impulses normal expression will somehow hurt the mother or the unborn child. One study has found that husbands as well as wives experience a gradual abatement of sexual desire as pregnancy progresses.[32] Most couples, it would seem, would not go too far wrong by merely attending to their own sexual urges. Couples in doubt could check with their physicians. They will probably find that doctors have far less rigid and restrictive rules than those dictated by superstition.

A source of difficulty more serious than failure to find a suitable sexual adjustment during pregnancy is the couple's failure to make a satisfactory sexual adjustment before pregnancy. This illustrates once again how the achievement of any one developmental task builds on those that have preceded it. For some women pregnancy is but a convenient excuse to avoid sexual relations they never really enjoyed. Some men are quick to blame their wife's pregnancy for their lack of satisfaction with sexual relations when in reality the cause lies deeper and the dissatisfaction existed even before their wife conceived. Professional help may be required to remedy conditions such as these, for frequently even a partial recognition of the true source of the difficulty is insufficient to enable the individual or couple to effect a real change in attitude or behavior.

SOURCES OF HELP FOR THE MARRIED PAIR

In the opening pages of this chapter we made the point that the developmental tasks facing the newly married pair are complex and challenging. Certainly many couples are able to meet these challenges and find them stimulating and enjoyable. There are others for whom one or more of the developmental tasks proves to be a stumbling block. A large proportion of the marriages that eventually end in divorce have begun to deteriorate at this first stage of the family life cycle. Many of these couples and many of those who somehow manage to blunder through marital life

[32] Landis and Poffenberger, *op. cit.*

without divorce but also without much happiness could be helped toward better achievement of their developmental tasks.

In most communities the resources for the married couple are more numerous than imagined. Most social welfare agencies, in addition to their better-known function of supplying temporary financial assistance, are prepared to help couples develop more satisfactory ways of managing their finances. The State Employment Office can be of real help in finding a job, or a different job, for the husband or for the wife if it seems desirable. Although their numbers are not large, in most large cities today there are professional marriage counselors associated with public and private social welfare agencies or in private practice. Mental hygiene clinics, not for the seriously mentally ill but for those with emotional problems they are unable to work out without help, are found in most large cities and in many county seats. In more and more communities the developmental tasks that arise with pregnancy do not have to be faced alone. Clinics and other groups sponsor classes and discussion sessions for prospective parents. Although it is manifestly unnecessary to be an expert in human embryology before becoming a parent, husbands and wives seem to appreciate the opportunity for learning more about the processes of pregnancy and childbirth, for having specific troublesome questions answered, and for sharing with other couples common problems and ways of meeting them.

In some communities, finding competent help for the married pair may be difficult or almost impossible. Greater difficulty, however, may be experienced in recognizing when help is needed and developing a willingness to seek asistance when it seems advisable. Whether with or without help, couples who successfully meet the challenges at the first stage of the family life cycle will be better prepared to meet those at the child-rearing stage to which we next turn.

SELECTED READINGS

BLOOD, ROBERT O., JR., *Anticipating Your Marriage* (Glencoe, Illinois, The Free Press, 1955), Ch. 10.

CHRISTENSEN, HAROLD T., "Family Size as a Factor in the Marital Adjustments of College Couples," *American Sociological Review*, Vol. 18 (June, 1952), pp. 306-312.

DUVALL, EVELYN M., *Family Development* (Philadelphia, J. B. Lippincott Company, 1957), Ch. 6.

————, *In-Laws: Pro and Con* (New York, Association Press, 1954).

FOOTE, NELSON N., "Changes in American Marriage Patterns and the Role of Women," *Eugenics Quarterly*, Vol. 1 (December, 1954), pp. 254-260.

FROMME, ALLAN, *The Psychologist Looks at Sex and Marriage* (Englewood Cliffs, New Jersey, Prentice-Hall, Inc., 1950).

GIANOPULOS, ARTIE, and MITCHELL, HOWARD E., "Marital Disagreement in Working Wife Marriages as a Function of Husband's Attitude Toward Wife's Employment," *Marriage and Family Living*, Vol. 19 (November, 1957), pp. 373-378.

GROSS, IRMA, and CRANDALL, E. W., *Management for Modern Families* (New York, Appleton-Century-Crofts, Inc., 1954).

HACKER, HELEN M., "New Burdens on Masculinity," *Marriage and Family Living*, Vol. 19 (August, 1957), pp. 227-233.

JACKSON, EDITH B., and TRAINHAM, GENEVIEVE, eds., *Family Centered Maternity and Infant Care* (New York, Josiah Macy Jr. Foundation, 1951).

JACOBSON, ALVER H., Conflict of Attitudes toward the Roles of the Husband and Wife in Marriage," *American Sociological Review*, Vol. 17 (April, 1952), pp. 146-150.

KENKEL, WILLIAM F., "Influence Differentiation in Family Decision Making," *Sociology and Social Research*, Vol. 42 (September-October, 1957), pp. 18-25.

KOOS, EARL L., *Families in Trouble* (New York, King's Crown Press, 1946).

KYRK, HAZEL, *The Family in the American Economy* (Chicago, University of Chicago Press, 1953).

LANDIS, JUDSON T., "Adjustments after Marriage," *Marriage and Family Living*, Vol. 9 (Spring, 1947), pp. 32-34.

LANDIS, JUDSON T., and POFFENBERGER, THOMAS and SHIRLEY, "The Effects of First Pregnancy upon the Sexual Adjustment of 212 Couples," *American Sociological Review*, Vol. 15 (December, 1950), pp. 766-772.

LANDIS, PAUL H., *Making the Most of Marriage* (New York, Appleton-Century-Crofts, Inc., 1955).

LEVY, JOHN, and MUNROE, RUTH, *The Happy Family* (New York, Alfred A. Knopf, Inc., 1938).

MYRDAL, ALVA, and KLEIN, VIOLA, *Women's Two Roles* (London, Routledge and Kegan Paul, 1956).

NEWTON, NILES, *Maternal Emotions* (New York, Paul B. Hoeber, Inc., 1955).

PINK, LOUIS H., "Housing the Middle Income Family," *Marriage and Family Living*, Vol. 17 (May, 1955), pp. 152-154.

CHAPTER | 16

Developmental Tasks at the
Child-Rearing Stage

MANY FAMILIES find that there is a child in the home during half or more than half of the entire family life cycle. There is good reason, therefore, to attempt to make some division of the long child-rearing stage of the family cycle. The period can be divided according to the stage of development of the oldest child; we can speak of families with an infant, families with a young child, and families with an adolescent. Divisions also could be made according to the times when the need for new learnings arise with particular force, such as birth of the first child, his start to first grade, his completion of high school, and, finally, the stage when the last child in the family leaves the parental home.

Dividing the child-rearing stage into too many segments is likely to obscure the continuity of the developmental tasks of the various family members. We prefer, therefore, to treat as a whole the admittedly long years from the time a child is added to the family until his adolescence. In discussing the developmental tasks of children and parents during this stage, we will take occasion to point out how the nature of the various tasks changes with progression in the family life cycle. In this manner we will be able to see that there are some basic developmental tasks associated with parenthood and some broad developmental learnings of children which, change as they will and as they must, nevertheless are found throughout the child-rearing stage.

The developmental tasks of the family members at the child-rearing stage of the family life cycle have been ordered in the following manner. We first investigate the tasks of children, arranged in a manner that emphasizes the importance of the tasks rather than the details of their nature. In a complementary manner the developmental tasks of the adults as parents are next discussed. Following this we look into the developmental tasks of the man and woman of the family as husband and wife; these are the tasks that continue from the previous stage of the family cycle. We conclude by discussing the total developmental strivings first of the woman and then of the man, attempting in both cases to draw together the tasks associated with their various roles as spouse, individual, parent, and homemaker or provider. This discussion should allow us to understand how the various developmental tasks fit one with the other and why at times they may conflict.

DEVELOPMENTAL TASKS OF CHILDREN

Although at no time in his life is the individual free from developmental tasks, the entire pre-adult stage of life is characterized by continual and fairly rapid change and thus the need for many and frequent new learnings.[1] There are several ways of ordering the many developmental tasks of children. They can be classified, first of all, according to the nature of the learnings required and discussed as physical skills, mental abilities, and attitudes. Some kind of chronological classification also can be used, in which the pre-adult period is broken down into fairly small periods and an attempt is made to delineate the various tasks facing the child at each particular sub-stage. Although this method has the advantage of allowing us to see at a glance the many new learnings facing a child at a particular time in his life, it may obscure to some extent the continuity of developmental strivings and the manner in which the developmental tasks build one upon the other. A third way of ordering developmental tasks of children is to relate them to the end product of pre-adult development. This method should make it easier to see how the many developmental tasks of childhood, which arise at various stages, are related to what the child is and what he is to become. This type of classification implies that we know at least the broad outlines of the abilities we expect to find in a normal, healthy, adult member of our society and that we have some understanding of the way in which these abilities are learned. Although our knowledge is more meager than we would like, the approach nevertheless shows promise of allowing us to look more meaningfully at the vast array of developmental tasks that arise between infancy and adolescence.

There are many ways of visualizing and describing the ultimate goal in the development of children. Concepts like "healthy personality," "maturity," and "good adjustment" immediately come to mind. A new and

[1] For other discussions of the developmental tasks of children see Robert J. Havighurst, *Human Development and Education* (New York, Longman's Green & Co., Inc., 1953), Chs. 2, 3, and 4; and Evelyn M. Duvall, *Family Development* (Philadelphia, J. B. Lippincott Company, 1957), Chs. 8, 9, and 10.

intriguing approach to human behavior is contained in the concept of *interpersonal competence*.[2] This concept takes cognizance of the fact that something more is desired in human development than the absence of unhealthy symptoms, than adjustment, or even than happiness. It recognizes that individuals differ in their ability to deal effectively with the objects, ideas, and people in the world about them. This capability "to meet and deal with a changing world," as Foote and Cottrell phrase it, is seen as interpersonal competence.[3] "Competent personalities," they continue, "in contrast to adjusted ones have the qualities, skills, and orientations which ideally enable them to cope with whatever confronts them, insofar as any human being can do so."[4] Although interpersonal competency is viewed as the totality of acquired abilities for effective interaction, six components of competency have been designated as (1) health, (2) intelligence, (3) empathy, (4) autonomy, (5) judgment, and (6) creativity. In the section that follows we will investigate these components in more detail and for each will outline the developmental tasks of children that are related to the development of competence. The lists of developmental tasks that follow each element of competence are admittedly incomplete; they are merely suggestive of the kinds of new learnings that would facilitate the development of interpersonal competence.

1. Health

As a component of competence, health includes more than the absence of disease and disorders. Developmentally it would include the progressive maximization of the potentialities of the organism to perform its physiological function and "to achieve its maximum of sensory acuity, strength, energy, co-ordination, dexterity, endurance, recuperative power, and immunity."[5] Health, in the sense of this definition, quite obviously is related to interpersonal relations and is not simply a state or condition of an individual organism. Health forms part of the basis for the achievement of many developmental tasks at various stages of the family life cycle. To play the roles of normal adults in the family, men and women need endurance, energy, sexual potency, and other abilities that have as part of their basis the sense of physical well-being implied in this conception of health. Some

[2] For the development of this concept see Nelson N. Foote and Leonard S. Cottrell, Jr., *Identity and Interpersonal Competence* (Chicago, University of Chicago Press, 1955).
[3] *Ibid.*, p. 49.
[4] Nelson N. Foote and Leonard S. Cottrell, Jr., *Identity and Interpersonal Competence* (Chicago, University of Chicago Press, 1955), pp. 61-62. Copyright 1955 by the University of Chicago.
[5] *Ibid.*, p. 52.

important developmental tasks of children relating to the maximization of health would be the following:

Infancy and Early Childhood
1. Achieving physiological stability and establishing rhythms of rest and activity.
2. Learning to eat; involves learning to suck and swallow and later to take solid foods and to enjoy new textures and tastes in food.
3. Learning to handle one's body effectively; developing eye-hand and hand-mouth co-ordination, learning to reach, handle, pull, crawl, walk, and run.
4. Learning to control bodily elimination; learning to recognize the need for elimination, learning to control the processes, and accepting responsibility for performance of them.

Middle Childhood
1. Learning to take increasing responsibility for personal health and safety; learning to recognize when he is tired and hungry, gaining complete mastery in toilet training, getting adequate sleep and food, taking responsibility for bodily cleanliness.
2. Developing a rudimentary knowledge about the human body; learning elementary facts about the structure of the body, the functions of its parts, and the digestive, reproductive, and re-cuperative processes of the human organism.
3. Growing in strength and in bodily control; developing the large muscle system by running, climbing, and using appropriate play equipment; increasing manual dexterity and developing skill in such things as buttoning, cutting, and manipulating small objects.

2. Intelligence

The usual definition of *intelligence* is an inborn capacity to learn. Competency in interpersonal relations requires more than being born with normal learning ability. The developmental conception of intelligence emphasizes the maximization of mental potentialities so that the greatest amount of skill is reached in such abilities as reflective thinking, perceiving relationships among events, symbolic reasoning, and drawing generalizations.[6] Every normal individual has the potentialities for these sorts of intellectual skills, although probably few operate close to the peak of their abilities. The developmental conception of intelligence stresses the

[6] Cf. *ibid.*, p. 53.

experiences, the learnings, and the practices necessary to awaken and utilize intellectual potentialities. In the developmental sense every normal person has intelligence and probably everyone's intelligence could be increased, despite the fact that the individual capacity to learn sets a limit on what can be achieved. The tasks of children that lead to and enhance intellectual competence include the following:

Infancy and Early Childhood
1. Learning to talk; involves learning to recognize objects and people by name, learning non-verbal communication, building a repertory of sounds learning and using words and, later, forming sentences.
2. Beginning to understand and to build up a store of knowledge about the nature of the world about him, what things are and how and why they work.
3. Developing the capacity for abstract thinking through learning simple concepts like good, round, large, animal, and cold.

Middle Childhood
1. Developing fundamental skills in reading, writing, and calculating.
2. Expanding his ability to reason and to understand cause and effect relationships.
3. Increasing his capacity to abstract, to symbolize concrete and vicarious experiences, and to manipulate symbols into generalizations.
4. Building his store of knowledge of the world about him and learning to apply generalizations.

3. Empathy

Empathy consists of the imaginative projection of one's self into the being of another person. To the extent that this projection approaches completeness, the empathic person is able to interpret correctly the attitudes and intentions of others, to perceive situations accurately from another's point of view, and to predict and anticipate the behavior of others.[7] Clearly some degree of empathic ability is an absolute necessity for adequate social interaction. Without empathy there would be confusion, misunderstanding, and misinterpretation of one another's behavior. It is equally clear that people differ in empathic ability. Less well understood

[7] Cf. *ibid.*, p. 54. See also Leonard S. Cottrell, Jr., and Rosalind F. Dymond, "The Empathic Processes," *Psychiatry*, Vol 12 (November, 1949), pp. 355-359.

are the kinds of experiences, in the family and other situations, that enhance the development of this important component of competence. Although it would seem that achievement of the developmental tasks that follow would aid in the development of empathy, greater empathic ability would depend on the degree to which performance of the tasks focuses on understanding the roles of others.

Infancy and Early Childhood
1. Learning a basic attitude of trust through affectionate, consistent, and satisfying responses to his early needs.
2. Learning to love and be loved; responding affectionately to family members and later to others.
3. Learning to share parents with other children and gradually learning to see the necessity for so doing.
4. Beginning to control impulses, to share toys and equipment, to take turns, and gradually to see the reason for so doing.
5. Developing habits of giving within the family and later within a wider circle.

Middle Childhood
1. Developing a greater appreciation of the need for rules and the necessity for give-and-take in the family, among peers, and in other group situations.
2. Seeing the need for assuming some responsibility within the family.
3. Recognizing the differences between his family's customs and standards and those of other families, and trying to appreciate the right of his family and others to their uniqueness.
4. Learning to understand why individuals need such things as privacy, solace, and companionship.
5. Learning attitudes toward the many individual and group differences that exist in his society and the broader world which would facilitate interaction and co-operation without threatening his own loyalties or values.

4. Autonomy

In the adult world people expect one another to be capable of acting as independent agents, making their own plans and decisions and carrying them out without continuous supervision. It is expected that an adult will have the insight into his abilities necessary to know what he can do and the self-confidence to do it. He is expected, furthermore, to have internalized a stable set of norms and values so that he is capable of directing and controlling his own behavior. Abilities such as these are all included in the concept of autonomy.[8] Individuals quite clearly differ in this element of competence, and there is some professional concern over whether most people in our society have sufficient autonomous ability to be considered competent *individuals* in the strict sense of the term.[9] Autonomy, with its elements of self-respect, self-confidence, and self-control, is a learned ability. It is acquired gradually through experiences in independence that begin in early childhood. A people truly valuing autonomy will stress and help their children to achieve developmental tasks like those that follow:

Infancy and Early Childhood
1. Learning that he is basically a good child, worthy of the love and respect of others.
2. Learning to be comfortable away from his parents.
3. Accepting increasing responsibility for dressing himself and for caring for himself and his belongings.
4. Learning to do increasingly more things, at play and around the house, at a rate that allows him to appreciate his own abilities.

Middle Childhood
1. Learning to plan the use of his time, to choose friends, and otherwise to begin to achieve independence of his parents and other adults.
2. Developing a conscience by internalizing the expectancies of his family and society.
3. Learning to handle himself in potentially dangerous situations or in situations requiring caution.
4. Learning the social and other skills necessary to prevent feelings of inadequacy, self-consciousness, or shyness.

5. Judgment

As a component of competence, judgment refers to "the ability, which develops slowly in human beings, to estimate and evaluate the meaning and consequences to one's self of alternative lines of conduct."[10] It involves choosing among values and deciding among competing lines of

[8] Cf. Foote and Cottrell, *op. cit.*, p. 55.
[9] Robert Linder, *Prescription for Rebellion* (New York, Rinehart & Company, Inc., 1953).
[10] Foote and Cottrell, *op. cit.*, p. 56.

action. Conceived in this manner, the capacity for sound judgment is different from intelligence. Judgment involves more than knowledge and the possession of factual information, for it implies the weighing of available facts and the reaching of a satisfactory conclusion on what kind of action is called for by the situation. The ability to judge and decide is constantly required in many phases of personal and social living. It is certain that this capability is not sufficiently developed in many people to allow for adequate, let alone optimum, living. Many are those who are tortured by indecision or who find difficulty in making choices or in living comfortably with them once they have been made. There are a number of developmental tasks, arising at different times during childhood, the successful completion of which would aid in developing judgment ability.

Infancy and Early Childhood
1. Learning through simple examples in his world of toys, clothes and food that a variety of situations call for choice or decisions.
2. Beginning to learn that alternative choices have implications beyond the immediate situation.
3. Expanding the area of activities in which he can practice choosing and deciding.

Middle Childhood
1. Learning more complex concepts of decision-making behavior, such as the need for an exhaustive investigation of alternatives, the anticipation of the consequences of alternatives, and the irrevocable nature of some decisions.
2. Learning to make wise spending decisions; learning to relate what he wants to what he has and to his available resources; learning the satisfactions of saving for larger purchases.
3. Taking a more active and decisive role in family discussions, plans, and decision making.
4. Learning to make independent judgments in an increasingly wider range of situations and circumstances as his skill and readiness indicate.

6. Creativity

As an ingredient of interpersonal competence, *creativity* is defined as "any demonstrated capacity for innovations in behavior or real reconstruction of any aspect of the social environment."[11] It involves the ability to invent combinations or arrangements of ideas and objects not before

[11] *Ibid.*, p. 57.

in use. Creativity includes the capacity to deviate from routine by originating alternative behaviors or roles. It involves endowing new meaning to that which has been known before or discovering that which existed but was unknown. The ability to invent, to improvise, to discover, to devise, and to originate in the area of interpersonal relations all seem to be part of what Foote and Cottrell term *creativity*.[12] Close to this kind of creativity would be spontaneity, adaptability, and flexibility of outlook and action.

Despite the inability to define precisely this concept, creativity of the kind we have been describing can be recognized readily as a valuable capacity. It is the sort of thing that is frequently associated with leadership or with scientific ingenuity, but it is not here considered as a rare ability of the few. People everywhere and in all walks of life face dilemmas that call for new ways of thinking and acting and find the need for going beyond the accustomed routine. Although creative ability is much praised in the abstract, it seems that conformity, uniformity, and routinized behavior are more frequently taught and encouraged in contemporary American society.[13] To the extent that creativity is valued, it can be nurtured and developed. Accepting the worth of and stressing developmental tasks such as the following would seem to be favorable to the expansion of the child's capacity for creativity.

Infancy and Early Childhood
1. Becoming increasingly able to accept changes in routine, in place, and in persons attending him.
2. Learning to enjoy simple games and toys requiring trial, experimentation, and originality.
3. Gaining practice in such childhood creative activities as coloring, making up stories, and naming toy or real animals.

Middle Childhood
1. Increasing his variety and range of experiences of all sorts to provide a richer base for creativity.
2. Learning to test his inventiveness in such situations as cooking foods, repairing toys and equipment, and choosing gifts for others.
3. Accepting new and uncharted situations as challenges to his ingenuity rather than occasions for seeking directions.

Reviewing our discussion of the six components of competence and the developmental tasks associated with them, one may argue that some tasks have been "misclassified." It may also be pointed out that success

---

[12] *Ibid.*
[13] Cf. Linder, *op. cit.* See also our remarks, pp. 242-243.

in meeting a number of the developmental tasks would lead to several different abilities and that, therefore, some tasks should have been listed more than once. But our purpose was not taxonomic. We have attempted to make some order out of the profusion of new learnings facing children by setting up a framework that provides criteria for evaluating the relative importance of these developmental tasks and the reasons for their importance. Whether or not the competence framework continues to be accepted, we will have need for some such framework for delineating developmental tasks. It is conceivable that as our knowledge increases, we will be able to cast the developmental tasks of persons of all ages and at all stages of the family life cycle into a single generalizing framework that will provide us with a sound rationale for determining the really important new learnings of life.

DEVELOPMENTAL TASKS OF PARENTS

The simplest way of describing the developmental tasks of adults as parents would be to state that they should do everything necessary and possible to assure that their children accomplish their developmental tasks. Although this statement is true enough as it stands, it is also begging the question. It tells us little of the intricacies and complexities of being an adequate parent. Let us accept, nevertheless, our simple statement of the all-important developmental task of parents. Rather than describe minutely what exactly parents should do as they help their child to achieve his developmental tasks, our intention is to discuss the more general learnings of parents that set the stage for, and in a sense determine, their performance of the specifics of child rearing.

Developing a Philosophy of Child Rearing

In Chapter 11 we investigated several lines of evidence on the relationship between the nature of child-rearing practices and the personality outcome for the child. In the same chapter we also saw that currently various "systems" of child rearing are in vogue and that parents are bombarded from all sides by myriads of articles, lectures, and helpful hints on this or that aspect of how they should rear their child. When we say, therefore, that young parents need to develop a philosophy of child rearing, we are not suggesting that an intellectual excursion into metaphysics and aesthetics is necessary before one can be an adequate parent. We mean, rather, that there is a need for a certain amount of thinking-through on such matters as the things that they consider important in child rearing, their general approach to child rearing, and the implications of their approach for the personality of the child. The state of our knowledge on the importance of child-rearing practices is such almost to demand that parents come to grips with general problems such as these. What is more, accomplishing this task of developing a general orientation toward child rearing should make the job of parenthood easier. Day-to-day decisions on such matters as child care, discipline, and the purchase of equipment could be made within a framework of agreed-upon child-rearing goals and would not be seen as unrelated problems that arise to harass parents.

A fundamental part of developing an orientation to child rearing is the decision concerning the relative emphasis parents will place on individual development. Whether we like it or not, each child will have his uniqueness, and just as certainly everyone must learn a certain amount of conformity to group standards. Parents have a right to know, however, that within limits they have a choice in the direction in which they will move in child rearing. They need to know the nature of the broad choice that lies before them and its implications for child-rearing techniques and for the end product of their child rearing, the personality of the child they have reared.

The philosophy of child rearing that stresses individual development takes cognizance of the uniqueness of the child. It recognizes that not everyone, child or adult, is able to fit into the rigid sort of sex, age, and other roles sometimes demanded. It encourages experimentation, trial, and innovation in order for the individual to discover what is best for him. Rather than encouraging the child to step into new roles as he would a ready-made suit of clothes, parents emphasizing individuality want the child to try out new age roles, altering them here and there, accepting what he finds good and disregarding the rest. Within the framework of what is socially approved, the child is encouraged to develop his potentialities to the fullest. The opposite of this is to foster in the child values of conformity to rather rigid role definitions. Such a philosophy stresses the orderly progression through the age-graded roles of society and encourages behavior that is well within the appropriate sex role.[14] Parents emphasizing conformity appreciate the comfort that some find in the lack of confusion over what they should do and when they should do it.

In order to make an intelligent and realistic choice between whether to stress individual development or conformity, parents should be aware of the full implications of the choice that lies before them. The development of abilities like autonomy, creativity, and judgment exact a price.[15]

[14] Cf. Clifford Kirkpatrick, *The Family* (New York, The Ronald Press Company, 1955), p. 88.

[15] Cf. Robert O. Blood, "Consequences of Permissiveness for Parents of Young Children," *Marriage and Family Living*, Vol. 15 (August, 1953), pp. 209-212.

If parents truly value creativity, for example, they must encourage it from an early age. The young child's toys and play space must allow him to be free to experiment, bound only by the fewest possible rules concerning what he can and cannot do. This means, to be sure, that the personality outcome must be valued higher than the physical equipment or the standards of housekeeping perfection. Picture-book versions of little children's rooms do not have chairs piled on tables and a three-year-old entangled in the chairs. Furthermore, a child does not gain self-confidence by learning through constant parental reminder that basically his knowledge is meager and his decisions unwise. Allowing the child to test his own wings and to discover just how well and how far he can fly, so to speak, may be more trying to parents than setting forth rules and giving detailed directions.

Although many parents dream and even state that their child will be "different" in some important respects from "the average," many of these same parents do everything they can to assure that their dreams will not come true. Conformity, like its opposite, creativity, can be taught in simple ways, for example by teaching the young child that chairs are made for sitting on and not for turning upside down to be used as boats or dungeons or whatever else the unharnessed imagination of the child wills them to be. Some children learn early in life that the chief reason they cannot do something, whether it is walking barefoot in the rain or standing on their heads on the sofa, is that "people just don't do such things." This simple explanation, repeated and applied to a variety of situations, gives the child a certain rationale for his behavior. The question is, of course, is it the best rationale? Parents have to try to determine just what they are attempting to accomplish in child rearing, and they need to search hard and long to determine whether they are really willing to do what is necessary to accomplish the broad goals they set for themselves.

What we have labeled a developmental task of parents is in actuality a three-fold task. It involves, as we have seen, (1) determining some sort of personality goals or developing a basic orientation toward child rearing, (2) assessing as completely as possible the implications of the choice and the various effects it will have on other family members and the home, and (3) attempting to put the goals, perhaps modified in the light of foreseen difficulties, into practice. We have emphasized the first two points to the seeming neglect of the third. This has been done partly because we believe that parents will experience less difficulty in determining how to put their philosophy of child rearing into action but mainly because there can be, and is, great variation in the ways in which the same philosophy can be transferred into action. Wealthy and poor parents alike, for example, can espouse the value of encouraging creativity and curiosity in their children. Both sets of parents can attempt to put this value into practice when selecting toys for a child, furnishing his room, planning a vacation, or deciding what to do on a Sunday afternoon. It is obvious that because of their differences in financial status the two families would come up with different sorts of plans and activities. Then, too, as we have seen in the developmental tasks of children, working toward full achievement of individual potentialities implies that experiences will be modified, re-evaluated, and enlarged as the child grows and develops.

There are various stumbling blocks in the way of developing and using a basic philosophy of child rearing. Many of these inhere in the personalities of the parents. It is easy to see, for example, that a certain amount of knowledge of child development is mandatory. Knowledge of the available choices is necessary before a choice can be made, and knowledge of the implications of the decision is also necessary. It seems that today, for example, many who claim that they want to be "permissive" parents do not clearly understand why they espouse permissiveness and are somewhat surprised to learn by experience that permissiveness has consequences for family routine, furniture selection, and perhaps even the basic design of the house. Putting values into practice, finally, requires knowledge and information. Parents need to gain a general understanding of the physical, social, and psychological development of a child and to enrich and enlarge upon this knowledge in keeping with the inevitable change in the child, the state of available knowledge, and the general family circumstances.

Knowledge is seldom enough for developing and using a philosophy of child rearing. Other traits and abilities of parental personality, perhaps more difficult to achieve and develop, are required before the necessary knowledge can be put to use. The parents themselves need to be relatively autonomous persons who are capable of making judgments and sticking to them even in the face of criticism from their own parents or from the community. To achieve this task best, therefore, the parents cannot be tradition-bound, for it may very well be that what has "always been done" in a certain family or locality will bear only faint resemblance to what is best for the child. Flexibility and adaptability are likewise necessary in order to perform the developmental tasks of parenthood. This would include the willingness to re-evaluate the basic philosophy, the ability to assess whether or not it is actually being put into practice, as well as the ability to change it if this seems desirable. Tenacity of convictions can be an extremely poor character trait indeed when it means holding doggedly to child-rearing practices and ideas that do not seem to work out in practice. Undoubtedly a deep sense of security and an inner feeling of self-worth is valuable in performance of the tasks of parenthood. Perhaps much of this is but an elaboration of the truism that competent, healthy adults make the best parents.

CONTINUING DEVELOPMENTAL TASKS OF THE MARRIED PAIR

Although new parents may sentimentally exclaim, "We don't know what we *ever* did before we had the baby," in their more realistic moments they are forced to admit that they had a life together and that this life continues. In our terms, we would say that many of the developmental tasks inherent in married-pair living continue into other stages of the family life cycle. Sometimes the nature of these tasks changes, and sometimes the demands of the new and changing family situation place added difficulties in the way of achieving the continuous developmental tasks. But always there continue the fundamental learnings associated with living together as man and wife.

One of the developmental tasks we singled out for discussion in Chapter 15 was labeled "achieving a satisfactory sexual relationship." The nature of this task, in the sense of basic attitudinal and other requirements, remains constant. The best preparation for continuing this task at the second stage of the family life cycle is to have come as close as possible to completing it before the first child was born. There are, however, conditions and characteristics peculiar to the child-rearing stage of the family life cycle that many interfere with the achievement of this task, despite the previous learnings.

Soon after childbirth the couple is faced with the decision of when to resume their sexual life. Most women are physically capable of sexual intercourse from four to six weeks after delivery. That is, usually by this time postpartum bleeding has ceased, the uterus and cervix have returned to their normal form, and any stitches in the perineum have healed. A woman may not be ready for intercourse, however, in other respects. The new mother who is breast-feeding her infant, caring for him, and performing many of the usual homemaking tasks might well be chronically tired. The experiences of motherhood are as intriguing as they are demanding, and the new mother may find that her interests and attention are centered more on her maternal than marital role. Part of the task facing the young mother, then, is to recognize that it is normal and healthy and desirable to resume sexual relations with her husband as soon as she is able to do so. Once she has accepted this idea, she will be better able to co-operate with him in finding ways to relieve her fatigue and otherwise remove the stumbling blocks in the way of a normal sexual life. The husband, on his part, needs to recognize that tiring demands are being made on his wife's energy and that a period of readjustment and relearning is frequently necessary after childbirth.

As the children grow, new situations arise which could interfere with the re-established sexual relationship. A good example is the greater need for privacy demanded by the presence of children. Decorum suggests that sex talk and the more obviously erotic forms of demonstration of affection should not take place "in front of the children." Some parents complain that these necessary restrictions rob their sexual life of the spontaneity and playfulness that once it had. Others find that major readjustments are necessary. Their preferred time for sexual relations may conflict with child-care activities or may be otherwise incompatible with the necessary routine of the growing family. To the need for the sorts of readjustments that arise with change in the family life cycle status, we should add those connected with the increasing ages of the spouses. There is good evidence that women reach the peak of their sexual drive years later than men and at the time, in fact, when the sexual appetite of many men actually has started to decline.[16] Generally at the middle and later stages of the child-rearing stage of the family life cycle, many husbands and wives will find it necessary to adjust to a growing disparity of interest in sexual activity, with the woman desiring intercourse more frequently than the man.

Even our few restricted examples should make it clear that the task of achieving a satisfactory sexual relationship takes on new requirements at the child-rearing stage of the family cycle. Recognizing that the task exists and being willing to work on it with intelligence should in most cases assure that the sexual side of marriage continues to be rewarding to both partners.

The task of learning to make family decisions also changes with the stage of the family cycle. With the new requirements are found different sources of interference with its successful completion. The child-rearing years are busy years, laden with things that have to be done to take care of the practical affairs of life. Since the mother has the primary responsibility for the care of the young child, there may tend to occur a more clear-cut differentiation in the roles of the spouses than was in force before the first child was born. Some amount of role reallocation is probably neces-

[16] Alfred C. Kinsey, Wardell B. Pomeroy, Clyde E. Martin, and Paul H. Gebhard, *Sexual Behavior in the Human Female* (Philadelphia, W. B. Saunders Co., 1953), pp. 353-354.

sary. It is possible, however, that the sheer force of all that has to be done may lead the couple into an ever-greater division of labor and responsibility and away from the sharing and planning patterns they had developed in the early years of marriage.[17] Since it may seem more efficient to divide responsibilities rigidly into "his" and "hers," couples may tend to become so concerned with the expedient that they neglect the important. Those who are aware of the tendency and its underlying reasons will strive to retain in their marriage the sense of partnership and the patterns of mutual planning that once it had.

At this stage of the family life cycle there arises a new developmental task associated with family decision making. It becomes the parents' responsibility to help the children to take an increasingly fuller role in family decision making. Much has been written about democratic family decision making, and for our purposes the best defense of it is that it seems to be the kind of experience that prepares children for the emergent adult roles in our society. For this reason family decision making is considered a developmental task. It is contended that children should learn the attitudes and skills called for by family decision making in order satisfactorily to play the kinds of roles expected in our society today. In a reciprocal manner, parents need to learn the values and skills necessary to encourage their children to take part in decision making that affects the entire family group. Parents may find this task anything but easy. For one thing, some of them come to this stage of the family cycle with more traditional notions about the child's place in the family and find it difficult to reconcile their ideas and their own family experiences with the newer conceptions of the role of the child.[18] Even those parents eager to learn the new practices may find more confusion than practical help. After digesting much of the literature on the subject, they may be left with the feeling that families cannot be democratic unless they organize themselves like a miniature United Nations, complete with council meetings, rotating chairmanship, voting rules, and a plethora of committees. Although some families find that a certain amount of formal structuring facilitates group decision making, it is by no means a requisite for all families that wish to behave democratically. All that is really necessary is a basic recognition of the worth and dignity of every family member, regardless of age or status in the family, and appreciation of the values of co-operative group

---

[17] Cf. Elizabeth H. Wolgast, *Economic Decisions in the Family* (Ann Arbor, Michigan, Survey Research Center, 1957), p. 9. (Mimeographed.)

[18] The tendency to re-enact in marriage the authority pattern and role arrangement of one's parental family has been noted by Ingersoll. See Hazel L. Ingersoll, "Transmission of Authority Patterns in the Family," *Marriage and Family Living*, Vol. 10 (Spring, 1948), pp. 36 ff.

action.[19] Within this framework of democracy, families have much leeway in working out their roles and tasks in group decision making.

It is easily understood that the developmental task of getting and spending the family income extends through all stages of the family life cycle. Sentimentality aside, no marriage and no family can live on love alone. It is equally true that the nature of this task changes along with changes in family cycle status. One of the important decisions facing couples at the child-rearing stage concerns the wife's employment outside the home. Perhaps the need for this decision arises more frequently in those families where the wife held a job before the first child was born. Many families find that the child-rearing years strain the family budget well-nigh to the breaking point and find it difficult, therefore, to eliminate a source of potential relief from the strain. They appreciate, at the same time, the really great demands placed on the woman as a homemaker and mother, particularly when the children are of pre-school age. In some families, of course, there is no choice, for absolute necessity demands that the wife seek employment. Many others must weigh and evaluate the gains and the losses and come up with an answer that is best for their family and all of its members.

The new developmental tasks concerned with spending the family income that arise at this stage have to do with the recognition of the child of the family as an economic consumer. Some would contend that he is a consumer *par excellence,* and hardly anyone would miss the point that child rearing costs money. Full recognition of the child as a consumer means that the parents must decide wisely how much of the family income should be devoted to the needs of the child. It is possible, of course, to spend both too much and too little on child rearing, and it is impossible to say which error is the more damaging to the real needs of the child. As the child grows older, recognition of him as a consumer implies that he be helped to make increasingly more of his own spending decisions. Living in modern American society demands considerable competency in making spending decisions. To the extent that parents have assumed the responsibility of helping to prepare their children for adult life, it becomes one of their tasks to provide the opportunities and practice for their children to develop the necessary abilities to make adequate spending decisions. Some parents find it difficult to relinquish a personal hold on the purse strings, and others experience extreme discomfort in granting their children the privilege of making their own mistakes. It is well to re-

[19] Cf. Christine Beasley, *Democracy in the Home* (New York, Association Press, 1954), Ch. 1.

ember that the unwise economic decisions of children generally are far less costly than those of adults.

DEVELOPMENTAL TASKS OF THE WOMAN OF THE FAMILY

At the child-rearing stage of the family life cycle there are many and complicated tasks facing the woman of the family.[20] With her husband she needs to work on those tasks associated with their life as a married pair. At the same time, special demands are placed on the woman as a mother, apart from the broad tasks as a parent she shares with her husband. She is also a homemaker. She has a responsibility to herself to grow as an individual. At times the developmental tasks associated with being a wife, a mother, a homemaker, and an individual neatly mesh with and complement one another. At other times they conflict and seem almost to be incompatible. But always these various developmental tasks face the woman, for they are necessary for optimum fulfillment at this stage of the family life cycle and for best preparation for the stages that follow.

In almost all cases the woman of the family, as a mother, must accept the fact that the major responsibility for care of the children is hers. This means that she must learn a host of skills and abilities. Although many women enter this stage of the family life cycle with some knowledge of child care, few are fully aware of what it means to have complete responsibility for a child. Specific skills like bathing and feeding the baby and recognizing when he needs to sleep certainly have to be learned and practiced. It is inherent in human growth, of course, that the nature of the mother's child-rearing tasks changes as the child develops. The need for some sorts of care drops out entirely, only to be replaced by other requirements. Rather than dwell on the many requisite skills of mothering, however, we can sketch the broad outline of this developmental task by stating that it requires accepting the responsibility for learning and performing the ever-changing skills associated with physical and psychological mothering. The mother must accomplish these tasks within the context of her and her husband's philosophy of child rearing and in such a way to insure the optimum opportunity for the child to accomplish his developmental tasks.

The woman of the family is also a homemaker. The exact nature of her duties varies according to the family's economic position, the number and ages of the family members, and the size of the home and the equip-

---

[20] See the discussion of the developmental tasks of the woman of the family during this stage of the family life cycle in Duvall, loc. cit.

ment in it. Certain broad areas of homemaking activities remain essentially the woman's sphere whether she does all of the physical work involved, part of it, supervises it, or arranges for its performance by others. Meal planning and preparing, laundering, cleaning, and the purchasing of many household items would be examples of the kinds of activities for which almost all homemakers have some responsibility at some phase in the planning-to-executing sequence. Clearly the performance of these responsibilities requires skill and knowledge, the nature of which changes as the family members increase in number and as they grow older. Modern household equipment and better-built homes have done much to relieve the physical burden of the homemaker, when, of course, these things can be afforded. At the same time, standards of homemaking have risen, with the result that considerable time still is spent on these tasks. The more that we learn about nutrition, for example, the harder it is to prepare meals that will meet the vitamin, calorie, and other requirements of each individual member of the family. With the advent of easily laundered fabrics and automatic washers and dryers have come new standards of cleanliness and new requirements for variety and style of clothing. All of this means, too, that the homemaker must constantly be re-evaluating her procedures and methods in the light of new knowledge. She is continually faced with choices of different techniques and competing styles and brands. These choices, furthermore, cannot be made on the basis of efficiency or desirability alone, but in making them the homemaker must accept realistically the limitations of the family's resources. The modern homemaker is far from being a switch-puller in an age of household automation. Many women approach the developmental tasks in these areas with originality and zest and find the new learnings challenging; others are chronically fatigued and find their role in the family boring and unimaginative. This difference in homemakers, which almost anyone can observe, is but another way of pointing out the difference between being able to recognize and meet the developmental tasks at this stage of the family cycle and not being able to do so.

"This above all, to thine own self be true," the poet tells us. In terms of a developmental task facing the woman of the family it means that she must recognize the need for continuing to develop as a person. Developmentally speaking, this is more a duty than a privilege, and more a necessity than something that would be "nice" to do if only she could find the time. The woman needs, first of all, to accept the fact that the performance of the tasks in this area is something she owes to her family and particularly to herself. She needs next to determine more specifically of what the tasks consist and how to go about working on them. Some women will continue to develop interests and hobbies they have always enjoyed, whereas others will prefer to go out on an entirely new line of activity. Some will find a role in civic and social organizations rewarding, and others will emphasize creativity in gardening, music, or ceramic art work. There is a great deal of flexibility in the actual performance of this developmental task. Modern living requires that there be an almost inflexible commitment to the value that some means of self-expression and continued self-development is necessary and desirable.

It is fortunate that the developmental tasks of the woman as a wife, mother, homemaker, and individual often complement and reinforce one another. The woman who is adequately developing her own interests and exploring avenues of self-expression, for example, is not just living fully at this stage of the family cycle and preparing well for later stages. In some respects she is also able to perform better her tasks as a parent, in this case particularly the tasks associated with helping the child increasingly to grow out of the family. Conversely, the woman who sees herself only as a mother may relinquish only with great difficulty the help and services children no longer need or want. The developmental tasks of the woman in her role as homemaker fit in with and converge upon tasks associated with her other roles. The efficient use of time devoted to housekeeping chores can help to give the homemaker more time to be a mother. The working-out of daily routines so that the necessary activities of the various family members get done with a minimum of friction will help to create an atmosphere conducive to relaxation and recreation with her husband. Although for some purposes it is well to categorize the various roles of the woman of the family and the developmental tasks associated with them, it is also necessary to see the interrelationship of the roles and the complementary nature of the developmental tasks.

The interrelationship of woman's several roles means also that there will be times when it is extremely difficult to reconcile their conflicting demands. It may be hard, for example, for a woman to fit her conception of an orderly and well furnished house to the needs of a young child for freedom of movement and expression. Although the home can be made relatively "childproof," the job of arranging and decorating it may become unimaginative and more routinized than it would need otherwise to be. The conflict between the demands on the woman as a wife and as a mother is well recognized. Undoubtedly the conflict is intensified when after the arrival of the first baby the mother realizes that she is also married to one, but even in the best of situations the scarce resources of the woman's time and energy may make some conflict inevitable. Conflicts may also arise because of what the woman wants or needs for self-development. This is most vividly seen when the woman desires employment outside the home. She may be the first to recognize the many good reasons why, for her, a job is desirable and the equally good family reasons why it is undesirable. So it is that co-ordinating her various developmental tasks and attempting to resolve their conflicting demands constitute a further developmental requirement.

DEVELOPMENTAL TASKS OF THE MAN OF THE FAMILY

The man of the family has several selves. He is the father to his children, the husband to his wife, and the one who has the primary responsibility for obtaining the family income. He has a role in the family as homemaker in that almost always he is expected to assume responsibility for some work around the home. The man also has developmental tasks associated with continuing to develop himself as an individual. If we take a closer look at the various developmental tasks of the man, we will be able to understand why at times they fit together well to form a co-ordinated whole, and at other times the tasks in one area conflict with those in another.[21]

The man's role of provider demands more than working as regularly as possible and bringing home a paycheck. At the child-rearing stage of the family life cycle he may need to re-evaluate the requirements of his job and the income it produces. If he is forced to conclude that the needs of the expanding family are not adequately met by his present income, then he is faced with a number of alternatives. He can take on overtime work, if it is available, he can seek additional work on a part-time basis, or he can prepare himself for a more remunerative position. Every day men change from one job to another or move from place to place in search of better job opportunities. As the provider for a family, the man needs to search out the alternatives available to him and relate the income and the time, travel, and other requirements of the job to the needs of his family. It is not always possible to work out a good solution to problems such as these, but attempting to work out the best possible solution under the circumstances constitutes the man's task as family provider.

Although some men may object to the designation, the man of the family usually must take a responsibility for some of the housekeeping chores of the family. In the past there was a fairly rigid distinction between man's and woman's work around the American home. Traditionally the

---

[21] A discussion of the developmental tasks of the man during the child-rearing stage can be found in Duvall, loc. cit.

man's job included such work involving greater physical exertion as shoveling snow, care of the furnace, and mowing the lawn and such lighter tasks as washing the car and repairing leaky faucets. Woman's work included such heavy tasks as mopping floors and scrubbing clothes and lighter tasks like dusting furniture and mending garments. Today, there is far less distinction between the man's and the woman's work in the home. Considerations of time, interest, energy, and ability are given more importance than mere sex in deciding who will do what. Thus the modern-day husband is required to do more than merely his share of the work around the house and yard. He needs also to develop a willingness to experiment in an effort to discover how, in the interests of himself, his wife, and his children, the necessary family chores can be divided. Although men have always had a housekeeping role in the family, some men will find the demands of the modern role difficult and will feel uncomfortable when hanging out the washing or watching their wives steer the power lawn mower around the small suburban lot. Undoubtedly much of the difference in the ability of men to meet the new challenges of this developmental task depends on their sense of security, their adaptability, their flexibility, and their appreciation of what is expected of them.

We have already seen that the man as a father shares with his wife some mutual developmental tasks of parenthood. Beyond accepting his share of these tasks, the father increasingly is expected to assume some responsibility for the care and training of the child. The father of younger children is expected to find a place for himself in the child-care routine, whether he bathes the baby, or feeds him, or whatever else he feels he can do both to get better acquainted with his infant child and to give his wife some help. As the child grows older, it is frequently the father who is better prepared to help both boys and girls learn such skills as swimming, throwing a ball, riding a bicycle, and, later still, driving an automobile. Learning skills such as these are important developmental tasks of children, and they help to build in the child a sense of security and self-worth.

Regardless of how interesting, how stimulating, or how giving of love a woman may be, there are some things she can never give to her children. It is the unique contribution of the father to serve as the symbol of masculinity for his children. Boys need a model with whom to identify, and girls need a model on which to build up a conception of masculinity and the role of the male in the family. The father is the first man the child comes to know and during the years of early childhood frequently the only one. Even later, from nursery school at least through grade school, the development of the child is entrusted to women. If the father fails to serve as an appropriate model of his sex, in other words, the job is usually left undone.

The man of the family, more frequently than the woman, stands also as a symbol of the world outside the family. It is he who daily leaves the home to manipulate the external environment and to interact with non-family members. By sharing these experiences with his children, he helps them learn about the society in which they live and how to interpret it. This, too, can be seen as a unique contribution of the father. As a developmental task, then, the father needs to learn and appreciate the fact that he has certain unique functions in the development of the child. He needs to learn that these cannot be performed by remaining aloof from the children or by waiting until they are older before attempting to be their companion and friend. These important developmental tasks of fatherhood can be some of the most challenging ones facing the man of the family—and some of the most enjoyable.

The man of the family needs also to recognize that he has a responsibility to himself to grow and develop as an individual. Usually he has less trouble in this respect than does his wife, for the man has the adult contacts at shop or office to help stimulate new interests or awaken old ones. His co-workers can be a ready set of companions with whom he can engage in sports or hobbies. In the complex workaday world with its fatiguing demands, perhaps the most difficult task in this respect is to recognize that the pursuit of self-interests is a necessary developmental task. It is good primarily because it is good for him as an individual, and not because it may also help him to be a better father or husband or provider.

Even our cursory treatment of his developmental tasks may appear overwhelming to a man with mere human qualities. The man who recognizes the developmental tasks that lie before him, however, may find that frequently he can act out his several roles at the same time. Yard work, for example, can be a chore that has to be done or it can be an opportunity for being with his wife or children. Children can learn manliness as well as cleanliness while helping their father wash the car or the windows of the house. At times, however, the many requirements placed on the man to be a successful husband-provider-father may be too great. Some of the most expensive child-care and home-maintenance work in the world is done by the American male, not in the sense of how much his time is worth but in the sense of the psychological toll it exacts from a man already overburdened by a demanding job and long hours of travel to and from work. Conflict between being a good provider and good family man is notorious. Determining how to allocate their scarce resources in time and energy proves difficult for many men, the more so when they must admit that regardless of how they work it out the optimum arrangement will be impossible to attain. All of this indicates that we must look upon the developmental tasks facing the man of the family as requiring learning and preparation and not as something that he automatically achieves as he moves into the child-rearing stage of the family life cycle.

As the various family members work out their developmental tasks during the child-rearing stage, the period may seem never-ending. But as the stage comes to a close, parents, in particular, may regret that it has been so short. Although the inclination to hold on to the familiar and the pleasant is natural enough, living means changing. Parents and children alike will have times for enjoying the memories of the satisfying child-rearing years. To the extent that they have met successfully their developmental tasks, they will be able to remember without regretting and to reminisce without longing to reverse the inevitable progress of time. They will be prepared, in other words, to meet the new challenges at the next stage of the family life cycle, and they will find that this stage also is good.

SELECTED READINGS

BEASLEY, CHRISTINE, *Democracy in the Home* (New York, Association Press, 1954).

BLOCK, JACK, "Personality Characteristics Associated with Father's Attitude toward Child Rearing," *Child Development*, Vol. 26 (March, 1955), pp. 41-48.

BLOOD, ROBERT O., "Consequences of Permissiveness for Parents of Young Children," *Marriage and Family Living*, Vol. 15 (August, 1953), pp. 209-212.

———, "A Situational Approach to the Study of Permissiveness in Child Rearing," *American Sociological Review*, Vol. 18 (February, 1953), pp. 84-87.

DUVALL, EVELYN M., *Family Development* (Philadelphia, J. B. Lippincott Company, 1957), Chs. 8, 9, and 10.

ELDER, RACHEL ANN, "Traditional and Developmental Conceptions of Fatherhood," *Marriage and Family Living*, Vol. 11 (Summer, 1949), pp. 98-101.

ENGLISH, O. SPURGEON, and FOSTER, CONSTANCE J., *Fathers Are Parents, Too* (New York, G. P. Putnam's Sons, 1951).

ERIKSON, ERIK, *Childhood and Society* (New York, W. W. Norton & Company, Inc., 1950).

FOOTE, NELSON N., and COTTRELL, LEONARD S., JR., *Identity and Interpersonal Competence* (Chicago, University of Chicago Press, 1955).

HAVIGHURST, ROBERT J., *Human Development and Education* (New York, Longmans, Green & Co., Inc., 1953), Chs. 2, 3, and 4.

LEVY, DAVID M., *Maternal Overprotection* (New York, Columbia University Press, 1943).

LINDER, ROBERT, *Must You Conform?* (New York, Rinehart & Company, Inc., 1956).

———, *Prescription for Rebellion* (New York, Rinehart & Company, Inc., 1953).

PORTER, BLAINE M., "The Relationship between Marital Adjustment and Parental Acceptance of Children," *Journal of Home Economics,* Vol. 47 (March, 1955), pp. 157-164.

STAPLES, RUTH, and SMITH, JUNE W., Attitudes of Grandmothers and Mothers toward Child Rearing Practices," *Child Development,* Vol. 25 (June, 1954), pp. 91-97.

STRECKER, EDWARD A., *Their Mothers' Sons* (Philadelphia, J. B. Lippincott Company, 1946).

CHAPTER 17

Later Stages in the Family Life Cycle

THROUGHOUT the child-rearing stage of the family life cycle, the child and his parents have in countless ways learned their roles, and they have played them in innumerable situations. Although the needs of the developing child have necessitated changes in the family interaction pattern, at the same time there has come to be a certain steadiness in the reciprocal roles of the parents and their child. The protection, help, and guidance by parents is not only anticipated but is needed and appreciated by the immature offspring. More or less suddenly there arises the need for a new relationship. The adolescent-child strives quickly to renounce childhood and to prepare himself for life outside the family. As the child's role changes, a corresponding change is required of his parents if the family is to settle down to a new interaction pattern. The onslaught of adolescence represents a milestone in the life cycle of the family just as surely as it is a junction in the personal life of the individual.

As the adolescent in the family passes through this transitory stage and on into adulthood, his middle-aged parents reach an eventful turning point in their lives. If he is the last or only child, the parents typically will be alone for the first time in many years. The new learnings required of them by the changing structure of their family group are accompanied by those brought on by their changing selves. In this chapter we will treat first the developmental tasks of the adolescent, at the same time touching on the reciprocal tasks of parents as they help him achieve adulthood. We will then turn to the married pair and the new and continued learnings required of them as individuals and as spouses. The chapter concludes with a discussion of the tasks facing the married couple as they pass from the intermediate stage into the final stage of the family life cycle.

DEVELOPMENTAL TASKS OF THE ADOLESCENT

Adolescence is a stage of transition. Indeed, its fundamental characteristic is that it overlaps both childhood and adulthood. The very ambiguity of the adolescent stage indicates the continuity in the process of human development. Adolescents face the same *general* life tasks as children and adults. But at this stage of life some tasks are considerably more pressing than previously they have been. Social, psychological, and biological forces converge at adolescence to produce a time of readiness for new learnings which must be accomplished before the person can be said to have become a competent adult.

An individual enters adolescence a child, and he should leave the period an adult. Perhaps the most obvious task facing him in the interim is the need to become an autonomous person, no longer emotionally dependent on his parents and freed from the need for direction from parents or other adults. Adolescents must reconcile societal demands, family expectations, and their own personality needs in such a manner that they emerge with a realistic masculine or feminine sex role. Adolescent boys and girls alike must come to grips with the economic realities of the society in which they live and select and prepare for a role in the economic system. Ultimately the normal adult is expected to be able to marry, so at the adolescent stage preparation for marriage and family living must be in the picture. A further developmental task involves the ability of the adolescent to find a place for himself among his age-mates.

Clearly the developmental tasks of the adolescent interpenetrate one another.[1] The young man or woman who is achieving emotional independence from his parents is at the same time, and through the same efforts, enhancing his adequacy both as a potential marriage partner and as a self-directing agent in the economic world. Learning an acceptable sex role is most assuredly linked with preparation for marriage and is related on a more immediate basis to finding a place for one's self in one's own generation. What we have done is to isolate several facets of the broad developmental tasks facing the individual at the adolescent stage so that through discussion we can better understand the complex new learnings in which the adolescent is involved. The length and definition of adolescence, as well as the specific nature of the tasks faced therein, exhibit a certain variation by social class, race, and ethnic status. At a more general level, all adolescents regardless of these characteristics are confronted with the same broad developmental tasks.[2] The nature of these tasks and the kinds of

[1] Cf. Douglas M. More, "Developmental Concordance and Discordance during Puberty and Early Adolescence," *Monographs of the Society for Research in Child Development*, Vol. 18, Serial No. 56 (1953), p. 21.

[2] Cf. Lawrence K. Frank and others, "Personality Development in Adolescent Girls," *Monographs of the Society for Research in Child Development*, Vol. 16, Serial No. 53 (1951), p. 10.

learnings they require should deepen our insight into the dynamics of family living at the third stage of the family life cycle.[3]

Achieving Independence

Modern American society demands a relatively high degree of autonomy on the part of its adult members. Our marriage pattern requires that the young couple establish and maintain their own home and that they rear their children with little help or supervision from parents. To be successful in our occupational system, a person needs to be able to move away from his parents, both spatially and socially. This is not to say that everyone who remains in his home town is either unsuccessful or immature, but, rather, that the autonomous adult would have the qualities and abilities to move if it seemed desirable.

Independence is not acquired solely during adulthood. When a youth enters the adolescent stage, ideally he has learned to make some of his own decisions and to take responsibility for his actions. In short, he has begun to be autonomous in the sense that previously we talked about this ability.[4] As an adult, it will certainly be possible for him to grow in self-respect, self-confidence, and self-control. During adolescence, however, there seems to be a demand for a relatively sudden spurt of growth in these abilities.

One of the first responsibilities of adolescents and their parents is to accept fully the necessity for achieving independence during the relatively short years of adolescence. By the time he is eighteen, for example, a boy is expected to have sufficient ability to make his own decisions and to manage his time and money to be able to serve in the armed forces of his country. An increasing number of girls of about the same age are choosing husbands, managing independent households, and preparing to bear and rear children. It is foolish to label these late teenagers "mere children" and to bemoan the fact that they are not being relieved of the responsibilities for which they are biologically capable. The fact remains that these are the kinds of responsibilities increasingly expected of adolescents in our society, and change in societal expectations, in the direction either of demanding more or less of its preadults, will come only gradually.

The adolescent needs to accept his share of the responsibilty for achieving independence. He needs to try to make his own decisions and gradually to relinquish the comforting aspects of control by parents or

[3] See the developmental tasks of adolescents in Robert J. Havighurst, *Human Development and Education* (New York, Longmans, Green, & Co., Inc., 1953), Ch. 16.
[4] See pp. 362-363.

other adults. He needs to learn that having one's own convictions, loyalties, and values means that one must necessarily reject some ideas and standards, even though they are held by his peers or his parents. The adolescent must increasingly come to lose the childish notion that somebody other than himself has the responsibility to keep him occupied. There is a part of most adolescents that cries out for independence in thought and behavior, but frequently there is also another part that longs for the familiar direction and help more suitable to a younger age. Although the first tendency may need to be tamed so that the person is truly self-directed rather than impulse-driven, the second tendency needs to be admitted and counteracted.

Parents can do much either to hinder or help the adolescent achieve his independence. Some parents, for example, manage to keep their adolescent economically naïve by retaining too tenacious a hold on the family purse strings. They teach him, by their policies more than by their words, that basically he is incapable of making purchasing choices and decisions. Other parents, conversely, work with their adolescent in evaluating his monetary needs and give him increasingly greater responsibility in financial matters. In this way the adolescent learns how to allocate his budgetary resources for clothes, refreshments, carfare, entertainment, and the like, and he gains the experience of making his own selections and purchases. Parents of adolescents further must learn to expect, to accept, and to look upon as desirable the fact that their child of a few years previous now has ideas and feelings different from their own. The tendency for parents to do otherwise is quite pronounced, and some parents become quite effective in squelching the least sign of adolescent originality or rudimentary self-direction.

Failure to achieve the learnings associated with gaining independence means that the person, despite his age, is not qualified for adulthood. Every clinician is acquainted with men and women who have never sufficiently freed themselves emotionally from their parents to be able to form an adequate marriage. Many such people do marry, of course, only to try to force their spouse into the role of parent substitute. Nearly everyone has had some acquaintance, too, with the pseudo-independent person who spends a life of constant rebellion against parents, authority figures, or social mandates generally. Such individuals are actually highly dependent on their parents, as much as are those whose binding tie is more obvious. In his compulsion for rebellion, the pseudo-independent negatively demonstrates how utterly he needs the very figures against whom he is rebelling. Whether dependency is expressed by blind submission to others or just as blind rebellion against them, it is scarcely an appropriate quality for an adult who must live in a world of adults. The time for making rapid strides toward emotional independence is adolescence.

Choosing and Preparing for an Occupation

Selecting his life's work and doing what is necessary to prepare himself for it are some of the more complex and important tasks facing the modern-day adolescent. Recent estimates show that there are over 50,000 specific occupations in our society, more than one hundred times as many as there were in 1870.[5] Every adolescent is most certainly not faced with 50,000 choices. Differential knowledge of possible occupations, differential ability, and, to a lesser extent, class background and race, all effectively help to determine what are realistic occupational choices for an individual. It is also true today that women cannot realistically expect to pursue some careers, although the number of jobs barred to women, or difficult for them to enter, is steadily decreasing. The sheer volume of occupational choices facing an adolescent of either sex is nevertheless staggering. Never before in our society has the range of possible choices been so extensive.

It is scarcely possible to overestimate the importance of making a wise occupational choice. It has been estimated, for example, that occupations requiring a college education will pay on the average $100,000 more over the individual's working life than jobs that do not require this much education.[6] Furthermore, there is considerable evidence that a sizable number of people somehow find themselves on jobs at which they are unhappy. They contribute to the high absenteeism and turnover rates in some occupations, or they stick doggedly to jobs they do not like, developing one psychosomatic complaint after the other. Some of these people are not very well prepared for any job; others would make good workers in some job other than the ones they have attempted. Both instances point to a failure to have met and solved the developmental task of choosing and preparing for an occupation.

Selecting and preparing for his life's work make many demands on the adolescent. Gradually he must build up a realistic picture of his capabilities and interests. A deep sense of security and a feeling of self-worth are clearly necessary before a person can reach the state of objective evaluation of his potentialities that is required. Some never reach this state and continue through life depreciating their abilities or failing to recognize their limitations. Once the adolescent has, in a general way, dis-

[5] *Job Guide for Young Workers: 1956-1957* (Washington, D.C., U.S. Government Printing Office, 1956).

[6] Paul C. Glick and Herman P. Miller, "Educational Level and Potential Income," *American Sociological Review*, Vol. 21 (June, 1956), pp. 307-312.

covered what he is able to do and what he wants to do, he needs to gain as much information and knowledge as possible about specific jobs and career fields. To do this effectively he must be able to seek and accept the counsel of parents, guidance officers, and others in a position to help him. Most frequently the adolescent is required to make at least a tentative selection of an occupation. He needs, finally, to do what is necessary to prepare himself for the occupation, whether this is gaining on-the-job experience, working summers to finance further education, or simply enrolling in the college of his choice. Today's adolescent male must keep in mind at the various stages of his career planning the necessity of satisfying his military service requirements. The odds are good that most healthy young men will sometime serve in the armed forces. It becomes the task of the adolescent to determine, within the choices he may have, when he should fulfill his military requirements and which of the various arrangements for so doing fits in best with his job and educational plans. To the extent that the adolescent has accomplished these many tasks he has done well, even though he may later revise his goals and change his course of preparation.

Parents of an adolescent play a significant role in helping him choose and prepare for his life's work. The first demand placed on parents is to accept their adolescent as a person with his own life's plans, his unique capabilities, and his individual interests. If they are able to do this, they will find it easier also to accept his early occupational choice as an experimental effort rather than an irrevocable committment. They will not depreciate his attempts to find his way in the adult world by calling his hopes "visionary" or otherwise make sport of what to the adolescent is, and should be, a serious matter. Parents need also to be realistic with their adolescent concerning how much help from home he can expect in furthering his education or in embarking on his career. The adolescent has a right to know whether the family budget can stand the cost of a "diesel rig," a college education, a business loan, or whatever else may be appropriate for his plans. It is an economic fact of life that many families can afford to give their child very little financial help, particularly if he is the eldest of many children. But surely the adolescent needs to know just what, in view of his family's limitations, he can expect. Although choosing and preparing for an occupation is a task that belongs to the adolescent, it is sometimes the parents who fail in the task.

Learning an Accepted and Satisfactory Sex Role

Male and female are biological concepts. Masculinity and femininity are cultural ones. All societies make a basic differentiation between the rights and duties of the sexes. Although sex-role differentiation is a funda-mental fact of human society, there is ample variation in the content of the roles of the sexes. In many, but not all, societies men are assigned those tasks that call for physical vigor and that involve periodic absence from the home.[7] Still as Linton has pointed out, Tasmanian women were the seal hunters, swimming out to the rocks, stalking the large animals, and clubbing them to death.[8] It is reported that Arapesh women are expected to carry heavier loads than men because women, by nature, have so much harder heads.[9] In our own society women are expected to be more "emo-tional" than men, to have deeper aesthetic appreciation, and to be more sympathetic.[10] In some societies these are manly qualities. From cross-cultural studies we can reach two conclusions. First, always and every-where there is a basic differentiation between the roles of the sexes. This role differentiation is almost always taken very seriously. It is defended and rationalized by various means, and it is taught with a vigor not found with many other aspects of social conditioning. Second, there is a wide variation among societies concerning what is considered appropriate be-havior for males and females.

The boy in American society will always be male; he must learn to become masculine. Similarly, there is no way a girl can avoid being female, but there is no guarantee she will be feminine. Despite the cross-cultural relativity in the definitions of masculine and feminine roles, each American boy and girl must learn what *this* society expects of him as an adult repre-sentative of his or her sex. This task is by no means easy. In the present-day United States the learning is made more difficult by the changing societal conceptions of sex roles and the presence of competing definitions of what are the appropriate roles of the sexes. This may very well mean that the adolescent's parents, as representatives of a different generation, are not good models of their sex, in the sense of what is expected of the youth. When the adult of his own sex whom the adolescent knows most intimately cannot be emulated completely, we can begin to appreciate the difficulty the adolescent has in learning an appropriate sex role.

The masculine role in our society is not easy to define.[11] Masculinity traditionally stands for strength and vigor and the ability to meet the

[7] George P. Murdock, *Social Structure* (New York, The Macmillan Co., 1949), p. 7.

[8] Ralph Linton, *The Study of Man* (New York, Appleton-Century-Crofts, Inc., 1936), p. 117.

[9] *Ibid.*

[10] Mirra Komarovsky, "Cultural Contradictions and Sex Roles," *American Journal of Sociology*, Vol. 52 (November, 1946), pp. 184-189.

[11] Cf. Mary Frank and Lawrence K. Frank, *Your Adolescent at Home and in School* (New York, The Viking Press, Inc., 1956), pp. 117 ff.

outside world head on and to deal effectively with it. This aspect of the masculine role probably receives the most emphasis in our society. Few boys grow up not wanting to be men in this sense. The difficulty is that the stereotypical version of the masculine role can, and has, become exaggerated. Many boys and men simply are not constitutionally equipped to engage in the kind of sports, to have the degree of strength, or to possess the kind of physique demanded by the exaggerated version of masculinity. Because of the emphasis placed on these things in our society, it is almost normal for the boy to worry about being normal. In addition, the adolescent boy has to come to grips with his own physique and his own physical abilities. He needs to recognize what society expects of him in this aspect of his masculinity, and he needs to determine how far he is willing to deviate from these expectations and still remain acceptable, most of all to himself.

Masculinity also implies being a husband and a father. The modern version of these roles demands traits and abilities that may be at odds with the man's role among men. Strength and power and aggressiveness are not nearly as valuable qualities for the father as tact, understanding, and firm guidance. It is becoming increasingly less acceptable to speak of the superiority of the male in marriage. Modern marriage more frequently calls for the ability of the husband to meet his wife as an equal partner in a common venture. The very traits that spell success in one facet of the masculine role may be liabilities in others. The adolescent boy must somehow reconcile the competing conceptions of masculinity with one another and with his own capabilities and personality needs. Ideally he should work out a personal version of the masculine role that is both satisfying to himself and acceptable to society.

Not so many years ago an adolescent girl could be relatively certain of the part in life she was expected to play. Her parents, the group of men from whom she would choose a husband, and the rest of the meaningful others in her life were in basic agreement concerning the proper role of an adult woman. Few people, least of all girls and women, need to be reminded that today we are far from consensus on the role of the adult woman. On her uncharted course through the troubled waters of adolescence, the girl is faced with perplexing alternatives. Choose she must, and choose she does, but is the choice always the best one for her?

In our society, power, prestige, and importance are largely tied to the kind of pursuits traditionally reserved for men. Woman has been invited into this world, and she has been told that with few reservations she can compete for the one-time masculine rewards. This, of course, is part of what we mean by the "equality of the sexes." The big pitfall for the adolescent girl is to interpret the new equality to mean that she must abandon any claim to femininity. In his study of adolescent girls, Frank reports, for example, that there was "a notable absence of being happy or even satisfied to be feminine and little or no indication of positive expectations of becoming a woman."[12] Rejection of one's unalterable biological sex and the failure to find emotional gratification in one's sex are scarcely indications that normal adult heterosexuality is being achieved. It is in this very direction, however, that many girls feel pressured. To want truly to be feminine is not easy for a young girl. Much that is done to her conditions her otherwise, so much so that More claims that the adolescent girl best suited for modern-day society is the one who *acts as if* she were sexually mature, "but who does not allow herself to feel the emotions which she appears to be acting out."[13] To the extent that emotional nihilism is encouraged, the tragedy of the adolescent girl is a social rather than a personal one. It is little wonder that the adolescent girl finds almost unmanageable her life's task of feeling satisfied with her own sex and contented in her own sex role.

The parents of the adolescent girl have much to do with the success the girl meets in her task of accepting her sex role. Some parents manage to convey early in life that this is basically "a man's world," that woman's place in it is inferior, and that all in all her lot in life is not a pleasant one. By example and precept they teach their daughters that woman's sexual functioning and her role in reproduction are trials and curses that must be borne rather than normal functions that can be enjoyed. At puberty when her biological self almost demands to be recognized, everything possible is done to teach the girl not merely to hold her emotions in check but even to deny that she has them. Especially in these changing times parents need to help their daughter discover the rewards of being a woman. They can help her see that employment outside of the home, for example, does not demand that she render herself psychologically neuter. They *could* perform the heretofore unmentionable service of teaching her that female sexuality is enjoyable, although wisdom dictates waiting a few years for complete fulfillment. Parents who themselves are not at peace with their own role and how it relates to that of the other sex will find it difficult to pass on to their daughter anything but insecurity, antagonism, and discontent.

[12] Frank and others, *op. cit.*, p. 203.
[13] More, *op. cit.*, p. 117.

Learning to Be an Acceptable Member of One's Own Generation

Although the ability to feel comfortable with people of ages different from one's own is a mark of social competence, one must also find a comfortable role for one's self among one's peers. This task begins early in life, but its time of ascendancy is adolescence. There are many positive reasons why the achievement of this task during adolescence is important. There are also stumbling blocks strewn in the paths of the adolescent who is trying to find a place for himself in his own generation.

Very few adolescents are oblivious of the standards, the behavior, or the activities of their peers, and few are completely void of any desire to interact with their age-mates. The more troublesome task for the adolescent is finding a place for himself among his peers which does not demand that he negate his individuality. He needs to learn that group ideas and group goals are not necessarily ethically superior to his own. It is a paradox that many adolescents, while insisting that they be free from their parents, are busily engaged forging chains of emotional bondage to "the group."

Parents, as well as adolescents, need to recognize the positive values inherent in acceptance in the peer group. In the first place, there are the personal validation and sense of self-worth that are gained by being found likable by a group of one's peers. These inner feelings will stand the adolescent in good stead as he meets and attempts to solve others of his developmental tasks. Peer group activities provide the opportunity for testing a myriad rudimentary social skills and for developing new ones. Peer group activities, finally, are enjoyable. Few parents deny that they enjoy being with friends, but some of these same parents fail to appreciate fully that adolescents too have fun being together. As part of their developmental tasks as parents of adolescents, the mother and father need to recognize the positive and worth-while functions associated with their adolescent's finding a comfortable place for himself among his peers. The adolescent, too, needs to gain some insight into these functions. He needs to assume his responsibility for being accepted by his contemporaries and for accomplishing this task in a way that does not mean sacrificing autonomy for acceptability.

Preparing for Marriage and Family Life

The developmental tasks of adolescence that we have already investigated—achieving independence of parents and other adults, choosing and preparing for an occupation, learning to accept one's sex role, and finding a place for one's self among one's age-mates—are all clearly related to preparation for marriage. So it is that the adolescent is simultaneously working on related developmental strivings. However, readiness for marriage is not something that occurs merely with increasing age nor even after related developmental tasks have been achieved. There are some tasks faced by adolescents, in other words, directly related to preparing for marriage and family life, regardless of what other abilities he may have for living in the adult world.

Entire courses of study, at both the high school and the college level, are oriented directly toward preparing young people for marriage. There are, in addition, related courses in homemaking and child care. It is not difficult to understand, therefore, why in our discussion of the developmental tasks necessary for preparation for marriage we must be content with tracing the broad outlines and then only of a few of the tasks.

American society has done a fairly complete job of segregating the married from the unmarried segments of its population. Few adolescents, even those with older siblings who are married, are able to learn of the joys, the problems, and the complexities of marriage and the family through intimate acquaintance with married couples of their own generation. When we label the acquisition of such knowledge a developmental task, we must admit that its sources most often must be the more formal ones of books, courses, counselors, and special classes. Somehow a realistic understanding of marriage and family life needs to be acquired. These learnings are practically essential before the young person realistically can assess his own readiness for marriage.

It may, at first, seem unusual to consider dating as a developmental task for adolescents. Yet dating is an early stage in the progressive process which culminates in marriage. Viewed as a developmental task, dating can serve the function of allowing the person to know a variety of personalities and to test his personality with them. It can help the person gain competence in getting along with the opposite sex. It can provide him with the opportunity to test and develop skills in social situations at a time when others his age are faced with the same uncertainty and ineptness that he is. There is, finally, a "mental hygiene value" to dating. To be found likable by a member of the other sex is a worth-while achievement in and of itself. Dating is also fun, and so it must be understood as part of the adolescent pattern of recreation. When dating is viewed as a developmental task, a framework is provided for resolving various difficulties and problems associated with it. Questions about the frequency of dating, about when, if, or at what age to "go steady," and the like can be viewed against the functions that dating should serve. Although the solutions to such problems will not be immediate, they should, when they come, be meaningful.

One of the more difficult developmental tasks confronting the adolescent is learning about the emotions of love and sex. In a very few years he will be expected to determine whether the emotional and physical attraction he feels toward a person of the other sex is sufficient to form a basis for marriage. Meanwhile he must try to understand the differences among the various sorts and degrees of love he will normally experience from time to time. In discovering how to handle his love and sex impluses, he should learn to take into account his long-term life's goals and values so that his present behavior can be guided by these conceptions of what he hopes to be. The uncertainty and doubts of adolescents, as well as the guilt and regrets of adults, are testimony enough that many in our society fail to understand themselves and their emotions and find difficulty in settling on a pattern of behavior with which they can be reasonably satisfied.

Parents of adolescents are faced with the perplexing task of learning to understand the maturing sexuality and the early love experiences of their boy or girl. Even normal curiosity and the desire to learn all that he can about sexual practices is enough to frighten some parents. Although they may intellectually accept the fact that readiness for marriage demands a certain amount of sexual knowledge, some parents interpret their adolescent's strivings toward this knowledge as perversity or an indication that he is heading for a life of promiscuity. In a similar manner, parents have an important role with respect to the adolescent's early love experiences. Regardless of whether parents think of them as "mere infatuations" or "puppy love," they need always to remember that they are important emotional involvements to the adolescent. Ridicule, censure, and interference may very well alienate the adolescent from them and may have a lasting effect on his ability to love and be loved. Parents of adolescents have a serious responsibility in helping their children to work through their emotional problems so that they will become neither traumas nor lifelong tragedies. Quite obviously the adolescent needs his parents. His is not the helpless need of an infant, but it is a need nevertheless.

DEVELOPMENTAL TASKS OF THE MARRIED PAIR IN THE MIDDLE STAGE OF THE FAMILY LIFE CYCLE

What we term the middle stage of the family life cycle is reached when the last child of the family passes through adolescence and leaves the home. The status of the family changes with some abruptness from one in which there was at least one child to one in which the married pair is the essential unit. This stage can be thought of as the reciprocal of the child-rearing stage. The one stage takes its definition from the addition of a dependent member to the family group; the other begins when, now independent, he leaves the family circle. Both types of change require readjustments and new learnings on the part of the married pair.

As the last child leaves the home, the parents will find that for the first time in twenty, thirty, or even more years they alone are the family. Some of the developmental tasks facing the married pair at the middle stage of the family life cycle, therefore, have to do with the reworking of their life together. Others are concerned with the husband and wife as individuals and the challenges they face as they move into and through this stage of life. Some of these individual tasks actually are more related to physical and mental development, and thus to age, than to family life cycle status, for they arise whether or not a child has recently left the home, or for that matter was ever in it. Although there is a certain concordance between age and family life cycle status, it is well to recognize that among families rather marked differences can be observed. Parents who had their last or only child while they were still fairly young will enter the middle stage of the family life cycle between the ages of forty and forty-five. Other parents may be considerably older than this when their last child reaches adulthood.

Many parents will be between the ages of forty-five and fifty-five when they reach the middle stage of the family cycle. Our discussion of the individual developmental task of *learning to accept the physiological changes of middle age* is based on this consideration. The task which we have labeled *discovering new satisfactions in the husband-wife relationship* comes to the fore because of the change in family life cycle status, independent of age. The third developmental task which we will investigate, *planning for retirement*, has its source both in the ages of the married pair and their family cycle status. Some of the accomplishments are called for because retirement age is being approached. Other types of planning assume that at about this age the couple will be alone and can use their present life together as a point of departure for their later years as a married pair.

Learning to Accept the Physiological Changes of Middle Age

At all times of life change is occurring in the human body and its processes. At times, like childhood and adolescence, the change is marked and easily observable. In the years of young adulthood physical change is generally slower and less noticeable. With the approach of middle age physiological change once again becomes more marked, particularly for women. In addition, both sexes are required to admit, to accept, and to adjust to those other changes that have been gradually occurring.

Some of the metamorphoses of middle age are readily apparent. Middle age brings with it changes in hair color, in body form, and in various of the body organs. Normally, hair either begins to fall out or it turns gray, the skin loses some of its tone and begins to wrinkle, and the eyes and ears begin to lose their efficiency. There is a tendency for the abdomen, hips, and thighs to become more prominent. Individuals differ, of course, in the age at which these symptoms occur, the order of their appearance, and their degree of intensity. Sooner or later the inevitable life's processes will manifest themselves in these and other outward signs.

Generally between the ages of forty-five and fifty-five most women will reach the end of their reproductive period. Folk language calls this the "change of life." More technically it is known as the *climacteric*, which comes from the Greek word *klimakter*, meaning the rung of a ladder. Both the folk and the technical terms express vividly that one of life's major transitions has taken place. The final cessation of her menses indicates dramatically that the woman is no longer able to play a role in the reproduction of the species. With the male, the decline of reproductive ability generally comes much later in life. There is no sudden change in the output of sex hormones, so that the diminution of reproductive powers is a gradual affair. There is some dispute whether or not *climacteric* is the correct term for such a gradual change in the male's reproductive capacity; it is nevertheless certain that almost all men eventually will lose their ability to produce offspring.

The physical changes in the man and woman are manifestations of the normal and inevitable forces of life. The developmental tasks of the man and woman concern their acceptance of and adjustment to these irreversible processes and their signs. Probably the people who find these changes troublesome are those who have throughout their lives accentuated physical appearance and the appeal of one sex for the other.[14] A man or woman who has neglected his other potentials at the expense of his physical ones may well be at a loss when his appearance changes and his sexual attraction wanes. These are the people who turn to the market place with its skin preparations, hair dyes, and numerous tonics in their futile effort to stave off life's inevitable changes or at least to disguise their manifestations. On the other hand, it is undoubtedly beneficial to keep one's self well groomed and clothed in modern attire if these things are done

[14] Jeanne G. Gilbert, *Understanding Old Age* (New York, The Ronald Press Company, 1952), p. 61.

to enhance self-esteem and to maintain general attractiveness. Procuring visual and auditory aids to compensate for the decline in these functions is a sensible admission of life's changes. Realistic adjustment to the physical changes of middle age, in other words, may require compensatory attention to the body and its appearance. This does not mean that one should attempt to make one's self over in the image of youth.

Individuals meet the climacteric and the waning of sexual attractiveness with various reactions. Some women seem to feel that when they can no longer render a reproductive service to the species, life has lost its essential meaning. Others meet the change in their life as a challenge and set about to develop new potentialities and find new satisfactions. Some men and women attempt to deny to themselves their lessening sexual potency and attractiveness by engaging, sometimes promiscuously, in extramarital affairs. Others, while not relishing the gradual decline of something they found enjoyable, are able to find pleasure in their declining marital sex activity, unhampered by needless regrets and futile longings. This is the difference between meeting and failing to meet the developmental tasks of accepting and adjusting to the physical changes of middle age.

Discovering New Satisfactions in the Husband-Wife Relationship

After the last child has left the home, there lies before the couple a relatively long period during which they, rather than the children, will be the focus of family life.[15] It is normal enough for a couple to find that it takes time and effort to redevelop their relationship with one another. Throughout the busy years of child rearing, the demands made on the woman in her role as mother and homemaker may have meant that her role of wife slipped into secondary significance. Now the children are away from home, and the homemaking tasks consequently are greatly reduced. In a similar manner, the man of the family may find his responsibilities reduced. By this stage of their lives, many men have reached the peak in their occupational career. No longer is there the same struggle to "get ahead" occupationally, and no longer will overtime or additional work be necessary to keep up with the needs of the growing family. Maintenance and repair work around the home may drop off abruptly as the children reach adolescence and then leave the home. The husband and wife usually will find that they have more time for one another. What is more, they will need one another in many important ways.

[15] See the discussion of the developmental tasks of husband and wife at this stage of the family cycle in Evelyn M. Duvall, *Family Development* (Philadelphia, J. B. Lippincott Company, 1957), Ch. 13.

It is not always easy for a middle-aged couple to recognize what their spouses need from them or to discover what is required of them in order to strengthen their life together. The wife needs to appreciate what it means to her husband to be near the peak of his occupational career. Often enough at this stage the man is forced to admit that he will never reach the heights to which he once aspired. He may already be feeling the competition of younger and better-trained men, or he may be discovering that technological improvements are pushing his once valuable skills into obsolescence. For his sense of self-worth and importance, the man needs the support and encouragement of his wife. He needs to feel that as a man and as a husband she needs him, appreciates him, and respects him. On his part, the husband should try to understand the void created in his wife's life by retirement from mothering and partial retirement from homemaking. It is understandable that a woman at this stage of the family life cycle feels the need for reassurance from the important man in her life. She wants to know that he, above all others, needs her and appreciates her, as well as loves her.

Couples at the post-child-rearing stage of the family life cycle will find it desirable to strengthen the psychological togetherness that once, presumably, marked their marriage. It may be hard, at first, for the wife to rekindle her interest in her husband's work and its problems, and it may be just as hard for the man to share with her the hopes, the disappointments, and the more mundane occurrences in his world away from home. A husband who has been busy away from home for many years may find it difficult to become reabsorbed in his home as the center of his marital life and the locus of his wife's major interests. Efficiency may have suggested that both the major and minor problems of homemaking be shunted off toward the wife. Now there is time for him to share his wife's domain and in so doing to grow closer to her as his wife.

Undoubtedly the psychological togetherness sought by middle-aged couples can be fostered and strengthened by increasing their shared activities. The needs of the children no longer have to be taken into account in planning vacations, hobbies, or projects. The husband and wife are free to do what they want to do, and fortunate are they who are able to find new interests at which they can work and play together. Renewed togetherness and the psychological support each spouse receives from the other are some of the great satisfactions for the middle-aged couples. Those at or approaching this stage of the family life cycle need to recognize that these satisfactions do not come automatically as the older children leave the home. As with other developmental tasks, the rewards and satisfactions go to those who are able to recognize and to make the changes required of them by advancement in the family life cycle.

Planning for Retirement

Probably no couple at the post-child-rearing stage of the family life cycle is completely oblivious to the need for planning for the time when the husband retires from work. Not all are aware, however, of the really fundamental alterations in their lives that will take place and the consequent need for thoughtful preparation. Financial planning is a case in point. For couples who have not done so previously, middle age is the time to try to assess their financial needs during retirement and to estimate the resources they will have for meeting them. A careful review of their Social Security status, their savings and insurance, and a thorough study of any retirement benefits are demanded. It may well be necessary to obtain the help of a financial adviser, either privately or through the husband's place of employment, for not all people are sufficiently equipped to make the decisions that may be necessary. The best of planning will not assure that all couples will meet retirement with no financial problems. Social and economic conditions of our society are such that a certain proportion of the population are destined to a life of severe hardships in their later years.[16] Most couples will nevertheless benefit from adequate financial planning for retirement and will find that thoughtful preparation, at a time when something still can be done, will make a difference.

Planning for retirement should include consideration of the greater leisure time that will be available and the ways in which the couple would like to spend it. Perhaps there are trips they would like to make or hobbies they would like to pursue. Frequently middle age is the time to think about things such as these. With the man still employed and few urgent financial problems, expenses can be arranged so that the goals for later years are more likely to be achieved. A middle-aged couple may decide, for example, to move to a smaller and less expensive home so that the savings can be used for better vacations, either at present or after the husband's retirement. Another couple may decide that upon retirement they will move to a new community, and as retirement approaches they will investigate and travel to possible locations for their new home. Preparation for part-time employment for the husband or wife may be advisable for some couples, and others will begin to develop new hobbies that are neither too expensive nor too physically demanding to carry over with them into their later years. In

[16] For a comprehensive treatment of the economic problems of older people, see Floyd A. Bond and others, *Our Needy Aged* (New York, Henry Holt & Co., Inc., 1954).

planning ahead in these and other areas the thoughtful couple will assure that when retirement comes it will mean retirement *to* something rather than *from* something. Making the most of the later years of life frequently means that the most has been made of earlier years.

DEVELOPMENTAL TASKS OF THE COUPLE IN THE AGING FAMILY

Throughout the life cycle of the family, there occur certain events that signify the transition from one stage to another. Thus the family cycle begins with the marriage of the couple, is thrust into a new phase with the birth of the first child, and enters still another phase when the last child leaves the home. The cycle abruptly comes to an end with the death of either spouse. The earlier stages in the family life cycle are generally characterized by abrupt beginnings and ends, but most couples slide gradually into what we have termed the aging family. Although a family with the complete status of "aged" has certain clear-cut characteristics, it is frequently more difficult to recognize a family that is in the process of aging.

To classify a couple as "aging" solely according to their chronological age is unrealistic. Surely the sixty-eight-year-old couple who are healthy, who maintain an independent household, and in which the husband is regularly employed differ little from themselves four years earlier. But neither can chronological age be ignored completely. Retirement of the husband is not a totally acceptable criterion of an aging family. The man who continues to work until he dies at age seventy-five has obviously aged, and, more to the point, in his lifetime both he and his wife were faced with many of the same developmental tasks as are faced by older couples generally. The usual adult family is expected to be able to provide for the economic needs of its members and to maintain its separate and independent household. When an older couple permanently relinquishes these responsibilities and functions, it has clearly passed into a new phase of family life. The aging family consists of an older couple that is moving in this direction. Often the husband's retirement from work represents the first indication of the family's changing status, less frequently it is the wife's inability to maintain a home for the couple, and sometimes it is merely the increasing years of the couple that thrust upon them new developmental tasks.

Some of the developmental tasks of spouses in an aging family have their bases in the changed roles of husband and wife within and outside the family. Other tasks are more clearly associated with physical aging and the limitations this places on the person and the effects it has on his spouse.

The successful meeting of both sorts of tasks will allow the couple to find in their final days together as many satisfactions as are available to them. To the young adult the rewards of old age may seem few and none too sweet. Almost anyone will admit, however, that finding the satisfactions at any stage of life is better than missing them completely.

Finding Satisfactions as a Useful Person

In some societies when a person becomes too old to perform his usual adult role, he is put to death or allowed to die of exposure and starvation. In other places the older person holds a position of esteem and is respected for his wisdom in practical affairs. The status of the aged in American society falls between these extremes. Although we attempt to treat the older person with kindness and sympathy, basically we have no adequate and useful role for those in their later years.[17] When older people claim that they have "nothing to do" or express feelings of rejection, they are voicing a societal more than an individual problem. As difficult as it may be, it nevertheless becomes the task of the person in the aging family to develop for himself a role in which he can find satisfaction and a sense of usefulness. Undoubtedly those husbands and wives who have met successfully earlier tasks associated with their development as individuals will be the best equipped to meet the new tasks of their later years. At the same time, everyone owes it to himself as a person to attempt to face up to and meet the demands that arise as he passes into the final stage of the family life cycle.

In a society that defines usefulness largely in terms of economic productivity, the old person probably can best retain a feeling of self-respect and adequacy by keeping a paying job as long as he is able to do so.[18] It is paradoxical that at the same time that the proportion of the aged in our society has been rising, fewer and fewer of those over sixty-five manage to remain in the labor force. It may well require considerable ingenuity for the older person to find employment. Undoubtedly he will be helped in this task by a flexibility of outlook that allows him to accept a job with less prestige and lower pay than he may have held customarily. Realistically, however, we cannot expect that most people will be able to find gainful employment for many years after the usual retirement age. Jobs are too few, and eventually the person will find himself physically or mentally unable to work. Women who have seldom or never worked outside the home

[17] Cf. John F. Cuber, Robert A. Harper, and William F. Kenkel, *Problems of American Society*, 3rd ed. (New York, Henry Holt & Co., Inc., 1956), pp. 292-295.
[18] Cf. Gilbert, *op. cit.*, pp. 326 ff.

may find it almost impossible to enter the labor force in their later years. As rewarding as gainful employment may be, many older people will be forced to fulfill their need for useful activity in other ways.

The specific ways in which older people can and do find a useful role for themselves are numerous. Some secure volunteer work with civic and social agencies. Others, individually or with their spouses, manage to keep finding hobbies that absorb their interest and do not overtax their strength. Frequently the adjustment of the older person is helped if he identifies with those of his own age and joins their groups. The negative effects of admitting to one's self and others that one is old are usually more than balanced by the rewards of affiliation with one's peers. In older age groups the tempo of life is slower, there is usually a freer admission of the value of recreation and pleasure, and usefulness has lost much of its economic connotation. Whatever interests and activities an older person develops must be in keeping with his physical and mental abilities, and they must perforce change as his abilities decline. More important, the activities should bring him satisfaction as well as a sense of achievement and purpose. The lifelong developmental task of finding fulfillment as an individual assumes challenging proportions in the last stage of the family life cycle.

Accepting and Adjusting to the Limitations of Physical Aging

The signs of physical aging that begin to appear in middle age frequently become more pronounced in later years. What may have been the annoyances and inconveniences of middle age can become the incapacities of old age. Even if they do not reach such proportions, most older couples will find that definite readjustments are required in both their individual lives and their life together. Older people generally need to readjust their thinking about the amount of work they can accomplish and the speed with which they can work. In their avoidance of overfatigue, the older husband and wife may find it necessary to curtail their activities and perhaps even their services for one another. Most older women, for example, cannot continue to do all of the physical work connected with homemaking. Both husband and wife are required, in this case, to accept the change brought on by limitation on the wife, whether it means obtaining domestic help, moving to a smaller home, or giving up their home altogether.

Old age carries with it an ever-increasing inclination to illness and disease. What is more, the disorders of the aged are likely to be accompanied by long periods of disability and even complete helplessness. It has been estimated, for example, that at least half of the people who live to be seventy-five years old will be faced with a period of invalidism before they die.[19] If the invalid or disabled spouse remains at home, frequently he will need extensive nursing care. In addition, the entire burden of managing and running the household falls to the other spouse, himself or herself probably also burdened with some of the infirmities of old age. The wife in the aging family may have to learn new skills and may find her own strength overtaxed as she takes on the responsibilities formerly shouldered by her disabled husband. Attempting to carry out the unfamiliar tasks of homemaking is likely to prove difficult for an older man who is also providing personal care for an invalid wife. As the irreversible forces of physical aging increase, more and more drastic adjustments are required of the married pair. It is never too late for a person to learn what his age and the stage of his family life cycle require of him and to try to work out the best possible solution within the available alternatives. For this reason the person in an aging family is faced with developmental tasks just as surely as is the infant or the newlywed.

Admitting the Realities of Widowhood

Few healthy, normal people look forward to their own or their spouse's death with equanimity and lack of anxiety. In the aging family, when both spouses are faced with the incontrovertible facts of aging, it is difficult to escape the thought that their life together is drawing to a close. Although we cannot discuss the personal adjustment of the remaining spouse following the termination of the family life cycle,[20] it is well to recognize that certain tasks preparatory to widowhood need to be met while the pair is still together. These are not morbid tasks, or at least they need not be. They amount, rather, to facing up to the realities of life. There is the sheer statistical fact, for example, that most wives outlive their husbands.[21] The husband and wife who do not consider this possibility in their housing, financial, and other plans are simply avoiding one of the facts of life and death. A widow who although mentally and physically capable is unprepared to manage whatever financial assets are available to her and to make decisions concerning them has failed in a developmental task at an earlier stage. As we have indicated already, there are most assuredly satisfactions to be found in the last stage of the family life cycle. It by no means detracts from these satisfactions to admit that it is the last stage and to devote

[19] Havighurst, op. cit., p. 277.
[20] See Ruth S. Cavan, Ernest W. Burgess, Robert J. Havighurst, and Herbert Goldhamer, Personal Adjustment in Old Age (Chicago, Science Research Associates, Inc., 1949).
[21] Metropolitan Life Insurance Company, "Widows Increasing in Number," Statistical Bulletin, No. 36 (January, 1955), pp. 6-8.

some thought to the inevitable fact that one or the other will then experience a period of widowhood.

SELECTED READINGS

ALBRECHT, RUTH, "Relationships of Older Parents with Their Children," *Marriage and Family Living*, Vol. 16 (February, 1954), pp. 32-35.

CAVAN, RUTH S., "Family Life and Family Substitutes in Old Age," *American Sociological Review*, Vol. 14 (February, 1949), pp. 71-83.

CONNER, RUTH, JOHANNIS, THEODORE B., JR., and WALTERS, JAMES, "Family Recreation in Relation to Role Conceptions of Family Members," *Marriage and Family Living*, Vol. 17 (November, 1955), pp. 306-309.

CROW, ALICE, "Parental Attitudes toward Boy-Girl Relations," *Journal of Educational Sociology*, Vol. 29 (November, 1955), pp. 126-133.

DONAHUE, WILMA, and TIBBITTS, CLARK, eds., *Growing in the Older Years* (Ann Arbor, University of Michigan Press, 1951).

DUVALL, EVELYN M., *Facts of Life and Love for Teen-Agers*, rev. ed. (New York, Association Press, 1956).

————, *Family Development* (Philadelphia, J. B. Lippincott Company, 1957), Chs. 11-14.

FRANK, MARY and LAWRENCE K., *Your Adolescent at Home and in School* (New York, The Viking Press, Inc., 1956).

FREID, EDRITA G., and STERN, KARL, "The Situation of the Aged within the Family," *American Journal of Orthopsychiatry*, Vol. 18 (January, 1948), pp. 31-53.

GILBERT, JEANNE G., *Understanding Old Age* (New York, The Ronald Press Company, 1952).

GROSS, IRMA H., ed., *Potentialities of Women in the Middle Years* (East Lansing, Michigan State University Press, 1956).

HAVIGHURST, ROBERT J., and ALBRECHT, RUTH, *Older People* (New York, Longmans, Green & Co., Inc., 1953).

HAVIGHURST, ROBERT J., and others, *Adolescent Character and Personality* (New York, John Wiley & Sons, Inc., 1949).

HERMAN, ROBERT D., "The 'Going Steady' Complex: A Re-Examination," *Marriage and Family Living*, Vol. 17 (February, 1955), pp. 36-40.

HUMPHREYS, J. ANTHONY, *Helping Youth Choose Careers* (Chicago, Science Research Associates, 1950).

KOLLER, MARVIN R., "Studies of Three-Generation Households," *Marriage and Family Living*, Vol. 16 (August, 1954), pp. 205-206.

LANDIS, PAUL H., *Adolescence and Youth*, rev. ed. (New York, McGraw-Hill Book Company, Inc., 1952).

LEVINE, LENA, and DOHERTY, BEKA, *The Menopause* (New York, Random House, 1952).

MOORE, DENISE F., "Sharing in Family Financial Management by High-School Students," *Marriage and Family Living*, Vol. 15 (November, 1953), pp. 319-321.

MUELLER, KATE H., *Educating Women for a Changing World* (Minneapolis, University of Minnesota Press, 1954).

NYE, IVAN, "Adolescent-Parent Adjustment: Age, Sex, Sibling Number, Broken Homes, and Employed Mothers as Variables," *Marriage and Family Living*, Vol. 14 (November, 1952), pp. 327-332.

ROSE, ARNOLD M., "Factors Associated with the Life Satisfaction of Middle-Class, Middle-Aged Persons," *Marriage and Family Living*, Vol. 17 (February, 1955), pp. 15-19.

SCHOEPPE, AILEEN, HAGGARD, ERNEST A., and HAVIGHURST, ROBERT J., "Some Factors Affecting Sixteen-Year-Olds' Success in Five Developmental Tasks," *Journal of Abnormal and Social Psychology*, Vol. 42 (October, 1952), pp. 42-52.

TOWNSEND, PETER, *The Family Life of Old People* (Glencoe, Illinois, The Free Press, 1958).

WALLIN, PAUL, "Cultural Contradictions and Sex Roles: A Repeat Study," *American Sociological Review*, Vol. 15 (April, 1950), pp. 288-293.

WALTERS, JAMES, and OJEMANN, RALPH H., "A Study of the Components of Adolescent Attitudes Concerning the Role of Women," *Journal of Social Psychology*, Vol. 35 (February, 1952), pp. 101-110.

Part IV

THE PSYCHOANALYTIC STUDY
OF THE FAMILY

CHAPTER 18

Basic Psychoanalytic Concepts

Most INFORMED people have heard of psychoanalysis. Few people understand it. All of psychoanalysis is dismissed by some as a fantastic, somewhat shocking kind of therapy in which the emotionally disturbed unburden themselves of torturing thoughts, primarily those of a sexual nature. Others view psychoanalysis as nothing more than a weird parlor game, and still others, in opposition, consider it a panacea for all of the ills of the world. Most of those with more moderate views recognize that psychoanalysis deals with personality development, that it stresses the importance of the experiences of early childhood, and that, therefore, it would have some relevance for the study of the family. Before we can elaborate on the appropriateness of the psychoanalytic framework for the study of the family, it is clear that we must try to determine what psychoanalysis is and what it is not.

The Viennese physician Sigmund Freud is generally considered the founder of psychoanalysis.[1] In his early work with nervous disorders, particularly hysteria, Freud and his older colleague Breuer noted that various symptoms disappeared when the patient was made to recall in a waking state some forgotten experience that had been uncovered during hypnosis. Freud later abandoned hypnosis, for he discovered that the cure was only temporary and that one neurotic symptom would be replaced by another. Nevertheless the germ of psychoanalysis had been born; even those experiences, wishes, or ideas considered by a person himself to be forgotten can exert an influence on his contemporary behavior. Over the years and through his work with many patients, Freud found ample verification of the importance of that part of the mind of which the person is unaware, or the *unconscious* as it came to be called. Gradually there developed out

[1] For a brief history of psychoanalysis see Ernest Jones, *What Is Psychoanalysis?*, rev ed. (New York, International Universities Press, Inc., 1948), Ch. 2, and Calvin S. Hall, *A Primer of Freudian Psychology* (New York, The World Publishing Company, 1954), pp. 7 ff.

of these experiences an organized body of knowledge about the workings of the human mind, particularly its unconscious aspects.

The term *psychoanalysis* is used today in several senses.[2] Psychoanalysis is a special form of therapy, or medical treatment, devised by Freud for the cure of certain kinds of nervous disorders. Note that it is *one technique for treating* the emotionally disturbed, not just *any* technique. Psychoanalysis is also a procedure for the investigation of mental processes. In this meaning it is a special method for exploring the deeper layers of the human mind with the primary aim of understanding its intricate workings. It is thus *a method of research*. The term *psychoanalysis*, finally, is used also to describe the body of knowledge that gradually has been built up through the use of the research and therapeutic methods. Psychoanalysis is in this sense *a theoretical system* that attempts to explain the development and functioning of the human personality.

Psychoanalytic theory, as systematic knowledge about personality, is concerned both with normal development and functioning and the deviations from the normal that are wont to occur. In the remainder of this chapter we will discuss some of the major concepts and tenets of psychoanalytic theory. Following this we will be in a position to comment generally on the psychoanalytic approach to the study of the family and the insights it can provide into personality development and interpersonal relationships within the family. The remaining two chapters in this section each deal with specific phases of family life, and each utilizes and continues to build upon the basic tenets set forth in this chapter. Sequential reading of the chapters, therefore, is strongly advised.

BASIC CONCEPTS AND TENETS

Although the name of Sigmund Freud is irrevocably linked with psychoanalysis, many people are aware that there are today various psychoanalytic schools. Some of the founders of independent systems of psychoanalysis, for example, Jung and Adler, were originally adherents of the Freudian system. The leaders of other schools, such as Horney, Sullivan, and Alexander, were one or more steps removed from the direct influence of Freud. The major schools of psychoanalysis, of which there are many more than we have indicated, each consist of a theoretical system with its own major premises.[3] The conclusions on the nature of personality reached by

[2] Cf. Jones, *op. cit.*, p. 8, and Otto Fenichel, *The Psychoanalytic Theory of Neurosis* (New York, W. W. Norton & Company, Inc., 1945), pp. 7 ff.

[3] For an excellent critical review of the various schools of psychoanalysis, see Ruth L. Munroe, *Schools of Psychoanalytic Thought* (New York, The Dryden Press, Inc., 1955).

each school fit together in an integrated pattern. Obviously we cannot begin to investigate each separate psychoanalytic system. There are grave difficulties, on the other hand, in merely selecting concepts or conclusions from the different schools and attempting to apply the strange conglomerate to the study of the family. It is the familiar problem of specific parts becoming distorted or meaningless when taken out of context from their integrated whole.

Despite the divergency within the ranks of psychoanalysis, there is a certain common conceptual ground on which they meet. There are some basic premises, some concepts, and even some methods of therapy that are characteristic of all psychoanalysis rather than a particular school of psychoanalysis. It is these basic, common concepts that we need to investigate more thoroughly, for it is essentially these that will be applied to the study of interpersonal relations within the family. Otherwise, we have drawn on psychoanalytic literature which probably would be labeled *Freudian* or *neo-Freudian*.

The Unconscious

An extremely important concept of psychoanalysis is that there are mental processes and mental phenomena of which the individual is unaware. Stripped down to its bare essentials, the notion of an unconscious mind is not hard for most people to accept. Almost everyone, for example, has had the experience of not being able to recall a name that he "knew." Temporarily, at least, the name was in an inaccessible part of his mind and try as he would it could not be brought forth and pronounced. But the name was not completely gone, for "somehow" it suddenly came to the person, perhaps at quite an interval after he had despaired of remembering it. *Where* was the elusive name, and *how* did it manage to return from wherever it was? In this simple illustration we see that one has thoughts of which one is not aware or conscious and similarly that there is a movement, itself not under the conscious control of the person, from the level of unawareness to the level of awareness. The forgotten name, of course, was not really forgotten but for a time was not among the conscious thoughts.

Not everything that a person has ever experienced, or known, or feared can be recalled from the unconscious with the relative ease of most instances of forgotten names. The term *unconscious* generally is reserved for those mental materials and processes of which one cannot become aware save by special analytical procedures.[4] Materials not at such a depth but

[4] Sigmund Freud, *An Outline of Psychoanalysis* (New York, W. W. Norton & Company, Inc., 1949), p. 38.

not subject to immediate recall are said to be residing in the preconscious or foreconscious.[5] It is more accurate still to envision various degrees of consciousness and non-consciousness with the instantly recalled type of memory at one end of the scale and, at the other, the memory which only can be recalled with the aid of psychoanalysis. These posited levels of the mind are merely a kind of topographical analogy. There are no compart- ments in the human brain that mechanically hold the different types of memories. What determines the level of non-consciousness is the strength or intensity of countervailing forces that are acting upon a supposedly for- gotten thought. Another way of describing the true unconscious, therefore, would be to say that it consists of those mental materials against which strong forces stand opposing their entry into consciousness.

By definition, one cannot be aware of his unconscious mental proc- esses. Early childhood experiences, pleasant and unpleasant episodes of long ago, and a host of other types of forgotten memories nevertheless can continue to have an effect long after they have been pushed from conscious- ness. The simplest demonstration of the sometimes compelling force of unconscious motives can be found in the phenomenon of posthypnotic suggestion. Many people have either witnessed or read about a demonstra- tion in which the subject under hypnosis is told that at some specified time after he is awakened he will perform some act, like scratching his ears or winding a clock. When the subject does in fact carry out what was sug- gested to him while under hypnosis he will be the first to admit that he does not know *why* he is behaving as he is. Some compelling force of which he is not aware is nevertheless affecting his conscious behavior. So it is that thoughts and experiences that have reached the unconscious by more usual means than hypnosis can exert an influence without the person being aware of either the existence of the thought or the fact that it is affecting his actions.

The formulation of the concept of the unconscious is a major con- tribution of psychoanalytic theory. It has thrown open whole new avenues of research into human motivation. Recently advertisers have begun to give it more serious attention. In the technique of Precon, for example, a message is flashed on a motion-picture screen at such a speed that the viewer is unaware that he is seeing it. Frequently he acts as if he saw it, for he buys the soft drink or popcorn or whatever else was advertised. We are not sug- gesting that in choosing a mate or a job or doing anything else for that matter, one is influenced only by unconscious thoughts that somehow flash across a mental screen. Recognizing the importance of the unconscious

[5] *Ibid.*

means that in these and other situations motives of which one is unaware may be exerting significant influence.

Psychic Determinism

A second principle of psychoanalysis is that no behavior is purely accidental.[6] The simplest thing that a person does or says has a cause or a reason behind it. Gestures, slips of speech, dreams, forgetfulness, and so on, all have some explanation. It is not denied that reflex, habit, and conscious thought-control influence behavior outcome. Psychoanalysis gives considerably more emphasis, however, to the role of the unconscious. Accepting the view that all behavior is caused does not mean that the causes are immediately recognizable. If a newly married man, for example, mistakenly talks of his "moneyhoon," it does not necessarily mean that he is resentful of the financial toll of his wedding trip. It could possibly mean this or something akin to this, or it may have an entirely different meaning. It does mean *something*. Although a slip of the tongue or any other action is not without a cause or reason, the individual himself would have to be understood before its significance to him would be clear. It is in the parlor-game, not in psychoanalysis, that a single dream or a specific action is given an immediate and unequivocal "interpretation" out of context of the individual's personality and life history.

We have already implied that a single action may result from different causes operating simultaneously. Freudian psychoanalysts frequently use the term *overdetermination* to mean that the same behavior has multiple causes at different levels of consciousness.[7] Each of the influences may be interpreted meaningfully at its own level. A simple hypothetical example will illustrate the principle of overdetermination. A man may want to marry a certain woman because unconsciously he sees in her something of his mother. At the same time unconsciously he detects other resemblances to his older sister whom he long ago wanted to surpass and figuratively to master. If the man is an American, he will tell you he is marrying the woman because he is deeply in love with her, and no one is denying that he is. The man may also admit that his wedding plans have been influenced by a desire to avoid military service. There are thus multiple forces that together determine that he marries a certain woman at this time. It is not immediately apparent which forces have exerted the greater influence in his marital choice or which, for that matter, will have the most bearing on whether he can be happy with the woman after they are married.

[6] Cf. A. A. Brill, *Basic Principles of Psychoanalysis* (Garden City, New York, Doubleday and Company, Inc., 1949), pp. 19 and 41.
[7] Munroe, *op. cit.*, p. 54.

The principle that all behavior is caused, with its refinement of over-determination, greatly enlarges the area of human motivation that can be investigated, particularly when this principle is coupled with the concept of the unconscious. More complete insights into human behavior can be obtained by trying to discover the various forces which at different levels of awareness have exerted an influence. When a psychoanalyst delves into the symbolic meaning of dreams or seeming minutiae of everyday life, he is not ignoring the obvious or "simple" explanations, but he is attempting to discover also any unconscious forces that may be at work to a significant degree. He is striving to understand, or in the case of therapy to cure, an entire, complex personality with its myriad forces and counterforces.

The Genetic Approach

It is not just the poet who believes that "the child is father to the man." Although all of the behavioral sciences recognize the importance of early experiences for later personality organization, it is psychoanalysis that originally laid stress on the lasting effects of childhood experiences.[8] In psychoanalytic theory, the adult personality is not something to be studied in and of itself. Psychoanalysis emphasizes the theory that the basic personality patterns of an adult are the product of his growing experiences as he came into contact with and adapted to the outside world. By analogy, the plastic mass of personality took its basic shape in the early years of life, and the continuing experiences thereafter gradually hardened the mass and brought out the details of line and contour. This concern for the origin of personality and its development is what is meant by *the genetic approach* of psychoanalysis.

Freudian psychoanalysts conceptualize personality development in terms of relatively fixed stages through which the individual passes.[9] The stages gradually fade one into the next, and there is a considerable amount of overlapping among them. In terms of chronological age, there is a certain amount of individual variation with regard to when the various characteristics of a given stage will come into prominence. Despite the overlapping nature of the stages and the individual variations in reaching them, they can nevertheless be thought of as recognizable phases in the regular progression from infancy to adulthood. No stage is completely left behind, but always some of the characteristics of the earlier level are carried forward throughout the remaining stages. The personality of the normal adult, therefore, cannot be fully understood without reference to his earlier stages of psychic development. We will deal more specifically with the stages of

[8] *Ibid.*. p. 34. See also Jones, *op. cit.*, pp. 106-107.
[9] Cf. Hall, *op. cit.*, pp. 107-119, and Jones, *op. cit.*, pp. 41 ff.

development in the chapters that follow. For the present it is necessary to realize that the genetic approach of Freudian psychoanalysis utilizes the concept of stages of personality development. It is further held that psychological phenomena in the adult can meaningfully be understood in terms of the problems faced by the person in the early stages and the ways in which these problems were handled.

Although non-Freudian psychoanalysts deal with the consequences of early childhood experiences in different ways, there is basic agreement that the major directions of personality are set in early childhood and that the adult personality, therefore, can best be understood in terms of its development rather than in its contemporaneous existence.

If in the normal course of events a child's body reaches a permanent halt in its growth process, we speak of his growth as having been stunted. If an individual remains at a psychological stage inappropriate to the rest of his development, he is said to have become *fixated*.[10] Fixation is a relative matter, ranging from near-complete arrestment of development to only somewhat greater than normal retention of characteristics of an earlier stage. The causes of fixation are complex and include both too extreme frustration and too great satisfaction at a particular stage of development.[11] A common pattern in fixation is excessive satisfaction at one stage that allays the anxiety felt in connection with advancing to the new and unfamiliar stage.

A person's return to a stage in his psychic development through which he earlier passed is referred to as *regression*.[12] Too great disappointment or frustration at a given stage of development may give rise to a longing for an earlier period of life when experiences were more pleasant and satisfying. The longing may lead to a return if there was a certain amount of fixation at the earlier stage. Extreme dangers and sudden or intense threats can bring about regression even in those without an undue amount of fixation in their psychic history. Although the normal person occasionally may allow himself, as it were, to indulge in regressive behavior, full regression is pathological. Many of the bizarre symptoms of neurotics can be understood as a disguised acting-out of the impulses and fears of an earlier stage of development.

The Organization of Personality

Freud conceived of the total personality as consisting of three provinces which he called the *Id*, the *Ego*, and the *Superego*.[13] These three major

---

[10] Fenichel, *op. cit.*, p. 65.
[11] *Ibid.*, pp. 65-66.
[12] *Ibid.*, pp. 65-66, 159-160.
[13] Freud, *op. cit.*, pp. 43 ff. See also Hall, *op. cit.*, Ch. 2.

systems of the personality perform different functions and utilize different mechanisms and processes. In the healthy personality the three provinces fit together to form a co-ordinated totality. The individual is able to find satisfactions for his basic needs and wishes within the delimited features of his environment. At times, however, there may be conflict between the parts of the individual's personality and this conflict may give rise to symptoms like worry, anxiety, or regret. Needs go unmet and the individual is not at peace with himself or his environment. To understand a personality, it is necessary to know something about how the three provinces developed and how normally they relate one to the other.

The personality at birth exists in an undifferentiated form and has not yet developed the three major provinces. The personality of the infant consists almost entirely of a number of instinctual drives that demand gratification. These drives are known collectively as the Id. The Id operates on the pleasure principle, which consists of attempting to avoid pain and to seek pleasure. Its unorganized and diffuse energy strives for release without regard for the outside world or the people in it. The forces that make up the Id are asocial, amoral, and devoid of ethical considerations. Discomforts arising either from internal or external stimuli seek immediate relief. The primary purpose of the Id is to satisfy the instinctual needs, and in its undifferentiated state it strives to do so with persistence. The Id, like a spoiled child, wants what it wants when it wants it.

The personality of the infant does not long remain governed only by the undisciplined Id. In his long trek toward becoming a social being, the infant must learn that wishes cannot find immediate gratification. He must learn, in short, to relate his inner drives to the outside world and the outside world to his inner drives. This situation calls for a new type of personality mechanism. In response to this need there arises from the Id a system capable of acting in the position intermediary between the Id and the environment. This new system is the Ego. It will continue to retain the function of reconciling the demands of the Id with the realities of the environment. Whereas once unharnessed drives sought immediate satisfaction regardless of custom, order, or the needs of other people, now the Ego must find ways within these social realities for the demands of the Id to find expression. Whereas the Id operated on the pleasure principle, the Ego now attempts to inaugurate the reality principle, that is, the capacity to forgo the pleasure of immediate gratification in order to gain pleasure or avoid pain at some future time. The realities of social living demand that the pleasure principle be abandoned in favor of the reality principle.

Sheer efficiency would suggest that a way be found whereby the Ego would be relieved of the necessity for almost continually making judg-ments concerning the expression of impulses of the Id. There is a need, in other words, for a retention of the demands of the outside world in addition to the mere observation of them. To meet this need a part of the Ego splits off to form the third personality system, the Superego.

The main source of impulse gratification for the infant and his main source of impulse frustration are his parents. For all practical purposes, then, the outside world with which the young child's Ego must deal con-sists of his parents. So it is that the Superego begins as a retention of parental "do's and don't's." Originally it consists of the assimilation and in-ternalization of the codes and standards of parents. The actual authority of the parents is replaced by the child's inner authority. At this stage, im-pulses and wishes which seek expression must be related not only to the realities of the external environment but also to the collection of behavioral standards that are stored in the Superego.

It is useful to distinguish between two sub-systems of the Superego, the *Conscience* and the *Ego Ideal*. The internalized parental prohibitions are collectively thought of as the Conscience.[14] The child's Conscience develops as he is able to understand more of the parental prohibitions and to incorporate them into his own personality. The Conscience is further enlarged as teachers and others in a position to influence the child instill prohibitions of their own. This part of the Superego is thus essentially what has been incorporated of the restraints and prohibitions of other people.

The Ego Ideal arises in response to the felt deficiencies and limitations in one's self as one really is.[15] To compensate for these inadequacies, the child begins to construct a picture of himself as he would like to be. Into this picture go physical, moral, mental, and other sorts of traits and skills that the child has observed in his parents. Later, other people exhibit their personalities to the child and from the many traits which are modeled for him the child selects some to incorporate in his Ego Ideal. The construction of the Ego Ideal is not restricted to childhood. We see the adolescent trying to dress or act like a favorite movie star, and we see the underling aping the behavior of his superior. All through life various ego models exhibit their personalities, and from these are selected some traits which are incorporated in the image of the self one would like to be.

---

[14] A full treatment of the origin and development of the Conscience can be found in Edmund Bergler, *The Battle of the Conscience* (Washington, D.C., Washington Institute of Medicine, 1948).

[15] For a general discussion of the concept Ego Ideal see J. C. Flugel, *Man, Morals and Society* (New York, International Universities Press, Inc., 1945), p. 35.

In its totality the Ego Ideal represents a standard of perfection toward which an individual is striving.

The Ego Ideal and the Conscience have been described as opposite sides of the same moral coin.[16] As parts of the Superego, they share the function of controlling behavior. What a person is and does and what he allows or forces himself to strive for are intricately bound up in the prohibitions and demands of his Superego. It should be borne in mind, finally, that the Superego functions largely unconsciously. An individual is only partly aware of the many internalized prohibitions that guide his behavior. In a similar manner, he is only partly aware of the various aspects of his Ego Ideal. Forgotten or unknown qualities in the self that one would like to be can continue to exert an influence on behavior just as surely as can the more recognizable goals that form the conscious part of the Ego Ideal.

THE PSYCHOANALYTIC STUDY OF THE FAMILY

All marriage and family living requires interaction. It is the unique contribution of psychoanalysis to focus on the personalities of the family members engaged in interaction. Clearly the psychic equipment that the husband and wife bring to marriage is going to affect the way in which they interact with one another and just as surely will it affect the way in which they rear their children. The child, in turn, will come to interact with his peers; he will date, become engaged, and marry. To all of this interaction he brings a self that received its original mold in his family. Bringing into sharper focus the normal personality development of the individual is thus one method of gaining insight into the complex net of interaction among family members.

Even a cursory review of the basic concepts we have discussed in this chapter will allow us to illustrate more concretely the unique contributions of the psychoanalytic approach to the study of the family. Combining the concepts "unconscious," "psychic determinism," and "the genetic approach," we have already learned much about the influence of the family on the child. We see why, in the light of these concepts, the years of early childhood receive so much stress in psychoanalytic theory and elsewhere. What happens in these formative years is never really forgotten. To be sure, it is gone from consciousness, but it is not dead. Whether the influences were good, bad, or mediocre, they become a part of the personality of the adult. There are many factors that influence how a person chooses a mate, lives with her after marriage, and helps in the

[16] Hall, *op. cit.*, p. 26.

rearing of their children. According to the genetic or developmental theory, one important line of influence will be how as a child the person worked-through his love and hate and other emotions with his parents and his siblings.

Earlier we said that the concept of the unconscious is the keystone of psychoanalytic theory. That part of us of which we are not aware is the hidden but not silent partner in all of our interactions. In mate selection and in almost innumerable situations in marriage and family living this obscure partner makes his presence felt. To understand the nature and the power of unconscious forces is to understand more fully the interacting personalities in the family. Just as we miss the true dimensions of an iceberg if we fail to recognize the submerged portion, so we do not get a complete picture of personality and personality interaction unless we include that which lies beneath the level of immediate awareness.

Perhaps nowhere does psychoanalytic theory more clearly relate to the study of family interaction than it does with respect to the formation of the Superego. The Conscience of psychoanalytic theory does not "just happen." Its strength and its content reflect the early family experiences in no uncertain terms. When all is functioning well, the basic needs of the Id sooner or later find gratification in ways of which society approves and which the Superego will allow. Too harsh a Superego may foredoom a person to a life of inner tension and frustration. A Superego that makes it impossible for a person to have or to enjoy marital sexual relations, for example, is obviously malformed. An individual who is constantly tortured by the neurotic thought that somebody, somewhere, is having a better time than he can scarcely make an adequate spouse or parent, or for that matter a reasonable adult. We have ample evidence, on the other hand, of individuals who have failed to incorporate into their Consciences the usual prohibitions and rules of social behavior. True social living is impossible if the deviation is extreme, and even in less severe cases the person may find himself continually at odds with his society. How the Superego developed and who were the significant adults who influenced its development become matters of extreme importance.

The Ego Ideal sub-system of the Superego is likewise important to understand. Normally the child's first ego models are his parents. It is from his parents that he selects traits and characteristics to incorporate into the standard that becomes the self that he would like to be. According to psychoanalytic theory, the original content of the Ego Ideal, like all early experiences, is not strictly forgotten. It is, of course, overlaid with other experiences, and the abandoned selves of childhood may have been successfully obliterated from awareness. But they are not gone. In a later chapter we will see how in choosing a marriage partner the normal individual is guided unconsciously by the selves he cannot be and the selves he must be. The abandoned and retained aspects of the Ego Ideal are certainly not the only influences on mate selection. The fact that they do have an influence attests to the need for a better understanding of this phase of psychic life.

In the chapters that follow we will explore psychoanalytic theory more thoroughly. The relationships and effects that we have merely hinted at here should begin to take on meaning and should begin to "make sense" within the psychoanalytic framework. It has been our purpose in this introductory chapter to provide a background for that which follows by investigating some of the basic concepts that underlie psychoanalysis. In a most general way we have attempted also to demonstrate the unique approach of psychoanalysis to the study of the family. The two chapters that follow can be thought of as an elaboration of this latter point.

SELECTED READINGS

BLUM, GERALD S., *Psychoanalytic Theories of Personality* (New York, McGraw-Hill Book Company, Inc., 1953).

BRILL, A. A., *Basic Principles of Psychoanalysis* (Garden City, New York, Doubleday & Company, Inc., 1949).

FENICHEL, OTTO, *The Psychoanalytic Theory of Neurosis* (New York, W. W. Norton & Company, Inc., 1945).

FLUGEL, J. C., *Man, Morals and Society* (New York, International Universities Press, Inc., 1945).

FREUD, ANNA, *The Ego and the Mechanisms of Defense* (New York, International Universities Press, Inc., 1946).

FREUD, SIGMUND, *Collected Papers*, 4 vols. (London, Hogarth Press, Ltd., 1925).

———, *New Introductory Lectures on Psycho-Analysis* (New York, W. W. Norton & Company, Inc., 1933).

———, *An Outline of Psychoanalysis* (New York, W. W. Norton & Company, Inc., 1949).

———, *Three Contributions to the Theory of Sex*, 2nd ed. (New York, Nervous and Mental Disease Publishing Company, 1916).

HALL, CALVIN S., *A Primer of Freudian Psychology* (New York, The World Publishing Company, 1954).

JONES, ERNEST, *What Is Psychoanalysis?*, rev. ed. (New York, International Universities Press, Inc., 1948).

MUNROE, RUTH L., *Schools of Psychoanalytic Thought* (New York, The Dryden Press, Inc., 1955).

SEARS, ROBERT R., "Survey of Objective Studies of Psychoanalytic Concepts," *Social Science Research Council Bulletin*, No. 51 (1943).

WILBER, G. B., and MUENSTERBERGER, W., eds., *Psychoanalysis and Culture* (New York, International Universities Press, Inc., 1951).

CHAPTER 19

Family Experiences and Early
Psychosexual Development

ACCORDING TO the genetic principle of psychoanalysis, a person is the product of all of his experiences. He cannot erase completely a certain segment of his life and proceed onward as if it had not happened. When a young man and woman fall in love, marry, and begin to raise children of their own, each brings to this new family a relatively long history of love experiences.

To understand better the early portions of the individual's life history is the primary objective in this chapter. We will describe the normal pattern of development of the love-sex drive that culminates in the ability to love a person of the opposite sex and co-operate with him in the task of reproducing the species. Through the account of the normal development of the child, deeper insights should be obtained into the important influences of the parents and of the early family experiences on the child's personality. In addition, a better understanding of adult love and sexual drives should be derived from the investigation of their psychological forerunners. Although our focus will be on normal development and the family effects thereon, we will take occasion also to indicate the kinds of parental handling that may interfere with or make difficult the normal course of development.

The Sexual Drive

In Freud's conception, a drive has three aspects, its source, its aim, and its object.[1] The source of a drive is the state of tension or excitation within the body that produces a quantum of energy. The aim of all drives is to obtain pleasure by removing or reducing the state of tension. The object

[1] Sigmund Freud, *New Introductory Lectures on Psycho-Analysis* (New York, W. W. Norton & Company, Inc., 1933), pp. 132 ff.

of a drive is that through which it achieves its aim of tension reduction. The source and aim of a drive are considered to be part of the individual's normal biological equipment. The object of the drive is learned.

One entire category of drives Freud labeled *sexual*. All impulses connected with love in its broadest possible sense would be included in the sexual drive.[2] The sexual union of male and female is one important aim of this drive, but it is not the only aim. The love of a parent for his child, the love of a child for his parent, friendships, and even attachments or devotions to ideas and things, all would be considered as obtaining their energy from the broad sexual drive. Thus the Freudian sexual drive includes much more than is commonly thought of as "sexual."

Freud's conception of sex allows us to understand the love life of a child, a married person, a neurotic, and an ascetic. Although their observable behavior is quite obviously different, the source of energy which gives rise to their behavior is the same broad drive. Freud makes the point that the sexual drives are remarkable for their plasticity. They seem to have a great capacity for changing their aims and objects and even for being held in abeyance. Viewing the sexual drive genetically, one sees that it is present in the infant even though the infant is quite incapable of an adult sexual aim. Sexual energy is expended by the young child in a manner different from that of both the infant and the adult. Inherent in this conception of sexual energy, however, is the thesis that the heterosexual love life of an adult has been affected by and is in some ways related to his earlier love relationships.

Erogenous Zones

In order to understand the unfolding and developing of the sexual drive of the normal person, we need the concept *erogenous zone*. It was early noted by psychoanalysts that certain areas of the body are capable of giving pleasurable sensations. An area of the body where tensions tend to be focalized and where they can be removed by action upon the area is called an erogenous zone.[3] The principal erogenous zones are the mouth, the anus, and the genitals. In the normal adult, the pleasure-giving quality of the genitals greatly overshadows that of other zones, but in the infant and young child the other zones, at different times in his life, provide the principal sources of pleasure.

The end product of psychosexual development can be thought of as

[2] Cf. A. A. Brill, *Basic Principles of Psychoanalysis* (Garden City, New York, Doubleday and Company, Inc., 1949), pp. 17 ff.

[3] Sigmund Freud, *An Outline of Psychoanalysis* (New York, W. W. Norton & Company, Inc., 1949), p. 24.

the production of an adult in whom the principal source of sexual gratification is focused on the genitals and who is capable of selecting a person of the opposite sex with whom to complete the task of reproducing the species. The unfolding of the sexual drive can thus be considered in terms of the changes that take place in the shift of focus of the principal areas of pleasure.[4] The first stage in this gradual development takes its name from the dominant erogenous zone of infancy and is called the oral stage.

The Oral-Dependency Stage

When a baby is born, he begins immediately to experience displeasures or pain due to the external environment in which he finds himself. In his uterine world the temperature was always correct and constant, but now it is variable and may be too cold. The strange experiences of noise and light produce a certain amount of displeasure. Most of all, the infant soon experiences discomforts that arise from within himself. These inner tensions center about the upper part of the gastrointestinal tract because of the recurring need for nourishment. Because the mouth is so important to life itself at this stage, the dominant erogenous zone is the oral one. During this stage, which lasts for about the first year of life, the infant both experiences and expresses most of his desires through his mouth.[5]

Everyone knows that an infant needs food and that he cannot obtain or use it as would an adult. To meet his biological requirement for food, the infant is equipped with a sucking reflex. When the breast or bottle nipple is placed close, most infants immediately will grasp it with their lips and begin to suck. The observation of many infants has led to the conclusion that infants find pleasure in sucking in and of itself and apart from their desire to satisfy hunger. On the first day of life, for example, it is quite unlikely that an infant is hungry. He will nevertheless suck at his mother's breast, although at this time the mother is producing colostrum and not milk. It has often been observed, furthermore, that infants will suck their fingers, blankets, and other non-nutritional objects even after they have been fed. Levy observed that those infants tended to be finger suckers whose need to suck was not met in the course of their feeding.[6] If

---

[4] For a brief discussion of the development of the sexual drive, see Calvin S. Hall, *A Primer of Freudian Psychology* (New York, The World Publishing Company, 1954), pp. 107-119.

[5] For a brief description of the oral stage, see O. Spurgeon English and Gerald H. I. Pearson, *Common Neuroses of Children and Adults* (New York, W. W. Norton & Company, Inc., 1937), pp. 21-27.

[6] David M. Levy, "Fingersucking and Accessory Movements in Early Infancy," *American Journal of Psychiatry*, Vol. 7 (May, 1928), pp. 881-918.

the mother's milk flowed too freely or if the opening in the nipple of the bottle was too large, the infant's need to suck was not fully satisfied even though his need for nourishment was. This is the kind of evidence that demonstrates that a need or desire to suck exists apart from the desire to relieve the tensions of hunger.

Normally there is a certain amount of fusion of the tensions of hunger and those produced by the desire to suck.[7] Both are relieved by the process of nursing, and since they are relieved or reduced the infant finds nursing pleasurable. As the infant grows older he gradually learns that the source of his tensions is within himself, and the pleasure-giving reliever of tensions is external to himself. Through the periodic arising and abatement of tensions, he comes to realize that he has needs which his mother's breast can satisfy. Soon the mother herself is seen as the source of pleasure and the reliever of discomfort. He thus comes to need and to depend on his mother. A turning point in the infant's love life has been reached. He is beginning to love a person external to himself.[8]

At this stage of his life the infant has begun to separate himself from all of the non-selves in the world about him. He perceives that one of these non-selves, his mother, is capable of relieving his distresses, and he develops a dependency-type love for this person who provides him pleasure. Gradually he learns, too, that he himself is capable of eliciting gratification from his object of affection. When tensions arise, he can summon his mother by crying. The normal infant in the normal family is bound to learn that all of his distresses cannot be relieved as soon and as completely as he would like. Having identified his reliever of tensions, he now experiences the frightening thought that she may fail to meet his needs. Usually this thought is soon dismissed, because the mother does respond to his signal of distress and does comfort, feed, or otherwise reduce his discomfort. Through the periodic fear that his love object has deserted him and the subsequent removal of his fear the infant builds up a certain tolerance for anxiety.[9] Such a tolerance is utterly necessary if he is to cope with the many potentially anxiety-producing situations he will perforce meet in his later life. At the same time, through the repetition of the anxiety-relief sequence the infant develops an early, general interpretation of the capabilities of the people in the outside world to satisfy his needs. His experiences may teach him that the world is cold and hostile and unreliable, or, on the contrary, that basically people are warm and giving and able to gratify his needs. So it is that the first and most important

[7] Cf. English and Pearson, *op. cit.*, pp. 21-22.
[8] *Ibid.*, p. 24.
[9] *Ibid.*, p. 25.

activities of the infant are oral ones, and his experiences with respect to them have emotional as well as the more obvious physical ramifications.

When the infant is weaned from the breast or the bottle, his opportunity to obtain oral gratification is drastically reduced. Normally there comes about a realignment of his drives so that in the next stage these drives will find expression in other ways. Each stage in development seems to require its own time of completion. Although there is individual variation in the length of the stages, and thus the ages at which change occurs, the sequence of the stages is the same. Movement onward from the oral stage comes most readily when oral gratification has been optimal. If for some reason the child has met too severe frustration, he will find it hard to give up his infantile pleasures. To a greater or lesser degree he will tend to become fixated at this level. It will be as if he were continually striving to obtain gratification for the desires denied him in his early life.

In view of the emotional significance of the oral stage of development, it should begin to be clear why the early family experiences receive so great stress in psychoanalytic literature. It should be clearer, too, why such importance is attached to the feeding and weaning experiences of the infant. In these times of bottles and formulas, almost any responsible adult could satisfy an infant's need for food. Various systems of feeding would probably work equally well in the sense that the infant would not starve to death. However, psychoanalysis emphasizes that the child at this stage of life has important emotional needs that are met, or are left unmet, in the course of his feeding experience. It is for this reason that breast feeding is to be preferred to bottle feeding. Modern science allows us to simulate with some accuracy the nutritional value of mother's milk, but it has failed to make of the impersonal bottle a warm and loving person. The mother with her child at the breast is doing more than feeding him. She is at the same time assuring him of love and providing him the emotional sustenance that he needs as much as he needs the physical kind. If bottle feeding is necessary, the mother can help to meet the infant's dependency needs by holding him during feeding instead of leaving him in the crib with the bottle propped on pillows. The mother, through her methods of feeding, is helping to form the young child's conception of the outside world. He can develop a basic confidence in people and learn to expect them to be friendly, loving, and lovable. Just as surely the opposite lessons can be taught and learned through the infant's first contacts with a person outside of himself.

The currently accepted practice of "demand feeding" has much to recommend it psychoanalytically. According to this practice the infant is fed when he is hungry and he is allowed to eat his fill, as opposed to being given specified quantities at predetermined intervals. Demand feeding requires that the mother be in tune with the unique rhythm of her infant and that she be sensitive to changes in it. Because of the individual variations in the needs for food and sucking and because even in the same infant these needs vary from time to time, it is more likely that an infant will find optimum gratification for his needs if he is allowed to set his own pace.

There are many and varied manifestations in later childhood and adulthood of the failure to find optimum gratification for the oral-dependency needs of infancy. These outward signs and behavior patterns should not be viewed as isolated symptoms of unmet needs. The real meaning of the behavior can only be understood in the context of the functioning personality of the child or adult. In general terms, nevertheless, there are certain kinds of behavior patterns typical of those who have experienced too great frustration in early infancy. Such is the personality type, to which we have earlier referred, that finds it almost impossible to enter into meaningful and intimate relationships with others.[10] It is as if they were expending so much energy trying to be loved that there was no energy left with which to love.

Sometimes the unmet needs of early infancy find later expression in physical symptoms and disorders.[11] Those with a compulsion to overeat are thought to be responding to an unsatisfied need to be loved and to be dependent.[12] In an almost literal sense such individuals are hungry for love. Stomach ulcers and other gastrointestinal disturbances may likewise have their origins in the unmet infantile needs at the oral-dependency stage of development. There are still other ways in which a tendency towards fixation or a partial regression to the oral stage can manifest itself. Sometimes the symptoms are less obvious than the illustrations we have used, for since overdependency in the adult is not looked upon with favor the person may unconsciously construct a façade of independence and normality. Even the few illustrations we have provided should be sufficient to emphasize the importance of the early family experiences of the infant, in this case particularly the mother's handling of his feeding and weaning. According to psychoanalytic theory, these early love experiences can never be dismissed as forgotten and unimportant.

[10] See the discussion of unmet dependency needs in Irene M. Josselyn, *Psychosocial Development of Children* (New York, Family Service Association of America, 1948), pp. 41-46.
[11] *Ibid.* See also Helen Ross and Adelaide M. Johnson, *Psychiatric Interpretation of the Growth Process* (New York, Family Service Association of America, 1949), pp. 4-5.
[12] For a more general discussion of obesity in children, see Hilda Bruch and Grace Touraine, "Obesity in Childhood: The Family Frame of Obese Children," *Psychosomatic Medicine*, Vol. 2 (April, 1940), pp. 141-212.

The Anal Stage

Even after the child has left the oral stage the mouth will always remain capable of providing pleasant sensations, as witness the adult pleasures in kissing, gum chewing, and smoking. Normally, however, between the ages of one and two the young child is ready to give up many of his distinctly oral pleasures. Whether or not the infant's oral gratification has been optimum, he seems to be propelled onward to leave the oral stage, or at least to make an attempt in this direction. Gradually during the oral stage the infant has observed that parts of his body other than his mouth are capable of giving pleasant sensations. He begins to enjoy his body and everything associated with it. He finds pleasure in urination and defecation. These latter pleasures become more pronounced after he has been weaned and thus denied his major oral gratification. The dominant erogenous zone becomes the anal zone and the second stage in the young child's life is for this reason designated as the anal stage.[13]

The typical adult, because of his own inhibitions in these areas, finds it difficult to appreciate the amount of sheer pleasure the child finds in his excretory functions. In the first place, the *processes* of urination and defecation are enjoyable to the child.[14] It is not at all unusual to discover that a child will delay moving his bowels in order to obtain the added pleasure associated with almost uncontrollable urgency. To the displeasure of many adults, children exhibit their interest in the excretory processes by talking freely about them and by attempting to observe other children, adults, or animals urinating or moving their bowels.

At this stage of life the child is also engrossed in his excretory *products*.[15] He likes his feces. As many mothers will attest, the young child seems to enjoy handling his feces and smearing them around his crib or room. He is proud when his bowel movement has been large and will gladly exhibit it to any interested person. He feels a sense of accomplishment and pride in having produced something from his own body. The young child, too, finds pleasure in being able to control when and where he performs his excretory functions.

Within this period of the child's life, toilet training will be initiated. Although the child's interest in his excretory processes would seem to be an aid in his toilet training, the pleasure associated with these functions must also be taken into account. To the child, his parents are asking him to

[13] For a general discussion of this stage see Josselyn, *op. cit.*, pp. 52-63.
[14] English and Pearson, *op. cit.*, p. 28.
[15] *Ibid.*

give up his pleasures. They deny him the pleasure of deciding when and where to execute his functions, and they may perhaps compound matters by punishing him severely for attempting to cling to his infantile pleasures. On the other hand, the mother may seem to agree with the child that his feces are a valuable production, for she urges him to present them and rewards him when he does so. Confusingly enough, she then discards and flushes away this seemingly prized gift. Although this parental behavior can be perplexing to the child, he realizes that either he must relinquish his excretory pleasures or he must be prepared to accept the loss of his mother's approval.

Part of the psychological significance of toilet training lies in its opportunities for the expression of power and hostility.[16] Realistically, the infant had little to say concerning whether or not he was to be weaned nor was his co-operation actually required. Just about the only choices he had were to accept the proffered cup or starve to death. With toilet training the situation is otherwise. Unless the child co-operates with his parents, he will never be toilet-trained, their threats, praises, and punishments notwithstanding. With the realization of his sense of power comes the decision of whether or not or how to exercise it. Through repeated negative sanctions, either in the form of physical punishment or of withholding praise, the child may come to learn that the exercise of power carries a penalty, and perhaps a severe one. Thus through his toilet-training experiences the child learns his first important lesson about the use of his own strength and power.

The child's almost complete ability to control the toilet-training situation has implications for his learning about the emotions of hate and love. It is common for the child to feel a certain amount of hostility toward those who are asking him to relinquish his pleasure and who are attempting to invalidate his new-found sense of power. If he is at all perceptive, he will sense that he has a ready weapon with which to express his hostility, that is, his refusal to keep himself clean. At the same time, he needs the love of his parents and the security that stems from their love and acceptance. If he is to continue to receive the love of his parents, he must, in turn, love them and generously give them what they ask. These contradictory feelings are not easily reconciled by the young child. He begins to realize that he can both love and hate the same person. Normally, of course, the need for security and love eventually helps the child to acquiesce to the parental demands. Meanwhile he has learned important lessons about the primitive emotions of love and hate.

Various adult personality traits are thought to have their origin in

[16] Josselyn, *op. cit.*, p. 53.

the toilet-training experiences of the child.[17] Sometimes these are so pronounced or extreme that the individual has difficulty in functioning properly in the adult world, although more often he will differ to a less serious degree from the hypothetical normal personality. If his parents attach too great importance to toilet training, for example, the child may incorporate their attitudes. He may find it difficult to relinquish his interest in the excretory functions, as he must if he is to progress to the next stage of development. As an adult he may exhibit a preoccupation with excretion and with the proper functioning of his body generally. Such a person is the delight of the patent-medicine industry, as he may be a fond user of laxatives and other pills and nostrums that claim to keep his body functioning regularly. If the toilet-training methods are too severe, the child may be almost frightened into complying with his parents' wishes. He may overlearn their dislike of soiling. All kinds of dirtiness and disorder may become repulsive to him. Throughout his life such a person may be overclean and meticulous about details and order.

Sometimes the child's interpretation of severe parental measures in toilet training leads him simultaneously to acquiesce to the demands and to resist them. By refusing to move his bowels the child accepts the demand that he not soil himself while at the same time he defeats the broader purpose of toilet training. In adult life this refusal to give up what is asked of him may show itself in extreme stinginess, stubbornness, and the tendency to hoard. It is found in other cases, finally, that some difficulties in forming meaningful relationships with others can be traced to the tendency of the person to bring to such situations the mixed feelings of love and hate he held toward the person who forced him to relinquish his anal pleasures. Once again we must caution that the aforementioned personality traits or disturbances could stem from many causes, and that the life history of the individual is required before an adequate explanation for his behavior is possible. The fact that difficulties during the toilet-training period can and do have more or less lasting personality effects illustrates well the sensitive role of the parents as they handle this phase of the child's development.

The Oedipal Stage

The third stage of psychosexual development generally is designated as the Oedipal stage.[18] The name is obviously derived from Sophocles'

[17] Karl Abraham, "Contributions to the Theory of the Anal Character," in *Selected Papers of Karl Abraham* (London, Hogarth Press, Ltd., 1927), Ch. 22.

[18] For a discussion of this stage, see Freud, *An Outline of Psychoanalysis*, pp. 88 ff. See also Josselyn, *op. cit.*, pp. 64 ff.

tragedy in which the hero, Oedipus, unwittingly kills his father and marries his mother. In some ways it is unfortunate that another name could not have been used to designate this stage of development. Oedipus, as an adult, expressed emotions and feelings of which no child is capable. He experienced adult anger when provoked by an apparent stranger, he felt adult love and sexual desires toward a comely woman, and he expressed adult guilt and remorse when he came to learn that unknowingly he had violated a primary incest taboo. A certain amount of confusion has resulted from having used the name of an adult hero in a highly atypical, mythical situation to designate a stage in the normal development of a child.

As the worm is not the butterfly it will someday become, so a child is something different from a miniature adult. The young child is simply incapable of the sexual aims of an adult even though he has certain tensions which derive their energy from a more diffuse sexual source. It is particularly well to keep this in mind as we turn to the third stage in the child's psychosexual development. At the Oedipal stage the genitals become the principal erogenous zone. In addition, the child develops a new and different kind of love attachment toward his parent of the opposite sex. But he is neither experiencing adult sexual tensions nor adult heterosexual passions. According to the genetic approach, however, the love and sex life of the normal adult are shaped to some extent by the various experiences at the pre-adult stages of psychosexual development. Accordingly, we will attempt to describe what is entailed in the normal course of development at the Oedipal stage, and, also, some of the implications of the ways the problems at this stage are resolved.

The Oedipal stage is, in a sense, the child's first introduction into a bisexual world, and during it he first manifests that he is aware of his environment's inherent bisexuality. At the Oedipal stage the little boy develops a kind of love for his mother that is distinct from the affection and response he has previously expressed toward her. It is usually a more intense type of love, it is demanding, and it is possessive. He would like his mother's undivided attention, and he enjoys her caresses and other expressions of love. It is not uncommon for a boy of this age to tell his mother that he wants to marry her "when he grows up." This does not mean that the boy of three or four desires his mother sexually in an adult sense. It does mean that the little boy wishes that it were possible to have his mother always to himself.

Even while the young boy has the strong attachment toward his mother, he realizes that there is a rival for her affection in the household. What is more, the mother seems actually to prefer his father to himself. She sleeps with his father, she goes out with him alone, and she shows in other ways that at times she enjoys his exclusive company. The boy does not have to search hard for an explanation for this behavior of his love object. The father is more of a man than he is. The father is big while the boy is small, he is strong while the boy is weak, and he is sexually mature while the boy is not. All of these discrepancies between himself and his father the boy notices and sees in them the reason for his father's peculiar success as a rival for the mother's affection.

The young boy at the Oedipal stage loves his father. At the same time, he is jealous of him and defines him as a rival. This holding of contradictory feelings toward the same object at the same time is termed *ambivalence*. The boy may verbalize his hostile feelings and tell his father, "Go away, it's *my* Mama." More commonly he harbors wishes that he dare not express. Part of him wishes that his father were gone or, barring this, wishes that there were some way to reduce his father's appeal to the mother. If the boy could weaken the father and render him sexually less attractive, then the rivals would be on equal footing. These hostile thoughts frequently are projected by the boy onto his father by the simple logic that if the boy wants to destroy his father's masculinity, then it is only reasonable that the father should feel similarly about the boy. This fear of being emasculated, or *castration anxiety*, is thought to be widespread, judging from the material uncovered in the psychoanalysis of normal as well as sick persons. The castration anxiety is, of course, intensified if the boy's parents have threatened to cut off his penis if he masturbates, or if they have told him that it will fall off if he masturbates. If the boy has observed the female genitals, he may find reinforcement for his castration anxiety in his interpretation that some people in the world have somehow lost their penes. Thus the boy is troubled. The father whom he loves, he hates. The person whom he wants to hurt wants to hurt him. The mother whom he loves so much loves someone else more than himself. Somehow these conflicts need to be resolved.

There are several different processes, working for the most part on the unconscious level, that aid in the resolution of the boy's Oedipal conflicts.[19] The love he has for his father will help him to identify with his father and to incorporate into his own personality some of the behavior of his father. His envy is used constructively in that he strives to emulate the person who embodies the traits of which he is jealous. Through the mechanism of repression the boy removes from consciousness his intense strivings toward his mother. It is not uncommon for mothers of boys of this age to report that the small boy goes through a stage of strongly resisting her embraces, refusing to sit on her lap, and otherwise reacting

[19] Josselyn, *op. cit.*, pp. 66-67.

negatively to her overt expressions of affection. These things are resented for they would only serve to reawaken the desires which he is trying so hard to hold from consciousness. It has been suggested, too, that help in resolving the Oedipal conflict is obtained by the boy's fusing to some extent the personalities of both parents and turning his love to the family rather than to either individual.[20] Turning outside the family, finally, provides still another way in which the boy can escape the troublesome implications of the domestic triangle. Some of the intense love for his mother can find diffuse expression in the friendships the boy will begin to make. The hostile feelings toward his father will be expressed in the competitive strivings with his peers.

The Oedipal stage in girls in some ways parallels and in some ways is more complicated than that of boys. Like the boy, the little girl develops a new kind of attachment to her parent of the opposite sex and ambivalent feelings toward the parent of the same sex. Since in most families the mother has been the child's chief source of need gratification, both pre-Oedipal boys and girls are somewhat more strongly attached to their mothers than their fathers. At the Oedipal stage the boy retains his familiar object of affection and merely redefines the relationship. It is more difficult for the girl to shift her object of affection, and it is more troublesome for her to be faced with the jealous, hostile feelings she holds toward her mother. Not only does she love her mother but she needs her and knows full well that she needs her. The thought that if she hates her mother so must her mother hate her is thus quite frightening to the little girl.

Quite obviously the little girl, at this stage of development, cannot develop the type of castration anxiety we noted in the boy. The feminine counterpart of this anxiety is *penis envy*. If the little girl has had the opportunity to observe the male genitals, as most seem somehow to manage, she may define her own lack of a penis as a sign of inferiority. It is common for girls of this age to feel that the boy has a more desirable way of urinating, and mothers often report that their little daughters have tried to urinate in a standing position. Some little girls think that they once had a penis, which for some reason was removed, and others may believe that one will yet grow. As much as the little girl loves her father, he cannot reciprocate by giving her the organ she desires, and as much as she may blame her mother for depriving her of a penis, there is nothing that can be done about it.

The resolution of Oedipal conflicts in girls follows along the same lines we saw with respect to the boy. Gradually she de-emphasizes her

[20] Irene Josselyn, *The Happy Child* (New York, Random House, 1955), p. 87.

strong attachment for her father and may go through a brief period of refusing his attentions. She begins to identify with her mother and to see her less as a rival and more as a person worthy of emulation. The girl, like the little boy, turns some of her attention away from the family circle and thereby finds an outlet for some of her rivalrous and affectional strivings. Although the Oedipal period is normally one of conflicts and troubles, these difficulties are clearly not beyond resolution. Through the various mechanisms we have discussed, most children of both sexes manage to work through the problems of this stage without retaining serious psychological scars.

Importance of the Oedipal Period

When a person reaches early adulthood he is expected to be able to form an intimate and personal relationship with a member of the other sex. His love and sexual strivings should be of such a nature that he can marry, enjoy sexual relations with his spouse, and love and rear the children who are born of the union. These feelings and passions do not descend on a person in early adulthood. Many aspects of the child's early love experiences in the family are pushed from consciousness, but whether the problems met in these experiences were solved poorly or well and whether the general picture was one of optimal satisfaction or undue frustration, there remains in the unconscious a dynamic memory of these early feelings. At the Oedipal stage the child has his first true experience with heterosexual love. As he leaves this period of life, he will already have learned important lessons about his own sex and its relation to that of the other sex. He will have learned important lessons about love and hate. The fact that earlier and later stages of life carry their own influences on the love life of an adult by no means detracts from the significance of the Oedipal stage. For a better understanding of the love relationships of the adult, it becomes necessary to look at the sources of difficulties at the Oedipal stage and the kinds of problems that can result from them.

The normal child has the capacity to resolve satisfactorily the usual Oedipal situation. When things go wrong at this stage of development, whether more or less seriously, one must understandably look to the adult members of the emotional triangle. The personalities of the child's parents and their relationship to one another can play an important part in the way the child resolves his Oedipal conflicts. Some parents, for example, are confused, frightened, and perhaps even threatened when their child begins to act out the Oedipal situation. The parent of the same sex may find it difficult to accept the rebuffs of the child and his obvious preference for his other parent. Sometimes it is simply a matter of ignorance, that is, not knowing that this is a normal experience and that it should be no cause for concern for the child. At other times the parents' marital relationship is such that their own child is unconsciously seen as coming between them and weakening the none too strong emotional bonds of their marriage. Some parents are too insecure and threatened as individuals to accept the hostility that is directed toward them at the Oedipal period.

There are still other marital situations and parental personality problems that interfere with, or make difficult, the child's solution of his conflicts. An extremely severe and domineering father may provide so threatening a situation for the young boy that he dare not express his affection for his mother for fear of harsh reprisals. A woman who is unhappy in her love relationship with her husband may in subtle ways encourage the little boy's Oedipal attachment. This encouragement can be quite frightening to the boy, for it intensifies the possibility of retaliation by the father. In addition, his mother's attention makes it difficult for the boy to renounce his strong attachment as he will come to want to do. Marital unhappiness and bickering between the parents, particularly, but not only, if it culminates in divorce, can be extremely upsetting to the child in the throes of Oedipal conflicts. Consciously or unconsciously he may blame himself for his parents' marital difficulties because they are acting out, more seriously than he actually wished, what a part of him desired them to do. Marital situations and parental personalities such as we have described make it difficult for the child to do what he must do if he is to progress normally through the stages of development.

Freud spoke of the Oedipal situation as "the kernel of neuroses." Many of the difficulties that arise from the unsuccessful meeting of the problems of this period can be more generally thought of as disturbances in the person's heterosexual love life. Some people are never able to love completely, for when they love a part of them also hates. When others attempt to love, the Oedipal scene unconsciously is re-enacted and the prohibitions and fears associated with their first love affair are painfully reawakened. Sometimes the person finds it difficult to be an acceptable member of his own sex capable of forming an intimate attachment to someone of the other sex. A cold and harsh mother may almost literally force a boy to seek warmth and affection only from a member of his own sex, first, of course, from his father. If a girl fails to resolve her problems of penis envy during the Oedipal stage, she probably will never again consciously be jealous of the male's sexual apparatus. As an adult, however, she may be hostile toward men, jealous of them, or she may attempt through her choice of occupation, dress, and the like, to be as much like a man as she possibly can. Few, if any, adult males are consciously worried lest they be castrated. If their fears of punishment at the hands of their father were intense, however, they may carry over into adulthood a fear of and hostility toward authority figures generally. Fearful of stern rebuff if they express what they feel, they may not be able to function adequately in situations that call for expressing and defending their point of view or opposing the view of others. Conditions of all degrees of seriousness, of which we have mentioned only a few, provide ample testimony to the importance of the Oedipal stage and the significant role the parents have in its successful resolution.

LATENCY PERIOD

In the young child, as we have observed, there seems to be an inherent force propelling him along the progressive steps to maturity. Between the close of the Oedipal period and the first manifestations of puberty there seems to be a decided diminution in the rate of psychosexual growth. For this reason this time of life has been designated as the latency period. *Latency* is actually a misleading term, for it implies that no important changes are occurring in the child and that emotionally the child is more or less dormant. Although neither of these implications is accurate, the older term *latency* has been retained to designate the years of less rapid growth.[21]

During the latency period the child comes more into contact with the world about him and becomes more interested in it. As a result, his concept of reality expands, and he finds an increasing amount of gratification in the people and pleasures in the real world. The intense emotions of the Oedipal period become diluted and find expression in the friendships with other children and with adults. At the same time, these important people in the child's life will be used as referents for his expanding Ego Ideal. Although first it was his parents' personalities from which he selected traits for the self he wanted to be, now the child may have many ego models in the world outside the family. Through his experiences in the real world the child may be forced to reject some aspects of his previously formed Ego Ideal. He may find that some characteristics heretofore considered desirable are not in accordance with the role he is expected to play by virtue of his biological sex. It may be that the various selves he wants to be conflict one with the other, or perhaps his experiences outside the family circle

[21] Oddly enough, the latency period has been a somewhat neglected area of study. See, however, Fred S. Friedenberg, "Thoughts on the Latency Period," *Psychoanalytic Review*, Vol. 44 (October, 1957), pp. 390-400. See also Josselyn, *Psychosocial Development of Children*, pp. 75-92.

teach him that some of the aspects of his growing Ego Ideal are for him unrealistic. The child's Ego Ideal was formed in rudimentary fashion when he began to emulate his parent of the same sex in his attempt to resolve the Oedipal situation. It will continue to expand throughout adolescence. The latency period is nevertheless the time when the Ego Ideal is submitted to a certain amount of reality testing and accordingly is expanded and modified.

Near the close of the latency period there are manifestations of the maturing capacity to love that will become more pronounced after puberty. The older child is wont to develop a strong attachment for one or a few friends of his own sex. He may want to be with this close friend constantly and may talk incessantly of him. This is a normal phase in the process of growing up and constitutes the first step in the reawakening of intense emotional attachments, now directed to a person outside of the family. Because of its connotation for adults, it is confusing to refer to this period as the homosexual stage. To be sure the boy or girl is strongly attached to a person of the same sex, but his loves and passions are not yet those of an adult. The infant began his love life with the pleasures found in his own bodily processes and the dependency toward those who helped him to meet his needs. As a young child he developed an intense attachment for the parent of the same sex, and this attachment became diluted in the friendships of the early latency period. The attachment the older child now has for a person of the same sex is but another step in the relatively long development of heterosexual love.

SELECTED READINGS

BERGLER, EDMUND, *The Battle of the Conscience* (Washington, D.C., Washington Institute of Medicine, 1948).

BUHLER, CHARLOTTE, *The Child and His Family* (New York, Humanities Press, 1948).

ENGLISH, O. SPURGEON, and FOSTER, CONSTANCE, *Fathers Are Parents, Too* (New York, G. P. Putnam's Sons, 1951).

FRIEDENBERG, FRED S., "Thoughts on the Latency Period," *Psychoanalytic Review*, Vol. 44 (October, 1957), pp. 390-400.

JOSSELYN, IRENE M., *The Happy Child* (New York, Random House, 1955).

———, *Psychosocial Development of Children* (New York, Family Service Association of America, 1948).

JULES, HENRY and WARSON, SAMUEL, "Family Structure and Psychic Development," *American Journal of Orthopsychiatry*, Vol. 21 (October, 1951), pp. 59-73.

MEISS, M. L., "The Oedipal Problems of a Fatherless Child," *Psychoanalytic Study of the Child*, Vol. 7 (1953), pp. 216-229.

MULLABY, PATRICK, *Oedipus Myth and Complex* (New York, Hermitage Press, 1948).

Psychoanalytic Study of the Child. (Yearly since 1946.)

RIBBLE, MARGARET A., *The Personality of the Young Child* (New York, Columbia University Press, 1955).

ROSS, HELEN, and JOHNSON, M., *Psychiatric Interpretation of the Growth Process* (New York, Family Service Association of America, 1949).

SPERLING, MELITTA, "The Neurotic Child and His Mother: A Psychoanalytic Study," *American Journal of Orthopsychiatry*, Vol. 21 (April, 1951), pp. 351-364.

WINCH, ROBERT F., "Some Data Bearing on the Oedipus Hypothesis," *Journal of Abnormal and Social Psychology*, Vol. 45 (July, 1950), pp. 481-489.

CHAPTER 20

Adolescence, Mate Selection, and Marriage

In the preceding chapter we followed the psychosexual development of the child from infancy to early puberty. The metamorphoses that normally take place during these years constitute a significant prologue to the stages that follow. Childhood, although important, is not the only important time of life. In this chapter we will trace the outline of psychic development during later puberty. Following this we will turn to the young adult and the difficult phenomena of love and choosing a marriage partner. We conclude with some aspects of marital life on which psychoanalytic theory is uniquely capable of providing insight and understanding. Although the psychoanalytic overview of the life cycle provided in this and the preceding chapter is of necessity incomplete, it should be at least suggestive of the kinds of understandings of marriage and the family that can be gained through the application of the discipline.

ADOLESCENCE

Adolescence is a period when many demands for new learnings are thrust upon the individual.[1] Psychosexually, adolescence is also a complicated and important time of life. Concomitant with the spurt toward physical and sexual maturation that occurs at this time of life, there is a resurgence of sexual energy. During the latency period the Superego generally is sufficiently strong to keep in check the sexual energy, but now the sudden onslaught of a more intense drive threatens to break through the previously adequate barriers.[2] The adolescent's struggle between the demands of his Superego and the demands of his sexual drive cannot be avoided. It is a normal phase of life that must be dealt with if the person is to reach adult heterosexuality.

[1] See pp. 382-393.
[2] O. Spurgeon English and Gerald H. J. Pearson, *Common Neuroses of Children and Adults* (New York, W. W. Norton & Company, Inc., 1937), p. 46.

The rush of sexual energy that is encountered during adolescence occurs before the individual has learned to direct his sexual aim to those outside of his family. The familiar emotional triangle of the Oedipal period is consequently reawakened.[3] The inhibitions against falling in love once again with the parent of the opposite sex are usually strong enough to prevent any direct manifestations of the inner urgings. The adolescent, with his near-adult emotions and his near-adult body, cannot dare to express what unconsciously he feels. At the same time, the intense sexual drive seems to demand some attention. The mechanism of denial frequently is used to cope with the dual struggle against his inner urges and his Conscience. By denying that he is attracted to his parent of the opposite sex, the adolescent is spared the torturing guilt that would result if his inner thoughts were allowed to become conscious.

Successful repudiation of the adolescent's forbidden desires means that the denial be forcible and, in a sense, overdone.[4] The adolescent boy dare not be the kind of boy his mother wishes him to be, for he would run the risk of becoming her love object. The adolescent girl cannot take the chance of being loved too much by her father and accordingly must strive not to be the sort of woman her father prefers. In order to deny successfully what he really feels, the adolescent comes into conflict with both of his parents. He cannot please the parent of the opposite sex, for this is interpreted as a kind of love response to the parent. He cannot emulate the parent of the same sex, for in doing so he would become too much like that parent and, therefore, too close a rival for the affection of the other parent. By ridiculing his parents, belittling them, and behaving in direct opposition to their desires, the adolescent is helped to deny the feelings he has toward them.

The achievement of heterosexuality means that the unconscious strivings which the adolescent has toward the parent of the opposite sex must be directed toward someone of this parent's sex who is outside of the family. The adolescent's conception of someone of the other sex who is desirable usually is strongly flavored by the personality of his parent. To please such a person and to be found attractive by him would seem to imply that the young person be like the parent of his own sex. The adolescent, therefore, cannot entirely repudiate his parents, and he cannot disregard their wishes completely. To retain his sense of security, the adolescent is sorely tempted to accept fully the standards of behavior of his parents and to seek their advice at every turn. The struggle between

---

[3] *Ibid.*, p. 48.
[4] See the treatment of adolescent sexual conflict in Irene M. Josselyn, *The Adolescent and His World* (New York, Family Service Association of America, 1952), pp. 58-66.

striking out for independence and retreating to an earlier stage of dependency is not always successfully completed. Probably there is no adolescent as troublesome as the adult who emotionally has remained at this stage and is in perennial revolt against the parent figures in his society. Almost everyone has met, also, the eternal "daddy's girl" or "mother's boy" who was frightened back into a pre-adolescent dependency relationship or who otherwise is unable to leave home, at least emotionally. The normal person resolves the conflicts and ambivalences of the adolescence period and emerges with the ability to love and be loved intact and capable of transfer to a socially acceptable love object.

In still other ways is adolescence a time of struggle with the Superego.[5] It is as if the Superego to which the child fell heir by virtue of being reared by a particular set of parents is no longer completely serviceable to him as an independent near-adult. There are many examples of behavior which is prohibited for the child but allowed or even expected of the adult. To leave childhood psychologically, the adolescent must free himself from the shackles of his puerile Conscience. Along with the desire to be free from the demands of his Conscience exists a fear of this very freedom. As long as the childhood Superego is in control, there is a certain security in knowing that his behavior will meet with acceptance and approval. Caught between the desire to be free from the Superego and the equally strong desire to retain its comforting protection, the adolescent is apt to develop some kind of compromise. At the verbal level he may denounce every moral standard and virtue he has ever learned, whereas actually he may behave in strict accordance with the demands of his Superego. The parents, as symbols of his Conscience, may be attacked with a vigor that could not be used against himself. Rebelling against his parents personifies the inner struggle and brings it out into the open, where it can be waged in not too abstract a manner.

The adolescent's struggle with his Superego is a necessary part of his psychological growth process. The conflict nevertheless needs to be resolved before he can be considered a mature person capable of controlling his actions and taking responsibility for them. It is well to remember, however, that certain modifications of the Superego are absolutely required before psychological maturity is reached. The Conscience of childhood, for example, forbids heterosexuality. This notion must be modified in such a way that the individual can experience a strong passion for someone of the other sex and can marry. If because of childhood experiences all sexual activity continues to have unconscious overtones of incest, the individual is psychologically retarded. He will not be able to allow himself

[5] *Ibid.*, pp. 67 ff.

any heterosexual expression and will meet his sexuality with revulsion, denial, or frigidity. The struggle against the Conscience of childhood will have ended in retreat. In the usual course of events, the post-adolescent Conscience will not be dramatically different from the previously incorporated parental standards. Concessions and compromises will have to be made to allow him to function as an adult, but the guiding force of his Superego will permit him to function as a moral adult.

During adolescence the other system of the Superego, the Ego Ideal, also undergoes change. The young child, with his parents as ego models, began to build up a conception of himself as he would like to be. As other ego models crossed the scene, he selected with seeming lack of discrimination certain traits and characteristics to be incorporated into his Ego Ideal. Adolescence is a time when the Ego Ideal can be given a more perfect test of reality; he is nearly an adult and should therefore swiftly be becoming the self he feels he must be. To crystallize his Ego Ideal and to help himself live up to its demands, the adolescent may frantically reach out to an adult outside of his family who seems to him to be the kind of person he himself would like to be. We then encounter the familiar adolescent "crush."[6] If the person is of his own sex, the adolescent may imitate his behavior, his dress, or his mannerisms. If the crush is on someone of the other sex, the adolescent will try in his actions and thoughts to be the kind of person he believes his love object would like him to be.

Generally speaking, there is nothing "wrong" with adolescent crushes. Some parents, however, become disturbed over them or are threatened because the adolescent seems to prefer some other adult to themselves. If the adult is of the same sex as the young person, parents and others may read into the relationship a homosexual implication that in actuality does not exist. Difficulties may also arise because the person on whom the adolescent has a crush is not, by the parent's standards, worthy of emulation. He may be everything the parent is not, and everything the parent hopes his child will not become. The adult who is the object of the adolescent's affection quite clearly affects the outcome of the event. In response to his own needs, the adult may fan the emotions of the adolescent beyond normal proportions. The adult may be frightened by the relationship and withdraw suddenly or rebuff the young person. Although they can indeed present difficulties, adolescent crushes also can be valuable. As he gradually terminates the relationship, the adolescent will be that much closer to adult heterosexuality. He will have sharpened

[6] *Ibid.*, pp. 77 ff.

and crystallized his Ego Ideal, and he will have made strides in his ability to choose an appropriate love object.

MATE SELECTION

As the adolescent becomes an adult, he is expected to be able to love a person of the opposite sex and to choose a spouse with whom he will live out his life. How to explain who marries whom, and why, is as fascinating as it is perplexing. The man and wife who ponder about the couple next door and "what they see in each other" probably are vaguely aware that their own match is the subject of similar discussion.

The intriguing problem of how mates are chosen can be approached from various directions. Certainly the laws of a society have an effect on who marries whom. To the extent that racial, ethnic, religious, age, and class endogamy are followed, the group of persons from which one could choose a mate is substantially less than all of the unmarried persons of the opposite sex. The tendency of a person to choose as a mate someone who is spatially close to him, although not wholly distinct from some of the endogamous regulations, further delimits the group from which a mate is selected.[7] Even the seemingly less important folkways, such as the notion that the man should be taller than his wife, are not without their influence. Within a given society, these laws, mores, and folkways partially explain who marries whom.

Psychoanalytic theory is applied to mate selection on the personal level. It can help explain why from all of the eligible persons known to them a man and woman choose one another as husband and wife. Psychoanalytic theory can shed light on why some people seem destined to marry a person with whom they cannot be happy, and others seem unable to find a mate at all. In American society the basis for marriage is supposed to be a strong, personal attachment between the prospective spouses. Love and mate selection, in this society, are intricately intertwined. In explaining who loves whom and who marries whom, psychoanalysis focuses on the personalities of the individuals and how they have developed throughout the years. Unique to psychoanalysis is the stress on the unconscious, that is, those parts of the personality of which the individual himself is not aware. In our application of psychoanalytic theory to adult love and mate selection, we will deal both with the processes that take place in the normal individual and the vagaries that occur when

---

[7] Alfred C. Clarke, "An Examination of the Operation of Residential Propinquity as a Factor in Mate Selection," *American Sociological Review*, Vol. 17 (February, 1952), pp. 17-21.

the person unconsciously must reckon with the psychic wounds caused by disturbances in his earlier love relationships.

In an earlier chapter we introduced the concept of the Ego Ideal. We saw that it is that part of the Superego, largely unconscious, which consists of the conceptions a person has of the kind of person he would like to be. It was built up from personality characteristics exhibited by the child's parents and, later, by other ego models. These internalized conceptions of the ideal self serve the function of regulating behavior. The individual strives to fit his Ego Ideal, that is, he tries to be the kind of person and to have the traits and characteristics that are in accord with his conception of himself as he would like to be. For several reasons, it is almost impossible that a normal individual can as an adult come to personify his Ego Ideal.

Over the many years of its development, a host of characteristics have been incorporated into the Ego Ideal. The sheer number of these traits makes it unlikely that all of them can be achieved. Some aspects of the Ego Ideal, moreover, may be in conflict with others. Such a conflict may occur when in the early stages of development of his Ego Ideal, the child internalizes antithetical traits of his mother and of his father. Although a child may well admire the gentle submissiveness of his mother and the heavy dominance of his father, both cannot simultaneously be imitated. Sometimes the Ego Ideal is partly constructed of traits or ambitions that do not stand the test of reality. One man may have to renounce traits that in his society are designated feminine, and another may find that he is physically or psychologically unsuited to be the kind of person that he feels he must be. It is a harsh but realistic fact of life that many dreams of power, prestige, and fame simply cannot be fulfilled. Less dramatically, many quite prosaic goals can never be achieved, at least not by all of the people who aspire to them. In the normal course of events, then, the individual must come to abandon some aspects of his Ego Ideal. He is left, as it were, with two unconscious selves, the self he cannot be and the self he must be.

Since this part of the Superego is largely unconscious, a person is not completely aware of the abandoned and retained aspects of his Ego Ideal. Both "selves" nevertheless can influence behavior. It is only with regret that an individual forsakes treasured patterns of his Ego Ideal, and it is only with difficulty that he can meet the remaining demands. This dual source of frustration sets up tensions that amount at least to minor irritation at one's perceived imperfections and at most to severe feelings of guilt. To relieve this discomfort the person is tempted to project his Ego Ideal on to some one or more persons and thus be strongly attached to them.[8] A person is attracted to another who embodies the self that he himself can never be, and he is attracted also to someone who, by virtue of his own personality, allows or even helps him to be the person that he has to be. By hitching our psychological wagon to a star of proper proportions we can travel to the heights we believe we must without actually expending the energy necessary to do so. In a similar manner, we can love in someone else the traits that we would like to have but dare not or cannot have. Through the process of projection of the Ego Ideal one reaches one's goals while not reaching them. Despite the illogic of this situation, it serves to reduce the inner tensions resulting from a failure to conform to the patterns of one's Ego Ideal.

The sociologist Robert Winch has taken the psychoanalytic theory of the Ego Ideal and its projection and developed it more explicitly into a theory of mate selection.[9] Winch, furthermore, has brought his theory into testable form and has proceeded to test it with a sample of married couples. The theory rests on the assumption that the abandoned and retained aspects of one's Ego Ideal can be partially observed in one's personality needs. It was reasoned that since these needs press for fulfillment, a man, for example, is directed from within to love and marry the woman who shows the greatest promise of allowing him to meet his needs. Reciprocally, the love object he has selected will in turn love him if it seems likely that life with him will allow her to meet her strong personality needs. Mutual love and attraction is thus hypothesized to rest on the reciprocal nature of a pair's need patterns. A woman with a need to nurture would be attracted to a man who needed ministering, solicitous care, and he would be attracted to her. This is a simple example of what Winch terms *the theory of complementary needs* in mate selection.

The theory of complementary needs has been developed to take into account various ways in which the need patterns of spouses relate to one another. Complementariness in Winch's sense can include the absence of certain needs in both spouses as well as the presence, at a fairly weak level, of the same needs in each. The theory is thus more than a logical version of the adage "opposites attract." Using the various definitions of complementariness, Winch's studies of a small sample of recently married couples supported his theory of complementary needs. We are not stating that his studies fully tested and supported the psychoanalytic

---

[8] J. C. Flugel, *Man, Morals and Society* (New York, International Universities Press, Inc., 1945), pp. 174 ff. The symptoms of being "in love" also have been considered from the standpoint of projection of the Ego Ideal. See Edmund Bergler, *Divorce Won't Help* (New York, Harper and Brothers, 1948), pp. 56 ff.

[9] Robert F. Winch, *Mate Selection* (New York, Harper & Brothers, 1958), Chs. 4, 5, and 6.

conceptions of the Ego Ideal and its projection. It in no way detracts from Winch's studies to point out that he restricted himself largely to the conscious dimensions of personality. The psychoanalytic theory deals primarily with the unconscious levels of personality and secondarily with the layers more observable to the person himself and to others. Although Winch's findings do not oppose the psychoanalytic theories, they remain but a partial test of them. To the extent that the theory of complementary needs can be more generally applied than so far has been demonstrated, Winch's theory indicates that in mate selection couples are guided at least partly by the demands of their inner selves and that these two sets of pressures from within fit together to form a complementary whole.

The psychoanalytic theory of the Ego Ideal and its projection and the derivative theory of complementary needs demonstrate well the relationship between the early experiences of a child and the marriage he forms as an adult. It becomes easier to see that there is *some* meaning in the dictum that "marriages are formed in the nursery." After all, the parents were the child's first ego models, and in the course of family living they invited the child to be like themselves. To the extent that a person's Ego Ideal has a bearing on the kind of person he chooses as a marriage partner, parents do exert an influence on the mate selection of their children. In other ways, too, it can be seen that early family experiences have a bearing on mate selection. The admittedly unusual, even pathological, cases to which we will now give some attention provide a more dramatic illustration of the significance of the family experiences. Despite their atypicality, they tell us something about the typical, for there would seem to be no reason to assume that early family experiences are important only in cases of demonstrable pathology or that the importance of family experiences diminishes as we go from the less than normal to the near normal.

Since the Oedipal situation represents an important early stage in the young child's love life, it is to be expected that ramifications of this stage are to be noticed when once again he develops a strong attachment for someone of the opposite sex. Some individuals carry their Oedipal attachment to adulthood and seem compelled to fall in love with and marry someone who resembles their parent. It is as if the only person psychologically suitable as a mate is the parent of the opposite sex. Since the wish cannot be admitted to consciousness, it is expressed through seeking in marriage a parent substitute. It is ironic that the more successful is the pursuit of a substitute parent the more likely is it to be in vain. The closer a person comes to finding in his mate the psychological equivalent of his parent, the more likely it is that the resemblance will stir up the revulsions associated with incestuous marriage. The neurotic is compelled to seek as a mate a substitute parent, but when he finds her he cannot be happy precisely because he has done a good job of selection!

The resemblance between the unconciously sought-for parent and the lover who becomes his or her substitute is seldom obvious, particularly to the person himself. Various associative links connect the newer to the original love.[10] The similarity may be a matter of physical appearance, or it may be in the lover's name that the association is found. Some mannerism of his love object, her facial expression, or some seemingly trivial characteristic may be sufficient to remind a man unconsciously of the lover he really seeks. It is not at all unusual to observe women who are attracted only to men significantly older than themselves and who cannot seem to love someone who in terms of age would seem to make a more desirable spouse. Even if the person does not become aware that his spouse is but a substitute for his parent, marriages in which the search for a parent substitute is the dominant and pervasive theme may not work out satisfactorily. Just because the color of a man's hair, his voice, or his build reminds a girl of her first "childhood sweetheart," there is no assurance that his personality is in other ways such that she can live out her life with him as a husband. So brightly may have shone the traits that she was forced unconsciously to like that she was unable to see other characteristics that perhaps she could never learn to tolerate.

Sometimes the resemblance between the original and the later love object comes about through a repetition of the circumstances that surrounded the early love affair. A woman may find that repeatedly she falls in love with a man who is already married. Consciously she is perplexed at the injustice in her fate, but unconsciously she seems compelled to become involved in a triangular situation. Similarly, a man may be able to love only a woman who is married or engaged. An appreciation of the deeper meaning of such affairs can be gained from those cases in which the woman does break with her husband or fiancé, and her lover cannot bring himself to marry her. Her attractiveness, it would seem, was lost the minute she ceased to be, like his original love, "someone else's girl."[11] Much the same mechanism operates when in the choice of a love object some other kind of obstacle to marriage is substituted for the obstacle of an existing marriage or engagement. The man or woman who falls in love consistently with a person who is temporarily or permanently not in a position to marry, who must be wooed across continents, or who otherwise presents

[10] For an early treatment of associative links in mate selection, see J. C. Flugel, *The Psycho-Analytic Study of the Family* (London, The Hogarth Press, Ltd., 1921), pp. 104 ff.
[11] Cf. the case history reported in Victor W. Eisenstein, *Neurotic Interaction in Marriage* (New York, Basic Books, Inc., 1956), p. 119.

a barrier to marriage may complain of his chronic ill luck. It is not difficult to accept the fact that such a person unconsciously seeks out as a love object only those who cannot marry him. The similarity of the circumstances surrounding the original Oedipal attachment and the later love affair is once again evident.

There are still other ways in which severe difficulties over the Oedipal situation in childhood can leave their marks on the mate-selection tendencies of the adult. It is not too unusual to learn of men and women who seek out as a mate a person who is in some manner markedly inferior to themselves.[12] The man who falls in love with a prostitute or a women of low sexual morality would be a case in point, as well as would the woman who falls in love repeatedly with a known criminal, an alcoholic, or a ne'er-do-well. Sometimes the inferior person represents the parent's baser side invented by the child. In the throes of his Oedipus conflict the young boy may blame his mother for submitting to the advances of his father and may consider her akin to a fallen woman for doing so.[13] The girl, in turn, may believe that her father degrades himself by responding to the mother or making advances to her. At the same time, of course, the boy and the girl have a positive attachment to the parent of the opposite sex. If the idea of the parent of the opposite sex as someone low and base becomes fixed in the unconscious along with the positive feelings, it may lead the person to see in a socially disreputable person a substitute for the sought-for parent. In other cases the selection of a socially inferior person as a spouse is found among those who have not in any sense devalued the parent of the opposite sex and may even have idealized him. Only by marrying someone who is the antithesis of the cherished parent can the unconscious dread of incest be handled. Both motives for marrying a socially undesirable type of person represent disturbances in the usual development of love, which can have their geneses in the emotional triangle of childhood.

The many admittedly unusual motives in mate selection must be considered only as illustrative of the possible manifestations of a disturbed psychosexual development. The symptoms we have described, furthermore, are not to be thought of as having diagnostic value in and of themselves. Although the relationship between the early emotional disturbances and the later tendencies in mate selection we have described are the type that have been discovered in actual cases, it must be remembered that only a thorough understanding of the individual can lead to a discovery of a cause and effect relationship. As we saw above in the example of attrac-

[12] A number of such cases are reported in Bergler, *op. cit.*, pp. 17 ff.

[13] Cf. Emily H. Mudd and Aron Krich, eds., *Man and Wife* (New York, W. W. Norton & Company, Inc., 1957), pp. 61-62.

tion for a socially inferior person, the same symptom may result from different causes. It is likewise true that a similar childhood disturbance may manifest itself differently. One man who as a boy fixed on the idea of his mother's debasement in her response to the advances of the father may seek out other "fallen women" as his love objects; another man may attempt to compensate for the "unfaithfulness" of his first love with such a strong desire for virginity in his later love choices that regardless of the extenuating circumstances he cannot love a person who has had sexual relations with someone other than himself.[14] Although each person can only be understood in the light of his own developmental history, it is of value to see the kind of disturbances in love and mate selection that have been found to result from earlier difficulties. There can remain little room for uncertainty concerning the importance of the early family experiences.

SEXUAL ADJUSTMENT IN MARRIAGE

Although the foregoing discussion was focused chiefly on mate selection, it necessarily included some aspects of postmarital adjustment. We saw, for example, that some people are driven by neurotic impulses to marry a person with whom they are likely to be unhappy. We need now to direct our attention more specifically to the married pair. Frigidity and impotence are two marital problems that are fairly common, particularly if we recognize that these may be relative as well as absolute conditions. We cannot, of course, fully explain these phenomena. Nor should it be inferred that these are the only problems of marital life or the only ones subject to psychoanalytic appraisal. Sexual responsiveness in marriage nevertheless is an important aspect of marital interaction, and psychoanalytic theory is uniquely suitable for explaining the developmental causes of this responsiveness.

Frigidity

The first question to settle with respect to frigidity in women is just what is meant by the term. There are some women who view all kinds of sexuality with extreme disgust. So great is their revulsion to sexual intercourse that they cannot bring themselves to marry and to engage in that "horrid act." Other women marry, have sexual relations with some frequency, but frankly (or not so frankly) admit that they are in no way pleasurable. Still others enjoy the preliminaries to sexual intercourse and

[14] Flugel, *Psycho-Analytic Study of the Family*, pp. 115-116.

find intercourse itself pleasant but never or rarely experience orgasm. They may report, however, that all in all their sexual life is satisfactory. The types and subtypes of sexual responsiveness could be expanded almost without limit. How many of these women are frigid?

There is, unfortunately, no unanimity of opinion among the "experts" on what constitutes frigidity. Some psychoanalysts would consider as frigid any woman who is incapable of reaching orgasm during sexual intercourse. An orgasm, in turn, would be defined as pleasurable sensation in the vagina which culminates in the involuntary contractions of the vaginal muscles.[15] Other psychiatrists, as well as medical and other authorities, believe that the center of woman's sexual sensations is the clitoris and may even challenge the concept of vaginal orgasm. If clitoridean release is considered sufficient, the problem of definition of frigidity may shift to the degree of pleasure that is experienced through the clitoris. Even if one denies the orgasmic capacity of the vagina, one may still designate as frigid those women who find sexual relations pleasurable but who cannot claim that clitoridean orgasm or something approaching full clitoridean release has been achieved. We cannot, of course, settle the question of what "really" constitutes frigidity. In our discussion of frigidity we will use the term to describe those cases in which there has been found to be a clear and consistent inability to obtain pleasure in sexual intercourse. This definition is necessarily general, and it excludes women who by other definitions would be labeled frigid. Few would deny, however, that women who conform to our definition are frigid.

Therapeutic analyses of frigid women have uncovered many and complex causes of frigidity. Only a few of the causes can be dealt with here. It is frequently found that a frigid woman has a strong masculinity complex. She has never been able to work through her envy of men and bears an unconscious desire to take revenge on them.[16] In her frigidity she can settle the old problem that arose with the feeling that she had been robbed of a penis. Although not actually robbing the male of his penis, she can with her aversion to sexual intercourse rob that organ of its function. The wife who allows intercourse to take place only on infrequent occasions is demonstrating that the penis is after all a fairly useless organ. Sometimes in frigidity that has its origin in the wish to take revenge on the male, marital intercourse takes place with some frequency and the woman seems to anticipate it with enjoyment. Here the revenge is more subtle. The wife encourages her husband to expect that intercourse will

---

[15] Cf. Eisenstein, *op. cit.*, p. 105, and Bergler, *op. cit.*, pp. 79-81.

[16] A failure to master the envy of men can also lead to a desire to emulate the male and to assume the masculine role. See Helene Deutsch, *The Psychology of Women*, Vol. I (New York, Grune and Stratton, 1944), p. 318.

be a mutually satisfying experience and then repeatedly disappoints him by her obvious lack of enjoyment.[17] When frigidity does not have this revenge basis, on the other hand, some women will go to great lengths to feign pleasure and will try to simulate orgasm because they have learned that their husband's satisfaction is related to their own.

It has been found in other cases of frigidity that the woman too closely indentifies her husband with her father. Precisely because the woman has done a good job of finding a substitute for her father, she cannot have intercourse with him. Her aversion and disgust will prevent her from carying out her unconsciously perceived incest with her husband-father. In other cases where the husband and father are unconsciously confused, sexual intercourse is possible but not enjoyable. The long-sought alliance with the father is realized, but punishment for the "crime" is exacted through her inability to obtain any pleasure from it. Such a woman may seek passionless intercourse with her husband not, in this case, to disappoint him, but to disappoint and punish herself.

Still other instances of frigidity have been found to stem from a negative attitude toward sexuality that was learned early in life and reinforced throughout childhood.[18] If disgust, shame, and disapproval are all that the girl has been taught to associate with sex, it becomes difficult for the woman to make an exception for marital sex. Severe negative conditioning of this sort can result in long-lasting inability to find sexual relations pleasurable. Occasionally women are found who experience some pleasure in sexual intercourse itself but can find no enjoyment in sexual foreplay, and who after intercourse act is if it were an emotionally meaningless experience.[19] It is as if only for a brief interval can they allow themselves enjoyment in the tabooed, disgusting activity and must by their aloofness at other times deny that they have even this amount of interest.

The various cases of frigidity we have described have one feature in common. All of them stem from earlier disturbances in the woman's sex life. There is no reason why almost every woman could not find real pleasure in the act through which the reproduction of the species has been assured. Girls can be taught to enjoy the prospects of becoming a woman or to resent womanhood. They can be taught that sexual relations are base or dignified. They can be helped or hindered as they work through the early conflicts in love relationships, which occur as the ability to love in a mature, heterosexual manner gradually unfolds.

---

[17] Karl Abraham, *Selected Papers* (London, Hogarth Press, Ltd., 1927), p. 357.
[18] Mudd and Krich, *op. cit.*, p. 202.
[19] Abraham, *op. cit.*, p. 359.

Impotency

A man is considered impotent if he is unable to achieve and maintain an erection for a period of time sufficient to engage in and complete sexual intercourse. In a pronounced type of impotency, the male consistently fails to achieve an erection. Impotency is also applied to the conditions of premature ejaculation and retarded ejaculation. In the former disturbance an erection is achieved, but emission of the semen occurs immediately after, or even before, intercourse begins. With retarded ejaculation, a somewhat less common phenomenon, even sexual intercourse of a relatively long duration fails to result in an ejaculation. As with frigidity, the etiology of impotency involves the complex developmental history of the individual. We must necessarily be restricted to a few examples of the manifestations and causes of impotency.

One type of impotency is related to latent homosexuality.[20] Thus the condition that the young man may discover at the time of his marriage had its origin years before in his childhood. A father he was afraid to rival, a mother he could not love, or some combination of situations in the Oedipal period may have been the beginning of his partial retreat from heterosexual love. As a man he may never have conscious homosexual desires, but neither is he capable of acting out the part of the male in sexual intercourse. He may shun sexual relations entirely, or as an unconscious defense against experiencing them he may suffer from premature ejaculation. A man with this type of disturbance may be quite passive and "feminine." Sometimes he may be able to function sexually if married to a dominant woman who makes all of the sexual advances and in a sense seduces him.

A type of potency disturbance that may also be related to latent homosexuality is found in the promiscuous man who has conquered many women. Although he gives the appearance of a super-male, the promiscuous, Don Juan type is actually a sheep in wolf's clothing. He is not masculine enough to hold the love of a woman, and unconsciously he realizes it.[21] To ward off such disturbing thoughts the Don Juan engages in an endless series of seductions. The inner doubts of his masculinity are only temporarily quieted and need to be dispelled again and again. It is likely that many a Don Juan is incapable of seducing a normal woman or at least is afraid to try. His "victims" are frigid women who seek him out in the vain hope that as an apparent super-male he may waken their

[20] Eisenstein, op. cit., pp. 109-110.
[21] Theodor Reik, Psychology of Sex Relations (New York, Rinehart & Company, Inc., 1945), pp. 188-189.

sexuality.[22] The great seducer is actually seduced by a complementary neurotic trying to relieve her frigidity.

Another type of impotency is manifested by the inability to practice sexual relations even though an erection is achieved. In some cases this has been found to be due to an unconscious association between intercourse and a physical attack on the woman. Inserting the penis is unconsciously bound up with ideas of piercing or stabbing the woman or otherwise injuring her.[23] To guard against these aggressive desires, the penis quickly is rendered harmless by prematurely returning to a flaccid state. Premature ejaculation may also represent an unconscious hostility toward women. Revenge for the childhood disappointments in love experienced with the first woman in his life is obtained by denying his wife the pleasure of intercourse. Of course the unconscious cheater is likewise cheated, for men with a potency disturbance of this type frequently suffer dreadfully from a feeling of inadequacy.

Although impotency and frigidity are serious plagues to marital happiness, they are not the only disturbances in the love life of adults. The age-old problem of adultery is a case in point. In some cases an extramarital affair is sought and enjoyed precisely because it is forbidden.[24] The childhood prohibition against sexuality has never been forgotten, and marital sex suffers from the intolerable deficiency of being permissible. In our discussion of love and sexual disturbances we have purposefully avoided the bizarre and the extremely perverse. The cases that we have seen, however, provide ample testimony to the developmental concept of the ability to love. The pathologies that are exhibited in an unhappy marriage did not have their geneses on the wedding day. The adult can better be understood by his history than by his present. The child, indeed, is father of the man. More than this, when psychoanalytic theory is applied to love and marriage, the importance of the unconscious becomes manifest. Frequently the human mind is compared to an iceberg, with the large mass concealed beneath the surface of the water representing the unconscious. The unique contribution of psychoanalytic theory lies in the light it sheds on what is otherwise unknowable. In our brief treatment we have been unable to expose in detail the submerged portion of the human mind. But perhaps to trace the outlines of what lies in the murky waters below the surface is better than to ignore the mass entirely.

---

[22] See the treatment of the relationship between Don Juanism in males and frigidity in women in Bergler, *op. cit.*, pp. 85-93.

[23] Eisenstein, *op. cit.*, p. 109.

[24] Bergler, *op. cit.*, pp. 34 ff. For a more general treatment of the desire for forbidden activities see Flugel, *Man, Morals, and Society*, pp. 197-200.

SELECTED READINGS

ABRAHAM, KARL, *Selected Papers* (London, Hogarth Press Ltd., 1927).

ACKERMAN, NATHAN W., *The Psychodynamics of Family Life* (New York, Basic Books, Inc., 1958).

BERGLER, EDMUND, *Divorce Won't Help* (New York, Harper & Brothers, 1948).

———, *Unhappy Marriage and Divorce* (New York, International Universities Press, Inc., 1946).

BERGLER, EDMUND, and KROGER, WILLIAM S., *Kinsey's Myth of Female Sexuality: The Medical Facts* (New York, Grune & Stratton, Inc., 1954).

DEUTSCH, HELENE, *The Psychology of Women*, 2 vols. (New York, Grune & Stratton, Inc., 1944-45).

EISENSTEIN, VICTOR W., ed., *Neurotic Interaction in Marriage* (New York, Basic Books, Inc., 1956).

FLUGEL, J. C., *The Psychoanalytic Study of the Family* (London, Hogarth Press, Ltd., 1921).

HOLLIS, FLORENCE, *Women in Marital Conflict* (New York, Family Service Association of America, 1949).

JOSSELYN, IRENE M., *The Adolescent and His World* (New York, Family Service Association of America, 1952).

MARIANO, J. H. A., *A Psychoanalytic Lawyer Looks at Marriage and Divorce* (New York, Council on Marriage Relations, 1952).

MUDD, EMILY H., and KRICH, ARON, eds., *Man and Wife* (New York, W. W. Norton & Company, Inc., 1957).

SKIDMORE, REX A., and GARRETT, HULDA, *Marriage Consulting* (New York, Harper & Brothers, 1956).

SPIEGEL, L. A., "A Review of Contributions to a Psychoanalytic Theory of Adolescence," *Psychoanalytic Study of the Child*, Vol. 6 (1951), pp. 375-393.

YOUNG, LEONTINE R., *Out of Wedlock* (New York, McGraw-Hill Book Company, Inc., 1954).

Index

Kurland, Samuel, 182
Kvutza, 167
Kyrk, Hazel, 356

Landis, Carney, 276
Landis, Judson T., 280, 341, 351, 352, 354, 356
Landis, Mary G., 280
Landis, Paul H., 32, 308, 310, 356, 403
Langdon, Grace, 255
Lansing, John B., 325, 334, 343
Latency period, 433-434
Lavin, David E., 337
Lawrence, Henry W., 108
Leffingwell, Georgia W., 83
Legacy-hunting, in ancient Rome, 78-79
Levensohn, Lotta, 182
Levin, Harry, 244, 258
Levine, Lena, 403
Levirate duty, 46-48
Levy, David M., 380, 421
Levy, John, 347, 350, 356
Lichtenberger, James P., 317
Life cycle of families, *see* Family life cycle
Linder, Robert, 242, 363, 365, 380
Lindesmith, A. R., 234
Linton, Ralph, 12, 28, 29, 32, 36, 233, 234, 257, 388
Littman, Richard A., 247, 248
Locke, Harvey J., 237, 262, 263, 301, 314, 322, 340, 341
Love,
    development of, in infant, 422-423
    learning to handle, as developmental task, 393
Lowie, Robert H., 16, 23, 24, 26, 28, 29, 31, 289

Maccoby, Eleanor E., 244, 248, 258
Mace, David R., 57, 63
Maine, Henry S., 11, 19, 67, 74, 83
Maintenance family function, *see* Economic family function
Malinowski, Bronislaw, 37, 109, 110, 112, 113, 114, 115, 116, 117, 118, 119, 120, 123, 126, 127, 129, 130, 131
Marasmus, 237-238
Mariano, J. H. A., 451
Marital adjustment,
    and income, 295, 296-297, 340-341
    and sexual adjustment, 346-348
    effects on child, 307, 431-432
    in remarriage, 313-315
Marital sexual intercourse,
    during pregnancy, 354
    taboos on, 125, 127-128
    See also, Sexual adjustment

Marquesans, group marriage among, 28
Marriage,
    achieving adult status as motive for, 119, 120
    adoption of civil in post-Revolution Russia, 138
    age at, and divorce, 301
    age at, and premarital intercourse among females, 272-273
    ancient Hebrew conception of, 49
    ancient Roman legislation encouraging, 81
    and subordinate position of women, 139
    arranged, as deterrent to divorce, 288
    as status differentiation, 171, 172
    attitude toward, and remarriage, 310-311
    banns published in colonial period, 98
    by capture, 33-34
    by consent of principals, 36-37, 49-50, 69, 97-98, 138
    by purchase, 34-36, 50, 72
    by service, 36, 50
    changing conception of, 316-317
    common-law, among ancient Romans, 72
    common-law, in Russia, 154-155, 158
    companionship function in kibbutz, 172-173
    companionship function in Trobriand society, 119
    cross-cousin, 23-24, 114-116
    desire for children as motive for, 119
    duration of, and extramarital sexual intercourse, 268-269
    economic difficulties in, 296-297
    economic function of, 172
    economic motives for, in ancient Rome, 76-77
    economic motives for, in colonial period, 99-100
    economic motives for, in Trobriand society, 119
    endogamous rules, 22-24, 44-45, 69-70, 97, 114
    exogamous rules, 22, 24-27, 45-46, 96-97, 113-114
    forms of, 28-32, *See also*, Group marriage, Monogamy, Polyandry, Polygyny
    in ancient Rome, 68-72, 76, 80
    in Israeli kibbutz, 169-173
    in Russia, 132
    in Trobriand society, 117-120
    parental control of, 49-50, 69, 97-98, 138
    permanency of, *see* Divorce
    rates by age and sex, 308
    registration in colonial period, 98-99